Cases in Competitive Strategy

Cases in Competitive Strategy

Michael E. Porter

THE FREE PRESS
New York London Toronto Sydney Tokyo Singapore

The Free Press
A Division of Macmillan, Inc.
866 Third Avenue, New York, N.Y. 10022

Maxwell Macmillan Canada, Inc.
1200 Eglinton Avenue East
Suite 200
Don Mills, Ontario M3C 3N1

Macmillan, Inc. is part of the Maxwell Communication
Group of Companies.

Printed in the United States of America

printing number

9 10

Library of Congress Cataloging in Publication Data

Porter, Michael E.
    Cases in competitive strategy.

    "Designed to be used in combination with . . . Competitive
strategy"—Introd.
    Includes index.
    1. Competition—Case studies. 2. Industrial management—
Case studies. I. Porter, Michael E.
Competitive strategy. II. Title.
HD41.P667 1983   658   82–45034
    ISBN 0-02-925410-8   AACR2

To Agnes Porter

Contents

Preface and Acknowledgments

Over the past decade, I have been engaged in research on the economics of competition in industries and its implications for formulating competitive strategy. This work reached a milestone in 1980 with the publication of *Competitive Strategy: Techniques for Analyzing Industries and Competitors* (The Free Press), which presented a conceptual framework for competitive strategy formulation. The framework aims to combine economic theory with the practical concerns of individual companies.

The conceptual framework in *Competitive Strategy* is complex and demands a large quantity of data concerning industry structure and competitors to apply in practice. In order to teach about the framework to executives and students of business administration, I developed an extensive series of case studies on industries (and the companies within them). These case studies formed the foundation for a course, entitled "Industry and Competitive Analysis," that I developed and am teaching at the Harvard Business School. At this point, approximately half of the second-year MBA class enrolls in the course each year.

This book contains the case studies, drawn from eighteen different industries that were chosen to illustrate a range of the important issues in competitive strategy formulation. The case studies have the data necessary for sophisticated strategic analyses and provide a laboratory for the student to apply the framework in *Competitive Strategy* to current real world competitive situations in important domestic and international industries. Thus the cases form a critical bridge between a complex conceptual framework and the practice of strategy formulation.

As anyone who has attempted it quickly learns, the development of case studies on industry competition is both labor and capital intensive. One must become so thoroughly familiar with an industry and its competitors so as to be able to capture the essential issues in a case study of manageable length. A considerable amount of on-site interviewing of executives is also required to ensure that a case study captures reality and not a public relations view of competitors' strategies. Finally, a good case study contains not only the information managers actually considered in analyzing a competitive situation but also the information they *should have* considered. Only in this way can a case study be a vehicle to leading management practice rather than following it.

The development of the case studies in this book has necessarily involved the assistance of many people and required sustained and generous financial support. It is hard to imagine anywhere besides the Harvard Business School where this work could have been done. Dean Lawrence Fouraker and Associate Dean and now Dean John McArthur have provided vital support and encouragement, as have Professors Richard Rosenbloom and Raymond Corey in their capacities as Directors of the Division of Research. Professor Norman Berg also kindly consented to allow me to use the original Polaroid-Kodak case prepared by Glenn Merry under his supervision.

I have also had the very able help of a series of research associates in preparing many of the cases, all of whom are Harvard MBA's or doctoral students. Margaret Lawrence wrote the cases on the corn wet milling industry, the oil tanker shipping industry, the securities industry, and the fiber optics industry. Steven J. Roth prepared the case studies on Hospital Affiliates International and the Hospital Management Industry, Bendix Corporation, and Cramer Electronics and was also instrumental in preparing the note on the electronic component distribution industry with the assistance of Parmalee Eastman, Boon Koh, and Gustav Christensen. Kathryn Rudie Harrigan, now Assistant Professor at Columbia University, prepared the two cases on the problems of decline drawn from the vacuum tube and baby food industries. Mark Fuller, now Assistant Professor at the Harvard Business School, worked with me on the Polaroid-Kodak case series and the Sierra Log Home case. George Yip, also now an Assistant Professor at Harvard, prepared the SWECO case. Neal Bhadkamkar prepared the three case studies making up the series on the world television set industry. Jessie Bourneuf Dougherty wrote the EG&G case series. The chain saw industry case series grew out of a student research project by David Collis, James DeBelina, Jon Elsasser, James Hornthal, and R. Gordon Shearer, and I was also assisted by Susan Mayer in the preparation of the cases. The bicycle industry case benefited greatly from an earlier case prepared by Elisabeth Lyman Rachal under the supervision of Professor C. Roland Christensen and from work by Steven Sydness. Finally, the case study on large turbine generators drew heavily from an excellent two-volume research study prepared by Ralph G. M. Sultan, a former Associate Professor of Marketing at Harvard.

Preparing a case study is only the first step in making it into an effective teaching vehicle. A case usually gets repeatedly revised based on the experience gained in using it and on subsequent research. In this regard, I have benefited greatly from comments and insights by colleagues who have taught the cases. Professors Richard Meyer and John R. Wells, particularly, have made innumerable suggestions that have improved the cases in teaching the entire Industry and Competitive Analysis course with me. In addition, other colleagues have offered useful suggestions, including Joseph Badaracco, Christopher Bartlett, Joseph Bower, Richard Ellsworth, Kathryn Harrigan, Richard Hamermesh, Michael Lovdal (Temple, Barker and Sloane), John Matthews, John Rosenbloom (University of Virginia), Malcolm Salter and others both at Harvard and at other schools. Case preparation and revision also draw heavily on administrative support, and I have been extremely fortunate in having Emily Feudo, Sheila Barry, and Kathleen Svensson to help me in this respect. Kathleen Svensson has been particularly instrumental in helping me prepare this book.

A joy of case studies is that they are dynamic teaching vehicles in which the instructor can learn alongside the student. In the numerous times that I have taught these case studies at Harvard and elsewhere, I have often been stimulated to new insights by my MBA and executive students. To them I owe a debt of gratitude not only for their intellectual curiosity but also for their enthusiasm that made the long and arduous process of preparing this book worthwhile.

Finally, I would be extremely remiss if I did not include among those I thank the many companies and managers all over the world who gave generously of their time and data to make these cases possible. Bendix Corporation, Cramer Electronics Inc., EG&G, Hospital Affiliates International, Sierra Log Homes, and SWECO—all consented to allow the preparation of case studies bearing their names. Many other companies, most of whom prefer not to be identified, cooperated in the preparation of other case studies in the book. The case method of learning about management problems is paralyzed without the generous and open cooperation of managers. It is to all the managers that gave of their time and allowed me to study their competitive problems that I ultimately owe my greatest debt in the preparation of this book.

Introduction

This book contains in-depth case studies on eighteen industries (and the companies in them), representing a wide range of industry structures, states of maturity, and competitive situations. The case studies have been chosen to provide real-life settings in which to explore the range of analytical problems involved in the formulation of competitive strategy—the positioning of a firm (or business unit) relative to its competitors in an individual industry or industry sector.

The cases in the book aim to provide students with a laboratory in which to develop a working understanding of the fundamental determinants of competition in industries and the factors that shape the competitive success or failure of firms. The cases place the reader in the actual position of a firm or firms having to cope with competition. A prominent theme of the cases is that a firm can shape the rules of competition in its favor through strategy if it understands those rules in a sophisticated way.

The case book is designed to be used in combination with my book *Competitive Strategy: Techniques for Analyzing Industries and Competitors.* *Competitive Strategy* provides a comprehensive framework for competitive analysis and for translating this analysis into a competitive strategy. Other readings on industry structure and strategy formulation in industries can be used as supplementary readings as well.

The book can be used in a number of types of courses. The cases in the book can be the basis of an entire course on competitive strategy or industry analysis. At the Harvard Business School, the case studies in combination with *Competitive Strategy* make up a course entitled "Industry and Competitive Analysis," a second year elective course in which approximately one-half the students are enrolled. The book can also be used as a major segment of courses on business policy, strategic planning, or strategic management. Any course on the problems of strategy must contain some consideration of competition and how to deal with it.

The cases in the book can and have been used outside of policy courses, however, because they provide a laboratory in which to study the generic topic of competition, which is important in a number of other functional fields. For example, the book can be used in such courses as strategic marketing, security analysis, and corporate financial management. These are just a few functional areas where the fundamental determinants of competition and competitive position are essential to sophisticated analysis. Finally, the book can be used in courses on industrial organization and applied microeconomics to supplement the more traditional theoretical readings. The cases illustrate the way in which a wide variety of real markets behave and can be used to bring the economics of markets to life.

The choice of industries for inclusion in this book reflects two broad considerations. The primary criterion is that the industries portray a range of competitive situations that allow a thorough grounding for the reader in the conceptual framework contained in *Competitive Strategy*. The second criterion for inclusion is that the industry be one that is both interesting and important. Such important industries as fiber-optics, securities, oil field equipment, automotive components, television sets, and heavy electrical equipment are represented. The conceptual framework in *Competitive Strategy* is generic and applies to any industry, whether it be domestic or international, product or service, and populated by entrepreneurial companies or larger ones. The industries represented in the book reflect this. Companies and industries range from large to small, and the cases represent a wide diversity of industries along conventional industry classification schemes such as consumer, in-

dustrial, durable, nondurable, product, and service as shown in Figure I–1.

The Conceptual Framework for Industry Selection

The conceptual framework contained in *Competitive Strategy* suggests that for competitive strategy development there is a more important way to classify industries and competitive situations than conventional approaches such as consumer goods versus industrial goods. The conceptual framework consists of three building blocks. The first is "General Analytical Techniques," or generalizable conceptual tools for understanding competition that can be applied to any industry. These all stem from the concept of structural analysis of industries that models competition in any industry as the operation of five basic competitive forces and identifies their underlying determinants. The second building block, "Generic Industry Environments," consists of generalizations about competitive analysis in particular types of industry structures, such as emerging industries,

FIGURE I–1. Classification of Industries in the Book

	NONDURABLE	DURABLE
CONSUMER	Disposable diapers Baby foods	Bicycles Instant photography Chain saws Log homes TV receivers
INDUSTRIAL	*Raw Materials and Supplies* Auto components Fiber-optics Electronic fuel injection Receiving tubes Electrical connectors	*Capital Goods* Large turbine generator Oil field equipment

	PRODUCT	SERVICE
CONSUMER	Bicycles Instant photography Disposable diapers Chain saws Log homes Baby foods TV receivers	Securities Hospital management
INDUSTRIAL	Large turbine generators Oil field equipment Automotive components Fiber-optics Electronic fuel injection Receiving tubes Electrical connectors	Electronic components Oil tankers

declining industries, or global industries. The third conceptual building block is "Strategic Decisions," which develops the way in which to analyze all the important decisions that occur in the context of an industry, including entry, capacity expansion, vertical integration, divestment, and coalitions. Each decision has its own set of analytical issues.

General Analytical Techniques

The industries that are the subjects of the cases in this book allow a systematic investigation of the following important General Analytical Techniques:

- *Structural analysis.* The study of the five competitive forces influencing industry competition and their underlying determinants
- *Generic strategies.* The three internally consistent approaches to creating a defensible competitive advantage (The three generic strategies, their relationship to industry structure, their risks, and their organizational implications are a basic building block in the selection and analysis of strategic alternatives.)
- *Microeconomics of markets.* The basic microeconomic processes by which competitive markets reach equilibrium and adjust over time, including supply and demand curve analysis, elasticity of supply and demand, price formation and adjustment, and so forth
- *Product substitution.* The determinants of the extent and rate of substitution of one industry's product or service for another's, and how substitution can be influenced through strategy from either an offensive or a defensive standpoint
- *Strategy toward suppliers and buyers.* The strategic implications of the bargaining relationship between an industry and its suppliers and buyers
- *Entry/mobility deterrence.* The mechanisms by which firms can influence the ease or difficulty of entry into an industry (or mobility from one strategic position to another within the industry) and their strategic implications
- *Competitor analysis.* An in-depth framework for assessing competitors' positions and their likely behavior
- *Market signals.* Mechanisms by which information about competitors' goals and intentions is transmitted in industries

- *Competitive moves.* Game-theoretic principles for selecting offensive and defensive competitive moves, and executing them so as to maximize the chance of success
- *Strategic groups and strategic mapping.* The theory of strategic groups, which shows how structural analysis can be used to determine the fundamental strategic position of the individual firm (Strategic mapping is a tool with which the strategic position of firms can be displayed to facilitate analysis.)
- *Industry evolution.* The underlying determinants of changes in industry structure over time and their strategic implications

Generic Industry Environments

The generic industry environments examined in the cases in this book are derived from five basic dimensions of industry structure: degree of seller concentration; extent of product differentiation; rate of technological change; state of maturity; and degree of globalization. These five dimensions define continua on which any individual industry can be placed. The cases in this book examine industries that represent particularly interesting points on these continua.

The principle underlying the examination of these generic industry environments is that the ability to generalize about competition and strategic alternatives is limited by the intrinsic diversity of industry structures. By focusing systematically on important generic industry environments, we enhance our ability to go deeper in competitive analysis.

The particular generic industry environments emphasized by cases in this book are as follows:

- *Fragmented industries.* Industries with a low level of seller concentration and no clear market leader
- *Emerging industries.* New or reborn industries at the beginning of their growth and characterized by fluid industry structures and undefined rules of the competitive game
- *Transition to industry maturity.* Industries undergoing the often difficult transition from rapid growth to the much slower growth and changed competitive circumstances generally associated with maturity
- *Declining industries.* Industries that are in a state of decline, in which firms must make difficult decisions about endgaming

- *Global industries.* Industries where the relevant market is worldwide, and firms must compete with coordinated global strategies in order to be winners

Consideration is also given in the cases in this book to industries with undifferentiated products and industries characterized by high levels of technology and rapid technological change, though these cases consider other primary conceptual issues as well.

Strategic Decisions

Industries and companies examined in the cases in this book allow the reader to consider systematically the important types of strategic decisions that occur in the context of a single industry. The general analytical techniques are brought to bear in developing specific conceptual tools for analyzing each type of decision. In addition, each type of decision has its own economic and administrative issues that require examination.

The strategic decisions highlighted in cases in the book are the following:

- *Major capacity expansion.* The decision to commit resources to a substantial addition to firm capacity, whose success depends on future industry conditions and what competitors choose to do
- *Vertical integration.* The extension of the firm's scope of operation through either forward or backward integration
- *Entry.* The decision to enter a new industry through either acquisition or internal development
- *Divestment.* The often painful decision to withdraw from an industry
- *Coalition.* Agreements among firms in the same industry short of outright merger, including supply agreements, joint ventures, and cross-licensing

Some of the cases portray companies facing a particular decision, while in many other cases the analysis of a strategic decision is a secondary theme in material primarily addressing other topics.

Organization and Flow of the Cases

Each of the eighteen industries in the book can be analyzed using all three of the conceptual building blocks described above—the "General Analytical Techniques" apply to every industry; every industry is characterized by being in one or more "Generic Industry Environments," and some firms in every industry face one or more of the "Strategic Decisions." Thus the cases in the book cannot be organized along any one dimension. They are organized instead to allow cumulative examination of all three conceptual building blocks.

Early cases in the book place the greatest emphasis on "General Analytical Techniques" in the analysis, though beginning with the first case there should be secondary attention placed on learning about "Generic Industry Environments" and "Strategic Decisions." Later cases shift the emphasis of the analysis to "Generic Industry Environments," with cases interspersed throughout that highlight particular "Strategic Decisions." Table I–1 lists the cases in the book and relates them to the conceptual framework, giving the primary and secondary analytical issues each case is designed to highlight. The cases have been grouped into nine parts, reflecting their primary analytical themes.

Many of the cases are in multiple parts, designed to allow depth of analysis while making the preparation of a case manageable by breaking the industry and competitor data into blocks. A number of the cases involve sequential parts to allow practice in prediction of future competitive events followed by immediate feedback on the accuracy of such predictions. This book contains the initial case study, while subsequent cases are distributed by the instructor. Finally, several cases, notably Polaroid–Kodak, Disposable Diapers, EG&G, and TV Receivers, present data or events in a very undigested form in which the data or events occurred in practice. This reflects the view that learning how to use data in this form is crucial to formulating competitive strategy in practice.

How to Use the Book

While the cases in the book present interesting problems and examine important industries, the purposes of the book will be missed if the cases are treated as an end in themselves. The medium is not the message. The reader will gain the most from

TABLE I-1. Outline of Industries and Cases

Part	Industry	Cases	Primary Topic	Secondary Topic
I. Industry Structural Analysis				
1	Electric component distribution	Note on the Electronic Component Distribution Industry Raytheon Company—Diversification Cramer Electronics, Inc.	Structural analysis	Fragmented industries Vertical integration Entry
				Fragmented industries
2	Oil tanker shipping	The Oil Tanker Shipping Industry	Review of strategy identification Generic strategies Structural analysis of industries Microeconomics of markets	Fragmented industries Vertical integration Capacity expansion
II. Competitor Analysis				
3	Instant photography	Polaroid-Kodak Polaroid-Kodak Addendum	Competitor profiling Market signaling and competitive moves	Entry and entry deterrence
4	Large turbine generators	General Electric Versus Westinghouse in Large Turbine Generators	Determinants of competitive rivalry Market signaling and competitive moves	Competitor selection and optimal market configuration
III. Strategic Groups				
5	Bicycles	The U.S. Bicycle Industry in 1974	Strategic group theory	Industry evolution
IV. Entry and Entry Deterrence				
6	Disposable diapers	The Disposable Diaper Industry in 1974	Entry and entry deterrence Strategic cost analysis	Competitor selection and optimal market configuration Competitive moves Emerging industries
7	Oil field equipment	SWECO, Inc.	Entry Strategic group theory	Strategic cost analysis
V. Industry Evolution				
8	Chain saws	The Chain Saw Industry in 1974	Industry evolution Competitor profiling	Portfolio analysis techniques
9	Securities	The U.S. Securities Industry in 1979	Industry evolution	Government impact on industry structure
10	Hospital management services	Hospital Affiliates International, Inc., and the Hospital Management Industry	Transition to industry maturity	Industry evolution Product bundling

(cont.)

TABLE I-1. *(Continued)*

Part	Industry	Cases	Primary Topic	Secondary Topic
VI. *Buyers and Suppliers* 11	Automotive supply	Note on Supplying the Automobile Industry	Strategy toward buyers and suppliers	
VII. *Emerging Industries* 12	Electronic fuel injection systems	Bendix Corporation: Electronic Fuel Injection	Emerging industries Competitor selection	Scenarios Vertical Integration Forecasting potential entrants
13	Fiber-optics	The Fiber-Optics Industry in 1978: Products, Technology, and Markets The Fiber-Optics Industry in 1978: Competition The Fiber-Optics Industry in 1978: Corning Glass Works	Emerging industries High technology industries	Scenarios Market leadership Coalitions
14	Log home manufacturing	Sierra Log Homes, Inc.	Emerging industries Competitive strategy for smaller companies	Fragmented industries
VIII. *Decline and Divestment* 15	Receiving tubes	The Receiving Tube Industry in 1966	Declining industries	Divestment
16	Baby Foods	The Baby Foods Industry in 1965	Declining industries	Divestment
17	Electrical connectors	EG&G, Inc. (A) EG&G, Inc. (B)	Divestment	Strategic planning systems
IX. *Global Industries* 18	Television receivers	The U.S. Television Set Market, Postwar to 1970 The U.S. Television Set Market, 1970-1979 The Television Set Industry in 1979: Japan, Europe, and Newly Industrializing Countries	Global industries Coalitions	Industry evolution Market leadership

studying the cases in the book if he or she prepares them in combination with reading the appropriate sections of *Competitive Strategy*. The cases and conceptual material are mutually reinforcing. The cases will deepen the understanding of the conceptual material and how it can be applied, while the conceptual material will aid the student in analyzing and understanding the cases and how the lessons learned in one case can be transferred to other cases and to other industry situations.

In preparing a case, the reader will benefit from starting with a clear understanding of the type of industry structure being examined and the particular analytical issues that are at issue in the case. For example, is the industry in the case emerging or mature? Does the company face vertical integration or entry choices? Then the particular industry and company under examination can be studied, employing the conceptual tools available, in order to address the decision or decisions at hand. After the case has been prepared as discussed, the reader will benefit greatly by going back to the conceptual framework to review its principles and application. In addition, the reader will enrich his or her understanding of competitive strategy by attempting to link one case with another in order to form working generalizations about the field.

The cases in the book describe a diverse but finite number of industries, allowing in most instances only one or two chances to explore each important topic area in competitive strategy formulation. The reader is encouraged to draw on examples from his or her experience in other industries and from readings in the business press or other literature to provide additional insights into the analysis of competition. The conceptual framework in *Competitive Strategy* is detailed and the study of industries complex, which means that no one ever learns all there is to know about this subject—it is a field in which learning occurs throughout one's career. Thus the reader should view the cases in this book as only the beginning of a self-education process to be nurtured and developed through subsequent experience.

PART I
Industry Structural Analysis

The first four cases place primary emphasis on developing skills in the structural analysis of industries and translating a sophisticated understanding of industry structure into a strategic positioning for the firm through generic competitive strategies. The first two cases, "Note on the Electronic Component Distribution Industry" and "Raytheon Company: Diversification," are considered together. Raytheon must assess the fundamental attractiveness of the electronic component distribution industry as an entry target and decide how it would compete if it chose to enter. "Cramer Electronics" confronts the problems faced by a company that is among the leaders in the electronic component distribution industry and must either reaffirm or change its strategy. Finally, "The Oil Tanker Shipping Industry" portrays a glamorous but intensely competitive industry, raising questions about its fundamental profit potential, the vertical integration strategies of the major oil companies, and the strategic alternatives available to an independent tanker owner. The oil tanker industry also shows the process of market adjustment at work in a particularly graphic form and highlights some important principles of market adjustment processes.

CASE 1

Note on the Electronic Component Distribution Industry

The electronic component distribution industry was engaged in distribution of semiconductors, capacitors, resistors, connectors, and other electronic parts purchased from component manufacturers to a wide range of commercial and industrial customers in the United States and overseas. The industry had developed in parallel with the development of the electronics industry itself. Beginning with the vacuum tube, successive waves of product innovations in electronic components had been added to the distributors' product lines. Vacuum tubes were followed over time by the transistor, the integrated circuit, the large-scale integrated circuit, and, recently, the latest technological innovation, the microprocessor.[1] In 1975, approximately 23 percent of the electronic components sold passed through distributors, while the balance were sold directly by manufacturers (Exhibit 1–1).

The distribution industry had grown dramatically with the growth of electronics, with distributors' sales rising from $937 million in 1971 to $1.4 billion

[1] These developments will be discussed in more detail later in Case 1.

in 1974, an annual compound growth rate of 15 percent per year. However, 1975 proved to be a very bad year for the industry. Sales declined 21.4 percent to $1.1 billion from 1974's peak of $1.4 billion, and profits declined even more sharply. Despite the poor results in 1975, observers unanimously predicted a turnaround in 1976 as the recession ended, and forecast substantial long-term growth for the industry. The percentage of electronic component sales passing through distributors was expected by some observers to increase to 32 percent by 1985. Projections put the dollar value of distributors' sales at $5.6 billion in 1985 versus $1.1 billion in 1975, or an increase of about 18 percent per year.

These prospects were not without uncertainties, however. The projected sales increase hinged in part on expectations for the growth of the microprocessor and its accompanying equipment (Exhibit 1–2). How the microprocessor would affect distributors' operations was a major question facing the industry. In addition, the recent moves by certain electronic component manufacturers toward expanding their captive distribution operations and the potential effect of the expected entry of major Japanese electronic component manufacturers into the U.S. market increased the uncertainty faced by distributors.

Functions Performed by Distributors

Distributors served as the link between electronic components producers and the wide variety of components users. Distributors performed the following essential functions:

- *Hold and manage inventories.* Distributors carried from 25,000 to upwards of 300,000 different electronic components in inventory at any one time. Most items had a value of less than 50 cents, with individual items ranging from fractions of a cent to $20.00 for microprocessors. Generally the higher-priced items were the more complex recent devices, and the average unit cost of distributor inventories was increasing. The specific number of components maintained in inventory varied as a function of the distributor's business strategy and the tradeoff between maintaining high inventory turnover and minimizing the risk of stock outs. The distributor assumed the capital costs of holding component inventories. A typical broad-line distributor stocked components that it reordered from manufacturers every month, others that it reordered three or four times a year, and others where six months to a year would elapse before reordering. Inventory typically represented approximately 50 percent of a distributor's total assets, with supplier credit providing a major mechanism for financing it.

- *Hold and manage accounts receivable.* Almost 100 percent of distributors' business was transacted over the telephone, therefore involving the extension of trade credit to customers. Credit terms were normally 2/10 net 30; however, the normal terms were often overlooked for the smaller customers in an effort by the distributor to gain sales volume. Servicing accounts receivable involved the maintenance of between 10,000 and 40,000 individual customer accounts, with at least one order generally posted to one-third of the active accounts each month.

- *Provide fast service in meeting orders.* Providing requested items within twenty-four hours was the most critical function performed by the distributor. According to industry executives, the first question asked by customers was, "Do you have the part in stock right now?" The range of customer types was exceptionally broad, from one-person "basement operators" to multibillion-dollar firms, such as Raytheon and General Electric. However, when using a distributor the diverse customers shared a desire for instantaneous delivery. This was due, in part, to the cost of components versus their importance to the success of customers' projects. An item might cost only a few dollars, but without it expensive equipment and engineers remained idle.

- *Servicing of small orders.* The distributor filled orders that were too small for component manufacturers to be willing to fill directly. Typical distributors had average order sizes of $150 to $250, compared to minimum order sizes for manufacturers in the range of $2,500.

Some distributors also performed certain very simple assembly operations with electronic components called connectors, which were devices that joined two cables. The distributor modified a standard connector body by attaching the desired number of male and female leads to serve a specific application. This function was an accepted practice because large inventory savings could be achieved by holding unassembled connector parts instead of finished connector assemblies.

Product Lines

The electronic components handled by distributors fell in two broad general categories, active and passive. The two classifications will be discussed separately.

Active Components

In simple terms, active components have a specific effect on the electrical current passing through them. Certain components convert the electrical current from wave form to a digital (either 0 to 1) series, while other components serve to amplify the signal or modify its wave shape. Active components had progressed through several technological phases since the 1930s, reflected in five general product types:

Component Type	Year of Introduction
Vacuum tubes	1930s
Transistors	1947
Integrated circuits (IC)	1958
Large-scale integrated circuits (LSI)	1970
Microprocessors (MP)	1974

Each new technological phase had reduced the physical size of the components and increased the number of functions that could be performed per dollar. The first four product types had all followed a distinct product life cycle. This cycle was characterized by rapid standardization and rationalization of the component type over time as users became more experienced with the technology and with hardware and software configurations, and as component manufacturers strongly influenced by the learning curve philosophy sought to increase the size of market by forcing down unit production costs over time through standardization and lowering prices. Figure 1-1 shows the approximate position in the product life cycle of each of the five product types in 1976.

THE MICROPROCESSOR

The development of the microprocessor had resulted from the proliferation of LSIs, each of which

FIGURE 1-1. Relative Position of Five Leading Technologies on the Product Life Cycle Curve as of 1976

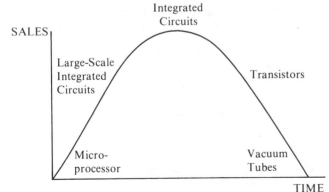

was designed and produced for a specific application. The design content of LSIs meant that their uses were limited to applications where the volume was large enough to justify the design costs involved. Rather than continue to design a specialized computer (LSI) for each new application, a general-purpose programmable microprocessor, a "computer on a chip," could be produced in a standard form and customized by the user. Operating instructions for any particular application could be stored in a memory circuit where changes could be made in seconds rather than having to wait for the design and production of a new LSI circuit. Industry observers (distributors, manufacturers, and user engineers) unanimously believed that the number of applications for microprocessors was limited only by the imagination. Intel Corporation was the first company to develop a working microprocessor in 1974 and until late 1975 had a virtual monopoly. All the major active component manufacturers had entered the microprocessor market by 1976.

Although the microprocessor had been in existence only since 1974, its growth was expected to be even more explosive than its predecessor components. From a market approximating $100 million in 1975-1976, sales of microprocessors were expected to reach $500-$1,000 million by 1980 (see Exhibit 1-2). The microprocessor differed substantially from earlier generations, because it did far more than simply affect an electrical current. It was a computer, and like all computers it required input/output linkages, memories, and programming languages to complete the system. Thus, three steps had to be taken before a microprocessor could be used in a particular application. First, it had to be linked to the input/output and memory units in what was called the "hardware configuration." Step two was designing, writing, and testing the "software" or computer language programs that caused the hardware configuration to perform the specific tasks desired by the user. In step three, the tested programs were written onto devices known as Programmable Read Only Memories (PROMs), which controlled the microprocessor's operation. These instructions could not be altered without using a special device to erase the PROM completely.

Some industry sources believed that the second step in preparing the microprocessor for use (programming it), represented an opportunity for distributors to increase their role in the electronics industry by providing services in educating and helping customers to perform this step more effectively. As a result, by 1975 about half of the top twenty-five distributors had set up microprocessor centers where a customer's engineers could come to set up a hardware configuration for microprocessor application studies and then to write and test the software. These centers each required an investment of approximately $30,000 each to establish and were expected to speed the introduction and development of the microprocessor. Some industry executives expected an additional benefit to the distributor to come when the customer bought from the distributor the microprocessors themselves, input/output devices, etc., for the application developed in the distributor's centers.

However, there were critics in the industry who argued that it was not the business of the distributors to educate the customers and that distributors had "fallen in love" with the microprocessor rather than view it objectively.

Passive Components

Passive components did not emit electrons themselves but influenced the behavior of electrons that had been emitted by active components. The four principal types of passive components were:

Component Type	Functions
Resistors	meter electron flows, convert electrical energy into heat energy, and control current
Capacitors	store electrical energy
Inductors and transformers	even out the flows of electric current and change the voltage level
Connectors	serve as a link between electronic devices, and transport electrical signals

All four types of passive components were simple to produce (relative to the manufacture of active components), had been on a technical plateau for many years, and were considered standard "off-the-shelf" items.

Product Standardization

A high degree of product standardization existed among the product lines of competing suppliers of both passive and active components. This standardization was especially pronounced in the passive component lines, where specifications had been fixed for many years. In the active component lines some technological differences existed near the upper performance limits of a specific electronic device. However, such differences among different suppliers' products were important only in a very small number of applications.

Customer Profile

The customer base served by distributors was exceptionally diverse. An individual distributor dealt with as many as 40,000 customers each year, with many purchasing only a few times per year. Customers tended to be small electronic firms that could not buy directly from component suppliers as a result of their small order sizes. However, even multibillion-dollar firms such as Raytheon, General Electric, and Westinghouse used distributors for rush orders and the purchase of certain low-volume items that suppliers preferred not to service themselves. Customers were located nationwide but tended to concentrate in a number of important centers for electronics industry activity (Exhibit 1-3). Most customers of distributors were original equipment manufacturers (OEMs) using electronic components in the manufacture of everything from burglar alarms to sophisticated missile guidance systems. A very large customer might account for 1 to 2 percent of the typical distributor's total sales, while the smallest customer might have placed only a single $25 order. There were a growing number of small customers in the industry as electronics technology spread to more and more applications.

Customers tended to be very knowledgeable

about the product, and components were usually standardized items bought to specifications. The buyer was primarily interested in price and delivery, and maximum retail prices were known to buyers, thanks to price books published by manufacturers. Buyer loyalty to a distributor was transient (one distributor described it as a "what have you done for me today?" attitude).

The particular buying procedure followed by customers varied according to the nature of the buyer firm. Buyers could be approximately grouped into three categories:

• *Large professionally managed companies with a separate purchasing department.* These companies used a professional buyer, who was usually required to solicit bids from distributors. This buyer was often solely responsible for component purchases and tended to be well informed about them. The number of bids solicited varied as a function of the dollar value of the order. For example, a $500 order might require two documented bids, a $1,000 order three documented bids, and so on up to the spending authority of the buyer. As a result of this process, large buyers tended to be very price-sensitive. Recently some large customers had moved toward annual buying contracts with a group of the larger distributors. Annual buying contracts did not guarantee a minimum level of purchases from any one distributor but guaranteed that all orders would be placed with one of the distributors on the approved buying list. The contracts also generally stipulated a rising rebate level as purchases increased. Large firms selected distributors based on the presence of local stocking locations, local sales offices, important supplier franchises (such as Texas Instruments, Fairchild or Motorola), product expertise, financial strength, and a "reasonably" thought-out plan for servicing the buying firm's needs.
• *Medium-size firms without an independent purchasing department.* In this type of company, orders were usually placed by a clerical or administrative employee who was not a specialist in component purchasing. The employee followed selection criteria specified by the chief engineer, production manager, or administrative manager. In these circumstances the process

was very mechanical since the buyer could not deviate from the instructions given. Quotes were then reviewed by the individual who initiated the request for bid before an order was placed.
• *Small companies.* In these instances the president and chief engineer themselves would request the bids and place the order. These firms often did the most shopping around for the best price.

Selling and Marketing

Distributors used a combination of field salespeople, product specialists, limited cooperative advertising, and product catalogs to promote their services.

The function of the field sales force was to call on current and potential accounts to push the services and product lines offered by their firm. The salespeople were not technically trained and had no formal technical background. They usually had previous sales experience that involved extensive client contact.

The product specialists were responsible for the marketing functions, such as pricing and promotion planning. Product specialists were typically former purchasing agents. They also received little or no formal training and had nontechnical backgrounds.

Cooperative advertising and product catalogs were the primary media used by the electronic component distributors. Advertising had just recently become an important promotion tool for the larger distributors.

No distributor employed an engineering staff to answer the technical questions raised by its customers. The distributors did disperse technical material supplied to them by the component manufacturers and referred customers to manufacturer technical personnel.

Distributor Operations

The day-to-day operations of a distributor consisted largely of order processing and shipping of components. Industry executives used terms such as "order/paper processing factory" to describe a distributor's home office operations. The order process flow could be generalized as follows:

- The request for a bid was received by an "inside salesperson"[2] over the telephone for a certain type, quantity, and mix of components. The salesperson looked up the current price for the components on the spot and gave a bid to the customers.
- If the bid was not accepted because of price, the salesperson could refer the customer to a manager for rebidding.
- If the bid was accepted, then an order to remove the components from inventory was prepared and forwarded to inventory control.
- Warehouse personnel selected the specified items from the thousands of cardboard boxes lining the shelves in the warehouse, placed the components in a plastic bag, and forwarded the order to packing and shipping. If an item was not in stock (because physical inventory frequently differed from stated inventory), then the sales representative was notified so that the customer could be informed and asked if another product was satisfactory.
- The packaging and shipping department shipped the orders.

The actual process varied a great deal depending upon the size of the distributor; in extremely small firms the president sometimes did all of the order-processing functions personally.

Order processing was made complex by the large number of small orders received by a distributor. Orders averaged approximately $150–$250 in size, with the average shipment approximately one-half the average order. Thus a $50 million distributor would process approximately 200,000 orders and 400,000 shipments per year. Order processing was further complicated by frequently changing prices on items held in inventory. This was more common for active components because of the pricing policies of firms following the learning curve in the hope of gaining additional market share, but it affected the entire product line.

Most distributors operated from a central ware-

---

[2] An inside salesperson was a distributor salesperson who was located at the distributor's home office and took customer orders over the telephone. The inside salesperson was authorized to initiate a sales invoice on behalf of the distributor. Less than 2 percent of the orders were submitted through the field sales force.

house facility plus a series of remote "stocking locations," as they were referred to in the parlance of the industry. A stocking location was a remote warehouse containing high-turnover components dedicated to a particular marketing area. Nonstocking locations were field sales offices without a dedicated warehouse. The number of stocking locations had declined in the several years prior to 1976, as the 1975 sales decline prompted distributors to close marginal stocking locations and the growth in computer-based order entry and inventory management systems permitted better coordination between a central warehouse and regional markets. Some distributors believed that a fully computerized system would theoretically permit a single warehouse facility to be used in conjunction with air freight shipping, though other distributors felt that the presence of a stocking location was an important marketing tool.

The bulk of the distributor's order-processing functions were handled by clerical-level personnel with minimal direct supervision. Most distributors had very lean management teams, often consisting of only the owners of the firm.

Industry observers believed that few economies of scale existed in the order-processing operation. Some economies of scale were thought to exist for the largest distributor within a specific product line. The economies resulted from higher inventory turns, improved expertise in the product line, and increased consumer awareness of the distributor as the leading source of information about the line and holder of the largest inventory of it.

Active Component Manufacturers

The active component (semiconductor) manufacturing industry was highly concentrated, as shown in Exhibit 1–4. Approximately 60 percent of the market was accounted for by Texas Instruments, Motorola, Fairchild Camera, and National Semiconductor. Texas Instruments and Motorola had total sales in excess of one billion dollars, while Fairchild Camera and National Semiconductor were somewhat smaller. All the major firms were growing rapidly.

Industry surveys indicated that distributors handled 15–30 percent of a semiconductor manufacturer's sales. Distributors were given "franchises" to sell a supplier's products either regionally or nationally. However, franchises did not give distributors exclusive rights to an area, nor did they provide any real protection for the distributor against competition. It was not uncommon for a supplier to set up competing franchises if individual distributors began to account for more than 10–15 percent of its sales through distributors in a given area. Recently, leading distributors, such as Cramer Electronics and Hamilton/Avnet, had begun to aggressively use cooperative advertising with major suppliers. This was a relatively new development in distributor–supplier relations in active components, and its long-term effects was still uncertain.

The semiconductor industry was strongly influenced by the presence of (and belief in) a strong learning curve effect, which meant that costs tended to decline as volume increased. It was estimated that costs fell 27 percent every time cumulative volume doubled. Semiconductor manufacturing was a process in which labor could be and was readily replaced by capital. Capacity additions in the industry tended to occur in large discrete chunks rather than spread evenly over time. Texas Instruments, the industry leader, was well known for its aggressive business strategy of bringing new capacity onstream in anticipation of future market demand to ensure that its total cumulative production volume was the highest. As long as the learning curve operated, this made its unit cost the lowest of all manufacturers. It was not uncommon for market shares in the industry to change rather often as manufacturers opened new and larger production facilities. Vigorous price competition was the rule in the industry.

In addition, the active component manufacturing industry had a history of rapid technological change. There was active technological competition among firms in the industry, and spinoff firms, founded when scientists and engineers left the larger, more established companies, were not uncommon. The most recent example of this was Intel Corporation. Formed in 1968 by one of the founders of Fairchild Camera, Intel invented the microprocessor and had seen its sales rise from $556,000 in 1968 to $130 million in 1974.

Passive Component Manufacturers

The suppliers of passive components were very different from the suppliers of active components. They were generally smaller, more conservative, and older. A major manufacturer of capacitors was Sprague Electric Company. Founded in 1926, Sprague had sales of $162 million in 1975, of which 90 percent was capacitors. The leading connector manufacturer was Burndy Corporation. Burndy manufactured more than 80,000 different types and sizes of electrical connectors, ranging from cast connectors weighing several hundred pounds to microminiature connectors weighing a few grams. Burndy had sales of $120 million in 1975, of which 90 percent was connectors. The leading resistor manufacturer, Allen-Bradley Corporation, was privately held. Industry sources estimated Allen-Bradley's 1975 sales of resistors at $150–$200 million.

Distributor–Supplier Relations

The operating relationships between distributors and suppliers varied depending on whether the suppliers were active or passive component manufacturers.

Active Component Suppliers

Many distributors believed that the active component suppliers had never really understood or appreciated the role of distributors in their sales effort. Distributors viewed these firms as run by individuals whose primary training and orientation were scientific and not as managers. Distributors complained that they were treated as a necessary evil rather than as an inexpensive and efficient method of servicing a national market without having to build or maintain a captive sales force. Active suppliers believed that their efforts had created the product, according to leading distributors, and that no one but themselves should receive the profits that resulted. This reasoning was used by distributors to explain the aggressive and sometimes hostile competition between the suppliers and the distributors. This conflict took a number of forms:

- As new components gained acceptance and moved into the growth stage of their product life cycles, the dollar value of the orders for them increased. At a certain point, suppliers began to compete directly against their own distributors for the larger orders, with the result that distributors were continuously losing the larger orders to suppliers.
- There was a lack of channel loyalty between suppliers and distributors. Suppliers transferred their franchises to other distributors if the existing ones did not measure up and created competing franchises if a distributor became too large in a given marketing region. Distributors stocked and promoted competing product lines. Supplier reaction to the industry's sales decline in 1975 was to aggressively open new franchises wherever they could find takers. Suppliers justified these actions as keeping production high and reducing unit costs, while the attitude of the distributors was that the suppliers "panicked."
- Suppliers published suggested retail price directories, which were sent to all component endusers. The price list established a firm price ceiling in the market place. However, minimum price levels were not guaranteed by the suppliers except for new products, and on these only for the first six months. In addition, distributors expressed the feeling that the "pricing breakpoints" at which volume discounts were given to customers, mandated by the suppliers, were irrational and were simply holdovers from the first pricing formula used for transistors. Distributors attempted to bargain with suppliers over their purchase price, which was based on the annual volume. The very largest distributors for a supplier might secure an additional discount of 1 percent from the price paid by other distributors.
- Distributors believed that it was the job of the suppliers to educate the market place when a new product was introduced or a new application for an older product was found. In many instances, most notably the microprocessor, distributors complained that the suppliers had not adequately performed this task. The resulting education gap had been left to the distributors to fill.

Passive Component Suppliers

Distributors' relations with the passive component suppliers were quite different from those with active suppliers. Passive suppliers were described by industry sources as more "mature" organization men who had been through several business cycles and were better equipped managerially to cope with bad times. While approximately 15–30 percent of the sales of a typical active supplier passed through distributors, as much as 75 percent of a typical passive supplier's output would be sold by distributors, and some very small passive suppliers sold all of their output through distributors. In general, relations between passive suppliers and distributors were described as cordial and businesslike.

Competition

The electronic component distribution industry comprised a few large national firms in addition to hundreds of small companies serving narrow regionalized markets based on personal business contacts. Smaller firms tended to have low fixed overhead and offered a high level of personal service to the customers based on technical support and product knowledge. They relied on a strategy of price-cutting to gain sales volume. However, these small regional distributors had been losing ground to the top twenty-five companies for the last ten years.

Exhibit 1–5 gives the total sales of electronic components sold by distributors and the share accounted for by the top twenty-five firms from 1971 to 1975 with estimates for 1976. In 1974 the top twenty-five firms accounted for 71 percent of the industry's sales, up from 35 percent ten years previously. The market share of the top twenty-five companies rose to 86.5 percent in 1975 despite the 21 percent decline in total industry sales, as small "garage" distributors went out of business.

Exhibit 1–6 presents data on the top twenty-five firms as of 1975. The range within the group was most dramatic. The two largest firms accounted for

29.7 percent of the industry's sales while the top five accounted for almost 46 percent. Industry financial characteristics and financial performance are given in Exhibits 1-7 and 1-8.

The industry, despite the increased concentration, did not have a true market leader. Industry executives believed that many of the problems of the industry, especially those involving reduced profitability due to price cutting, were entirely self-inflicted.

Competitive Strategies

Among the top twenty-five distributors a range of competitive strategies had been adopted. Four representative firms are briefly described below, and the financial performance of the three which were publicly held is summarized in Exhibit 1-9.

Jaco Electronics. Jaco carried a limited product line consisting almost entirely of passive components. It distributed from two stocking locations, supported by a sales force of eighty-eight individuals and a computerized order entry and inventory management system. Jaco usually purchased all or nearly all the production output of small suppliers.

Jaco attempted to minimize fixed costs, and its small number of locations reflected its desire to maximize control of inventory levels. Components were shipped by air freight to ensure delivery in twenty-four hours. Jaco's management team consisted of Joel and Allan Girsky, plus two field sales managers. The Girsky brothers maintained a very high profile in the industry and had gained notoriety for the passive component manuals they developed for the military.

Diplomat Electronics. Diplomat's product line consisted of 97 percent semiconductors. It distributed nationally from fourteen stocking locations but concentrated the bulk of its sales efforts in the New York Metropolitan region. Diplomat's sales effort was primarily directed toward other smaller distributors and original equipment manufacturers and was based on extensive knowledge of semiconductor product lines. Diplomat had no computer-based systems.

Cramer Electronics. Cramer Electronics was the second largest component distributor in the United States. Cramer stocked an inventory of approximately 265,000 items covering the entire spectrum of active, passive, and electromechanical components in addition to such items as pliers, soldering guns, and fuse boxes. Cramer maintained twenty-nine stocking locations throughout the United States and had subsidiary operations in the United Kingdom, Italy, Australia, and Canada. It had the largest outside sales force in the industry and had recently introduced computerized order entry and inventory management systems. Cramer also marketed the Cramer Kit (a microcomputer kit ready for assembly by the customer).

Hamilton/Avnet Corporation. Hamilton, the leading distributor in the industry, was a wholly owned subsidiary of Avnet Corporation. Hamilton stocked fewer items in its inventory than Cramer Electronics, but more than either Jaco or Diplomat Electronics. The largest portion of its sales was in active components and connectors, which had both been especially rapid growth lines in the 1970s. Hamilton stocked a variety of passive components and electromechanical devices, however. Hamilton was known for having one of the most aggressive sales programs in the industry with the largest number of stocking locations (thirty-two) and a field sales force of 225. Hamilton was also known in the industry to use price-cutting as a competitive weapon to gain sales. It used manual systems for order processing and inventory control.

Unconsolidated financial data for Hamilton were not available, but Hamilton's $206 million in sales (in 1975) provided 40 percent of Avnet's total sales. Hamilton was acquired by Avnet in 1972 and had gone from a position roughly equal to Cramer Electronics to a leadership position in the industry in terms of sales. Industry observers believed Hamilton was profitable and that the task of raising capital was made easier by its relationship with Avnet.

Recent Recession Experience

In 1975 the electronic components industry experienced its worst general recession. Distributors were caught with inventories far in excess of their immediate sales requirements and were hit by rapidly escalating fixed costs due to inflation. Therefore, the impact on profits and cash flow was even greater than the sales declines for most distributors. The actions of the manufacturers did not help the distributors. When confronted with already oversupplied channels of distribution, firms such as Texas Instruments sought aggressively to open new franchises. Passive suppliers reacted quite differently, working with their distributors to reduce inventories in the channels to a level sufficient to satisfy the reduced demand.

By mid-1976 distributors believed that the recession had run its course. Inventory levels in the industry had been reduced to a minimum, and a sales increase of 15 percent or more in 1976 was likely. Of immediate concern to the existing distributors was the effect of the "recession-born" franchises on the market. Some distributors believed that these new entrants would begin price-cutting to gain volume as the economic recovery got under way, with the possible effect of keeping profits at recession levels for the distribution industry.

Future Outlook

Capital Availability. Unless the industry could generate additional cash flow through improved profitability, the lack of adequate financial support at "livable" interest rates could impact the rapid rate of growth the industry had enjoyed in the past. This pattern could be accelerated by a move to more capital-intensive projects, such as computerized inventory control and order entry systems. Joel Girsky, Vice President of Jaco Electronics, made the following projections in a speech to an industry association:

> If we say distribution will gross 30 percent in that year [1980], and we won't, past history proves that; and we turn over inventories three times, and we won't, past history proves that; and we earn 2.5 percent net after (tax), and we won't, past history proves that; look at what we have in absolute numbers: an inventory of $980 million, receivables of $700 million and after-tax profits of $105 million. If we also say that the combined sales for years 1975–1979 equal $12.5 billion and the net after-tax profit reaches an average of 2.5 percent, and remember what I said about past history, the combined profits are $132 million. Add the $105

million for 1980, and we are short 360-some-odd million dollars to fulfill our obligations in inventory and receivables.

That is right, short over 360 million dollars. And that, my fine feathered friends, is being overaggressive in profits and inventory turns. If reality applied, the shortage number would be, in round numbers, 875 million dollars.

Supplier Integration. Texas Instruments began to move toward a system of company-owned and -operated distribution centers. While Texas Instruments had long had a captive distribution company, T. I. Supply, its role was expanding. In addition, Texas Instruments' stated objective was to build a viable consumer franchise for both its electronic components business and such consumer products as the electronic calculators and wristwatches by opening retail stores.

Services. There was a move among the distributors, going beyond supplier pressure, to perform more services. This was especially true with the advent of microprocessors. Customers were still unfamiliar with the technology of microprocessors and required help in configuring, programming, and testing them. Some distributors were packaging kits from components and selling them as an aid for OEMs and other customers to understand the technology of microprocessors. Initial evidence indicated that these kits had not gained the market acceptance first hoped for. Other distributors had gone into packaging digital clock kits, aimed primarily for the hobby market.

Management Infrastructures. The larger distributors were in the process of developing, testing, and installing modern computerized management information systems that they hoped would provide more control over their businesses. The main reason that the industry spoke of "margins" instead of "contribution" was not a lack of management familiarity with the terminology but a lack of useful information. Indeed, even with the computerized systems, determining the variable costs associated with each of the many thousands (up to 250,000 and more) of items sold would be a difficult task. One large distributor had spent approximately $6 million to $8 million and four years developing its computer system. The distributor projected annual operating (fixed) costs for the system at about $2 million.

Microprocessors. This innovation represented a third generation of electronics technology that was still in the early stages of its product life cycle. Distributors had enjoyed better than average margins on the microprocessor units they had sold.

Effects of the Japanese. It was anticipated that the large Japanese manufacturers of active electronic components would enter the United States market in the near future. It was estimated by industry sources that they could take as much as 15 percent of the market from major U.S. firms. The effect of such a broadening of the supplier base was a major question for the distributors.

The Japanese firms that had entered other U.S. industries (such as automobiles, radios, television and stereo components) began with a low-price, high-volume business strategy. Whatever the pattern of market entry to be followed by the Japanese semiconductor manufacturers, the role distributors would play was yet to be determined.

EXHIBIT 1-1. *Total U.S. Electronic Component Sales and Portion Sold by Distributors (thousands of dollars)*

	1968	1969	1970	1971	1972	1973	1974	1975	Estimated 1976	Estimated 1977	Projected 1985
Total U.S. sales	4,000	4,300	4,250	4,175	4,622	6,010	6,400	4,785	7,100	8,030	17,666
Sales by distributors	740	800	885	937	1,040	1,350	1,400	1,100	1,400	1,810	5,600
Percent sold by distributors	19%	19%	21%	22%	23%	17%	22%	23%	20%	23%	32%

SOURCES: National Credit Office and Cramer Electronics.

EXHIBIT 1-2. *Microprocessor Sales Projections*

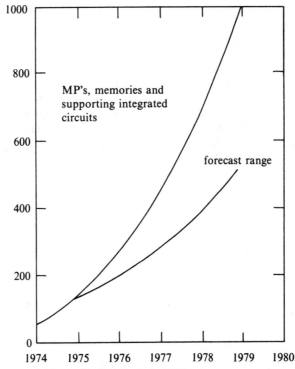

SOURCE: *Business Week,* March 1, 1976.

EXHIBIT 1-3. *Major Active Component Markets, 1975*

Area	1975 Sales (in millions)	% of Total
Total U.S.	$3,060.1	100%
By State		
California[a]	671.1	22
New York	569.3	19
Texas	316.9	11
Massachusetts	190.3	6.2
Ohio	174.3	5.7
Illinois	150.7	5.0
Pennsylvania	147.6	4.8
New Jersey	88.0	3
Florida	68.4	2.3
Michigan	69.3	2.3
Total of 10 largest states	$2,445.9	81.3%
By Region		
New England	225.6	7.37
Mid Atlantic	804.8	26.30
South Atlantic	217.7	7.11
South Central	443.1	14.48
East North Central	455.2	14.88
West North Central	140.1	4.58
Mountain	46.1	1.51
Pacific	727.5	23.77
Total	$3,060.1	100.00%

[a]California accounts for 43 percent of the U.S. integrated circuit market and 30 percent of the U.S. semiconductor market.

SOURCE: National Credit Office Study of the Electronic Component Distribution Industry, 1975.

EXHIBIT 1-4. *The Semiconductor Market*

TABLE A. Total U.S. Market for Semiconductors (*dollars in millions*)

1972	1973	1974 (est.)
$1,524	$2,017	$2,324

SOURCE: *Electronics,* January 10, 1974, p. 98.

TABLE B. Estimated Market Shares of Top Four Semiconductor Manufacturers in 1973

Firm	Market Share	Cumulative Market Share
Texas Instruments	22%–27%	
Motorola	15%–18%	37%–45%
Fairchild Camera	10%	47%–55%
National Semiconductor	5%–8%	52%–63%

SOURCE: H. C. Wainwright report, "Industry Review: Semiconductor Industry Trends," August 1973, p. 12.

TABLE C. Estimated Total Sales and Semiconductor Sales of Top Four Manufacturers in 1973 (*dollars in millions*)

Firm	Total Sales	Sales in Semiconductors
Texas Instruments	$1,287	$500
Motorola	1,437	325
Fairchild Camera	351	200
National Semiconductor	99	99

SOURCES: Company Form 10–Ks and annual reports.

EXHIBIT 1-5. *Distributor Sales and Importance of the Leading Firms (dollars in millions)*

	1971	1972	1973	1974	1975	Est. 1976
Total sales	$937	$1,040	$1,350	$1,400	$1,100	$1,400
Sales of Top 25 firms	500	604	855	1,000	951	1,000
Percent	53%	58%	63%	71%	86%	71%

SOURCES: National Credit Organization and Cramer Electronics.

EXHIBIT 1-6. *Top Twenty-five Distributors of Electronic Components*

Rank	Distributor	1975 Volume ($ mil.)	Market Share	Number of Stocking Locations	Number of Employees	Field Sales Force	Ownership
1	Hamilton Avnet	$ 206	18.7	32	1900	225	sub. of Avnet
2	Cramer Electronics	122	11.0	29	1300	280	public
3	Schrueber	62	5.6	16	500	80	private
4	Kierulff	60	5.5	15	560	70	sub. of Ducamman, Inc.
5	Wyle	55	5.0	6	400	50	sub. of Wyle labs.
6	Pioneer	45	4.1	18	400	50	publicly held
7	Arrow	41	3.7	14	321	107	div. of Arrow. Electronics
8	Newark	39	3.5	19	547	115	sub. of Premium Ind. Corp.
9	Hall Mark	33	3.0	18	338	118	public
10	Jaco Electronics	30	2.8	2	250	88	public
11	Sterling	28	2.5	12	1200	n.a.	div. of Sterling Elec. Corp.
12	TI Supply	25	2.3	19	n.a.	n.a.	sub. of Texas Instru.
13	Marshall	25	2.3	17	485	88	public
14	Harvey	21	1.9	5	240	36	public
15	Wiltshire	20	1.8	8	220	40	div. of Wiltshire Oil
16	Weltherford	15	1.4	11	200	38	public
17	Senicum Specs	15	1.4	16	160	35	private
18	Milgray	15	1.4	9	179	41	public
19	Powell	14	1.3	5	266	43	private
20	Allied	14	1.3	3	420	80	div. of Tandy Corp.
21	Diplomat	14	1.3	11	120	45	public
22	Bell	13	1.2	4	100	25	div. of Bell Industries
23	Artrex	13	1.2	12	450	20	div. of Artrex, Inc.
24	Laser Link	13	1.2	6	130	50	public
25	Zeus	12	1.1	3	85	22	private
	Total Top 25	951	86.5				
	Total Industry	1100	100.0				

SOURCE: *Electronic News*, December 1, 1975.

EXHIBIT 1-7. *Composite Income and Balance Sheet Data of Electronic Distribution Industry*[a], *1972*

Income Statement (*in percent of net sales*)

	Lower Quartile[b]	*Median*	*Upper Quartile*
Net Sales	100%	100%	100%
Cost of Goods Sold	75.8	73.8	70.8

Balance Sheet (Median Values) (*in percent of total assets*)

Assets		*Liabilities*	
Cash & Securities	4.9%	Accounts & Notes Payable, Trade	23.1%
Accounts Receivable Net	31.1%	Other Notes Payable, Due Within Year	5.4%
Inventory	51.7%	All Other Current Liabilities	7.4%
Other Current Assets	5.0%	Total Current Liabilities	35.9%
Total Current Assets	92.7%	Long Term Liabilities	8.9%
Fixed Assets Less Deprec.	4.9%	Total Liabilities	44.8%
All Other Non-Current Assets	2.4%	Total Net Worth or Equity	55.2%
Total Non-Current Assets	7.3%		
Total Assets	100.0%	Total Liabilities and Net Worth	100.0%

[a]Based on a survey of all industry participants.
[b]Ranked by profitability.
SOURCE: National Electronic Distributors Association study performed in 1972.

EXHIBIT 1-8. *Financial Performance Ratios of Electronic Distributors*[a], *1972*

Financial Ratio	*Lower Quartile*	*Median*	*Upper Quartile*
Asset management:			
· Net sales to average inventory	4.1	5.2	6.9
· Current asset turn	2.5	2.7	3.3
Financial management			
· Total debt to net worth (%)	47	31	131
· Total assets to net worth	3.7	4.9	7.1
· Current ratio	1.8	2.5	3.3
· Number of days payables outstanding	28	40	65
· Cash discounts and purchases as a % of purchases	.8	1.2	1.4

[a]Based on a survey of all industry participants.
SOURCE: National Electronic Distributors Association study performed in 1972.

EXHIBIT 1-9. *Financial Highlights of Selected Electronic Component Distributors ($000)*

	1975	1974	1973	1972	1971
Jaco Electronics					
Sales	31,755	29,513	20,644	12,220	8,860
Assets	15,484	13,787	8,620	5,648	4,033
Equity	6,396	5,671	3,761	2,955	2,519
Net sales to inventory	3.9	3.7	4.7	3.8	3.9
Current ratio	1.5	1.6	2.7	2.7	2.6
Debt to net worth (%)	97	54	54	27	2
Diplomat Electronics					
Sales	13,720	15,468	14,641	7,253	4,603
Assets	6,739	6,969	6,683	3,324	2,084
Equity	2,871	2,656	2,544	1,543	1,160
Net sales to inventory	4.1	4.8	4.9	6.2	6.9
Current ratio	2.2	2.0	2.0	2.0	2.2
Debt to net worth (%)	52	66	42	32	14
Cramer Electronics					
Sales	122,037	155,051	121,805	88,210	60,136
Assets	63,401	75,046	54,970	47,817	36,483
Equity	21,106	20,946	17,861	15,185	14,571
Net sales to inventory	3.5	3.4	4.1	3.4	3.2
Current ratio	1.7	1.6	1.8	1.9	2.6
Debt to net worth (%)	136	166	130	155	122

SOURCES: Company annual reports and Form 10–Ks.

CASE 2
Raytheon Company— Diversification

Raytheon Company, located in Lexington, Massachusetts, was the 124th largest U.S. company in 1975 with sales of $2.2 billion. While ten years previously Raytheon had been primarily engaged in the design and manufacture of sophisticated electronic equipment sold to the U.S. government for defense applications, the company had embarked on a program of diversification that had changed its character by 1975. Fully 63 percent of 1975 sales came from commercial sources, and diversification had played a major part in Raytheon's 15 percent growth in earnings per share over the previous decade.

In the context of its continuing diversification program, Raytheon was considering possible entry into the electronic component distribution industry. As both a manufacturer of electronic components and a substantial component purchaser for use in many of its divisions, Raytheon had long interacted with electronic component distributors. Raytheon's senior management viewed component distribution as a possible vertical extension of the company's operations, which also offered the po-

tential for substantial outside sales. Preliminary inquiries had suggested that a number of independent distributors were available for purchase. Before formal approaches were made to any of these companies, however, senior management wanted to assess the potential of electronic component distribution for Raytheon and to define the best strategy for entering the industry.

History of Diversification at Raytheon

In 1964 Raytheon was a producer of electronic systems and devices known primarily for its sophisticated engineering capability, with 82 percent of its sales to the U.S. government. In response to sluggish growth and increasing unease about its dependence on the government, Thomas L. Phillips, Raytheon's president, announced in May 1975 an ambitious set of goals for the corporation:

> For more than these [past] twelve months, but at a sharply accelerated pace during the past six, we have been bringing our combined management talents to

bear on the problem of a viable strategy for profitable growth. . . . We established objectives for 1970 which will guide the planning and actions of our key managers over the next five years:

1. Double our sales, both by internal development and acquisitions.
2. More than triple our total earnings, with a substantial improvement in earnings per share.
3. Achieve a non-government sales level at least as large as our government sales this year [1965].
4. Continue to grow our international sales proportionately to total company growth. [Annual Meeting of Stockholders, 1965]

These new goals were rapidly translated into action. In 1965 Raytheon acquired Amana Refrigeration, Inc., a manufacturer of appliances, and Dage-Bell Corporation, which produced educational television equipment. D. C. Heath and Company, a major book publisher, was acquired in 1966, and over the next several years Raytheon made a number of further acquisitions in the education field. Seismographic Services Corporation, engaged in seismographic exploration for petroleum and natural gas, was acquired in 1966. Another appliance manufacturer, Caloric, was acquired in 1967. And Badger Company and United Engineers and Constructors, both leaders in the design and construction of large manufacturing facilities, were acquired in 1968 and 1969 respectively.

Though Raytheon's foray into education had proved disappointing, Raytheon's diversification program as a whole met with substantial success.[1] By 1969 Raytheon had already exceeded all its goals for 1970. (See Exhibits 2-1 and 2-2 for a description of Raytheon's financial history, and Exhibit 2-3 for the historical balance between commercial and government sales.)

After two years of more modest improvements, Raytheon announced its next five-year targets:

For the past two years, your company has been essentially on a plateau. Now, we are ready for a new period of growth and have announced new management growth goals to be achieved by the end of 1975. These call for sales of $1.8 billion, earnings per share of $3.50, a sales mix 55 percent commercial with $1 billion of commercial volume, and overseas volume at 20 percent of the total. [1971 Annual Report]

[1] All Raytheon's educational units except D. C. Heath and Company had been disposed of by 1976.

With the help of only one further major acquisition, Iowa Manufacturing Company (heavy construction equipment) in 1972, Raytheon once again exceeded its goals a year ahead of schedule. While goals for 1980 had not been publicly announced as of mid-1976, Thomas L. Phillips commented on the need for further diversification in order to sustain the company's historic rate of earnings growth:

I believe a 15 percent annual profit growth will be difficult with our present mix, even though we have some very fine growth businesses. . . . To sustain a 15 percent rate of growth, I think we would have to rely in part on sound acquisitions. We continue to look for such acquisitions, but we're being very selective. [1975 Annual Meeting of Stockholders]

Diversification Approach

Exhibit 2-4 gives the broad objectives and criteria for Raytheon's acquisition program in 1976. Robert Seaman, Raytheon's Vice President for Planning, elaborated on the philosophy of Raytheon's diversification program:

We try to avoid highly structured diversification guidelines. Irrespective of what we currently do as a company, we look at a diversification opportunity as a separate business and judge it as such. We will operate in any business area that meets our criteria. Our criteria are not so much the ROI that a business is currently earning, though that is obviously part of it, but such things as whether a new business fits in with the family of other businesses we are in, whether it has a technological orientation, what it needs versus what we can contribute to it, and the intangible elements of its quality, image, corporate responsibility, and dedication to doing the "right things" for its employees, stockholders, and community.

While acquisitions in Raytheon's existing business areas were assimilated into the appropriate Raytheon division, diversifying acquisitions were established as independent subsidiaries reporting directly to Thomas Phillips, who headed the Commercial Group as well as serving as Chairman and Chief Executive Officer of Raytheon. (See Exhibit 2-5 for Raytheon's organization chart.) Phillips as well as most of Raytheon's other senior managers had engineering backgrounds, and Phillips had been a general manager in one of Raytheon's high technology electronics divisions.

Raytheon's organization structure was built on the principle of autonomy. According to one Raytheon executive:

> We are a very decentralized company. The real decisions are made at the division and group levels, not here in Lexington. In fact, the total cost of running the corporate headquarters, including the senior executives and vice presidents, is not more than $20 million a year—for a company the size of over $2 billion in sales that's not a big deal.

The lean corporate staff reflected the character of the Raytheon organization, which was sometimes discussed by managers in terms such as "no frills," and "hard work and attention to detail."

Reflecting the policy of decentralization, subsidiaries were given a great deal of autonomy in management. While subsidiaries were required to comply with Raytheon's accounting format, prepare five-year plans, and secure corporate approval for major capital expenditures, senior management did not become involved in operations except in emergencies. In the words of Robert Seaman:

> We believe in protecting those attributes that made the subsidiary attractive at the outset. We provide those resources promised. We look for quality companies with quality management, and do not change managements after the acquisition. Monthly performance reviews are held with Raytheon senior management, but there is no day-to-day "interference."

Subsidiaries had access to Raytheon's corporate staff (Exhibit 2–5) for assistance in solving operating problems. In the past senior corporate staff specialists had been detached to deal with particular subsidiary problems and had also served a coordinating role in finding the best people in the company to aid the subsidiary. While the process sometimes worked slowly because operating managers were reluctant to give up good people, transfers of technology between Raytheon units had occurred.

Electronic Components

Raytheon's principal business areas in 1976 are described in Exhibit 2–6. Raytheon's Semiconductor Division manufactured a variety of electronic components for sale both inside and outside the company. Inside sales accounted for a substantial fraction (though not the majority) of the division's sales, while the balance of its output was sold direct, via sales representatives and through independent distributors. The share of division sales through distributors was relatively small. The division had not been an important profit contributor to Raytheon and was not a major factor in the semiconductor manufacturing industry. Industry observers described the division as not being on the forefront of semiconductor technology. In addition to its U.S. operations, Raytheon had semiconductor manufacturing facilities in Europe, India, and Japan.

Raytheon's Microwave and Power Tube Division produced components for microwave applications, a large proportion of which were for in-house use. Microwave components were quite specialized and more expensive than electronic components generally, and the large majority of Raytheon's outside sales of microwave components went direct to the end user.

As shown in Exhibit 2–6, most of Raytheon's divisions were users of electronic components. The component applications within Raytheon ranged from simple uses of passive components in the appliance subsidiaries to sophisticated uses of microprocessors in the manufacture of "intelligent" or interactive computer terminals. Some divisions actually made prototype components for new uses, and Raytheon possessed the engineering capability for a broad range of component applications.

As a result of this heavy use of electronic components, Raytheon was one of the largest purchasers of components from distributors in the United States. In addition to substantial direct purchases from manufacturers, Raytheon purchases $8 million to $10 million in components from distributors annually. In 1976 Raytheon had ten electronic component distributors under long-term contract to supply components to Raytheon divisions at prices that reflect the purchasing volume of the company as a whole rather than the volume of its individual user divisions.

Electronic Component Distributors

On the basis of discreet inquiries through third parties, Raytheon was aware that a number of electronic component distributors were available for ac-quisition in 1976. These included both large and smaller distributors among the top 25 firms in the industry. While 1976 was proving to be a good year for distributors, they had typically suffered from relatively low stock market valuations since the in-dustry was little understood by the financial com-munity and far from glamorous. As a result, the market value of the stock of leading distributors was approximately at book value or somewhat below in mid-1976, with price-earnings ratios for distributors in the 1 to 5 range.

EXHIBIT 2-1. Ten-Year Operating Summary ($ and shares outstanding in 000's)

	1975	1974	1973	1972	1971	1970	1969	1968	1967	1966
Operating Results										
Net sales	$ 2,245.4	$ 1,928.9	$ 1,590.5	$ 1,465.0	$ 1,347.1	$ 1,298.4	$ 1,332.0	$ 1,255.6	$ 1,188.1	$ 960.9
Income before taxes	122.0	103.9	85.6	73.6	70.5	70.2	77.0	68.5	61.8	51.1
Income after taxes:										
before extraordinary items	71.0	57.7	46.2	41.2	38.4	37.0	38.8	34.9	32.9	25.7
after extraordinary items	71.0	57.8	46.2	37.9	38.4	33.6	38.8	33.6	32.9	25.7
Earnings per common share:										
fully diluted—after extraordinary items	4.65	3.84	3.02	2.37	2.37	2.03	2.31	2.00	1.97	1.56
Return on sales before extraordinary items	3.2%	3.0%	2.9%	2.8%	2.9%	2.8%	2.9%	2.8%	2.8%	2.7%
Return on stockholders' equity before extraordinary items	16.4%	15.2%	13.4%	12.3%	12.3%	12.5%	13.9%	13.9%	13.9%	12.7%
Financial Position at Year End										
Assets: Current	$ 751.7	$ 692.6	$ 512.8	$ 449.3	$ 442.3	$ 405.7	$ 403.6	$ 361.2	$ 364.5	$ 301.4
Property, plant and equipment (net)	230.0	186.7	148.6	136.2	128.7	133.2	116.3	91.1	78.2	63.9
Total (including other noncurrent)	1,030.7	917.8	705.8	631.1	612.5	577.3	538.8	465.7	460.0	382.0
Working capital:										
Net working capital	275.8	262.1	247.1	236.1	207.8	130.1	158.0	160.4	148.0	122.9
Ratio of current assets to current liabilities	1.58	1.61	1.93	2.11	1.89	1.47	1.64	1.80	1.68	1.69
Financial structure:										
Total debt	114.9	115.6	128.2	115.9	146.0	156.6	116.2	116.2	115.1	140.4
Common stockholders' equity	464.2	403.2	356.1	336.0	292.4	265.4	259.8	225.6	220.9	161.0
Common stockholders' equity per share (2)	30.54	26.85	23.79	21.59	19.41	17.69	16.57	14.93	13.48	12.48
Debt to equity ratio	.25	.29	.36	.34	.50	.59	.45	.52	.77	.87
General Statistics										
Total backlog	$ 2,458.6	$ 2,647.2	$ 1,421.1	$ 1,008.6	$ 936.6	$ 817.3	$ 751.3	$ 786.5	$ 699.3	$ 410.3
U.S. Government funded backlog included above	657.7	644.6	653.3	642.3	446.2	386.9	299.0	429.1	380.3	354.4
Number of employees	52,692	54,410	51,081	48,338	45,750	46,201	53,300	51,588	50,146	41,821
Research and development (company-sponsored)	42.3	41.6	35.4	30.6	32.5	28.2	29.6	26.2	22.6	19.5
Depreciation and amortization of property, plant, and equipment	48.4	36.7	29.8	28.3	27.2	26.3	22.1	19.6	16.7	12.4
Capital expenditures for property, plant, and equipment	95.5	72.8	41.0	32.3	27.1	47.1	48.1	33.3	26.5	26.6
Shares outstanding: common	15,201.5	15,014.7	14,971.6	15,564.6	14,136.8	13,766.8	14,423.5	14,347.1	14,123.9	12,115.4
preferred	—	—	—	—	932.4	1,239.2	1,259.3	770.4	788.9	792.0

SOURCE: Annual report.

EXHIBIT 2-2. *Ten-Year Balance Sheet History ($ in millions)*

	1975	1974	1973	1972	1971	1970	1969	1968	1967	1966
Assets										
Cash	8.6	12.9								
			22.4	27.2	30.0	24.7	21.4	25.7	24.3	19.9
Securities	122.2	50.4								
Receivables (net)	184.6	165.3	141.0	121.5	176.3	147.9	139.2	123.0	138.4	123.9
Contracts in progress	222.3	225.5	175.6	163.8	109.4	108.2	120.0	108.6	89.5	81.9
Inventory	208.3	232.1	167.7	132.2	115.5	117.0	115.1	110.8	107.0	99.9
Prepaid expenses	5.8	6.5	6.2	4.6	5.1	6.9	7.9	8.3	5.3	6.1
Total current assets	751.8	692.7	512.9	449.3	442.3	404.7	403.6	376.4	364.5	331.5
Long-term receivables	24.8	17.0	20.9	24.5	20.1	18.1	–	–	–	–
Investments	4.0	5.4	5.2	8.2	8.3	8.8	6.1	7.2	9.1	9.8
Property, plant and equipment (net)	229.9	186.7	148.6	136.2	128.7	133.2	116.3	91.8	78.3	69.5
Deferred charges and other assets	20.2	16.0	18.4	13.1	13.2	12.6	12.8	6.8	8.0	8.9
Total Assets	1,030.7	917.8	706.0	631.3	612.6	577.4	538.8	482.2	459.9	419.7
Liabilities										
Notes payable	14.9	27.8	41.0	31.0	57.4	117.3				
							82.8	79.5	112.5	102.0
Current portion of long-term debt	9.5	3.7	3.2	3.0	3.0	3.0				
Advance payments less contracts in progress	193.0	185.2	18.2	25.1	20.9	12.6	18.8	26.8	5.4	5.9
Accounts payable	91.6	103.4	87.6	64.3	63.8	59.6	54.6	49.7	37.7	41.3
Accrued salaries, wages	49.8	46.5	39.3	33.4	29.5	28.5	60.0	54.4	43.0	36.8
Federal and foreign taxes	50.7	19.1	21.6	10.5	22.8	17.5	29.3	(.1)	17.8	11.6
Other accruals	66.5	44.7	54.6	46.0	37.1	37.1	–	–	–	–
Total current liabilities	476.0	430.4	265.5	213.3	234.5	275.6	245.5	210.3	216.4	197.6
Long-term debt	90.5	84.2	84.4	81.9	85.7	36.4	33.5	39.3	42.6	45.5
Stockholders equity	464.2	403.2	356.1	336.1	292.4	265.4	259.8	232.6	200.9	176.6
Total liabilities	1,030.7	917.8	706.0	631.3	612.6	577.4	538.8	482.2	459.9	419.7

SOURCES: Annual reports and Form 10K's.

EXHIBIT 2-3. *Relative Sales to Government and Commercial Customers (percentages)*

	1964	1965	1966	1967	1968	1969	1970	1971	1972	1973	1974	1975
Commercial sales	18	25	34	45	42	45	50	51	52	52	59	63
Government sales	82	75	66	55	58	55	50	49	48	48	41	37

SOURCE: Company annual reports.

EXHIBIT 2–4. *Raytheon's Acquisition Program*

Objectives	• To broaden activities in existing fields and to gain entrees into new areas • To achieve above-average growth in earnings and return on investment
Acquisition criteria	
General	• Strong position in an industry with potential and desire for above-average growth • Able to benefit from Raytheon's broad technological base, products, present channels of distribution, and/or financial strengths • Quality name in its field • Management team willing to join with Raytheon and continue to run and extend their business
Financial	• Sales $25-$250 million in a business area new to Raytheon • Sales $3-$50 million in a business area supplementing our present commercial activities

SOURCE: Company documents.

EXHIBIT 2–5.   *Table of Organization*

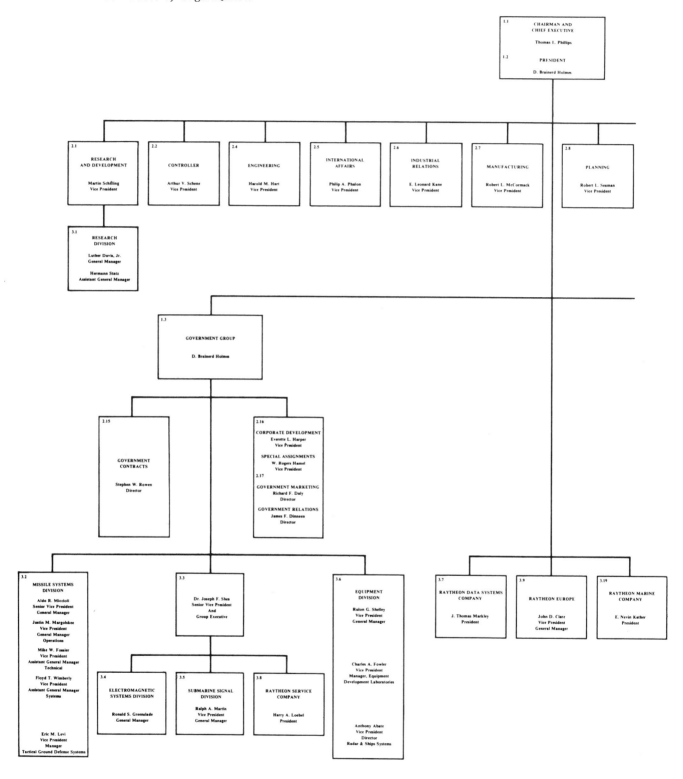

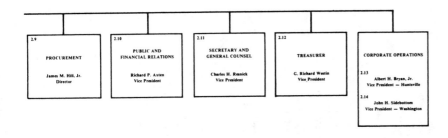

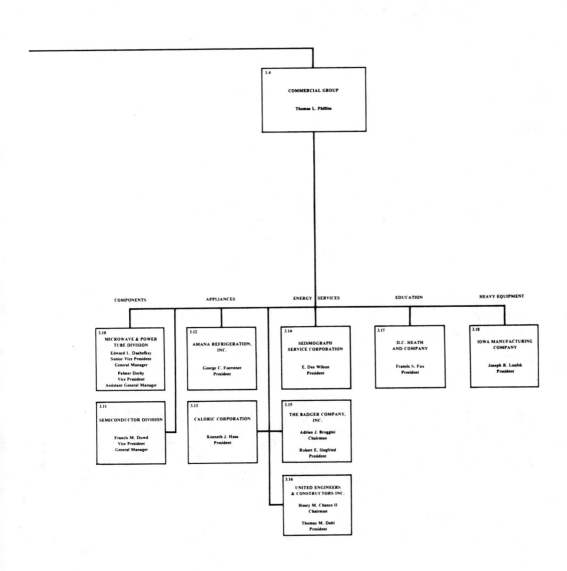

EXHIBIT 2-6. *Principal Business Areas and Products*

Business

Electronic Systems and Devices (Sales $1,233 Million in 1975)

ORGANIZATION	MICROWAVE AND POWER TUBE DIVISION[a]	SEMICONDUCTOR DIVISION[b]	RAYTHEON DATA SYSTEMS CO.[a]	RAYTHEON MARINE CO. SORENSEN CO.[a]	MISSILE SYSTEMS DIVISION[a]	ELECTROMAGNETIC SYSTEMS DIVISION[a]	EQUIPMENT DIVISION[a]
Principal Products	Microwave tubes Microwave ferrite devices and materials Microwave solid state devices and components Microwave industrial heating equipment Special microwave and electronic equipment Pulsed modulators and power supplies Magnetic devices (transformers, etc.) Rare earth magnetics High dielectric ceramics X-ray tubes and accessories X-ray image intensifiers X-ray subsystems X-ray patient handling equipment Large and small power tubes Industrial tubes Control knobs and electronic hardware Cathode ray tubes Storage tubes and display tubes Microelectronic modules Laser machining equipment Infrared detectors Receiving tubes Heat transfer devices Plastic molded products Nuclear medical scanners, cameras, data systems and gamma sample changers	Transistors Diodes Integrated circuits Monolithic memories Beam lead semiconductors Special semiconductor assemblies High frequency power modules Semiconductor chip elements	Telecommunication systems and products Commercial and scientific data processing systems Data display and switching systems Teleprocessing systems and terminals Programmable terminal systems Mini-computers Seismic data processing systems Information management systems Airline reservation and ticketing systems Digital microwave radio systems Credit verification systems Brokerage transaction systems Airline departure control systems Text editing systems Data entry systems Remote job entry systems Process control systems Fast fourier array transform processors	Marine radio telephones Depth sounders and recorders Navigational aids Radars Power supplies and regulators Ultrasonic grinders and welders	Air-to-air missile systems Surface-to-air missile systems Air-to-surface missile systems Ballistic missile guidance systems Anti-tank missiles Bomb, projectile and mine fuze systems Avionics Airborne radar systems Sparrow missile systems Hawk missile systems SAM-D missile systems Sidewinder missile systems Chaparral missile Dragon missile Missile fire control systems Fuze production Electro-optical systems Special support test equipment Missile telemetry	Electronic countermeasures Reconnaissance systems Electromagnetic warfare simulators Antennas Infrared systems Specialized receivers	Shipboard and ground radars Fire control systems Shipboard electronic systems integration Range instrumentation sensors and systems Air traffic control systems Air traffic control radars, displays, navaids and communications Over-horizon detection systems Ballistic missile guidance electronics Aerospace data systems and computers Military communications systems Photogrammetry and mapping services Wire wrap and other manufacturing services Industrial support services Laser radar and fire control systems

28

EXHIBIT 2-6. *Continued*

Electronic Systems and Devices (Sales $1,233 Million in 1975)

SUBMARINE SIGNAL DIVISION[a]	RAYTHEON EUROPE[a,b]	RAYTHEON OVERSEAS, LTD.	AFFILIATED COMPANIES[a,b]	RESEARCH DIVISION[a]
Sonar systems	Air traffic control radar video-processing and display equipment	International sales of electronic systems and devices	Entertainment tubes	IR domes and windows
Sonobuoys	Precision secondary radar		Power tubes	Surface wave devices
Acoustic communication systems	Airborne SSR transponders		Power supplies	Microwave semiconductor materials
Oceanographic instrumentation	Airborne/shipborne IFF		Diodes	Materials R and D
Acoustic signal analyzers	Airborne tacan, and instrument landing systems		Transistors	Optical and IR
Electrographic recording systems	ILS, VOR, and IFF test equipment		Ferrites	Semiconductor
Pollution control instrumentation	VHF/UHF ground-air communications		Integrated circuits	Magnetic
Coastal and harbor bottom surveys	Marine radar, loran, omega, and weather facsimile			Dielectric
Environmental impact surveys	Special military electronic systems			Refractories
	Digital display terminals			Component R and D
	Reservation systems			Microwave semiconductors
	Computers			Surface acoustic wave
	Oscilloscopes			Electro-optic and lasers
	Electric power, instrument and communication cables for industrial and military use			Radomes
	Ultra-fine wire and cables			Microwave
	Magnet (enamelled) wire			Medical electronics
	Oxygen free copper wire			
	Electrical wiring installations			
	Cable EST-sets			
	Stabilized power supplies			
	Silicon controlled rectifiers			
	Thyristors			
	Transistors			
	Diodes and rectifiers			

EXHIBIT 2-6. Continued

Energy Services ($613 million)			Major Appliances ($241 mil)		Other Lines ($159 million)		
SEISMOGRAPH SERVICE CORPORATION[a]	THE BADGER CO., INC.	UNITED ENGINEERS & CONSTRUCTORS INC.	AMANA REFRIGERATION, INC.[a]	CALORIC CORPORATION[a]	RAYTHEON SERVICE COMPANY[a]	D.C. HEATH AND COMPANY	IOWA MANUFACTURING COMPANY
Seismic exploration services to the petroleum industry Radio positioning Oil well logging services Analytical instrumentation Communications equipment Contract manufacturing	Design and construction services for process plants: Petroleum Petrochemical Chemical Phosphates Fertilizers	Design and construction services for: Electric power generating stations Steel plants Chemical plants Industrial buildings	Refrigerators Freezers Room air conditioners Radarange® microwave ovens Radarange® cooking controls Trash compactors Dehumidifiers Commercial Radarange® microwave ovens Central air conditioning and heating	Ranges—gas & electric Dishwashers Disposers Portable gas cooking equipment Patio grills Kitchen ventilating hoods	Field engineering Installation Operation Maintenance Training Replacement parts System analysis Operation research Systems integration Operation: Systems engineering System safety Human factors/training Security systems Quality assurance Communications: Engineering Propagation studies Site selection Surveys Facilities engineering Transmission, video, and control systems engineering Air traffic control systems: Planning and implementation Installations Relocations Modifications Retrofits On-the-job training Follow-on support Publications: Proposals Technical manuals Writing and editing Presentations Technical and creative art Photography Composition Printing	Textbooks General interest books Films, tapes and records	Complete portable and stationary aggregate processing plants Jaw crushers Roll crushers Impact breakers Hammermills Limemills Vibrating screens Fedders Belt conveyors Complete asphalt pavement mixing plants Asphalt mixing units Asphalt aggregate drier units Asphalt aggregate feeders Asphalt paving machines Air pollution control systems

[a]Electronic Component User.
[b]Electronic Component Manufacturer.

SOURCE: Raytheon Company literature.

30

Cramer Electronics, Inc.

Cramer Electronics, Inc., headquartered in Newton, Massachusetts, was by 1976 the second largest distributor of electronic components to industrial customers in the United States. Cramer's growth in sales had been dramatic from the mid-1960s to 1970, with sales increasing at a compound growth rate of almost 22 percent per year. Since 1970, however, Cramer's record of sales and earnings had been erratic. Difficulties were experienced as a result of the acquisition of Electronic Wholesalers, Inc., in 1971, and the general recession in 1975 saw Cramer's sales falling 19 percent and profits falling 96 percent from 1974 levels. In the first half of 1976 Cramer's sales and profits had risen considerably, spurred by a combination of improved general economic conditions, better inventory management procedures, and reduced operating expenses.

T. X. Cronin, Cramer's President and Treasurer, was optimistic that Cramer would return to its previous pattern of steady improvement. He predicted that growth would continue at 15–20 percent annually for the electronic component distribution industry and that Cramer would be able to grow at least as fast as the industry. As Cramer came out of the 1975 recession it was faced with the question of how it might best capitalize on the substantial growth opportunities electronic component distribution offered. A specific question facing Cramer was what its future policy regarding the microprocessor should be. The microprocessor was the latest technological innovation in active electronic components and represented an important potential source of sales and profits if properly managed. Cramer had experimented with the Cramer Kit, a self-contained microcomputer laboratory introduced in the fall of 1975, but the results had not been encouraging.

History

Cramer Electronics began as Hatry & Young, Inc., in the very early days of electronics. Hatry & Young was a small firm selling replacement parts to radio repair shops from a single location in downtown Boston, until Al Cramer bought the company in 1945 and renamed it Cramer Electronics. Mr. Cramer was characterized by members of present management as being "always good for a deal." He instituted an aggressive growth strategy for the company that included the philosophy of selling every electronic component or accessory he possibly could. Mr. Cramer began buying up odd lots of electronic components on a distressed basis (usually obsolete or surplus inventory of other distributors or original equipment manufacturers). These components were sold at profit margins substantially better than normal for a distributor. Mr. Cramer also expanded the company's market from retail customers to industrial concerns.

By 1962 Cramer Electronics had sales of $5.4 million and was large enough to warrant moving to larger quarters in Needham, Massachusetts, and to interest the capital markets in supplying Cramer with equity financing. In December 1961 Cramer sold 250,000 shares of stock to the public at $8 per share. However, the occasion was saddened by the untimely death of Mr. Cramer. At only forty-nine years of age, Mr. Cramer suffered a fatal heart attack while working at his desk in September 1961. Mr. Cramer's brother became president but lacked Al Cramer's leadership ability and lost the faith of the Cramer family in his ability to manage the business. The decision was made to begin looking for a new chief executive officer, and Cramer Electronic's investment banker was selected to carry out the search.

Timothy X. Cronin was Executive Vice President and Chief Operating Officer of Radio Shack when the search committee found him. Radio Shack was a major retail and industrial distributor of electronic components. Mr. Cronin was receptive to the idea of accepting Cramer's top management position, believing that his advancement at Radio Shack was blocked by recent strategic changes made by Radio Shack's president. He recalls:

> I liked Cramer because the fragmentation and dysfunctional competition which characterized the electronic component distribution industry offered an excellent opportunity for me to build a company which would be a major force in the business. My plan for doing this was through consolidating several of the large regional distributors into one national concern. The idea was to merge six to eight distributors into one firm with sales of $60–70 million which would maintain one large central inventory of components in Chicago or Kansas City, link regional sales offices together with a computer-based telecommunications system, and use airfreight transportation to meet a twenty-four-hour delivery goal. If I could do this, the combined company would have greater bargaining power with suppliers, would have better access to financing at lower interest rates, and would permit us to reach a "critical mass." In this industry there is a critical mass which is approximately $70 million in sales. This is the point at which a company can justify the need for and afford to develop and maintain sophisticated internal management and control systems. I thought the component manufacturers would welcome such a consolidation because of their desire to see a healthier distributing system develop.

Cronin developed pro forma financial statements for the combined entity and visited the target companies that were to be a part of it. Unfortunately, his vision was not seen as clearly by others. It was not without a trace of bitterness and regret that Cronin described the reactions of the company presidents he spoke with:

> One guy told me he "didn't need help from anybody to grow his company into the industry leader." Another one "couldn't even imagine giving up control of his business." After this experience, I decided to build Cramer itself into a dominant force in the industry.

Cramer set out to achieve sales growth through geographic expansion into new markets. The strategy called for an orderly national rollout from Cramer's historical area of strength: New England. New stocking locations would be opened in new markets adjacent to existing markets until all significant U.S. markets were covered. Cronin believed that this would permit Cramer's management to exercise maximum control over the business while it was growing. Cramer's first expansion move was into the New York City and Connecticut electronics markets. In 1965, to take advantage of what Cramer's management felt was the best available opportunity, the company expanded its operations into Florida. If a particular market proved too competitive for Cramer to enter entirely on its own, the company acquired existing local or regional distributors in attractive competitive situations. For example, three small firms were acquired in 1969, one medium-size firm was acquired in 1971, and another small firm was acquired in 1972.

During the middle and late 1960s Cramer's growth strategy yielded rapidly improving financial results. From 1966 to 1970 sales grew from $20.5 million to $54.3 million and net earnings from

$658,000 to $1.5 million, representing compound annual growth rates of 21 percent and 17 percent respectively. However, despite increased sales in 1971 and 1972, Cramer's profits declined substantially to $851,000 in 1971 and $600,000 in 1972. Profits recovered somewhat in 1973 and 1974, but reached only 2 percent of sales after tax, well below the 3 percent rate experienced in the 1966–70 period. This modest success was short-lived, with 1975 proving to be Cramer's worst year for profits in over a decade. See Exhibits 3–1, 3–2, and 3–3 for a summary of Cramer's financial performance.

Cramer's management offered a number of explanations for the fluctuations in its financial results. First, the acquisition of Electronic Wholesalers was supposed to expand Cramer's profile in the growing Southeast U.S. market for electronic components. However, Electronic Wholesalers had been losing money during the five years before it was acquired, and turning its operations around proved to be a slow and expensive process for Cramer. One senior manager blamed excessively slow inventory turnover for the earnings difficulties, while another senior manager believed that Cramer had simply overcommitted its small management staff in trying to turn around a firm as large as Electronic Wholesalers, which meant that less attention was given to the rest of its business.

A second cause for fluctuating results identified by management was a lack of emphasis on maintaining proper control of the business during Cramer's rapid growth phase. Until Cramer reached Cronin's $70 million sales threshold, few problems in handling the paperwork necessary to support the growing sales had developed. Difficulties in control became evident in 1972, however, while management was still involved in the turnaround of Electronic Wholesalers. The problems included an inability to obtain relevant gross margin information on product lines; mounting delays in order processing, which resulted in delayed shipments to customers; haphazard inventory management requiring time-consuming telephone calls between stocking locations to determine what inventory was at hand; and rising operating expenses relative to sales. Cramer attacked the control problem on two fronts. First, management sought to streamline existing manual methods for order processing and inventory control wherever

possible. Second, work was begun on developing a computerized system that could integrate the order-processing, inventory management, and accounts receivable functions.

The 1975 recession had caught Cramer somewhat off guard, partially because of delays encountered in developing the computer system. During the 1973–1974 business upturn inventory had grown faster than necessary to support sales. Cronin expressed the feeling that 1975 had provided an opportunity for Cramer finally and thoroughly to "clean house":

> The recession finally provided the stimulus for us to cut all operating expenses to bare minimums. We phased out over 500 clerical employees in operations during the year, and with the computer ready to come "on-line" in 1976 the size of clerical staff will not increase as sales pick up. We also closed out some of our unprofitable or marginal stocking locations, and raised the sales volume required to justify a stocking location from $2 million to $4 million.

Cronin was confident that as Cramer moved out of the recession it was in an excellent position to maximize its future profits.

> With excess inventories finally worked off, the computer system rapidly becoming operational, operating expenses reduced as far as possible and a new $30 million secured, three-year term loan successfully negotiated with a consortium of banks, we are looking forward to renewed 15 percent-a-year growth in sales, a return to stable profitability, and improved cash flow from operations.

Product Line

Cramer handled the largest, broadest line of components of all distributors. There was unanimity among senior management about the long-term value of the broad-line concept to Cramer's growth, its profits, and its ability to differentiate itself from other electronic component distributors. The broad-line concept was expressed by key executives as "one-stop shopping." Cramer's goal was to provide everything a customer would need to complete an electronic assembly. Therefore, Cramer carried everything from microprocessors and Programmable Read Only Memories to resistors, connectors, spools of wire, fuse boxes and fuses, soldering guns, and solder (Exhibit 3–4). A recent addition to the line was a complete microcomputer kit assembled by Cramer and called the Cramer Kit. In total, Cramer carried some 265,000 unique items purchased from 76 suppliers and divided into 96 distinct product lines. The price range of components in the line varied from a low of 1,000 screws for $2 to a high of $20 to $200 for a microprocessor. The average value of an item carried in inventory was 25.7 cents.

Cramer's management believed that the strategy of being a broad line distributor yielded it the following competitive advantages:

- *Customer service.* Management believed that the buyers were more likely to call Cramer knowing that they could satisfy a greater percentage of their buying needs at Cramer than at any other distributor. This was cited as a very important selling point used by the field sales force to encourage buyers to call Cramer, assuming that its prices were in line with the market. Cronin and other senior managers explained the concept as being similar to a supermarket. The customer who bought a low-margin traffic-building component would also buy a higher-margin accessory item.
- *Differentiation.* Since distributors all sold essentially the same or very similar products, the broad-line concept enabled Cramer to differentiate itself from its competitors. Management believed this differentiation would result in greater customer awareness of Cramer's name and, therefore, more telephone calls asking Cramer for quotes on component orders.
- *Opportunities for growth.* Cramer's management believed that while smaller, more specialized distributors could show high returns for a few years, they quickly outgrew the particular market segment in which they operated and were forced to broaden their product line. As evidence of this trend, Albert J. Dinicola, Executive Vice President for Sales and Marketing, cited the recent case of Jaco Electronics, Inc. Jaco, which had begun as a specialist in capacitors, had, according to Dinicola, expanded its product line to allow it to continue sales growth. Management believed that Cramer's broad line gave it access to a wider range of markets than

other distributors, which improved growth potential.

Of the 96 product lines, 26 were lines of major electronic components such as microprocessors, integrated circuits, capacitors, resistors, and connectors. These 26 lines represented about 80 percent of Cramer's sales volume. The 70 supplemental lines included such items as ground lugs, nuts, bolts, fuse boxes, pliers, and wire. These 70 lines were stocked only at the main warehouse facility in Newton, Massachusetts.

Customers

Cramer sold electronic components to approximately 45,000 different customers in 1975. Cramer's broad client base included everything from industry giants such as General Electric and Raytheon to two-person engineering firms operating out of a garage or basement. Cramer's largest single customer accounted for about 2 percent of sales, with one hundred other firms purchasing more than $100,000 each in components annually. The remaining customers purchased from $100 to more than $30,000 per year.

Customer purchasing behavior reflected the size and resources of the individual firms. In general, however, purchasing agents did not receive specific training for the job. Cramer's management characterized them as people with a high school education who had begun in the shipping room and had been promoted to purchasing. The larger, higher-volume customers had better access to market information through visits by sales representatives, the ability to support professional purchasing agents for components, and the requirement that multiple bids be solicited on most orders over $500. The larger customers had been moving toward selective purchasing agreements with a few distributors over the last five years. Cramer's management was divided on how to react to this trend. Al Dinicola and Louis Backe felt that while the 15 percent gross margins typical on large customers' business were below the usual 25 percent, the business was available and accounts such as General Electric were "too important to lose." Others, including Cronin, believed that the purchase agreements gave everything away to the customer, yielding little or no profit to Cramer after considering inventory carrying charges, operating expense, and corporate overhead.

The medium-size customers tended to be less concerned with price and more interested in the distributor salesperson's knowledge of the product line and profit availability. Management believed that this was due to the lack of specific product information available to the buyer of a medium-size firm. In addition, these individuals were often clerical employees who received no training whatsoever. It was with this type of buyer that Cramer's management felt personalities played a key role. Customers tended to develop a close personal relationship with Cramer's employees and often placed orders with Cramer for this reason.

The smaller customers were often as price-sensitive as the largest ones, since it was frequently the president or chief engineer who called Cramer to place the order. They also required more time and effort in extending and controlling credit privileges. Small accounts had to be monitored regularly to ensure prompt payment, to establish and adjust credit limits and negotiate extended credit terms if and when Cramer's management decided such extensions were warranted.

The last category of customer was termed the "walk-in." These were individuals who came to Cramer's "will call" counter and purchased a bag full of components. One Cramer executive stated: "These people are a nuisance. Servicing these accounts [less than 1 percent of sales] creates work flow, accounting, and inventory management problems not offset by profits this business generates."

Mr. Cronin described what he believed were unique features of Cramer's long-term business relationship with customers:

> As a customer's sales grow so does the volume of components he purchases. As the purchases grow larger it becomes more economical to buy directly from the factory and use Cramer for only the smaller rush orders. Cramer always loses the bulk of its customers' business, as they grow larger, to the manufacturer.

Suppliers had order size maximums above which a distributor could not service an order without the supplier's involvement or, at minimum, his knowledge. Cramer management believed that it needed the cooperation of the supplier in large orders to ensure help in meeting delivery dates. In addition, the suppliers were allowed to see where Cramer's sales of their products had been and would find out about large customers themselves. Mr. Cronin added a final consideration: "The customers will not let us get too big. Even in New England, our home area, we are only 30 percent of the market. The manufacturers want to have multiple distributors to compete for their business."

Suppliers

Cramer purchased components from the widest variety of suppliers in the industry, ranging from multibillion dollar semiconductor firms to small wire producers. Its policy was to carry the products of all major components suppliers, regardless of any overlap in their product lines. Cramer's management believed that its relationships with its suppliers were as vital to Cramer's long-term success as its relationship to its customers. The current status of these relations was described as a state of friendly aggression. Suppliers awarded and supported franchises, established a book price which tended to be the maximum, provided funds for cooperative advertising, and participated in joint sales calls on the more promising customers. Suppliers were also valuable sources of information about future price fluctuations, changes in product lines, and the status of their competition. Cramer's management frequently talked to and visited the marketing and production managers of firms such as Texas Instruments and Sprague Electronics.

In the early 1970s Cramer had taken serious steps to trim its supplier base. These moves reduced the number of suppliers from 300 to 76. The majority of the suppliers terminated by Cramer were smaller manufacturers of passive components. Management believed that the passive component product lines had been firmly established as a commodity-type item in the mind of the customer. Therefore, Cramer saw no need to inventory the products of any but the most well-known manufacturers. The decisions to discontinue product lines were made by Cramer's senior managers based on such factors as current demand for the product. T. X. Cronin had been surprised by the reaction of some of the suppliers after Cramer informed them that their product line was to be discontinued. Suddenly several of these companies were prepared to give Cramer a higher gross margin and more flexible payment terms to make their lines profitable enough to ensure that Cramer would not discontinue them. Renegotiations resulted in retaining a number of suppliers who offered the best terms.

In 1975 Cramer's two largest suppliers were Texas Instruments and Motorola. Both of these firms were suppliers of active components, and each accounted for 10 percent of Cramer's sales. Cramer's top twenty suppliers accounted for 73 percent of its sales and also included Intel among the active suppliers (Exhibit 3–5). Franchises simply gave Cramer the official right to stock and sell a supplier's product. Cramer's franchise agreements were not actual contracts specifying terms such as exclusive territories, volume minimums, and advertising support, although such items were often agreed to after informal negotiations.

Cramer was vulnerable to losing its franchise agreements with suppliers, and in one specific instance Cronin felt that Cramer's competitive position had been hurt by the loss of a franchise. In 1970, prior to Cronin's general reduction in the supplier base, Fairchild Semiconductor had dropped Cramer in response to Cramer's decision to carry the product line of Texas Instruments. Fairchild proved to be one of the more dynamic growth companies in the active component industry and the largest single product line of Cramer's primary rival, Hamilton/Avnet Corporation.

Cramer's policy of carrying several suppliers' product lines for the same type of component resulted in a significant inventory duplication, especially in the passive component lines. While the extent of the duplication was hard to pinpoint, management estimated that about one-third of the inventory was redundant. Management believed that the duplication was justified by some customers' preference for one product over another, even though they had identical or almost identical performance characteristics. This preference was manifested in orders being placed for a specific supplier's component and not for the component's performance specifications per se. One Cramer executive said, "Certain companies have had good

experience with a particular manufacturer and want to use only his components."

Distributor–supplier relationships were different for active and passive components. According to Cramer's management, passive component suppliers were more flexible and cooperative than the active suppliers. The relative stability of the passive product lines resulted in slower price changes, fewer new product introductions, and less requirement for customer support from Cramer's sales force and product specialists. Cramer's management believed that the passive suppliers had a better understanding of the services provided by distributors than the active suppliers. The active manufacturers, on the other hand, were fiercely competitive, and constantly falling prices plus the flow of new products in active components created business risks and management problems that Cramer did not feel it was being properly compensated for. In addition, the active suppliers were more insistent that the distributor maintain a local inventory of their components in each selling area and were more aggressive in competing with distributors for larger orders than were passive suppliers.

Prices were often negotiable, though within a fairly narrow range. One Cramer executive stated, "They say 15 cents apiece, we look at each other in shock and say 14.2 cents apiece, and two hours later we agree on 14.6 cents." Cronin believed that a supplier might shave the price of a component for a distributor who was important enough. Cramer's management was hopeful that the new computer would provide the management information necessary to improve its bargaining position vis-à-vis the suppliers. This information was to include items such as gross margins and movement of components by stocking location.

Selling

Cramer employed some 170 field ("outside") salespeople divided into eight regions and twenty-six divisions. Each division and region was supervised by a sales manager. The outside salespeople spent 90 percent of their time calling on the approximately sixty companies assigned to each of them. Cramer visited each of its 45,000 customers at least once during the year, with the 10,000 customers who bought something every month visited more frequently. Large customers such as Raytheon Corporation received even more intensive attention.

Cramer's outside sales representatives did not take orders, nor did they quote prices, a procedure also followed by most firms in the industry. An outside salesperson promoted Cramer's product lines, its position as a broad line distributor, and its twenty-four-hour delivery capability. Mr. Cronin described the sales representative's role as follows: "The sales representative is someone who serves as a goodwill ambassador, taking buyers to dinner and ballgames, maintaining an open, two-day communication between Cramer and the market, and serving as an expediter for the customer." Sales representatives were compensated with a salary plus a commission based on the total order volume placed by their accounts.

T. X. Cronin and Albert Dinicola both believed that an aggressive sales force was a key to gaining market share. In Dinicola's opinion one of the primary reasons for the recent success of Hamilton/Avnet was that it had the most aggressive sales force in the business. Cronin was anxious to provide the sales force with more and higher-quality sales training. He spoke admiringly of the professionalism and thoroughness of the IBM sales representatives he had come in contact with. The average Cramer sales representative had a high school education and some previous experience.

The "inside" sales force was where 99 percent of Cramer's orders were initiated, and was equal in size to the outside sales force at 170 people. Each stocking location had its own inside sales force. The primary responsibility of this group was responding to bid requests that came over the telephone from their accounts. Prices for components, especially active components, changed rapidly in response to technological advances, price cutting by suppliers, and Cramer's "deal-making" ability in the buying of components for inventory.

Cramer's management believed that the inside sales force was as important to Cramer as was the field sales force. Cronin said:

The inside sales force's knowledge of the line and mastery of the mass of minor information about the line makes these individuals invaluable to our marketing effort. This knowledge of the line is the ability to serve as a reliable information resource to the customer about such topics as what other components can perform the same functions for less money, which suppliers have been experiencing quality control problems recently, what future price changes might be, and what new products are scheduled to be released.

The inside sales force was divided by specific customer accounts, as was the outside sales force. This organizational structure was very similar to that of other distributors and had been in use at Cramer for some time. The inside sales force had little or no technical education or experience and received limited training at Cramer. Like the outside salespeople they were required to service the entire scope of Cramer's product line.

Cramer's management believed that the ability of the inside salesperson to know the intricacies of the product line formed the foundation of the subjective and personal reasons certain customers placed orders with Cramer. The specific needs of the customers were manifested in the nature of the phone calls with the inside salespersons. Small accounts frequently required more of the inside salesperson's time than did medium or large accounts. Compensation for the inside sales force was primarily salary, although small commissions were given based on percent of volume placed by the individual and achievement of the sales budget for particular product lines.

Cramer also employed a staff of sixty product specialists responsible for managing the profitability of each product line. The product specialists controlled decisions such as what level of inventory to maintain, the proper mix of items within the product line to order, when to reorder components, and, within strict limits set by top management, how much gross margin to trade away for sales volume. The product specialists were not engineers and had received little specific technical training. They were usually former buyers who gained knowledge through many years of business experience with a particular component line. Product specialists were paid primarily on straight salary with some opportunity for bonuses.

The product specialists were occasionally used to mobilize retaliation against a competitor's moves.

Dinicola cited Jaco Electronics to illustrate the point:

> Jaco decided that since capacitor technology was very stable and well defined, capacitors should be treated exactly like a commodity. They adopted the philosophy that a "capacitor was a capacitor" and began filling orders for a particular manufacturer's capacitor with anything that equaled that component's technical specifications. To the surprise of many industry people, including us, the customers accepted this practice because of Jaco's low prices. In reaction to Jaco's competitive threat, Mr. Cronin found an executive with many years' experience in the capacitor business, hired him as our capacitor product manager, and placed responsibility for combating Jaco on his shoulders.

Promotion and Advertising

The promotion and advertising activities of Cramer fell into three general categories: the Cramer catalog, price promotions, and trade magazine and newspaper advertising. Every year to eighteen months Cramer published a 700-page buyer's guide, which listed most of the products it sold. Cramer's management felt that the catalog was very useful in supporting the company's image as a broad-line distributor. Catalogs were given to customers by Cramer's field sales force and mailed to customers, if requested, from the Newton office.

Promotions were held frequently to push the product line of one particular supplier or to strengthen sales of a weak product line. For example, Cramer and Motorola would plan a month-long promotion designed to boost sales of Motorola semiconductors to Cramer's customers. Manufacturers supported the promotion with independent advertising and cooperative advertising. Promotions were usually accompanied by banners, slogans, and occasionally hats for the inside salespeople to wear. When answering the telephone the salesperson would say, "Hello, Cramer-Motorola." The inside salespeople would try to encourage accounts to purchase Motorola products if at all possible. Normally only one promotional campaign was held at a time.

Advertising at Cramer was almost entirely cooperative advertising with the major component suppliers. The manufacturer established a cooperative advertising fund equal to one-half of 1 percent of its sales through Cramer. For the majority of Cramer's suppliers, sales volumes were too small to generate an advertising budget large enough to be useful. Most ads were placed in the large industry publications such as *Electronic News* with prior approval of the supplier. Mr. Dinicola said:

> The role of advertising in distribution is to create enthusiasm for the company and convey a sense of activity to the customer. The specific benefits of advertising are hard to measure, but I feel sure that putting Cramer's name before the public is a positive move for the company.

Exhibit 3–6 gives a sample Cramer ad.

Pricing

Pricing was a particularly sensitive area for Cramer, and indeed all distributors. The suggested Book Price Lists, published by both the active and passive component manufacturers, set the maximum price a distributor could normally charge for the component. Mr. Dinicola says, "The inside salespeople are often tempted to give the components away at a 15 percent gross margin to make the sale. Insuring that a sufficient gross margin is recovered on each sale is vitally important to Cramer's profitability, and a prime target for improvement." A computer program was designed to help protect the gross margin of every item Cramer sold by rejecting any order that fell below the prescribed minimums. Before a rejected order could be booked the salesperson would have to receive authorization from a more senior member of Cramer's sales or product management group. This program was expected to be operational in the very near future.

When an order became large enough to command the interest of a component supplier the bidding became very competitive. In some instances Cramer and a supplier would work together bidding against another distributor/supplier team, with Cramer getting a certain amount of price protection from the supplier. The process was usually initiated by Cramer when a customer received a bid at a price too low for Cramer to match. Cramer then contacted a competing manufacturer and asked if they wanted to "buy" the business at the reduced price with Cramer acting as the sales agent. If the manufacturer agreed and the Cramer team won the bid, then the manufacturer billed the customer at the reduced price, and the difference between Cramer's normal price and the actual sales price was credited to Cramer's account against future purchases. Cramer's management estimated that its margins on the large orders were only around 15 percent. In general, Cramer sought to match competitors' prices but not undercut them, with Cronin believing that the component market was not particularly price-elastic.

Operations

Cramer was a paper factory processing some 1 million orders and shipping some 2 million packages per year. Cramer had been hurt by its inability to process orders efficiently, and this was the primary reason for the investment in automation currently being made.

The warehouse system was an integral part of Cramer's order-processing operations. Cramer maintained two major stocking locations, twenty-nine smaller stocking locations and four centers for connector assembly. Fifty percent of Cramer's inventory was located in Newton, Massachusetts, 25 percent was in Irvine, California, and 25 percent was spread over the twenty-nine regional warehouses. The inventory carried by the regional warehouses was limited to the twenty-six major product lines. The remaining product lines were stored primarily at Newton (a small quantity was kept at Irvine) and sent to either the customer or a regional warehouse upon request.

Cramer was currently in the process of establishing a computer-based communication system linking all of its stocking locations. The system would be able to track every component in Cramer's inventory, show the inside salespeople exactly what was available for shipment, and reorder a component once its inventory dropped below a minimum level.

Cramer's experience with computers had not been trouble-free. Once the decision to computerize had been made in 1970, Cramer contracted with its accounting firm, Arthur Anderson and Company, to do the system development work. It quickly became apparent to Cramer's management that

Arthur Andersen's design could not support the type of system they wanted. After negotiations between Cramer and Arthur Andersen's consulting group, the decision was made to terminate the contract and begin the systems development process all over again.

After this rather disappointing and unfortunate initial experience Cramer's management decided to build an internal systems and programming capability and to maintain strict control over the systems development effort. It tooks three years before Cramer was able to finish its in-house systems development effort and begin to feel the impact of computerization in its daily operations. The computer system cost between $1.5 million and $2.0 million per year to operate.

Financing

Cramer was one of the few major distributors of electronic components that was publicly held. Ownership of Cramer's stock was divided among several major groups and the general public. The Cramer family held 21 percent, most of this by Mr. Cramer's widow. Another 23 percent was held by Loeb, Rhoades & Co., who maintained a position on the Board of Directors. Of Cramer's top management, Timothy Cronin owned 6 percent and Albert Dinicola owned 15,000 shares (or 0.7 percent). The remaining 49.3 percent of Cramer was publicly held but very thinly traded. Interestingly, a large block of Cramer's stock was held in the Midwestern section of the United States because of the efforts of one stockbroker who actively followed and supported Cramer's stock.

In early 1976 Cramer's stock had been trading at about $3 per share, as against the initial offer price of $8. Cramer's management anticipated the Cramer family would eventually have to sell all or part of their holdings for tax and estate purposes. The specific timing of such a move would depend somewhat on Mrs. Cramer's health and age. Matthew Burns reflected on the difficulties distributors faced with the financial markets: "Our low stock price is indicative of the fact that the distribution industry has never been a stock market favorite and that industrial distribution is even less understood than distribution in general."

In October 1975 Cramer had entered into a three-year revolving loan and security agreement with a four-bank consortium, with First National City Bank acting as the lead bank. The agreement permitted Cramer to borrow up to $30 million in short-term debt at the rate 2.75 percent above Citibank's prime commercial lending rate. The loan was backed by all of Cramer's inventory and accounts receivable and certain cash accounts. In addition, the loan placed certain restrictions on Cramer's business flexibility. Stephen C. Stuntz, Assistant Vice President, Finance, had been the individual most involved in negotiating the details of the loan agreement and was responsible for interfacing with First National City Bank on a continuing basis. He commented on the loan agreement:

> The loan agreement has been as much of a learning experience for the banks as for Cramer. The banks had limited experience with and understanding of distribution in general and industrial distributors specifically. We have to file daily sales, inventory, and accounts receivable reports with the bank in addition to weekly and monthly summary reports. I am hopeful that as the banks become more familiar with us and our business, the loans will move from a secured to an unsecured basis, adding some flexibility to our financing alternatives.

The subject of improved inventory management as a source of funds was of great importance to Cramer. If the investment in inventory relative to sales could be reduced over the next five years, bank debt would be reduced, interest charges would drop, and profits would increase. In Burns's words, "In this business inventory turns are where the action is." It was Cramer's hope to use the computerized inventory management system it had been developing to increase inventory turns from 2.8 to 4 times per year over the next five years.

Competition

Cramer's management found it difficult to pinpoint any single distributor as being Cramer's competition. Dinicola believed that all distributors were competitors because of Cramer's broad-line strategy and geographic dispersion. Cronin also believed that Cramer competed with a wide group of firms: "We compete with other broad-line distributors on service and product availability, with regional firms

on sensitivity to the needs of the local market, and with specialized distributors on price and expertise on a specific product line." However, Hamilton/Avnet was the distributor most carefully followed by Cramer because of the similarity of some elements of its strategy to Cramer's and Hamilton/Avnet's very dramatic growth in the early 1970s.

Until 1972 Hamilton and Cramer had been approximately the same size, but by 1975 Hamilton had sales of $206 million versus Cramer's $122 million. Cramer's management attributed Hamilton's success to a number of factors. Mr. Dinicola believed that Hamilton's association with Avnet resulted in the following advantage: "Avnet has given Hamilton easier access to capital, thereby permitting Hamilton to expand more rapidly. The extra aggressiveness of Hamilton's sales force may well be due in part to Hamilton's reduced financial exposure."

Cramer's management also credited Hamilton's success to the fact that Hamilton was more specialized in semiconductors and connectors than Cramer. These two lines were very important for very different reasons. Semiconductors had been the fastest growing segment of the business over the past five years and now accounted for about 55 percent of Hamilton's sales. Connectors had always been a profitable product line for distributors because of the assembly work done by the distributor. Hamilton did some $20 million of connector business in 1975, while Cramer did not do very much business in connectors. T. X. Cronin also credited Hamilton's success to its operating philosophy, geographic concentration, and size:

> Hamilton has always paid excellent attention to the control side of its business and had avoided some of the problems we encountered. As far as I know, Hamilton still uses a manual system and has had no plans to computerize. Their ability to control is aided by the fact that they carry fewer lines than we do. Tony Hamilton [Hamilton's president] is basically a "simple guy" who runs an uncomplicated business. He has found an excellent match between his personality and distribution since this is a business of fundamentals.

Hamilton also did some $50 million of semiconductor business in National and Fairchild components, which Cramer did not carry in 1975.[1]

[1] In July of 1976 Cramer resumed selling Fairchild semiconductors.

Hamilton had concentrated on the larger markets for electronic components, especially semiconductors, such as Southern California, Chicago, and Dallas–Houston. Cronin believed that as a Southern California–based company, Hamilton had been able to capture a dominant market share in the fastest growing semiconductor market in the U.S. In contrast, Cramer was far more spread out across the country. In 1975 less than 1 percent of Cramer's sales had come from the Dallas–Houston area, which was one of the Big Eight electronics markets. Cronin hoped to correct this situation in the very near future. Finally, Hamilton was often a manufacturer's number one distributor and used its size to gain purchasing leverage. For example, Cramer believed that Hamilton gained almost a full 1 percent additional purchase discount from suppliers. In addition, Hamilton would occasionally negotiate a "very good" price on a large order for a customer. Hamilton would then buy more items than the customer needed and place the surplus in its own inventory for resale at the higher market price.

Cronin believed that Hamilton would continue to be a leader in the electronic distribution industry following essentially the same strategy as before, though Cramer's management anticipated some broadening of Hamilton's product line over the next few years. Cronin's outlook for most of the other top twenty-five distributors was far less optimistic. He expressed his opinion as follows:

> I expect concentration in the industry to continue and perhaps accelerate, forcing more smaller firms out of the business. The business will probably stabilize with four-five large broad-line national distributors pulling away from the pack, some regional firms in the larger markets and a few product line specialists. A lot of the smaller firms have yet to be tested at the $70 million threshold. Some just won't be able to make the transition. I wouldn't be surprised to see several mergers occur.

However, Cronin did not see the end of the small "garage" distributors in the industry. The low investment in plant and equipment meant that people could always enter as long as they were able to find a source of components. Cramer's management felt that such firms would be an annoyance and little more. With respect to the expected Japanese semiconductor manufacturers' entrance into the U.S. electronics market, Cronin said, "They are not here yet."

The Microprocessor

The microprocessor presented a major strategic question for distributors in 1976, and Cramer reflected the indecision in the industry. Cramer was hopeful that this latest technological innovation would be a principal source of sales growth in the years ahead. The growth would come from both direct microprocessor and auxiliary hardware component sales as well as the increased use of electronic versus mechanical devices in existing products. However, Cramer's management was divided on the role of a distributor for a $20 item against what was traditionally a 20-cent item.

Dinicola and Backe pointed to the microprocessor as a singular opportunity to use creative marketing in the distribution industry. Dinicola believed strongly that if Cramer could find a way to bring some degree of standardization to the microprocessor's usage they could gain a dominant position in this newest and fastest-growing product line. After considerable thought and the help of an outside consultant, Dinicola decided on the concept of the Cramer Kit. The kit was to be a complete microcomputer laboratory including microprocessor, packaging board, memories, and other necessary peripheral devices, testing and debugging programs, documentation and schematics, software, microcomputer dictionary, and two free hours at any one of a series of Cramer microcomputer design centers to be established across the country.

The kit was priced to sell at just under $1,000 as compared to a cost of $1,750 if all the pieces were purchased separately. In late 1975 the first advertisements for the Cramer Kit were run in the leading industry journals. The initial response was far greater than any one at Cramer would have believed possible. Some 55,000 people sent in the response card included with the ad.

Dinicola decided to follow up each response card with a visit by a field salesperson. The sales force suddenly found itself dealing with professional engineers rather than purchasing agents, who asked technical questions that went far beyond the ability of the salesperson to answer. In addition, a sales call often lasted several hours, resulted in no Cramer Kit sales, and caused the sale force to fall behind in its regular activity. The follow-up calls were terminated very shortly after they began. The 55,000 responses resulted in sales of only 500 Cramer Kits. Dinicola was disappointed with the response:

> I made a mistake in not screening the responses before spending the salespeople's time on site visits. I had forgotten how "gadget happy" the electronics industry was. However, my initial feelings about the kit remain unchanged and I think this first attempt at creative marketing was a good learning experience for me.

In the late spring of 1976 Dinicola went back to the consumer with the fourpage color advertisement and a formal screening procedure to process inquiries. "Although I can't quantify it, Cramer has gained substantial publicity from the kit," he says. "I am convinced that additional business has resulted and will result from the kit as the electronics community learns more about us."

Mr. Cronin held a very different opinion. He viewed the kit as a good idea that was wrong and a distraction for the company:

> Cramer has done little more than put together a "sack of parts" and try to sell it using a sales force that could not and would not be able to back it. The $100,000 we invested in setting up microcomputer centers has been a waste. I would probably faint if I ever saw an engineer in the Newton microcomputer center.

Cronin had definite opinions about the future of the microprocessor:

> Cramer should treat the microprocessor the same as any other electronic component. Distributors were in the business of selling pots and pans, not ovens, and our microprocessor adventure was most definitely a distraction for management. I did not feel that the task of customer education can be shouldered by the distribution industry. I want to see the manufacturers of microcomputer components invest money in education; that is where the investment should come from.

For the present Cronin was willing to let Cramer continue promoting the Cramer Kit. However, progress of the kit was to be measured on a continuous basis until a reevaluation was completed. Cronin summarized his opinions: "The microprocessor was so revolutionary that the industry fell in love with its potential. But now that so many companies, big and small, have lost so much money try-ing to promote its use we have to rethink our position."

Future Plans and Goals

Cramer's goals for the next three to five years were to return the business to stable and growing profitability, resume sales growth at about the industry rate of 15 percent per year, keep the fixed costs (especially personnel) from rising as sales volume increased, and continue the gradual phasing in of additional computer applications. Cronin stated Cramer's goals in greater detail:

> Our goal is to increase Cramer's profit after tax from its average level of the last five years of about 1.2 percent of sales to 4 percent. I think this profit goal is obtainable if Cramer can accomplish a number of tasks. First, we need to complete the computerized margin monitoring and inventory management systems. Second, I plan to hire a strong chief financial officer. Third, we need to improve the effectiveness of the sales force by more professional sales training. Fourth, we must improve the productivity of the inside sales and support personnel through a careful examination of every facet of Cramer's operations, and then develop and implement a plan of action designed to correct or improve the deficiencies. Finally, we have got to improve the product management group. We are not as good as Hamilton in this area, and I wanted to see a much more aggressive and dynamic group develop in the next few years.

Cramer's management was considering several major strategic alternatives for the future, which they did not believe were mutually exclusive but would each demand considerable management input to be successfully carried out.

Market Penetration Versus Market Expansion

Cramer was a national distributor but had not achieved the presence it felt it should have in all of the major United States electronic markets. Cronin recalled that at the very beginning of his career in distribution he was told that the eight largest markets were the key to success. Cramer had stressed geographic coverage in the past and could continue to follow this strategy by selectively making additional acquisitions in new market areas. Cramer was in the process of trying to increase its share of the larger markets through special sales campaigns and the opening of new stocking locations and sales offices. Cramer's management believed that to gain market penetration in such markets could require a long and costly effort. The stiff competition that characterized business in Boston, Los Angeles, or Chicago made "buying market share" expensive, while it was easy to buy a location in Seattle.

Future Status of Regional Stocking Locations

The computer system, Cramer's WATS line telephone network, and the growth in cities serviced by air transportation seemed finally to permit Cramer to realize Cronin's concept of fourteen years earlier of a national distributor with one central inventory. However, the willingness of Cramer's customers to accept the change was still debatable. Cronin said:

> There is a cult that holds regional is beautiful and national is nasty. Some customers are comforted by the knowledge that their distributor has a local inventory, and the regional distributors play this for all it's worth. The customer always wants to know he can have his order delivered today even though he doesn't need the parts for three days.

Cramer was uncertain if its competitive position would be damaged by converting its regional stocking locations to just regional sales offices sometime in the near future.

Private Label Branding

Cronin was eager to explore the possibility of entering into a contractual agreement with a passive component manufacturer to bring out a product line bearing Cramer's name:

> Passive components such as capacitors have very stable technology and are enough of a commodity item to permit this concept of work. We would buy components at the traditional discount given to Original Equipment Manufacturers, about 20 percent below what we buy them for, and then sell them for 5 percent less than the other capacitor lines we carry. In this fashion we could keep the 15 percent difference plus our standard margin, with little further investment required. This strategy has been most successful

for supermarkets, and I don't see why it couldn't be transferred to the distribution of industrial components. No manufacturer could refuse to accept a single order for $3 million in capacitors from a major national distributor.

Purchasing Management Company

Cramer had discovered growing interest among the larger purchasers of electronic components to negotiate long-term supply contracts with distributors. Dinicola was very interested in seeing Cramer become more active in this new business area:

> Our real expertise is in the buying, holding, and shipping of high-unit-cost, low-weight items. These supply contracts are a natural extension of our skills. The new computer system would permit the inventory related to a specific supply contract to be segregated with relative ease.

Cronin was rather uneasy about the benefits of these contracts. While they provided a relatively stable sales and profit base, the companies usually forced a very hard deal on the distributors. Cronin was uncertain about taking a 15–20 percent margin even if the level of sales was high.

Such contracts might involve either a larger purchaser of electronic components desiring to consolidate its distributor base, or a company that paid a fee for Cramer's ability to buy, hold, and deliver the components needed to meet its production schedule. In the former case, a firm such as General Electric would seek to decrease the price it paid for components purchased from distributors by dealing exclusively with six or seven national firms. In the latter case, a smaller manufacturer would be seeking to minimize working capital by purchasing components only as they were needed for production.

Vertical Integration

Cronin was interested in exploring the possibility of selective vertical integration at some future date:

> To take an example, why shouldn't we have our own wire plant? This would entail some risk and require management skill that we don't presently possess. But if distributors in other businesses could successfully vertically integrate, then we should be able to do as well.

EXHIBIT 3–1. *Cramer Electronics Ten-Year Income History ($000; years ending September 27)*

	1975	1974	1973	1972	1971	1970	1969	1968	1967	1966
Net sales	122,038	151,051	121,805	88,211	60,137	54,261	43,653	33,007	24,338	20,036
Cost of sales	92,249	113,769	91,766	67,631	44,886	40,367	32,564	24,646	18,241	15,383
Gross income	29,789	37,282	30,039	20,580	15,251	13,898	11,088	8,360	6,097	4,653
Selling, general and administrative	26,033[a]	27,551	22,544	17,876	12,493	10,038	8,022	6,045	4,366	3,356
Operating income	3,756	9,731	7,495	2,703	2,758	3,860	3,066	2,315	1,732	1,297
Interest expense	3,518	3,340	1,880	1,550	1,197	1,088	502	309	176	111
Income before federal income tax	238	6,391	5,615	1,153	1,561	2,772	2,564	2,006	1,556	1,186
Federal income tax	117	3,239	2,875	553	710	1,261	1,281	991	733	565
Net income	121.0	3,152	2,740	600	851	1,511	1,283	1,015	823	621

[a]Includes a $126,000 loss on currency translation from foreign operations.

EXHIBIT 3-2. *Consolidated Balance Sheet History ($000; years ending September 27)*

	1975	1974	1973	1972	1971	1970	1969	1968	1967	1966
Assets										
Current assets:										
Cash	2,776	2,773	1,429	1,167	432	777	1,265	840	462	571
Accounts rec. (net)	18,247	22,936	11,950	16,979	13,220	10,256	7,036	4,265	2,902	2,377
Amounts due from vendor	696	–	–	–	–	–	–	–	–	–
Inventory (FIFO or market)	35,366	44,671	29,671	25,656	18,734	16,302	12,865	8,518	6,195	4,443
Prepaid expenses	540	172	495	368	419	721	449	158	101	92
Total current assets	57,625	70,552	51,545	44,170	32,805	28,055	21,615	13,779	9,661	7,983
Property, plant & equipment:										
Land	1,083	1,078								
Buildings	3,894	2,536	2,302	2,283	2,277	2,264	793			
Furniture, equipment	2,268	1,983	1,736	1,728	1,510	942	922			
	7,245	5,597	4,039	4,011	3,787	3,206	1,741	690	454	374
Less: accumulated dep. & amortization	(1,940)	(1,587)	(1,326)	(1,230)	(975)	(495)	(387)	(268)	(158)	(113)
Net property, plant and equipment	5,305	4,007	2,713	2,782	2,812	2,711	1,327	422	296	261
Goodwill	204	241	277	323	209	296	388	–	–	–
Other assets	268	247	247	542	657	111	125	138	32	37
Total assets	63,401	75,047	54,971	47,817	36,483	31,173	23,455	14,340	9,988	7,782
Liabilities and stockholders' investments										
Current liabilities:										
Notes payable to banks	18,765	23,853	14,083	14,000	8,500	8,500	5,453	3,250	2,550	1,850
Current maturities of long-term debt	1,539	490	619	498	87	92	39	–	–	–
Accounts payable	11,863	17,869	10,445	8,129	3,540	4,136	4,330	2,711	1,560	1,172
Accrued liabilities	1,439	1,440	787	604	457	297	348	216	179	128
Accrued income taxes	79	1,417	2,500	–	–	506	655	466	568	411
Total current liabilities	33,684	45,068	28,384	23,231	12,584	12,531	10,825	6,643	4,857	3,561
Long-term debt (net):	8,567	8,902	8,508	9,129	9,165	5,275	4,570	1,750	750	750
Excess of underlying book value of net assets of subsidiary acquired over cost of parent's investment	44	130	217	272	163	–	–	–	–	–
Stockholders' investment:										
Common stock	2,166	2,105	2,045	1,977	1,894	1,675	1,389	624	576	541
Premium paid in common stock	9,118	9,027	8,834	8,444	7,705	5,926	2,754	1,474	823	627
Retained earnings	10,380	10,469	7,704	5,501	5,532	5,398	4,622	3,848	2,982	2,293
	21,634	21,601	18,583	15,922	15,731	12,999	8,766	5,947	4,381	3,471
Less:										
Treasury stock (at cost)	(267)	(262)	(250)	(250)	–	–	–	–	–	–
Deferred compensation	(291)	(393)	(471)	(486)	(559)	(632)	(705)	–	–	–
Equity	21,106	20,947	17,862	15,186	14,572	12,367	8,060	5,947	4,381	3,471
Total liabilities and stockholders' investment	63,401	75,047	54,971	47,817	36,483	31,173	23,455	14,340	9,988	7,782

EXHIBIT 3-3. *Cramer Electronics, Inc. and Subsidiaries: Consolidated Statements of Changes in Financial Position For the Five Years Ended September 27, 1975*

	1971	1972	1973	1974	1975
Working capital was provided by:					
Operations –					
Net income	$ 851,015	$ 600,195	$2,740,085	$ 3,151,898	$ 120,993
Depreciation and amortization not requiring the use of working capital..................	317,797	352,909	375,414	405,659	451,899
Utilization of acquired tax loss carry-forwards	85,118	205,378	40,517	–	–
Amortization of the difference between the book value of subsidiaries acquired and the cost of parent's investment, net.....................	(23,800)	(48,852)	(48,852)	(51,027)	(49,200)
Total from operations	$1,230,130	$ 1,109,630	$3,107,164	$ 3,506,530	$ 523,692
Proceeds from long-term debt	4,000,000	132,348	–	884,569	1,357,200
Fair value of shares issued in connection with purchased business...	1,269,856	161,772	–	–	–
Working capital and other net assets acquired in excess of cost of purchased business..............	188,069	–	–	–	–
Proceeds from the exercise of stock options	20,358	38,116	–	–	–
Total working capital provided..	$6,708,413	$ 1,441,866	$3,107,164	$ 4,391,099	$ 1,880,892
Working capital was used for:					
Additions to property, plant and equipment	$ 330,968	$ 234,583	$ 218,853	$ 1,606,581	$ 1,673,710
Reduction of long-term debt	109,740	168,565	620,671	491,279	1,691,826
Purchase of treasury stock........	–	250,000	–	11,890	5,000
Other	183,046	71,003	161,546	(40,358)	53,296
Total working capital used	$ 623,754	$ 724,151	$1,001,070	$ 2,069,392	$ 3,423,832
Net increase (decrease) in working capital...................	$6,084,659	$ 717,715	$2,106,094	$ 2,321,707	$ (1,542,940)
Increase (decrease) in working capital:					
Cash......................	$ (345,115)	$ 734,967	$ 262,285	$ 1,343,185	$ 3,802
Accounts receivable, net........	3,267,799	3,758,941	2,971,434	2,985,842	(4,689,137)
Amount due from former vendor ..	–	–	–	–	696,320
Inventory..................	2,432,266	6,921,518	4,015,366	15,000,162	(9,305,615)
Prepaid expenses............	(218,031)	(50,621)	151,499	(322,977)	367,717
Increase (decrease) in current assets	$5,136,919	$11,364,805	$7,400,584	$19,006,212	$(12,926,913)
Notes payable to banks and current maturities of long-term debt	$ (5,618)	$ 5,910,848	$ 204,259	$ 9,641,226	$ (4,039,226)
Accounts payable	(595,545)	4,588,556	2,316,581	7,423,201	(6,005,939)
Accrued liabilities	129,529	116,521	293,791	652,953	(1,001)
Accrued income taxes	(476,106)	31,165	2,479,859	(1,032,875)	(1,337,807)
Increase (decrease) in current liabilities	$ (947,740)	$10,647,090	$5,294,490	$16,684,505	$(11,383,973)
Net increase (decrease) in working capital...................	$6,084,659	$ 717,715	$2,106,094	$ 2,321,707	$ (1,542,940)

EXHIBIT 3-4. *Major Product Areas,*
Cramer Electronics

Integrated Circuits and Semiconductors
Tubes
Controls
Resistors
Capacitors
Transformers
Relays
Switches
LEDs
Miniature Lamps
Hardware
Connectors
Batteries and Fuses
Wire and Cable
Racks and Cabinets
Chemicals and Tools
Panel Meters
Test Instruments

EXHIBIT 3-5. *Top Twenty Suppliers in 1975,*
Cramer Electronics

Advanced Micro Devices
Allen Bradley
Alpha Wire
Amphenol
Augat
Bourns
Burndy
Cambridge Thermonic
Corning Glass Works
General Electric
Intel
ITT
Motorola Semiconductor Products
North American Philips
Potter & Brumfield
RCA
Rotron
Sprague Products
Texas Instruments
TRW

EXHIBIT 3-6. *Advertisement from 1976 Buyer's Guide*

At 10:43 a.m. Peter Doucet, Inside Salesman at Cramer/Newton, got into analytical instruments.

Peter didn't have to get into them that weekend. He *wanted* to. You see, Pete's typical of Cramer's dedicated professionals.

Service comes first. "Sorry, closed for annual inventory" comes second. So when the call from Baird Atomic (Scientific and Nuclear Instruments manufacturer) came in, Pete went right into action.

Baird Atomic needed 3 power transistors for three very expensive systems due to be shipped that day. But they *had* to be Motorola transistors. And they *had* to be received that same day.

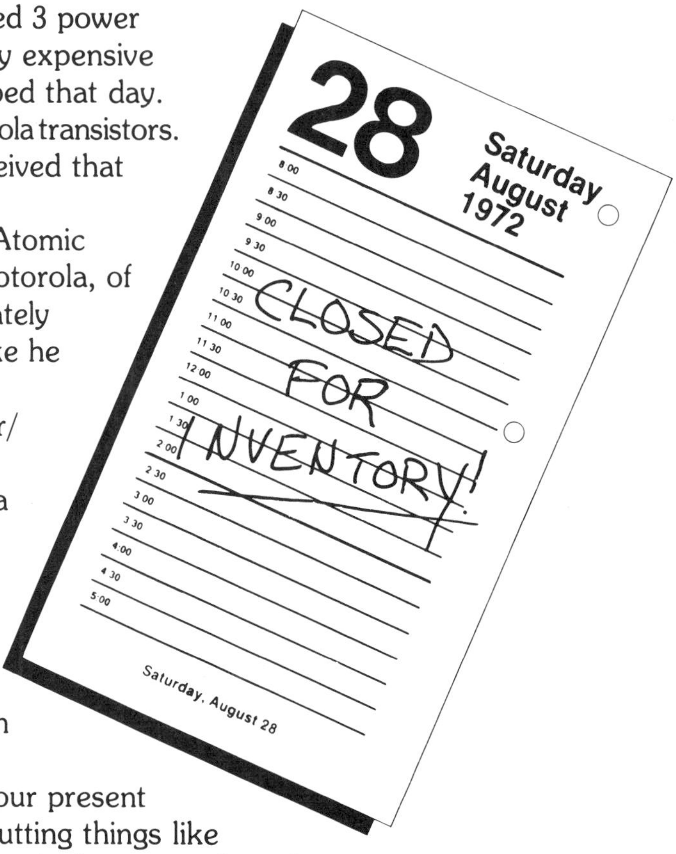

Hours later, Baird Atomic had their transistors. Motorola, of course. Because fortunately Pete knows his stock like he knows his customers.

Naturally, if Cramer/ Newton did not have a quality line like Motorola in stock, Pete would have automatically called another nearby Cramer distribution center in our $40,000,000 inventory network for an immediate air shipment.

So if you feel like your present component supplier is putting things like "sorry, we're closed" ahead of your needs, call us. You'll always come first. No matter if you're large or small. Computer, communications or aerospace manufacturer. Name it. We've got 1,400 more around the country like Pete Doucet ready to get into your business.

cramer
Our most important component is service.

CASE 4
The Oil Tanker Shipping Industry

The world oil tanker fleet traveled the seas transporting crude oil between oil-producing and oil-consuming nations, a trade that amounted to approximately 1.8 billion tons of oil in 1977. Sudden and unpredictable changes in the supply and demand relationship for oil tankers made the industry a never ending game of chance, which had been described as "the world's largest poker game." The chips in this game consisted of tankers costing millions of dollars, some of which were almost as long as the Empire State Building was tall; the players included some of the world's wealthiest and most colorful figures as well as the major multinational oil companies, international banks, and huge shipyards. The "stakes" were measured in tens if not hundreds of millions of dollars.

In 1978 the oil tanker industry was in the midst of the longest and most severe period of overcapacity and depressed rates in its more than thirty-year history.[1] Recent improvements in "spot" market rates for tankers had led some experts to predict the end of the crisis, which had begun in 1973 when the

oil-producing nations of the Middle East had tripled the price of crude oil. However, changes in the patterns of oil consumption and the severity of this crisis had led others to believe that the way business was done in this industry would never be the same again.

The Oil Tanker Fleet

The world shipping fleet comprised three principal types of vessels: tankers, bulk carriers, and liners, the latter also known as liners or general cargo vessels. Tankers could be differentiated from liners because liners carried many different types of cargo and maintained fixed schedules between designated ports of call, while tankers and bulk carriers carried a single cargo and were hired to carry this cargo between ports of call designated by the hirer. Bulk carriers and tankers were larger, required fewer crew members, and could be loaded and unloaded in less time than general cargo vessels. However, tankers could carry only one commodity, while bulk carriers were able to transport several different types of commodities—coal, iron ore, grain, and so forth—but not oil. A new category of vessel known as the

[1] Although the first ship specifically constructed to carry oil was built in Germany to transport oil along the Rhine River, the world oil tanker industry had begun with war surplus ships after World War II.

combination carrier could carry either dry bulk or liquid cargoes, including oil. The combination carrier fleet was 12 percent to 14 percent of the size of the oil tanker fleet in number and tons respectively.

Within each broad category of vessel were some specialized varieties of ships. In the tanker category there were oil tankers (the larger group); "product carriers," which could usually carry only refined petroleum; liquid natural gas tankers; and chemical tankers. These latter vessels tended to be smaller and more costly to build and operate than oil tankers. Although they did not compete directly, product carriers and oil tankers transported the same basic product in different forms. In 1978 most petroleum was shipped in the form of crude oil. However, there was some speculation that the OPEC nations would build refining capacity; if this happened, more product carriers and fewer tankers would be needed.

The oil tanker fleet represented some 55 percent of the world's shipping capacity in 1978. Oil tankers were designed to maximize carrying capacity and minimize both operating expenses and loading/unloading time. The main distinction among oil tankers was their carrying capacity, which was measured in deadweight tons (DWT).[2] The largest class of tankers were called supertankers and included very large crude carriers (VLCC) with a capacity between 200,000 and 300,000 DWT, and ultra large crude carriers (ULCC) with capacity exceeding 300,000 DWT. At the other extreme, the smallest category (called handy-size tankers) ranged in size from 20,000 to 35,000 DWT, while tankers between 70,000 and 80,000 DWT were called MST (medium size tankers). Panamax tankers were somewhat smaller and the largest tankers capable of traversing the Panama Canal. Exhibit 4–1 lists the size distribution of the existing tanker fleet in October 1978.

Other significant performance specifications for oil tankers included length, beam (width), and draft (allowable depth). Typical dimensions of tankers in the various classes are illustrated in Exhibit 4–2. In general, since tankers carried the same commodity, one tanker could be substituted for another. The size of the tanker required was determined by the size of the shipment, though two smaller tankers could almost always be substituted for one larger vessel or shipments could be consolidated for shipping in one large tanker. Tankers had a useful life of approximately twenty years. Since there had been few changes in tanker design, age alone was not a major distinguishing factor from the customer's point of view. The important components of tanker operating cost were wages, repair, maintenance, fuel, and insurance. While wages and fuel costs were independent of the age of the vessel, repair and maintenance costs rose gradually over the life of the vessel. Fuel costs were generally a function of maintenance standards, and to some extent the age of the vessel, since newer vessels had made fuel efficiency a higher priority. For insurance purposes, tankers were required to have a "special survey" every four years (in some cases 5 years), which verified their seaworthiness. Insurance premiums increased with each survey and jumped abruptly after the fourth survey.

The most important difference among tankers was their size: The draft of the large VLCCs and ULCCs limited their ports of call to deep-water harbors. In 1978 fifteen harbors could accommodate vessels of up to 500,000 DWT and twenty-two others could accommodate vessels of up to 300,000 DWT. Although a supertanker facilities was being built in the Gulf of Mexico, the largest U.S. port facilities, at Ferndale, Washington, and Richmond, California, could accommodate tankers of only up to 150,000 DWT. In addition, some vessels had specialized equipment on deck, including oversize or automated booms (for loading and unloading). Since on-shore loading and unloading facilities varied somewhat, this equipment made some vessels more suitable for certain harbors than others. Finally, crews of certain nationalities were considered more skillful, and some shipowners were known in the industry to be more reliable than others.

A recent history of accidents and oil spills involving millions of gallons of crude oil had focused public attention on the safety and environmental aspects of tanker transportation. In 1979 a number of measures addressing these issues had been ratified by the member nations of the Intergovernmental Maritime Consultative Organization (IMCO), an agency of the United Nations. These pro-

---

[2] The "deadweight" of a ship was defined as the full cargo capacity in tons, including water, fuel, and stores. A deadweight ton of cargo capacity equaled 7.3 barrels of crude oil.

posals included provisions designed to reduce the oil pollution created in the normal course of loading and unloading cargo, and pollution resulting from accidents at sea. These measures called for specialized equipment and design standards which would increase the cost of new construction and require an investment of approximately $1 million per vessel for upgrading the existing fleet. A plan that would require oil tankers to designate part of their cargo capacity for use only when carrying the sea water required for ballast on voyages where the tanker was otherwise empty, the alternative to retrofitting with specialized equipment, would reduce world tanker capacity by an estimated 20 percent. These measures were being phased in to go into effect in 1981. Industry observers believed that some but not all of these proposals would eventually become effective. In much the same way, environmental concern had stimulated government and industry efforts to create funds to cover the cost of cleaning up large oil spills.

Tanker Economics

The dominant factor in tanker economics was the decline in the cost of carrying a barrel of oil associated with tanker size. This decline resulted in part from simple geometry. An oil tanker could be thought of as a large cylinder. The surface area of a cylinder does not increase in direct proportion to its volume. As a result, a 200,000 DWT tanker was only about twice as long, broad and deep as a 20,000 DWT tanker but could carry ten times the cargo. Since construction costs varied in relation to the surface area of the cyclinder and not its volume,

construction costs were substantially reduced for larger vessels. On a per-ton basis, a 200,000 DWT tanker could be built for one-third the cost of the 20,000 DWT tanker. In 1978 a tanker of between 70,000 and 90,000 DWT cost approximately $16,000,000 at a Japanese shipyard. In addition, the size of the engine and the complexity of the machinery that ran the ship did not grow in direct proportion to ship size, and this resulted in proportionally more efficient use of fuel and power in larger vessels. Similarly, larger vessels did not require substantially larger crews than smaller ones. Construction costs for oil tankers ranged from $666 to $165 per/DWT.[3] Costs of new tankers also fluctuated with market conditions, as shown in Exhibit 4-3, and also to some extent with the number of ships a particular owner had or was likely to purchase.

An estimated breakdown of tanker operating costs is illustrated in Table 4-1.

These economies of scale associated with tanker construction and operation had led to a steady increase in the average size of tankers, as illustrated in Table 4-2.

Supertankers, the newest and largest type of tanker, had been developed to bring crude oil from the Middle East to Europe and Japan. A major impetus in the demand for these larger ships had come from the closing of the Suez Canal in 1967, which had greatly increased the distance oil had to travel in the Middle East trade. In addition, U.S. oil imports from the Middle East had increased rapidly in the early 1970s, increasing the anticipated demand for

[3] In addition to reflecting differences in size and market fluctuations, this range also reflected differences in production costs among shipbuilders, which will be discussed later in Case 4.

TABLE 4-1. Tanker Operating Costs

	Tanker of 50,000 DWT Capacity (%)	Tanker of 250,000 DWT Capacity (%)
Port charges, wages, repair, etc.	10–20	5–15
Fuel	45	36
Insurance	5–10	10–15
Capital Cost	30	40
	100	100

SOURCE: Estimates provided by a major oil company.

TABLE 4–2. Average Tanker Size

	1956	1964	1967	1973	1978
Average Tanker Size (thousand DWT)	16.2	25.3	35.0	64.0	103.0

Source: H.P. Drewry, *Shipping Statistics and Economics.*

supertankers, although draft restrictions in U.S. ports at the time limited the size of tankers that could be used. Most of the existing fleet of supertankers had been delivered since 1971, and they represented 74 percent of total existing tonnage in 1978.

The trend toward the use of larger tankers had resulted in a sharp decrease in the average cost of tanker transportation, as illustrated in Table 4–3.

The economies of scale in tankers were believed to be exhausted at about 500,000 DWT. Vessels in excess of 500,000 DWT would require larger engines, offer lower fuel economy, and create the risks of massive accidents that raised insurance costs. There were also practical limits to the ultimate size of tankers, which were determined by the infrastructure necessary to support them. This included the size and adequacy of repair facilities, the requirement for large enough docking facilities, and the need for adequate land-based capacity to store and transport the oil as it arrived. It took about five years to upgrade a port facility to handle supertankers.

Although they generally cost 15 percent more to build than ordinary tankers, the operating cost for combination carriers was roughly similar to that of oil tankers. The main difference between the two was that if a suitable cargo was available, a combination carrier could carry cargo on the return or "ballast" leg of the voyage. Combination carriers could be converted from oil to dry bulk cargo use in three days. Although they were designed to be con-

TABLE 4–3. Average Cost of Tanker[a] Transportation
(typical 11,000-mile voyage)

	1954	1960	1965	1970	1974
Dollars/barrel	2.25	1.60	1.05	0.95	1.00

[a] Largest class in use at time.
Source: Estimates provided by a major oil company.

TABLE 4–4. Estimated Increases in Oil Tanker Operating Costs in 1973

Crew Costs	+30%
Insurance	+15% to 30%
Stores	+30
Repairs	+40
Fuel	+250%

Source: Estimates provided by a major financial institution.

verted frequently, in practice combination carriers tended to be run as either oil carriers or bulk carriers, with conversion taking place only when oil tanker rates reached a sufficient level.

Operating costs for all sizes of ships had begun to increase at an unprecedented rate in the 1970s, reflecting the high rates of inflation generally. Table 4–4 contains one bank's estimates of the increase in operating expenses just in the year 1973, and inflation had continued throughout the 1970s.

Inflation had also significantly affected tanker construction costs over the 1970s.

Demand for Oil Tankers

The demand for oil tankers was a function of demand for oil and the distance between the sources of oil and the ultimate consumer. Oil was a major energy source, and energy demand had historically been closely related to world economic growth. World energy consumption had grown at a historical rate of approximately 5.5 percent since 1965. In 1978 one typical projection by a major oil company had energy consumption growing at an annual rate of 3.9 percent through 1985. This projection assumed slower future world economic growth as well as plans to conserve energy. The demand for oil would grow at an annual rate of 2.5 percent according to this same source, from 46 million barrels per day in 1978 to 76 million barrels per day in 1990, with oil dropping from 53 to 48 percent of the world's total energy consumption.

The average shipping distance for oil had increased from 3,520 miles in 1966 to 5,560 miles in 1978, an increase of 4 percent annually. The increased distance reflected the increased importance of trade between the Arabian Gulf and Western Europe, Japan, and the United States, as shown in Exhibit 4–4. Efforts to reduce oil imports could reverse this trend, as would any changes in the source of crude oil supply that shortened the distance that oil had to travel between production and consumption. Increased oil production in Mexico, Alaska, the North Sea, and China would reduce Mideast oil trade and reduce the demand for tanker transportation. In addition, expansion of the Suez Canal to accommodate ULCCs, scheduled for completion in 1984, would shorten the distance between the Arabian Gulf and Western Europe, thereby significantly reducing the demand for tankers. A proposed fivefold increase in pipeline capacity in the Middle East would also reduce demand for tankers of less than 250,000 DWT by allowing tankers that normally traveled through the Suez Canal[4] to pick up oil in the Mediterranean instead of in the Persian Gulf.

Though the demand projections cited above were representative, there were as many demand scenarios as there were industry participants. The oil company's figures cited illustrate the assumptions that had to be made in projecting demand. The movement of oil was affected by unpredictable events such as the severity of winter weather, sudden slowdowns in the economy, strikes, and political upheavals in the Middle East.[5] Finally, most projections dealt with aggregate demand, while the need for transportation between any specific points could be absolutely predictable or totally unexpected, depending on whether the oil was obtained from company-owned fields, obtained under long-term contract, or purchased.

Finally, the demand for oil tankers tended to be seasonal, peaking in the late fall, when oil was moved to meet the demand for heating oil, and in winter, when winter weather slowed down ships. Since OPEC oil price increases were usually announced for the spring, the winter months were also used to build inventory.

The Supply of Tankers

As shown in Exhibit 4–5, the oil tanker fleet consisted of 3,150 vessels with a capacity of

[4] The Suez Canal could accommodate tankers up to 250,000 DWT.
[5] The closing of the Suez Canal in 1967 had increased tanker demand by approximately 25 percent.

325,241,000 DWT in October 1978, with an additional 19,639,000 DWT tons of capacity scheduled for delivery within the next three to five years. The fleet of combination carriers represented an additional 45,000,000 DWT of capacity in October 1978, with 45 percent of this capacity then in use for oil transport.

The world tanker fleet had grown at an average annual rate of 12 percent since 1963. As shown in Exhibit 4–6, orders for new ships had shown a marked increase in 1973. The total of ships on order in 1974 represented a 76 percent increase in the size of the fleet, and delivery time for new vessels reached five years.

Owners had historically ordered similar types of vessels, when the spot market for tanker services was high. Government policies influenced investment decisions in the tanker industry. For example, Norwegian owners were permitted to write off up to 25 percent of the cost of a new vessel in the year in which a building contract was signed. Delivery would come to five years later, during which time the owner would have paid only the initial installment of 5 percent of the contract cost.

Scheduled tanker deliveries could be altered in three ways—slippage, conversion of an order into a contract for a new type of vessel, or cancellation. Slippage referred to the delay in the scheduled delivery of a vessel, which resulted from constraints on available shipyard capacity, steel shortages, and labor problems. In periods of depressed demand for tanker capacity, slippage tended to increase because of lower use of overtime and less pressure to meet schedules. In 1978 slippage was running 20 percent annually; that is, one out of every five vessels was scheduled for delivery one calendar year later than originally anticipated.

Scheduled deliveries could be canceled by mutual agreement between shipyard and owner at no cost. When mutually agreeable to owner and builder, tanker orders could also be converted into orders for different types of vessels. Most conversions had been from tanker to bulk carrier. However, outright cancellation of a tanker at the owner's request resulted in a penalty charge of 20 percent of the original contract price, a figure that could rise as much as 40 percent. Cancellations could damage the reputation of a shipowner who wished to place orders at some future date and were once considered an unlikely course of action. However, in 1975 cancellations had reached the all time high of 7.5 percent of the total tonnage on order. Most of these cancellations had involved supertankers.

Effective tanker capacity could be varied in the short run through changes in ship operating practices. By "slow steaming," a vessel could economize on fuel: Slowing down a VLCC by two knots[6] resulted in a 25 percent savings in the cost of fuel. This represented a savings of $150,000 on a round trip between Europe and the Arabian Gulf. The cumulative effect of slow steaming was estimated by one industry source to produce a 20 to 30 percent reduction in fleet capacity during periods of overcapacity. Tankers could also be used as "floating storage"—for a minimum fee, loaded tankers waited to unload crude oil at the convenience of the oil companies. Tankers could also be laid up. Though finance charges continued, many (though not all) variable expenses were eliminated. It cost an estimated $750,000 to prepare a VLCC for layup, and $70,000 a month more to maintain the vessel. Exhibit 4–7 gives a three-year summary of the inactive tanker tonnage.

Tankers were normally sold for scrap at the end of their useful life. When tanker demand was high, vessels otherwise destined for scrap would enter the market for "one last voyage." Scrap prices also varied, and equaled $90 per ton in Europe and $65 per ton in the Far East, down from a high of $180 (Far East) in 1973. Tankers were also bought and sold secondhand. Exhibit 4–8 presents some data on the sales of secondhand ships.

The supply of tankers exceeded demand by about 30 percent in 1978. One major oil company's estimate of future supply/demand relationships for tankers is illustrated in Exhibit 4–9.

The Market for Tanker Capacity

Two types of markets existed for oil tanker services, the *spot market* and the *period market*. In the spot market the shipowner agreed to carry a single cargo between two specified ports in the near future, usually from one or two days to two weeks from the date on which the agreement was made. Spot rates

were expressed in terms of an industry index called "Worldscale." The index was designed to compensate for the cost differences in operating on different routes, to allow prices on different routes to be compared. At a given Worldscale rate, the shipowner theoretically received exactly the same revenue per day no matter what the voyage. Worldscale rates were based on a standard ship size operating under standard conditions. On each tanker route, the rate per ton of oil delivered was expressed in terms of the cost of a round trip voyage for a 19,500 DWT tanker traveling at 14 knots. Worldscale 100 represented the cost of fuel, port charges, and canal tolls for this "standard" ship, plus $1,800 per day. This base rate was adjusted periodically to reflect changes in port charges and exchange rates.

Trading in the spot market was based on bids using the Worldscale index. A bid of Worldscale 60 represented a price 60 percent of the Worldscale 100 rate for a given route. Conversely, a Worldscale 200 bid equaled twice the Worldscale 100 rate. Exhibit 4–10 shows how the Worldscale rate had changed over time.

Ships could also be hired on a longer term basis, under four types of contractual arrangements:

1. *Timecharter.* The charterer leased the cargo-carrying capacity of the ship at a fixed dollar rate per dead weight ton per month for a fixed period of time (typically three months to fifteen years).
2. *Bareboat charter.* Like a timecharter, except that the charterer undertook to operate the ship at his/her own expense (crew, maintenance, repairs, etc.), whereas under a timecharter the owner absorbed these expenses, leaving the charterer only those expenses associated with the voyage itself (fuel, port charges, canal charges, extra insurance, etc.).
3. *Contract of affreightment.* Here the owner undertook to transport a certain quantity of a given commodity per year between two or more specific points using any ship he or she desired within given size limits. Remuneration was set at a fixed dollar amount *per ton transported.* Contracts might vary in duration from one to ten years.
4. *Consecutive voyages.* The owner undertook to provide a specific ship (sometimes with substitution options) for consecutive voyages at a given rate per ton of cargo transported. In tankers, the rate was usually stated in terms of Worldscale plus or minus a percentage. The duration of the con-

[6] Normal cruising speed was 15 nautical miles/hour.

tract might be stated in terms of a number of voyages or years, with the owner undertaking to maintain a certain average speed in transit.

Some charter agreements included escalator clauses to compensate for the effect of inflation on an operator's costs. Although almost 80 percent of the world oil tanker fleet typically was either owned outright or operated under some form of charter arrangement, all vessels were offered in the spot market whenever they had space available. Exhibit 4–11 gives historical charter rates for several types of vessels.

The rates obtainable for charters were largely a function of the current spot rate and market expectations about the future. As can be seen from Exhibit 4–10, the spot market was extremely volatile. It was an industry quip that one tanker too many in the Persian Gulf could send spot rates plummeting, while one tanker too few sent rates soaring. An example of the extreme volatility of the spot market was the drop in the rate of VLCCs from Worldscale 410 to Worldscale 57 within three weeks during October 1973. This drop represented a difference of a startling $8 million in the gross revenue for a single voyage from the Arabian Gulf to Western Europe. The period market was less volatile, but the rate per ton could vary by several dollars per month between peaks and troughs.

Industry Participants

The main participants in the oil tanker industry were the oil companies, the independent shipowners, shipping brokers, bankers, and the shipbuilding industry. These players were remarkably different in their characteristics and their approaches to doing business.

The Oil Companies

The oil industry comprised a relatively small number of large, multinational, vertically integrated firms. Since oil reserves, refineries, and markets were dispersed throughout the world, transportation was a necessary part of the oil business. Historically transportation cost had represented 50 percent of the cost of imported crude oil; by 1978 it was about 10 percent.

Transportation executives of major oil companies often referred to shipping as "a necessary evil." The responsibility for managing tanker transportation was typically assigned to a group within the "supply and procurement" division of an oil company. This division had overall responsibility for assuring a supply of crude oil for company refineries. Oil refineries were continuous process operations, which were difficult as well as extremely costly to shut down. Although refineries had some storage facilities for crude oil, transportation was a vital link between crude oil procurement and refining. Transportation also tied up capital in oil inventory while the vessel was in transit.

Oil companies were the main purchasers of oil tanker services and also owned about 40 percent of world tanker tonnage themselves, as shown in Exhibit 4–12. To supplement their internal tanker fleets, oil companies utilized both chartered and spot vessels, as shown in Exhibit 4–13. The mix between ownership and charter activities varied among companies, with companies owning from 10 to 80 percent of their transportation requirements in 1978. The average proportion of vessels owned had risen from 33 percent in 1972.

Oil companies sought to minimize the cost of transportation. Most believed that they could purchase and operate vessels as efficiently as the independent shipowners. In addition, ownership bought control over the skill of the crew and the maintenance of the ship. Investments in tanker capacity typically required the approval of executive-level investment committees.

Oil companies tried to plan their transportation needs very carefully. They had charters of varying lengths, in part relating to the duration of the anticipated need for transportation on that route. Oil companies also entered into long-term charters that essentially covered the expected lifetime of a chartered vessel and utilized the spot market when owned or chartered vessels were unavailable. The transportation departments of oil companies were organized as cost centers; they maintained large research staffs whose primary function was to amass and analyze data on oil supply/demand relationships and transportation requirements. Transportation departments were generally considered to be outside the mainstream activities of an oil company, though sometimes managers in these departments were rising executives on rotation who were destined to assume responsibility in other areas of the corporation. Most of these managers had no previous shipping experience. Some major oil companies evaluated their transportation managers annually on the basis of the total net present value of the average transportation cost of oil on a per barrel basis. The net present value summed the average cost per barrel of spot voyages during the year, the discounted average cost per barrel of all outstanding charter agreements, and the discounted average cost per barrel of operating the company-owned fleet over its useful life.

The Independent Ship Owners

There were about 1,100 independent shipowners in 1978. Included among them were fabled names like Onassis, Stavos Niarchos, Sigval Bergesen, Sir Y. K. Pao, and C. Y. Tung, to name but a few. The owner built a fleet by assessing the future market for tankers and deciding on the size and type of ship likely to be in demand. The shipowner could perhaps obtain a long-term charter before deciding to build a ship, or before any substantial payments on the ship were due. On the strength of such a charter, long-term financing could be arranged for up to 80 percent of the cost of the ship. Once long-term financing was assured, interim financing could also be obtained to cover the remaining balance, if necessary.

Shipowners frequently were family firms that encompassed several generations and by and large maintained very small staffs. For the independent shipowners shipping was a way of life, and business was done on the basis of playing hunches, having a feel for the business, and having the nerve to take big risks when necessary. Many shipowners professed to have very little use for sophisticated analytical techniques. They preferred to act quickly and decisively, to follow their instincts. One Norwegian tanker operation had its office in a little building in the corner of the owner's garden. It was across the road from a nursery school. In this office one evening in May 1973, the owner made a deal

worth $80 million. The deal involved a single long distance telephone call. As one Greek shipowner put it, "Business—I know nothing about business, I only know how to make money."

Shipowners had a number of options in running their fleets, ranging from operating all ships only under long-term charter agreements to running an entire fleet on the spot market. At any given time approximately 60 percent of the independently owned fleet was on term charter. Shipowners could charter other independently owned tankers; during periods of rising rates some particularly "bullish" independents had chartered additional tankers, which they in turn had run on the spot market. Depending on their circumstances, owners could operate under flags other than their own countries.

Shipowners were spread throughout the world. However, leading groups of owners were located in Scandinavia, Greece, and Hong Kong. Although there were variations within each group, shipowners of the same nationality tended to operate their fleets in a generally similar way. Because of high construction and operating costs, the United States was not a significant factor in the international tanker business.[7] Only two U.S. companies, the Overseas Shipholding Group and Gotas Larsen, a subsidiary of IU, Inc., participated in the international tanker business. Both of these companies were diversified into bulk and specialized shipping. Overseas Shipholding was exclusively in domestic and international shipping, with 80 percent of its fleet run on the international market.

THE SCANDINAVIANS

The Scandinavian shipowners were diversified into all types of shipping, including general cargo liner operations, specialized shipping businesses such as container cargo shipping, liquified natural gas (LNG) shipping, and offshore drilling rigs, as well as oil tankers. They were highly respected in the shipping business and were known as the most technologically sophisticated owners in the industry. Scandinavian ships were very well maintained, and

---

[7] In recognition of this disadvantage, U.S. law (the "Jones Act") excluded foreign-flag ships from any trade in which cargoes were both loaded and discharged at U.S. ports. This protected the U.S. shipping industry, which was required to use U.S.-built vessels and U.S. crews, from foreign competition.

Scandinavian crews were considered the most skillful in the world.

However, the Scandinavians had high operating and investment costs. The Norwegians, the dominant force within the Scandinavian group of shipowners, were required by law to operate their ships under the Norwegian flag. As a result they paid higher crew costs than owners who ran their ships under flags of convenience, typically Liberian or Panamanian. In addition, Norwegian owners ordered one-third of their ships from Scandinavian shipyards, which had the highest construction costs in the world. The Scandinavians were the only group of shipowners subject to taxation. The Scandinavians paid high marginal income taxes (both personal and corporate, up to 60 percent) but could take advantage of liberal depreciation and reinvestment options.

The Scandinavians were considered gamblers among the gamblers in the shipping industry. They had placed more early orders for VLCCs and ULCCs than other nationalities and ran large portions of their fleet on the spot market. The Norwegians, for example, owned only 15 percent of the world tankers but accounted for nearly 50 percent of the tonnage on the spot market. The Scandinavians had invested heavily in new capacity during the bull market in 1973–1974, and these new ships were coming on stream in the 1976–1978 period. Because the Norwegian shipowners were having difficulty meeting operating expenses and paying for these new ships, the Norwegian government had guaranteed all outstanding shipping debts. This move came too late to save Hilmar Reksten, one of shipping's most colorful figures, from bankruptcy —Reksten had committed his entire fleet, including VLCCs, to the spot market.

THE GREEKS

The Greek shipping community comprised a number of closely knit family firms, many of which were related by marriage. Greek firms were smaller than the Scandinavian firms and typically were exclusively in oil tanker operations. Most Greek ships were smaller and older than the Scandinavian ships and had been purchased secondhand. Over the years the Norwegians had traded-up their fleets,

and many of their older ships had been bought by Greeks, who could run them with less expensive labor. A few of the larger Greek shipowners had ordered their first supertankers in 1973.

The Greeks generally followed a policy of seeking time charters on their newer, larger vessels. They placed only their older, usually smaller vessels on the spot market. The Greeks typically had very large cash reserves and were frequent buyers and sellers of used ships.

THE HONG KONG CHINESE

The Hong Kong Chinese operated ships exclusively on long-term charter to the Japanese. Japan had huge maritime transportation requirements, and to meet this need Japan had built up the largest fleet of all nations in the free world, with the exception of flag-of-convenience countries. Japan owned and operated approximately 9 percent of the world's merchant fleet as of 1978 and 10.5 percent of the world's oil tankers.[8] The Japanese tanker fleet met only half of Japan's total marine transportation requirements. To meet additional requirements, the Japanese entered into what was called a "shikumisen transaction" with the Hong Kong Chinese, whereby the Hong Kong Chinese owner simultaneously accepted a long-term charter with a Japanese oil company, ordered a tanker from a Japanese shipyard, and arranged for financing through the Japanese Export-Import Bank. From the point of view of the Japanese, the shikumisen transaction resulted in lower transportation costs because the Hong Kong Chinese operators could hire less expensive Chinese or Indonesian crews, saving $300,000 to $400,000 per year in operating costs, and because by selling the tankers to foreign nationals the Japanese shipyards "earned" foreign currency.

Financing Tankers

Financing was a major requirement for the tanker industry since high leverage was a common practice even for the most conservative shipowner. A rough rule of thumb in ship financing circles was that if the

---

[8] Classified by number of ships.

total of outstanding mortgage debt on a fleet represented 40 percent or less of the current market value of the ships, a shipowner was considered financially solid. If debt exceeded 60 percent, this was cause for concern. Larger, financially secure owners commanded better terms despite the secured nature of the loan and its tie to a long-term charter. This is because if the owner's financial condition deteriorated he could not afford to operate the ship to generate the revenues, leaving the lender no recourse other than to liquidate the ship whose value would probably be depressed by market conditions.

Debt financing was sometimes provided by governments or government agencies of shipbuilding countries. The financing was made available either through shipyards or directly from the government. Conventional financial institutions also provided financing, usually in the form of loans secured by a first mortgage on the ship involved. However, because banks were hard pressed to meet the favorable terms offered by governments, they financed only a very small portion of the new building.[9] They did, however, finance most of the secondhand tankers. Bankers typically considered the following criteria in evaluating a loan: the ship (its age, condition, special features, etc.); the existence of long-term charter agreements; the quality and reputation of the management; the overall financial condition of the owner; the condition and mix of the rest of the owner's fleet; and the estimated residual value of the ship.

Numerous U.S. banks had discovered the shipping industry's appetite for capital during the boom period of the early 1970s. Merchant banks in London formed syndicates that made it easy for the newcomer bank who knew very little about the shipping industry to invest in what looked like a sure thing. The depressed market of the mid-1970s caused most of these banks to withdraw from the business abruptly, and only a very few major international banks with specialized personnel remained in ship financing. These banks tended to make loans very conservatively, considering charter agreements to be a key determinant of long-term profitability.

---

[9] In 1978 the Brazilian government had reportedly offered a financial package consisting of 90 percent financing at 7.5 percent to be paid back over a ten-year period.

Bankers were viewed as a disruptive force within the industry by other participants, who cited frequent instances where bankers had forced shipowners to accept disadvantageous charter agreements in order to meet their financial obligations.

Brokers

Brokers were intermediaries who served as the interface between buyers and sellers of tanker services. When in need of a tanker, an oil company contacted a number of brokers, who in turn contacted shipowners. The broker's objective was to force an agreement between the oil company and the shipowner at a mutually acceptable price. For this the shipowner paid the broker at 1.25 percent commission. Brokers also arranged purchases of ships in both the new and secondhand markets.

Although there were some brokers in Greece and Scandinavia, the majority were found in the financial capitals of major oil-importing countries, specifically in New York, London, and Tokyo. Since five of the seven major petroleum companies were located in New York, most of the business originated there. Four New York brokers did about 80 percent of the New York business. Business was done quickly and always by telephone. Within five minutes the entire shipping community would know, through their brokers, that an oil company needed a tanker. A negotiation process would start, on a deal often involving several million dollars, sometimes to be completed within a half hour. The annual phone bill for a large brokerage house was well in excess of one million dollars.

Although oil companies usually dealt with a number of brokers, they could and did exercise preferential treatment when contacting brokers. Favored brokers were called first, giving them the edge in contacting shipowners. Brokers also had to convince the shipowner that they were protecting the shipowner's interests and provide critical information to both parties on rates and recent transactions in the spot and charter markets.

Because of the international nature of the industry, brokers worked literally night and day, and traveled extensively to meet "buyers" and "sellers." Brokers believed that it took at least ten years to learn the business. Although brokers come from diverse backgrounds, many had once worked in oil company transportation departments.

Shipyards

The world maritime fleet was built by shipyards located all over the globe. In 1976, the latest year for which these statistics were available, world shipyards delivered 60 million DWT of shipping capacity of which approximately 45 million DWT were tankers. World shipping was characterized by an increasing emphasis on specialized vessels designed to achieve economies in operating and in loading and unloading. At one end of the spectrum were the very simple ships: tankers and bulk carriers, which held one product, and loaded directly into an open hold. At the other end of the spectrum were increasingly sophisticated ships, including liquified gas carriers and containerized cargo vessels. Production of general purpose vessels had declined.

Shipbuilding was basically a mature technology and extremely labor-intensive. However, recent developments had influenced the industry. Some shipyards had reduced production costs substantially during the 1960s through improved techinques in fabrication. By constructing ships in large sections and using building berths (the large scaffolding which once housed the ship during the entire construction process) merely for welding completed sections together, berth time was reduced from a year to about two months.[10] In addition, use of standardized designs and of computers for scheduling increased shipyard efficiency. The ability of the shipbuilding nations of the world to compete in 1978 was influenced by the degree to which they had achieved these production efficiencies and how they had reacted to the trend toward specialization.

Nations around the world considered shipbuilding a vital industry for a variety of reasons: to supply a naval defense force; to supply a domestic commercial fleet; to improve the balance of payments by eliminating the need to import ships; and to earn foreign currency. Since shipbuilding was considered

of strategic significance to the nations involved, government involvement in the industry was a major factor in international competition in shipbuilding in 1978. In some nations, shipbuilding had been nationalized; in all nations the government had a major influence on competition.

Financial assistance from governments to their shipbuilding industries took a number of forms: (1) direct subsidies for either construction or operation of ships; (2) tax allowance programs for shipowners or shipyards, including generous depreciation allowances, low taxes or customs rates, tax deferments, and customs rebates for imported materials; (3) credit assistance, including loans, interest subsidies, and loan guarantees made available to the purchaser of a ship through the shipyards. Exhibit 4–14 summarizes the various government supports to the maritime industry in some major shipbuilding nations.

The supply/demand balance in the shipbuilding industry reflected trends in world shipping. Since oil accounted for nearly half the seaborne transportation requirements, developments in the oil tanker industry set the pace for shipbuilding. In the face of reduced demand for oil tankers, overcapacity in the shipbuilding industry was estimated to be 50 percent in 1978.

The major shipbuilding nations of the world could be divided into four groups: EEC countries, Japan, and less-developed countries (LDCs) and the Communist bloc. Traditionally, the great seafaring nations of the world had dominated shipbuilding, and the industry had a cultural as well as economic significance to the oldest and at one time greatest shipbuilders in the world: Great Britain, Sweden, and Norway. In 1978 the largest and most competitive shipbuilding nation was Japan, which had increased its yearly production capacity some 900 percent since 1960. However, during the 1970s the LDCs (Korea, Brazil) and the Communist bloc countries (Poland, USSR) had increased production by approximately 80 percent. Trends in orders for ships placed in the mid- to late 1970s indicated that these newer participants, which had access to cheap labor, were becoming a significant force in international shipbuilding. Since building tankers was a less complex process and required less technology but more unskilled labor than building

---

[10] The entire construction process took about eighteen months for an oil tanker.

newer types of ships, competition from low-wage countries had the greatest impact on oil tanker construction. The shipbuilding industries of the major international builders of tankers are briefly profiled below.

JAPAN

Japan had the largest and most competitive shipbuilding industry in the world. Japan supplied all of the ships for its domestic fleet, and exports of ships represented 10 percent of total Japanese export revenue in 1978. The Japanese had adopted streamlined ship construction techniques, computerized scheduling, purchasing, and inventory control. Japanese shipworkers were the most productive in the world, and the Japanese had access to the cheapest steel in the world. The Japanese had recently begun to switch to production of smaller, more sophisticated vessels.

The seven largest Japanese shipbuilders accounted for 80 percent of industry production, and most firms were part of large, vertically integrated conglomerates including Hitachi, Honda, and Kawasaki. Shipbuilding was coordinated through the Ministry of Transport, and there was a great deal of cooperation among builders. The Japanese supplied the best credit terms in the world, with up to 95 percent financing available through the Japanese Shosha or "trading houses," which arranged the actual sale of ships.

Worldwide overcapacity had brought pressure on the Japanese from the EEC countries to cut back on ship construction. In 1977, under the direction of the Ministry of Transport, the Japanese industry agreed to cut back operating levels to 65 percent of peak 1974 levels. Japan thus became the only country of the world to implement a voluntary cutback.

SWEDEN

Sweden was the world's second-ranked shipbuilder and a major exporter of ships. Swedish shipyards made large investments in innovative production methods for constructing increasingly large bulk carriers and tankers. Sweden's large shipyards sought to compete with Japan in building larger ships despite the constraints of high labor costs; high social benefit costs such as comprehensive health insurance, pension plans, etc.; and the fact that Swedish shipyard productivity per man had been level since the mid-1960s. The large Swedish shipyards were profitable in the 1960s, when they enjoyed technological advantages, but Japanese competition and tanker overcapacity ultimately jeopardized the very existence of Swedish shipbuilding. By 1978 the government had virtually taken over the industry and ordered cutbacks of at least 30 percent of capacity. To ease the transition of resources to other industries, the government was building ships for inventory.

NORWAY

The Norwegian shipyards had made an early commitment to the construction of large tankers. In spite of high social benefit costs the Norwegians had efficient production methods and productive workers, but they were at a disadvantage in international competition because harsh winters hampered production. Seventy percent of the Norwegian industry's output was delivered to Norwegian shipowners, who had to import an additional two-thirds of their tonnage requirements from foreign yards.

LDCs AND COMMUNIST BLOC COUNTRIES

Brazil, South Korea, Yugoslavia, and Poland were the newest entrants in the world shipbuilding industry. Although their current market share was small, less than 5 percent, they had grown two to three times as fast as the rest of the industry. New capacity, centralized planning, and low labor costs led some industry observers to consider these countries major potential competitors, particularly in the production of oil tankers where their lower labor costs would have the greatest impact. Recent statistics on contracts for new tankers had shown that significant tanker orders had been placed in Brazil.

EXHIBIT 4-1. *Estimated Tanker Fleet Ownership by Vessel Size, September 1978*

Ship Size (DWT)	Total Existing Fleet		Ships on Order	
	Number	000 DWT	Number	000 DWT
10–19,999	433	6,805	29	450
20–29,999	434	10,471	16	389
30–49,999	551	20,276	28	974
50–69,999	275	16,006	32	1,862
70–99,999	379	31,975	42	3,848
100–124,999	136	15,506	8	885
125–174,999	201	28,846	22	3,256
175–224,999	146	31,026	5	967
225–299,999	484	123,639	8	2,088
300–000+	111	40,700	13	4,920
Total	3,150	325,241	203	19,639

SOURCE: H. P. Drewry, *Shipping Statistics and Economics*, October 1978.

EXHIBIT 4-2 *Relative Sizes of Tankers*

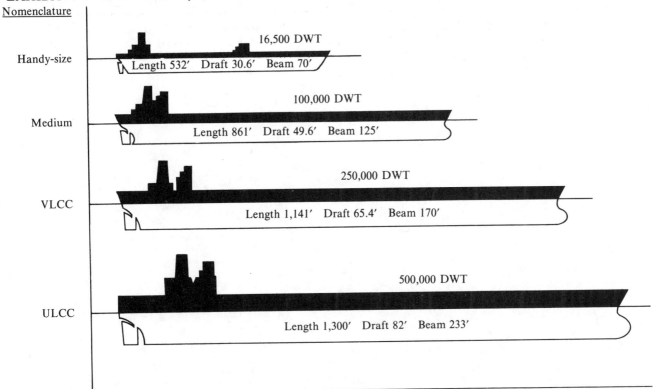

Nomenclature

Handy-size
16,500 DWT
Length 532′   Draft 30.6′   Beam 70′

Medium
100,000 DWT
Length 861′   Draft 49.6′   Beam 125′

VLCC
250,000 DWT
Length 1,141′   Draft 65.4′   Beam 170′

ULCC
500,000 DWT
Length 1,300′   Draft 82′   Beam 233′

SOURCE: Exxon Corporation, *Very Large Crude Carriers,* Exxon Background Series, November 1975.

EXHIBIT 4-3. *Prices for New Tankers, 1970-1977 (prices in million dollars at the end of the year)*

	1970	1971	1972	1973	1974	1975	1976	1977
30,000 DWT prod. tanker	10.0	11.2	11.4	17.5	20.0	18.0	15.0	15.0
87,000 DWT tanker	17.0	17.3	15.0	25.0	28.0	22.0	16.0	16.0
210,000 DWT tanker	31.0	33.5	31.0	47.0	42.0	38.0	34.0	32.0
400,000 DWT tanker	—	—	51.0	78.0	65.0	62.0	56.0	45.0
96,000 DWT combination carrier	23.0	23.7	21.0	29.0	33.0	30.0	23.0	21.0

NOTES: The prices refer to time of contracting. Up to 1975 the prices are based on West European yards' quotations, while in 1976 and 1977 Japanese yards' prices are used. Prices are for cash payment at delivery including financing costs prior to delivery. Tankers are priced without SBT.

SOURCE: Drewry, *Shipping Statistics and Economics.*

EXHIBIT 4–4. *Principal Crude Oil Movements by Sea**

1962

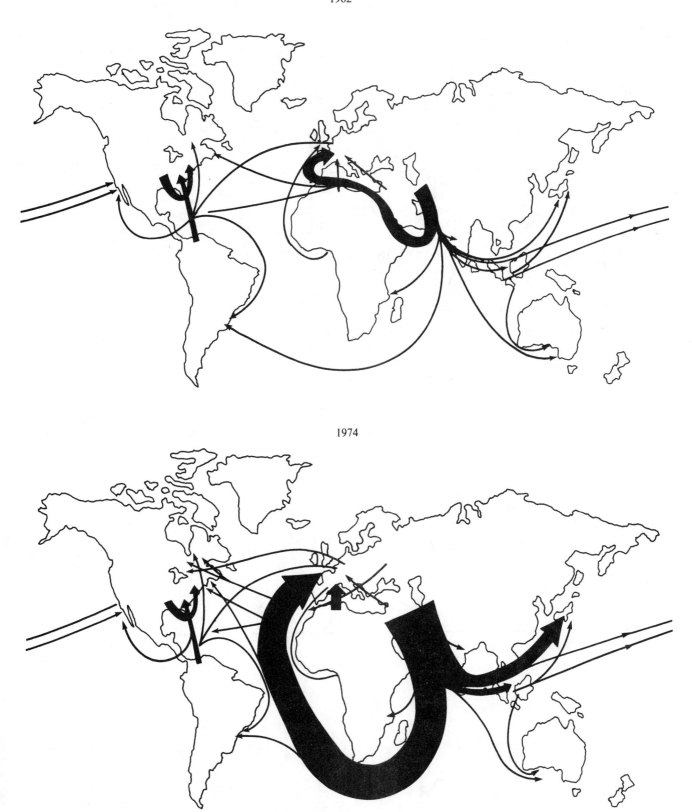

1974

*Size of arrows is proportional to the volume of oil transported.
SOURCE: Exxon Corporation, *Very Large Crude Carriers.*

EXHIBIT 4-5. *World Tanker Fleet and Future Deliveries, End-September 1978*

A. Future Scheduled Deliveries (000 DWT)

Ship Size (DWT)	Current Fleet	2nd Half 1978	1st Half 1979	2nd Half 1979	1st Half 1980	2nd Half 1980	1981+	Total on Order
10–19,999	6,805	203	45	16	78	36	72	450
20–29,999	10,471	166	50	74	49	50	—	389
30–49,999	20,276	609	133	70	162	—	—	974
50–69,999	16,006	1,285	296	281	—	—	—	1,862
70–99,999	31,975	1,813	626	259	457	198	495	3,848
100–124,999	15,506	685	100	100	—	—	—	885
125–174,999	28,846	1,504	443	570	150	289	300	3,256
175–224,999	31,026	389	—	389	189	—	—	967
225–299,999	123,630	1,260	276	552	—	—	—	2,088
300,000+	40,700	3,498	391	711	—	320	—	4,920
Total	325,241	11,412	2,360	3,022	1,085	893	867	19,639
Cumulative total	325,241	336,653	339,093	342,035	343,120	344,013	344,880	

B. Future Scheduled Deliveries (Number of Ships)

Ship Size (DWT)	Current Fleet	2nd Half 1978	1st Half 1979	2nd Half 1979	1st Half 1980	2nd Half 1980	1981+	Total on Order
10–19,999	433	14	3	1	5	2	4	29
20–29,999	434	7	2	3	2	2	—	16
30–49,999	551	18	4	2	4	—	—	28
50–69,999	275	22	5	5	—	—	—	32
70–99,999	379	20	7	3	5	2	5	42
100–124,999	136	6	1	1	—	—	—	8
125–174,999	201	10	3	4	1	2	2	22
175–224,999	146	2	—	2	1	—	—	5
225–299,999	484	5	1	2	—	—	—	8
300,000+	111	9	1	2	—	1	—	13
Total	3,150	113	27	25	18	9	11	203

SOURCE: Drewry, *Shipping Statistics and Economics.*

EXHIBIT 4–6. *Measures of Maritime Activity, World Shipbuilding and World Fleet, 1970–1976*

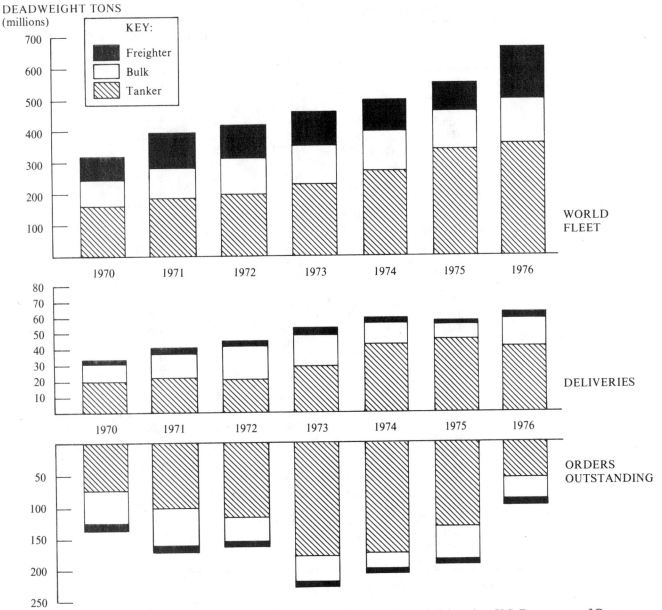

SOURCES: *Merchant Fleets of the World* and *New Ship Construction,* Maritime Administration, U.S. Department of Commerce.

EXHIBIT 4-7. *Inactive Tonnage, 1976-78*

Year	Month	Tankers		Combined Carriers	
		Number	000 DWT	Number	000 DWT
1976	January	516	43,989	60	6,494
	February	516	45,049	61	7,089
	March	523	47,228	64	7,276
	April	538	48,041	64	7,435
	May	506	46,172	54	6,016
	June	490	44,223	53	5,851
	July	466	41,602	48	5,337
	August	466	39,935	46	5,256
	September	407	34,918	43	4,630
	October	424	35,090	38	3,909
	November	389	32,700	36	3,494
	December	379	32,794	40	4,133
1977	January	351	31,011	35	3,387
	February	329	28,387	40	4,094
	March	337	30,158	44	4,857
	April	318	28,184	35	3,717
	May	309	27,690	37	3,833
	June	340	35,248	37	3,558
	July	339	37,880	45	4,489
	August	354	39,488	56	5,762
	September	350	40,440	59	6,416
	October	353	40,166	57	6,192
	November	338	36,744	63	6,787
	December	311	33,024	61	6,674
1978	January	312	34,487	60	7,022
	February	316	37,436	61	7,034
	March	337	41,684	61	7,306
	April	344	43,841	71	8,527
	May	339	44,642	69	8,456
	June	356	47,093	71	8,867
	July	354	48,433	72	9,517
	August	359	46,009	67	8,708
	September	327	42,074	56	7,646
	October				
	November				
	December				

SOURCE: Drewry, *Shipping Statistics and Economics.*

EXHIBIT 4-8. *Average Values of Secondhand Tankers, 1967–1974*

		Prices in Millions of Dollars at End of Year							
DWT	*Built*	1967	1968	1969	1970	1971	1972	1973	1974
15/16,000	1951/52	0.7	0.5	0.5	0.9	0.5	0.4	1.5	0.5
18,000	1952/53	0.9	0.8	0.8	1.5	0.8	0.7	1.9	0.8
19/20,000	1959/60	1.7	1.2	1.4	3.3	2.0	2.0	4.0	2.7
25,000	1958/59	2.0	1.8	1.9	4.0	2.2	2.2	5.0	3.0
35,000	1958/59	2.4	2.4	2.6	6.0	3.5	3.5	7.5	3.5
50,000	1963/64	4.4	4.2	4.5	10.0	7.0	6.0	13.0	7.0
60,000	1964/65	5.3	5.5	5.8	12.0	8.5	7.5	16.0	8.0
80,000	1966/67	—	7.7	8.0	19.0	12.0	10.5	25.0	9.5
100,000	1967/68	—	—	12.0	26.0	16.0	13.5	30.0	11.0
200,000	1969/70	—	—	—	40.0	30.0	30.0	52.0	23.0
300,000	1971/72	—	—	—	—	—	42.0	78.0	36.0

SOURCE: Estimates provided by major financial institution.

EXHIBIT 4-9. *Industry Tanker Outlook*

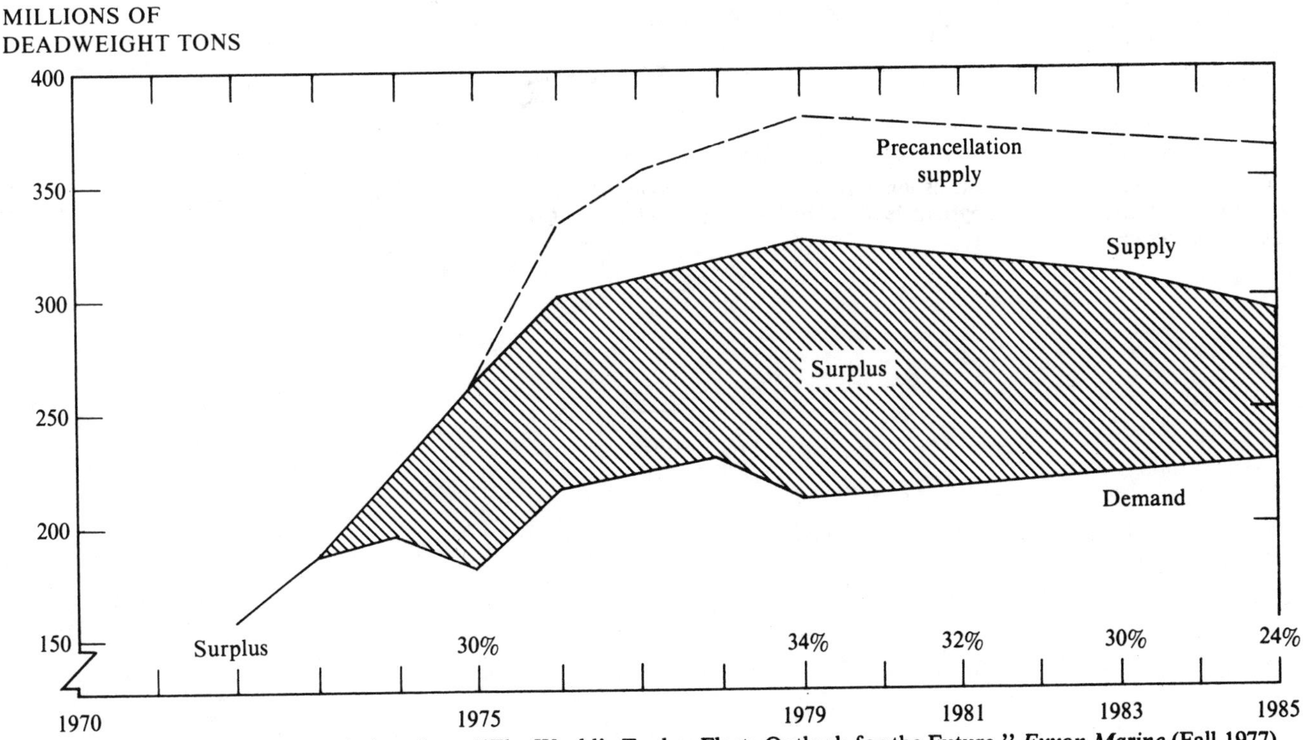

SOURCE: Reprinted, with permission, from "The World's Tanker Fleet: Outlook for the Future," *Exxon Marine* (Fall 1977).

EXHIBIT 4–10.   *Tanker Rates—Average Freight Rate Assessments (AFRA)**

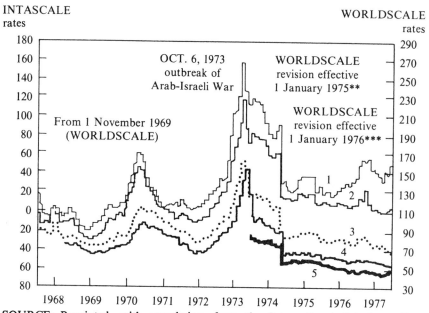

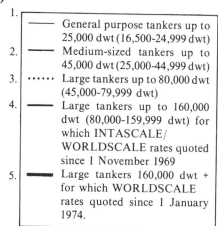

1. —— General purpose tankers up to 25,000 dwt (16,500-24,999 dwt)
2. —— Medium-sized tankers up to 45,000 dwt (25,000-44,999 dwt)
3. ······ Large tankers up to 80,000 dwt (45,000-79,999 dwt)
4. —— Large tankers up to 160,000 dwt (80,000-159,999 dwt) for which INTASCALE/ WORLDSCALE rates quoted since 1 November 1969
5. ▬▬ Large tankers 160,000 dwt + for which WORLDSCALE rates quoted since 1 January 1974.

* AFRA for each month is awarded on the first of each month and includes fixtures reported up to the middle of the previous month.
** From 1 January 1975, WORLDSCALE rates adjusted to reflect increases in Bunker prices in 1974.
*** From 1 January 1976, WORLDSCALE rates adjusted to reflect increases in Bunker prices for 1975.

SOURCE: Reprinted, with permission, from the *International Petroleum Encyclopedia,* Vol. 2, p. 311. Copyright 1978 by the Petroleum Publishing Company, Tulsa, Oklahoma.

EXHIBIT 4–11. *Indicative Tanker Timecharter Rates*[a]

WORLDSCALE 1978

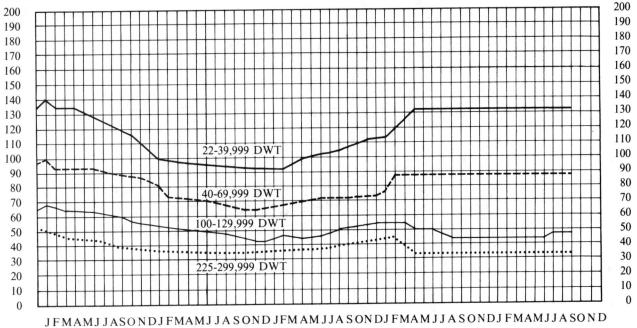

JFMAMJ JASONDJ FMAMJ J A SOND JFM AM JJA SONDJ FMAM J J A SOND J FMAMJJASOND

1974   1975   1976   1977   1978

[a] Based on a five-year timecharter. When no five-year timecharter fixtures have been reported in the size category, the rate has been estimated. The estimate has been based on the last similar reported fixture plus trends in the rates for other ship sizes and for other charter periods. All sales have been converted to a January 1978 Worldscale equivalent basis.

SOURCE: Drewry, *Shipping Statistics and Economics*.

EXHIBIT 4-12. *Estimated Tanker Fleet Ownership, September 1978*

Ship Size (DWT)	A. Existing Fleet						B. Ships on Order					
	SEVEN MAJORS		OTHER OIL COMPANIES		INDEPENDENTS		SEVEN MAJORS		OTHER OIL COMPANIES		INDEPENDENTS	
	Number	000 DWT	Number	000 DWT	Number	000 DWT	Number	000 DWT	Number	000 DWT	Number	000 DWT
10-19,999	37	656	275	3,825	139	2,324	—	—	21	889	8	111
20-29,999	127	3,083	120	2,852	187	4,536	—	—	16	389	—	—
30-49,999	99	3,689	175	6,621	277	9,966	8	259	11	422	9	293
50-69,999	40	2,340	59	3,194	176	10,472	—	—	7	394	25	1,468
70-99,999	37	2,906	85	7,176	257	21,893	2	160	25	2,455	15	1,233
100-124,999	16	1,816	36	4,164	84	9,526	—	—	2	220	6	665
125-174,999	4	528	69	9,949	128	18,369	2	330	13	1,972	7	954
175-224,999	35	7,429	8	1,629	103	21,977	—	—	4	778	1	189
225-299,999	118	30,991	76	19,316	290	73,323	1	260	5	1,340	2	488
300,000+	42	15,143	8	3,272	61	22,285	—	—	4	1,536	9	3,384
Total	555	68,572	893	61,998	1,702	194,671	13	1,009	108	9,845	82	8,785

SOURCE: Drewry, *Shipping Statistics and Economics.*

70

EXHIBIT 4-13. *Tanker Charters by Charterer and Duration of Charter, September 1978[a]*

Charterer	To 6 Months No.	To 6 Months 000 DWT	7-12 Months No.	7-12 Months 000 DWT	13-24 Months No.	13-24 Months 000 DWT	25-48 Months No.	25-48 Months 000 DWT	49-72 Months No.	49-72 Months 000 DWT	73+ Months No.	73+ Months 000 DWT	Total No.	Total 000 DWT	Of Which Combined Carriers No.	Of Which Combined Carriers 000 DWT
BP	—	—	—	—	—	—	—	—	—	—	—	—	—	—	—	—
Exxon	2	660	—	—	—	—	—	—	—	—	—	—	2	660	—	—
Gulf	2	310	1	106	—	—	—	—	—	—	—	—	3	416	—	—
Mobil	—	—	—	—	—	—	—	—	—	—	—	—	—	—	—	—
Royal Dutch/Shell	1	40	—	—	—	—	—	—	—	—	—	—	1	40	—	—
Socal	2	56	—	—	—	—	—	—	—	—	—	—	2	56	—	—
Texaco	—	—	—	—	—	—	—	—	—	—	—	—	—	—	—	—
Total Majors	7	1,056	1	106	—	—	—	—	—	—	—	—	8	1,162	—	—
Amoco	2	485	—	—	—	—	—	—	—	—	—	—	2	485	—	—
Ashland	1	260	1	269	—	—	—	—	—	—	—	—	2	529	—	—
Conoco	2	190	—	—	—	—	—	—	—	—	—	—	2	190	—	—
Elf	4	1,363	—	—	—	—	—	—	—	—	—	—	4	1,363	—	—
Fadi	3	610	—	—	—	—	—	—	—	—	—	—	3	610	1	110
GSSK	2	299	—	—	—	—	—	—	—	—	—	—	2	299	1	154
Hess	3	226	—	—	—	—	—	—	—	—	—	—	3	226	—	—
INA	1	210	—	—	—	—	—	—	—	—	—	—	1	210	1	—
Latsis	1	220	—	—	—	—	—	—	—	—	—	—	1	220	—	—
MSG	2	420	—	—	—	—	—	—	—	—	—	—	2	420	—	—
Pontiol	—	—	—	—	—	—	1	253	—	—	—	—	1	253	—	—
Soponata	1	340	—	—	—	—	—	—	—	—	—	—	1	340	—	—
Total	1	210	—	—	—	—	—	—	—	—	—	—	1	210	—	—
Japan Petroleum Corp.	—	—	—	—	10	2,307	—	—	—	—	—	—	10	2,307	1	214
Others	13	495	1	21	—	—	—	—	—	—	—	—	14	516	—	—
Total others	35	5,328	2	290	10	2,307	1	253	—	—	—	—	49	8,178	4	688
Total	43	6,384	3	396	10	2,307	1	253	—	—	—	—	57	9,340	4	688
Of which combined carriers	3	474	—	—	1	214	—	—	—	—	—	—	4	688	—	—

[a]Includes combined carriers fixed for trading in oil. Duration of charter does not include options to extend period.

SOURCE: Drewry, *Shipping Statistics and Economics.*

EXHIBIT 4-14. *Summary of Government Supports to Maritime Industry*

	Japan	*Sweden*	*United Kingdom*
Construction subsidy	None.	None. However, interest-free loans to yards in financial difficulties are made. Additionally, major price increases recently accepted by numerous customers on orders firmly under control.	None.
Loans & interest, domestic sales	Government-backed. 70% maximum 10 years—interest moratorium years. Interest rates subsidized.	Loans guaranteed to 50% of ship value. Credit period 15 years. Interest as of current bond markets.	None unique.
Loans & interest, foreign sales	Conform with OECD understanding on export credit for ships. Essentially, 8 year term. 7.5% interest rate; 20% of price paid on delivery, 70% of value covered.	Loans available from Export Credit Association. Terms in accord with OECD agreements.	None special. Certain circumstances of unconditionally guaranteed loans result in lower interest rates.
Depreciation	For domestic trade, 16-year maximum rate, 13.4% annually—for foreign trade, complex formula, resulting in less than 16 years.	Flexible and liberal. 30% per year or complete writeoff on 5 years. Ships recently delivered qualify for special investment allowance in addition to 100% depreciation allowance.	"Free," i.e., may be taken at any rate up to 100% first year.
Tax aids	Complex—corporate tax minimized for operators who continue fleet improvement. Credits against foreign trade earnings. Deferred capital gains tax on ship sales.	40% of pre-tax net income to tax-free future investment, with 54% of this available to current working capital. Tax free capital gains from ship sales.	2% relief from taxes on shipbuilding costs. Imported materials exempt from customs duty.
Replacement program	"Scrap and build." Government-backed favorable loans.	None formal.	None formal.
Operating subsidies	Annual and varied—first 5 years service on cross trades and special ones—up to 8% on revenue.	None on foreign trade.	None on foreign trade.

SOURCES: As interpreted by Shipbuilders Council of America, October 1976. Primary: Maritime Subsidies, May 1974, U.S. Dept. of Commerce, Foreign Maritime Aids, December 1974, Kapian and Hatfield. Secondary: Various news items through June 1975.

PART II
Competitor Analysis

The next two cases focus on the in-depth analysis of competitors and the translation of this analysis into predictions about competitive behavior, the interpretation of market signals, and the selection of offensive and defensive competitive moves. "Polaroid–Kodak" examines the impending confrontation between Polaroid and Kodak in the instant camera industry, given that Kodak has decided to enter what has been an exclusive Polaroid preserve. Both firms must interpret each other's behavior, and Polaroid must formulate a defensive strategy while Kodak must formulate an offensive one. "General Electric Versus Westinghouse in Large Turbine Generators" portrays two competitors locked in a bitter and protracted price war. The underlying factors causing the breakdown in industry equilibrium must be identified, and the options available to General Electric to improve industry conditions can be explored.

CASE 5
Polaroid–Kodak

Introduction

On April 20, 1976, Eastman Kodak Company announced that it would challenge Polaroid Corporation's twenty-eight-year-old monopoly of the instant photographic field. At a press conference held that day in the grand ballroom of the Pierre Hotel in New York City, Walter A. Fallon, president of Kodak, personally demonstrated two new cameras and an instant film, which he spoke of as offering "remarkable color quality" to the consumer. Dr. Albert Sieg, leader of the company's seven-year-long development effort, stated that the chemistry of the new film was "fundamentally new."

The earliest responses from Polaroid Corporation were varied. Several days prior to the Kodak announcement one Polaroid employee was quoted in the press as saying, "I've seen it. It's primitive, but it works." Later, on the afternoon of the Kodak demonstration, Polaroid issued a formal statement:

We have had a chance to make a brief comparison between the Polaroid instant picture system and the new Kodak system. The comparison renews our confidence that our leadership in the field of instant photography remains unchallenged.

At the Polaroid annual meeting, held one week after the Kodak announcement, Edwin Land, founder, director of research and chairman of the board of the company, informed his stockholders that their company had filed suit in Federal Court charging Kodak with the infringement of ten Polaroid patents. In an emotion-laden session, during which there were periods of prolonged applause from the crowd, Land commented on the situation:

"This is our very soul that we are involved with. This is our whole life. For them it's just another field. . . . The only thing that keeps us alive is our brilliance, and the only thing protecting our brilliance is our patents. . . . We will stay in our lot and protect that lot [it is] an overlap of their way onto our way. How serious this is remains to be seen. That's for the courts to decide."[1]

Land continued, in a session that some reporters described as a strange blend of ridicule and outrage, to comment that since the introduction of the Kodak system Polaroid had been "in a state of euphoria"; that Polaroid's real fear had been that Kodak's product "might incorporate some of the

[1] *New York Times,* April 28, 1976.

really brilliant ideas we've had but never incorporated ourselves''; and that ''the new guys would like to confine its use to cocktail parties.''[2]

Other events at the Polaroid annual meeting centered on several new products now in the late planning or preproduction stages, among them: instant color transparencies; instant color movies; an 8-by-10-inch instant camera and film; and, finally, a camera the size of a room for making full color, instant, life-size copies of museum paintings that, in Land's words, ''will change the whole world of Art . . . make great paintings available in every high school . . . (and) bring museums into the home.''[3] Land also demonstrated an improved SX-70 film incorporating a coating to reduce surface reflections as well as the ability to develop properly over a wider temperature range.

Polaroid Corporation

Origins and Growth

In 1949, the first full year of sales for the Polaroid camera (a 5 pound, $90, revolutionary product that produced brown and white pictures one minute after exposure), the firm's sales more than quadrupled (to $6.7 million) over those of the previous year. Twenty-seven years later the company's sales broke the $800 million mark, proving to all the skeptics that what they had considered a mere ''fad'' was, in fact, one of the most dramatic achievements in the history of photography. In the twenty-eight-year period, from 1947 to 1975, Polaroid's sales grew at an average annual compounded rate of over 25 percent (see Exhibit 5–1), while profits and common stock price advanced by more than 17 percent per year (see Exhibit 5–2). In an accomplishment matched by only a handful of companies, Polaroid's average price-earning's ratio during this entire period was 44. By 1969 each dollar invested in Polaroid common stock in 1948 had grown to more than $500. This consistent and clearly outstanding financial performance could be broken down into several distinct phases.

Although for most people the story of Polaroid began in Boston, Massachusetts, in November 1948 with the first retail sales of the now famous ''picture in a minute'' Polaroid Land Camera, in reality Polaroid (or more accurately Edwin Land) had been in business for almost twenty years by that time. Land's initial research, begun when he was a freshman at Harvard University in 1926, was with means of polarizing light. In 1932 he and an associate created the Land-Wheelwright Laboratories, Inc., to develop, manufacture and sell light-polarizing filters. The company's first product was the ''Polaroid'' filter; the name Polaroid was derived from the fact that the filter was composed of celluloid material which polarized light.

The first two customers of any great size for Land-Wheelwright were Eastman Kodak Company, which signed a contract in 1934 for the purchase of ''Polascreens,'' and American Optical Company, which signed a contract in 1935 for the purchase of filter material to be used in ''Polaroid Day Glasses'' (sunglasses). The money from these contracts provided the young company with funds to continue its development of Polaroid filter products. An additional $750,000 supplied by two investment banking firms in 1937 (in the form of a private placement) enabled the company to continue its search for profitable applications for the filter. At that time the most promising applications appeared to be in 3D movies (which required special polarized glasses to be worn by each viewer) and automobile headlights and windshields (where it was thought the product could reduce the glare from the headlights of oncoming vehicles at night).

Polaroid's sales grews from $142,000 in 1937 to $1,481,000 in 1948[4], most of the increase represented by sales of Polaroid filter material for use in sunglasses. The company was never successful with its plans to have polarizing filters used in movies, automobiles, and elsewhere to the extent originally envisioned. This resulted in a much smaller company than Edwin Land appeared to be comfortable with. Late in 1943 Land began working on the ideas that would form the basis for an ''instant'' photographic process and camera. His first patent application on the topic appears to have been made

---

[2] *Wall Street Journal,* April 28, 1976.
[3] *Boston Globe,* April 28, 1976.

[4] The casewriter has excluded sales made to the government during World War II.

in June 1944, and by that time work on the "Land Camera" must have been under way at Polaroid. In 1945, by means of a rights offering to existing stockholders, $2 million was raised by the company.

From 1947 to 1962 Polaroid's revolutionary instant photographic product was essentially a black-and-white print system for amateur use. While as first introduced the product was far from perfect in comparison with conventional materials, it did offer the consumer a way of making pictures that was truly unique. Until 1950 the large and bulky roll film camera could produce only Sepia (brown and white) pictures of sometimes uneven quality from a film of comparatively low ASA speed. In May 1950, however, the company introduced a true black-and-white film with an ASA speed of 100. In 1955 panchromatic films with ASA speeds of 200 and 400 were introduced. In 1959 a black-and-white film with an ASA speed of 3000 was introduced. This last improvement in the company's film was three times as "fast" as any other black and white print film available to amateurs at the time. It allowed most pictures to be taken with existing light, even those taken indoors at night.

In 1960 the development time to obtain a finished print was reduced for all films from the original 60 seconds down to 10 seconds. Also in 1960 the company introduced its first camera with automatic exposure control. By the end of 1962 the company had sold 4 million Polaroid cameras in its fifteen-year history as a photographic products company. See Appendix A for information on the market for amateur photographic products.

Major Strategic Policies

During its exploitation of the market for its black-and-white instant photographic system, Polaroid's financial strategy appeared to be always to preserve capital for investment in the aspects of its business that would yield the highest possible returns. Plants and equipment were usually rented or leased; camera manufacture was always subcontracted to others; and negative material, although developed by Polaroid itself, was always purchased under long-term contracts from Eastman Kodak. Capital investments were made only in the critical or truly proprietary aspects of manufacturing. The company never made any significant use of long-term debt.

In the marketplace, the company reached out directly to the consumer by advertising. Dealers and distributors were looked upon merely as means to deliver the product to the consumer; passive rather than active participants in the sales cycle. Industry observers were always amazed by the company's willingness to have its products sold at nearly cost by outlets that used them to build retail traffic. The company shied away from distributors and concentrated on direct sales to large retailers. Moreover, the company never appeared to be concerned over the high turnover in its sales staff, which, in the opinion of many observers, it treated more as "order-takers" than as true salesmen. Rarely, if ever, did the company utilize sales incentives for dealers in the form of co-op advertising programs, mixed-case discounts, or introductory specials. In terms of the product itself, the company frequently surprised the market with sudden introductions of improvements in the product. Generally available on an allocated basis to dealers during the first few months following their introduction, these improvements quite often left dealers with merchandise they had to dispose of as best they could before they were able to replace it with the newer form.

With respect to the other companies in the industry, Polaroid remained apart. It never licensed others to manufacture cameras for its highly profitable films. Indeed, the company built an extensive wall of patent protection about its camera designs and diligently defended its position as the sole manufacturer of instant cameras and films in any form whatsoever.

Perhaps most important, the company never appeared to be interested in diversification at all. Every product introduced since 1948 related solely to the photographic process in its instant form. The company never gave any public indication of interest in any other activity.

An important aspect of Polaroid was always Edwin Land's total involvement in and identification with his company, of which he owned about 20 percent during the early 1960s. Land's management style seemed to some outsiders to be almost more a form of philosophy than anything else. Annual meetings at Polaroid were always a unique experience for stockholders; sales and earnings figures were hardly ever mentioned. At typical meetings Land would demonstrate one or more new products or processes he and his large research team had developed. Most often these demonstrations, which in many cases were much like seminars or lectures, were totally unrelated to the products the company intended to introduce in the future. From time to time Land would remind his stockholders why Polaroid existed: "Our function is to sense a deep human need . . . then satisfy it. . . . Our company has been dedicated throughout its life to making only those things which others cannot make. . . . We proceed from basic science to highly desirable products."

Results by 1962

By 1962 Polaroid's financial success over the preceding fifteen years had been impressive. Since 1947 sales had grown by an average of 42 percent per year compounded, profits by 25 percent per year. The common stock price had advanced at a rate of some 41 percent per year. By the end of 1962 Polaroid had become the second largest photographic products company in the United States. However, also by this time sales had remained almost level for the third year in a row, implying that Polaroid had perhaps saturated the market for its black-and-white product in all its forms (amateur roll films, professional sheet films, x-ray film and transparencies) and that the total market was not growing very rapidly.

The Introduction of Instant Color

On January 28, 1963, the stock market analysts' dreams were answered: Polaroid introduced a color print film with a development time of sixty seconds. First sold on a limited basis in the Miami area, the film was compatible with all existing Polaroid cameras. As with the earlier black-and-white system, this product was another major technological achievement for the company. Prior to "Polacolor," color film processing and printing required more than twenty steps and ninety-three minutes. The new Polacolor film not only offered color to

the owners of Polaroid cameras, it also produced its own protective plastic coating as a part of the development process. At that time all of Polaroid's black-and-white films required the application of a protective coating by hand, a messy and often difficult procedure for many amateur photographers.

In June 1963 the company introduced film in convenient "packs," in both the ASA 3000 speed black-and-white print and Polacolor types, designed to be used with a new automatic exposure "Colorpack" camera, the "Automatic 100," priced at $100 retail. Following much the same strategy it had used with black-and-white, the company gradually reduced the prices of its cameras. In 1964 a lower-priced version of the Colorpack was introduced at a suggested list price of $75, followed a year later by a full line of cameras carrying suggested full prices ranging from $50 up to more than $150. In 1967 a second generation of Colorpack cameras was introduced with slightly lower prices overall. In April 1969 the company introduced its first truly low-priced camera, the $29.95 Colorpack. All of these cameras used Polacolor film, ASA speed 75, in the same easy-to-load pack size.

During this same period the company began to emphasize foreign sales of its products, where selling strategy closely followed that employed domestically. See Exhibit 5–1.

In an effort to gain distribution for its products in drugstores, supermarkets, and other unconventional photo outlets, in 1965 the company introduced its "Swinger" camera and film. Swinger was a $19.95 (list price) semi-automatic exposure, fixed-focus, plastic bodied camera that used a low-cost black-and-white roll film which did not require coating after processing. Several million of these cameras were sold in just three years. In 1968 the company completely phased out the Swinger by introducing its "Big Swinger" at a suggested list price of $24.95. The Big Swinger was identical in every respect to the previous model, with the exception of price and the fact that it used ASA 3000 speed film in the same packs as Polaroid's other cameras. In 1969 the introduction of the Colorpack camera, which listed for only $5 more than the Big Swinger, virtually halted all sales of the latter. The Colorpack offered fully automatic exposure and the ability to use Polacolor film at a retail price differential of about $3 on the average. By 1970 all traces of the

Swinger and Big Swinger had been removed from retailers' shelves. Even the roll film for the original Swinger became almost impossible to obtain.

Results by 1972

As with the previous success in black-and-white, color caused explosive growth at Polaroid. By 1969, however, the company was facing softness in the demand for its products once again as may be seen from Exhibit 5-1. Fortunately for the company, during this period foreign sales expanded rapidly as a result of the gradual introduction of the same products that had given the company its growth in the domestic market during the 1960s.

The SX-70 System Is Introduced

In November 1969 Polaroid, through a rights offering to existing stockholders, raised $99 million. The prospectus stated that the company was about to undertake another step in its search for the absolute form of one-step photography: The money was to be used to help finance the research, development, and manufacture of a totally new instant color film and camera system. Just a little more than three years later, in November of 1972, the first SX-70 cameras and film went on limited sale in the Miami area. The camera, available in only one model, carried a suggested list price of $180, six times that of the company's Colorpack model, while the film was priced at $6.90 (list) for ten exposures, compared with $5.49 for Polacolor pack film's eight exposures.

Shrouded in the greatest of secrecy from the beginning of its design, the SX-70 system was another truly revolutionary product. The company had designed a product that was intended to alter the fundamentals of the industry and eventually make obsolete both earlier instant camera systems, i.e. roll and pack film types. In Land's own words, "Photography will never be the same. . . . With the Gargantuan effort of bringing SX-70 into being, the Company has come fully of age." With a romantic flair that only Land could have fully appreciated, the name SX-70 was chosen because it

had been the code name of the original camera project in 1944.

From the consumer's point of view the SX-70 was indeed a different kind of Polaroid camera and film. What had previously generated large quantities of chemically coated waste paper, e.g. used negative material and related paper goods, was now a totally litter-free system. Of perhaps equal importance, there was now no need to time the development of the picture. Other features included automatic ejection of the picture from the camera by a small electric motor (powered by a fresh battery present in each film pack), single lens reflex viewing and focusing, a folding design that allowed the camera to be carried conveniently in a large pocket or purse and less need for periodic cleaning of critical mechanical components inside the camera. See Appendix B for a more detailed explanation of the differences between the Colorpack and SX-70 systems.

The SX-70 Program

As originally conceived, the SX-70 program was designed to accomplish two major changes at Polaroid. The first was the total integration of the company. All of the manufacturing for SX-70 would be carried out within Polaroid. Toward this end a color negative manufacturing plant and camera assembly plant were designed and built. The program also required an expansion of the firm's existing chemical production facilities and film packaging operation. The total cost of these additions to plant and equipment were estimated, by most observers in 1969, to be about $150 million, including the cost of research and engineering for the SX-70 camera and film.

Although the company never formally disclosed the cost of the SX-70 program, Land once referred to it in an interview as "a half-billion-dollar investment." Some outside estimates have placed the actual figure at much more than that. Speculations as to the source of the $350 million additional investment requirement have centered on two items. First, the company admitted publicly that it was not until January of 1974 that the SX-70 product was breaking even on a variable manufacturing cost basis. It was not until early 1976 that most outside observers felt that the product was profitable in a conventional "normal" accounting sense. Several estimates of the total cost of these manufacturing-related expenses center on a figure of about $250 million over the entire period from 1969 to 1976. Second, some outside observers have concluded that the design and development costs of the film and, most notably, the camera were much higher than anticipated. Both of these factors were related to the second major change SX–70 was intended to bring to Polaroid: the perfection of photography.

For Edwin Land, SX–70 was the realization of a dream, not merely a new product. He often referred to it as "absolute one-step photography." As he stated in a booklet entitled "The SX–70 Experience" (included with the annual report for shareholders in 1974):

> . . . a new kind of relationship between people in groups is brought into being by SX–70 when the members of the group are photographing and being photographed and sharing the photographs: it turns out that buried within us—God knows beneath how many pregenital and Freudian and Calvinistic strata—there is a latent interest in each other; there is tenderness, curiosity, excitement, affection, companionability and humor; it turns out, in this cold world where man grows distant from man, and even lovers can reach each other only briefly, that we have a yen for a primordial competence, for a quiet good-humored delight in each other; we have a prehistoric tribal competence for a non-physical, non-emotional, non-sexual satisfaction in being partners in the lonely exploration of a once empty planet.

Thus at age sixty-three Edwin Land brought into existence his highly personalized message to civilization in the form of the SX–70 system.

The design criteria for the SX–70 had been very straightforward: The photographer must have only to compose his picture and press a button—the photographic process was to be totally segregated from the creative act. In real terms this philosophical task created a number of problems for designers. Rather than use the company's successful $30 Colorpack camera as a starting point, Land ordered his engineers to start from scratch on a totally new design. The parameters of the camera were startling: It must fold to a size appropriate for a pocket or purse; it must be a single lens reflex viewing and focusing design; it must focus from less than a foot to infinity; and, it must be totally automatic (exposure, processing, etc.) and litter-free.

The result, after more than three years of intense development work, was a $180 masterpiece of design. The reflex viewing system alone cost millions; a single mirror, one of three in the camera, took more than two and one-half years of full-time computer work to engineer. The eyepiece design alone cost $2 million to develop. Company sales projections of at least several million cameras (up to 5 million by some accounts) to be sold the first year alone were used as the basis for capacity decisions in the plants under construction during the design stage. Long before the camera design was finalized the company's color negative pilot plant began turning out finished packs of SX–70 film.

Marketing the SX–70

In 1973, the first full year of sales for the SX–70 system, 470,000 cameras and 4.5 million packs of film were sold. The company reported that the system had contributed $75 million to its sales that year. During the year the company grappled with several technical problems. The camera factory, still in its infancy, was turning out a disturbing number of defective cameras even though it was operating at only a fraction of its capacity. At one point the company began to open Polaroid "Service Centers" in large cities across the United States in an effort to help consumers with their problems.

A more troublesome technical problem was encountered when it was discovered that fumes from the battery present in each film pack (this had been done to eliminate the need for a yearly battery change on the part of users) were seriously degrading the color quality of the pictures. Related in part to this problem was the fact that the battery had a shelf life of only several months at best. After a considerable period of time, during which the company worked with the company that manufactured the batteries, Polaroid made the decision to build a plant and produce its own batteries. Within a few months the shelf life of the film was extended to six months and color quality improved dramatically.

By far the greatest problem facing Polaroid by the end of 1973 was the fact that camera sales were nowhere near the projected level. Both camera and film manufacturing operations were running at only a small fraction of their rated capacity. Although the company sold about 4 million Colorpacks and an estimated 100 million packs of Polacolor film in 1973, both negative and camera manufacturing for this product line were subcontracted to others.

In 1974, in an attempt to stimulate SX-70 sales, the company introduced an SX-70 Model II camera. Identical to the original in every respect except for price ($140 suggested retail) and exterior finish (all plastic verses chrome-plated plastic and genuine leather for the original), it was estimated by trade sources that this model helped to boost SX-70 camera sales during 1974 to about 750,000 units. The casewriter's estimate for factory sales of the SX-70 system in 1974 was $100 million domestically.

Faced with continuing resistance to the product from consumers, in May 1975 the company introduced an SX-70 Model III camera, which carried a suggested list price of $99. The Model III abandoned the reflex viewing arrangement of the other two models and replaced it with a conventional, and far simpler, viewfinder type. The company reported that it sold a total of about 1 million SX-70 cameras during 1975. The casewriter's estimate for the 1975 sales volume of the SX-70 system was $150 million, about 80 percent from domestic sales.

In 1975 the company reported that it had sold about 4 million Colorpack cameras for the third year in a row. In March 1975 the company introduced its "Supershooter" Colorpack camera at a suggested retail price of $24.95. Also in March the company introduced "Polacolor II" Colorpack film, which offered the consumer excellent color in an instant product for the first time. Prior to Polacolor II instant prints had tended to be somewhat subdued and lacked saturation as compared to conventional color prints and slides. Both Supershooter and Polacolor II were manufactured by Polaroid in its own plants.

In January 1976 Polaroid introduced a Model IV

SX-70 called the "Pronto!" Pronto! was a non-folding, nonreflex, molded-plastic body camera with a suggested list price of $66. This model was widely discounted by retailers to $49 (only a few dollars over cost), and by late April 1976 sales and advance orders of Pronto! had exceeded 400,000 units. Industry observers began predicting that during 1976 as many as 2 million SX-70 cameras might be sold.

Polaroid in April 1976

As of April 1976 the suggested retail and common discount prices of the most popular models in each of Polaroid's instant systems were as presented in Table 5-1.

There were three significant differences between these systems. First, in terms of pricing, while the Supershooter sold for less than half of the price for Pronto!, the cost per print was about 25 percent higher because Colorpack film had eight exposures per pack versus ten for SX-70 film. Second, the color quality of the pictures made from Polacolor II film was far superior to that possible with SX-70 film.[5] Polacolor II prints rivaled conventional color prints in quality. Finally, in terms of camera operation, while all the Pronto! user did was to focus and press a button, after which the motor in the camera ejected the print, which developed automatically in about twelve minutes with no litter, the Supershooter user had to pull each exposure from the camera, time the development for sixty seconds, and then find a place to dispose of the used negative (which was covered with a highly alkaline processing jelly).

In terms of manufacturing costs the systems had contrasting patterns. While both SX-70 film and Polacolor II film were essentially identical, in that they both required a negative, processing reagent,

---

[5] Or the new Kodak instant film. (Casewriter's personal judgment, and assessment of industry opinion.)

TABLE 5-1.

System	Camera Prices		Film Prices	
	LIST	DISCOUNT	LIST	DISCOUNT
SX-70 (Pronto!)	$66.00	$49.00	$6.99	$5.50
Colorpack (Supershooter)	$28.00	$23.00	$6.75	$5.50

and print material, each SX–70 pack also required a battery to power the camera's flash, exposure, and print ejection motor. From the perspective of cameras, however, the Pronto! was essentially a Supershooter with a mirror and an electric motor added. These facts led industry observers to speculate as to the actual source of profits from each system as well as to try to predict the degree to which prices could be changed if necessary.

By April 1976 Polaroid had about 25 million Colorpack cameras in use worldwide, as compared with an estimated 2 million SX–70s. Most industry observers agreed that the Colorpack system was the more profitable of the two, contributing at least 95 percent to the company's earnings. See Exhibit 5–3 for a five-year summary of Polaroid's financial statements, including full data for 1975.

Eastman Kodak Company

Origins and Growth

George Eastman had a bit of a jump on Edwin Land; he marketed his first camera in 1888. Kodak's motto, "You press the button, we do the rest," and the ubiquitous "yellow box" were revolutionary developments of their time, sweeping America and the world for 60 years before the first Land camera appeared. Kodak was the world's first integrated photographic firm, so fully integrated at one point that it owned its own stockyards so that it could control the quality of the source for its large needs of photographic-grade gelatin.

As any trip to the average corner drugstore in the United States would reveal, Kodak products, film and cameras, clearly dominated the market for conventional amateur products in 1976. Most estimates of Kodak's market shares were 90 percent for film and 85 percent for cameras at that time. The firm's share of the expenditures for processing and printing of amateur films was only about 15 percent, largely a result of a 1954 consent decree with the U.S. Justice Department which stipulated that Kodak would sell its films and processing separately. However, when the dollar value of the print paper, chemicals, and processing equipment the company sold to independent photofinishers was

added in, the company's effective market share for processing was probably closer to 50 percent overall.

Kodak was active in many more markets than those for conventional amateur still films, cameras, and processing. For example, through its Eastman Chemicals Division (1975 sales $1 billion) it sold a wide variety of chemicals, fibers, and plastics to industrial customers. The company's domestic and foreign photographic divisions (1975 sales $4.5 billion combined) marketed a wide range of products including amateur movie films and equipment, professional still and motion picture films and equipment, medical and industrial x-ray films and equipment, various graphic arts and audiovisual products, and microfilm and other business products. Kodak was, with rare exceptions, the leader in each market in which it competed. Compared to Agfa-Gavaert of Belgium, the only other full-line photographic products company in the world, Kodak was a giant; its photographic sales alone were three times those of Agfa in 1975. See Exhibit 5–4 for a ten-year summary of Kodak's sales and earnings.

Major Strategic Policies

Kodak's dominance of the photographic industry seemed to most observers to stem primarily from its leadership in film technology. To Kodak's competitors the firm's complete mastery of all aspects of the photographic art was a mighty barrier. Since the introduction of Kodachrome (ASA speed 10) in 1935, the first color film for amateur use, Kodak had managed to keep ahead of every other company in almost every aspect of photography. It was Kodak that foresaw and nurtured the color slide and color print for the amateur market. It was not until 1954, when the Justice Department forced it to sell film and processing separately, that other companies were even allowed to participate in Kodak's lucrative color products. In the twenty-year period in which it captured all the profits from both film manufacturing and processing (a situation *all* film manufacturers agree is the ideal), it also prevented the formation of independent photofinishing laboratories equipped to process color products sold by its competitors. The net effect of the tied-in sale of processing was thus to retard the dispersion of color film technology and to allow Kodak to become the dominant company in amateur color photography.

Even after 1954 Kodak was able to capitalize on its previous success by constantly forcing competitors to upgrade the quality of their color film products. Most firms simply did not have the expertise in the research laboratory to continue the fight. During the 1950s Kodak effectively displaced all foreign and domestic competitors from the U.S. market. In addition it successfully defended itself against inroads from formidable would-be competitors. In the early 1960s a joint venture between Bell & Howell[6] and Dupont, which had been formed in the late 1950s, failed completely. Dupont described its color film research program as an exasperating effort in which each time it was able to improve its film to meet Kodak's high quality, Kodak film mysteriously became even better. In 1961, when Dupont's film was finally ready for introduction, at a total cost to both companies estimated by some to be in the tens of millions of dollars, Kodak responded to the threat with "Kodachrome II," a color slide film with an ASA speed of 25 and far better color quality than the original against which the Dupont entry was targeted. The Dupont product was withdrawn before it ever reached the market.

For a time some competitors attempted to increase their share of the market by lowering their prices slightly. The response from consumers was nil, indicating what was interpreted to be an unwillingness to accept less quality, or less assurance of quality, under almost any circumstance. In 1976 most competitive color film products were sold for a slight premium over Kodak's prices. What appeared to be responsible for the survival of most of Kodak's competitors was the existence of a small "following," those who wished to avoid the supersaturated colors, extremely high resolution, or mass market image of Kodak's color films. Although Kodak had always manufactured a full line of cameras for its films, the company's early success in dominating the amateur color film market was almost solely a direct result of the firm's expertise in color film technology.

---

[6] At the time Kodak's film and camera business alone was about ten times the size of Bell & Howell's total sales.

1963: The First Kodak System

Since the introduction of the company's "Instamatic" camera and film products in 1963, however, Kodak's emphasis in the amateur photographic market had been on "systems"—unique film formats packaged in a cartridge or magazine usable only in cameras designed expressly for that configuration. On February 28, 1963, the Instamatic system was introduced with complete availability of the product on that day to 75,000 retailers in 147 countries supported by major advertising in eight languages. Prices for the camera, available in five models, ranged from $20 up to over $100 (list). Ten million Instamatic cameras were sold in the twenty-six months following their introduction.

In that same year Kodak also introduced "Kodachrome-X" (ASA speed 64) color slide film for 35 mm and Instamatic cameras and the "Super 8" film and camera system for the amateur movie market. The main feature of the Super 8 and Instamatic systems was that the films were cartridge-loaded into cameras equipped, in most models, with automatic exposure. For the first time in conventional amateur photography consumers were relieved of two major obstacles to their picture-taking: the manual dexterity required for loading roll-film cameras, and the decision-making problem of setting proper exposure. The Instamatic cameras also featured a more convenient flashbulb device, the "Flashcube," which provided four flash bulbs in an easy-to-insert configuration (including a disposable reflector for each bulb). Previous to the Flashcube, flashbulb devices tended to be rather bulky and unreliable.

As one might have predicted, both systems resulted in not only a dramatic increase in the sales of Kodak's cameras but also an equally impressive increase in the rate with which film was used in these by consumers.

1972: The Second Kodak System

In May 1972 Kodak introduced its "Pocket" Instamatic system in a manner similar to that used in 1963 with the original system. The main improvement for consumers purchasing the Pocket Instamatics was the dramatic reduction in the size of the camera, which was about one-third that of the original model. Prices for the camera, available in five models, ranged from $25 up to more than $200 (list).

Also in May of 1972 Kodak introduced its "XL" Super 8 amateur movie system. The principal feature of this product was that it allowed the user to film under most existing light conditions. For example, the light from a single candle on a birthday cake was, in most instances, adequate for proper exposure of subjects within several feet of the cake. In the fall of 1972 Kodak added a line of sound movie cameras to its XL Super 8 line, bringing the total number of Kodak Super 8 movie cameras to five, ranging in price from $35 to $200 (list).

In April 1975 Kodak introduced a new generation of Pocket Instamatics, the "Trimlite" series. The chief improvement in this version of the Instamatic was the use of a small piezo-electric crystal to generate electricity to fire a new form of flashbulb, the "Flipflash." One of the cameras in the line was also equipped with a telephoto lens, which could be brought into position by moving a small slide at the top of the camera. Industry observers were quick to note that the name, as well as the fact that the most expensive camera in the line was equipped with a provision to use an ASA 400 color print film, was indicative of the fact that Kodak was close to bringing out its long-awaited "XL" still camera color film, which would dispense with the need for flashbulbs entirely.

Industry Reactions

The effect of the two Instamatic waves on the conventional amateur market was significant. By the end of 1975 it was estimated that Kodak had sold more than 60 million Instamatic cameras in just a little more than a decade. During this same period all of Kodak's competitors combined had sold, by most estimates, no more than 10 million Instamatic-type cameras. By surprising the industry with radical changes in both camera structure and film requirements the company was able to consolidate its position in the market place. Independent camera manufacturers were faced with a need to invest in increasingly complex production equipment to remain competitive in terms of price with Kodak. Kodak's expanding use of precision plastic optics,

integrated circuits and piezo-electric type devices left many manufacturers dumfounded. Film manufacturers were equally amazed by Kodak's ability to push film technology to new limits by the use of smaller negatives and higher ASA speeds in both color print and transparency films without significant reductions in quality. Independent processors were forced to buy new processing equipment and learn new techniques to stay in business. And always, all of Kodak's competitors had to face the fact that Kodak's product would be on sale for a year or more before they were able to react effectively.

To counteract some of the criticism it was receiving from other manufacturers, Kodak freely licensed its systems. For Kodak the benefits were twofold. First, of course, it probably lessened Kodak's vulnerability to antitrust suits. More important, perhaps, Kodak benefited from the fact that licensing increased the number of cameras in use that could use its highly profitable films. In the still film amateur market, the Pocket Instamatic format, which used a negative only 25 percent of the size used until that time, had substantially eliminated all but one or two of Kodak's film sales competitors.

All of this success for Kodak in the market place made more than one company seek restitution elsewhere. In 1973 Bell & Howell filed a private antitrust suit against Kodak charging that the Pocket Instamatic and XL Super 8 systems were introduced in such a way that competing manufacturers were prevented from marketing their own products. The suit also charged that the practice of marketing systems was restricting competition in the amateur photographic products market. Kodak settled the suit by offering to give Bell & Howell eighteen months' advance notice prior to the introduction of any new conventional amateur systems.

Also in 1973 Berkey Photo, Inc., filed a private antitrust suit against Kodak charging the firm with restrictive marketing practices and asking for treble damages of $300 million, advance disclosure of new products, free patent licenses, free know-how and technical advice, and a general break-up of Kodak into separate companies. At the time this case was written the suit was still pending.

In 1974 GAF Corporation filed a private antitrust suit charging Kodak with marketing systems, changing the components of systems to adversely affect competitors products, disclosing new systems far in advance of the actual intended date of introduction to discourage sales of competing products, and the use of huge advertising budgets to ensure the dominance of Kodak in various markets. The GAF suit, in the pretrial stage at the time of this writing, sought treble damages of proven losses, free know-how and technical advice, the break-up of Kodak into ten separate companies, and the dedication of the trademark "Kodak" to the public domain.

Also in 1974 Pavelle Corporation filed suit against Kodak charging that the company had test marketed, at the same time as Pavelle, a color print paper and related chemicals at prices below which Pavelle could profitably sell these, causing Pavelle to file bankruptcy. In addition to most of the charges mentioned in the other suits against Kodak, Pavelle specifically sought the divestiture by Kodak of its color print and chemical businesses. At the time of this writing, this suit was still pending.

Kodak has not always been the defendant, however. Since 1972 the company had been challenging certain Polaroid patents in foreign countries (most notably Britain, Canada, Germany, Australia, and Japan) in an apparent attempt to clear a path for an instant camera and film of its own. While such challenges were not technically legal actions, they could become the basis for evidence to be submitted in the event a U.S.-based patent infringement suit was ever filed against Kodak by Polaroid. Such a suit was in fact filed by Polaroid at 4:59 P.M. on April 26, 1976, the day before the annual meetings of both companies.[7]

Kodak's Instant System

As stated previously, on April 20, 1976, Eastman Kodak publicly demonstrated its own instant photographic product for the amateur market. In February of 1976 the company had announced that sometime in April it would make that demonstration, but it was not until the day of the demonstration that the company revealed that its product would go on sale first in Canada, on May 1, 1976, and in the United States on July 5, 1976. While rumors of a Kodak instant product had been circulating in the industry for more than a decade (peaking at one point in 1969 when leaks of a Kodak–Polaroid agreement to allow the former to market a Colorpack compatible film of its own by sometime in 1975 were reported in various publications), it was not until early 1970 that Kodak formally announced that work on a Colorpack type film was under way.

In its 1973 annual report, however, Kodak indicated that it had altered its research goals somewhat:

> In the field of rapid-access photography the basic decisions have . . . made feasible a film that will yield dry prints of high quality without waste, to be used in equipment priced for a wide spectrum of consumers.

This announcement by Kodak left some industry observers puzzled as to whether Kodak's film was still intended for use in Colorpack type cameras. In 1974's annual report the company clarified its statement further: "During the year, Kodak completed the design of its own instant cameras and finalized the format and characteristics of a litter-free film for instant prints."

Thus Kodak had, within a comparatively brief period, moved away from the idea of making a film for existing cameras. It now intended to market a system of its own design.

In its 1975 annual report the company devoted a total of four pages to a detailed explanation of its progress in instant photography, as well as two full pages describing its new "Ektaprint 100" Xerox-type copier, which had been on limited sale since October 1975.

Some observers, noting that most of Polaroid's "basic" patent protection had run out by 1969, were concerned at the seemingly ponderous method by which Kodak finally reached the market with an instant product of its own. But others, as they compared the Kodak system with its competition (see Exhibits 5–5, 5–6, and 5–7), were more impressed by Kodak's decision to bring out a completely new

---

[7] Polaroid was also involved in other legal actions. In 1975 it sued Berkey Photo for the infringement of patents relating to the SX-70 camera. Berkey had introduced a camera that used SX-70 film. In a cross-action Berkey was charging Polaroid with the monopolization of the instant photographic market, held that the patents in question were invalid, and was seeking a cancellation of the trademark "Polaroid." Also in 1975 Bell & Howell and Polaroid had become involved in a dispute relating to the production of instant movie camera equipment by B&H for Polaroid. As of the time of this writing the Berkey suit was outstanding, and the Bell & Howell conflict had been settled out of court.

system and the company's stated intention of freely licensing others to build cameras that could use the film. With respect to licensing the production of film cartridges and film itself for its instant product, however, Kodak was silent. But one executive of a competing film manufacturing company commented, "It would take us three to five years and a lot of money to come up with a film for that camera."

Kodak's Annual Meeting

At the Kodak annual meeting held one week after the introduction of the Kodak Instant, and coincidentally on the same day as Polaroid's annual meeting, Walter A. Fallon, Kodak's President, responded as follows to several stockholder questions about the new product:

> There will be no time for resting on laurels, however. I can tell you that the curtain will rise on yet another member of the Kodak instant family within the coming year. This will be the Kodak EK8 Instant Camera, a folding model designed and built at the Kodak Camera Works in West Germany.

Fallon went on to say that expressions of interest in the Kodak Instant from the trade were "at a high and very positive pitch." When asked if Kodak planned to introduce an under $20 "EK2" instant camera, Fallon declined to comment. At that point, however, he did confirm that the EK8 would "probably" be available by early fall 1976 and that it would carry a suggested retail price of "about $140."

Later on the day of the annual meeting, at a luncheon held for security analysts, Fallon commented on the Polaroid patent suit by saying, "We believe that our patent position is sound. We don't knowingly infringe anybody else's valid patents."

See Exhibit 5–8 for Kodak's financial statements for 1975.

EXHIBIT 5–1. *Polaroid Corporation, Summary of*

SALES VOLUME
(Millions of dollars)

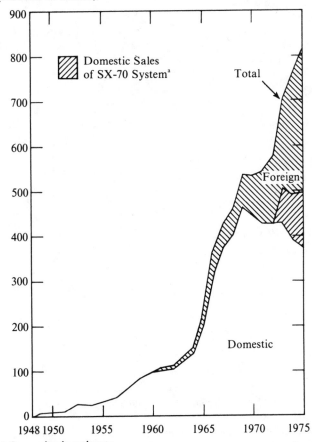

^a Casewriter's estimate.
SOURCE: Company annual reports.

EXHIBIT 5-2. *Polaroid, Summary of EPS and Stock Price, 1948-1975*

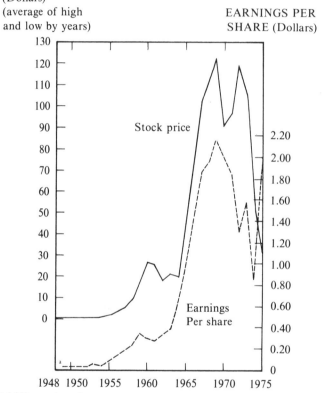

SELLING PRICE
PER SHARE
(Dollars)
(average of high
and low by years)

EARNINGS PER
SHARE (Dollars)

[a] (.32) per share loss.
SOURCES: Company annual reports. Merrill Lynch, Inc.,
historical library.

EXHIBIT 5-3. *Polaroid Corporation*

A. Consolidated Financial Statements, Year Ending December 31, 1975 (in millions of dollars)

Income Statement		Balance Sheet	
Net Sales	813	*Assets*	
		Current:	
Less:		Cash	22
		Marketable securities, at cost	158
Cost of goods sold	468	Receivables	181
Advertising expense	52	Inventories	244
Research & development	64	Prepaid expenses	26
Administrative expenses	121	Total current assets	631
Operating Profit	108	Fixed	
		Property, plant & equipment, at cost	435
Less:		Less accumulated depreciation	232
		Net property, plant & equipment	203
Interest expense	1	Total Assets	834
Plus:		*Liabilities & Equity*	
		Current Liabilities:	
Interest income	9	Notes payable to banks	12
Other income (expense)	7	Payables and accruals	80
		Taxes payable	53
Profit Before Tax	123	Total current liabilities	145
Less:		Stockholder's Equity:	
		Common stock at par value	33
Income taxes	61	Additional paid-in capital	122
		Retained earnings	534
Net Profit	62	Total stockholder's equity	689
Cash dividends paid	10	Total Liabilities & Equity	834

(*cont.*)

EXHIBIT 5–3. *Polaroid Corporation (cont.)*

B. Five-Year Financial Review (in thousands, except per share and employee data)

Summary of Operations	1975	1974	1973	1972	1971
Net sales	$812,703	$757,296	$685,536	$559,288	$525,507
Cost of sales	467,934	485,158	358,046	260,075	243,575
Selling, advertising, research, engineering, distribution and administrative expenses	236,995	239,347	251,628	236,741	180,934
Total costs	704,929	724,505	609,674	496,816	424,509
Profit from operations	107,774	32,791	75,862	62,472	100,998
Other income	16,772	13,425	14,277	13,574	16,074
Interest expense	1,272	1,098	316	836	346
Earnings before income taxes	123,274	45,118	89,823	75,210	116,726
Federal, state and foreign income taxes	60,684	16,731	38,005	32,676	55,708
Net earnings	$ 62,590	$ 28,387	$ 51,818	$ 42,534	$ 61,018
Earnings per share[a]	$ 1.91	$ .86	$ 1.58	$ 1.30	$ 1.86
Cash dividends per share	$ .32	$ .32	$ .32	$ .32	$ .32
Average number of shares	32,855	32,855	32,853	32,844	32,837
Financial position at year end					
Working capital	$485,666	$412,600	$390,734	$352,432	$330,908
Net property, plant and equipment	203,351	224,341	228,334	224,535	213,272
Stockholders' equity	689,017	636,941	619,068	576,967	544,180
Other statistical information					
Additions to property, plant and equipment	$ 21,829	$ 39,951	$ 40,265	$ 44,560	$ 60,167
Depreciation	39,151	39,614	35,326	32,018	22,329
Number of employees, end of year	13,387	13,019	14,277	11,998	11,654
Payroll and benefits	$225,896	$223,154	$191,315	$160,247	$136,741

[a]Per share earnings based on average number of shares outstanding during the year.

SOURCE: Polaroid Corporation 1975 Annual Report.

EXHIBIT 5-4. *Eastman Kodak Company: Summary of Sales and Earnings, 1966–1975*

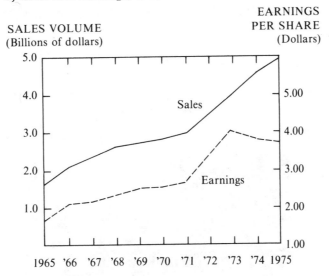

NOTE: Approximate percentage of total sales contributed by divisions (including interdivisional sales) were as follows:

Division	1966	1975
U.S. & Canadian Photographic	60%	50%
International Photographic	21%	31%
Eastman Chemicals	19%	19%

SOURCE: Casewriter's estimates from data in company annual reports.

EXHIBIT 5-5. *Polaroid and Kodak Instant Cameras Compared*

Aspect	Polaroid Pronto!	Kodak EK6 Instant Camera
List Price	$66.00	$69.50
Exposure System	Fully Automatic	Fully Automatic
Focusing Range	3′ to infinity	3½′ to infinity
Focusing Method	Estimation	Rangefinder, zone symbols
Film counter	Yes	Yes
Method of Film Ejection	Automatic	Automatic (manual in EK4)
Weight	15 ounces	29 ounces
Size	Small, Irregular Shape	Medium, Rectangular Solid Shape
Carrying Strap	Yes, for Wrist	Yes, for Neck
Flashbulb Type	Flashbar, 10 Shots per bar	Flipflash, 8 Shots per bar
Lens	3 element plastic, 116 mm	3 element plastic, 137 mm
Shutter Speeds	1 second to 1/125th	1/20th to 1/300th
Warranty Period	1 year	3 years
Flash Distance	3 to 12 Feet	4 to 10 feet
Fill Flash Capability	Yes	No
Flash Warning Light	No	Yes
Camera Power Source	From battery in film pack	From batteries in camera, change yearly
F-Stop Range	F9.4 to F22	F11 or F116

SOURCES: Company publications and news articles.

EXHIBIT 5-6.   *Polaroid and Kodak Instant Cameras and Films Compared*
I. Cameras

Photograph courtesy of *Modern Photography*

II. Films

Characteristic	Polaroid SX-70	Kodak PR-10
Type	color print film	color print film
Format	square	rectangular
ASA speed	100	150
Image size	3.13″ by 3.13″	2.63″ by 3.56″
Image area	9.77 sq. inches	9.35 sq. inches
Development time	about 12 minutes	about 10 minutes
Color quality[a]	good	good
Color stability[a]	good	good
Exposures per pack	10	10
List price per pack	$6.99	$7.45
Average retail price	$5.50	$5.50
Exposed through	front	rear

[a] From published specifications and casewriter's personal judgment and assessment of industry opinion.

EXHIBIT 5-7. *Price Comparison of Polaroid and Kodak Instant Systems*

	List Price	Average Retail Price[a]
Polaroid		
Camera: Pronto!	$66.00	$49.00
Film: SX-70	6.99	5.50
Flash: Flashbar	3.28	1.89
Cost per picture:		
available light	$ .70	$ .55
flash	$ 1.03	$ .74
Reprints (by mail from Polaroid, $.88 handling charge per order):		
wallet size	$ .39	same
same size	$ .49	same
5 by 5 inches	$ 2.25	same
8 by 8 inches	$ 5.50	same
11 by 11 inches	$ 9.95	same
Kodak		
Camera: EK4	$53.50	$39.00
EK6	69.50	49.00
Film: PR-10	7.45	5.50
Flash: Flipflash	2.30	1.19
Cost per picture:		
available light	$ .75	$ .55
flash	$ 1.04	$ .70
Reprints (available from any Kodak dealer)		
same size	$ .85	$ .68
3½ by 4½ inches	$ 1.00	$ .80
5 by 7 inches	$ 2.25	$ 1.80
8 by 10 inches	$ 5.35	$ 4.28
11 by 14 inches	$10.75	$ 8.60

[a]Based upon interviews with camera dealers in the greater Boston area in May 1976.

SOURCE: Casewriter's fieldwork.

EXHIBIT 5-8. *Eastman Kodak Company, Consolidated Financial Statements, Year Ending December 31, 1975 (in millions of dollars)*

Income Statement		Balance Sheet	
Net Sales	4,959	*Assets*	
		Current:	
Less:		Cash	76
		Marketable securities, at cost	672
Cost of goods sold	2,927	Receivables	804
Advertising expense	a	Inventories	986
Research & development	313	Prepaid expenses	82
Administrative expenses	632	Total current assets	2,620
Operating Profit	1,087	Fixed	
		Property, plant & equipment, at cost	4,438
Less:		Less accumulated depreciation	1,970
		Net property, plant & equipment	2,378
Interest expense	15		
		Total Assets	5,056[b]
Plus:		*Liabilities & Equity*	
		Current Liabilities:	
Interest income	40	Payables and accruals	688
Other income (expense)	(6)	Taxes payable	246
		Dividends payable	143
Profit Before Tax	1,106	Total current liabilities	1,077
Less:		Other Liabilities:	
		4½% convertible debentures, due 1988	66
Income taxes	493	Other long term liabilities	75
		Deferred income taxes	129
Net Profit	613	Total Liabilities	1,347
Cash dividends paid	332	Stockholder's Equity:	
		Common stock at par value	404
		Additional paid-in capital	268
		Retained earnings	3,037
		Total stockholder's equity	3,709
		Total Liabilities & Equity	5,056

[a]Not reported separately, included with "Administrative expenses."
[b]Includes 58 of miscellaneous assets.
SOURCE: Eastman Kodak Company 1975 Annual Report.

APPENDIX A

A Brief Note on the Amateur Photographic Products Market

Because of the highly concentrated nature of the photographic industry it was very difficult to come by precise data on the size and character of the segments that made up the total market for amateur photographic products. Most firms treated their market data with the same degree of secrecy as their film and camera designs. This note is a composite picture made from a wide variety of public sources.

The Market in 1962

In 1962 the total U.S. domestic market for amateur photographic products was about $1.4 billion at the retail level. In that year about 2.2 billion snapshots were taken by amateur photographers.

The total U.S. domestic factory sales of Eastman Kodak for all of its photographic products was estimated to be $600 million at that time. Polaroid Corporation's reported domestic sales were $100 million in 1962, about 40 percent of this volume related to film sales.

In terms of consumer patterns in 1962, about half of the pictures taken were in color, half in black and white. The average consumer used about four rolls of film per year. Sixty percent of the pictures taken were taken by women.

The Market in 1969

In 1969 the total U.S. domestic market for amateur photographic products was about $3.5 billion at the retail level. About 4.5 billion snapshots were taken by amateur photographers that year.

Kodak's domestic sales for all of its photographic products were about $1.5 billion that year. Polaroid reported domestic sales of $466 million that same year. Kodak's domestic sales of still camera films to the amateur market were about $265 million at the time, about $140 million of this from sales of Kodacolor film, about $100 million from Kodachrome and Ektachrome, and about $25 million from its black-and-white films. Polaroid's domestic sales of film to the same market were estimated to be $240 million, about $135 million of this from Polacolor and about $105 million from ASA 3000 speed film. The Kodak figure excluded the company's sales of processing services and its sales of equipment and supplies to the photofinishing industry.

Kodak, by doing all of its own manufacturing for film and camera products, enjoyed an estimated pretax profit margin on these items of about 70 percent. Polaroid, which subcontracted both negative and camera manufacturing, was thought to gross about 45 percent pretax on its cameras and films.

The Market in 1975

In 1975 the total U.S. domestic market for amateur photographic products was about $6.6 billion at the retail level. In that year about 7 billion snapshots were taken by amateur photographers.

Kodak's domestic sales for all of its photographic products was estimated at $2.5 billion. Polaroid reported total domestic sales of $500 million. An analyst's estimate of Kodak's and Polaroid's film sales to the domestic amateur still film market was "about 500 million dollars for each," which was obviously a bit high for Polaroid.

In terms of consumer patterns in 1975, about 90 percent of the pictures taken were in color, 10 percent in black and white. The average consumer used about eight rolls of film per year. 60 percent of the pictures were taken by women. Market data suggested that 92 percent of America's homes owned at least one conventional camera, 49 percent owned at least one Polaroid camera. Surveys taken by Kodak suggested that as many as 24 million American homes would buy an instant camera with "improved features."

In 1975 the total world market for amateur photographic products was about $14 billion at the retail level. Worldwide sales of cameras and films were estimated at $2 billion for Kodak, $800 million for Polaroid and $2 billion for all other companies combined. About $1 billion in retail sales was related to "sophisticated" equipment.[8] Of the remaining $8 billion or so the majority was related to the photofinishing industry, which was composed of the multitude of retail outlets and processing laboratories worldwide.

Retailing Amateur Products in 1975

Sales of "sophisticated" equipment excepted, the average photographic products dealership made its money primarily from processing services. The use of film and cameras of all types as traffic builders and loss leaders had consistently forced dealer margins on both of these items down to minimal levels, in many cases to no more than 5 or 10 percent above cost. Retailers, however, seemed to be holding the line on processing prices where margins of 25 percent or more were common.

---

[8] "Sophisticated" equipment included cameras, projectors, and various accessory items, which were usually only available in stores where more than 50 percent of sales came from photographic products. Prices for this equipment were much higher than those for "mass market" items.

APPENDIX B
Major Differences Between the Colorpack and SX–70 Systems

Film Configuration

The general form of all Polaroid instant photographic materials was as follows:

A. The Negative. Whether a color negative or black and white, it contained all of the basic components of what would become the image in the final print. However, the negative *itself* never became the actual print.

B. Processing Chemistry. In both color and black-and-white processes a highly viscous, alkaline reagent was employed to extract the latent image from the negative and transfer it, by simply diffusion, across a very thin layer of the reagent to a "receiving" surface. In all cases the reagent was stored in air-tight "pods," which were broken open by rollers in the camera.

C. The Print. In all cases the function of what was to become the print was identical. It was always a "receiving" surface which became the final print, i.e., a surface that received the image migrating from the negative and retained it (at which time processing was complete). In the case of the Colorpack film this surface was present on a paper-based card, separated from the negative and reagent to halt processing. In the case of SX–70 film, the surface was present on the interior face of a transparent Mylar sheet, which was permanently bonded to the nega-

tive material at the edges to prevent reagent from leaking out.

Camera Design

Several differences existed in the operation of the cameras and films of the two systems. First, because the SX–70 print was to be viewed from the same direction in which it was exposed, the image reaching the film needed to be reversed by the camera. In the case of the SX–70 camera a mirror was used to achieve this. Second, because the negative and chemistry were to become a permanent part of the print in SX–70 film, all of the products of the various chemical reactions needed to be inert with respect to the final image as it resided on the interior surface of the Mylar sheet. Third, because the SX–70 print developed outside of the camera it needed to be shielded from light from the moment it was ejected from the camera. This was accomplished by the use of an "opacifier," a chemical layer that prevented light from reaching the negative during processing but which allowed the color forming dyes to migrate through it to reach the Mylar-supported surface.

As to the operation of the two systems, except for the litter associated with the Colorpack and the need to clean the camera's rollers periodically, there were, in the casewriter's opinion, virtually no differences between the two systems.

CASE 6
Polaroid–Kodak Addendum

I. Industry Data

The Photo-finishing Market

Photo-finishing had boomed in the 1960s and 1970s, breaking $1,000,000,000 in 1971 and $1,500,000,000 in 1975 for processing alone. Along with hundreds of other companies, Kodak participated in the boom by processing film directly.[1] More significantly, the company supplied other photo-finishers with photographic paper, sensitized materials, and photo-finishing equipment. Industry analysts conceded Kodak's preeminent positions in both sensitized materials and finishing equipment sales. Although the company did not release market share data, experts believed Kodak was responsible for more than 50 percent of the multibillion-dollar market in sensitized materials and almost 100 percent of finishing equipment market.[2]

Over the years, although Kodak's percentage of direct photo-finishing had declined, absolute dollar sales had risen. Since Kodak accepted only color film for processing, its potential market was limited, but as photographers increasingly abandoned black-and-white film the limitation became insignificant. In 1975 Kodak claimed 9.5 percent of the total photo-finishing market (10.6 percent of color photo-finishing), down from a high of 16 percent in 1967.[3]

Kodak had recently faced some decline in share in the "sensitized materials" market. While Kodak was still the undisputed leader in the field, since 1967 seven major companies—Ilford, 3M, Ciba, Turaphot, Fuji, Konishiroku, and Mitsubishi—had entered the color print market. Fuji, in particular, had encroached on traditional Kodak preserves by offering a similar quality product at prices 10 to 20 percent below Kodak's. Harvey Berkey, President of Berkey Photo, explained the change: "Five years ago we used 95 to 98 percent Kodak paper. But today we use 20 percent Kodak. The primary reason is that we can now buy other paper cheaper that is

[1] *The Wolfman Report* (1976), p. 65. The *Report* estimated that there were 875 professional processing laboratories in the United States. Major Kodak competitors included Berkey Photo, Fox-Stanley, Fotomat, and Colorcraft Division of Fuqua Industries.

[2] *Fortune*, September 1976, p. 123; *Business Week,* June 20, 1977, p. 70.

[3] *Advertising Age,* August 1, 1977, p. 10.

as good in quality.''[4] Kodak company estimates revealed that its share of the U.S. amateur color paper business had dropped from 98 percent in 1965 to 60 percent in 1976.

Company executives expressed Kodak's resolve to fight for this important segment of its photographic sales.[5] Without ruling out price competition, Kodak management stressed its preferred strategy—advertising to expose to consumers the fact that many film processors were not using Kodak products.

The Home Movie Market

According to the industry annual, *The Wolfman Report*, ''The movie market remains the dilemma of the photographic industry.'' Despite the introduction of ''truly sophisticated, easy-to-use'' hardware, the American public continued to be apathetic to home movies. Only 12 percent of U.S. households owned a movie camera, and only 1 percent purchased a new system in 1976. Indeed, 1976 unit sales of home movie cameras stood at less than half those of 1958, the peak year for home movie sales. Sales of 8 mm movie projectors fell 34 percent between 1971 and 1975. Studies indicated that most of the new units sold went to existing movie-taking amateurs as replacements for older equipment. Nonetheless, processing movie film remained a $100,000,000 business, and some observers predicted a bright future. Most, however, agreed with the *Wolfman Report*:

> Near-term outlook for the movie market remains mixed—odds are that as movie cameras and projectors become more versatile and easy to use, more people will be attracted to movie making, but there will probably be no more than a moderate increase in the total market.[6]

Eastman Kodak was well established in the amateur movie field. The company's XL Super 8 System, introduced in 1971, had become the ''standard'' of the industry. In 1973 Kodak added sound. During 1976 Kodak planned expenditures of more than $4,000,000 advertising amateur movie products.

Although Kodak's sound cameras proved popular with the public (and with dealers because of their generally high margins), overall sales of Kodak movie cameras were declining in 1976. Slumping silent movie system sales more than offset any gains recorded by newer sound models. While projector purchases also fell off, ''satisfying gains'' were posted in movie film sales.

As a company, Eastman Kodak preferred to shroud its market share data in secrecy. Nonetheless, recent court battles had forced the disclosure of some corporate estimates. In the color movie film market, Kodak's market share approached monopoly, and since 1967 its share had run between 88 percent and 90 percent. In movie cameras and projectors, Kodak had experienced declining market shares in shrinking markets. In movie projectors, Kodak's share had varied from a low of 17 percent in 1972 to a high of 30 percent in 1974. In 1975 Kodak's percentage stood at 27 percent.[7] ''Given these facts,'' a Kodak spokesman commented, ''it's obvious why we're concentrating elsewhere.''[8]

II. The Instant Camera Market

When Kodak introduced its instant camera line in April 1976, industry analysts remarked at the complexity of the new cameras' design. With more than 250 parts, the EK 4 and EK 6 inherently required far greater labor input than Polaroid's Pronto!, which contained twelve snap-together plastic pieces. Notwithstanding this, Kodak priced its instants to yield dealer net prices that were the same as the far simpler Tele-Instamatic 608. Analysts remained convinced that Kodak was selling the cameras below their cost of manufacture. One estimated that the EK 6 cost over $100.00 to make shortly after its introduction. Another forecast Kodak's cumulative operating loss on the instant program at

---

[4] One source estimated that one-half of Kodak's 1975 sales of $4,900,000,000 came from film paper and other sensitized materials.

[5] *Business Week,* June 20, 1977, p. 73.

[6] *The Wolfman Report,* 1976–1977, pp. 10, 12.

[7] *Advertising Age,* August 1, 1977, p. 10.

[8] *Newsweek,* May 9, 1977, p. 77.

$120,000,000 for 1975–1976.[9] In response to these allegations, a Kodak spokesman commented, "As a basic policy and practice, we don't make and market hardware without the expectation of a reasonable profit."

III. Company Data

Polaroid and Kodak Senior Management in April 1976

As of April 1976, Polaroid's founder, Dr. Edwin H. Land, continued to direct the corporation's destinies.[10] While Dr. Land remained chairman of the board, chief executive officer, and director of research, he had relinquished Polaroid's presidency in February 1975. Land was succeeded as president and chief operating officer by William J. McCune, Jr. A Polaroid employee since 1939, McCune had participated closely in the development of the original Land camera system in the late 1940s. Named corporate vice president of engineering in 1954, McCune subsequently rose to vice president and assistant general manager in 1963 and executive vice president in 1969.

Kodak's top management in April 1976 consisted of two men: Walter A. Fallon and Colby H. Chandler. Fallon, who originally joined Kodak in 1941 as a chemist in film quality control, subsequently served as a color emulsion researcher at Kodak Park. He became assistant manager of the film emulsion and plate manufacturing organization in 1961, and divisional general manager in 1966. In

February 1970 Fallon was elected vice president, and three months later he assumed control of Kodak's U.S. and Canadian Photographic Division (USCPD) which was then embarking on a renewed effort to develop an instant camera. When President Gerald B. Zornow succeeded Dr. Louis K. Eilers as chairman of Kodak in May 1972, Fallon was named Kodak's president and chief executive.

Chandler, a Kodak employee since 1950, started his career as a quality control engineer with the Kodak Park Division. After holding a number of technical and supervisory posts at Kodak Park, Chandler was promoted to general manager of the Color Print and Processing Division in 1971. Later in the year he became director of Photographic Program Development for USCPD, which included direction of Kodak's massive instant camera research program headed by Dr. Albert Seig. In 1972 Chandler was named assistant vice president and, on the death of Robert W. Miller in early 1974, took over as general manager of UPCPD. In February 1974 Chandler became Kodak's executive vice president.

Both Kodak and Polaroid managements were known throughout the photographic industry for their taciturn style. Corporate executives rarely discussed company plans or expectations, but when they did, their reports had a reputation for scrupulous accuracy and precision. Both companies shared an internal style where events proceeded, in the words of a Kodak executive, "at a very orderly, structured, and deliberate pace."

Performance of Kodak and Polaroid Stock

During 1975 and early 1976, Kodak and Polaroid experienced disappointing stock price movements (see Exhibit 6–1.)

---

[9] *New York Times,* April 24, 1977, p. F9, *Images,* January 1977, pp. 8, 11.

[10] As of December 31, 1976, Dr. Land owned 13.76% of Polaroid's outstanding voting shares.

EXHIBIT 6-1. *Polaroid and Kodak Stock Price Performance*

	Kodak Stock Price[a]	Polaroid Stock Price	Dow Jones Industrial Average
Jan. 1975	72 1/2	20 1/4	703.69
Feb. 1975	87 3/4	21 1/8	739.05
Mar. 1975	92 1/4	24	768.15
Apr. 1975	104 1/2	30 7/8	821.34
May 1975	105 1/4	32 1/8	832.29
June 1975	103 1/4	37	878.99
July 1975	95 3/4	38	831.51
Aug. 1975	93	35	835.34
Sept. 1975	90 3/4	34 1/8	793.88
Oct. 1975	100 3/8	36 5/8	836.04
Nov. 1975	107 1/2	36 5/8	860.67
Dec. 1975	106 1/8	31	852.41
Jan. 1976	113	37 7/8	975.28
Feb. 1976	108	37 3/4	972.61
Mar. 1976	118 3/4	37 3/8	999.45
Apr. 1976	107	33 7/8	996.85

[a]Prices are closing prices the last day of month on which business was transacted.

SOURCE: *Bank & Quotation Record.*

General Electric Versus Westinghouse in Large Turbine Generators

In early 1963 General Electric Company (GE) and Westinghouse Electric Company were reeling under the effects of a protracted period of depressed prices in the approximately $400 million large turbine generator market. After reaching a peak in 1957 and 1958, industry prices had fallen nearly 50 percent by 1963. Industry capacity utilization was low, and competitors were being forced to lay off highly skilled workers who would be very difficult to replace. Extremely difficult industry conditions had driven the historical number three competitor, Allis-Chalmers, to announce its exit from the turbine generator market on December 20, 1962.

At the same time the industry was still being rocked by litigation resulting from the so-called electrical conspiracy price-fixing case in which seven electrical executives had gone to jail for actions involving large turbine generators among other electrical products. A consent decree involving pricing behavior had been signed in 1962. However, civil treble-damage suits and out-of-court settlements with customers had already cost GE and Westinghouse in excess of $100 million each, and lawsuits and settlement negotiations were continuing.

Product

A large turbine generator was a highly sophisticated device for converting steam into electrical power, as shown in Exhibit 7-1.[1] Turbine generators were used to produce more than 80 percent of the power generated in the United States. Costing from several million dollars to $15 million apiece, turbine generators were sold to electrical utilities and represented by far the most expensive single item of electrical equipment in a power plant. Ancillary

---

[1] Much of the information in this case is taken from Ralph G. M. Sultan, *Pricing in the Electrical Oligopoly,* Volumes I and II (Division of Research, Harvard Graduate School of Business Administration, 1975).

equipment to complete the power plant was based on the characteristics of the turbine generator, and the efficiency of the turbine generator in large part controlled the plant's operating costs.

Each turbine generator was highly engineered to meet the customer's particular specifications, with up to 10 percent of the cost of an order representing engineering costs specific to that order. There were many complex design tradeoffs, which meant that few turbine generators were exactly alike. Turbine generators differed in kilowatt capacity, thermal efficiency in converting fuel to electrical energy, design philosophy, accessories, and numerous other dimensions. Continuous technological change had led to increases in the kilowatt capacity of turbine generators and improvements in efficiency, which had reduced utility capital cost per kilowatt for turbine generators and reduced operating costs (see Table 7–1). These improvements in turbine generators had allowed electric utilities to lower their prices for electric power continuously.

Technological development in turbine generators was the result of large-scale expenditures by competitors on engineering development, which amounted to more than $30 million per year in the early 1960s. Progress was based on incremental improvements rather than completely new breakthroughs and seemed to be largely a function of spending levels.

There were various designs for large turbine generators, which differed in their sophistication and performance. The increases in maximum steam temperature and pressure that had boosted fuel efficiency of turbines in the 1950s were getting increasingly difficult to accomplish in the early 1960s, and technological emphasis was shifting toward more rapid increases in turbine size. Larger turbines tended to be more sophisticated in design and technology, and improvements in the state of the art of turbine design tended to extend the size limits of turbines that manufacturers could produce. Size limits had increased at an unprecedented rate beginning in the late 1950s, with turbine generators rated in excess of 500,000 kilowatts being produced by 1962, as against maximum ratings of less than 200,000 kilowatts in 1955.

Manufacturers offered a wide range of turbine generator sizes and design configurations. Simple designs with higher operating costs were generally available only on smaller units. The price per kilowatt of a turbine generator declined with the size of the unit but generally at a decreasing rate. The manufacturer price-size curve was different for the more sophisticated "cross-compound" turbine generators than it was for the simpler "tandem-compound" design (Figure 7–1).

Buyers

Buyers for large turbine generators were primarily investor-owned and government-owned electric utilities. The top twenty-five utilities accounted for approximately 55 percent of the U.S. turbine generator market in 1960 as shown in Exhibit 7–2. Investor-owned utilities accounted for about three-quarters of U.S. generating capacity, with 99 percent of this accounted for by 212 operating companies. Some of these were part of twenty-eight utility holding companies, leaving 143 independent decision-making entities. Federal government-owned utility organizations accounted for approximately 13 percent of generating capacity, with by far the largest being the Tennessee Valley Author-

TABLE 7–1

Year	Utilities Constant Dollar Capital Cost per Kilowatt[a]	Year	Average Pounds of Coal per Kilowatt Hour
1946	$27.31	1925	2.029
1950	25.06	1935	1.439
1955	24.46	1945	1.302
1960	20.92	1955	0.954
1965	16.59	1960	0.876
		1965	0.858

[a] Based on General Electric orders.

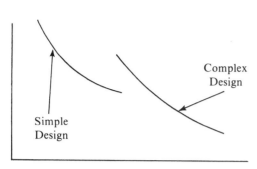

PRICE
(Dollars per
Kilowatt)

Complex
Design

Simple
Design

RATING IN KILOWATTS

FIGURE 7–1.

ity. Finally, there were nearly 500 small municipal power systems and so-called Rural Electrification Agencies (REAs). While these accounted for one-quarter of the turbine generator units sold to utilities, most units purchased were small. A small number of turbine generators was also sold to industrial firms.

The impact of the government-owned utilities on the turbine generator market was greater than their capacity share would imply. Government-owned utilities had been formed in the 1930s Depression amid great opposition from the privately owned utilities. The major electrical manufacturers had sided with the privately owned utilities, and relations with government-owned utilities still remained cool. Government-owned utilities (including municipal utilities) also purchased through soliciting sealed bids on orders with published product specifications. Orders were awarded by law to the lowest qualified bidder, and all bids were posted for all to see. This differed greatly from the highly private negotiations characteristic of the privately owned utility business.

Utilities ordered turbine generators based on their forecasts of the growth in electrical demand. There was a substantial delay, averaging two years, between the time a utility placed an order and when the turbine generator was actually shipped. This reflected engineering and building time of a year to eighteen months, and the manufacturer's order backlog.[2] A further period of six to twelve months was necessary after the unit was shipped before it came on line. The turbine generator was usually the bottleneck component determining how quickly a new power station could be constructed.

Utility orders for turbine generators were highly cyclical, as shown in Exhibit 7–3. Utilities ordered turbine generators to meet peak load electrical demand. Since electricity costs were lower with large-capacity turbine generators, utilities purchased large units infrequently rather than make more frequent purchases of smaller size units. The high capital cost of turbine generators coupled with rapid technological change in turbine design discouraged utilities from investing very far in advance of actual expected power needs. Future needs were forecast by extrapolating historical growth in peak electrical power demand. Utilities' expectations regarding growth in peak power loads tended to be revised upward or downward together. While different utilities operated in different markets with differing demand conditions, some uniformity in expectations was imposed by the state of the national economy. More important, though, utility executives closely communicated among themselves about future power growth, aided by extensive data collection and dissemination efforts by the Federal Power Commission and the utilities' own Edison Electric Institute. Utilities seemed not to accelerate their orders of turbine generators to take advantage of low prices in the turbine generator market, but they would accelerate the timing of orders if order backlogs were lengthening in order to "get in line."

Larger utilities and utilities in power pooling arrangements tended to order the larger turbine generators. Large-size units could be accommodated only by utilities with relatively large incremental power capacity needs, a function of utility size and rate of growth. Also, the size of turbine generators purchased could only reach a percentage of total system load that the utility could risk losing in the event of an accident or serious failure.

Large utilities also tended to be the most likely to adopt new technologies in turbine generators. They tended to be more willing to take risks, had larger and more competent engineering staffs, and greater financial resources. Their larger systems allowed larger utilities to integrate new units without undue risk to total generating capacity.

Buying Process for Turbine Generators

The buying process for turbine generators was both protracted and complex. A major distinction ex-

---

[2]Some orders took as much as four or five years when manufacturer backlogs extended.

isted between publicly owned utilities and private utilities, because public utilities purchased on the basis of sealed bids. These bids were opened at an appointed time, and the order went to the low qualified bidder. The bids themselves were available for inspection by the public.

The buying process for private utilities was a great deal more complex. Negotiations were conducted at high levels and under conditions of secrecy and incomplete information on both sides. Competitors did not have access to each other's bids, and utility purchasing agents provided only selective information to competitors about each other's proposals in the negotiating process. Much information came only in the form of hints or innuendos. Information was incomplete even once an order was signed. Utility purchasing agents would usually tell the losing competitor only the approximate price at which the order was won, while the winning competitor would rarely be told how close its rivals had come in price.

Utility purchasing agents also had incomplete knowledge of the prices at which turbine generators were being sold in the market. They relied partly on the trade press, engineering consultants, and informal communications with other utilities for information on the prices at which orders had actually been awarded by other utilities. Much information had to come from competitor salesmen, however, and even the veracity of information coming from other utilities were tempered by their desire to protect what they saw as their price advantages. Thus no one in the market, neither buyers nor sellers, knew the averge market price with any assurance, and what information they had was often not up to date.

A typical negotiation for an order began when a utility invited firms to submit bids on a turbine generator or generators with specifications outlined by the utility. Each manufacturer then computed a book price for the unit using its so-called price book, a manual that contained formulas for computing the price of a turbine generator based on its specifications. There was often room for interpretation in how the book price should be computed, even though the manual existed, because of the myriad technical tradeoffs and options available. Either the book price or a price which was discounted from the book was then quoted by the manufacturer. However, the effective price of the turbine generator to the customer was also affected by a wide variety of other items in the bid, which could represent a significant fraction of the total value of the deal. For example, the bid often included a stock of spare parts, the price of which was negotiable. Other negotiable items included accessories and minor variations in the technical specifications of the turbine generator, such as changes in turbine blades to improve thermal efficiency or small improvements in the guaranteed kilowatt rating. There were also discounts for ordering multiple units.

Final negotiations themselves were conducted by top-level utility executives and often involved a series of proposals and counterproposals. Manufacturers not infrequently accepted verbal commitments to put turbine generators into the factory schedule long before final technical specifications were settled or before any negotiation occurred, and sometimes such orders never materialized. Price was *the* negotiating variable at the bargaining table, while product performance and postpurchase service were important but less a part of the bargaining process.

At any given time, this process resulted in widely varing order prices relative to book prices for different customers. The discounts off book at which turbine generators were sold by the same competitor differed greatly from customer to customer, even for similar units. Thus while average price levels in the industry moved up and down over time, the dispersion of prices at any one time was always great.

Marketing

Turbine generator producers marketed their products through the use of technically skilled sales forces that called on utilities and carried out the bidding and negotiating process. Competitors maintained price books, which served the function of price lists, allowing the salesperson to determine the price of a turbine of various sizes and specifications (though use of the price book did not always allow the computation of a single unambiguous price because of the myriad interpretations.)[3] Price books were also widely disseminated to customers for use

---

[3]Such differences in prices calculated from the price book for the same unit could be significant.

in planning purchases. Westinghouse (and prior to 1963 Allis-Chalmers) utilized price books that were virtually identical to General Electric's, the industry leader.

Book prices were periodically adjusted to reflect cost changes and changes in marketing conditions. Price changes were announced by first sending salesmen to call on all utility customers, then by sending a press release to the wire services, and finally by publishing the new price sheet. Competitors knew about each other's price changes within hours.

Competitors went to great lengths to justify price increases as "fair" and based them publicly on increases in costs. Also, utilities had come to expect reductions in the cost per kilowatt of turbine generators. Competitors stressed the increased value of a turbine generator due to technological improvements rather than the absolute price of the unit.

Manufacturing

The manufacturing of turbine generators was of a job shop nature and involved a relatively small number of customized units produced to specifications. Production consisted of parts fabrication and assembly of purchased and internally fabricated parts. Turbine generator manufacture employed highly skilled labor; used large, sophisticated machine tools; and required a great deal of manufacturing space. While some turbine generators, particularly smaller units, were relatively standardized, nearly all units required at least some modification. The direct cost of manufacturing was high, representing approximately 65 to 75 percent of sales revenue. The largest single item in costs was materials, which were approximately half of direct costs, while direct labor was approximately a third. At any given time, direct costs were relatively constant with the output of turbine generators produced until factory utilization became very high. After approximately 85 percent of normal capacity was reached, overtime premiums in bottleneck operations, reworking of mistakes, excessive waste, and hiring of less-skilled employees sent costs rising modestly.[4]

Competitors added manufacturing capacity in order to maintain their market positions and ensure that order backlogs and consequent delivery delays did not become excessive. Delivery time could be important in increasing the probability of winning an order, particularly during periods of lengthy backlogs. Production capacity of turbine generator competitors was increased by making additions to existing facilities rather than constructing entirely new facilities, and capacity had increased by more than 400 percent in the 1946 to 1963 period at a cost of more than $150 million. Capacity additions were announced in the trade with maximum press coverage for maximum impact on utility customers. Competitors' plans for capacity expansion were rather wellknown throughout the industry as a result of lead times in ordering machine tools and the efforts of the trade association, which surveyed capacity expansion intentions. It was common among industry participants to underreport capacities, however.

Manufacturing costs of turbine generators had declined over time for a variety of reasons. Newly built capacity incorporated more modern machine tools and other facility improvements. In addition, the state of the art in manufacturing improved in such areas as materials and forging technology. Competitors had cost reduction programs that yield savings on the order of 2 to 8 percent per year through cost-saving ideas, increases in worker productivity, and the like. Finally, product innovations that increased turbine generator size reduced manufacturing costs per kilowatt. Manufacturing technology improvements could not be kept entirely proprietary but many were. Worker and management productivity and cost reduction declined during prosperous times in the industry, while productivity and cost reduction programs showed the greatest gains when the market was low and there was idle time in the shop.

Competition

Competition in the turbine generator industry coupled with demand conditions produced wide swings in book prices, actual prices, orders, backlogs, and

---

[4]Capacity in the industry was viewed as relatively elastic, depending on lead times, the size of engineering staffs, and other factors besides the amount of bricks, mortar, and

machine tools. Capacity also depended on the product mix, as large turbine generators required proportionally less facilities and equipment per kilowatt produced.

capacity. Exhibits 7-4, 7-5, and 7-6 plot these variables for the postwar period.

The turbine generator industry consisted of two domestic competitors in early 1963, GE and Westinghouse. Allis-Chalmers had decided to leave the industry in 1962 after many years of marginal results. In addition to domestic firms, Brown Boveri of Switzerland and Parsons of England had been attempting to penetrate the U.S. market. Brown Boveri and Parsons had won 13.3 percent of the domestic orders in 1959, and Brown Boveri had won 3.8 percent of domestic orders in 1961. Both episodes had been met by bitter price cutting by both GE and Westinghouse, as well as lobbying based on the threat to national defense if U.S. utilities relied on foreign-made turbine generators. While neither foreign firm had succeeded in winning orders in other years, they were viewed with great concern by U.S. manufacturers.

GE had long dominated the turbine generator market. Exhibit 7-7 shows historical market shares in the industry, and Exhibit 7-8 gives historical competitor backlogs.

General Electric

General Electric was a diversified manufacturer of electrical and electrical-related products in 1963, with 1962 sales of $4.8 billion. Heavy capital goods accounted for 23 percent of 1962 sales, of which turbine generators were estimated to be approximately one-fourth. GE sold turbine generators primarily to the domestic market but sold some units outside the U.S. and Canada. GE reported excess capacity and depressed market conditions in 1962, citing large reserves of excess power generating capacity enjoyed by most utilities. A summary of overall GE financial results is shown in Exhibit 7-9, along with detailed historical operating statistics in turbine generators.

GE had historically been the technological leader in turbine generators and had pioneered most innovations in the industry. As a result, GE had the largest share of its sales in the large, sophisticated units. Over time, GE had followed a policy of reducing prices of the larger, advanced-technology turbine generators while raising prices on its smaller, lower-technology turbine generators. This

policy had become more pronounced since the late 1950s.

GE had also historically been the price leader in the market, with competitors matching its changes in book prices. GE tended to negotiate a more consistent discount from book price, while Allis-Chalmers and Westinghouse were more prone to switch back and forth from deep discounting to selling at list price as competitive circumstances changed. GE offered its greatest discounts on very large turbine generators. In periods of rising industry demand and increasing backlogs, GE consistently increased its prices less rapidly than Allis-Chalmers and Westinghouse. When the market was declining GE tended to charge a premium price relative to competitors.

GE enjoyed an unusually high market share among the Federal agencies and large utilities, and a low market share among municipal and REA utilities. GE had by far the largest share among customers who purchased from only one supplier.

GE had spent over $100 million for capacity additions since World War II and tended to add capacity a year or two ahead of Westinghouse. GE's main turbine generator facility, at Schenectady, specially designed for turbine generators, was constructed in the late 1940s. Its capacity had been expanded a number of times since then, the most recent expansion having been recently completed.

Westinghouse

Westinghouse was also a diversified electrical products producer in 1963, with 1962 sales of $1.95 billion. Turbine generators accounted for an estimated 8 percent of corporate sales. Westinghouse sold turbine generators primarily in the domestic market, but also had some international sales. Exhibit 7-10 gives a summary of Westinghouse's overall financial results as well as detailed historical operating data in turbine generators. Westinghouse's turbine generator operations had been severely affected by a ten-month strike in 1956–1957.

Westinghouse was generally regarded as a technological follower to GE in turbine generators. However, over the years Westinghouse had developed some alternative technological strategies to GE. In the early 1950s, Westinghouse aggressively created a number of standardized turbine generator units in frequently ordered sizes. This led to a significant improvement in Westinghouse performance in the mid-1950s when standardized units accounted for almost 30 percent of total units, but these units had waned sharply in popularity by the latter part of the 1950s. As this was happening, Westinghouse launched an aggressive $25 million program to standardize components, its so-called building block approach. Certain key turbine generator components were frozen in design and manufactured in batches, to be assembled later into turbine generators suitable to a specific customer's needs. This program was substantially complete by 1959 but almost immediately ran into great resistance from utilities.

Westinghouse had a core group of utilities that had purchased only Westinghouse turbine generators and did unusually well among municipal utilities. Its greatest market penetration was among the medium and smaller utilities, and it held only a 30 percent average share of large (over 10 billion kilowatt) utilities over the 1948 to 1962 period. Westinghouse charged relatively high prices to the larger utilities, particularly those that purchased only Westinghouse equipment, but was known to discount deeply to win particularly sought-after orders.

Westinghouse manufactured most of its turbine generators in South Philadelphia and had invested $53 million in capital expenditures there since 1948. The facility was adapted after being leased from another firm in the early 1950s. The most recent expansion of the Philadelphia facility, costing $21 million, had been completed in 1961.

Allis-Chalmers

Allis-Chalmers had struggled as the number three competitor in turbine generators until 1962. It was behind GE and Westinghouse technologically, and its financial results had been erratic, as shown in Exhibit 7–11. Allis-Chalmers had achieved its greatest penetration among small utilities, though it had made some spectacular (and costly) forays into large turbine generators for large customers. Allis-Chalmers's delivery schedule had been much more erratic than either GE or Westinghouse. It had been hurt the most by the order declines since the late 1950s and finally succumbed.

The Situation in 1963

The depressed prices in early 1963 were causing even more concern in view of GE's ill-fated attempt at boosting prices in March 1961. Prices then were averaging 35 percent below book prices. After a strategy study, GE had concluded that it could stem the decline if it lowered book prices 12 percent and announced a new policy of quoting only book prices on all orders. By July, however, discounting had not stopped, and market prices were 25 to 30 percent below the *new* book prices. Soon afterward these discounts widened to 30 to 35 percent, led by Westinghouse and Allis-Chalmers.

Utilities had unusually large reserve capacity in excess of peak needs in 1963, caused by overly optimistic forecasts of electric power growth, which had caused major expansion in the late 1950s. While turbine generator demand was beginning to pick up, it would take a major and sustained increase to overcome industry excess capacity.

EXHIBIT 7-1. *A Large Turbine Generator*

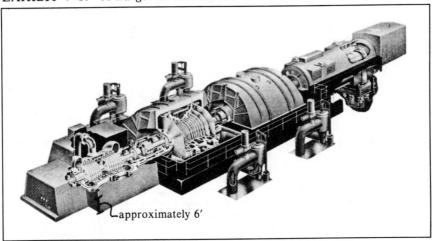

approximately 6′

EXHIBIT 7-2. *Largest Turbine Generator Customers in 1960*

Electric Utility	Estimated Percent of Total Annual Market for Turbine Generators
Tennessee Valley Authority	8.8%
American Electric Power	4.4
Southern California Edison	3.5
Middle South Utilities	3.4
Houston Lighting & Power	3.4
Florida Power & Light	3.1
Pacific Gas & Electric	2.2
Commonwealth Edison	2.1
Texas Electric Service	1.9
Consumers Power	1.8
Duke Power	1.8
Virginia Electric Power	1.7
Georgia Power	1.6
Public Service Electric & Gas	1.6
Dallas Power & Light	1.6
Detroit Edison	1.5
Gulf States Utilities	1.4
Consolidated Edison	1.3
Florida Power	1.3
Central Power & Light	1.2
Oklahoma Gas & Electric	1.1
Union Electric	1.1
Texas Power & Light	1.1
Albama Power	1.1
Tampa Electric	1.1
	55%
Total Market Additions to Thermal Capacity	100%

SOURCE: Electrical litigation materials, *Ohio Valley Electric* v. *General Electric*, Civil Action 62 Civ. 695 (S.D.N.Y. 1965). (S.D.N.Y. is the U.S. Second District Court of New York.)

EXHIBIT 7–3. *Turbine Generator Orders and Backlogs, in Kilowatts, and Index of Order Price*

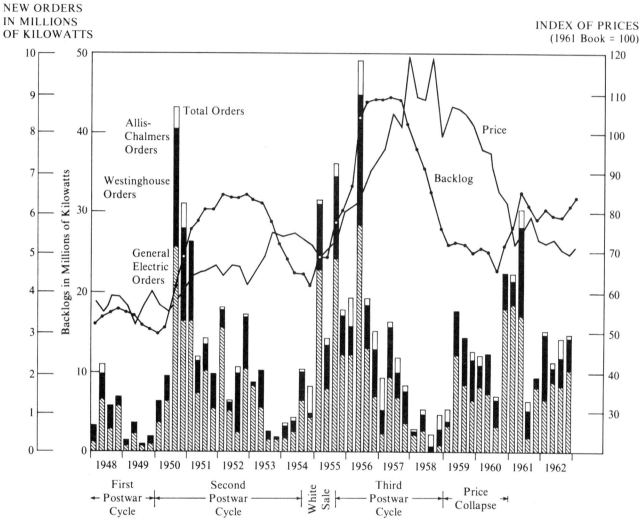

NEW ORDERS
IN MILLIONS
OF KILOWATTS

INDEX OF PRICES
(1961 Book = 100)

SOURCE: Exhibit material, *Ohio Valley Electric* v. *General Electric.*

EXHIBIT 7-4. *Turbine Generators, Capacity, 1948–1962*

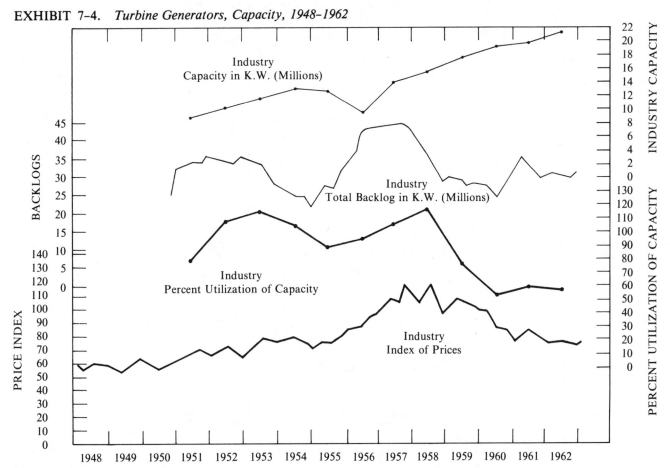

SOURCE: "Defendants' Pre-Trial Brief," *Ohio Valley Electric* v. *General Electric.*

EXHIBIT 7–5. *Estimated   Annual   Manufacturing Capacity: Domestic Turbine Generator Manufacturers, 1946–1962* (*in kilowatts per year*)
MILLIONS OF
KILOWATTS
PER YEAR

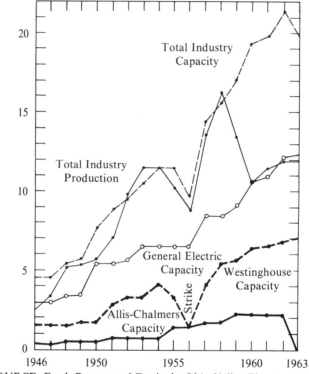

SOURCE: Ford, Bacon, and Davis, in *Ohio Valley Electric* v. *General Electric.*

EXHIBIT 7-6.   *Index of Turbine Generator Book Prices and Actual Order Prices, 1948–1962*

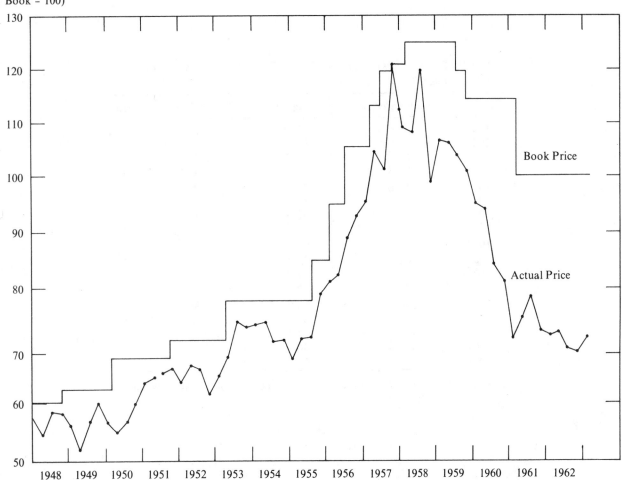

SOURCE: Reconstructed from ''Plaintiffs' Trial Brief,'' and other exhibit material, *Ohio Valley Electric* v. *General Electric.*

EXHIBIT 7-7. *Market Share of Turbine Generator Orders (aggregate kilowatts basis)*

	General Electric	Westinghouse	Allis-Chalmers	Foreign
1946	63.0%	35.0%	2.0%	0%
1947	57.0	38.0	5.0	0
1948	59.7	35.2	5.1	0
1949	56.2	39.1	4.7	0
1950	58.6	38.1	3.3	0
1951	62.4	35.1	2.5	0
1952	63.3	32.6	4.1	0
1953	73.7	23.2	3.1	0
1954	60.0	24.7	15.3	0
1955	62.9	33.4	3.7	0
1956	59.4	27.9	12.7	0
1957	48.5	38.1	13.4	0
1958	48.8	25.9	25.3	0
1959	52.5	25.5	8.7	13.3
1960	62.4	32.8	4.8	0
1961	55.2	26.4	14.6	3.8
1962	63.6	35.2	1.2	0

SOURCE: Tabulation of Electrical Equipment Antitrust Actions data, filed at S.D.N.Y.

EXHIBIT 7-8. *Backlogs of Unshipped Orders: General Electric, Westinghouse, and Allis-Chalmers (Quarterly Data), 1951–1962*

BACKLOG AT
BEGINNING OF
PERIOD IN
KILOWATTS
(Millions)

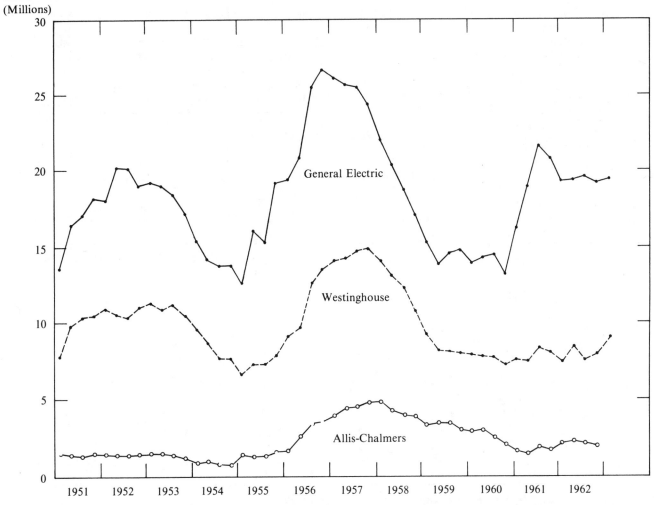

EXHIBIT 7-9. *Financial and Operating Data: General Electric*

A. Overall Corporate Results (*millions*)

	1958	1959	1960	1961	1962
Net Sales	$4,120.8	$4,349.5	$4,197.5	$4,456.8	$4,792.7
Heavy capital goods (%)	24	22	25	24	23
Consumer goods (%)	26	26	24	21	25
Components/materials (%)	26	27	29	30	28
National defense (%)	24	25	22	25	24
Net profit	242.9	280.2	200.1	242.1	265.8
Current assets	1,407.9	1,567.4	1,478.5	1,452.5	1,556.5
Total assets	2,420.9	2,561.5	2,551.3	2,704.5	2,840.6
Long term debt[a]	306.3	278.0	250.5	229.6	223.4
Shareholders' equity	1,311.0	1,457.7	1,513.4	1,603.2	1,722.3
Return on sales (%)	5.89%	6.44%	4.77%	5.43%	5.54%
Return on equity (%)	18.5%	19.2%	13.2%	15.1%	15.4%

[a]Includes long-term notes payable.

SOURCE: General Electric annual reports.

B. Turbine Generator Department

Year	Sales Billed	Direct Cost[a]	Overhead Expense[b] (incl. R&D)	Research and Development (millions)	Operating Profit Pretax	Operating Profit After-Tax[c]
1947	100.0%	83.2%	30.5%	$N/A	(17.9%)[d]	(8.9%)
1948	100.0	71.3	21.6	8.0	9.0	5.2
1949	100.0	75.0	19.9	8.3	4.6	1.8
1950	100.0	66.7	13.3	9.1	16.4	10.0
1951	100.0	65.9	12.1	12.0	23.9	8.4
1952	100.0	66.7	12.2	12.2	24.7	7.7
1953	100.0	62.6	14.5	14.4	26.9	8.2
1954	100.0	61.8	16.3	16.4	27.3	11.5
1955	100.0	62.1	11.9	19.1	26.4	11.7
1956	100.0	63.4	14.1	23.9	21.3	9.2
1957	100.0	67.5	14.1	24.1	18.6	7.6
1958	100.0	64.4	14.0	22.7	21.8	9.6
1959	100.0	58.5	13.8	21.3	27.9	12.8
1960	100.0	52.4	15.8	21.2	32.2	14.8
1961	100.0	54.5	16.4	20.5	29.7	12.9
1962	100.0	57.4	17.3	20.6	26.2	10.5

[a]Includes direct labor, materials, components, and indirect factory expense.
[b]Includes engineering, marketing, administration, employee relations, finance expense.
[c]After federal taxes and other assessed financial charges (e.g., interest).
[d]Parentheses indicate operating loss.

NOTE: Items may not add to 100 percent because of special expense items.

SOURCE: Exhibits submitted to the court, *Ohio Valley Electric* v. *General Electric.*

EXHIBIT 7-10. *Financial and Operating Data: Westinghouse*

A. Overall Corporate Results (*millions*)

	1958	1959	1960	1961	1962
Net sales	$1,895.7	$1,910.7	$1,955.7	$1,913.8	$1,954.5
Apparatus/general products (%)	N/A	54	55	54	51
Consumer products (%)	N/A	28	25	26	28
Atomic/defense products (%)	N/A	18	20	20	21
Net profit	74.8	86.0	79.1	45.5	57.1
Current assets	928.2	999.3	993.6	952.4	939.3
Total assets	1,411.5	1,498.1	1,521.1	1,531.8	1,516.5
Long-term debt	327.3	327.1	321.0	305.9	290.9
Shareholders' equity	870.3	924.3	964.1	971.3	970.9
Return on sales (%)	3.9%	4.5%	4.0%	2.4%	2.9%
Return on equity (%)	8.6%	9.3%	8.2%	4.7%	5.9%

SOURCE: Westinghouse annual reports.

B. Turbine Generator Business

Year	Sales Billed	Direct Cost[a]	Overhead Expense (incl. R&D)	Research and Development (millions)	Operating Profit Pretax[b]	Operating Profit After-Tax
1946	100.0%	103.1%	32.5%	N/A	(35.6%)	(18.0%)
1947	100.0	76.7	21.1	N/A	2.3	1.2
1948	100.0	66.9	20.8	$ 4.3	12.4	6.5
1949	100.0	55.0	17.1	3.6	27.9	10.6
1950	100.0	55.6	15.7	4.6	28.7	12.3
1951	100.0	65.7	17.2	5.8	17.1	6.0
1952	100.0	69.2	18.2	7.4	12.6	3.9
1953	100.0	83.7	25.1	10.1	(8.9)	(3.0)
1954	100.0	73.0	17.3	11.5	9.8	4.4
1955	100.0	77.9	18.8	10.1	3.2	1.6
1956	100.0	79.6	59.0	11.9	(38.6)	(18.5)
1957	100.0	80.5	23.6	18.0	(4.1)	(2.0)
1958	100.0	75.0	16.3	16.8	8.6	4.1
1959	100.0	72.9	23.9	16.0	3.2	1.5
1960	100.0	65.0	25.0	14.7	10.0	4.9
1961	100.0	58.6	24.8	15.4	11.8	5.9
1962	N/A	N/A	N/A	12.8	N/A	N/A

[a]Westinghouse operations were on strike from the beginning of 1956 through the spring of 1957.
[b]Parentheses indicate operating loss.

SOURCE: Exhibits submitted to the court, *Ohio Valley Electric* v. *General Electric.*

EXHIBIT 7-11. *Financial and Operating Data: Allis-Chalmers's Turbine Generator Business*

Year	Sales Billed	Direct Cost	Overhead Expense (incl. R&D)	Research and Development (millions)	Operating Profit	
					Pretax	After-Tax
1946	100.0%	117.0%	71.1%	N/A	(88.2%)[a]	(44.0%)
1947	100.0	106.0	30.5	N/A	(36.5)	(18.2)
1948	100.0	100.4	18.9	$ .14	(19.3)	(10.0)
1949	100.0	77.2	18.1	.30	4.8	2.0
1950	100.0	75.9	16.9	.19	7.1	3.2
1951	100.0	68.8	25.4	.29	5.8	2.4
1952	100.0	69.7	23.1	.27	7.2	3.2
1953	100.0	81.6	28.2	.26	(9.8)	(3.9)
1954	100.0	75.5	31.1	.27	(6.6)	(3.0)
1955	100.0	72.6	35.2	.81	(7.8)	(3.7)
1956	100.0	74.0	45.0	.27	(19.0)	(9.1)
1957	100.0	79.6	24.3	.48	(3.9)	(1.9)
1958	100.0	82.1	10.0	.55	12.2	6.1
1959	100.0	79.9	8.1	.62	11.5	5.8
1960	100.0	74.8	13.8	.97	17.5	8.6
1961	100.0	66.6	22.2	1.45	29.2	14.6
1962	100.0	75.8	75.6	1.42	(51.5)	(24.8)

[a]Parentheses indicate operating loss.

SOURCE: Exhibits submitted to the court, *Ohio Valley Electric* v. *General Electric.*

PART III
Strategic Groups

The case of "The U.S. Bicycle Industry in 1974" treats the topic of structure *within* an industry. The case centers on the identification of strategic groups within the bicycle industry and on assessing the relative position of firms in different strategic groups in view of the industry changes that are occuring. In order to diagnose strategic groups, the technique of strategic mapping can be employed to display graphically the competitors in an industry along axes that best reflect the competitive barriers in the industry. "The U.S. Bicycle Industry in 1974" provides the information necessary to construct a strategic map and to diagnose its implications for the strategies of firms such as Huffman, Murray Ohio, and AMF.

While only one case is primarily directed at exploring the concepts of strategic groups and strategic mapping, these techniques can be employed in many subsequent cases later in the book.

CASE 8
The U.S. Bicycle Industry in 1974

The American bicycle industry owed its decades of obscurity and its recent overwhelming prosperity to its cousin, the automobile industry. The invention of the automobile at the turn of the twentieth century forced the bicycle from its position as the prestigious and primary form of transportation in America to the realm of a toy, a Christmas gift for children, and a tool of the trade for newspaper delivery boys. Ironically, seventy years later, ecology- and health-minded Americans, tired of pollution-filled air and flabby waistlines, turned to bicycling in droves. American bicycle manufacturers scrambled to expand production facilities in order to meet the new adult demand and to fend off the threat of rapidly growing foreign competitors striving to make inroads in the domestic market.

From 1970 to 1973 annual sales of new bicycles rose from 6 million units to 15.2 million units. During the same period, manufacturers' annual revenues from bicycle parts and accessories increased from $350 to $750 million while annual industry profits climbed from $14 to $30 million. In 1970, for the first time since World War I, Americans purchased more new bicycles than new cars. According to the Bicycle Institute of America, there were more than 70 million bicycles in use in the United States in 1973, as against 93 million registered passenger cars.

Types of Bicycles

There were four distinct categories of bicycles: (1) coaster brake bicycles, (2) three-speed English racers, (3) lightweight derailleur models, and (4) specialty bicycles.

The *coaster brake bicycle* was identified by its single speed, coaster brakes, conventional diamond frame, heavy tires, mattress saddle, and upright handlebars. The average coaster brake bike weighed around 42 pounds, cost less than $70, and was desirable only for short trips on flat surfaces. Coaster brake bikes were able to withstand much abuse and were thereby suitable for children.

The *three-speed English racer* was equipped with caliper (hand-operated) brakes, mattress saddle, upturned handlebars, sturdy frame, fenders, and three-speed gears that facilitated hill climbing. The English racer was lighter in weight (37 pounds), and easier to operate than the coaster brake model. The average price of a three-speed English racer was $65, with the most expensive models retailing in the range of $100.

The *lightweight derailleur bicycle* was identified by its drop (racing) handlebars, much lighter frame and tires, narrower saddle, absence of fenders, and derailleur-operated ten-speed gear changing mechanism (there were five- and fifteen-speed combinations as well). The derailleur bike offered a wide variety of riding choices since the correct gear ratio made even the hilliest terrain a pleasure to ride. The better ten-speed bicycles had high-grade steel frames, aluminum-alloy components, and precision-machined hubs, headsets, cranks, and chain wheels. The least expensive models could be purchased for under $100, while the middle range went up to $250. Professional racing and custom frame bikes retailed for as high as $900.

Most derailleur bikes weighed between 20 and 36 pounds. Racing lightweight bicycles weighed less than 23 pounds. Touring lightweights—what most people rode—were slightly heavier than racers and could be equipped with fenders, chain guards, mattress seats, touring handlebars, and other accessories.

Specialty bicycles included adult tricycles, tandems, folding bicycles, and exercisers. Adult tricycles were designed for older persons with balance problems or for persons riding on slippery suraces. They were popular as shopping vehicles. Tandem bicycles were recreational bicycles requiring two or more riders. Folding bicycles were designed for commuters, and exercisers were used in homes, physical therapy clinics, and health clubs.

Bicycle Technology

The average bicycle was a complex piece of machinery consisting of 1,500 or more parts. Five categories of components made up the typical bicycle as shown in Figure 8–1: (1) frame; (2) steering mechanism; (3) transmission; (4) wheels/tires; and (5) brakes.

FIGURE 8–1. Men's Lightweight Derailleur Bicycle

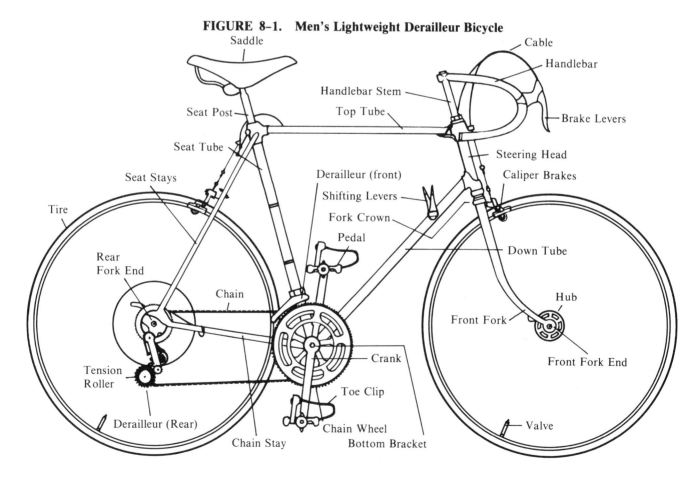

Frame. The bicycle frame, the most important part of the bike, was identified by its design, size, materials, and construction. There were three configurations: men's, women's, and "mixte." The men's diamond frame, in the form of two triangles (Figure 8–1), was the strongest unit and most popular.

Bicycle tubing was made from metal alloys. Finer tubing had lower carbon content and was lighter, more resistant to corrosion, and higher in tensile strength. Inexpensive bicycles were made with seamed tubing, where a steel strip was shaped into tubing with a welded seam. Better bicycles were made with extruded seamless tubing that was lighter, stronger, and consistent in shape. On the finest bicycles, stress points were made of seamless tubing that was thicker than that at the center, thus providing increased frame strength at the joints without sacrificing lightness.

Frames were identified as "lugless" (welded steel) or "lugged" (brazed alloy) according to how the tubing was joined together. The tubing members in a lugless frame were melted together, resulting in a stiff and heavy frame with smooth joints. In a lugged frame, the tubing members were soldered with brass by a low-heat process. The lugged frame was stronger and more resilient than the lugless frame and was characteristic of most fine imported bicycles.

Steering Mechanism. The steering mechanism consisted of the handlebars and saddle. The two major types of handlebars were upright and drop bars. The upright bar was usually associated with heavy, practical bicycles. Drop bars, found on more costly bicycles, enabled a streamlined riding position, lower wind resistance, and increased efficiency of muscular effort.

Transmission. The transmission took the push and pull of the cyclist's legs to the pedals and applied that force to the rear wheel. Pedals were of two basic designs and followed somewhat the relationship between the handlebars and saddle. Rat-trap pedals had an open metal frame and were characteristic of lightweight bicycles. Toe clips and straps could be added to enable the rider to keep his feet in the pedals better and to exert pressure on the upswing—a technique called "ankling." Block

pedals had solid rubber treads and were the rule on heavier, coaster brake bikes.

The crank was a lever that attached the pedal to the chain wheel that turned the rear wheel. Cotterless cranks were found on the finest bicycles and were often made of a lightweight aluminum alloy. A large bolt was used to attach the crank to the axle. Lower-priced bicycles had steel one-piece cranks and axles—a less sophisticated, weaker design.

The sprocket was the metal wheel with teeth that grabbed the chain and pulled it along while the bicycle was in motion. The bicycle chains were attached to the front and rear sprockets. Simpler one- to three-speed bikes had a heavy chain with a safety link, which permitted easy removal for cleaning. The more sophisticated five- to fifteen-speed bicycles had lighter, narrower chains with no safety links.

Wheels/Tires. Bicycle wheels consisted of rims, spokes, and hubs. Rims were of two types: steel and alloy. Steel rims held up much better than alloy rims for rough riding or carrying loads, while alloy rims were lighter. The hub was a loose term which applied to everything in and around the center of the wheel. The hub consisted of flanges to which the spokes were attached and a shell that connected those flanges. The axle and its bearings were inside the hub. Inexpensive bicycles with coaster brakes had bolted-on heavy steel hubs: better multigear bicycles had quick-release light aluminum-alloy hubs.

The three-speed or English hub, developed by Sturmey-Archer of England about 1900, was the first gearing system. It was a complex, internally geared system containing approximately 100 moving parts. Campagnolo of Italy introduced an alternative to the fixed chain and movable gears in a three-speed system called the "derailleur." The derailleur was a simple linkage system made up of movable arms, which "derailed" the chain from one series of sprockets and "rerailed" it on another, thus expanding the number of gear ratios.

Brakes. There were two types of brakes, coaster and caliper. For many years the standard braking system was the coaster brake, located within the hub of the rear wheel. Reverse pressure from the pedal was brought to bear on the axle through a large number of metal disks inside the hub, slowing the axle's rotation. The coaster brake was a simple, reliable system requiring no routine adjustment or maintenance. Caliper brakes were operated with two hand levers on the handlebars, one for the front and one for the rear brake. Squeezing the hand levers pulled on the cable that brought the two braking levers with their rubber pads into contact with the rim.

Accessories. In addition to these five categories of parts, accessories were an important part of the bicycle. Accessories could easily cost as much as the bicycle itself. A minimum list of accessories included front and rear lights (a legal requirement in many areas), reflectors on the front, rear, and sides of the bicycle and on the pedals, a tire pump, a tire repair kit, an inexpensive set of tools for simple road repairs and maintenance, and a small saddle bag. For touring, accessories might also include a rear metal carrier, a set of side baskets, a handlebar bag, and toe clips and straps for the pedals. Other popular accessories were locks, bike flags, rear view mirrors, bike carriers for cars, horns or bells, kick stands, fenders and chain guards. Also, there was a wide variety of clothing and shoes designed for cycling.

Industry History

Americans had been infatuated with the bicycle since the introduction of the European-made "Ordinary" bike at the U.S. Centennial Exposition in 1876. Despite their expense ($150 on average in the late 1800s), bicycles skyrocketed in popularity. Bicycle clubs were formed in many cities, and many were elite social groups with luxurious facilities. Fashions were developed especially for cycling. Bicycle racers became the sports heroes of the day.

The popularity of the bicycle was overshadowed by the invention of the automobile in 1902. Viewed first as a "toy" for touring and racing, the automobile soon replaced the bicycle as the principal mode of transportation in America. The bicycle assumed the reputation of "father of the automobile and grandfather of the airplane." Aviation pioneers Wilbur and Orville Wright originally were bike makers, as were auto manufacturers

Henry Ford, Glen Olds, George Pierce, and others. Nearly every modern improvement on the automobile—pneumatic and cord tires, ball bearings, differential steering, seamless steel tubing, and expansion brakes—could be traced to developments begun on the bicycle. Mechanical tools and assembly methods used for bicycle production were readily applied to automobile manufacturing.

For fifty years the bicycle was relegated to the realm of a toy. Although Americans continued to ride bicycles, the market changed in emphasis from expensive adult vehicles to inexpensive, sturdy, balloon-tired children's bicycles. The American bicycle industry plodded along in relative obscurity, composed of small family-owned or family-managed firms whose annual shipments increased slowly and erratically from 1.2 million units in 1900 to 2.0 million units in 1950. In contrast, sophisticated bicycle development in areas such as the lightweight lugged frame, the three-speed gear hub, and the derailleur gear system was still in progress in Europe.

From 1950 to 1970 the American bicycle industry began to gain momentum. Bicycle shipments increased from 2 million to 5 million units, and imported units from 68,000 to 2 million units. Concerned with flabby waistlines and weak hearts, adults begun to seek new forms of exercise. Gone were the atrociously heavy bikes with fat tires that made pedaling a chore rather than a pleasure. Instead, there were lightweight European three-speed bikes for adults and the new High-riser[1]—a radical change in fashion and design—for children.

Beginning in 1971 ecology- and health-minded Americans suddenly became obsessed with bicycling. Annual bicycle sales rose from 6.9 million units in 1970 to 15.3 million units in 1973. Manufacturers' annual revenues from bicycles, parts, and accessories increased from $350 to $750 million and industry profits climbed from $14 to $30 million. Table 8–1 illustrates the growth of the bicycle industry from 1960 to 1973.

The bicycle boom led to a dramatic shift in the industry from a children's market (83 percent of new bicycles in 1970) to an adult market in which 65 percent of the users of new bicycles were adults in 1974.

---

[1] The High-riser was a children's bike with a banana-shaped saddle, small wheels (typically 20 inches in diameter), and upright handlebars.

TABLE 8-1. Growth of the American Bicycle Industry

Year	Total Sales U.S. and Imports (millions/units)	Bicycles/ 1,000 Persons	Bikes in Use[a] (millions)	Estimated Users (millions)
1960	3.7	21.0	23.5	35.2
1965	5.6	29.1	32.9	49.3
1968	7.5	37.3	42.3	63.4
1969	7.1	34.9	47.7	71.5
1970	6.9	33.6	50.0	75.3
1971	8.9	42.7	53.1	79.6
1972	13.9	66.3	61.2	91.9
1973	15.3	71.9	70.0+	100.0+

[a] Estimate based on estimated bike life multiplied by a unit sales factor. Rentals and other multiple-use situations were factored into the figures for estimated users.
Source: Bicycle Institute of America.

While children's High-riser bicycles had been the rage of the 1960s, lightweight bicycles had become the rage of the 1970s. As American manufacturers struggled to expand their facilities and to change their model mix, foreign bicycle firms made substantial inroads into the American market. Table 8-2 highlights the model change over the ten-year period preceding 1974.

Bicycle Demand

Bicycle manufacturers attributed the surge in bicycle sales in the 1970s to a variety of factors. The bicycle was a form of recreational activity that consumers could afford despite swings in the business cycle. From 1970 to 1973 the annual rate of GNP growth in current dollars averaged 9.1 percent, yet bicycle sales increased at an average annual rate of 32 percent. The U.S. Department of Commerce reported that the annual growth in bicycle dollar sales since 1967 had averaged 26 percent versus 11 percent for consumer expenditures on recreation. The trends toward shorter work weeks and less labor-intensive jobs allowed many adults the physical capacity and free time to enjoy new recreational activities. Expenditures on recreation were projected to grow at an annual rate of 9 percent over the latter half of the 1970s.

U.S. demographic trends in the 1970s also seemed to have a favorable impact on bicycle sales. In 1970, 71.5 percent of the U.S. population of 211 million people fell in the over-fifteen age group, which roughly constituted the adult bicycle market. By 1980 the U.S. Department of Commerce projected that 77 percent of the population of between 222 and 231 million would fall in the fifteen and over age group. The Census also reported that the

TABLE 8-2. Composition of Total U.S. Bicycle Market Shipments (000)

Year	Total	Lightweight	%	High-rise	%	All Other	%
1973	15,228	10,563	69%	3,821	25%	844	6%
1972	13,906	9,384	67	3,549	26	973	7
1971	8,858	3,819	43	4,020	45	1,019	12
1970	6,998	1,424	20	4,436	63	1,138	17
1969	7,060	980	14	4,637	66	1,443	20
1968	7,500	969	13	4,797	64	1,734	23
1967	6,298	893	14	3,334	53	2,071	33
1966	4,222	1,069	25	0	0	3,153	75

Source: Bicycle Institute of America.

population was becoming increasingly concentrated in urban areas. In 1960, 70 percent of the population lived in urban areas[2] versus 74 percent in 1970, and 30.4 percent resided inside the central cities. Participation in active sports was on the rise as well.

The surge in bicycle sales had also occurred because legions of adults who had once considered the bicycle strictly a toy for children suddenly became cyclists themselves. Adult enthusiasm for bicycles grew out of an increasing national interest in physical fitness, the environmental movement, and the appeal of cycling as an inexpensive family-oriented activity.

The national concern for physical fitness dated from the 1950s. When President Eisenhower suffered a serious heart attack in 1955 his coronary expert, Dr. Paul Dudley White, the "Dean of Cycling," recommended bicycling as a way to prevent such attacks through promoting "good muscle tone and circulation, proper breathing, weight control and a generally improved outlook on life."

Bicycling had also come to be regarded as an activity that an entire family could enjoy. Its requirements were minimal: modest cost, no special facilities, and a small degree of athletic prowess and physical strength. An A. C. Nielsen survey in 1973 rated bicycles second to swimming in popularity of recreational activities for children, third for adult women, and seventh for adult men. While bicycle touring dated from the late 1800s in Europe, the idea of extended group bicycle trips did not catch on on a large scale in the United States until the 1970s. Bicycle racing on the road or on indoor tracks grew increasingly popular in the U.S. as well, having long been a major sport in Europe.

End-User Markets

There were three categories of end-user markets for bicycles: adult, children, and specialty. The children's market dominated bicycle industry sales in the 1960s thanks to the popularity of the High-riser. The adult market dominated the industry in the 1970s because of the rise in popularity of the lightweight bicycle. In 1973, 65 percent of all new

[2] Urban areas were defined as towns or densely settled urban fringes with a census of 2,500 or more people.

units sold went to adults, 34 percent to children and 1 percent to the specialty market.

Industry participants loosely defined children's bicycles as those used by persons below the age of fifteen who had not yet attained their full growth. The emphasis in the children's market was on durability, since the bicycles were subject to heavy usage, abuse, and accidents. Many children's bikes, particularly for young children, were made from seamed and welded, heavy-gauge steel tubing. Replacement of a children's model occurred when the child damaged the bicycle beyond repair or outgrew it, or when the fashion in terms of models, colors, or designs changed. The High-riser style bicycle was popular with young children in 1974, while teenagers preferred lightweight bicycles.

The use of adult bicycles differed from that of children's bikes, because there was little chance that adult bicycles would be outgrown or subjected to a major accident. Sturdiness became less important, while serviceability and adjustment became more important. Adults purchased bicycles with a definite purpose in mind, and manufacturers provided a wide range of specialized adult bicycles to fit a range of needs. The most popular types of adult bicycle were three-speed English racers and ten-speed lightweight touring bicycles.

Safety

The Consumer Product Safety Commission placed bicycles at the top of its index of hazardous consumer products in 1974, reflecting an increase in bicycle accidents. The agency estimated that more than a million injuries were attributed to bicycles in 1973, of which 419,000 persons were hurt seriously enough to be treated in hospital emergency rooms. The agency reported that 63 percent of the injuries involved a loss of control by the riders and 17 percent involved mechanical or structural failure. Most accidents occurred in the five-to-fifteen age group.

In an attempt to curb the rising number of bicycle accidents the Federal Government issued mandatory safety standards in July 1974, imposing minimium strength and performance requirements on brakes, steering systems, frames, and other bicycle components sold in the United States after January 1, 1975. As of the spring of 1974, 212 state bills pertaining to bicycle standards were pending in state legislatures. The new federal standards required manufacturers to provide wide-angle reflectors on fenders, wheels and pedals to increase visibility at night, chain guards, and protective coverings on fender edges and protruding bolts and chains, among other things. The Bicycle Manufacturers Association had developed its own voluntary safety standards in 1971, described by some as "stricter" than the new federal requirements. The recent bicycle boom had witnessed foreign bicycles of inferior quality imported into the American market in vast numbers. With the recent federal standards and rise in state bicycle safety legislation, bicycle recalls appeared likely. The federal standards gave bicycle retailers, in addition to government officials, the authority to recall defective bicycles, at the manufacturers' expense.[3]

Bicycle Riding Facilities

On August 13, 1973, the Federal Highway Act was signed into law, heralding a new era for bicycle safety. The Act declared communities responsible for the design, construction, and maintenance of bicycle riding facilities, which ranged from bike routes (roadways to be used by cars and bikes), to bikeways, or pathways designed exclusively for bicycle traffic which did not parallel a street or highway. Additions to the act promulgated in 1974 provided for the construction of bicycling and pe-

[3] Stelber Industries, Inc., was the first American bicycle manufacturer to face this problem. A substantial number of its bicycles imported from an overseas facility had been recalled in 1973 and 1974 because of fork durability deficiencies.

destrian facilities on a 70/30 matching funds basis, with $120 million set aside for bikeway construction over three years.

The first bikeway had been inaugurated in Homestead, Florida, by Dr. Paul Dudley White in 1962. By 1974 more than 300,000 miles of bikeways had been developed, costing anywhere from $8,000 to $18,000 a mile, depending upon the terrain and surfacing.

Distribution

The sales of 15.3 million bicycles in 1973 were distributed evenly between independent outlets (largely bicycle dealers) and mass merchandisers, as shown in Table 8–3. Sales through bicycle dealers represented 30 percent of all bicycle units sold in the United States in 1973. All Schwinn bicycles, some higher-priced American-made bicycles, and most expensive lightweight foreign-made bicycles were sold by bicycle dealers. Bicycle dealers generally sold higher-quality products and emphasized the availability of service, parts, and accessories. Selling was heavily based on brand loyalty and personal selling, and price cutting was limited. There were an estimated 3,500 bicycle dealerships in the United States. Raleigh and Schwinn were the only firms that had developed full-concept authorized dealership programs. Dealers' markups ran 30–40 percent.

The remaining 70 percent of bicycle units sold in the United States were marketed through mass volume retail outlets: national department stores such as Sears, discounters such as K-Mart, regional chains such as Winn-Dixie, and independent de-

TABLE 8–3. Bicycle Distribution, 1973

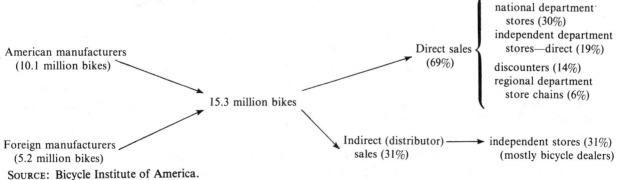

SOURCE: Bicycle Institute of America.

partment stores such as Jordan Marsh of Boston. Many mass volume retailers used bicycles as traffic builders and sold them practically at cost. Contracts between bicycle manufacturers and retailers were renegotiated each year, and price was a determining factor, along with credit terms, delivery time, and the quality of the merchandise. Most mass merchandisers did not provide servicing, parts, or accessories, although several large companies such as Sears had implemented new bicycle service programs. Bicycles sold through mass merchandisers were generally sold in kit form rather than assembled, as with bicycle dealers, and manufacturers that sold bicycles to those channels attempted to prepare the bicycle for easy assembly by the purchaser by including an explicit instruction manual in the shipping container.

Production

The bicycle production process was a complex assembly operation using a mixture of purchased and manufactured parts. Bicycle manufacturers had long been largely assemblers and marketers, purchasing the majority of components from outside suppliers. While this was the case prior to the 1960s, the trend was toward increasing vertical integration in bicycle production. By 1974 most firms were manufacturing a significant portion of bicycle components internally. Machined parts, such as the frame, handlebars, and fenders, were generally produced internally, while more intricate and sophisticated components such as hubs, brakes, and derailleurs were purchased. The most important criteria for the make–buy decision were the capital intensity of the component manufacturing process and the level of technological expertise required. Table 8–4 shows the split between internally produced and purchased parts for a typical major U.S. firm.

In 1974 most U.S. manufacturers had comparable levels of vertical integration. Although their sales volumes differed considerably, most firms were large enough to self-manufacture the typical internally produced components listed in Table 8–4 while no firm was large enough to bring production of the purchased components in-house.

On high-quality bicycles sold through dealers, materials accounted for approximately 50 percent

TABLE 8–4. Vertical Integration of a Typical U.S. Manufacturer

Produced Internally	Purchased
Frame	Tires
Chain gear	Spokes/nipples
Sprocket	Saddles
Crank	Grips
Handlebars	Coaster brakes
Rims	Derailleur
Fork	Front hub
Fenders	Reflectors
Kick stand	Hand brakes
	Pedals
	Chains
	Handlebar stems

of production cost, labor 16 percent, and manufacturing overhead 34 percent. Production costs for less expensive bikes produced for the mass market were approximately 57 percent materials, 6 percent labor, and 37 percent manufacturing overhead. Purchased parts represented about 30 percent of the total material cost in both cases. Transportation costs were also a significant cost element.

Most firms produced a wide variety of models. It was possible for a manufacturer to produce an entire line of bicycles from one or two basic frame varieties by making a series of increasingly costly variations on them. Bicycle quality could also be upgraded by increasing the quality of the components. Particularly with ten-speed derailleur bikes, the brand name of the components used in the bike became as important as the name of the frame builder. For example, a Campagnolo headset (a bearing assembly joining the fork frame and stem) was much prized and was available on high-quality bicycles assembled by manufacturers the world over, all of whom purchased the component from its Italian designer and producer.

Suppliers

The bicycle parts supply industry was populated by a large number of relatively small, highly specialized firms serving the world market. Table 8–5 shows the number of domestic and foreign firms producing components.

Prior to 1970–1974, purchasing arrangements

TABLE 8-5.   Number of Domestic and Foreign Suppliers of Component Parts

Component	Domestic Suppliers	Foreign Suppliers
Tires	2	20
Spokes/nipples	1	10
Saddles	3	20
Grips	3	30+
Coaster brakes	0[a]	5
Derailleurs	0	4
Front hubs	2	10
Hand brakes	0	10
Pedals	3	20
Handlebar stems	1	7
Chains	0	9

[a] One U.S. company had coaster brake operations overseas.
SOURCE: Industry interviews.

had tended to be stable, with many components made to the specifications of individual manufacturers. By 1974, however, there were worldwide shortages of most components, particularly tires, chains, and plastic parts. To further exacerbate the problem, international exchange rates had become increasingly volatile. This had raised the cost of some components to U.S. manufacturers by as much as 100 percent or more in the 1971–1974 period.

Foreign-made parts represented about 30 percent of the parts on a typical U.S.-made bicycle in 1974 and made up approximately 35 percent of the dollar imports in the bicycle industry. Sourcing of foreign parts had originally developed because of the advantages of cheap labor costs abroad. U.S. manufacturers, trying to compete with cheap imported bicycles, turned to foreign sources as a way to keep their costs down. While a number of U.S. bicycle manufacturers were seeking to reduce their dependency on foreign suppliers, either through further integration or by encouraging domestic vendors to begin to supply parts, the long-term loyalties and dependencies involving foreign suppliers were difficult to break off. Foreign suppliers were also ahead of domestic suppliers in components for sophisticated, lightweight bikes as a result of the comparatively recent growth of demand for lightweight bikes in the U.S. market.

Most foreign parts manufacturers specialized in one or two component areas and sold worldwide. Tooling costs were large, and learning curves were significant for the more complex parts. By 1974

Japan had assumed the position of leading supplier of parts and had managed to capture a 66 percent share of the U.S. component business. France followed with a 10 percent share, West Germany with 9 percent and the United Kingdom with 4 percent of the component market.

U.S. Manufacturers

There were eight domestic bicycle manufacturers in the United States in 1974, accounting for 25 percent of worldwide production. Operating at full capacity they had produced 11.0 million units, consisting of 6.48 million lightweights, 2.97 million High-risers, and 1.55 million others. Overall, a 20 percent increase in capacity was planned by U.S. manufacturers in 1974. Summary financial data for the four publicly held firms appears in Exhibit 8–1, and comparative sales and production data on selected firms is given in Exhibit 8–2. Exhibit 8–3 gives data on the distribution channels of the eight U.S. firms as well as imports.

The market shares in units of the eight U.S. firms in 1968 and 1973 are shown in Table 8–6.

Murray Ohio Manufacturing.   Murray Ohio was the largest producer of bicycles in the United States in 1974. Located in Tennessee, Murray produced a wide variety of tricycles, pedal cars, trucks, tractors, and other types of riding toys in addition to bicycles. The company also produced electric fans, which were sold exclusively to Sears under the Ken-

TABLE 8-6.   Market Share Distribution (unit sales), American Firms

COMPANY	Production (million units) 1968	Production (million units) 1973	Share Among U.S. Firms 1968	Share Among U.S. Firms 1973	Share of Total U.S. Industry 1968	Share of Total U.S. Industry 1973
Murray Ohio Manufacturing	1.4	2.4	24.1%	23.8%	20.0%	15.7%
Huffman Manufacturing	1.0	2.3	17.2	22.8	14.3	15.0
AMF, Inc.	0.7	1.8	12.1	17.3	10.0	11.4
Schwinn Bicycle Company	1.0	1.5	17.2	14.5	14.3	9.6
Stelber Industries, Inc.	0.3	0.6	5.2	6.2	4.3	4.1
MTD Products, Inc.	0.7	0.6	12.1	5.9	10.0	3.9
Chain Bike Corp.	0.4	0.5	6.9	5.0	5.7	3.3
O. F. Mossberg	0.5	0.5	5.2	4.6	4.3	3.0
Total	6.0	10.1	100.0%	100.0%	82.9%	66.0%

SOURCE: Arthur M. Louis, "How the Customers Thrust Unexpected Prosperity on the Bicycle Industry," *Fortune,* March 1974, pp. 117–121.

more name. Murray also manufactured a full line of push and self-propelled rotary lawn mowers, though it was not a market leader. Management was actively considering the addition of a line of riding mowers as well. The breakdown of Murray's corporate sales by line of business is shown in Table 8-7.

Murray sold a wide line of standard-quality bicycles primarily through mass merchandisers. Eighty percent of Murray's bicycles and wheel goods were sold under private labels, as were 70 percent of its lawn mowers and 100 percent of its fans. Murray was chief bicycle supplier to Sears, the single largest U.S. bicycle retailer with an estimated 15 percent of the market. The two companies had been doing business for fifty years, and at one point Sears owned 15 percent of Murray's stock. Sears accounted for 26 percent of Murray's sales in 1974. It was suspected in the industry that Murray was producing bicycles on a "known cost basis" for Sears. Under such an arrangement Murray would divulge its production cost data to Sears when negotiating a

TABLE 8-7.   Murray Ohio Sales by Product Line

	1973	1972	1971
Bicycles and wheeled goods[a]	79%	78%	73%
Lawn mowers, Wheel goods, & Others	21%	22%	27%
Total	100%	100%	100%

[a] Bicycles were estimated at approximately 62 percent of total sales in 1973.

contract. Murray also was a supplier to Western Auto, J. C. Penney, Gamble-Skogmo, and other private label accounts.

Murray maintained the position as the low-price manufacturer. Competitors labeled Murray "tougher than hell" on price and always the one to follow. Murray management also emphasized customer service and quality control. Murray sold a selection of parts and maintained repair service centers. The Sears organization also provided service outlets for Murray bikes. Murray maintained a staff of seven full-time designers and eight product engineers and planned to spend approximately $2 million on R&D in 1974. Murray had registered several firsts in product development including the 1958 introduction of the middleweight bicycle and the 1966 introduction of the "Elimination" (multispeed derailleur) version of the High-rise bike.

Murray produced bicycles in a single, nonunion plant that utilized some shared machining operations with other Murray products. Murray did not have sufficient volume to clear the next hurdle on vertical integration, and its level of vertical integration was comparable to the other large U.S. manufacturers.

Murray management reported that 1974 would be the fourth consecutive year of record sales and profit for the company, but expected 1975 to be a difficult year because of conditions in the general economy. Sales were forecast to decline 14 percent. There was no family involvement in Murray management, and no officer owned a significant fraction of company outstanding shares.

Huffman Manufacturing Company. Huffman produced bicycles, push and riding lawn mowers, and outdoor power equipment such as tillers and power edgers. Huffman's power equipment business was growing, but Huffman held less than a 10 percent share of the U.S. market. All its engines were purchased from Briggs & Stratton. Huffman also manufactured automotive equipment such as metal gasoline containers, pouring spouts, drain pans, and mechanics' creepers. The company also manufactured a full line of engine-powered mini-bikes. Sales by product area are shown in Table 8–8.

Huffman produced a wide line of bicycles, of which about 60 percent were lightweights and 45 percent were ten-speed models. Huffman had aggressively pursued product development. In 1963 Huffman was the first manufacturer to offer the High-rise bicycle. Although other firms quickly followed, Huffman benefited significantly from the rapid growth that followed the introduction.

Huffman's sales were divided 55–45 between private label and sales under the Huffy brand. Huffman's three largest accounts were Sears, J. C. Penney and S. S. Kresge. Huffman did not operate repair service centers, although some private label outlets like Sears would service bicycles sold under its brand.

Huffman produced bicycles in three locations. Bicycles and lawn mowers were produced in a Richmond, Indiana, plant that opened in late 1969. Bicycles were also produced in a Celina, Ohio, plant and in Azusa, California. Capacity was being expanded at Celina through moving inventory storage to a new warehouse. Huffman imported parts from France, Italy, Japan, Germany, and other foreign countries for complex or specialized components, and characterized its parts imports (30 percent of purchases) as similar to other U.S. manufacturers. Huffman had another plant in Delphos, Ohio, that

produced the automotive line. Corporate headquarters were located in Dayton, Ohio.

The Huffman family was active in management. The family plus Mr. Smith, the chairman, owned approximately one-third of the outstanding shares. Management was optimistic for 1975 and termed the outlook good for continued earnings growth.

AMF, Inc., Wheel Goods Division. AMF was a worldwide producer of leisure time and industrial products with total sales in 1973 of $962 million. Leisure products accounted for $605 million, of which vehicles (motorcycles and bicycles) were $325 million and the most rapidly growing product area in the company. AMF had acquired two industrial products companies in 1973 as part of a campaign to balance leisure and industrial sales.

The Wheel Goods Division produced juvenile wheel goods (tricycles, wagons, pedal cars), mopeds, and exercise bicycles in addition to bicycles. Bicycles were made exclusively in the Little Rock plant, with the other products coming out of Olney, Illinois. Although AMF also manufactured Harley-Davidson motorcycles, there was no relationship between the motorcycle division and the Wheel Goods Division. Harley-Davidson was an independent profit center and operated autonomously. The Wheels Goods Division had manufacturing facilities in Little Rock and in Olney. Division headquarters was located in Olney, with corporate headquarters in White Plains, New York.

AMF marketed approximately 60 percent of its wheel goods output under the AMF brand, with the balance sold under private labels. AMF favored major mass merchandise accounts and sold a large percentage of its branded bicycles to this channel. The Wheels Goods Division benefited from AMF corporate advertising, which was heavy and was directed two-thirds to consumers and one-third to the trade.

The Wheels Goods Division had six full-time designers as well as several product managers, who were assisted by corporate research and development. AMF's corporate philosophy called for high-quality products, and the Wheel Goods Division was no exception. In addition to following strict quality control procedures, the division offered bicycle repair services at Sunbeam Consumer Appliance Service Centers in sixty U.S. communities.

TABLE 8–8. Huffman Sales by Product Line

	(millions)	
	1973	1972
Bicycles & accessories	$ 83.8	$ 62.9
Outdoor power equipment	16.1	14.8
Automotive & other	5.2	4.8
Total	$105.1	$82.4

Manufacturing facilities in Olney and Little Rock were being substantially enlarged to meet increased demand.

Schwinn Bicycle Company.   Schwinn was unique among U.S. bicycle manufacturers in being a family-run, one-product business. Operating out of one plant in the Chicago area, the company had seen four generations of Schwinns in management since 1895.

Schwinn produced more bicycle models than any other manufacturer—365 in all—sold exclusively through its own authorized dealers. The 1,650 dealers were selected, trained, and monitored by corporate headquarters. Schwinn refused to make private label bicycles for mass merchandisers, selling 100 percent of its output under the Schwinn brand.

Schwinn had long established the reputation for high quality and durability that was manifested in a high material content relative to other U.S. manufacturers. Schwinn bicycles retailed at prices comparable to those of the high-quality imports, ranging from $42 to $677. Even a single-speed Schwinn bike cost as much as $88 at retail, as against competitors' prices in the $50-$60 range. Schwinn ten-speeds started at over $100, contrasted with the average U.S.-made ten-speed which retailed at $70. Schwinn invested heavily in product development and new model introduction.

Schwinn bikes were generally a little heavier than the competitive brands because of a special frame construction. This technique was aimed at producing bicycles built to last under rugged conditions with trouble-free service requirements. Unlike the other domestic firms, Schwinn guaranteed its bicycle parts indefinitely. Should service be required, each of the authorized dealers was well equipped to meet the need.

Schwinn assumed more of a "craftsman" approach to bicycle production and was believed to make more of the intricate components in-house than its competitors. However, the extent of this integration was limited and was not believed to produce an appreciable advantage for Schwinn. Schwinn had been responsible for many of the advancements in bicycle manufacturing technology.

Stelber Industries.   Stelber manufactured bicycles in a network of international plants, as well as distributed bicycles and accessories made by others. Four divisions—Plasco Corp., State Distributors, Scheuer-Shapiro Ltd., and Saf-Tee Products—were all involved in distribution, with Scheuer-Shapiro the second largest importer of European bicycles to the United States.

Stelber was also involved in chrome plating. Its Grand Chrome Plating Corp. had one of the finest automatic chrome plating facilities on the East Coast. In addition to plating for its sister divisions, Grand Chrome sold to outside customers. Stelber was also marginally involved with the entertainment industry through MBC Industries and Aura Recording, Inc. Combined, these two companies contributed less than 10 percent to Stelber's sales. Management intended to divest MBC in the near future while holding Aura for later sale.

Stelber was the only U.S. company in the industry that undertook the development of an international manufacturing network. Stelber had manufacturing facilities in New York, Austria, and Canada. The company planned plant additions in other areas to minimize transportation costs and supply sufficient product on short notice to meet regional demand. Stelber's New York plant had a capacity of 450,00 units per year. The Austrian plant, rebuilt after a 1971 fire, had single-shift capacity of over a million bicycles. The Canadian plant was acquired in 1972 and produced children's bicycles.

Stelber manufactured bicycles under its own Iverson label as well as for private labels. Stelber had an extensive distribution network through its subsidiaries. The Iverson line was sold primarily through small chain stores and as a fill-in line for major accounts, offering very low prices. Stelber did not operate a service network. Stelber had been plagued by quality problems, and in 1973 and 1974 a substantial number of Stelber's imported bicycles had to be recalled due to fork durability deficiencies.

Stelber possessed insufficient volume to achieve any significant scale or integration advantages over other U.S. firms, even though it manufactured on a worldwide basis. Stelber relied on ready access to foreign sourcing through its international operations as a competitive advantage.

Columbia Manufacturing Company. Columbia, the bicycle subsidiary of MTD Products, was the nation's oldest bicycle manufacturer, having begun production in 1877. In recent years, the firm had undergone severe management difficulties. In addition to bicycles, Columbia manufactured tubular school furniture.

Columbia sold private label bikes in regional and other smaller chain stores, as well as bikes under its own factory label "Columbia." The Columbia line was inexpensive and positioned as a fill-in line in bicycle shops.

Chain Bike Corporation. Chain was a family-run enterprise located in Pennsylvania. Chain marketed its bicycles exclusively in New England. Most of Chain's output was marketed under the "Ross" factory label. Chain was a less expensive bicycle and promoted primarily as a fill-in line to small chains and bicycle dealers.

O. F. Mossberg Company. Mossberg was also a family-run business located in Connecticut. Mossberg distributed principally through hardware store outlets. Mossberg had recently purchased H. P. Snyder Company and took over Snyder's distribution of Rollfast bicycles.

Imported Bicycles

The early 1970s saw foreign bike makers increase their share of the U.S. market. Many U.S. retailers found imported bicycles appealing because they were priced below the American models, despite tariffs ranging from 5 percent to 16 percent.[3] At the

[3] Tariffs were 5.5 percent on bicycles weighing less than 36 pounds and 11 percent on heavier bikes. The tariff laws were originally written to protect American manufacturers from competition by foreign coaster brake bikes.

same time, high foreign tariffs discouraged U.S. manufacturers from exporting bicycles. Table 8–9 shows the share of foreign-made bicycles in the American market over the 1960 to 1973 period.

With successive devaluations of the dollar that began in August 1971, most foreign-made bicycles had lost their price advantage by 1974. However, foreign companies continued to hold one-third of the U.S. market in unit sales since U.S. firms still found themselves in the humiliating position of importing bicycles to satisfy the needs of their regular customers. The U.S. Department of Commerce reported that in 1967 the average manufacturers' price of domestic bicycles was $29.20, versus $18.40 for imports. By 1972 the gap had closed to $38.30 and $37.80, respectively; and by 1973, the average domestic bicycle was slightly cheaper at $42.30 than foreign models at $42.40. The pattern of bicycle imports by country is shown in Table 8–10.

In the first six months of 1974 the number of imported bicycles dropped by 52 percent from the same period in 1973. The drop reflected a sharp decline in the sale of inexpensive foreign units, which had earned a bad reputation because of their poor quality and mechanical difficulties. The countries most affected by the recent drop in demand are shown in Table 8–11.

Asian imports varied greatly in quality. Taiwan and Korea produced inexpensive bicycles, which were sold as private label products in the U.S. market. Japanese bicycles, which for years had been the cheapest bicycles on the market, had undergone a major metamorphosis in the late 1960s. With a new quality image and the most modern plants in the world, Japan had become a significant force in the world bicycle market. No longer were Japanese bicycles sold under private labels. They were imported under their own distinct names, such as Fuji, Itoh, Nishiki, and Panasonic, and were ac-

TABLE 8–9. Foreign and Domestic Sales Percentage Breakdown in the U.S. Market

	1973	1972	1971	1970	1969	1968	1965	1960
Total sales (millions of units)	15.3	13.9	8.9	6.9	7.1	7.5	5.6	3.7
% Domestic	66%	63%	74%	73%	72%	80%	82%	70%
% Import	34	37	26	27	28	20	18	30

SOURCE: Bicycle Institute of America.

TABLE 8-10. Foreign Bicycle Import Patterns

Wheel Diameters 25" and Under	1965		1969		1973	
	% of Total[a]	Mfg. Price/Unit	% of Total[a]	Mfg. Price/Unit	% of Total[a]	Mfg. Price/Unit
United Kingdom	5.6%	$26.53	2.3%	$24.20	3.0%	$37.88
West Germany	36.2	14.14	29.0	16.88	5.4	29.79
Austria	3.8	17.10	11.5	15.96	5.9	29.13
Portugal	–	–	1.7	15.60	7.8	22.73
Italy	4.4	15.19	7.7	17.11	6.3	28.89
Taiwan	–	–	6.5	16.09	54.5	19.73
Japan	32.9	15.05	31.0	18.62	3.8	35.98
Other	17.1	–	10.3	–	13.3	–
Total	100.0%	$15.05	100.0%	$16.48	100.0%	$23.87

Wheel Diameters over 25"	1965		1969		1973	
United Kingdom	42.3%	$22.42	50.6%	$24.15	10.0%	$49.66
Netherlands	–	–	–	–	2.1	59.20
Belgium	–	–	–	–	1.4	62.56
France	2.3	30.24	3.2	37.00	11.2	63.64
West Germany	6.9	17.21	1.7	24.87	9.8	38.89
Austria	18.7	20.17	22.4	21.43	16.7	39.47
Italy	1.0	33.58	1.0	34.77	5.8	51.78
Taiwan	–	–	–	–	13.7	35.80
Japan	27.1	18.36	17.1	21.18	19.2	50.00
Korea	–	–	–	–	4.6	36.25
Other	1.7	–	4.0	–	5.5	–
Total	100.0%	$20.68	100.0%	$23.32	100.0%	$46.61

[a]Percentages below 1% not indicated.

SOURCE: U.S. Department of Commerce.

tively advertised and promoted. Most Japanese firms sold a narrow line of high-quality ten-speed lightweight bicycles through dealers at prices well over $100. Fuji Bicycle Company, for example, devoted its production almost exclusively to beautifully crafted and finished racing models outfitted with high-grade components. There were approximately ten Japanese bicycle manufacturers exporting to the United States. Japanese manufacturers relied on purchased components just as U.S. firms did and enjoyed close proximity to the strong Japanese component supply industry.

TABLE 8-11. U.S. Imported Bicycles by Countries (000)

Country	6 mos. 1974	1973	1972	1971	1970
Japan	368	836	1,213	686	532
Taiwan	198	1,125	712	104	55
Austria	269	671	606	346	375
United Kingdom	181	447	566	496	374
France	171	465	509	215	51
Italy	29	290	374	116	91
West Germany	17	445	516	197	319
Other	362	788	560	63	90
Total	1,595	5,155	5,156	2,340	1,948

SOURCE: Bicycle Institute of America.

European bicycle firms, like Asian manufacturers, produced units of varying quality. More than 150 firms ranging from custom and specialty shops to large factories operated in sixteen European countries. West Germany and Austria were the largest European exporters of inexpensive bicycles to the United States. The number of imported bicycles from Austria was high because of Stelber's Austrian-based production facility and because Sears imported many Austrian-made bicycles. Many of the Austrian-imported bicycles were three-speed and coaster brake models. Most West German bicycles were sold as private label bicycles, manufactured either for American distributors or for discount and department stores.

England, France, and Italy sold mostly high-quality branded bicycles to the U.S. market. Italian bicycles were generally the most expensive bikes on the U.S. market, and Italians had the reputation for producing the finest bicycles in the world, mostly by hand and in small quantities. The most famous handcrafted bicycle was the Cinelli, which was priced at $495 and up. Other fine Italian brands were Atala, Frejus-Legnano, Bottechia, and Bianchi.

French bicycle manufacturers offered a somewhat broader price range and product line than the Italians. Peugeot, Motobecane, and Gitane dominated the French market and, by extension, the French exports to the United States. As a group they shipped 300,000 bicycles into the United States in 1973, distributed through relatively unsophisticated dealership systems, offering parts, accessories, and services on a very limited basis. Other well-known French manufacturers were Mercier, Jeunet, and Lejeune. Most French bicycles sold in the American market were ten-speed units, averaging $150 or more in price, although the French did sell children's bicycles and specialty bicycles on a limited basis.

Raleigh Industries, Ltd. Raleigh was the foreign manufacturer that had most aggressively entered the U.S. bicycle market. Raleigh established a subsidiary, Raleigh Industries of America, Inc., in 1964, and by 1968 Raleigh had developed a nationwide network of sales office/warehouses and dealerships. In 1974, the company had begun to assemble Raleigh bicycles on American soil with the intention of full U.S. manufacturing of bicycles by mid-1975.

Raleigh Industries, Ltd., was the world's largest bicycle manufacturer, selling to 140 markets and producing bicycles in its twelve plants throughout the world. In 1973 it sold 500,000 bicycles through Raleigh Industries of America, Inc., and ranked as the chief foreign supplier of bicycles to the U.S. market. Raleigh offered the most extensive line of bicycles of all foreign suppliers and specialized in the lightweight market, where it had earned its reputation for superb craftsmanship and lightness. Raleigh was the only foreign company to have developed a "full concept" marketing approach in the U.S. market, involving a deep product line and availability of service, parts, and accessories through an extensive system of authorized dealers. Raleigh bicycles were high priced and were renowned for their quality and dependability.

Raleigh Industries, Ltd., was a highly integrated company, producing many of its own components for standardized bicycles and supplying a variety of parts to American manufacturers as well as for their own use. Raleigh's most direct competitor in the American market, particularly in terms of distribution and marketing program, was Schwinn; its major competitors in terms of product line were high-priced foreign-made bicycles such as Peugeot, Motobecane, Gitane, and Fuji.

The Future

The biggest question facing the bicycle industry in 1974 was how long the new prosperity would continue. Most industry leaders were convinced that the adult market would endure, but because it was such a new phenomenon there were many unknowns. The consensus among manufacturers was that their products would last between five and eight years, assuming normal wear and tear. But until the 1970s normal wear and tear had been at the hands of children. It was entirely possible that adults would keep their bicycles much longer. With proper care and maintenance, a bicycle could last a lifetime.

Another uncertainty concerned the strength of the secondhand bicycle market. To date that market had been practically nonexistent. Most children's bicycles wore out or were discarded because they were inexpensive items. The question remained as to whether adults would do likewise, or simply store their bicycles once they were no longer in use. The possibility for trade-ins and a secondhand market was also an unresolved issue.

The 1973–1974 energy shock further complicated speculation on prospective bicycle sales. Logically, the crisis was considered a boon to bike makers; with gasoline in short supply, more people were apt to turn to the bicycle for transportation. However, the energy crisis touched off an explosion of bike sales in a number of other countries besides the United States—notably Japan and Britain. There was serious doubt among bicycle makers about whether there would be enough capacity to go around, partly because of high foreign demand and partly because of the global shortage of key industrial materials. About 30 percent of a bicycle was purchased from suppliers, mostly foreign. All the multispeed gear systems, 80 percent of the tires and 75 percent of the bicycle chains used by U.S. bike manufacturers were produced abroad.

Despite the unknowns, U.S. manufacturers remained fairly optimistic about their future. The widely held view was that bike sales would rise to 15.5 million units during 1974—a gain of 300,000, or about 2 percent, over 1973—and that the market would stabilize around 16 million units for the following two or three years. U.S. manufacturers also expected to make a dent in the share of imported bikes, thanks to their increased capacity and the demand for bikes in other countries, which would keep the foreign companies busy. However, the U.S. industry had not been distinguished for its foresight. One company president remarked, "No one really knows what the demand for bicycles will be. We've even forecast as late as the third quarter of the year and have been way off. There is no scientific basis for what we predict."

EXHIBIT 8-1. *Comparative Financial Data*

	1973	1972	1971	1970	1969
Murray					
Net sales ($mm)	$133.5	$117.6	$ 89.1	$ 66.4	$72.4
Net income ($mm)	5.9	4.9	3.5	2.4	2.1
Net income/sales	4.4%	4.1%	3.9%	3.7%	3.2%
Dividend payout	0.28	0.25	0.35	0.5	0.59
ROE	16.4%	15.2%	11.9%	8.9%	8.0%
Total assets ($mm)	$ 72.2	$ 58.2	$ 50.6	$ 44.0	$ 39.5
Current ratio	2.6	3.4	2.8	3.2	4.4
Debt/equity	0.28	0.35	0.25	0.23	0.25
Working capital ($mm)	$ 31.0	$ 28.8	$ 21.9	$ 19.9	$ 18.9
Net property, plant, equipment	$ 17.9	$ 16.1	$ 13.8	$ 13.9	$ 13.8
ROA	8.4%	8.4%	6.8%	5.5%	5.3%
Depreciation/sales	0.96%	1.0%	1.3%	1.7%	1.7%
Net sales/total assest	1.9	2.0	1.8	1.5	1.7
Capital expenditures ($mm)	$ 3.5	$ 3.6	$ 1.0	$ 1.2	$ 1.7
Huffman					
Net sales ($mm)	$105.1	$ 82.4	$ 63.7	$ 55.4	$ 57.0
Net income ($mm)	2.0	1.5	0.5	0.8	2.2
Net income/sales	1.9%	1.8%	0.8%	1.4%	3.9%
Dividend payout	0.38	0.12	1.59	1.38	0.46
ROE	9.6%	8.3%	2.9%	4.4%	14.9%
Total assets ($mm)	$ 59.1	$ 43.6	$ 34.3	$ 34.3	$ 31.1
Current ratio	2.3	1.9	2.5	2.7	4.5
Debt/equity	0.61	0.38	0.44	0.47	0.46
Working capital ($mm)	$ 28.0	$ 16.3	$ 14.9	$ 15.2	$ 18.6
Net property, plant, equipment	$ 9.7	$ 8.8	$ 9.4	$ 9.6	$ 6.5
ROA	3.4%	3.4%	1.4%	2.2%	7.2%
Depreciation/sales	1.4%	1.5%	1.9%	1.6%	1.0%
Net sales/total assets	1.8	1.9	1.9	1.6	1.8
Capital expenditures ($mm)	$ 2.3	$ 1.2	$ 1.0	$ 4.0	$ 3.2
AMF					
Net sales ($mm)	$962.0	$928.9	$756.2	$646.7	$612.9
Net income ($mm)	57.8	55.6	43.7	37.3	33.9
Net income/sales	6.2%	6.0%	5.7%	5.6%	5.5%
Dividend payout	0.35	0.35	0.39	0.43	0.47
ROE	20.3%	20.1%	18.5%	18.1%	18.4%
Total assets ($mm)	$796.1	$688.3	$595.5	$511.8	$489.7
Current ratio	1.7	1.9	2.0	2.3	2.3
Debt/equity	0.6	0.57	0.62	0.75	0.83
Working capital ($mm)	$224.4	$220.2	$194.1	$191.6	$186.5
Net property, plant, equipment	$148.7	$138.1	$114.5	$ 97.4	$ 91.4
ROA	7.3%	8.1%	7.3%	7.3%	6.9%
Depreciation/sales	3.2%	3.0%	3.5%	3.9%	4.0%
Net sales/total assets	1.2	1.3	1.3	1.3	1.3
Capital expenditures ($mm)	$ 53.1	$ 60.1	$ 60.9	$ 30.4	$ 32.6

EXHIBIT 8-1. *Continued*

	1973	1972	1971	1970	1969
Stelber					
Net sales ($mm)	$ 71.4	$ 36.8	$ 29.6	$ 21.6	$ 15.8
Net income ($mm)	2.6	1.3	0.6	0.09	0.5
Net income/sales	3.7%	3.6%	1.9%	0.3%	0.3%
Dividend payout	—	—	—	—	—
ROE	3.5%	18.0%	11.3%	1.9%	13.3%
Total assets ($mm)	$ 69.1	$ 30.6	$ 17.9	$ 15.2	$ 11.4
Current ratio	1.3	1.2	1.2	1.3	1.4
Debt/equity	0.71	0.67	0.68	0.53	0.06
Working capital ($mm)	$ 9.5	$ 3.6	$ 1.8	$ 2.1	$ 2.6
Net property, plant, equipment	$ 18.3	$ 10.1	$ 4.2	$ 3.5	$ 1.4
ROA	0.9%	4.4%	3.1%	0.6%	4.8%
Depreciation/sales	1.1%	1.1%	1.1%	1.8%	2.5%
Net sales/total assets	1.0	1.2	1.7	1.4	1.4
Capital expenditures ($mm)	$ 11.4	$ 3.3	$ 1.1	$ 2.4	$ 0.6

SOURCES: Corporate 10K forms and annual reports.

EXHIBIT 8-2. *Comparative Financial Data on the Big Three U.S. Manufacturers*

1973	Murray	Huffman	AMF
Bicycle sales[a] ($000)	$105,437	$88,056	$83,000 (est.)
Bicycle units sold (millions)	2.4	2.3	1.75
Total market share	15.7%	15.0%	11.4%
% Business in large accounts	65	45	75
% Private label	80	55	40
Number of basic branded models	37	35	49
FOB factory price range:			
Adult lightweight	$38–76	$43–80	$41–99
High-risers	39–58	30–45	37–60
Specialty	27–48	110	33–125
Production capacity (million units)	3.0	3.0	2.2
Offerings by manufacturer:			
Accessories	No	Yes	Yes
Parts	Yes	Yes	Yes
Repair service centers	Yes	No	Yes

[a]Bikes, parts, accessories.

SOURCE: Corporate records.

EXHIBIT 8-3. *Estimated Distribution Patterns in the U.S. Bicycle Market, 1973 (millions of units)*

U.S. Firms	Dealers	Mass Merchandising Outlets	Imports	Dealers	Mass Merchandising Outlets
Huffman	0.2	2.2	Taiwan	—	1.2
Murray	0.25	2.15	Japan	0.5	0.4
Schwinn	1.4	—	France	0.4	0.1
AMF	0.3	1.1	Austria	0.3	—
MTD	0.3	0.6	Italy	0.5	—
Mossberg	0.1	0.4	United Kingdom	0.5	—
Stelber	—	0.7	West Germany	0.1	0.4
Ross	0.1	0.4	Others	0.4	0.5
TOTAL	2.65	7.55	TOTAL	2.7	2.6
% of Total	25.73%	74.27%	% of Total	51%	49%

Grand Totals:[a] Dealer — 5.35 million units (34.5%); Mass Merchandising
Outlets — 10.15 million units (65.5%)
Total Bicycles — 15.5 million units

[a]The estimated total was believed to be slightly high.

SOURCE: Estimates by industry official.

PART IV
Entry and Entry Deterrence

The next two cases focus on the analysis of entry into an industry and entry deterrence, two sides of the same coin. ''The Disposable Diaper Industry in 1974'' portrays the situation facing Procter & Gamble's dominant Pampers brand of disposable diapers as a number of large, credible entrants are attacking its position. The analysis centers on Procter & Gamble's defensive strategy against the new entrants but can be turned around to consider how an entrant might most successfully attack Procter & Gamble.

''SWECO, Inc.'' shifts the attention from defense to offense and examines the situation of a relatively small firm considering entry into a new industry against a number of large competitors. SWECO must decide whether entry into the drilling mud-processing equipment industry is attractive at all, and choose among a wide variety of entry strategy options. Strategic mapping can be employed to consider alternative entry strategies.

CASE 9
The Disposable Diaper Industry in 1974

The disposable diaper industry had emerged since 1966 as one of the largest consumer products in the United States, with manufacturer sales of an estimated $370 million in 1973. Enjoying sales growth in excess of 25 percent per year, disposable diapers had already become the single largest brand at Procter & Gamble, the firm that was credited with pioneering the large-scale use of disposable diapers and that remained the industry leader with an estimated 69 percent market share. Given the huge stakes involved, positions in the disposable diaper industry were being hotly contested in 1974. Kimberly-Clark had already captured approximately a 15 percent share and was driving to achieve national distribution in 1974 after a six-year rollout. Colgate-Palmolive's Kendall subsidiary was marketing an improved new disposable diaper. Johnson & Johnson had committed to a massive diaper production facility in Park Forest, Illinois, in 1971 that had recently begun production. Union Carbide was testing an innovative new disposable diaper in Bangor, Maine, and seemed ready to begin a national rollout. Scott Paper was testing a new disposable diaper to replace its Baby Scott line, which had been discontinued in 1971. Finally, a number of firms, including Weyerhaeuser and Georgia-Pacific, were manufacturing private label diapers, and a number of other potential entrants into private label production were known to be studying the market.

Industry History

As long as there had been babies, there had been the need for diapers. Prior to 1966 the great majority of diapers used in the United States were cloth diapers made of cotton, which were laundered and reused. Some families laundered their own diapers at home or at laundromats, while others made use of commercial diaper services that picked up soiled diapers and delivered clean ones on a regular basis. The leading manufacturers of cloth diapers had been Kendall Company[1] (Curity brand) and Johnson & Johnson.

[1] Kendall had since been acquired by Colgate-Palmolive.

Diaper delivery services handled approximately 7 percent of cloth diapers in 1966, producing revenues in the $100 million range. Diaper delivery services were not available to all consumers but covered the majority of households located in urban areas. Diaper service firms made up a highly fragmented, regional industry consisting of some 400 participants. There had been repeated allegations of price fixing in the diaper services industry in particular markets, and several cases of price fixing had been successfully prosecuted.

Disposable diapers had been on the market in the United States prior to 1966, but their market penetration had been minimal. Disposable diapers had been marketed through drugstores for some time by Chicopee Mills[2] (Chux brand), Kendall (Curity brand), and Parke-Davis. These early disposable diapers were quite expensive (with prices in excess of 10 cents apiece) and crude in design, consisting of a number of layers of tissue paper with a front and backing sheet. Early disposable diapers were sold primarily for use in traveling.

Disposable diapers had enjoyed considerably more success in Europe in the early 1960s, particularly in Sweden. Disposable diapers had been used in Sweden since the late 1940s and began spreading throughout Europe in the mid-1950s. Unlike the early U.S. varieties, European disposable diapers were two-piece in construction employing a reusable plastic pant combined with a disposable inner liner.

The seeds of the dramatic growth in the U.S. disposable diaper industry were sown in 1966 when Procter & Gamble (P&G) began national expansion of its Pampers brand diaper. P&G had become interested in disposable diapers in the mid-1950s. According to the popular story, the nun in charge of the nursery at a Cincinnati Catholic hospital had complained to some P&G personnel about the need for a disposable diaper that would eliminate the sanitary problems with cloth diapers. P&G engineers developed some prototypes and reportedly had a pilot diaper-making machine in 1956. P&G was also interested in the tissue paper market at this time. Both the tissue paper and diaper efforts gained momentum with P&G's acquisition of the Charmin Paper Company in 1957. Charmin became

[2] A unit of Johnson & Johnson.

the base for P&G's national expansion in bathroom tissue, paper towels, and facial tissue, as well as for its diaper business.

After further development work, P&G began its first test market of disposable diapers in 1962 in Peoria, Illinois. Its product, priced at 10 cents per diaper, consisted of approximately a dozen layers of tissue paper that had been mechanically embossed to hold them together, backed with a polyethylene plastic outer sheet and a porous rayon facing sheet (facing the baby). P&G assembled the product using purchased tissue and other components. While the new product, named Pampers, was highly rated by consumers, it did not achieve significant market penetration but rather proved to be a specialty item for use by travelers and high-income buyers.

Faced with these results, P&G concluded that the problem was high cost. At 10 cents each, Pampers cost far more than the estimated 3–5 cents per diaper charged by diaper delivery services and the 1–2 cents per diaper that it cost to launder cloth diapers at home, even including depreciation of the diapers themselves. P&G engineers went back to the drawing boards and developed a highly sophisticated block-long continuous-process machine that could assemble diapers at speeds of up to a remarkable 400 per minute. The new process allowed P&G to reintroduce Pampers at 5.5 cents per diaper in a second major test in Sacramento, California. This test proved to be a huge success, and full national distribution was begun in the Midwest in 1966.

Meanwhile, as early as 1962 Scott Paper Company had begun working on an entirely different disposable diaper based on the two-piece principle that had become the standard in Europe, and using snaps as closures instead of the pin that was required with Pampers. By early 1966, the year of the Pampers rollout, Scott was test marketing Baby Scott's in Denver, Dallas, and Minneapolis. Borden had also begun testing a two-piece disposable diaper under the White Lamb brand in 1965.

Kimberly-Clark had done research on disposable diapers for hospital nurseries in the early 1950s. The project had been unsuccessful but was rejuvenated in the late 1950s and early 1960s. Kimberly-Clark's development efforts in diapers were based on different technology, using what was known as fluff pulp. Fluff pulp was a highly absorbent material that Kimberly-Clark utilized in its feminine napkin products. Kimberly-Clark calculated that fluff pulp was inherently cheaper per unit of absorbency than tissue. It capitalized on this cost saving by designing a diaper with built-in adhesive tapes as fasteners rather than pins. Kimberly-Clark's diapers also employed a unique shape to improve their fit. After extensive development efforts with hospital nurseries, Kimberly-Clark began test marketing its disposable diaper in Denver in 1968 and went into a national rollout soon after.

Another competitor, International Paper (IP), had begun marketing two-piece disposable diapers in Canada in the mid-1960s through its Facelle division, which also produced other tissue paper products. In 1968 IP announced its entry into the U.S. market in both disposable diapers and tissue products, and began construction of a joint plant for the entire line in Los Angeles that came on stream in 1970. Weyerhaeuser announced its entry into disposable diapers in August of 1970, with a new plant to be operational in 1971. Several other private label producers entered the industry at about this time as well, producing for accounts such as Sears, Penney, and the major supermarket chains.

Johnson & Johnson had long been in disposable diapers through its Chicopee subsidiary, but the Chicopee product (Chux and later Chix) was far behind those of the new entrants since efforts had been concentrated on defending the cloth diaper businesses. By 1971, however, the Chicopee cloth diaper had been discontinued and the Chicopee disposable diaper was fading from the market. After years of development work, Johnson & Johnson announced in 1971 that it would enter disposable diapers under the Johnson's brand through its Domestic Operating Company. The product had been developed some years earlier, but patent difficulties with P&G had delayed entry. A large plant was begun in Park Forest, Illinois, to produce the new Johnson & Johnson diaper, a premium product using fluff pulp and a unique inner liner sheet. Johnson & Johnson had tested the new disposable diaper with great success in Denver and Fort Wayne, Indiana.

A final entrant, Union Carbide, had begun testing disposable diapers in 1973. Carbide's product had a unique, patented hydrophobic[3] inner liner made of plastic that allowed liquid to only go one way and thus keep the baby drier than other brands.

P&G had continued to develop its disposable diaper business while these entries were occurring. National distribution was achieved in 1969, and Pampers had been modified to incorporate some of the key features of competitors' products. P&G began converting from tissue to fluff pulp in 1972 and incorporated adhesive tape tabs on its diapers during 1972 and 1973. All the while P&G had been engaged in heavy advertising of its Pampers brand as well as extensive sampling and couponing and had maintained a commanding share of the market.

Despite the explosive growth of disposable diapers, by 1974 several entrants had called it quits. Borden had discontinued its White Lamb disposable diaper around 1970. Scott discontinued Baby Scott in the U.S. in 1971, when the two-piece design proved unsuccessful in the U.S. market. International Paper discontinued its Flushabye line of disposable diapers as well as its entire consumers paper products business in the U.S. in 1972, following after-tax losses of $7.5 million in 1971 and $5.6 million in 1972. Chicopee's Chux brand diapers were all but off the market as well, though Chicopee continued to produce diapers for private label.

Product

Disposable diapers were one-piece triangular or rectangular pads consisting of three layers. The outer layer of the diaper was a waterproof plastic film, which contained any moisture inside the diaper. The bulk of the diaper was a highly absorbent cellulose-based filler material. In 1974 most diapers had an absorbent layer of fluff pulp, replacing the tissue or creped wadding in earlier generations. Fluff pulp offered greater absorbency for its weight. The inner layer of the diaper next to baby was made of a hydrophobic material. Most inner liners were made of a weblike rayon fabric, or rayon and polyester mixture. By 1974 all disposable diapers were of one-piece construction, with the two-piece design consisting of a disposable liner and reusable plastic

[3] A hydrophobic material let moisture pass through it without absorbing the moisture and becoming wet itself.

pants having proved a failure in the U.S. market-place.

Most diapers (including Pampers and Johnson's) were rectangular and pleated, with the pleats allowing expansion when the diaper was put on the baby to yield a better fit; some of the low-price, private-label brands were not pleated. Kimbies was not pleated but had a unique triangular fold, designed to improve fit. While earlier generations of diapers had required safety pins as fasteners, by 1974 all brands had adopted the built-in adhesive tape fasteners that had been pioneered by Kimberly-Clark.

All manufacturers offered diapers in at least three and sometimes up to five sizes, designed for babies of different sizes and for daytime versus overnight use:

Diaper Varieties

Newborn	Babies up to 11 or 12 pounds[4]
Daytime	Babies from 12 to 22 pounds
Overnight	Babies from 12 to 22 pounds, with extra absorption capacity
Toddler	Babies over 22 or 23 pounds
Toddler overnight[5]	Babies over 20 pounds, with extra absorption capacity

The number of diapers in a box varied with the type of diaper, with fewer diapers per box typical for the large sized diapers. Some manufacturers offered large, economy size boxes as well.

The performance characteristics of diapers included absorbency, strikethrough and rewet of the inner liner, softness, fit, fastening system, shedding, ability to double up, and ease in disposal. Strikethrough was the speed at which liquid passed through the inner liner, and rewet was a measure of the percentage of liquid that would come back through the liner from the absorbent pad. Fit referred to the ability of the diaper to conform to baby's shape, the ability of the diaper to fit snugly, and whether the cover over the adhesive had to be thrown away or not. Shedding referred to the problem some diapers had in leaving a fuzz on baby's skin, which though not harmful was deemed a disadvantage. Doubling up referred to the practice by some parents of using two diapers together to cut down on wetness, especially at night. Ease of disposal referred to the ability of the diaper's absorbent layer to disintegrate easily in water when disposed of through household plumbing. Disposal in this manner was not recommended for most households, however, because of the load on the plumbing system.

Appendix A gives *Consumer Reports* ratings of the various diapers on the market in 1967, 1970, and 1974 as well as average retail prices as determined by *Consumer Reports* shoppers. Parents' choices of disposable diaper brands were highly performance-sensitive, and a diaper that performed poorly would soon lose market position dramatically.

Demand

The potential market for disposable diapers was huge by almost any firm's standards. With more than 3 million babies born each year in the United States who stayed in diapers for approximately 24–27 months and needed an average of 50–60 diapers per week, the potential market was an incredible 15–20 billion diapers per year or more. Demand for disposable diapers had grown rapidly since P&G's product introduction in 1966 (Table 9-1)

The rapid increase in disposable diaper sales was all the more remarkable because it had occurred in the context of generally declining births in the United States. Furthermore, disposable diapers were more expensive than the two alternatives: commercial diaper services and home laundering of cloth diapers. The estimated unit cost of disposable diapers in 1973 was 5.3 to 5.7 cents, compared to 4.5 to 5.5 cents for diaper services and 1 to 2 cents for home laundering (including depreciation but excluding a charge for labor).[6] A further indication

---

[4]The exact suggested weight cutoffs varied slightly by manufacturer.

[5]Some manufacturers also offered a premature and a professional newborn size. These were produced in small quantities as a convenience to hospitals and pediatricians.

[6]A disposable diaper was more absorbent than a cloth diaper, and thus somewhat fewer disposables were used per week than cloth diapers (approximately 60 per week versus 80 per week).

TABLE 9–1. Growth in Demand for Disposable Diapers

	1966	1967	1968	1969	1970	1971	1972	1973
Manufacturer's sales (millions)	$10	$20	$60	$90	$130	$200	$280	$370
Percent penetration of diaperable babies	1%	2%	7%	11%	15%	22%	35%	42%
Number of births (millions)	3.64	3.56	3.54	3.63	3.74	3.56	3.26	3.14

SOURCES: Bruce Kirk, *Disposable Diaper: Its Investment Potential,* Pressprich & Co., Inc.; L. J. Wilkerson, *Johnson's Diaper: Bottom Line Impact,* White Weld; U.S. Department of Commerce, Bureau of the Census; and casewriter estimates.

that cost was not the determining factor in parents' decisions to use disposable diapers was the fact that the less expensive European-style two-piece disposable diaper (2.5 to 3.5 cents per diaper) had been a failure in the United States despite significant outlays on the part of Scott Paper and International Paper to develop it.

The rapid penetration of disposable diapers in the United States was attributed to a number of factors. Perhaps the most important was the increasing number of working mothers, who returned to work sooner and valued the convenience of disposable diapers. Mothers were also increasingly older, as many families had postponed having children, and better educated. Families had also become more affluent during the late 1960s and early 1970s, and increasingly mobile.

Paralleling these trends had been dramatic and relatively continuous improvement in the quality of disposable diapers since the pre-1966 days. There had also been heavy advertising of disposables by competitors and wide exposure of mothers to disposable diapers in the hospital when the baby was born. The highest penetration of disposable diapers in 1973 was in metropolitan areas and among apartment dwellers and mothers of their second or later child. Home laundering had been affected more than diaper services by the growth in disposables.[7] Some estimates suggested that sales of diaper services actually improved in absolute terms during the early years of post-1966 disposable diapers, more recently leveling off or perhaps declining. Disposable diapers had become by far the largest product category in the baby care area by 1973 (Table 9–2). Disposable diapers had also sur-

[7] Cotton cloth diapers had increased significantly in price since 1966 as well.

TABLE 9–2. Retail Sales of Baby Care Products[a] (millions)

	1972	1973
Disposable diapers and liners	$415.1	$554.6
Baby medicaments	$141.7	$147.9
Baby supplies and equipment (excluding disposable diapers)	$145.4	$147.2
Total	$702.2	$849.7

[a] These estimated retail sales of disposable diapers cannot be exactly reconciled with the figures for manufacturer's sales from a different source given earlier coupled with estimated retail margins on diapers.
SOURCE: Frost and Sullivan, *Baby Care Market.*

passed or nearly equaled the sales of other major consumer paper products such as paper napkins ($160 million at retail in 1970), paper towels ($470 million in 1970), and bathroom tissue ($535 million in 1970).

Estimates for the rate of future growth of disposable diapers varied, but all observers agreed that growth would continue. Growth estimates were a function of forecast births, disposable diaper penetration, and the number of diapers consumed per baby. While there was considerable disagreement about future births, most observers expected the birthrate to continue to decline slowly until the late 1970s. It was expected that increases in the number of women of childbearing age would begin to offset the declining birthrate in the latter 1970s and that the absolute number of births would begin to increase by 1976 or 1977. By the late 1970s and early 1980s births could be increasing by as many as 300,000 to 500,000 per year and be at a level of up to 3.9 million by 1980. The penetration of disposable diapers was expected to increase as well. Most estimates forecast penetration at 70–75 percent of diaper changes or more by 1980. The usage rate of diapers was dependent on future product improvements that might make diapers more absorbent.

Distribution

While disposable diapers had been sold primarily through drugstores before P&G's entry, most diapers were sold through supermarkets by 1973. Drugstores had been steadily losing market share in disposable diaper sales, though their absolute sales of disposables had been gaining slowly. Mass merchandisers also sold disposable diapers, among them Sears, Penney's, Ward's, K–Mart, and others (Table 9–3). Supermarkets' share of disposable diaper sales was expected to continue to increase.

Gross margins on disposable diapers ranged from 10 to up to 28 percent of retail selling price, with a median of around 18–20 percent. These margins were considerably lower than other baby care products but high compared to other tissue products and approaching the level of female sanitary products. Disposable diapers represented 63 percent of the sales and 50 percent of gross profit of baby care products in supermarkets. Disposable diapers were the single most important product in supermarket health and beauty aid dpeartments in terms of both sales and gross profit (7.8 percent and 7.1 percent respectively). Health and beauty aids represented 7.6 percent of total supermarket sales in 1973.[8]

Retailers had allocated a significant amount of shelf space to disposable diapers despite the bulk of diaper boxes, because of the high volume and heavy store traffic that diapers generated. Disposable diapers were recognized as a fast-growing item, and sales per square foot were greater than similar sized paper towel or bathroom tissue products.

TABLE 9–3. Estimated Sales of Disposable Diapers by Retail Channel

	1971	1973
Drugstores	32%	26%
Supermarkets	60%	70%
Mass merchandisers	8%	4%
	100%	100%

Source: Frost and Sullivan, *Baby Care Market.*

[8] All figures taken from *Chain Store Age*, Supermarketing Edition, July 1974. They refer to supermarkets with sales in excess of $1 million.

Most retailers carried two or more branded diapers. Some major retailers also had contracted wth suppliers for private label products, offered at prices 10–12 percent below the leading branded lines and in more limited styles and boxing configurations. Private label products were inferior to the branded lines in 1973, but their quality was improving. Private label brands accounted for approximately 8 or 9 percent of disposable diaper sales in 1973 and had been increasing their share.

In the battle for diaper shelf space, retailers looked for aggressive support of a line by its manufacturer through sampling programs, consumer advertising, and promotional allowances to the trade. P&G was the least generous in trade promotional allowances, and retailers were anxious to find alternative diaper brands that could neutralize P&G's power. Nevertheless, a new brand had to provide incentives to get its product on the shelf such as giving the retailer a free case of diapers for every three cases that were purchased. Most manufacturers sold to retailers through brokers who received a fixed commission on sales, while some manufacturers had their own sales forces that handled disposable diapers.

Marketing

Marketing of disposable diapers was extremely complex and involved a wide variety of vehicles. One important vehicle was extensive sampling. Sampling began in the hospital, where branded manufacturers attempted to reach 2/3 to 3/4 of mothers with free samples of their products, which also included a coupon for the first purchase. Sample diapers were part of a larger kit of products the new mother received. The cost of hospital sampling was estimated at $1 per sample. P&G had locked up the premier hospital kit firm, Gift Pax, and competitors either used other firms or ran their hospital sampling programs in-house. Sampling sometimes continued once the baby went home.

Couponing was another vehicle for diaper marketing, widely practiced throughout the period the baby was in diapers. All major manufacturers purchased baby lists that gave the name and address of families with babies as well as the baby's date of birth. Coupons offering cents-off on purchases of diapers were mailed to parents when the baby reached the age to move to a larger-size diaper. Companies trying to break into the market used coupons and samples to induce trial, and coupons were also used to try to improve sales in problem markets.

The other major marketing vehicle for disposable diapers was consumer advertising. Advertising employed all the major media: network and spot television, radio, local newspapers, and specialized magazines such as *American Baby*. Exhibit 9–1 gives available data on historical diaper advertising spending. Network television was available only to nationally or near-nationally distributed firms and offered 20–40 percent lower cost per household than spot TV. However, even national brands used a spot TV overlay to reinforce sales in problem markets. Local newspaper advertising was used primarily for "coupon carrying," or offering the consumer a coupon giving a discount on purchases of diapers. Local newspaper advertising accounted for less than 5 percent of media budgets, though the cost of redeeming the coupons themselves was more significant.

All manufacturers engaged in extensive test marketing of new diaper entries or significant product changes. The typical test market lasted six months to a year.

Manufacturing

The manufacture of disposable diapers involved a highly complex, high-speed continuous process assembly operation using specialized diaper machines. The process began when rolls of fluff pulp in sheet form were fed into a hammer mill. In a separate room for dust and noise control, the hammer mill mechanically chopped up the pulp with rotating hammers or teeth. The pulp was then carried as a loosely formed batt by a stream of air to a diaper-forming machine. The forming machine cut the fluff batt into sections, and laminated it to the plastic outer sheet of the diaper, which was folded over the ends of the batt.[9] Then the inner liner and tape system were attached, and the diapers were folded, counted, and packaged.

---

[9] Sometimes the fluff batt was laminated to the inner liner first.

Diaper machines were several hundred feet in length and staffed by four complete crews so that they could be operated twenty-four hours a day and seven days a week. A well-running machine operated 80 percent of the week, and this percentage was termed machine efficiency. Diaper machines could reach speeds of an incredible 400 diapers per minute. The speed of the machine was a function of both engineering improvements and the complexity of the diaper. The folding operation was particularly important in setting the speed of the machine, and complex folds slowed machines down. It took months and even years to build up the speed and efficiency of a newly installed machine or an extensively redesigned machine, which operated at approximately 100–150 diapers per minute. Manufacturing costs were also affected by the amount of rejects and scrap in manufacturing, because scrap and rejects could not be reprocessed in diaper manufacture. Manufacturing diapers was so difficult that virtually all firms had experienced problems in mastering the process.

Diaper machines could be purchased from outside suppliers, but virtually all the major diaper manufacturers made major and costly proprietary modifications to machines in order to achieve competitive machine speeds and to produce their particular variety of diaper. A basic diaper-forming machine cost approximately $300,000 in 1974 and a complete line including the building in which it was housed represented an investment of $2 to $4 million. An efficient scale diaper plant required a minimum of three to four machines to achieve efficient use of buildings, maintenance crews, and other overhead. Maintenance requirements for maintaining machines at peak operating efficiency were substantial. There was a lead time of 12–18 months in ordering, installing, and modifying a machine. Table 9–4 gives estimated unit costs of disposable diapers for a producer of the scale of P&G.

Some diaper manufacturers were integrated into fluff pulp. Fluff pulp was also sold on the open market by such firms as Weyerhaeuser, International Paper, Rayonier, and Buckeye Cellulose (a P&G division). There was a tight supply of fluff pulp in 1974, and prices had been increasing. Most firms purchased the plastic outer liner. The inner liner for the diaper was made by some firms and

TABLE 9-4.   Estimated Diaper Unit Cost

	Dollars per Unit	Percent of Total
Raw materials		
Fluff pulp	$.006	15.0%
Cover sheet	.005	12.5%
Backing sheet	.001	2.5%
Packaging	.003	7.5%
Manufacturing labor	.003	7.5%
Depreciation and maintenance	.001	2.5%
Utilities	.001	2.5%
Total manufacturing costs	$.020	50.0%
Freight	.004	10.0%
Selling, general and administrative costs	.006	15.0%
Pretax profit	$.010	25.0%
Manufacturer sale price	$.040	100.0%

purchased by others from suppliers such as Kendall, Johnson & Johnson, Stearns & Foster, and Dexter Corporation. There were some though not large economies due to purchasing scale.

Because diapers were bulky, transportation costs were significant. Transportation amounted to approximately 10 percent or more of the total selling price, dictating regional plants to minimize cost. Significant savings could be obtained by manufacturers able to ship carload lots, either of diapers only or of diapers combined with other products shipped to the same channels. Only P&G could reap the benefits of full carload and even trainload shipments in 1974. Packaging costs were also a significant part of diaper costs and were rising in 1974.

Exhibit 9-2 gives the plant configurations and level of integration of major disposable diaper producers at the end of 1973.

Research and Development

All major diaper manufacturers engaged in heavy research and development (R&D) spending for both product improvements and improvements in their manufacturing processes. Industry sources estimated that leading firms spent at least $10 million annually on R&D. Any significant change in the diaper itself required additional major capital outlays to change over diaper machines, since the machines were highly specialized to the particular diaper configuration being produced. Machine changeovers usually led to a sharp drop in machine performance, and diaper manufacturers had to build up machine efficiency and operating speed slowly once again.

Competition

A variety of competitors were challenging P&G's strong position in disposable diapers in 1974, though some of the early challengers had already decided to throw in the towel. The firms with entries in disposable diapers in 1974 are listed in Table 9-5. Borden had discontinued its disposable diaper operations around 1970, and International Paper had discontinued diapers in 1972. Scott Paper was back in test market with a one-piece diaper after having abandoned its original two-piece entry (called Baby Scott) in 1971. Exhibit 9-3 gives estimated market shares for the leading firms over the 1967 to 1973 time period.

Only P&G was fully national in 1974, having achieved national distribution in 1969 after a three-year rollout. Kimberly-Clark was nearing national distribution in 1974 after some six years of rollout. Diaper manufacturers introduced their products one region at a time in conjunction with building a new plant in the region, which accounted for the long time required to reach national distribution.

Profiles of the leading branded competitors in

TABLE 9-5. Firms Producing Disposable Diapers

Branded	Branded—In Test Market	Private Label
P&G[a] (Pampers)	Union Carbide (Drydees)	Weyerhaeuser
Kimberly-Clark[b] (Kimbies)	Scott Paper (Scott Tots)	IPCO Hospital Supply
Johnson & Johnson		Georgia Pacific
Kendall/Colgate[b] (Curity)		

[a] National distribution.
[b] Nearly national distribution.

disposable diapers are given below, with a summary of their financial positions shown in Exhibit 9-4. Briefer profiles of several other firms, including the leading private label producer, are given as well.

Procter and Gamble (P&G)

P&G was the leading manufacturer and marketer of consumer products in the United States, 88 percent of its products sold to households and the balance representing closely related products sold to institutional or industrial users. P&G divided its businesses into four areas:

Laundry and cleaning products: detergents, soaps, fabric softeners, cleaners, and cleansers
Personal care products: bar soaps, toothpastes, mouthwash, deodorants, shampoos, paper tissue products, and disposable diapers
Food products: shortenings, oils, cake mixes, peanut butter, potato chips, and coffee
Other products: cellulose pulp, chemicals, and animal feed ingredients

The breakdown of P&G sales by product area is shown in Table 9-6. International operations contributed approximately one-fourth of total sales and a somewhat higher percentage of total profits, and involved the marketing of similar household products in Europe, Great Britain, Canada, and

parts of Latin America, Asia, and Africa. P&G's research and development spending totaled $115.8 million in 1973.

Disposable diapers, originally patented in 1961 and introduced in 1966, were part of the Paper Products Division that included Charmin bathroom tissue, Bounty paper towels, and White Cloud and Puffs facial tissue. P&G had entered the household paper products business in 1957 with the acquisition of the Charmin Paper Company. All its lines of paper products had been aggressively developed by P&G to occupy strong positions by 1974. Charmin and to a lesser extent Bounty were close to nationally distributed in 1974, while White Cloud and Puffs reached about 50 percent of the United States. Pampers was believed to be the single largest P&G brand in 1974 and to have enjoyed high profitability at least through 1972, when it was effectively the only major disposable diaper brand. P&G was constructing two plants in 1974 to support the entry of Pampers into the Canadian and West German markets.

P&G's diaper line included newborn, daytime, overnight, and toddler sizes in regular size packages as well as a larger package containing thirty diapers in the daytime size. P&G was testing a large Convenience Pak that contained a several-week supply of diapers. P&G had recently modified its Pampers diaper by phasing in adhesive tape tabs over the

TABLE 9-6. P&G Sales by Product Area

	1967	1968	1969	1970	1971	1972	1973
Laundry and cleaning products	45%	45%	46%	45%	44%	43%	43%
Personal care products	19%	21%	23%	25%	26%	27%	27%
Food products	24%	23%	22%	23%	24%	23%	23%
Other[a]	12%	11%	9%	7%	6%	7%	7%

[a] Includes Clorox liquid bleach sales until divestiture on January 2, 1969.
SOURCE: SEC Form 10K.

1972–1973 period and was also in the process of changing to fluff pulp instead of creped tissue for the absorbent layer. Both changes had required time-consuming (measured in years) and costly equipment changeovers. P&G had also modified its liner, going from rayon to a rayon-and-polyester mixture.

P&G aggressively marketed its diapers with the full range of marketing approaches. Its use of premiums and cents-off deals had increased significantly since 1972. Pampers were sold by the approximately 400-strong Paper Products Division sales force, which also sold the other P&G paper products. P&G had threatened patent action against Johnson & Johnson's planned Johnson's brand disposable diaper entry in the late 1960s, delaying it several years. P&G had also initiated patent infringement action against Weyerhaeuser, a private label diaper producer.

As shown in Exhibit 9-2, Pampers were produced in four plants located in Mehoopany, Pennsylvania; Albany, Georgia; Cheboygan, Michigan; and Cape Girardeau, Missouri. A fifth plant in Modesto, California, was planned. P&G obtained a portion of its fluff pulp needs from its Buckeye Cellulose facility in Alberta, Canada, and purchased the rest from outside suppliers.

Kimberly-Clark

Kimberly-Clark was a leading producer of consumer and industrial paper products and forest products, both in the United States and abroad. Kimberly-Clark businesses could be divided into a number of lines in 1973:

U.S. consumer and service products: Kleenex facial tissue, bathroom tissue, table napkins, and kitchen towels; Kotex sanitary napkins and tampons; Kimbies disposable diapers; Teri towels; bathroom tissue; disposable hospital paper products; towel wipes; interior packaging materials

U.S. paper and forest products: communication papers, including newsprint and coated papers for magazines, books and other printing applications; business papers, writing papers, and copying papers; industrial and specialty papers including thin papers (such as cigarette papers and condenser tissue) and saturated or coated papers; softwood and hardwood lumber and products made therefrom.

Operations outside the United States: production and sale of the same consumer products that Kimberly-Clark sold in the United States in overseas markets.

Kimberly-Clark's sales and operating profit were distributed among the lines of business as shown in Table 9-7.

Kimberly-Clark had enjoyed its best year ever in 1973, buoyed by strong results in paper products. The profitability of paper products had offset a price-cost squeeze in consumer products where pulp price increase could not be passed on. Kimberly-Clark was also facing heavy sales promotion cost in the hotly contested towels and tissue area where P&G was intent on building share. Kimberly-Clark held 35 percent of the facial tissue market and 12 percent of the paper towel market in 1973.[10] Kimberly-Clark had bet heavily on its new Terri line of paper towels with only moderate success. Kimberly-Clark was also bearing the costs of introducing several new lines of feminine sanitary products in the market to counteract competitive erosion of its traditionally dominant Kotex line.[11] Johnson & Johnson and Playtex had nearly eclipsed Kimberly-Clark's number one market share by being leaders in the newer tampon and beltless segment of the market.

Kimberly-Clark was making a strong effort as a company to expand its international operations and to boost its return on stockholders' equity to a goal of 14 to 15 percent established in 1971. To reach the latter goal Kimberly-Clark had eliminated four marginal paper mills in 1971 and discontinued some smaller consumer product lines that lacked promise. Research and development expenditures totaled $12.7 million in 1973, and capital expenditures had been distributed as shown in Table 9-8.

Kimbies, the new Kimberly-Clark disposable diaper, was the single largest investment program in the company in 1973. It was estimated that Kimberly-Clark's startup costs in disposable diapers had totaled more than $100 million through 1974. Kimbies were being rolled out nationally through the addition of one new diaper machine every six weeks and had achieved 85 percent national distri-

---

[10] Kimberly-Clark's tissue sales were estimated at $215 million in 1972, $100 million of which were Kleenex facial tissue. See Kirk, op. cit.

[11] Kimberly-Clark's sales in feminine hygiene products were estimated at $115 million in 1972. See Kirk, op. cit.

TABLE 9-7. Kimberly-Clark Sales and Profits by Line of Business

	1969		1970		1971		1972		1973	
	Sales	Operating Profit	Sales	Operating Profit	Sales	Operating Profit	Sales	Operating Profit	Sales	Operating Profit
U.S. consumer and service products	42%	54%	41%	56%	40%	63%	41%	53%	39%	35%
U.S. paper products	} 38%	} 30%	} 36%	} 19%	} 36%	} 12%	25%	} 22%	26%	} 33%
U.S. forest products							6%		6%	
Operations outside the U.S.A.	20%	16%	23%	25%	24%	25%	28%	25%	29%	32%

TABLE 9-8. Kimberly-Clark Capital Expenditures by Line of Business

	1970	1971	1972	1973
U.S. consumer and service products	21%	35%	47%	51%
U.S. paper and forest products	21%	23%	18%	20%
Operations outside the U.S.A.	50%	33%	30%	26%
Research and miscellaneous	8%	9%	5%	3%

bution by the end of 1973. The Kimbies line was reportedly ahead of schedule, and market share growth had met management's objectives. Management had stated that its ultimate goal was a 33 percent market share. Kimbies were assigned to the Consumer Products Division and sold through the Kimberly-Clarks sales force numbering some 650 sales personnel in 1973. Disposable diapers under the Kleenex brand were also being tested in West Germany and France.

Kimbies were one-piece diapers using a fluff pulp absorbent layer, adhesive tape tabs, and a unique triangular shape with a contour fold. The contour fold was quite difficult to manufacture at high speeds. Kimberly-Clark manufactured Kimbies in five plants in 1973, located in Memphis, Tennessee; Fullerton, California; Neenah, Wisconsin; New Milford, Connecticut; and Beech Island, South Carolina. Manufacturing startup had benefited from Kimberly-Clark's long experience in producing feminine sanitary products and facial tissue. Kimberly-Clark produced its own inner liner material but purchased fluff pulp and other key diaper components from outside suppliers.

Johnson & Johnson (J&J)

J&J was a leading manufacturer and marketer of prescription and nonprescription health care products as well as some specialized industrial products. J&J businesses in 1973 were as follows:

Health care: prescription and nonprescription drugs; diagnostic, therapeutic, contraceptive products; surgical dressings; ligatures and sutures; surgical instruments; surgical specialties and related items; toiletries and hygienic products, including baby care items; and veterinary products. This line of business included the activities of the following

domestic divisions and subsidiaries: Arbrook, Inc.; Cellulose Products Corporation; Codman & Shurtleff, Inc.; Ethicon, Inc.; Jelco Laboratories; Johnson & Johnson Baby Products Company; Johnson & Johnson Dental Products Company; Johnson & Johnson Domestic Operating Company; Johnson & Johnson International (Export Division); McNeil Laboratories, Incorporated; Ortho Pharmaceutical Corporation; Personal Products Company; Pitman-Moore, Inc.

Industrial and other: industrial tapes, adhesives, textiles, paper products and other items sold primarily to the apparel, textile, health care, agricultural, food, and other industrial markets. This line of business included the activities of the following major domestic divisions and subsidiaries: Cel-Fibe; Chicopee Manufacturing Company; Devro, Inc.; Permacel.

International: international sales of the products described above, manufactured in thirty-five countries outside the United States and sold in most countries in the world

J&J sales and operating profits were distributed among these lines of business as shown in Table 9-9. Worldwide sales are divided another way in Table 9-10.

J&J was organized into highly autonomous operating subsidiaries and was known to be highly secretive. The company had a distinctive corporate culture stressing basic business values of product quality, hard work, and intense company loyalty, one manifestation of which was the J&J creed chiseled into the marble wall at the entrance to corporate headquarters. Research and development expenditures in 1973 were $70.9 million.

J&J was the dominant producer of nonfood baby care products other than disposable diapers, and its name was synonymous with babies. J&J produced baby shampoo, baby lotion, baby powder, and other baby care products. J&J had reorganized its baby products into the Johnson & Johnson Baby

TABLE 9–9. Distribution of Johnson & Johnson Operating Profits

	1969		1970		1971		1972		1973	
	Sales	Operating Profit	Sales	Operating Profit	Sales	Operating Profit	Sales	Operating Profit	Sales	Operating Profit
Domestic health care	48.9%	46.2%	53.3%	51.2%	55.7%	55.8%	55.7%	56.3%	55.0%	55.8%
Industrial and other	11.6%	6.8%	13.5%	8.8%	13.2%	8.3%	14.7%	10.5%	16.8%	14.6%
International	39.5%	47.0%	33.2%	40.0%	31.1%	35.9%	29.6%	33.2%	28.2%	29.6%

TABLE 9-10. Johnson & Johnson Worldwide Sales

	1969	1970	1971	1972	1973
Prescription and nonprescription drugs, diagnostics, therapeutics, contraceptives, and veterinary products	18.1%	19.2%	20.2%	21.6%	22.3%
Toiletries and hygienic products, including baby care items	27.2%	28.0%	28.7%	27.7%	30.7%
Surgical dressings, ligatures and sutures, surgical instruments, surgical specialties, and related items	34.7%	34.8%	34.5%	33.7%	32.1%
Industrial tapes and adhesives, textiles, paper products, and other	20.0%	18.0%	16.6%	17.0%	14.9%

Products Company in 1972. Woven diapers, bibs, crib sheets, and baby pants had been produced in Johnson & Johnson's wholly owned Chicopee Manufacturing Company subsidiary, which also made Chux and Chix disposable diapers. All but disposable diapers had been discontinued by Chicopee in 1972.

Chux and Chix brand disposable diapers were being phased out in favor of the new Johnson's disposable diapers produced by the J&J Baby Products Company.[12] Johnson's brand disposable diapers had been in test market since mid-1972 and had achieved considerable sales success, primarily at the expense of Pampers. J&J's product was of premium quality and had a superior, patented inner liner and adhesive tape tabs. The inner liner was thick and spongy, giving it an unusually soft feel and providing some absorbent capacity. Two pricing approaches had been used by J&J in its test markets: one matched Pampers' and Kimbies' prices, and the other priced Johnson's diapers up to 20 percent higher than competitors'. Johnson's diapers were offered in newborn, overnight, and daytime sizes and were sold using a sales force dedicated primarily to disposable diaper sales.

J&J had opened a large, 400,000-square-foot diaper manufacturing and distribution facility in Park Forest South, Illinois, near Chicago, in 1973. J&J had also announced the start of construction of a second disposable diaper plant in Montgomery Township, New Jersey, with production expected to begin in 1975. J&J produced its own proprietary inner liner material on very costly machines developed in conjunction with the Honshu Paper Company of Japan. Each was estimated to cost in excess of a million dollars. J&J's diaper machines were more complex than competitors' and were correspondingly more costly. It was rumored that J&J was still having difficulty producing diapers at sufficient gross margins.

Union Carbide

Carbide was a leading producer of chemicals, plastics, industrial gases, batteries, and related products both in the United States and abroad. It operated in the following business areas:

Chemical: Carbide had been a pioneer in the development of the petrochemical industry and produced such products as ethylene, ethenol, ethylene oxide, ethylene glycol, latexes and solvents used in coatings; acetic acid and derivatives; intermediates for producing polyurethane plastics, agricultural chemicals; intermediates for producing biodegradable detergents; chemicals used in aerosol sprays and in refrigeration systems; chemicals used in brake fluids and synthetic lubricants; a variety of silicone products; and intermediates for synthetic textiles.

Plastics: A broadly diversified line comprised eleven principal plastic materials. It was a major producer of thermoplastics, including polyethylene, vinyl plastics, and polystyrene. Carbide was also an important supplier of phenolic resins.

Gases and related products: Carbide produced oxygen, nitrogen, argon, acetylene, hydrogen, helium, and specialty gases.

---

[12] Chicopee would continue to produce disposable diapers for private label.

Metals and carbons: Carbide metal and carbon products included ferroalloys such as ferrachromium, ferromanganese, and ferrosilicon, which were important additives used in the manufacture of steel; CARVAN vandium alloy and special alloys for the aluminum and iron foundry industries; mining and processing uranium ores; vanadium and tungsten; industrial carbon products including graphite electrodes, used in the production of electric furnace steel and foundry iron, and carbon electrodes, used in the production of phosphorous, calcium carbide, and ferroalloys; carbon and graphite refractories, carbon brushes, anodes, and carbon fiber products; electronic components including tantalum and other capacitors; electronic materials, including alumina powers, laser rods, and sapphire substrates for semiconductors.

Consumer and related products: Carbide consumer lines included Eveready batteries, flashlights, and lamps; Prestone antifreeze and car care products; the Glad line of household products (including plastic wrap, bags, and drinking straws); 6–12 PLUS and SPORTSMATE insect repellents, and Linde stars and other simulated jewels.

International: Carbide produced many of the same products internationally through 100 consolidated international subsidiaries and thirty international affiliated companies.

Carbide worldwide sales were distributed among these businesses as shown in Table 9–11.

Carbide's sales and earnings in 1973 had been all-time records. While Carbide had long been viewed as a commodity chemical producer, in 1974 the company was involved in an ambitious program to make Carbide a bigger factor in consumer products and other areas outside its traditional line of business. It had reportedly been looking to enter a consumer products category that would reach $1 billion by 1980. Faced with prodigeous appetites for capital in many of its businesses, Carbide was also attempting to redeploy assets into businesses with high potential and business where its products could have superior performance characteristics over competitors'. It had established more than 150 Strategic Planning Units (SPUs), and about 60 percent of its sales were represented by SPUs categorized as growth businesses. Research and development expenditures were $76.8 million in 1973.

Carbide's line of disposable diapers, called Dry-

dees, were being test marketed in 1974 in Bangor, Maine. Drydees were part of the newly formed Home and Automotive Products Division that also produced Glad Bags and Prestone antifreeze, among other products. Carbide had developed a unique patented plastic-based inner liner for its diaper and also produced the outer plastic liner for the diaper in-house. Carbide's product was believed by many to have superior performance characteristics to Pampers and had reportedly captured a major market share in the test market. Carbide sold Glad Bags to supermarkets through brokers and was expected to do the same with its Drydees line. Manufacturing disposable diapers bore some relation to making Glad Bags, which involved assembly and heat sealing layers of plastic at approximately 100 bags per minute.

Colgate-Palmolive (Kendall)

Colgate produced disposable diapers through its Kendall Company subsidiary, acquired in 1972. Colgate was a leading producer of consumer goods that operated in the following business areas:

Consumer laundry and cleaning products: laundry detergents, dishwashing detergents, cleansers, presoaks, bleaches, and spray starch

Personal care and cosmetics: toothpaste, bar soaps, hair products, shaving creams, skin creams, fragrances, eye and cheek colorings, razors and razor blades, bandages, gauze, cotton balls, elastic stockings and supports, food care products, aerosol medications, oral antiseptics, body powders, premoistened towelettes, and lipsticks

Other consumer products: plastic bags and food wraps, cloth and disposable diapers and other baby products, sporting goods, food items, kitchen towels, nonliquid heating substances, moth control products, furniture polish, and glue sticks

Professional products: surgical dressings and packs, obstetrical pads and underpads, urological products, surgical gowns and drapes, and prescription pharmaceutical products

Industrial and institutional: woven and nonwoven fabrics, specialty cotton, rayon products, industrial tapes, and a wide variety of cleaning and related products

Worldwide sales were distributed among these product areas as shown in Table 9–12. Fifty-five

TABLE 9-11. Union Carbide's Worldwide Sales by Line of Business

| | 1969 | | 1970 | | 1971 | | 1972 | | 1973 | |
	Sales	Operating Profit	Sales	Operating Profit	Sales	Operating Profit	Sales	Operating Profit	Sales	Operating Profit
Chemicals	28%	30.7%	27%	16.5%	27%	22.0%	28%	33.8%	27%	38.7%
Plastics	12%		13%		13%		14%		15%	
Gases and related products	14%	38.1%	14%	51.9%	14%	43.3%	15%	39.0%	15%	36.9%
Metals and carbons	25%		24%		23%		21%		22%	
Consumer products	21%	31.1%	22%	31.6%	23%	34.7%	22%	27.2%	21%	24.4%

percent of sales originated in areas outside the United States in 1973, up from 47 percent in 1969. Research and development expenditures were $38.1 million in 1973.

Kendall's Consumer Products Marketing Group sold two lines of disposable diapers in addition to its preeminent cloth diaper line and Curad bandages. Kendall had sold Curity brand disposable diapers for many years and had introduced an improved prefolded version in 1968. Kendall also sold Curity Tape-Tab disposable diapers, introduced in 1971. Kendall had enjoyed strong demand for its disposables from 1969 to 1972, though sales had reportedly plateaued in 1973.

A portion of Kendall's 300-strong consumer products sales force marketed the Curity line. Food brokers were used for the sale of consumer products in supermarkets. Kendall was also actively marketing disposable diapers overseas in 1974 in Europe and Great Britain. Kendall manufactured inner liners for use in its own disposable diapers and for sale to other diaper manufacturers.

Other Competitors

Scott Paper. Scott was a leading integrated manufacturer of paper and related products, including a broad line of tissue, facial tissue, paper towels, paper napkins, food wraps, and a line of feminine hygiene products. Packaged paper products accounted for 58 percent of 1973 sales of $931 million. Scott's paper products line had been under attack by P&G's Charmin Division.

Scott had been an early entrant into disposable diapers with its Baby Scott line of two-piece diapers. After a significant investment, the Baby Scott line was discontinued in 1971, with the two-piece style so popular in Europe failing to compete against the one-piece style popularized by P&G, despite the fact that Scott had nearly achieved national distribution.[13] The 1971 discontinuance resulted in an after-tax writeoff of $5.5 million. Scott had developed a one-piece diaper, Raggedy Ann and Raggedy Andy, which was tested unsuccessfully in 1972 and withdrawn. In 1974 Scott was testing another one-piece disposable diaper, named Scott Tots. The two-piece Baby Scott line was being sold overseas.

Weyerhaeuser. Weyerhaeuser was a leader in the forest products industry, with 1973 sales of $2,302 million and net income of $348 million. Principle products were lumber (24.9 percent of 1973 sales); paperboard containers and cartons (22.6 percent); pulp and paper (15.2 percent); plywood, veneer, and doors (11.6 percent); and other forest products (25.7 percent). Weyerhaeuser had begun making disposable diapers for the private label market in 1971. Management termed the entry into diapers the first step in the company's entrance into consumer markets, and the culmination of a major corporate marketing and development research effort. By 1974 Weyerhaeuser was the main factor in the private label market and had three diaper plants in operation. It was the only diaper producer that was fully integrated into fluff pulp, going all the way back to the tree. Other key components were purchased from outside suppliers. Weyerhaeuser had a brand name, Quik Fit, but the brand had not been advertised.

[13] Scott Paper had had a poor year overall in 1971 and had elected a new chief executive in 1971 upon the retirement of Harrison F. Durning in June.

TABLE 9–12. **Colgate-Palmolive Worldwide Sales**

	1969	1970	1971	1972	1973
Consumer laundry and cleaning products	39.7%	40.1%	38.2%	37.6%	37.2%
Personal care and cosmetics	37.6%	37.6%	37.6%	38.8%	39.3%
Other consumer products	6.8%	6.8%	8.1%	8.2%	8.9%
Professional	4.3%	4.4%	4.6%	4.6%	5.0%
Industrial and institutional	11.7%	11.0%	11.6%	10.7%	9.6%

SOURCE: SEC Form 10K.

EXHIBIT 9-1. *Media Advertising of Disposable Diapers*[a] *1966–1973 (thousands of dollars)*

		1966	1967	1968	1969[b]	1970	1971	1972	1973
Borden	Total	$ 12.6	$ 115.3	$ 171.4	—	$ 0.1	—	—	—
	Network TV	—	—	—	—	—	—	—	—
	Spot TV	—	115.3	171.4	—	—	—	—	—
	Magazines	12.6	—	—	—	—	—	—	—
Colgate-Polmolive	Total	—	—	—	—	—	—	$ 846.6	$1370.0
	Network TV	—	—	—	—	—	—	—	—
	Spot TV	—	—	—	—	—	—	846.6	1370.7
	Magazines	—	—	—	—	—	—		—
International Paper	Total	7.2	35.8	129.7	$ 54.1	787.7	$ 880.0	121.0	60.1
	Network TV	—	—	—	—	—	—	—	—
	Spot TV	—	29.4	112.0	—	741.8	828.4	102.4	57.2
	Magazines	7.2	6.4	17.7	54.1	45.9	51.6	18.6	2.9
Johnson and Johnson	Total	56.0	6.7	0.3	139.9	0.2	6.2	168.8[h]	159.5
	Network TV	—	—	—	—	—	—	—	—
	Spot TV	—	6.7	0.3	—	—	6.2	168.8	159.5
	Magazines	56.0	—	—	139.9	0.2	—	—	—
Kendall	Total	313.5[e]	181.0[e]	166.1[e]	155.7[f]	261.5[f]	504.1[f]	—[g]	—
	Network TV	—	—	—	155.7	59.0	—	—	—
	Spot TV	—	—	—	—	202.5	504.1	—	—
	Magazines	313.5	181.0	166.1	—	—	—	—	—
Kimberly-Clark	Total	—	—	51.8	49.7	78.6	307.9	1296.0	6529.1
	Network TV	—	—	—	—	—	—	—	1087.3
	Spot	—	—	39.7	—	40.1	225.8	1100.3	4929.7
	Magazines	—	—	12.1	49.7	38.5	82.1	195.7	574.2
Procter and Gamble	Total	18.5	1348.6	5032.1	618.5	4852.0[c]	6383.4	8478.2	8927.7
	Network TV	—	—	—	473.0	3487.4	4124.1	2559.7	2747.4
	Spot TV	—	1327.2	4884.7	N/A	1199.5	2020.8	4859.2	5085.8
	Magazines	18.5	21.4	147.4	145.6	165.0	238.5	1019.3	1094.5
Scott Paper	Total	27.8	52.5	195.0	23.2	2394.7[d]	790.1	37.7	27.1
	Network TV	—	—	—	—	—	37.2	—	—
	Spot TV	—	36.4	191.5	—	2394.7	752.5	37.7	27.1
	Magazines	27.8	16.1	3.5	23.2	—	—	—	—
Union Carbide	Total	—	—	—	—	—	—	—	4.8
	Network TV	—	—	—	—	—	—	—	—
	Spot TV	—	—	—	—	—	—	—	4.8
	Magazines	—	—	—	—	—	—	—	—

[a]Data does not include local newspaper or radio advertising.

[b]Data for 1969 does *not* include spot television.

[c]*Forbes,* December 15, 1970, reported that P&G was spending $16 million per year on advertising, with one-half for media ads and one-half for samples.

[d]*Advertising Age,* October 1970, reported that Scott was spending $6 million on diaper advertising in 1970.

[e]Data for Kendall is for Curity cloth diapers, rather than disposable diapers.

[f]Curity disposable diapers.

[g]Kendall acquired by Colgate-Polmolive.

[h]Advertising split approximately one-half for Johnson brand diapers and one-half for Chicopee Mills diapers.

SOURCE: Leading National Advertisers, Inc., *National Advertising Investments,* various years.

EXHIBIT 9–2. *Manufacturing Capacity of Major Diaper Manufacturers in 1973*

Company (Brand)	Procter & Gamble (Pampers)	Kimberly-Clark (Kimbies)	Johnson & Johnson (Johnson's)	Weyerhaeuser (Private Label)	Ipco (Private Label)
Fluff pulp	Integrated (Buckeye Cellulose) and some purchased	Purchased	Purchased	Integrated	Purchased
Inner liner	Purchased (Kendall, Johnson & Johnson, Stearns & Foster, Dexter)	Integrated	Integrated	Purchased Dexter	Integrated (previously Kendall)

Plants:
  Operating
  Announced
	4
	5
		5
		5
			1
			2
				3
				3
					3
					3

Estimated number of machines: December 1973	80+	20	N/A	6+	11
Estimated machine output rate	350–400/min.	250–275/min.	N/A	N/A	N/A
Estimated annual sales rate per machine	$5.5–$6.0 mil.	$4.0–$4.5 mil.	N/A	$3.0–$4.0 mil.	$3.0–$4.0 mil.

SOURCE: Bruce Kirk, *Disposable Diaper Investment Potential*, R. W. Pressprich and Co., Inc.

EXHIBIT 9-3. *Estimated Sales and Market Shares of Leading Disposable Diaper Competitors (dollars in millions)*

		1967	1968	1969	1970	1971	1972	1973
Total manufacturer's sales		$20	$60	$90	$130	$200	$280	$370
Procter & Gamble								
	Dollars	$10	$50	$80	$120	$170	$225	$225
	Market share	50%	83%	89%	92%	85%	80%	69%
Kimberly-Clark								
	Dollars	—	—	—	—	$ 5	$ 20	$ 62
	Market share	—	—	—	—	3%	7%	17%
Johnson & Johnson brand								
	Dollars	—	—	—	—	—	—	$ 8
	Market share	—	—	—	—	—	—	2%
Other brands[a]								
	Dollars	$10	$10	$10	$ 10	$ 20	$ 10	$ 10
	Market share	50%	17%	11%	8%	10%	4%	3%
Private label								
	Dollars	—	—	—	—	$ 5	$ 25	$ 35
	Market share	—	—	—	—	3%	9%	9%

[a]Includes Scott Paper, Kendall (Colgate), Borden, International Paper and Johnson & Johnson's Chicopee Mills brands (Chux and Chix). Union Carbide (Drydees) also had a diaper entry in test markets.

SOURCES: Casewriter's estimates based on Kirk, *Disposable Diaper Investment Potential,* Mitchell-Hutchins, Inc.; and interviews.

EXHIBIT 9–4. *Financial Performance of Selected Disposable Diaper Competitors, 1969–1973 (dollars in millions)*

	1969	1970	1971	1972	1973
Colgate-Palmolive					
Sales	$1383.0	$1463.0	$16.04.0	$1906.0	$2195.0
Depreciation	18.7	20.2	29.6	33.4	37.2
Net income	48.1	50.1	54.4	69.3	88.8
Return on sales (%)	3.5%	3.4%	3.5%	3.6%	4.0%
Return on equity (%)	15.4%	14.8%	11.9%	12.4%	14.4%
Marketable securities	91.3	92.0	104.4	129.3	112.8
Long- and short-term debt to equity	.18	.12	.17	.20	.22
Capital expenditures	28.2	29.0	48.0	55.4	60.6
Dividend payout	.37	.38	.36	.37	.39
Johnson & Johnson					
Sales	$ 901.0	$1002.0	$1140.5	$1317.7	$1611.8
Depreciation	29.7	31.8	35.9	41.6	49.0
Net income	69.4	83.7	101.8	120.7	148.4
Return on sales (%)	7.7%	8.4%	8.9%	9.2%	9.2%
Return on equity (%)	15.1%	15.7%	16.3%	16.5%	17.1%
Marketable securities	84.4	118.2	142.0	162.9	212.9
Long- and short-term debt to equity	.04	.03	.02	.06	.05
Capital expenditures	55.5	52.8	67.9	76.4	102.5
Dividend payout	.22	.22	.24	.21	.20
Kimberly-Clark					
Sales	$ 834.7	$ 868.7	$ 938.0	$1010.5	$1178.0
Depreciation	37.7	40.5	43.3	39.7	42.6
Net income[a]	49.9	38.3	(10.8)	55.6	81.7
Return on sales (%)	6.0%	4.4%	(1.2%)	5.5%	6.9%
Return on equity (%)	9.0%	6.7%	deficit	10.0%	13.4%
Marketable securities	49.0	13.0	10.1	24.0	34.6
Long- and short-term debt to equity	.35	.39	.41	.40	.36
Capital expenditures	70.1	94.9	87.1	67.5	57.1
Dividend payout	.47	.71	deficit	.50	.36
Procter and Gamble					
Sales	$2708.0	$2979.0	$3178.0	$3514.0	$3907.0
Depreciation	—	—	—	64.8	71.9
Net income	187.4	211.9	237.6	276.3	302.1
Return on sales (%)	6.9%	7.1%	7.5%	7.9%	7.7%
Return on equity (%)	16.1%	16.7%	17.0%	17.6%	17.2%
Marketable securities	274.0	316.0	307.0	393.0	381.0
Long- and short-term debt to equity	.13	.13	.11	.16	.16
Capital expenditures	149.0	128.0	188.0	265.0	271.0
Dividend payout	.56	.51	.48	.44	.42
Union Carbide					
Sales	$2933.0	$3026.0	$3038.0	$3261.0	$3939.0
Depreciation	250.0	236.4	229.3	245.2	245.2
Net income	186.2	157.3	157.8	205.2	290.9
Return on sales (%)	6.3%	5.2%	5.2%	6.3%	7.4%
Return on equity (%)	10.5%	8.7%	8.6%	10.6%	13.8%
Marketable securities	95.2	88.0	42.9	161.9	469.0
Long- and short-term debt to equity	.31	.54	.51	.53	.52
Capital expenditures	322.2	393.7	335.2	243.9	288.7
Dividend payout	.65	.77	.77	.59	.43

[a]After extraordinary items of $4.8 million in 1973 and ($42.5 million) in 1971.

APPENDIX A

Consumer Reports Magazine's Ratings of Disposable Diapers for 1967, 1970, and 1974[14, 15]

Ratings for 1967

✔ PAMPERS (Procter and Gamble Co., Cincinnati). Small ("Newborn"), 30 for $1.49 ($4.98); medium ("Daytime"), 15 for 89¢ ($5.93) and 30 for $1.63 ($5.43); large ("Overnight"), 12 for 89¢ ($7.40). Pleated.

✔ CHUX (Johnson & Johnson, New Brunswick, N.J.). Small ("Newborn"), 36 for $1.59 ($4.42); medium ("Regular"), 24 for $1.59 ($6.63); large ("Toddler"), 18 for $1.59 ($8.83). According to the manufacturer, all sizes are also available in "weekly" supply packages. Pleated.

FLUSHABYES (Facelle Co., Ltd., Toronto, Canada). Small ("Newborn"), 24 for 99¢ ($4.13) and 48 for $2.19 ($4.56); medium, 12 for 59¢ ($4.92), 24 for $1.35 ($5.63) and 48 for $2.39 ($5); large ("Toddler"), 12 for 73¢ ($6.08), 24 for $1.39 ($5.79) and 48 for $2.39 ($5). Pleated. No waterproof outer layer, but may be used with any waterproof pants. Tissue-type inner liner.

The following two models cannot be fastened with pins; they must be inserted into waterproof pants specially designed for them and bought separately. Listed in order of increasing price.

BABY SCOTT (Scott Paper Co., Philadelphia). Small (9 ½ × 5 in.) 30 for 86¢ ($2.87), to be used with "A" or "B" pants, 96¢; large (12 × 5 in.) 30 for 97¢ ($3.23), to be used with "C" or "D" pants, 96¢. No waterproof outer layer. Pants made of plastic-coated knit fabric, judged somewhat more durable than those for *White Lamb,* following.

WHITE LAMB (Borden Co., NYC). Small ("Newborn," 13 × 5 in.), 24 for 99¢ ($4.12), to be used with "Small" pants, 49¢; large ("Regular," 14 × 5 in.), 24 for $1.15 ($4.80), to be used with "Medium," "Large" or "Extra Large" pants, 53¢. No waterproof outer layer. Pants made of plastic film. Large diaper may be used with "C" and "D" pants for *Baby Scott,* preceding.

[14] Prices are the average of those paid by *Consumer Reports* shoppers. The calculated cost per 100 diapers is shown in parenthesis.

[15] Models are check-rated when *Consumer Reports* judged the samples to be of high overall quality and appreciably superior to non-check-rated models tested for the same report.

The following models were judged somewhat lower in overall quality than those preceding. Differences between adjacent models were judged very small.

WARDS TINY WORLD (Montgomery Ward). "Jumbo" pack, *Cat. No. 661*, $8 plus shipping; carton, *Cat. No. 662*, $2.88 plus shipping. The Jumbo pack contains 324 of the small size ($2.47); 216 of the medium ("Large," $3.70); or 180 of the large ("Extra Large," $4.44). The carton contains 108 of the small ($2.67), 72 of the medium ($4) or 60 of the large ($4.80). Tissue-type inner liner.

PARKE, DAVIS BAY'S (Parke, Davis Co., Detroit). Small, 36 for $1.98 ($5.50); medium, 24 for $1.99 ($8.29); large, 18 for $1.98 ($11).

CURITY (Kendall Co., Chicago). Small, 36 for $1.98 ($5.50); medium ("Large"), 24 for $1.89 ($7.88) and 72 for $4.98 ($6.92); large ("Extra Large"), 18 for $1.84 ($10.22).

SEARS (Sears, Roebuck). "Travel Pack," $2 plus shipping; carton, $2.88 plus shipping; "Hamper Box," $8 plus shipping. The travel Pack contains 72 of the small size, *Cat. No. 123* ($2.78) or 48 of the medium ("Large"), *Cat. No. 124* ($4.16). The carton contains 108 of the small, *Cat. No. 153* ($2.67); 72 of the medium, *Cat. No. 154* ($4); or 48 of the large ("Toddler"), *Cat. No. 155* ($6). The Hamper Box contains 324 of the small, *Cat. No. 167* ($2.47); 216 of the medium, *Cat. No. 168* ($3.70); or 144 of the large, *Cat. No. 169* ($5.56). Tissue-type inner liner.

Ratings for 1970

✔ PAMPERS (Procter & Gamble Co., Cincinnati). Newborn (birth to 11 lb.), 30 for $1.59 ($5.30); Daytime (11 lb. and over), 15 for 95¢ ($6.33) and 30 for $1.79 ($5.97); Overnight (11 lb. and over) 12 for 95¢ ($7.92). Resistance to pin tearing, relatively high. Judged less apt to tear, bunch and lump than most. Judged best in conforming to baby's body. Prefolded, with pleats tacked down in center. Scented.

✔ KIMBIES "THROW AWAY DIAPERS" (Kimberly-Clark Corp., Neenah, Wis.). Newborn (under 12 lb.), 30 for $1.59 ($5.30); Daytime (over 12 lb.), 15 for 95¢ ($6.33) and 30 for $1.79 ($5.97); Overnight (over 12 lb.), 12 for 95¢ ($7.92). Absorption capacity relatively high. Tended to shred and stick to skin less than most. Judged softer and better than most in conforming to baby's body. Tape fasteners; needs no pins. Prefolded in triangular shape, with pleats not tacked down. Scented.

✔ CHUX 630 (Chicopee Mills, Inc., NYC). Newborn 01 (up to 12 lb.), 24 for $1.29 ($5.38); Regular 02 (12 to 22 lb.), 18 for $1.29 ($7.17); Toddler 03 (over 22 lb.), 14 for $1.29 ($9.21). Tape fasteners; needs no pins. Not prefolded.

The following two models, which must be used with plastic pants, were judged approximately equal in overall quality.

BABY SCOTT (Scott Paper Co., Philadelphia). Newborn (5 to 12 lb.), 30 for $1.49 ($4.97); Regular (over 12 lb.), 30 for $1.59 ($5.30); Extra Absorbent (over 12 lb.), 12 for 89¢ ($7.42). No waterproof layer; must be used with specially designed plastic pants that cost 69¢ and come in sizes A (5 to 12 lb.), B (13 to 17 lb.), C (18 to 25 lb.) and D (26 lb. and over). Absorption capacity, relatively low. Needs no pins because plastic pants hold diaper in place. Prefolded with pleats tacked down at one end.

WARDS TINY WORLD (Montgomery Ward). Prices plus shipping: Medium (under 22 lb.), *Cat. No. 666*, 48 for $2.39 ($4.98); Toddler (23 to 32 lb.), *Cat. No. 648*, 48 for $2.59 ($5.40). No waterproof layer; must be used with plastic pants. Absorption capacity, relatively low. Judged rougher than most. Prefolded, with pleats not tacked down.

The following models were judged somewhat lower in overall quality than those preceding. Quality differences between models were judged very small.

SEARS prefolded (Sears, Roebuck). Prices plus shippings: Newborn (under 12 lb.), *Cat. No. 2250*, 108 for $3.69 ($3.42) and, *Cat. No. 2254*, 216 for $6.99 ($3.24); Super-Daytime (over 12 lb.), *Cat. No. 2251*, 72 for $3.69 ($5.13) and, *Cat. No. 2255*, 154 for $6.99 ($4.54); Overnight (over 12 lb.), *Cat. No. 2252*, 60 for $3.69 ($6.16) and, *Cat. No. 2256*, 128 for $6.99 ($5.47). Absorption speed, relatively low. Judged less apt to lump and bunch than most. Pleats tacked down in center.

CURITY (The Kendall Co., Chicago). Newborn (up to 12 lb.), *No. 2195*, 36 for $1.69 ($4.69); Regular (12 to 22 lb.), *No. 2329*, 24 for $1.69 ($7.04); Extra Large (over 22 lb.), *No. 2444*, 18 for $1.69 ($9.39). Prefolded, with pleats tacked down in center. Claimed to be medicated.

PENNEYS Cat. No. 0294 (J. C. Penney). Prices plus shipping: Newborn (up to 13 lb.), 24 for $1.18 ($4.92); Regular (14 to 22 lb.), 18 for $1.18 ($6.56); Toddler (over 22 lb.), 14 for $1.18 ($8.43). Resistance to pin tearing, relatively high. Tended to shred and stick to skin more than most. Judged rougher than most. Not prefolded.

DURASORB (Parke, Davis & Co., Detroit). Bassinet Bunch (under 12 lb.), 36 for $1.98 ($5.50); Crib Crowd (12 to 22 lb.), 24 for $1.98 ($8.25); Sandpile Set (over 22 lb.), 15 for $1.98 ($13.20). Absorption capacity and speed, relatively high. Resistance to pin tearing, relatively low. Judged more apt to lump and bunch than most. Difficult to use two at once, because plastic layer doesn't separate easily. Not prefolded. Available only in pink and blue.

The following model was judged somewhat lower in overall quality than those preceding.

SEARS (Sears, Roebuck). Prices plus shipping: Small (up to 13 lb.), *Cat. No. 2200,* 108 for $2.99 ($2.78) and, *Cat. No. 2204,* 324 for $7.99 ($2.47); Large (15 to 26 lb.), *Cat. No. 2201,* 72 for $2.99 ($4.16) and, *Cat. No. 2205,* 226 for $7.99 ($3.70); Toddler (27 to 37 lb.), *Cat. No. 2202,* 60 for $2.99 ($4.99) and, *Cat. No. 2206,* 180 for $7.99 ($4.44). Absorption capacity, relatively low; absorption speed, relatively high. Resistance to pin tearing, relatively low. Judged more apt to lump and bunch than most. Not prefolded.

Ratings for 1974

Parents expressed the highest overall preference for the following model.

✔ PAMPERS (Procter & Gamble Co., Cincinnati). Newborn, 30 for $1.80; Daytime, 14 for $1.07; Overnight, 12 for 96¢; Toddler, 12 for $1.31. Advantages: High absorption capacity and rate. Tape fasteners held better than most. No throwaway cover on tape fastener, a convenience. Conformed to babies' bodies better than most. Judged softer than most.

Parents expressed a high overall preference for the following models.

KIMBIES (Kimberly-Clark Corp., Neenah, Wis.). Newborn, 30 for $1.67; Daytime, 15 for $1.09 and 30 for $1.92; Overnight, 12 for $1; Toddler/Daytime, 24 for $1.85; Toddler/Overnight, 12 for $1.30. Advantages: High absorption capacity. Tape fasteners held better than most. Conformed to babies' bodies better than most. Judged softer than most. Disadvantages: Padding tended to lump together in toilet disposal. Difficult to double up.

JOHNSON'S (Johnson & Johnson, New Brunswick, N.J.). Newborn, 30 for $1.78; Daytime, 24 for $2; Overnight, 18 for $1.89. Advantages: High absorption capacity. Judged softer than most. Disadvantages: Plastic film not folded back into diaper on sides. Difficult to double up. Comments: Available only in the Midwest and in Denver.

Parents expressed a lower overall preference for the following models than for those preceding.

CURITY (The Kendall Co., Chicago). Newborn, 30 for $1.73; Daytime, 30 for $1.93; Overnight, 12 for $1.10; Toddler, 24 for $1.99. Advantages: High absorption capacity. Tape fasteners held better than most. Disadvantages: Difficult to double up. Comments: Widely available except in Los Angeles, New York, and a few other metropolitan areas.

K-MART (S. S. Kresge Co., Detroit). Newborn, 60 for $3.09; Daytime, 60 for $2.97; Overnight, 40 for $3.07; Toddler; 40 for $3.09. Advantages: Shredded less than most. Disadvantages: Difficult to double up Daytime and Overnight sizes.

SEARS (Sears, Roebuck), prices plus shipping: Newborn, *Cat. No. 2221,* 172 for $7.60; Daytime, *Cat. No. 2222,* 144 for $7.60; Overnight, *Cat. No. 2223,* 108 for $7.60; Toddler, *Cat. No. 2224,* 96 for $7.60. Advantages: High absorption capacity. Disadvantages: Lumped and bunched in use more than most.

A&P (A&P Stores). Newborn, 30 for $1.36; Daytime, 30 for $1.79; Overnight, 12 for 78¢; Toddler, 12 for $1.18. Disadvantages: Tape fasteners did not hold as well as most. Difficult to double up Overnight and Toddler sizes.

PENNEYS (J.C. Penney), prices plus shipping. Newborn, *Cat. No. 0559,* 180 for $7.80; Daytime, *Cat. No. 0567,* 180 for $9.50; Overnight, *Cat. No. 0575,* 180 for $11.45; Toddler, *Cat. No. 0930,* 144 for $12.40. Disadvantages: Lumped and bunched in use more than most. Conformed to babies' bodies less well than most. Difficult to double up Daytime size.

Parents expressed the lowest overall preference for the following models.

TRULY FINE (Safeway Stores). Newborn, 30 for $1.37; Daytime, 14 for 87¢ and 30 for $1.70; Overnight, 12 for 86¢. Advantages: Disintegrated in toilet disposal faster than most.

SITTING PRETTY BY FRUIT OF THE LOOM (Handico, Inc., NYC). Newborn, 30 for $1.67; Daytime, 30 for $1.83; Overnight, 12 for 95¢; Toddler, 12 for $1.22. Advantages: Except in Overnight size, no throwaway cover on tape fastener, a convenience. Disadvantages: Low absorption capacity. Tape fasteners did not hold as well as most.

WARDS (Montgomery Ward), prices plus shipping. Newborn, *Cat. No. 663 Size 20,* 192 for $8.88; Regular, *Cat. No. 663 Size 21,* 160 for $8.88; Toddler, *Cat. No. 663 Size 22,* 120 for $8.88; Overnight, *Cat. No. 663 Size 23,* 120 for $8.88. Advantages: Disintegrated in toilet disposal faster than most. Disadvantages: Low absorption capacity. Shredded, lumped, leaked, and stuck to babies' skin more than most. Judged less soft than most. Pleats not tacked down.

GRANTS (W. T. Grant Stores). Newborn, 24 for $1.53; Daytime, 60 for $3.35; Overnight, 40 for $3.52; Toddler, 40 for $3.35. Advantages: Disintegrated in toilet disposal faster than most. Disadvantages: Low absorption capacity. Shredded, lumped, tore, and leaked more than most. Judged less soft than most. Pleats not tacked down.

TABLE 9-13. Cost of 100 Disposable Diapers – 1974[a]

	Newborn	*Daytime*	*Overnight*	*Toddler*
Pampers	$6.00	$7.10	$ 8.00	$10.90
Kimbies[b]	5.60	6.40[c]	8.30	7.70
Johnson's	5.90	8.30	10.50	—
Curity	5.80	6.40	9.20	8.30
K-Mart	5.20	5.00	7.70	7.70
Sears[d]	4.40	5.30	7.00	7.90
A&P	4.50	6.00	6.50	9.80
Penneys[d]	4.30	5.20	6.40	8.60
Truly Fine	4.60	5.70[c]	7.20	—
Sitting Pretty	5.60	6.10	7.90	10.20
Wards[d]	4.60	5.50[e]	7.40	7.40
Grants	6.40	5.60	8.80	8.40

[a]Based on mid-1974 prices, rounded to the nearest 10 cents.
[b]Also comes in Toddler Overnight size; cost of 100 is $10.80.
[c]Based on average price of package of 30; based on package of 15, cost for Kimbies would be $7.30, for Truly Fine would be $5.80.
[d]All prices plus shipping.
[e]Size corresponding to Daytime is called Regular.

SWECO, Inc.

Well, we've done it. You and I know the process works and the equipment works, but it won't be easy to convince the old-timers who have drilled all their lives without it. That includes the people in my own company.

With these words in November 1972, Dr. Peter Hamilton of the production research department of a leading international oil company encouraged Les Hansen of SWECO, Inc., to enter the oil field equipment industry with a new piece of oil well drilling equipment that SWECO had developed, partly at the former's instigation. SWECO called the new product a "sand separator," though it was known in the industry as a "mud cleaner."

SWECO, Inc.

SWECO was founded in 1917 as the Southwestern Engineering Corporation. During the 1930s Southwestern went bankrupt. The Miller family, owners of some of the stock, assumed management control of the company to protect their position. Under new leadership, SWECO began to concentrate its efforts on the manufacture of heat exchangers and the engineering and construction of refineries and other process plants. This proved to be a highly competitive, and thus not very profitable, field.

In 1947 an event occurred that would completely change the nature of SWECO's business, an event described by Howard Wright, Jr., SWECO's president, as the most important event in the history of the company. This was the acquisition of the so-called Meinzer Motion patent, a technique for inducing vibration of process equipment in three dimensions rather than two. This patent provided the basis for SWECO to enter into the production of vibratory machines for use in industrial screening, finishing, and grinding processes. In 1972 nearly all of SWECO's business came from the manufacture of vibratory equipment based on the "Meinzer Motion" principle. SWECO had sold off its last nonvibratory business in 1969, a sale that had reduced the company to one-third of its previous size. However, looking back, all of SWECO executives thought that that sale had been an excellent decision.

Business Areas

In 1972 SWECO's revenues of just under $15 million came from three divisions: Process Equipment, Finishing Equipment, and Environmental Systems. Foreign sales accounted for approximately 15 percent of total sales. Exhibits 10–1 and 10–2 give SWECO's income statement and balance sheet.

Process Equipment Division. The Process Equipment Division accounted for more than 50 percent of revenues and was the oldest division. It had two major product lines. The first and most important was the Vibro-Energy Separator. This performed the function of screening solid particles from liquids or other solid particles. SWECO supplied separators to firms in many different industries throughout the world. More than 15,000 SWECO separators were in use in 1972 in such industries as chemicals, food, ceramics, pulp and paper, and other major process industries. Some of the materials screened included cereals, detergents, sugar, clay, fertilizer, sand and gravel, salts, plastic pellets, wood chips, soybeans, paint, and apple juice.

SWECO separators were vibratory screening devices with from one to four decks (layers) of screens of various mesh. The material to be screened was fed to the top layer. As vibratory motion forced the material to the periphery of the screen, the smaller particles or liquids passed through the screen. The larger particles were funneled off from the periphery. Further passes through lower, finer screens served to remove progressively smaller particles.

A vibratory separation machine consisted of a large metal cylinder with layers of screen cloth inside and spouts for inflow and outflow of materials. Units ranged up to 6 feet in diameter and were built with a variety of special configurations and custom features. In addition to selling separators, SWECO also sold replacement screens and spare parts. These areas were a continuing and profitable source of follow-on business. In 1972 SWECO separators ranged in price from $1,000 to $10,000, while replacement screens sold for between $50 and $400 apiece.

The second product line in the Process Equipment Division was the Vibro-Energy Grinding Mill, used for reducing the size of wet or dry particles. A grinding mill was loaded with the material to be ground, together with a special grinding medium (e.g., cyclindrical aluminum pellets). The combination was vibrated at a high frequency producing a grinding action. Applications of the grinding mill included the processing of ceramics, pharmaceuti-

cals, cosmetics, paints, foods, electronic memory cores, powdered metals, and pesticides.

The Finishing Equipment Division. This division manufactured Vibro-Energy Finishing Mills, which deburred or polished metal parts by vibrating them together with an abrasive compound. Customers for this equipment were many diverse metalworking industries.

The Environmental Systems Division. This division manufactured a Centrifugal Wastewater Concentrator that used a fine-mesh centrifugal screening process to purify liquids. The concentrator was used in municipal applications for removing a high percentage of the floatable, settlable, and suspended solids from raw sewage. It was also used in industrial processing plants, such as in paper, textiles, meat packing, food canning, or poultry, where the concentrator could recover large amounts of usable material while cleaning up plant effluent.

Product Technology

Nearly all of SWECO's major product lines depended on vibration. The vibratory products were based on the "Meinzer Motion" process, which used three-dimensional vibration rather than side-to-side vibration. Many benefits flowed from the added dimension of movement in the Meinzer process. It added more ways in which the materials undergoing separation could be shaken and allowed great force to be exerted on particles. This greatly improved the control of the separation process, its capabilities for discriminating among different particles, and the rate of throughput. Second, the three-dimensional vibrating movement allowed the use of round rather than rectangular screens. This led to two advantages. A round screen allowed the use of an entire screening surface without having to worry about materials becoming trapped in corners. Also, the efficient mounting of the screens was vastly improved. A key feature of an efficient screen was that it be as taut and even as possible to guard against materials concentrating at uneven spots. Rectangular screens had the problem that the mounting points on the framing rim exerted uneven pressures on the screen cloth. In contrast, the mounting points for a round screen exerted exactly even pressures. The greater resulting tautness and freedom from irregularities increased both the screening efficiency and the life of a round screen.

SWECO had also developed a patented self-cleaning device for its screens. A major problem in screening was that after operating for a while, parts of a screen would clog up with materials, an effect known as "blinding." SWECO's self-cleaning device minimized this problem.

SWECO separators combined three-dimensional motion, round screens, and the self-cleaning device to produce a machine with great advantages over competitors using rectangular screens. For example, 3 square feet of a SWECO screen was more efficient than 6 square feet of rectangular screen.

SWECO operated only in the "fine" segment of the screening business and was not usually cost-effective in screening particles larger than $\frac{1}{2}$ inch. Most of SWECO's production was of screens with 80 mesh or finer. An 80 mesh screen had 80 openings per linear inch (6,400 openings per square inch). Large screen (coarse mesh) separators were based on a totally different applications technology than were small screens. The larger screens were also incorporated in relatively low-value-added equipment, and there were many qualified competitors in this market.

There were about a dozen other fine screen manufacturers in competition with SWECO. Because of SWECO's many technological advantages, these competitors tended to supply separators and screens for less demanding uses. SWECO had maintained its technological lead despite the fact that the Meinzer Motion patent had expired in 1959. To do so SWECO spent heavily on research and development, with an annual product development budget of about 2 percent of sales. Spending was even heavier on applications engineering to find new uses for its equipment.

SWECO estimated that in 1972 it held a 50 percent share of the U.S. market for fine screens. Its three major competitors, all small independent companies (Kason, Inc., Midwestern, Inc., and Derrick, Inc.) had combined 1972 sales of $6 million to $7 million. Kason and Midwestern had been started by ex-SWECO sales representatives and also used round screens. SWECO did not consider their equipment to be as high quality. Derrick competed with a special retangular fine screen design. There were also about ten minor competitors, whose influence was primarily in the highly profitable replacement screen business, where they competed with low-cost regional strategies.

Roughly one-third of SWECO's revenues came from the sale of complete units (separators, finishing mills, etc.). Total unit sales in 1972 were approximately 1,000 units, at an average price of $5,000 each. The balance of revenues came from replacement parts and screens.

Operations

In 1972 SWECO had about 325 employees, the majority located at City of Commerce, California, near Los Angeles. Most of SWECO's manufacturing was done at the Los Angeles plant, which had 100,000 square feet of space and an average daily output of three units. Production was essentially a batch process. SWECO also had assembly plants in Toledo, Ohio; Marietta, Georgia; Little Ferry, New Jersey; Cincinnati, Ohio; Toronto, Canada; and Nivelles, Belgium. In addition SWECO had subsidiaries in Germany and Italy and was in the process of setting up others in Spain and Mexico. The company was also constructing an 80,000-square-foot plant in Florence, Kentucky. Manufacturing employees totaled about 200.

Manufacture of a separator unit comprised the following principal stages: steel sheet, light plate, structured shapes and bars were cut, rolled, shaped, and welded into equipment components. Metal components were joined with manual and automatic feed welding, conventional metal arc welding, and specialized submerged arc welding. Parts for specialized motors were machined from castings, and the motors were assembled. Screen cloth was stretched and bonded to rings via spot welding or special epoxy bonding techniques. Completed units were assembled from these components as required. Manufacturing costs were divided approximately as follows:

Materials	57%
Direct labor	13
Manufacturing overhead	30
	100%

SWECO manufactured virtually all fabricated steel components, electric drive systems, and cast polyurethane components in-house. It purchased woven wire cloth, nuts and bolts items, raw steel sheet and plate, motor bearings, rubber parts, and castings. Most of these purchases were made through local suppliers (although the woven wire cloth came from West Germany or Switzerland). Few volume discounts were available from suppliers.

Manufacturing overhead consisted of plant management; production control; scheduling and administrative personnel; plant costs such as rent, power, supplies, etc.; depreciation on equipment; and special tooling.

The division existed for marketing and administrative purposes, while manufacturing, engineering, and accounting remained independent functions. The divisions and head office together had forty marketing and sales employees, thirty-five management and general administrative employees, twenty-five engineering employees and twenty-five accounting employees.

The compensation system consisted of hourly pay for direct labor employees, salary for most other employees. Management also received a profit-based bonus, and there was a discretionary bonus for other employees. Salesmen received salary and commission. There was also a profit-sharing retirement fund for salaried employees.

The chairman of the board was Robert P. Miller, Jr., fifty-four years old, a member of the Miller family, which owned a majority portion of the company. Miller had recently been appointed chairman and had previously been vice president of the Vibro-Equipment Division. Miller had joined SWECO six years ago, from running a graphite mining business of his own. Howard W. Wright, Jr. fifty years of age, had joined the company in 1956 as vice president of the Separator Division and had been SWECO's president since 1963. Howard Wright was Robert P. Miller, Sr.'s son-in-law. Zack Mouradian, forty-seven years of age, had recently been appointed group vice president, coordinating the marketing activities of SWECO's three operating divisions. Mouradian, who joined the company in 1957, had previously headed the separator division for seven years. SWECO's organization structure is shown in Exhibit 10–3.

The Sand Separator/Mud Cleaner

Background

Early in 1971 Zack Mouradian, the group vice president, received a phone call from Dr. Peter Hamilton of the production research unit of a leading international oil company. Hamilton told Mouradian that the oil company had been experimenting with conventional fine screens in the separation of sand from the drilling fluid (mud) used in the drilling of oil and gas wells. The oil company now wished to conduct additional experiments and had contacted SWECO because of its reputation as the leading industrial fine screen separator manufacturer.

SWECO had made two aborted attempts to enter the oil field service business, with a SWECO industrial separator to be substituted for a shale shaker.[1] Both attempts, in the late 1940s and in the late 1960s, had failed. In retrospect, SWECO thought that it had made two fundamental errors. It had thought that it could just sell the equipment without providing service and maintenance. Also, the equipment had been too light-duty for oil field conditions and could not handle the high flow rates encountered in drilling.

Mouradian decided to assign Les Hansen to work with Dr. Hamilton on this recent effort. Hansen had joined SWECO in 1970 in the development engineering laboratory. Hansen was twenty-seven years of age, and his previous business experience was limited to his year with SWECO as an applications engineer and process trouble-shooter. Hansen's education included some engineering training and a degree in economics. He was also attending law school on a part-time basis at the time.

Solids Control Equipment

In drilling for oil and gas, a slurry (called drilling mud) of liquid, solids, and chemicals was pumped through the drill pipe in order to wash away the cuttings created by the drill bit and to bring them to the surface. Depending on the depth of the hole and

---

[1] A shale shaker was a standard type of mud cleaning equipment, to be described below.

other factors, the liquid used would be water or oil. Generally, the deeper the hole the greater was the required density of the drilling fluid. Hence at depths of about 10,000 feet or greater, a high-density material called barite (barium sulphate) was added to the drilling mud. Barite's specific gravity was 4.2, compared to only 2.6 for typical rock formation solids.

The drilling mud coming out of a well needed to be cleaned to remove the cuttings or "drill solids" before it could be recirculated downward into the well. While no process could eliminate all the drill solids from a mud system, maximum removal was highly desirable. Reduced drill solids content of muds improved bit life and minimized drilling problems such as pipe sticking. At their worst, mud problems could stop drilling altogether.

Unfortunately, existing processes for removing fine drill solids in 1972 also removed the barite. Barite was so expensive that the cost of weighted mud often represented 10 to 15 percent of drilling costs. Conventional approaches for handling drill solids included chemical treatment, dilution, settling pits, and mechanical removal techniques. The suitability of particular techniques depended largely on the weight of the mud. The oil company that had contacted SWECO was working on the problem of solids control in heavier muds.

Three types of mechanical devices for removing drill solids were currently used in oil fields: shale shakers, hydrocyclones, and centrifuges. A shale shaker was similar in principle to industrial separators, with materials separated through a vibratory screening process. Generally a standard shale shaker could remove solid particles larger than 500 to 1,000 microns.[2] More efficient fine screen shakers could remove particles as small as 177 microns, using an 80 mesh screen.

Hydrocyclones (also called "desanders" and "desilters") removed smaller particles in the 10 to 60 microns range using a different principle—centrifugal force. Hydrocyclones rotated the mud at high speeds in a cone-shaped container. Lighter, cleaned drilling mud would exit from the top of the cone while the heavier solids gravitated to the bottom of the cone, where the rotation speed was the highest. However, unlike the shale shaker, de-

sanders and desilters[3] could deal only with unweighted muds. For muds above about 10 lbs. per gallon (i.e., weighted with barite) an excessive amount of the barite was discharged and lost in the cleaning process, because small, heavy barite particles would discharge from hydrocyclones as fast as smaller and lighter fine drill solids. A desilter operating on mud weighted with barite would have discarded $7 worth of barite a minute on a continuous basis.

Centrifuges used a similar principle to hydrocyclones, but for smaller volumes and using higher G-forces. Centrifuges could remove very small particles, in the 3-to-5-micron range, and could be used with very heavily weighted muds (those above 13 lbs. per gallon), but they could not remove solids in the larger size range.

Thus, there was a gap in fine solids removal between the capabilities of shale shakers and of centrifuges. The problem, on which Dr. Hamilton of the oil company was working, was how to remove drilled solids from weighted mud in the 74-to-177-micron range. Particles this size were out of reach of shale shakers or centrifuges but impractical for hydrocyclones.

The Solution

In mid-1971 Hamilton came to SWECO's laboratory in Los Angeles and, working with Les Hansen, began to experiment with techniques to remove drill solids in the size range of the 74-to-177-micron gap while retaining barite. The arrangement was that the oil company and SWECO would each bear its own costs in these experiments. The oil company hoped to stimulate development of a product that would reduce drilling costs.

The process selected was one that combined a shale shaker, hydrocyclone, and SWECO fine screen separator in three stages. First, the mud flowed through a shale shaker, which removed large-size solids. The mud then passed through second-stage hydrocyclones, which separated the mud into low-density and high-density materials. The low-density material returned to the mud system. Third, the high density material containing

---

[2] 25 microns = 0.001 inch.

[3] De*sand*ers and de*silt*ers handled progressively finer particles.

barite and fine drill solids flowed through a smaller screen, which passed the fine barite but rejected the drill solids larger than about 74 microns.

The first-stage shale shaker was a conventional unit of the type already in use in oil fields, not a SWECO product but rented or purchased by the operator from any of a number of suppliers. The (second) hydrocyclone stage was performed by a desilter, also a standard product, though built into the SWECO unit. SWECO purchased desilters from Pioneer Centrifuge Co., Inc., a small manufacturer of solids control equipment. The third stage was provided by a specialized variant of SWECO's industrial separator, which was a higher-technology unit than separators currently in use in oil field applications. A bank of the Pioneer hydrocyclones was combined with a SWECO fine screen separator into one unit, referred to as the "sand separator" (see Exhibits 10–4 to 10–6).

SWECO ran several field trials, with a number of progressively improved prototype machines at a number of drilling sites over a twelve-month period in conjuction with Hamilton's company. These experiments showed that the fine screen separator had to run 50 percent faster than the speeds of SWECO's industrial separators, which meant that the vibration-induced stresses were about five times greater than normal. The oil field unit also had to be more rugged than SWECO's industrial products because of its treatment by the oil field workers—or "roughnecks." A SWECO machine installed in a food processing plant, for example, was well maintained and treated with care; in the oil field trials SWECO sand separators were sometimes unloaded from the delivery truck by tying a chain around the unit, attaching the chain to the drilling rig, and driving the truck out from under the separator.

By the fall of 1972 data from the field tests had been compiled from several drilling sites. In one controlled test in a deep well in Louisiana, round-the-clock operating data proved that the separator was able to remove drill solids while saving barite. In addition, its use had prevented downtime from stuck drill pipe, common on such wells, by providing superior solids removal. Hamilton's oil company estimated that there were combined savings of more than $100,000 on the well from using the mud cleaner. The oil company was now satisfied with the technique and suggested SWECO should market the mud cleaners on a commercial basis. By this time SWECO had spent approximately $100,000 in the development effort.

SWECO calculated that each sand separator unit would cost about $5,000 to manufacture in regular, large-scale production, broken down as shown in Table 10–1. SWECO thought that the sand separator could be rented at the same daily rate as a centrifuge, $100.

In addition, each unit would also require an electric or diesel-powered pump. SWECO could assemble these from purchased components for $3,000 and $6,000, respectively. Similar units were used by many drilling contractors to drive other pieces of solids control equipment and typically rented for about $30 and $40 a day, respectively.

In operation, the sand separator wore out its fine screen every ten days or so. SWECO sold replacement screens of a similar nature for between $100 and $200 to its existing industrial customers.

The Oil Field Service Industry

In 1972 a major boom in the oil and gas industry was under way and was expected to continue over the next several years. In 1971 almost 26,000 oil and gas wells were drilled in the United States, both onshore and offshore. This number was expected to increase to 27,000 in 1972, and by at least 1,000 additional wells per year over the next five years. The average depth of these wells was 5,000 feet, with an average drilling cost of $19 per foot, increases of 17 and 48 percent respectively over a ten-year period. Drilling costs varied with the geographic location of the well, the type of formations penetrated, and the depth. In 1972 drilling costs ranged from $15 for shallow wells to $45 per foot for wells drilled up to 15,000 feet in depth, in the United States. Average

TABLE 10–1. Projected Production Costs of SWECO Sand Separator

	Materials	Labor	Other	Total
Vibrating Screen	$1,000	$ 400	$ 800	$2,200
Skid	200	100	300	600
Motor Starter	400	—	—	400
Hydrocyclones	1,800	—	—	1,800
	$3,400	$ 500	$1,100	$5,000

depths were expected to continue to increase as part of the process of increasing exploitation of more "difficult" locations of oil and gas.

Drilling activity in the United States was geographically concentrated, with six states accounting for the bulk of wells (Table 10-2). Almost 80 percent of world drilling activity took place in the United States, and only 1 percent in the Middle East. U.S. wells were much deeper on average than wells in other parts of the world, and therefore made much greater use of weighted drilling fluids and solids control equipment.

In the United States most wells were drilled by drilling contractors under contract to the operator (oil company).[4] There were many hundreds of drilling contractors, most very small businesses. Approximately 90 percent owned five drilling rigs or less. The drilling contractor was responsible for putting together a basic package of the necessary equipment to drill a well. It was standard practice in 1972 for the contractor to be paid a flat day rate by the operator. The operator then paid for the rental of special equipment and services, such as drilling mud and solids control equipment. Standard practice was for the contractor to own some of such equipment and for the operator to rent additional equipment. Thus contractors did not rent, and operators did not buy.

TABLE 10-2. Geographic Distribution of U.S. Oil Drilling Activity

State	Number of Wells in 1971[a]
Texas	7,315
Louisiana	3,806
Oklahoma	2,490
Kansas	2,413
California	2,157
Ohio	1,157
	19,338
Other	6,513
Total	25,851

[a] Exploratory and development wells, both onshore and offshore.
SOURCE: American Petroleum Institute and the American Association of Geologists, published in *Basic Petroleum Data Book: Petroleum Industry Statistics,* 1978.

[4] The term "operator" applies to the oil company owning the hole. Actual drilling operations were carried out by the drilling contractor.

The key piece of equipment was the drilling rig itself. There were about 1,100 active rigs in the United States in 1971, and these were generally expected to increase in number by about one hundred per year over the next few years. While the drilling contractor owned the rig, suppliers provided specialized pieces of purchased or rented ancillary equipment, as well as many other services used in drilling. These suppliers constituted the oil field service industry, with revenues of about $3 billion in 1972.[5]

Oil field services included:

- Well logging: the measurement of drilling parameters such as depth, weight on the drilling bit, torque, pump pressure, pump rate, and geological statistics
- Drill bits
- Cementing of holes after drilling to prepare for regular production of oil or gas from the holes
- Down-hole tools; such as stabilizers and directional tools
- Drilling mud
- Rental equipment, including solids control equipment

Rental equipment included maintenance on a twenty-four-hour on-call basis as a major part of the service.

Drilling Mud

Barite-weighted drilling mud was used in most deep holes, and solids control equipment was needed to keep this mud clean of drill solids. Deep holes were those deeper than 10,000 feet. About 1,500 such holes had been drilled in the United States in 1971. In 1971 about 900 of the 1,100 active drilling rigs were capable of drilling more than 10,000 feet. They were distributed as follows:

Texas	280
Louisiana	240
California	50
Alaska	10
All other	320
	900

[5] The total U.S. oil and gas production industry had expenditures of more than $10 billion in 1972, split about evenly among exploration, development, and production.

Of these 900 rigs only about 400 were significant users of solids control equipment, because of the characteristics of the areas in which they were drilling: high drilling mud costs; soft sand formations; high waste disposal costs; high logistics costs; deep holes. The chief suppliers of drilling mud were the Magcobar Division of Dresser Industries, the Baroid Division of NL Industries, and the IMCO Services Division of the Halliburton Company. Precise estimates of market size were difficult to obtain, but the annual market for drilling mud was approximately $500 million in the United States and $150 million overseas in 1972.

Marketing of drilling mud was primarily through the use of a sales force that called on drilling contractors and oil companies. The oil drilling industry was well known for being a tight-knit community. Business in the oil field service market was typically sold on a per-hole basis. Advance knowledge from personal contacts of when and where holes would be drilled was crucial. It was necessary to sell both to the head office and the local office of the oil company owning a hole and to the contractor drilling the hole. Personal contacts and relationships were crucial in the selling process.

As part of the drilling mud service, all the companies also provided "mud engineers," who were responsible for maintaining the mud in a suitable condition during drilling operations. A "mud engineer" spent a great deal of time on-site and was virtually a member of the drilling contractor's team.

Solids Control Equipment

The market for solids control equipment was approximately $40 million domestically and perhaps $10 million overseas in 1972. About 85 percent of the domestic market for equipment was rental, with the remainder new equipment or aftermarket sales. The principal items of equipment are shown in Table 10–3. The power unit comprised the motor and pump that fed the desander and the desilter. A closely related piece of mud control equipment was the degasser, which separated unwanted gases from the mud. Degasser revenues were equivalent to about one-third of total solids control revenues. Of the U.S. rig population in 1972 of about 1,200 active rigs, perhaps 85 percent used shale shakers, 50

TABLE 10–3.   Rented Solids Control Equipment

	% of Rental Market (Rental Revenues)
Shale shaker	24%
Desander (hydrocyclone)	7
Desilter (hydrocyclone)	13
Centrifuge	17
Power unit	38
	100%

percent degassers, 25 percent desanders, 60 percent desilters, and 10 percent centrifuges. Daily rental rates were on the order of $40 for all units except the centrifuge, which had a rental rate of about $100 per day.

The effectiveness of solids control equipment was very difficult to judge precisely. The benefits of the equipment were:

- Reducing mud costs
- Reducing drilling time
- Reducing downtime from pipe sticking
- Improving drill bit life
- Saving wear and tear on pumps (owned by the contractor)

However, none of these benefits could be readily quantified, because the amount of barite used, drill bit life, and downtime were all subject to many factors besides solids control. Thus drilling contractors and operators tended to rely on the reputation of the supplier in purchasing solids control equipment. Also, the performance of solids control equipment was generally similar among existing suppliers, since the technology was well known. More crucial was the level of service. Each hour of downtime cost the operator hundreds of dollars onshore, and thousands offshore. Contractors were not directly motivated to avoid downtime because they were paid a flat daily fee. They were, however, motivated to minimize their load of activities and equipment, since they were responsible for its operation. Thus contractors tended not to be receptive to new types of equipment unless the associated benefits were fairly obvious.

Problems with oil field equipment were frequent because of the nature of the drilling process, the typically adverse operating conditions, and rough treatment in the hands of roughnecks. Suppliers of equipment had to provide twenty-four-hour on-call service over a very wide area. Sunday morning at 3 A.M. seemed the most frequent time for breakdowns! Despite the importance of minimizing downtime, drilling contractors did not place solids control equipment high on their list of priorities because of the innumerable other problems they faced.

Solids control equipment was generally rented rather than sold, because there were significant variations in the type of equipment needed for each particular well. The service component generally accounted for more than one-third of the rental fee.

Solids control equipment suppliers maintained service networks consisting of a number of service centers, located near drilling areas. A prime area might have up to one hundred rigs requiring solids control equipment. A minimum-size service center might service an area of approximately 200 miles in radius and be staffed by five people, a service center manager and four service reps. Such a center cost about $150,000 to maintain annually in 1972, excluding the cost of the rental equipment, with half of that cost being salaries. Such a service center could support $500,000 in rental revenues a year, based on a 50 percent utilization of its rental equipment. An average rental period per hole was about six weeks, although there was great variation in the period from hole to hole.

Suppliers depreciated their equipment over about a seven-year period. Over this period there would be extensive refurbishment of the equipment. Perhaps as much as 7–10 percent of rental revenues would be plowed back as refurbishment.

Competition

The solids control equipment business was led by the SWACO division of Dresser Industries, the Baroid Division of NL Industries, and a number of other firms including Baker Industries, Brandt, and Pioneer.

Dresser Industries

Dresser Industries had revenues of $905 million and pretax earnings of $66 million in the year ending October 1972, broken down by business segment as in Table 10–4.

Petroleum Group. The Petroleum Group provided a wide range of products and services for the exploration, drilling, production, and marketing segments of the oil and gas industries, as well as to mining and other industries. The principal products and services of the group included drilling mud additives, well logging and completion services, drill bits, down-hole tools, and other oil field equipment. The group also manufactured gasoline pumps and allied equipment for gasoline service stations.

Drilling mud and solids control equipment accounted for about $100 million, or one-third of this group's revenues, of which drilling mud represented approximately $90 million. Drilling muds and related services were marketed under the Magcobar trademark. The services included Magcobar engineers, who provided on-site, round-the-clock analysis and advice.

The SWACO division manufactured equipment for use in drilling, including shale shakers, desilters, and degassers. Although SWACO and Magcobar were organizationally separate, they shared the same sales force. SWACO had the largest market share in the solids control equipment market (which excluded degassers), about 30 percent. SWACO had very high visibility among operators and contractors and was widely recognized as the market

TABLE 10–4.   Breakdown of Dresser Industries Revenues, 1969–1972

	% Revenues				% Pretax Earnings			
	1969	1970	1971	1972	1969	1970	1971	1972
Petroleum Group	36%	37%	40%	35%	33%	30%	32%	32%
Machinery Group	26	26	24	26	16	13	15	13
Refractories and Minerals Group	21	20	18	16	28	34	23	18
Industrial Specialties Group	17	17	18	23	23	23	30	37

leader. SWACO had twenty-five to thirty oil field service locations in 1972.

Machinery Group. This group produced compressors, blowers, pumps, and engines for municipal water systems and for the oil, gas, chemical, refining, paper, water pollution control, and other industries. Other activities included air pollution control and materials handling.

Refractories and Minerals Group. This group mined and processed barite, bentonite, and lignite and supplied these to the Petroleum Group for use as drilling mud. The group also mined industrial sand, kaolin, and metallic sulfide ore. The other major activity was the mining, manufacturing, and marketing of refractories, which were nonmetallic mineral products used chiefly to line industrial high-temperature vessels.

Industrial Specialties Group. This group manufactured a broad line of pneumatic tools for various industrial uses, and hand tools for light service trades and home use. The group also manufactured abrasives, grinding wheels, coated abrasive cloth, and related equipment. Other products included gauges, thermometers, switches and valves for instrumentation or control of processes in the refining, chemical, petrochemical, electric power generation, and fire protection industries.

NL Industries

NL Industries (formerly National Lead) had revenues of $1,014 million in 1972, with pretax earnings of $62 million, divided as in Table 10–5.

Chemicals Group. This group supplied the petroleum industry with drilling mud additives and specialized water-treating and corrosion-inhibiting chemicals for the petroleum industries. It also furnished extensive engineering services and equipment for well logging and testing.

The Baroid Division represented about 55 percent of 1972 revenues of the Chemicals Group and had supplied drilling mud for almost fifty years. It had entered the solids control equipment business in the 1950s. The same sales force sold both drilling mud and mud control equipment. Approximately 80 percent of Baroid's revenues came from selling mud, 10 percent from solids control equipment, and 10 percent from other oil field service activities. Baroid maintained oil field locations, service reps, and mud engineers worldwide. Baroid purchased a great deal of its solids control equipment from other manufacturers. For example, desilters were purchased from Demco, screens from SMICO, and centrifuges from Bird.[6]

The other principal activity of the Chemicals Group was the production and sale of anticorrosive pigments, stabilizers, flame retardants, extender pigments, castor oil derivatives, and chemical specialties for use by the plastics, paint, ink, and adhesives industries, and of gellants for paint, grease, pharmaceuticals, and cosmetics producers.

Industrial Specialties Group. This group produced zirconium and titanium chemicals for the ceramic and electronic industries, and made process alloys for the aerospace industry. It also produced and distributed radio-pharmaceuticals to hospitals and doctors for use in nuclear diagnostic medicine. NL was also the contract-operator for one of the

[6] These companies were all manufacturers of process equipment for a variety of industries.

TABLE 10–5. Breakdown of NL Industries Revenues, 1969–1972

	% Revenues				% Pretax Earnings			
	1969	1970	1971	1972	1969	1970	1971	1972
Chemicals Group	17%	19%	19%	20%	19%	27%	35%	32%
Metals Group	29	30	27	29	12	15	7	8
Pigments Group	23	23	23	21	33	27	9	24
Fabricated Products Group	23	20	21	21	29	25	39	30
Industrial Specialties Group	3	3	3	3	4	3	1	3
Other activities	5	5	7	6	3	3	9	3

U.S. Atomic Energy Commission's feed materials production centers. The group also sold Dutch Boy paints.

Others. The metals group produced lead products, precious metals products, and zinc and aluminum products. Its customers included the electronic, jewelry, photographic, aerospace, and railroad industries. The pigments group was a leading producer of titanium pigments used principally by the paint, paper, plastics, and rubber industries. The fabricated products group manufactured custom die castings for use as components in the production of automobiles, trucks, electrical appliances, office machinery, hand tools, and hardware.

The Brandt Company

Brandt was believed to be the third largest supplier of solids control equipment, with an approximately 7 percent market share. Brandt's total revenues in 1971 were less than $3 million. Brandt sold shale shakers only and had been in business for less than five years. Brandt emphasized the ruggedness and simplicity of its equipment and had a much smaller service operation than other suppliers. Brandt sold its equipment directly to drilling contractors and was not in the rental business. Thus Brandt did not maintain any service centers.

Baker Oil Tools, Inc.

Baker Oil Tools had revenues of $151 million and pretax earnings of $10 million in 1972. International operations accounted for just under 40 percent of revenues. Baker's revenues came from the segments listed in Table 10-6.

Drilling Products. In 1971 Baker had acquired Milchem, Inc., for $12 million, thereby entering the drilling fluid business. Milchem sold both drilling mud and solids control equipment, with the revenue from mud approximately 95 percent of sales. Other components of Baker's Drilling Products group manufactured and marketed hole expanders, drill pipe controls, and well-logging equipment. Milchem's products and services, along with other Baker petroleum products and services, were distributed primarily through Baker's 140 oil field service locations.

Other Products. Baker also manufactured products used in lining holes to convert them from exploratory to production wells, and products used to restore maximum production to mature or aging wells. Baker had recently developed computer-controlled automated systems for controlling oil or gas production processes. Baker also marketed to petroleum refineries a line of precision instruments and a line of process control instruments. Through its Galigher Division, Baker manufactured processing equipment used in the mechanical and chemical extraction of metals from mined ores. Baker had also adapted for other industries some products originally designed for the petroleum industry. These other industries included cryogenics, paper pulp, chemicals, and food processing.

Pioneer Centrifuging Company

Pioneer was a small privately held company specializing in solids control equipment: centrifuges and

TABLE 10-6.   Breakdown of Baker Oil Tools Revenues, 1969–1972

	% Revenues			
	1 9 6 9	1 9 7 0	1 9 7 1	1 9 7 2
Petroleum industry				
Drilling	7%	7%	13%	35%
Completion and production	67	59	55	40
Remedial work and stimulation				
(of existing wells)	22	18	15	11
Other	1	3	4	4
Total petroleum	97%	87%	87%	90%
Mining industry	—	7	8	7
Other industries	3	6	5	3
	100%	100%	100%	100%

hydrocyclones (desanders and desilters). Its revenues in 1972 were estimated at between $2 million and $3 million. Pioneer had a reputation for high-quality products, and SWECO had used Pioneer hydrocyclones as part of its experimental mud cleaners. Pioneer maintained three service centers.

Halliburton Company

Although it did not supply solids control equipment, Halliburton was a leading supplier of drilling mud through its IMCO Services Division and was a leading oil field service company via IMCO and other divisions.

Halliburton had revenues of $1,422 million in 1972, with pretax earnings of $108 million. These revenues and earnings did not include $93 million of premiums and $6 million of net income from an unconsolidated fire and casualty insurance subsidiary. The breakdown by business segment of Halliburton's businesses is shown in Table 10–7.

Oil Field Services and Products. Halliburton performed a wide range of specialized services relating to drilling and production of oil and gas wells both onshore and offshore. Services included pumping services offered in conjunction with cementing wells, hydraulic fracturing and chemical treatments, testing, logging and perforating services, specialized remedial services for high-pressure producing wells, and the supply of cement, drilling muds, fracturing sands, and other bulk materials for both new and existing wells. In addition, Halliburton manufactured and sold a broad line of subsurface equipment, tools, and controls used in oil and gas production.

The IMCO Services Division was one of six Halliburton operating units providing oil field services

and products. The IMCO Services Division had been formed from IMC Drilling Mud, Inc., whose acquisition by Halliburton had been completed in January 1972. Halliburton had paid $4 million for the remaining 50 percent interest belonging to International Minerals & Chemical Corporation. IMCO sold drilling mud and related chemicals via distribution facilities in the United States, Canada, and the North Sea area. Its 1972 revenues were estimated at between $20 million and $40 million.

Engineering and Construction Services. These included industrial construction (principally refineries, petrochemical and petroleum facilities, pulp and paper mills, and power plants) and marine construction (principally the fabrication of offshore drilling and production platforms and the laying of submarine pipelines). Engineering and other construction consisted primarily of project management, maintenance services, and engineering and civil construction.

Specialty Services and Products to General Industry. Many of these involved industrial applications of techniques first developed for the oil and gas industry. These services included cleaning of petroleum refining and other industrial plants. Halliburton also manufactured specialty products, including hydraulic cushioning devices for railway cars, pneumatic handling systems, pipeline testing devices, solid state relays, and a digital pressure monitoring system for oil field production automation.

The Decision

In November 1972 SWECO had to decide what to do about the sand separator. Should it enter the oil field service business, and if so how? Les Hansen

TABLE 10–7. Breakdown of Halliburton Company Revenues, 1969–1972

	% Revenues				% Pretax Earnings			
	1969	1970	1971	1972	1969	1970	1971	1972
Oil field services and products	27%	26%	23%	28%	46%	58%	56%	61%
Engineering and construction services	66	69	73	68	48	37	41	37
Specialty services and products to general industry	7	5	4	4	6	5	3	2

and the other SWECO executives could see many factors against their success. The problems of entering the oil field service business seemed enormous. Les Hansen had estimated that a full-scale effort by SWECO would require revenues from at least two service centers to support the overhead costs of setting up an oil field service division. Also, SWECO had found that the mud cleaner process was not patentable, nor could Dr. Hamilton guarantee that his company would rent any units.

In addition, management wondered how SWECO could overcome these problems if they followed Dr. Hamilton's advice not to promote the sand separator. He had said to Howard Wright: "If you go ahead, be careful. Don't promote it. Let the machine sell itself. If someone calls you up to ask about it, say that you don't know if it will work. Tell them to ask me. Bite your tongue if they ask you whether it will work."

EXHIBIT 10-1. *Consolidated Statement of Earnings, SWECO*

	1972	1971	1970
Sales	$14,843,096	$11,889,643	$13,664,527
Cost of sales	7,964,294	6,391,671	8,237,809
Gross operating profit	6,878,802	5,497,972	5,426,718
Selling, administrative and general expenses	5,647,004	5,064,099	5,043,605
Operating Income	1,231,798	433,873	383,113
Other Income:			
Gain on the translation of foreign currencies	–	25,887	–
Earnings from unconsolidated corporate joint venture	11,188	20,877	–
	1,242,986	480,637	383,113
Interest expense, net	10,357	48,051	146,107
Earnings before income taxes	1,232,629	432,586	237,006
Income taxes	594,720	197,157	98,500
Net earnings	$ 637,909	$ 235,429	$ 138,506
Earnings per common share	$ 9.96	$ 3.63	$ 2.14

SOURCE: Annual reports.

EXHIBIT 10–2. *Consolidated Balance Sheet, SWECO*

	1972	1971
Assets		
Current assets:		
Cash	$ 855.608	$ 591,014
Receivables	2,897,518	2,623,654
Inventories	3,467,034	2,989,192
Prepaid expenses	169,316	169,385
Total current assets	7,389,476	6,373,245
Investments	52,685	92,497
Long-term receivables	17,494	36,312
Property, plant and equipment:		
Land	20,723	20,723
Buildings	264,976	246,957
Equipment	2,030,016	1,698,099
Leasehold improvements	367,006	332,430
	2,682,721	2,298,209
Less accumulated depreciation and amortization	1,402,886	1,162,130
Net property, plant & equipment	1,279,835	1,136,079
Patents	1,618	26,589
Deferred charges	2,581	14,295
	$8,743,689	$7,679,017
Liabilities		
Current liabilities:		
Notes payable to banks	350,371	594,231
Long-term lease obligation, amounts due within one year	10,114	19,932
Accounts payable	1,236,656	883,908
Accrued expenses	891,828	608,407
Income taxes	331,146	146,824
Total current liabilities	2,820,115	2,253,302
Long-term lease obligation	182,546	191,446
Unrealized gain on translation of foreign currencies	30,187	24,019
Stockholders' equity:		
Common stock	259,208	259,208
Additional paid-in capital	41,137	41,137
Retained earnings	5,445,371	4,909,905
	5,745,716	5,210,250
Less treasury stock	34,875	–
Total stockholders' equity	5,710,841	5,210,250
	$8,743,689	$7,679,017

SOURCE: Annual reports.

EXHIBIT 10–3. *Organization Chart, SWECO*

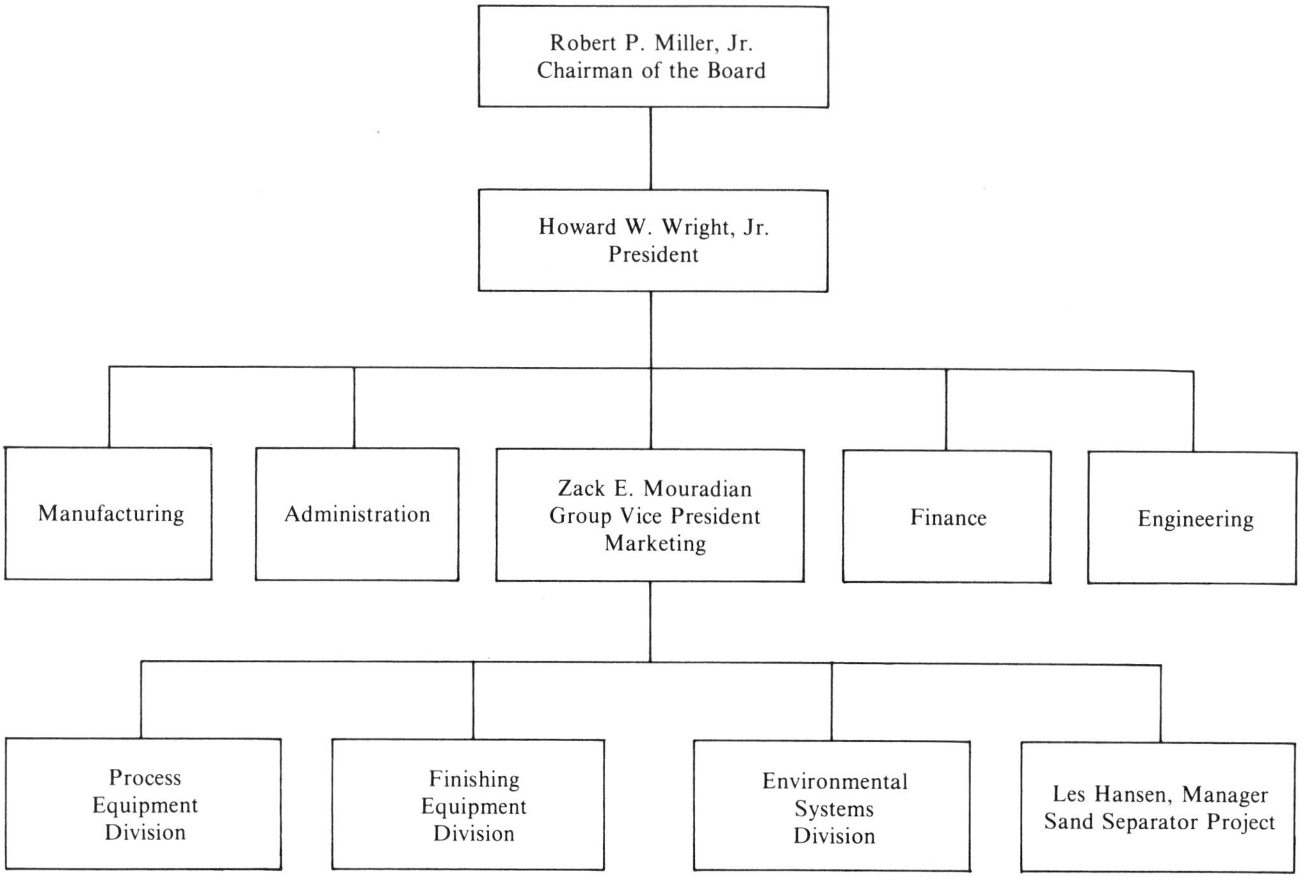

EXHIBIT 10–4. *Diagram of SWECO Sand Separator/Mud Cleaner*

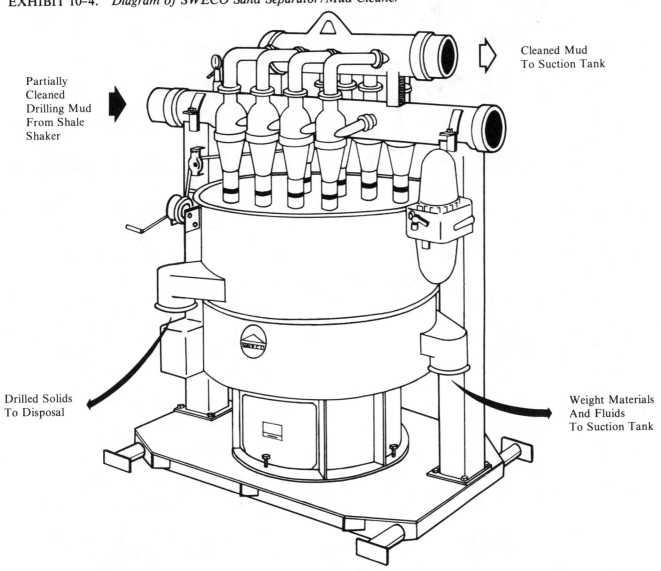

Cleaned Mud
To Suction Tank

Partially
Cleaned
Drilling Mud
From Shale
Shaker

Drilled Solids
To Disposal

Weight Materials
And Fluids
To Suction Tank

EXHIBIT 10–5. *Sand Separator/Mud Cleaner Specifications*

How mud cleaner fits in

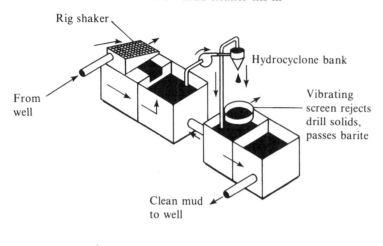

Rig shaker

From well

Hydrocyclone bank

Vibrating screen rejects drill solids, passes barite

Clean mud to well

SWECO sand-separator specs

Overall weight	2,600 lb.
Overall dimensions	7'5" high, 6'0" long, 4'0" wide
Construction	Epoxy-coated carbon steel
Hydrocyclones	
Size	4-in.
Number	8
Manifold	6-in.
Vibrating screen	
Screen diameter	48 in.
Screen mesh	150 mesh, or 200 mesh or finer for special applications
Motor	Explosionproof 2½-hp, 230/460-v, 60-cycle

Two key mud-cleaner components

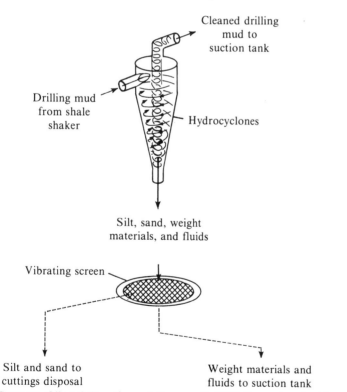

Cleaned drilling mud to suction tank

Drilling mud from shale shaker

Hydrocyclones

Silt, sand, weight materials, and fluids

Vibrating screen

Silt and sand to cuttings disposal

Weight materials and fluids to suction tank

Flows on one field test

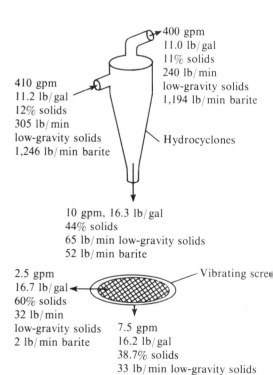

400 gpm
11.0 lb/gal
11% solids
240 lb/min low-gravity solids
1,194 lb/min barite

410 gpm
11.2 lb/gal
12% solids
305 lb/min low-gravity solids
1,246 lb/min barite

Hydrocyclones

10 gpm, 16.3 lb/gal
44% solids
65 lb/min low-gravity solids
52 lb/min barite

2.5 gpm
16.7 lb/gal
60% solids
32 lb/min low-gravity solids
2 lb/min barite

Vibrating screen

7.5 gpm
16.2 lb/gal
38.7% solids
33 lb/min low-gravity solids
50 lb/min barite

SOURCE: *Oil and Gas Journal,* January 7, 1974. Reproduced with permission.

EXHIBIT 10–6. *Diagram of Self-cleaning Screen Used in SWECO Separators*

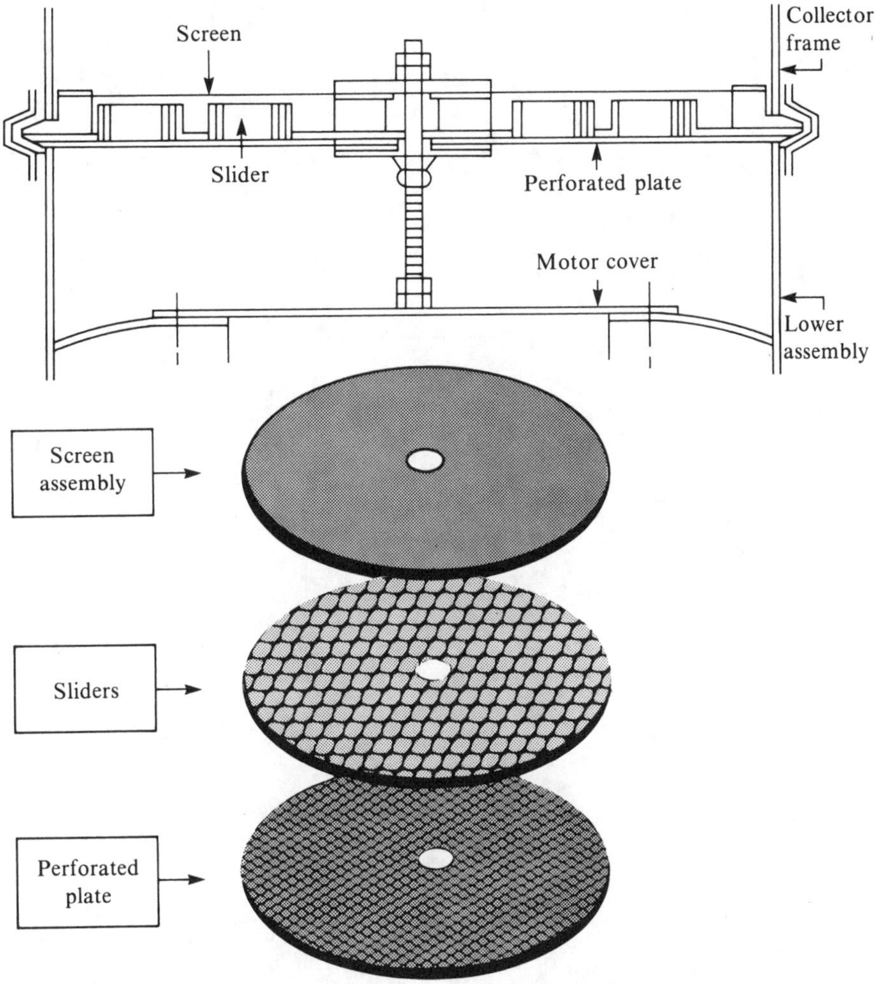

SOURCE: *Oil and Gas Journal,* January 7, 1974. Reproduced with permission.

PART V
Industry Structural Evolution

The next three cases examine industries undergoing major structural change. The focus of the required analysis is to predict the path of industry evolution and develop competitive strategies to cope with it. "The Chain Saw Industry in 1974" portrays the chain saw industry at the beginning of what is certain to be a discontinuity—a period of very rapid growth. Each of the major competitors must forecast what the future industry structure will look like, what its rivals will do, and what its competitive strategy should be. Strategic mapping will prove useful in this analysis, as in the other cases in Part V. "The U.S. Securities Industry in 1979" examines an important industry that has been buffeted by change, partly a result of the removal of government regulations. The fundamental forces driving the industry's evolution must be assessed in order to forecast the likelihood of further changes and to develop implications for the strategies of investment bankers and brokerage firms. "Hospital Affiliates International and the Hospital Management Industry" describes the situation of the industry leader in the hospital management contracts industry, who is facing the potential maturity of its business. Hospital Affiliates must decide whether and how its industry will soon mature and then formulate competitive strategy accordingly. This case, then, explores the problems of transition to industry maturity.

CASE 11
The Chain Saw Industry in 1974

After a long period of relative stability, the U.S. chain saw industry was experiencing rapid growth in early 1974, stimulated by increased consumer interest in chain saws as a result of the energy crisis and a trend toward back to nature and self-sufficiency. Long dominated by Homelite in the mass market and the German company Stihl in the premium segment, the industry faced other changes in the early 1970s. Two major companies in the industry had recently been acquired by large parents, and many other participants had taken a renewed interest in the industry as a result of the upsurge in growth.

The Product

Chain saws were motorized devices for cutting wood, which were sold to a wide range of industrial, commercial, and household buyers. There were two basic types of chain saws, which differed in the nature of their power unit (power head). Gas saws were free-standing units powered by an internal combustion engine of 2 to over 8 cubic inches of displacement. Electric saws utilized an electric motor, fed by a cable, which had to be connected to an electrical socket. Domestic U.S. sales of chain saws[1] over the 1949–1973 period are shown in Table 11-1.

Exhibit 11-1 shows a typical chain saw, identifying its major parts. Besides the basic nature of the power head, chain saws differed in two important dimensions. The horsepower of the power head varied from 1.5 to approximately 8.5. More powerful saws were designed for heavy-duty uses such as logging and construction, while less powerful saws were sufficient for the cutting of firewood and light clearing of land that the homeowner was likely to require. Chain saws also differed in the length of their cutting bar (from 10 to over 24 inches), with long bar saws designed by and large for heavy-duty applications.

These differences translated into the availability of a wide variety of chain saw models, with some manufacturers producing more than twenty different saws. Prices for chain saws reflected this wide range of products (Table 11-2). Chain saws had a useful life of approximately five years of regular use.

[1] The U.S. market for chain saws was approximately as large as the rest of the world combined.

TABLE 11–1. Historical Domestic Chain Saw Sales *(thousands of units)*

Year	Gas Saws	Electric Saws[a]	Total Saws
1949	40	—	40
1950	60	—	60
1951	95	—	95
1952	111	—	111
1953	150	—	150
1954	220	—	220
1955	248	—	248
1956	277	—	277
1957	248	—	248
1958	321	—	321
1959	363	—	363
1960	340	—	340
1961	340	—	340
1962	375	—	375
1963	381	—	381
1964	453	—	453
1965	501	—	501
1966	515	—	515
1967	518	—	518
1968	554	—	554
1969	613	—	613
1970	633	NA	633+
1971	750	NA	750+
1972	899	175	1064
1973	1400	312	1712

[a]Sales of electric saws were very small before 1970.
SOURCES: Manufacturer interviews; for pre-1972 data, Walter J. Williams, "The United States Chain Saw Market," unpublished manuscript, Amos Tuck School, Dartmouth College.

Markets

Industry participants had traditionally segmented end-users of chain saws into three categories: professional, farmer, and occasional or "casual" user. The *professional* used a chain saw as one of the primary tools of his trade. Along with professional loggers, the "pro" segment included commercial

TABLE 11–2. Chain Saw Retail Price Segmentation[a]

		1970	1971	1972
Less than	$140	12%	20%	22%
	$140–170	12%	27%	26%
	$170–300	} 76%	49%	47%
	$300–700		4%	5%
		100%	100%	100%

[a] Based on number of units in the price segment.
SOURCES: Chain Saw Manufacturers Association; dealer and manufacturer interviews.

TABLE 11–3. Farm Uses of Chain Saws

Specific Farm Use	% of Survey Respondents that Reported Use
Tree maintenance	54.1%
Land clearing	49.8%
Fence posts	49.4%
Firewood cutting	28.8%
Timber	26.2%
Pulpwood	1.3%

SOURCE: *Kansas Farmer.*

and government buyers who used chain saws as an auxiliary tool of their trades, such as building contractors, municipal employees, and local park district workers. Industry sources estimated that the great majority of pro users purchased saws with cubic inch displacements of 4.5 or greater.

The *farmer* used a chain saw for a variety of activities on his land, as shown in Table 11–3. Farmers purchased saws in the 2.7 cubic inch to 4.5 cubic inch displacement range, with some purchasing even larger saws.

Both professional and farmer users tended to make heavy use of chain saws and required regular service and repair for their saws. They were also frequent purchasers of replacement chain.

The term *casual user* referred to the homeowner or camper who used a chain saw for cutting firewood, tree trimming, pruning, or clearing storm damage. The casual user segment was a very diverse group with a wide variety of needs, and saw usage rates within this segment varied accordingly (Table 11–4. Not infrequently, the casual user's need for a

TABLE 11–4. Segmentation of Casual Users by Type of Use

Primary Type of Use	% of Casual User Market
Fireplace (occasional wood cutting)	60–70%
Home heating (heavy user)	10–15%
Camping	10–15%
Suburban Acreage (light clearing work)	5–10%
Nonuser (gift, etc., put immediately on the shelf)	5–10%
	100%

SOURCE: Manufacturer and distributor interviews.

TABLE 11–5. Chain Saw Sales by Price Range

	Percent of Total Saws Sold to Farm and Professional Users	*Percent of Total Saws Sold to Casual Users*
Less than $100	3%	23%
$100–200	7%	67%
$200–250	33%	8%
$250 or more	57%	2%
	100%	100%

SOURCES: Chain Saw Manufacturers Association; manufacturer interviews.

chain saw was very transient, such as a one-time tree-clearing project. After this use the saw might be used very lightly if at all. Other casual users were regular users of saws.

Most casual user saws were estimated to have power heads with less than 2.7 cubic inch displacement and bar lengths of less than 16 inches. Most casual users purchased saws that cost less than $200 (see Table 11–5). The estimated breakdown of unit sales of chain saws by end user segment is shown in Table 11–6.

Once a purchaser of a chain saw becomes a regular user, there was a tendency to trade up to a saw with either more power or more features. Chain saws in regular use required service, repairs, and the purchase of replacement saw chain. Professional users consumed from five to thirty 7-to-8-foot loops of saw chain per year, and farmers typically used three to five 4-to-8-foot loops if they were regular saw users. Pro and farm users also typically replaced the guide bar two or three times and the sprocket three to five times over the life of the saw. Usage of chain varied markedly in the casual user segment, and there was little reliable evidence of how much chain the average casual user consumed, though it was believed to be less than one 4-foot loop per year. A 4-foot loop of replacement chain

TABLE 11–6. Domestic Gas Chain Saw Sales by Primary Segment (*thousands of units*)

	1972	*1973*
Professional	259	315
Farmer	210	282
Casual user	430	803
Total	899	1400

SOURCES: Chain Saw Manufacturers Association; manufacturer interviews.

cost approximately $10, while bars and sprockets were somewhat more expensive, though the cost varied by size and manufacturer.

While pro and farmer segments had long been the dominant markets for chain saws and still dominated the market in terms of dollar sales because of their much higher average prices, the casual user segment had begun to emerge as a rapidly growing segment in the chain saw industry. Prior to 1963 the gas saws were sold almost exclusively to professional woodcutters. In 1963 a leading competitor, Homelite, introduced its lightweight XL-12 saw priced under $200, soon followed by McCulloch with a similar model. The unprecedented combination of light weight and low price was cited by observers as stimulating the birth of the casual user market. Industry sources attributed the recent spurt in casual user sales to a number of factors, among them increased use of fireplaces and wood-burning stoves as a result of the "energy crisis," social trends emphasizing back to nature and escape from urban living, ownership of second homes, and increased leisure time all coupled with wider availability of lower-priced saws, some costing less than $100.

The casual user market was expected to continue to grow rapidly for at least the next five years. The pro and farm segments were primarily replacement markets by 1974, though they were expected to grow at approximately 10 percent per year. Pro and farmer sales tended to be somewhat cyclical, in keeping with the cycles in their end user industries.

Distribution

Chain saws reached end users through a complex array of two- and three-stage distribution channels.

Exhibit 11-2 gives a schematic diagram of chain saw distribution and indicates the most important channel of distribution for saws in 1974.

Servicing chain saw dealers were the most important retail channel in the chain saw market. Chain saw dealers were full service outlets carrying broad lines of chain saws and offering extensive customer purchasing assistance. There were some dealers who sold only chain saws, but most were lawn and garden stores or building contractor supply outlets. Chain saw dealers were franchised to carry the brands of individual manufacturers, and approximately 25 percent of the dealers carried only one line. However, most dealers carried the product lines of more than one manufacturer, averaging approximately two such lines. Multiple-line dealers generally carried only one of the lines of the two major manufacturers, Homelite and McCulloch, and identified themselves with these firms.

Approximately 45 percent of chain saw dealers were in rural areas, while 35 percent were in urban areas and 20 percent in suburban areas. Dealers provided service, sold replacement chain and accessories, and had an average sales volume in chain saw and related products of $150 thousand to $200 thousand per year. Many were owned by former gasoline engine mechanics. Sales were seasonal, at their highest levels in the summer months. Dealers advertised primarily through local newspapers and radio, and many manufacturers had cooperative advertising programs that shared advertising costs with dealers on a 50-50 basis. Dealer margins for chain saws ranged from 20 to 40 percent, with margins on service and accessories significantly higher. Margins were lowest on the lower-price saws, and some dealers claimed to sell saws at or near cost and make their profit on service and accessories.

Other retail channels for chain saws were as follows:

Lumber and Home Centers. Both independent and chain stores, catering to homeowners and contractors, offered a limited line of saws without service and with limited accessories. Saws were sometimes bought directly from manufacturers but usually through distributors. Chain saws were not a major item for these outlets in 1974.

Farm Stores. Both independent and chain stores supplied farmers with a wide line of farm products,

including feed, equipment, fertilizer, and so forth. Examples of farm store chains included Agway (500 stores), Tractor Supply (250 stores), and Quality Farm and Fleet (23 stores). Most farm stores carried a full line of chain saws and accessories, purchased either direct from the manufacturer or through distributors. Some of the chains handled private label as well as several lines of branded saws. Independent farm stores usually offered service on chain saws, and these outlets resembled the chain saw dealer. Farm store chains were much less likely to offer service. Farm stores were concentrated in the West and Midwest and sold to professionals and casual users as well as primarily to farmers. Sales of chain saws in this outlet were growing, but more slowly than the market as a whole.

Department Stores. Major department stores sold chain saws, particularly the large national chains (Sears, Montgomery Ward, and J. C. Penney). Some of the smaller department stores carried chain saws, offering relatively few models and little or no service. The three large chains were major outlets for saws, and all sold moderately full lines of saws and accessories. They did not carry expensive, high-quality saws because of the difficulty of the sales task. Sears and Ward had their own service, while Penney referred customers to the nearest manufacturer-authorized service center. All three offered credit, which was an effective marketing tool that many other channels for chain saws did not have. The three leading department store chains as well as some other department stores had significant catalog sales of chain saws as well as over-the-counter sales. The Big Three sold an estimated 20-30 percent of their saws through catalog operations.

The major department store chains sold both private label and brand name saws, purchased directly from manufacturers in large volumes. Total sales of chain saws to the top three chains was estimated at several hundred thousand units in 1973. Sears and Ward sold only private label saws, while Penney sold brand name saws, though it had sold private label saws in the past. Ward and especially Sears required their suppliers to redesign products to give them a distinctive line.

Hardware Stores. Both local independent stores and chains that carried a full line of hardware products offered moderately wide lines of saws, including products of several competing manufacturers. Many offered service and a full line of accessories for the saws, but generally service was limited in scope compared to chain saw dealers. Hardware stores were characterized by a high level of customer purchase assistance.

While hardware stores purchased from independent chain saw distributors, an important volume of their chain saws was purchased through wholesale hardware buying groups such as HWI, American Hardware, Ace Hardware, and Cotter and Company. Chain saws represented a minor fraction of the sales of hardware stores, and hardware stores as a group represented less than 10 percent of chain saw sales in 1973.

Catalog Sales. Aside from catalog sales through the major department stores, there were some very limited sales of chain saws through exclusively catalog firms such as Aldens. These firms typically carried models from many manufacturers, with the focus on smaller saws and related accessories. No service was offered, and customers were referred to the nearest service center.

Other Outlets. In addition to these major channels for chain saws, there were two other kinds of outlets that had recently added chain saws to their line in some cases. A few mass merchandisers such as K-Mart had begun to carry very limited lines of lower-priced chain saws, with limited accessories and no service. These were purchased directly from manufacturers. In addition, some of the major auto store chains such as Western Auto had begun limited sales of chain saws on essentially the same basis. These firms bought either direct or through cooperative buying groups.

The breakdown of dollar volume sold through all channels in 1973 is shown in Table 11–7.

TABLE 11–7. Estimated Chain Saw Sales by Channel

Servicing dealers	50–65%
Department stores	20–25%
Farm stores	10–15%
Hardware stores	5–10%
Others	<10%
	100%

SOURCE: Manufacturer interviews.

Wholesale Channels

There were three types of wholesale channels for chain saws. By far the most important was wholesale distributors owned by or exclusively affiliated with the chain saw manufacturers. Most manufacturers had between twenty and fifty distributors, who sold to dealers in the various categories described above. In a few cases the distributors sold direct to large professional or industrial end users.

In addition to regular chain saw distributors, there were catalog distributors and dealer cooperatives (or buying groups) involved in wholesaling chain saws. Catalog dealers purchased direct from manufacturers and resold saws to smaller distributors who did not specialize in chain saws. Buying groups were arrangements by which a group of retailers banded together to secure favorable terms from manufacturers in purchasing. These were most important in hardware stores.

Manufacturing

Chain saw manufacturing involved a complex assembly operation using a variety of fabricated parts. Parts could be divided into two main categories: those relating to the power head, and attachments (bar, chain, and sprocket). Parts fabrication included machining, die-casting, forging, heat treatment, plating, and metal-stamping operations. Of these, die-casting involved the most significant investment and degree of difficulty and required extremely close tolerances. Exhibit 11–3 lists the major parts of a chain saw along with an estimate of the percentage of total costs represented by each part for a gas chain saw model with annual production volume of 100,000 units. There were economies of scale in the production of most of the significant components of the saw. There were also cost savings due to automation, particularly in machining and assembly. The total tooling investment required to produce all these parts (except saw chain, guide bars, and sprockets) for a chain saw model was estimated at approximately $300,000–$500,000 in 1972.

Chain saw manufacturers varied greatly in their level of vertical integration, with the manufacturer shown in Exhibit 11–3 having approximately an average level of integration. The very largest manufacturers were almost completely integrated, though they usually purchased some saw chain, bars, and other specialized parts. Saw chain and bar manufacture required significant investment and involved quite sophisticated and often proprietary technology that had been mastered by specialist outside suppliers. Medium-size firms purchased attachments as well as die-castings and sometimes forgings, doing most of their own machining and then assembly. There were some very small manufacturers that were solely assembly operations. Industry participants believed that integration lowered unit costs if the volume of parts produced internally was large relative to volumes produced by specialist outside suppliers. Specialized suppliers existed for all the major chain saw components, and many had been supplying the industry for decades. In carburetors, for example, there were specialized outside suppliers with such great annual and accumulated volumes that no chain saw manufacturer produced carburetors in-house. An approximate breakdown of costs for a typical chain saw manufacturer is shown in Table 11-8.

It was estimated that an efficient, highly integrated chain saw manufacturing facility with two production lines required a capital investment in excess of $15 million for a productive capacity of 600 saws per day. A less integrated plant had a lower minimum efficient scale and capital cost.

The Electric Chain Saw Market

Electric chain saws had a number of characteristics that made them quite different from gas saws. The majority of electric saws sold for less than $50 and were capable of only low horsepower levels.[2] Horse-

TABLE 11-8. Costs of Chain Saw Manufacture

Purchased parts and material	45-70%
Direct labor	7-10%
Indirect labor and overhead	24-40%
Total manufacturing costs	100%

SOURCE: Estimates based on manufacturer and supplier interviews.

[2] The cost of a long heavy-duty extension cord added $10-20 to the cost of an electric saw for a customer who did not already have one.

power of electric saws was inherently limited by the amperage capacity of conventional electrical wiring.

Electric saws were sold primarily to the construction market, where the flammability of gasoline posed a safety hazard, and to casual users who had very low power requirements. The average casual purchaser of electric saws was generally believed to have some differences from the casual gas saw buyer in 1974. Electric saw purchasers were believed to be extremely price-sensitive and in some cases also less "outdoorsy" and less comfortable with tinkering with gasoline engines. Some observers also noted that electric saws were often purchased by women as gifts. Distribution of electric saws was primarily through contractor supply outlets, hardware chains, and home centers as part of the electric tool line. Almost no electric saws were sold through servicing dealers, who had little expertise in electric motor repair. Electric saws required little service, partly because of reliability of the electric motor and also because electric saws tended to be used less intensively than gas saws.

Competition

There were approximately a dozen major manufacturers of gasoline chain saws in 1974. Some of these also produced electric saws, but the markets for gas and electric saws were quite distinct. There were major competitors in electric saws who did not produce gas saws, and vice versa. The largest firms and their estimated market positions are shown in Table 11-9.

Stihl and Solo were German companies; Jonsereds, Husqvarna, and Partner were based in Sweden; Echo was based in Japan and Pioneer was based in Canada. Each was a significant producer outside the United States.[3]

European firms had been the early pioneers in the chain saw industry and still maintained technological leadership according to most observers. The other major competitors were U.S. firms (Pioneer was based in Canada), having grown up largely

[3] In addition to the non-U.S. firms listed, a number of other producers such as Danarm, Dolmar, and Alpina exported minor volumes to the United States. None were considered significant factors in the market.

TABLE 11–9.   Estimated U.S. Market Shares of Gas Chain Saws[a] *(in units)*

	1970	1971	1972	1973
Homelite	35%	31%	28%	28%
McCulloch	33%	33%	27%	27%
Remington/DESA			8%	12%
Beaird-Poulan			8%	
Stihl			7–8%	6%
Roper			6%	
Pioneer			4%	
Skil			3%	
Echo (entered 1972)			1%	

Very Small Share in the United States:
  Husqvarna
  Jonsereds
  Partner
  Solo

[a] Omitted figures were not available.
SOURCE: Manufacturer interviews.

since World War II. Homelite and McCulloch sold outside the United States as well as domestically, exporting 10–20 percent of their volume to other countries, while the other U.S. companies were largely domestic competitors only. Stihl had a relatively small but stable share in the United States, and Echo had recently entered the U.S. market (1972). The other non-U.S. firms had very small shares in the U.S. markets, met exclusively through exports. Tariffs on chain saws were significant in the United States as in other countries, in the range of 5 to 15 percent. The estimated 1972 domestic dollar sales of chain saws of the leading U.S. firms is shown in Table 11–10.

A profile of each of the major competitors is given below. Exhibit 11–4 summarizes their product lines, Exhibit 11–5 their prices, Exhibit 11–6 their advertising spending, and Exhibit 11–7 their corporate financial results.

TABLE 11–10.   1972 Manufacturer Sales in U.S. Market

	(millions)
Homelite	$30
McCulloch	30
Remington/DESA	11
Beaird-Poulan	9
Roper	6
Pioneer	4
Skil	3

SOURCE: Industry interviews.

Homelite

Homelite was a division of Textron, Inc., having been acquired in 1955. Textron had more than thirty divisions in many diverse businesses, which were overseen by a corporate staff of fewer than 100 people. Divisions were managed very autonomously but were measured and compensated based on strict annual return-on-investment criteria. A group vice president monitored division results and consulted on major decisions but did not interfere with operations.

Homelite had been the leader in the U.S. chain saw industry for many years, and had been one of Textron's most successful divisions, though its market share had declined slightly in recent years. The division was one of the top Textron profit contributors. In addition to chain saws, the Homelite Division produced lawn and garden equipment, snowblowers, and some construction equipment such as pumps and generators. While chain saws were by far the largest part of division sales, Homelite's other businesses were being expanded through new product introductions.

Homelite produced a very wide product line in chain saws with a large number of models and engine sizes. It sought to produce a high-quality product, which was marketed to all the major market segments through an extensive network of servicing dealers. Homelite sought to segment the market and offer saws aimed at all the significant customer groups. Separate marketing managers directed activities in the consumer and professional markets. Homelite had been a pioneer in producing lightweigh chain saws in the 1960s, but in 1973 its products were not known as leaders in safety and comfort features.

Homelite was unique in the industry in its policy of in-house distribution. Homelite had more than forty in-house distributors, and these distributors served more than 10,000 authorized dealers. Homelite was particularly strong in hardware stores and farm stores and sold Homelite-brand saws to J. C. Penney. Homelite did not sell through mass merchandisers or for private label. Homelite spent heavily on advertising, including some consumer advertising of the Homelite brand name using television, magazines, and radio, as well as dealer-oriented advertising and advertising directed toward the farmer. Homelite also utilized occasional price promotions on selected models.

Homelite manufactured chain saws in two plants in North and South Carolina, constructed in 1957 and 1959. Homelite was not integrated into die-casting but manufactured its own bars and purchased saw chain from its sister division, Townsend, which manufactured precision metal parts. Townsend had entered into saw chain manufacturing in 1971 in a South Carolina facility.

McCulloch Corporation

McCulloch had long been a highly regarded manufacturer of chain saws and other products using small, two-cycle gasoline engines, and had been a pioneer in the U.S. chain saw industry. Until 1973 McCulloch had been privately held, and its chairman was Robert McCulloch, who was also chairman of McCulloch Oil. He had long been heavily involved in R&D and had worked on designing products ranging from electronic ball cups for golf greens to diesel aircraft engines. Bob McCulloch had also gained some notoriety for being instrumental in moving the London Bridge to Arizona and had shifted some McCulloch chain saw operations there to provide an employment base as well. Robert McCulloch had made several attempts in the previous decade to diversify the company into other areas. Ventures in outboard motors, snowmobile engines, and other products had proved unsuccessful, however. By 1973 McCulloch was in serious financial difficulty (due in part to some bad real estates ventures), even though its overall sales had grown from $41 million in 1963 to $75 million in 1973. Top management attention to the chain saw business had lagged.

McCulloch was acquired by Black & Decker in September 1973. The acquisition was immediately challenged by the Justice Department, and the matter was pending in early 1974. Black & Decker had been actively seeking entry into new markets from its strong base in power tools. Black & Decker's business was divided approximately as follows in 1974:[4]

U.S. power tools	35%
International power tools	50%
McCulloch	15%

[4] William P. Maloney, "An Analysis of Black and Decker Manufacturing Company," C. S. McKee & Company.

The power tool market in the United States was mature, with an estimated growth rate of 5–8 percent per year. Black & Decker had approximately a 40–45 percent market share in the power tool industry, well ahead of Sears with an estimated 25 percent and Skil Corporation with an estimated 8–10 percent. Black & Decker was known for extremely strong financial controls, a cost-conscious manufacturing orientation, and a product policy that ruthlessly weeded out less profitable lines. The company was known to have used the Boston Consulting Group for strategic advice and had followed an aggressive strategy in leading the power tool industry.

McCulloch offered a wide line of chain saws sold through a large network of servicing dealers to all the major market segments. It had more than twenty-five distributors nationwide, three of which were company-owned, and approximately 8,000–10,000 dealers. McCulloch had begun selling to mass merchandisers in 1973, the only major manufacturer to do so. Its market share had been increasing until recently as a result of its leadership in introducing lighter, less expensive chain saws, though its position in the professional segment had been eroding. McCulloch had been a technological leader in manufacturing techniques for chain saws.

McCulloch had a relatively integrated manufacturing facility in Los Angeles, California, producing its own die-casting and bars. The facility had been in operation for many years, and McCulloch had established a new facility in Arizona, where chain saw manufacturing operations were being gradually moved.

Desa Industries (Remington)

The chain saw division of Desa Industries had formerly been a unit of Remington Arms until its sale in August 1969. Desa was a mini-conglomerate that purchased troubled companies, and Remington had been in that category when Desa purchased it. In 1973 Desa was known to be in serious financial difficulty and short of capital.

Chain saws were sold under the Remington name. Remington had a moderately wide line of saws. A major portion of its output went to Montgomery Ward and John Deere under private label, and most of the rest was sold to other large chain accounts through a sales force of thirty-five manufacturers' reps (who represented other noncompeting manufacturers). Remington had little penetration of servicing dealers. It had a relatively strong position in electric chain saws.

Remington had a manufacturing facility most observers regarded as less efficient than those of the industry leaders, with a very low level of vertical integration and a low level of automation and use of special purpose machinery.

Beaird-Poulan

Based in Louisiana, Beaird-Poulan had been an independent manufacturer of chain saws until its acquisition by Emerson Electric in 1972. Emerson, with 1973 sales of $937 million, had more than twenty divisions producing a wide range of consumer and industrial products, including commercial and industrial components and systems, consumer goods, and government and defense products. Many of Emerson's products were in the electrical and electromechanical area, such as electric motors, controls, drives, and heating, ventilating, and air conditioning equipment. Emerson divisions were managed with considerable autonomy but were measured on growth and return on invested capital. Corporate targets were 15 percent growth in sales annually, with return on invested capital of at least 20 percent. Emerson placed extremely strong emphasis on planning and the setting of detailed objectives, and also emphasized cost reduction. Incentive payments based on performance could be a large part of division management compensation. Emerson had an annual cost reduction program with specific cost reduction goals at each division. The company had a stated goal of being the low-cost producer in each of its markets. Divisions that could not meet Emerson's goals were divested.

Beaird-Poulan offered a moderately wide line of chain saws, which were sold primarily to the private label market, and to a lesser extent under its Poulan brand to large accounts. Beaird-Poulan products were of acceptable but not premium quality and were sold at low prices. There had been little emphasis on safety features or product innovation. Aside from low price saws, Beaird-Poulan had some strength in professional saws designed for pulpwood logging, which was practiced heavily in the Southeast United States. Beaird-Poulan's major customers were Western Auto, Quality Farm and Fleet, Sears, and other large chains. It had recently joined Roper as a private label supplier to Sears, supplying Sears with its small 1.9-cubic-inch saws. Beaird-Poulan also had a network of servicing dealers, which accounted for less than 25 percent of sales. Poulan dealers, who numbered less than 3,000, were strongest in the South and generally smaller and less established than Homelite or McCulloch dealers.

Beaird-Poulan manufactured chain saws at a longstanding facility in Shreveport, Louisiana. It purchased most die-castings, saw chain, and bars from outside suppliers.

Stihl

Stihl was the world's leading producer of chain saws in 1973. Correctly named Andreas Stihl Maschinenfabrik, Stihl was a privately controlled firm headquartered in Germany. Stihl employed more than 2,000 people in 1972 and had more than 60 percent of the West German market. Stihl exported 80 percent of its production to more than one hundred countries, including approximately 70,000 units to the United States. Its world wide corporate sales had been $56 million in 1972 and had risen to $124 million by 1974. Stihl also produced gasoline-powered industrial cutting saws. While Stihl had exported saws for sale in the United States for decades, it had also begun limited assembly of one model of saw at a U.S. facility in Virginia in the fall of 1974.

Stihl produced a very wide line of premium quality saws for sale primarily to the pro and farmer market segments. Its products were universally acknowledged as the quality standard of the industry, and Stihl had long offered safety and comfort features just now being introduced by U.S. firms.

Stihl sold its products only through servicing dealers, a policy to which it adhered strictly. Its dealer organization was large in relation to the other non-U.S. firms, and Stihl dealers were known to be particularly knowledgeable and loyal to Stihl. Industry observers readily admitted that Stihl's dealer organization was also first in quality of servicing.

Stihl promoted heavily in the trade journals and at industry trade shows, stressing its leadership in the industry and its commitment to the servicing dealer.

Stihl manufactured most of its saws in Germany, though it also had a plant in Brazil in addition to the new U.S. assembly operation. Stihl was the most fully integrated of the chain saw manufacturers, producing all engine parts, most of its own bars and sprockets, and all of its saw chain. Stihl had also developed proprietary special machinery and processes for magnesium die-casting of engine parts and for machining operations and had its own tooling group, which designed and manufactured the machinery used in Stihl production facilities. Stihl's production strategy was characterized by observers as being one of extremely high quality and relatively high cost. No sacrifices in quality were made in the interests of cost. Stihl saws were also heavier than competitor saws for any given cubic inch displacement and bar length. Stihl's new U.S. assembly facility assembled only its smallest 015 model saw, which was designed for the casual user segment of the market.

Roper Corporation

Roper Corporation had been a major supplier to Sears for more than forty years, with Sears accounting for more than half of Roper's sales. Roper supplied Sears with electric ranges, gas ranges, and other hardgoods, and Roper's Outdoor Products Company supplied Sears with chain saws. Sears' employee pension fund owned 40 percent of Roper's common stock.

Until 1971 Roper had been the sole supplier of chain saws to Sears. Sears had worked with Roper over the years to develop competitive chain saws and to improve and update Roper's product line. In 1963, when Homelite introduced the XL-12 lightweight saw, Sears pressured Roper to follow. Roper had developed the new 3.7-cubic-inch engine for saws, which went on the market in 1968, and had purchased the design for a 1.9-cubic-inch engine in 1969.

When Sears first bought saws from another supplier (Beaird-Poulan) in 1971, Roper began thinking about selling saws to others. Until 1973 Roper's ouput went exclusively to Sears, but in that year Roper began selling saws under its own brand name

and to other private label accounts. Roper was making efforts to develop a servicing dealer network, though it had as yet achieved little increase in its dealer network by early 1974.

The Roper product line was limited and focused on the middle horsepower range, reflecting its heavy emphasis on Sears. Roper had little or no brand recognition. Roper products were serviced by Sears's service organization. In 1973 Roper had established a new chain saw production facility in Nogales, Mexico, which replaced its Illinois facility and increased capacity 100 percent in the process.[5]

Jonsereds

Jonsereds was the leading Swedish saw in terms of U.S. sales. The company was part of a large privately held Swedish holding company, about which information was scarce. Jonsereds' corporate sales were approximately $30 million in 1973, and the company produced woodworking machinery and tools and hydraulic loaders in addition to chain saws.

Jonsereds produced high quality saws primarily for the pro and farmer market segments. It sold a relatively small number of models, though it covered a relatively wide horsepower range. Swedish loggers generally used smaller saws than loggers in the United States. Distribution for Jonsereds in the United States was handled by two companies: Tilton Equipment in the East, and Scotsco in the West. Tilton, owned by two aggressive ex-Homelite salesmen, accounted for the great majority of Jonsereds's U.S. sales. It had four stocking locations. Jonsereds's saws were distributed to servicing dealers. The company had no marketing personnel of its own in the United States and promoted exclusively through the trade press.

Jonsereds manufactured all its saws in Sweden and was not integrated into bars or saw chain. It purchased these items from Canadian and U.S. suppliers.

Skil Corporation

Skil was a major producer of power tools, with 1973 sales of $107 million and an estimated market share

---

[5] Tariffs for importing chain saws into the United States from Mexico were nominal.

in power tools of 8–10 percent. Skil distributed power tools through 300 distributors to 25,000 retail outlets, primarily in hardware and home improvement, and through 4,000 industrial distributors to a wide variety of industrial customers. Skil had seventy-five Factory Service Centers nationwide and more than 350 authorized service agents.

Skil had a small line of high-quality chain saws, both gas and electric, which were sold through its power tool distribution channels. Approximately 50 percent of its outlets carried its chain saws. The primary target market was contractors.

Kioritz Corporation of America (Echo)

Kioritz Corporation, a Japanese company, was one of the world's largest manufacturers of two-cycle gasoline engines, and had a reputation for being a high-quality engine producer. It sold its engines to OEM's and had a large share of the market for snowmobile motors. Kioritz also manufactured a successful line of gas-powered products such as snow blowers, power scythes, power dusters, and misters for sale worldwide. Its products were sold under the Echo name. Kioritz's sales were in the $20 million to $40 million range.

Kioritz entered the U.S. chain saw market in 1972 using the Echo name. Echo's product line was initially composed of a relatively small number of models covering a wide horsepower range. Echo was aggressively seeking to build a servicing dealer network, offering high dealer margins, but it still had a very small network in early 1974. Echo was also pursuing private label sales. A major portion of Echo's sales were currently private label saws sold through John Deere's network of farm equipment stores. Echo was known to be trying to sell saws to Sears and Montgomery Ward and had sold saws to Sears in 1973, when Beaird-Poulan could not manufacture enough 1.9-cubic-inch saws to meet demand.

Echo saws were manufactured in Japan.

Husqvarna

Husqvarna was a Swedish firm that exported chain saws for sale in the United States. It also produced a variety of other products including refrigerators, motorcycles, sewing machines, and lawn mowers. Chain saws represented approximately 20 percent of total worldwide revenues of approximately $140 million. Husqvarna had recently been in financial difficulty because of soaring wage and benefit costs, which were prevalent in Swedish industry.

Husqvarna sold premium quality chain saws at premium prices primarily to the pro and farmer market segments. It had a company-owned sales subsidiary located in New Jersey and sold its products through five exclusive distributors to a network of servicing dealers. Its products were known for their excellent safety features. Promotion was solely through trade publications.

Husqvarna manufactured all its saws in Sweden. It was not integrated into saw chain, bars, or engine castings.

Solo

Solo was a German firm that manufactured a range of gasoline-powered equipment including mopeds, mist blowers, rototillers, and chain saws, with sales of approximately $25 million in 1973. Although Solo was one of the leading European manufacturers of small gasoline engines, rivaling Stihl, chain saws were not a major product for the company. Solo's chain saw product line was quite similar in size and appearance to Stihl's, though Solo had a narrower product line than Stihl. Observers termed Solo's strategy "me-too" with regard to Stihl.

Solo had no manufacturing or marketing subsidiary in the United States, exporting a small number of saws for sale through servicing dealers. Its European production operations were not integrated into the production of saw chains or bars.

Partner

Partner was a Swedish firm with sales of approximately $17 million in 1973, which produced chain saws and cutting machinery. It sold large, powerful saws primarily for the pro and farmer segments. It had no manufacturing or marketing facilities in the United States and exported saws for sale in the United States through a small network of servicing dealers. Partner manufactured two large saws (3.4 and 4.0 cubic inch) for Skil, which were used to round out Skil's product line. Skil, in turn, manufactured smaller saws used by Partner to round out its European product line.

Pioneer

Pioneer, a Canadian firm, was a unit of the Outboard Marine Corporation (OMC), having been acquired by OMC in 1965. OMC produced marine outboard motors, lawn mowers, and other products, and had sales of $472 million in 1973 with a return on equity of 16.3 percent. Chain saws represented 2.3 percent of OMC sales in 1973, or $10.9 million.

Pioneer offered four models of chain saws primarily directed at the farm and professional buyer. It sold exclusively through specialty chain saw dealers. Its market position in Canada was relatively stronger than that in the United States, and it had a significant position in Europe as well, with a well-developed dealer organization there.

Competition in Electric Chain Saws

The market for electric saws was quite distinct from the gas saw market. While Skil, McCulloch, Homelite, and a number of other gas saw companies also produced electric saws, Remington, Wen, and Singer dominated the electric chain saw market. Wen was an independent company producing a range of portable power tool products. Singer manufactured electric chain saws for Sears, along with a line of other electric tools. Neither Wen nor Singer manufactured gas saws. Remington had the Ward account for electric saws and sold to other chains.

EXHIBIT 11-1. *Diagram of a Gas Chain Saw*
Diagram of a Gas Chain Saw

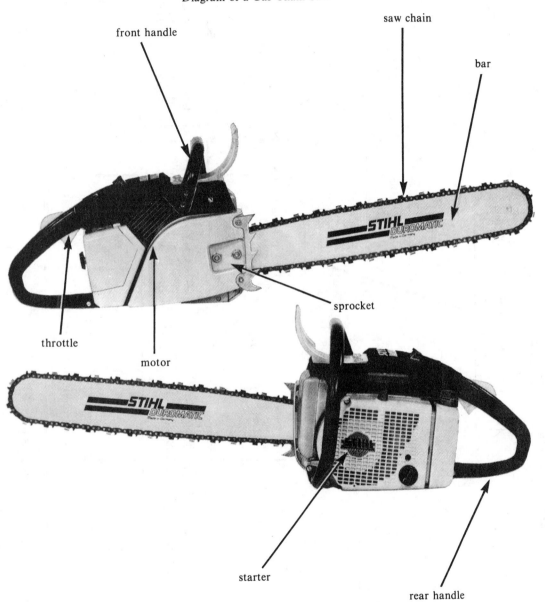

EXHIBIT 11-2. *Distribution Channels for Chain Saws*[a]

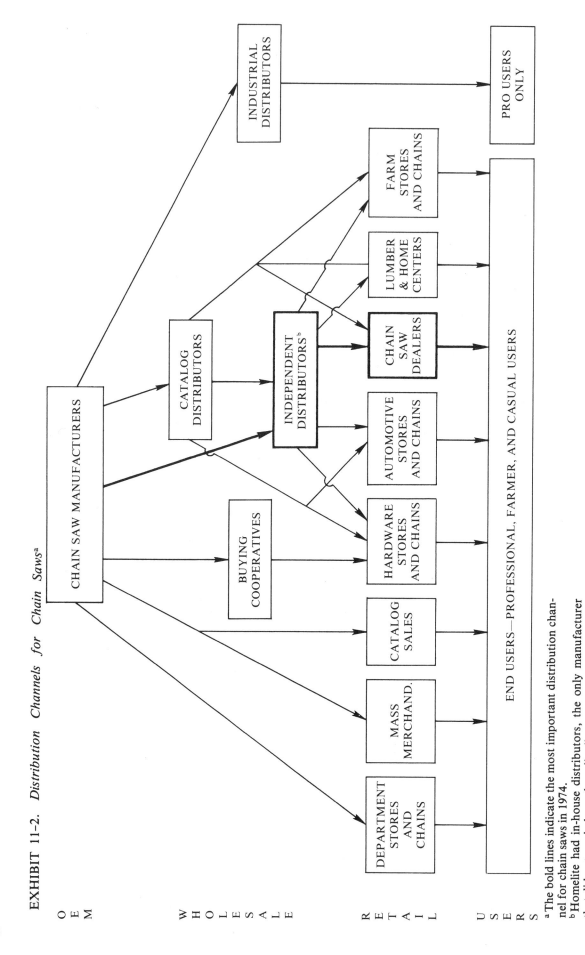

O
E
M

W
H
O
L
E
S
A
L
E

R
E
T
A
I
L

U
S
E
R
S

[a] The bold lines indicate the most important distribution channel for chain saws in 1974.

[b] Homelite had in-house distributors, the only manufacturer
that did not use independent distributors.

SOURCE: Manufacturer, distributor, and retailer interviews.

EXHIBIT 11-3. *Chain Saw Manufacturing Costs*[a]

	Percent of Unit Costs
Purchased Parts:	
Guide bar, saw chain, and sprocket	16.1
Carburetor	6.0
Ignition	6.0
Starter	6.6
Clutch	1.1
Piston	2.1
Total purchased parts	37.9%
Magnesium & Aluminum Die-Castings:	
Crankcase cover	4.5%
Rear handle	1.1
Oil tank cover	1.1
Sprocket cover	0.6
Cylinder	2.7
Total die-casting	10.0%
Plastic Parts:	
Various	3.1%
Forgings:	
Crankshaft	1.5%
Connecting rod	0.8
Stampings:	
Muffler, brackets, etc.	1.5
Bearings, Gaskets, Seals:	
Various	3.2
Miscellaneous	6.7
Total material	64.7%
Labor Costs:	
Die-cast machining	2.7%
Forging machining	2.8
Heat treatment	0.1
Chrome and copper plate	2.7
Subassembly[b]	1.6
Final assembly[b]	4.0
	13.9%

[a] Manufacturing cost of gas chain saw, assuming annual production volume of 100,000 units and average level of vertical integration for the industry.
[b] May include some overhead.

SOURCE: Testimony of DESA Industries, preliminary antitrust hearings against Black & Decker, 1972.

EXHIBIT 11-4. *Product Lines of Major Chain Saw Competitors, 1972–1973*

Cubic Inches

Company	1.0	2.0	3.0	4.0	5.0	6.0	7.0	8.0	9.0
Homelite (1 electric)	X	X XX	X / X X / X	XG X / XG XX	XG	XG / X X			
McCulloch (1 electric)	X / X X / X		X / X X X	XG / X X	XG / X	XG / X	X		
Stihl	XX / XX	X	XG / X X / X	X / X	X	XG / X		X	
Beaird-Poulan (1 electric)	X	X / X	X / X / X	X / X XG	XG / X				
Jonsereds		X / X	X X X X X	X		X			
Husqvarna			DATA NOT AVAILABLE						
Remington (3 electric)		X X / X X / X	X X	X / X	X / X X				
Roper (2 electrics)	X / X		X / X / X						
Skil (3 electrics)		X / X / X		X / X					
Echo	X	X	XX X	X		X			
Sears (3 electrics)	X	X / XX	X / X / X / X						

NOTE: X = gas chain saw model; X's aligned vertically are models with the same cubic inch engine.

SOURCES: Company product literature and manufacturer and retailer interviews.

EXHIBIT 11–5. *Comparative Manufacturer Prices in 1972*

PRICE PER CUBIC INCH
OF DISPLACEMENT

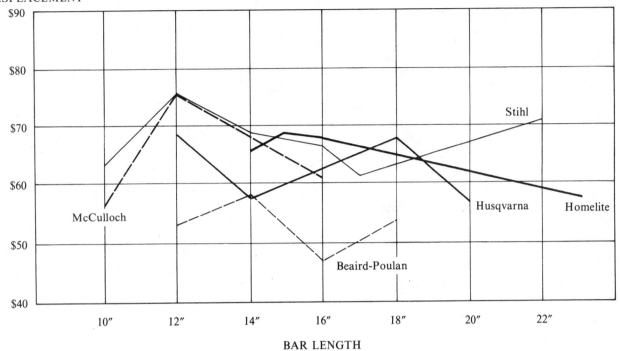

PRICE PER CUBIC INCH
OF DISPLACEMENT

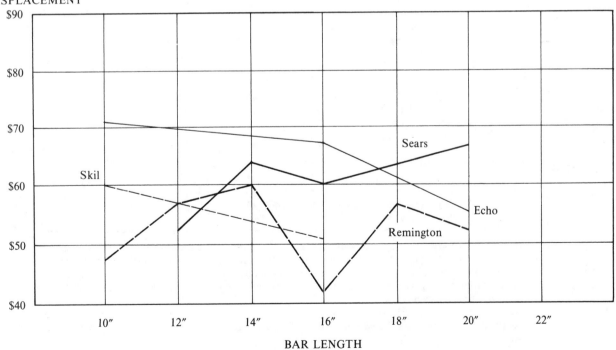

EXHIBIT 11-6. *U.S. National Consumer Advertising of Chain Saws by Leading Chain Saw Manufacturers, 1969-1973*[a] *(thousands of dollars)*

	1969	1970	1971	1972	1973
Beaird-Poulan[b]					
Total	—	$ 62.2	$ 109.8	$261.9	$ 399.5
Magazines	—	59.6	76.4	166.9	121.9
Network television	—	—	—	48.2	238.3
Spot television	—	1.3	32.4	46.0	38.6
Desa Industries (Remington)					
Total	$ 29.7	31.1	25.2	—	47.2
Magazines	29.7	30.1	24.8	—	46.0
Network television	—	—	—	—	—
Spot television	—	—	—	—	—
Husquarva					
Total	—	—	—	—	—
Magazines	—	—	—	—	—
Network television	—	—	—	—	—
Spot television	—	—	—	—	—
Jonsereds					
Total	—	—	—	—	—
Magazines	—	—	—	—	—
Network television	—	—	—	—	—
Spot television	—	—	—	—	—
McCulloch[c]					
Total	119.5	484.2	788.1	973.3	1340.8
Magazines	119.5	176.6	114.0	109.5	238.1
Network television	—	—	—	456.8	743.7
Spot television	—	307.5	659.8	377.4	289.2
Roper					
Total	—	—	—	—	0.4
Magazines	—	—	—	—	—
Network television	—	—	—	—	—
Spot television	—	—	—	—	0.4
Stihl					
Total	92.2	49.6	93.6	167.7	329.7
Magazines	92.2	49.6	44.7	73.1	53.4
Network television	—	—	—	—	246.9
Spot television	—	—	48.9	93.9	29.0
Homelite (div. of Textron)					
Total	825.5	864.5	1288.2	958.7	1025.9
Magazines	555.5	360.7	361.8	170.2	223.4
Network television	270.0	322.1	568.7	643.9	595.4
Spot television	—	168.7	338.8	141.2	164.2

[a] Advertising figures are for advertising of chain saws only. The data omit cooperative advertising by retailers, the cost of which is shared with manufacturers. Cooperative advertising, significant in the industry, was believed to be the highest as a percent of total advertising for pro-oriented firms such as Stihl. For Stihl cooperative advertising was as much as 50 percent of total advertising.
[b] Acquired by Emerson Electric in 1972.
[c] Acquired by Black & Decker Manufacturing Company in 1973.

SOURCE: Leading National Advertisers, Inc., *National Advertising Investments,* January–December 1969, 1970, 1971, 1972, and 1973.

EXHIBIT 11-7. Selected Corporate Financial Information for Publicly Held Chain Saw Manufacturers (millions of dollars)

	1964	1965	1966	1967	1968	1969	1970	1971	1972	1973
Black & Decker										
Sales	$101.0	$121.5	$146.8	$168.6	$189.7	$221.8	$255.4	$286.7	$345.7	$427.0
Net income	8.8	11.0	13.0	14.3	15.4	17.6	19.5	22.0	26.6	33.3
Return on sales (ROS)	8.7	9.1	8.9	8.5	8.1	7.9	7.6	7.7	7.7	7.8
Debt/equity (%)	—	.1	.2	.4	.4	.3	.3	.2	.1	.1
Return on equity	15.8	18.1	19.2	19.0	18.4	19.0	18.4	16.3	15.7	17.0
Capital expenditures	—	6.8	9.7	10.7	5.6	7.7	16.7	16.1	20.1	29.2
McCulloch Corporation (acquired by Black & Decker in 1973)										
Sales						45.4	43.2	50.6	58.9	73.1
% Chain saws									86%	81.6%
Net income						2.7	0.4	(4.4)	(0.6)	1.1
Market value of shares paid by Black & Decker										66.7[a]
Emerson Electric										
Sales	$219.3	$252.7	$348.0	$395.2	$522.0	$628.4	$657.0	$656.4	$764.7	$936.6
Sales of consumer products						217.8	239.7	254.1	290.0	317.9
Net income in consumer products						17.4	18.5	19.1	22.3	21.0
ROS—consumer products						8.0	7.7	7.5	7.7	6.6
Net income	15.0	17.6	26.4	30.2	39.5	49.9	54.6	56.1	63.6	75.9
ROS	6.8	7.0	7.6	7.7	7.6	7.9	8.3	8.6	8.3	8.1
Debt/equity (%)	6.5	5.4	13.8	20.5	17.0	14.1	11.9	12.6	10.7	9.9
Return on equity	15.2	16.1	18.3	18.7	18.2	17.8	17.3	16.6	16.5	17.0
Capital expenditures	6.3	9.4	17.1	12.2	19.4	23.9	20.5	21.4	26.6	40.8
Roper Corporation										
Sales	$108.2	$125.4	$164.9	$177.9	$200.2	$205.4	$204.3	$212.6	$251.7	$293.9
Net income	3.3	4.5	4.8	4.2	6.1	5.0	4.7	5.4	6.9	7.5
ROS	3.0	3.6	2.9	2.4	3.0	2.4	2.3	2.5	2.7	2.6
Debt/equity (%)	19.8	28.8	56.7	58.1	85.4	81.0	90.6	84.7	98.2	132.6
ROE	10.5	13.1	10.6	8.8	11.2	8.6	7.8	8.4	9.7	9.8
Skil Corporation										
Sales	$33.5	$39.7	$48.4	$51.2	$63.2	$68.9	$61.6	$74.3	$94.8	$106.8
Net income	2.6	3.1	3.7	2.4	3.1	3.2	.9	2.1	4.3	2.1
ROS	7.8	7.8	7.6	4.7	4.9	4.6	1.5	2.8	4.5	2.0
Debt/equity (%)	—	18.9	31.7	77.4	97.1	99.2	120.1	116.9	63.0	122.8
ROE	15.4	16.7	17.8	11.1	13.0	12.4	3.7	7.7	12.1	5.8
Textron										
Sales	$720.2	$851.0	$1132.2	$1445.0	$1704.1	$1682.2	$1611.9	$1603.7	$1678.4	$1858.4
% sales—consumer products					24%	26%	27%	31%		
% pretax net income—consumer products					37%	40%	40%	48%		
Net income after taxes	22.1	29.1	43.9	61.5	74.0	76.1	66.7	71.8	82.1	100.8
ROS (%)	3.1	3.4	3.9	4.2	4.3	4.5	4.1	4.5	4.9	5.4
Debt/equity (%)	34.9	25.0	25.1	18.3	31.5	27.8	36.5	28.8	37.2	33.7
ROE (%)	13.3	16.0	18.6	16.7	16.0	15.7	13.2	13.7	14.1	15.1
Capital expenditures	19.3	22.3	38.5	41.2	47.1	48.6	41.6	36.7	42.8	64.5

[a] Of this purchase price, $39.4 million was represented by the value of McCulloch Oil shares acquired.

CASE 12
The U.S. Securities Industry in 1979

The U.S. securities industry played a crucial role as an intermediary in the flow of capital in the U.S. economy. In the most general sense, the industry fulfilled three basic interrelated functions. First, it provided a mechanism to collect and channel capital from surplus, or savings sectors of the economy, to deficit, or investing sectors. Second, the industry facilitated the trading of securities among buyers and sellers and in so doing influenced the ability of industries and firms to expand and diversify. Finally, the industry provided investors with a wide range of investment vehicles with various degrees of liquidity as well as risk/return characteristics. Fulfilling these functions involved two different types of activity: the issuing and placement of new securities (known as investment banking), and the transfer of previously issued securities (known as secondary market activity).

The investment banking process was one in which the investment banker acted as agent for corporations or government bodies in the acquisition of long-term capital from individual or institutional investors (pension funds, insurance companies, etc.) In return for this capital the corporation or government issued a security, which could take the form of debt or equity. This security entitled the holder to dividends or interest and either the eventual repayment of the investor's principal or a permanent equity participation in the company.

In the securities brokerage process, the firm acted as agent for individual and institutional investors in the purchase or sale of investment products. Investment products included stocks, bonds, options, commodity futures, and mutual funds. Both investment banking and securities brokerage activity took place in securities markets, which included the New York Stock Exchange, the American Stock Exchange, regional stock exchanges, and the "Over-the-Counter Market."

Buyers and Sellers

CORPORATIONS

The securities industry assisted corporations in the acquisition of long-term capital. This was a complex process which depended on structuring a deal that would raise the required capital at the lowest cost and in a form most advantageous to the corporation. The deal, or issue, could take the form of debt or equity, either publicly or privately placed. Publicly placed securities were sold to investors through an exchange, while privately placed securities were sold directly to one or a small group of investors. There was an almost infinite range of variations within these broad categories, and each issue had a unique price and/or interest rate. Stock issues were the most standardized. If a company had previously "gone public," the price of the issue was based on the current market value of the stock. Bond issues, on the other hand, varied according to interest rate, maturity, protective covenants such as "call protection," and sinking funds. Hybrid securities such as convertible bonds exchangeable into stock were the most complex, because the value of such an option could not be definitely known. In addition, bonds or hybrid securities could contain covenants or special provisions that increased their value to potential investors.

The range of options in issuing securities was so broad that the investment banking process could be considered highly creative. The main determinants of the form an issue took were the state of the securities markets and the financial conditions of the issuer. The securities markets were constantly changing and subject to the influence of pervasive but subtle sociopolitical factors such as the "state of the economy," "investor psychology," present and anticipated inflation rates, government spending, and so on. Because of this, each issue was unique, and a thorough knowledge of the state of the financial markets was critical to the success of an issue. In addition, the process had become considerably more complex because of increased regulation.

There had been a sharp acceleration in the dollar volume of new corporate issues from $12 billion in 1963 to more than $54 billion in 1978. The mix of issues between public and private placement and debt versus equity had varied somewhat during this period, reflecting conditions in the various markets for these financial assets. Exhibit 12-1 presents the volume and type of corporate financing for the years 1968–1978. The rapid rise in the dollar value of corporate offerings had been accompanied by a significant decline in the number of issues being brought to market, from more than 4,000 in 1969 to 1,600 for the first eleven months of 1978. As a result the average size of an issue increased from approximately $5 million in 1965 to almost $35 million in 1978. Many observers believed that these larger issues were also more complex.

Exhibit 12-2 presents data on the volume and type of securities by type of issuer. Regulated industries such as utilities, transportation, and communication had accounted for 40 percent of new securities offerings in 1977, the latest date for which this information was available. Table 12-1 shows the number and size of new issues by type of issuer in 1977.

Wide distribution had become increasingly important in corporate security issues in the 1970s. Experience in the 1960s had shown that when a small number of institutions held large portions of a company's stock, the price of the stock and by implication the financial well-being of the company became extremely sensitive to these institutions' investment decisions. When stock was distributed among a large number of investors, however, price

TABLE 12-1. Average Size and Total Number of Issues in 1977 by Type of Issuer

	Total Number	Average Size (millions of $)	Total Volume (millions of $)
Manufacturing	513	$24	12,225
Extractive	124	21	2,589
Electric, gas and water	302	44	13,199
Transportation	61	27	1,641
Communication (primarily telephone)	77	56	4,353
Sales and consumer finance	74	27	2,016
Financial and real estate	266	36	9,549
Commercial and other	391	9	3,386

SOURCES: *S.E.C. Statistical Bulletin,* February 1979; casewriter's calculations.

fluctuations were less extreme, and it was believed the company would also be less vulnerable to takeover attempts.

Corporate issuers varied a great deal. Principal differences among corporations included size, profitability, the nature of business, and the sophistication of the financial officer, as well as investors' views of their growth potential and future profitability. These factors not only determined a firm's ability to raise capital and the cost and complexity of its issues but also resulted in differences in the frequency with which a corporation needed to enter the securities markets. Some corporations issued new securities once or twice a decade, while others did so two or three times a year. In general, corporate financial officers appeared to be gaining in sophistication as a generation of MBA-trained executives entered increasingly senior levels.

Raising capital was an ongoing process at most corporations. A single new issue could be completed within one month or could take as long as five years from conception to execution. Public issues were the most complex. A security could not be sold to the public until a prospectus or registration statement containing data on the issuer's business operations, competition, financial condition, and the purpose of the offering had been filed with the Securities and Exchange Commission. Since a prospectus did not become effective until thirty days after it had been submitted to the SEC, a public issue took at least thirty days. When the prospectus could be prepared by updating a previous prospectus, it could take less than a day to prepare. However, when the investment banker had to prepare an entirely new prospectus it could take as long as six months. Discussions on the specific form of an issue and special conditions such as covenants took additional time. Finally, corporations and their investment bankers watched the financial markets very closely to determine the best time to offer the issue. It was believed that the fluid nature of the securities markets made timing a key factor determining the success of an issue. Within limits, the issuing process could be sped up or slowed down to take advantage of favorable market conditions. The immediacy of an issuer's need for capital influenced its timing. When the need was not pressing and the financial markets were unfavorable, an issuer could wait out an entire economic cycle

before making a public offering. Private placements did not require a prospectus and could be completed within days.

Assistance in the acquisition of long-term capital was only one of a number of investment banking activities. Corporations also used investment bankers for financial counseling in such areas as capital structure, employee stock option plans, dividend reinvestment programs, lease financing, and advice on mergers and acquisitions, to name but a few.

Decisions on investment banking relationships were made at the highest level of a corporation, and the process of evaluating an investment banker was more or less continuous. The nature of the relationship between the corporation and its investment banker was both tangible and intangible. A survey done by *Fortune* magazine in 1971 indicated that personal relationships and the fact that a company had always used a specific firm were the chief factors in the choice of an investment banker. Historically, most investment banking relationships had been considered long-term. In fact, in the case of oil companies, railroads, and large industrial corporations such as General Motors and American Telephone & Telegraph, investment banking relationships were rooted in the nineteenth century, much to the benefit of so-called old line investment banking firms such as Morgan Stanley, First Boston, and Dillon, Read. Relationships were so close that investment bankers frequently sat on the boards of directors of client corporations. However, in the 1970s the nature of the relationship had begun to change as corporations began to switch to investment bankers or more likely to utilize a number of different bankers at once. The image or prestige associated with investment banking relationships was being supplanted by a relationship based more on service or performance.

As corporations increased in size and acquired increased financial sophistication, they were beginning to find new ways to attract capital without an investment banker's assistance. In 1978 corporations raised approximately $1 billion of capital through dividend reinvestment programs. Approximately 15 percent of all private placements were arranged through commercial banks or directly between the corporation and an institutional investor. Finally, in 1977 Exxon Corporation had issued over $50 million worth of debt securities through a "Dutch Auction." Institutional investors bid against securities firms, who competed only for the opportunity to distribute the securities.

GOVERNMENT

In 1978 the local, state, and federal governments issued $45 billion worth of new bonds. Government financing, also called municipal financing, took one of two forms: general obligation bonds or revenue bonds. General obligation bonds were backed by the issuer's ability to levy taxes and usually needed to be approved by taxpayers through referenda. Revenue bonds were repaid from the income of particular projects and were used to obtain funds for special projects such as hospitals, housing, solid waste disposal projects (these issues were known commonly as "sh-t" bonds), and so forth. Revenue bonds were also often issued under the sponsorship of a government agency on behalf of private corporations for the financing of pollution control or energy conservation projects. The primary difference between government and corporate debt securities was that interest paid on government issues was tax-free. The average size of government issues had increased from $5 million in 1965 to more than $30 million in 1979, and the proportion of government bonds represented by revenue bonds had increased from 32 percent in 1965 to approximately 60 percent in 1978.

INSTITUTIONAL INVESTORS

Institutional investors included private or corporate sponsored pension funds, public pension funds (state and local government employees' retirement funds), and insurance companies (life and casualty). As shown in Table 12-2, pension funds and insurance companies held 82 percent of all institutionally held corporate equities, 61 percent of institutionally owned government bonds, and 91 percent of institutionally held corporate bonds in 1977. Their total assets represented 53 percent of total institutional assets in 1977. Other institutions were

TABLE 12-2. Securities Holdings of Major Classes of Institutional Investors as of December 1977

	Dollar Holdings (billions)	*Percent of Total Assets*	*Dollar Holdings (billions)*	*Percent of Total Assets*
	LIFE INSURANCE COMPANIES		PRIVATE PENSION FUNDS	
Corporate equities	$ 33	10%	$102	55%
Government bonds	10	3	7	4
Corporate bonds	141	41	46	25
Other[a]	156.5	46	30.5	16
Total assets	$ 340.5	100%	$185.5	100%
	STATE AND LOCAL GOVERNMENT EMPLOYEE RETIREMENT FUNDS		OTHER INSURANCE COMPANIES (FIRE AND CASUALTY)	
Corporate equities	$ 30	23%	$ 17	16%
Government bonds	14	11	52	48
Corporate bonds	75	58	17	16
Other[a]	11	8	22.8	20
Total assets	$ 130	100%	$108.8	100%
	TOTAL INSTITUTIONAL SECTOR (INCLUDES SAVINGS AND LOAN ASSOCIATIONS)			
Corporate equities	$ 222	14%		
Government bonds	120	7		
Corporate bonds	309	19		
Other[a]	980	60		
Total assets	$1,630	100%		

[a] Includes cash, T-bills, mortgages.
SOURCE: Board of Governors of the U.S. Federal Reserve, Flow of Funds Accounts, August 1978.

such entities as savings and loan associations and mutual savings banks, whose assets consisted primarily of real estate mortgages.

The investment decisions of institutional investors had a significant impact on the U.S. capital markets. Decisions by each of these groups to increase their holdings of equity resulted in what industry observers termed the "institutionalization of the securities markets" in the 1960s. During this same period institutional investors also increased their rate of trading in the secondary market. Institutions' asset turnover, the portion of their portfolios traded for different securities during a year, increased from 15 percent in 1960 to a high of 35 percent in 1971–1972, while the average asset turnover in the securities markets as a whole rose from 12 to 20 percent during the same period. After a sharp decline in 1973–1974, institutions' asset turnover had risen again to more than 20 percent since 1975. Institutional trading of securities listed on the NYSE had risen from 30 percent of total trading volume in 1960 to 60 percent in 1979.

Historical changes in the behavior of institutions reflected changes in theories of portfolio management. The marked increase in institutional holdings of equity had reflected the belief that equity had the best long-term growth potential. Increased asset turnover reflected the belief that by trading equities frequently it would be possible to increase returns further by picking stocks that would outperform the market as a whole. However, by 1979 institutional portfolio management practices had changed somewhat in light of the fact that between 1969 and 1979 the average annual rate of return on bonds had been 5.8 percent, as against only 3.2 percent for stocks. In addition, proponents of the "efficient market theory" advised investors that price adjustments in the stock market occurred so quickly that it was impossible to outperform the market by actively trading stocks. As a result there had been a trend to less active portfolio management, less trading, and diversification away from equity.

For institutional investors money management was a full-time, professional activity. This activity could be handled by an in-house staff, by a bank trust department, or through investment management companies, some of which were subsidiaries of securities firms. Large insurance companies and publicly sponsored pension funds generally managed their funds in-house. Most corporate pension funds were managed by bank trust departments. Investment management companies generally had smaller staffs than bank trust departments, and because of this they were considered to be more flexible. They were also generally quicker to adopt more progressive techniques for portfolio management. Professional investment managers, including bank trust departments and investment management companies, also managed portfolios of wealthy individuals. Finally, investment management companies frequently managed mutual funds, municipal bond funds, and other similar investment vehicles designed to be sold to small individual investors. The total assets controlled by the ten largest institutional money managers were approximately 23 percent of the total holdings of insurance companies and pension funds.

Professional investment management organizations' staffs comprised a number of specialists including portfolio managers, research analysts, and traders. The portfolio manager was responsible for assembling or maintaining a portfolio to meet the investment objectives of the portfolio's beneficiary. Portfolios could be designed to maximize growth, maximize current income, or minimize risk. Research analysts were responsible for investigating different companies and industries to determine their investment potential. Institutional traders were responsible for arranging the actual purchase and sale of securities.

Within institutions, securities transactions took place constantly, and trading was an intense, highly professional activity. Institutional traders came to know their counterparts in other institutions. Institutional traders also had a thorough knowledge of the capabilities of the institutional trading departments of securities firms. They knew who could be counted upon to execute a tough trade, who would be willing to take substantial risks in block positioning, and whose advice could be trusted. Conversely, traders in securities firms came to know the preferences of institutional traders, their personalities, and the investment philosophies that motivated them.

INDIVIDUAL INVESTORS

The financial assets of individual investors included cash, real estate, and savings accounts as well as securities. According to flow of funds data, corporate equities, pension reserves, and life insurance accounted for 32, 21, and 5 percent of total individually owned financial assets respectively in 1977. At an estimated $734 billion, individual ownership represented over 75 percent of total ownership of corporate equity. On the other hand, the $65 billion worth of individually held corporate bonds represented less than 18 percent of total corporate bond holdings. The composition of individuals' portfolios had changed somewhat over time. Since 1962 individuals had been net sellers of equity, reducing the portion of their assets devoted to stock ownership. During this same period individuals increased the portion of their assets invested in pension benefits.

Other, newer types of financial assets were also being added to individual portfolios in the 1970s. The most noteworthy new investment vehicle was the stock option. By trading options (or promises to buy and sell stocks rather than trading stocks themselves) investors could take advantage of short-term fluctuations in the market value of a security while restricting their investment and potential capital loss to a fraction of the underlying value of the security. Options had a maximum maturity of nine months. The total value of options traded in 1979 was $18 billion, up from $10 billion in 1977 and $0.4 billion in 1973, when trading in options first began. Individuals accounted for 90 percent of options trading. The popularity of this type of investment led to the creation of different types of contracts including money market futures.

Mutual funds were another product designed for smaller individual investors. By pooling receipts into a large portfolio of securities, mutual funds enabled the small investor to diversify risk and gain the benefits of professional investment management. Mutual funds were typically invested in equity and had been very popular in the 1960s. However, common stock mutual fund redemptions had exceeded sales since 1970. The mutual fund concept had been recently applied to the creation of money market funds, tax-free bond funds, and the like, which were being aggressively marketed to individuals in the 1970s.

Individual participation in the securities markets reflected distribution of wealth among the population. Less than 15 percent of the population, approximately 26 million people, owned securities. The wealthiest 10 percent of the population owned more than 80 percent of the individually held common stock and the wealthiest 0.1 percent owned more than 40 percent. A New York Stock Exchange (NYSE) survey of individual owners of NYSE listed securities indicated that the average holder was fifty-two years old and had an annual income of $38,000. Individual holders of securities were geographically dispersed and typically bought and sold securities in small amounts. Industry observers suggest that only 10 percent of individual stock owners transacted enough business to generate $1,000 or more in annual commission revenue. Annual asset turnover rates for individual portfolios averaged about 12 percent in 1979.

Individual investors tended to be very risk-averse and relied heavily on the advice of the retail sales representative at their brokerage firm. They needed very specific advice—either to sell or to buy—and judged the quality of this advice entirely on the basis of results. A study of the individual investor done by the NYSE revealed that most investors, including the holders of large portfolios, felt that they did not understand the securities markets and did not know much about investing.

Securities Exchanges

Whenever corporations sold new securities to the public or investors wished to buy or sell securities, the transaction took place on a securities exchange. The securities exchanges included the New York Stock Exchange, the American Stock Exchange, the National Stock Exchange, and the regional stock exchanges. In these exchanges the securities firm acted as the agent for the buyer and seller in the transaction. Formalized securities exchanges performed an important function in the U.S. capital markets. They centralized trading in a security, concentrating all buyers and sellers in one market. As a result trading activity could be watched very closely both for the purpose of regulation and to publicize the prices at which transactions occurred. Publicizing prices established a market value, which reflected the supply and demand relationships reasonably accurately, and publicity assured the buyer a fair price.

Corporations paid a fee to have their securities listed on an exchange, and brokers paid fees for the privilege of transacting business on an exchange.

Participating brokers and corporations also had to abide by regulatory requirements established by the exchanges. Securities trading was influenced by a complex combination of variables, including the state of the economy and the world and national political situation. Price fluctuations in these markets assumed an almost mystical quality in spite of numerous theories that purported to "explain" their behavior. The volume of transactions and the rise or fall of prices on these markets were watched closely.

THE NEW YORK STOCK EXCHANGE (NYSE)

The first official U.S. stock exchange was formed on May 17, 1792, when a group of New York brokers, who had been doing business under a buttonwood tree on Wall Street, signed the Buttonwood Agreement. It began: "We the Subscribers, Brokers for the Purchase and Sale of Public Stock, do hereby solemnly promise and pledge ourselves to each other, that we will not buy or sell from this day for any person whatsoever, any kind of Public Stock, at less than one quarter of one percent Commission on the Specie value and that we will give preference to each other in our Negotiations."[1]

Most of the early trading on the NYSE was in bonds that had been issued to finance the American Revolution. Brokerage activities took place in a coffee house. In 1817 the group adopted the name New York Stock and Exchange Board and at the same time adopted a constitution providing for the election of officers, rules of conduct for members, and a system for admitting new members. Subsequent growth and development paralleled the industrial and economic history of the nation. By 1977 the NYSE, called the "Big Board," had 1,366 individual members. The market value of stocks sold on the NYSE in 1977 was $157 billion and represented 89 percent of the value of all stocks traded on registered exchanges. The NYSE also traded bonds and warrants. The par value of bonds traded on the NYSE amounted to $4.9 billion in 1977. Nine new issues of warrants[2] having a market value of $103

million were listed as of the end of 1977. Corporations listed on the NYSE accounted for more than 30 percent of the total assets, more than 40 percent of sales and more than 70 percent of the total net income of all U.S. corporations in 1979.

The NYSE required that corporations wishing to have securities listed on the Exchange meet certain minimum requirements, including net tangible assets of $16 million, publicly held shares having a market value between $8 million and $16 million, and demonstrated earning power under competitive conditions of $2.5 million before taxes for the most recent year, and $2 million for each of the preceding two years. Listed corporations also had to agree to release quickly to the public any information that might reasonably be expected to affect the market value of its securities. This required that information on earnings, dividends, acquisition, mergers, tender offers, and major changes in management be given to the media on an immediate release basis.

The NYSE was a so-called two-way auction market. According to NYSE Rule 390, all trades in listed securities had to be transacted orally on the floor of the Exchange, and the highest bid and lowest offer took precedence. Trading posts where buyers and sellers of a specific security could meet were established on the floor of the Exchange. "Specialists" who maintained an inventory of a designated security were also located at the trading post. About one-fourth of all Exchange members were specialists—so called because they specialized in making markets for specific stocks assigned to them according to NYSE Rule 104. The role of the specialist was to maintain liquidity by participating in securities transactions as either a buyer or a seller. In order to do so the specialist was allowed to trade for his or her own account on the floor of the Exchange. Other Exchange members were not permitted to do so. The specialist also assisted in the execution of large orders by helping to locate interested buyers or sellers or by handling all or part of the order personally. Orders to buy or sell stock at specific prices known as "limit-orders" were also left with the specialist.

NYSE members had to meet a series of requirements including a minimum net capital requirement of $100,000 in 1979. Members were admitted to the Exchange as individuals, although the vast majority were partners or voting stockholders of securities

---

[1] Frank B. Zarb and Gabriel T. Kerkles, eds., *The Stock Market Handbook* (Homewood, Illinois: Dow Jones, Inc., 1970), p. 72.

[2] Warrants were certificates sold or issued by corporations giving the holder the right to purchase securities at a specific price within a specified period of time.

firms allied with the Exchange as member firms. Member firms belonged to the Exchange by virtue of the fact that individuals within the firm had an Exchange membership and by agreeing to abide by the Exchange's rules of conduct and financial disclosure. Member firms were required to submit detailed financial information annually, and new members of the Exchange had to submit detailed personal information as well as recommendations from existing members. Memberships, called "seats," could be bought and sold with Exchange approval and were worth between $35,000 and $95,000 in 1977. The price of a seat in the Exchange had fallen steadily from a high of $515,000 in 1969. The number of member firms was 473 in 1977.

THE AMERICAN STOCK EXCHANGE (AMEX)

The AMEX, founded in 1849, was once known as the New York Curb Exchange because at one time its members actually traded securities in the street. The Curb Exchange moved indoors in 1921 and adopted its present name in 1953. The AMEX traded fewer securities and its listed companies lacked the size and stature of NYSE listed companies. The market value of securities traded on the AMEX in 1977 represented 5 percent of the total value of the securities traded on all registered exchanges. In addition to trading securities of listed companies, the AMEX traded stock options and commodities. The AMEX began trading stock options in 1975, just two years after the options market was born in the Chicago Board Options Exchange. In 1979 it traded options in sixty-nine stocks, nearly all of them stocks listed on the NYSE. In 1978 the AMEX had opened the AMEX Commodities Exchange (ACE) which traded contracts on Government National Mortgage Association (GNMA) futures, and had applied to the Commodity Futures Trading Commission for permission to trade contracts on U.S. Treasury bills, notes, and domestic bank Certificates of Deposit. As these investments gained popularity, the AMEX began to acquire greater importance within the financial community. When the SEC prohibited new listing of stock options in 1977, the AMEX gained a valuable competitive edge over the NYSE. Until the SEC completed its study of the op-

tions market, the AMEX would be the only national exchange with a full range of options trading activity. The AMEX and the NYSE had at times discussed the possibility of a merger, but as of 1979 a merger in the near future seemed unlikely.

THE REGIONAL EXCHANGES

Securities were also traded in ten regional exchanges. These exchanges traded dually listed securities (securities that were also listed on another exchange) as well as so-called regional listings. Standards for regional listings varied considerably among the regional exchanges. However, listing requirements were much less rigid than those of the New York Exchanges, and companies listed on regional exchanges were smaller and frequently younger than companies listed on the national exchanges.

THE OVER-THE-COUNTER MARKET (OTC)

The over-the-counter market consisted of a network of about 4,000 dealers and brokers linked by an extensive communications system. These dealers and brokers traded securities that were held in inventory by dealers who were said to "make markets" in specific securities by virtue of their willingness to buy and sell these securities from inventory. As reported by the National Association of Securities Dealers (NASD), an industry association representing OTC dealers, OTC trading involved 2,400 securities. In 1978 almost 3 billion shares were traded. This represented 24 percent of total U.S. shares traded, but total market value of less than 15 percent. The issuers in the OTC market varied in size and stature. The largest issuer was the Federal Government—all government securities were traded OTC. Virtually all the debt and equity of banks, insurance companies, and most utilities were also traded OTC.

Prices of OTC securities were quoted on a centralized electronic quotation system, and a record of recent transactions was available nationwide. Prices of OTC securities were not reported on the basis of the last sale, as was the practice on the Exchanges. Prices were quoted on the basis of a bid price and an ask (offer) price. Since a number of dealers often made markets in the same security, a buyer or seller checked the bid prices of all dealers and approached a single dealer for final negotiations. If the transaction involved a buyer or seller dealing directly with a broker, the final price included consideration of the costs of the transaction. When dealing through a broker who did not make a market in that security, the buyer or seller paid a commission that was negotiated.

A segment of the OTC market known as the "third market" consisted of a number of dealers who bought and sold securities listed on the NYSE. The third market was used by institutions wishing to trade large blocks of securities. Before May 1, 1975, a major difference between third market and Exchange trading was that commissions on sales in the third market could be negotiated, whereas commissions in the NYSE were fixed. Since most block transactions on the NYSE were brought to the floor only when both a seller and a buyer had been found "upstairs," third market trading and block trading on the NYSE were not markedly different once the NYSE abolished fixed commission rates. However, the third market continued to thrive.

Activities in the OTC market were governed by the NASD, a self-regulated organization of over-the-counter brokers and dealers established by special legislative amendment to the Securities Exchange Act of 1934.

THE COMMODITIES EXCHANGES

There were approximately fifty different commodities traded on twelve commodity exchanges. Commodity exchanges operated very much like stock exchanges. The largest commodity exchange was the Chicago Board of Trade (CBT). The CBT had recently expanded the scope of its activities to include trading in stock options (1975) and financial futures, both rapidly growing areas.[3]

The Securities Transaction Process

The purchase or sale of a security involved three steps: execution (finding a buyer or seller at a

[3] The National Stock Exchange was founded in 1962 by members of the New York Mercantile Exchange, a commodities exchange. Members of the Mercantile Exchange hoped to increase income and stature within the financial community by offering securities trading facilities. Its volume of trading was quite small.

mutually acceptable price), billing, and transferring ownership of the security. Whether accomplished on the floor of an exchange or over the counter, the execution was reasonably straightforward. The process began when an investor called his or her broker, who in turn telephoned or telegraphed the firm's trading department, where the order was filled directly or forwarded to a clerk on the floor of an exchange. The trade would be executed when a willing buyer or seller was found. News of the completed transaction reached the investor by the reverse process. The primary pieces of written documentation were a simple form known as an "order ticket" filled out at the trading department, and a "floor ticket," which was filled out by the partner handling the transaction on the floor of the exchange. The broker representing the buyer and the broker representing the seller each filled out floor tickets. The floor ticket contained only the name of the broker and the agreed-upon price. The entire process took less than thirty minutes.

While execution was relatively simple, the other phases of the purchase or sale could take up to two weeks and involved clerical procedures so complex that industry observers estimated that up to seventy different people were involved in completing a single transaction. Billing procedures were roughly similar to billing in other types of business. Transfer of ownership was somewhat more complex, because technically the buyer of a security had purchased a piece of paper and was entitled to possession of it. Securities could be endorsed like checks, notarized, and exchanged between parties. The company that had issued the security had to be notified so that dividends could be paid and annual reports, proxies, and other material could be sent to the appropriate parties.

Most securities were owned under a "street name," which meant that they were in the name of a securities firm that either owned the security or held it for an investor. The securities firm forwarded dividends, proxies, annual reports, etc., to the actual owner. When a transaction involved two firms (a broker representing the buyer and a broker representing a seller) exchanging a security held under street names, only the net amount of all the transactions of that specific security in a day needed to be transferred between firms. Nonetheless, the transfer process was extremely complicated. The brokers had to acknowledge that a valid transaction had taken place by matching floor tickets. The transfer process was done through clearinghouses operating in conjunction with the securities exchanges. All changes in securities ownership had to be recorded by the securities firm even when the transaction did not involve the exchange of a security with another firm. The process was the same whether the transaction involved 100 or 10,000 and more shares.

Industry participants were all too well aware of the complexities of the execution and transfer process. As trading volume had grown during the 1960s, the volume of paperwork generated by increased trading volume had finally exceeded the industry's capacity to process transactions manually, in a series of events in 1968 known as "The Paperwork Crisis," or the "Back-Office Crisis." Overwhelmed by the volume of trading, some firms found themselves unable to keep track of transactions, to trace the original seller, or to deliver securities to settle accounts with other brokers. In order to meet its obligations to other firms they had to purchase new securities. The delay caused by the need to purchase new securities meant that the firm to whom the securities were to be delivered was unable to complete the transaction for the purchaser. As a result the buy-side firm could not collect payment from the investor. Ultimately every firm in the industry was affected by the crisis, either through its own inability to meet its commitments to transfer securities or through the failure of other firms to honor theirs. The crisis ended only when trading volume dropped sharply in 1969–1970. However, in response to the crisis a large number of firms increased their investment in computers and automated office equipment during the late 1960s and early 1970s. By 1979 most securities firms had standardized their back-office procedure and believed that they were prepared to handle substantial increases in trading activity. However, the "back office" remained labor-intensive, and the industry as a whole had been unable to solve totally the problem of high turnover and a chronic shortage of skilled personnel for the back office.

Regulation of the Securities Industry

Activities within the securities industry were regulated by a number of organizations, including the national and regional securities exchanges, the Federal Reserve Board, each of the fifty states, and the Securities and Exchange Commission (SEC), an agency of the federal government. The most important regulatory body was the Securities and Exchange Commission, which was responsible for enforcing securities laws enacted by the U.S. Congress. The most important federal laws pertaining to the securities industry were the Securities Act of 1933 and the Securities Exchange Act of 1934. These were part of a series of laws designed to correct the abuses that were believed to have led to the stock market crash of 1929.

The Securities Act of 1933, often referred to as "the truth in securities law," required that a registration statement be filed with the SEC before offers for the sale or purchase of any corporate security could take place. The registration took the form of a prospectus, which had to include information on the use of the proceeds, the distribution spread, the plan of distribution, a description of the company's capital structure, earnings, organization, pending legal proceedings, remuneration of officers, and so forth. Information contained in the prospectus would allow the investor to assess the soundness of the investment, and the prospectus was reviewed by the SEC for the adequacy of its content. The law prohibited false statements or the omission of material facts in a registration. Unless the underwriters had exercised "due diligence" to ascertain and disclose all material facts in the registration statement, they could be sued along with the issuer for misrepresentation. Only private placements and intrastate offers (where the company sold securities only to residents in the state in which it did business) were exempt from the registration requirements.

The Securities Exchange Act of 1934 established the authority of the SEC over the securities exchanges and the brokerage community. It also established regulations controlling the amount of credit allowed in securities transactions, required periodic financial reporting by publicly held companies, and prohibited insider trading[4] in securities

---

[4] Insider trading took place when securities were bought and sold on the basis of information which was not publicly disclosed. Insiders could be employees or officers of the corporation. Securities firms that had access to confidential information in the course of doing business with a corporation were also considered "insiders."

of publicly held companies. Since 1934 the SEC has had a strong impact on the financial community, particularly in the areas of insider trading and due diligence.

The first important change in securities regulation came in the 1970s. In 1971 the SEC completed a major investigation called "The Institutional Investor Study." This report analyzed the impact of institutional investors on the securities markets and resulted in the legislation that changed the commissions on the sale of securities as well as the passage of the Securities Acts Amendment of 1975.

Historically, the commissions on securities sales were fixed. The minimum commission was determined according to the value and volume of shares traded. While the calculation of the minimum commission was complex, the important feature was that the charge did not decline as the number of shares increased. On April 5, 1971, by order of the Securities and Exchange Commission, New York Stock Exchange commission rules were changed to allow negotiated commissions on orders exceeding $500,000. In April 1972 the breakpoint was lowered to $300,000. On May 1, 1975, the SEC abolished fixed commissions on all exchanges. Since that time, known in the industry as "May Day," each securities firm has been free to establish its own commission schedule and to negotiate with customers on an individual basis. Since that time commissions on sales of large blocks of securities had declined almost 50 percent.

In June 1975 the U.S. Congress passed the Securities Act Amendment, which directed that the SEC "facilitate" the implementation of new procedures for securities trading that would allow the investor, regardless of size and geographic location, to buy and sell securities at the best price available. The SEC's broad but somewhat vague mandate was to create a "national market system." The progress that had been made toward a national market system by 1979 will be discussed later in this case.

Securities Firms

Securities firms earned income on underwriting and investment banking, trading securities, market-making, and lending in connection with securities transactions. The relative importance of these activities is illustrated in Exhibit 12–3. Securities industry revenues were extremely volatile. NYSE members firms represented approximately 80 percent of the total industry in terms of gross revenue. The remaining 20 percent consisted of small, independent securities firms. NYSE members earned $416 million on revenues of $6.7 billion in 1977, the latest date for which these figures were available.

UNDERWRITING AND INVESTMENT BANKING

Investment banking involved providing financial services to corporate and government clients. Corporate financial services included underwriting new securities issues and financial advisory services, such as private placements, mergers and acquisitions, etc., all of which could be considered "investment banking." Investment banking's special status in the financial community could be traced to the nineteenth century, when investment bankers invested their own capital or acted as agents in attracting European capital to finance a rapidly industrializing nation. Before uniform reporting and public disclosure requirements gave investors reasonably accurate information on the financial condition of a company, an investment banker's willingness to act as agent for a client was an important guarantee of the soundness of an investment.

Income from underwriting new public securities issues accounted for an estimated 40 percent of the income earned from investment banking activities in 1979, as illustrated in Exhibit 12–4. The underwriting process actually involved three distinct phases: management, underwriting, and selling. The manager advised the client on the structure of the issue, handled the legal requirements surrounding the process, and arranged for the underwriting and distribution of the issue. Actual underwriting was done by a group of firms called the underwriting syndicate. The underwriters, which included the manager, purchased the entire issue from the issuer. The issue was then sold to the public by a "selling group." The selling group included the underwriters and, if necessary, additional firms to augment the underwriters' distribution capability. The selling group did not have to commit any capital to participate in the distribution process. Underwriting and selling groups were based on traditional informal alliances among securities firms. Different members of the syndicate were allowed to underwrite different amounts of an issue. The size of a firm's participation was determined largely by tradition but also reflected a firm's ability to commit capital, (in the case of the underwriting syndicate) and distribution capability (in the case of the selling group).

The process of issuing and distributing new securities could take one of two forms: negotiated or competitive. When an issue was negotiated, the issuer chose an investment banker to design the issue and handle underwriting and distribution. The payment for this service was negotiated. Seventy-five percent of all public offerings were negotiated. When an issue was competitive, it was designed in-house by the issuer and given to the underwriting syndicate that offered to pay the highest price. In this latter case syndicates were formed to compete for the opportunity to distribute the issue. In competitive issues the winning syndicate was not chosen until the very moment that the issue went on sale. Because of this, competitive issues received no advance sales effort, and competitive bidding was practiced only when issues were highly marketable. Competitive bidding was used primarily for public utility issues and general obligation bonds where competitive bidding was required by law. Other corporations never used the competitive bidding option, and in especially difficult market conditions utilities and municipalities had obtained special permission from their regulatory authorities to use the negotiated bidding.

Payment for the investment banking, underwriting, and distribution service took the form of a discount on the selling price of the offering. The difference between the price paid by the underwriters and the price at which it was offered to the public was called the "gross spread." The spread on competitively bid debt was approximately 0.875% of the value of the offering in 1979, while it was 3 to 5 percent for publicly offered corporate equity. The managing underwriter generally received 20 percent of the spread; 30 percent was divided among the underwriters according to how much of the issue they had underwritten; and the remaining 50 percent was divided among the members of the selling group in proportion to the number of shares they had distributed. If a firm managed, underwrote, and sold a portion of the issue, the firm earned income from each of these activities.

Once an issue was offered to the public, slight im-

balances between supply and demand could begin to exert downward pressure on the original offering price. In order to maintain the original asking price of an issue, the syndicate was allowed to engage in stabilization. That is, they were allowed to buy back the new securities if the price began to fall. By offering to buy back securities at their original price, the syndicate could hold the price up at least long enough to overcome temporary problems caused by the influx of new securities into the market. If downward pressure continued, the price would have to be reduced. When this happened the gross spread was reduced or eliminated entirely. In 1979 the practice of stabilization, also known as the fixed price offering, was surrounded by controversy.

A related controversy was raised by the "Papilsky case." In 1971 Papilsky, a shareholder of a mutual fund, sued the fund's investment manager, Lord, Abbett & Co. Papilsky's attorneys alleged that Lord, Abbett & Co. had a legal responsibility to its shareholders to reduce commission costs and that the company could have reduced the commissions it paid on the purchase of new securities by joining the selling group. In 1976 a New York district court ruled in favor of Papilsky. Although the decision had been appealed, the entire investment banking community believed that the fixed price offering was under serious attack. If institutions were allowed to join the selling group on new issues, securities firms believed that they would be forced to offer discounts on new issues to all institutional customers. Stabilization prevented the awarding of concessions to large institutional investors on new issues and thus was closely related to the concerns implicit in the Papilsky case.

Within the securities industry the volume of managed underwriting was considered an important indicator of a securities firm's success. A leading position in the underwriting "sweepstakes" was considered a valuable new business tool for selling related services. Serving as a company's managing underwriter was an excuse to maintain contact and suggest other client services. Underwriting managerships also enabled the firm to secure a steady flow of "product" for the firm's sales personnel. Finally, the volume of managed underwritings was also an important determinant of the firm's standing in the underwriting syndicate structure. This standing not only influenced the volume of securities allocated by other managers when the firm participated in underwriting syndicates, but it also determined the firm's position in the "tombstone" advertisements used to announce new securities offerings. Tombstones were considered tangible evidence of status within the financial community and were considered a valuable tool for new business development. Exhibit 12-5A illustrates a "typical" tombstone. The order of placement divided the firms into the "special," "major," "major–out of order," "mezzanine," and "submajor" brackets. Each of these brackets was assigned progressively smaller participations in the syndicate. As Exhibit 12-5B illustrates, the underwriting hierarchy as symbolized by the "tombstone" had changed substantially between 1971 and 1978. Exhibit 12-6 shows the positions of the leading securities firms in the various types of securities issues.

Upon occasion an issuer requested that a firm be included in an issue or be named a co-manager. Issuers would do this if they believed that a firm could be influential in distributing the company's securities or if the firm had rendered it special service in the past. For example, Merrill Lynch's rise to the special bracket was based in part on recognition of its ability to distribute an issue. It was said that Merrill Lynch had been outspoken in asking issuers to see that Merrill Lynch was included in an issue. The use of co-managers had risen from 46 percent of all negotiated corporate financings (other than utility and telephone companies) in 1974 to 57 percent in 1977, according to industry sources.

Other investment banking services were paid for on a transaction basis. When an investment banker completed a successful transaction such as a private placement or an acquisition, the fee was a negotiated percentage of the total value of the transaction. The fee on a private placement was estimated to be 1 to 3 percent. Information on payment for other types of transactions was not readily available.

According to industry observers, substantial changes had occurred in investment banking since the mid-1960s. The size of corporate finance staffs within the investment banking firms increased, as illustrated in Exhibit 12-7, and corporate finance came to include specialists in tax-free issues, mergers and acquisitions, pollution control financing, lease financing, and so forth. By 1979 most investment banking firms believed that they had to offer a full range of specialized corporate financial services or risk losing clients to other firms. Professionals dedicated to new business development and marketing were added to corporate finance staffs. A number of firms emulated Goldman, Sachs's system for blanketing the top 5,000 U.S. corporations with regular visits by corporate finance professionals operating out of regional offices. A number of firms made major efforts to build their expertise in international finance (see below). Finally, firms began to emphasize their distribution capability to potential investment banking clients. Merrill Lynch, the largest retail distributor, used its capability in retail distribution to build an investment banking business. Merrill's push into investment began in the late 1960s, and by 1979 Merrill Lynch had become one of the most powerful investment banking firms in the industry. Other larger retail firms such as Dean Witter, Reynolds had tried to emulate Merrill Lynch's strategy. The strategy was most successful with utility companies that issued new securities frequently and depended on retail distribution to place them. Firms with strong institutional distribution capabilities, such as Salomon Brothers, also began to compete for corporate clients based on their ability to place issues with institutions.

BROKERAGE

Securities firms also earned commissions through the sale of securities to retail and institutional customers. According to the SEC, commission revenue for NYSE member firms had declined 13 percent because of the advent of negotiated rates. Because securities commissions reflected both volume and market value of the shares traded, it was difficult to isolate the impact of negotiated rates in the commissions revenue stream. However, commission rates for institutional sales had declined an estimated 48 percent, while commission rates on sales to individuals fell 18 percent. Commissions on small orders (less than 200 shares) placed by individuals had actually risen. Exhibit 12-8 contains recent statistics on the distribution capability of selected securities firms.

Institutional Brokerage. Institutional investors were served through a small number of sales offices located in major money market centers, including Boston, New York, and Chicago. Institutional salespeople were highly professional and knew their customers well. This involved being aware of the types of portfolios managed by their customers as well as their personal investment preferences. The most successful institutional traders made it their business to know their products well, including familiarity with the issuer and a thorough knowledge of the security itself, including any of its special features, such as call protection. Because of legal restrictions on insider trading, this knowledge was based on the prospectus. Although the prospectus was available to the customer, the institutional salesperson was expected to discuss its contents with the customer.

Institutional investors were concerned with the quality of execution. The quality of an execution reflected the institutional broker's ability to find a buyer or seller at the best price available within a very short period before the price of the security changed. Institutional investors were also concerned with minimizing the sales commission. Institutions typically contacted a number of brokers who competed for a particular piece of business. Trades could be more or less difficult depending on the size of the transaction, the frequency with which the security was usually traded, and its current popularity among investors. A trade was very difficult when it involved a large block of shares, was not frequently traded, or was not popular among investors. Institutional customers tended to favor brokers who could deliver under these conditions, and often rewarded these brokers by asking them to handle other, more attractive transactions.

Since institutional portfolios were typically quite large, decisions to change the mix of securities within a portfolio often necessitated the purchase or sale of large numbers of shares. Because institutions did not want their decisions to purchase or sell a security to increase or decrease its market value, the ability to arrange for the purchase or sale of large blocks of securities, known as block trading, was an important aspect of institutional brokerage. Block trading typically involved more than 10,000 shares of stock. Trades of large blocks of securities could be transacted either on the floor of securities exchanges, over the counter, or by arrangement with another institution. Whatever the method, ar-

rangements had to be made quickly and discreetly. When engaging in block trading the securities dealer frequently purchased a large block that was held in inventory until a purchaser could be found. The dealer assumed the risk of fluctuations in the price of the security during the period between purchase and resale. Several securities firms, including Salomon Brothers; Goldman, Sachs; Donaldson, Lufkin, Jenrette; Jefferies & Weeden Co., were known to be willing to purchase large blocks of securities for the convenience of institutional customers.

Institutional investors also used research provided by securities firms. For this purpose securities firms employed analysts, called sell-side analysts. Sell-side analysts were typically paid higher salaries than their buy-side counterparts, and they also had higher expense budgets and followed fewer companies. As a result they were able to supplement the buy-side analysts' research with more in-depth information. Sell-side analysts were expected to produce reasonably accurate information on a company's projected earnings, financial health, and management. They were also expected to interpret the significance of their company's press releases and any fluctuation in the stock price. Research analysts were rated annually in a poll published by the *Institutional Investor*. Known as the II All-American Research Team, the list was based on confidential information supplied by the institutions. It was considered an important indication of a successful analyst.

Research services were rarely paid for in cash. Before 1975 the institutions rewarded research by trading securities through the firm supplying the research or by requiring that securities firms that handled their transactions give up part of the commissions earned on these sales to a firm that supplied research. Institutions had evolved a complex system wherein buy-side analysts were responsible for allocating commission dollars to firms employing their favorite analysts. In the 1960s a number of firms known as "research boutiques" specialized in institutional research and survived entirely on commissions from directed sales. These included Mitchell-Hutchens; Wainwright Securities; and Auerback, Pollach & Richardson, to name but a few. After the demise of fixed commissions and the decrease in commissions dollars that resulted, research service became less important in securing commission revenue. Most of the research boutiques eventually went out of business or were acquired. Perhaps the most notable acquisition was that of Mitchell-Hutchens by Paine Webber in 1977. The absolute number of sell-side analysts decreased, and those who remained found employment in recently created or expanded research departments such as at Morgan Stanley (1973) and the full services houses such as Merrill Lynch and Goldman, Sachs. In 1979 research staffs were considered cost centers. However, there was intense competition among firms for the small number of "good" analysts. Bonuses such as Rolls Royces were used to lure analysts to new positions. In 1979 Merrill Lynch and Paine Webber had the largest complement of All-American analysts. Exhibit 12–9 contains the latest *Institutional Investor* All-American Team.

Retail Brokerage. Individual investors were served through a network of approximately 4,000 retail offices staffed by approximately 50,000 account executives (brokers). Since May Day, competitition for retail business had increased substantially. A number of firms had augmented their retail capability through acquisition. By 1979 acquisitions for this purpose included Clark Dodge by Kidder, Peabody; Harris, Upham by Smith, Barney; Reynolds Securities by Dean, Witter; and Hornblower Weeks by Loeb Rhoades. Since individual investors tended to be loyal to their account executives rather than to the firm, there was intense competition for successful account executives. The average commission revenue generated by an account executive was $85,000. However, top salespeople could generate between $750,000 and $1 million or more in commission revenue annually. Top producers could expect generous up-front cash bonuses and perquisites such as chauffeured limousines if they chose to change firms. As one story goes, in order to obtain the services of a certain broker producing more than $1.5 million in commissions annually, an unidentified securities firm canceled plans for a branch office in Greenwich, Connecticut, and opened instead a Westchester office at a location of the broker's choosing. As a rule, the industry preferred to hire trained account executives. Training took as long as two years and cost $14,000–$20,000 annually per

trainee. Only one trainee in four eventually became a successful producer. Merrill Lynch, the largest retailer in the industry, trained more than 1,200 salespeople annually. In 1977 Merrill Lynch raised its commission payouts to brokers from an average of 20 to 28 percent in the hope of reducing its very high turnover rate. Average commission payouts in the industry were 40 percent.

Securities firms seemed to be broadening the scope of their retail products. Merrill Lynch, for example, had begun to offer life insurance, a cash management service which enabled customers to earn interest on cash balances left with the firm, and a "sharebuilder plan" through which investors could purchase stocks through monthly installments as low as $25.00.

In 1979 retail brokers were worried about the recent apparent success of newly formed discount brokerage firms. These were no-frills operations offering retail customers discounts of up to 40 percent on commissions. These firms did not employ account executives and did not offer any investment advice.

MARGIN LENDING

Securities firms also earned revenues through margin lending. Securities could be purchased either for cash or "on margin." When purchased on margin, the securities firm loaned the customer a portion of the purchase price up to a limit determined by the Federal Reserve Board regulations and held the securities as collateral. In 1979 the customer was charged an interest rate on this loan, which was based on the firm's own interest rate plus an amount ranging from 0.75 to 2 percent, depending on the size of the account. The securities firm could loan the customer up to 50 percent of the market value of the securities held as collateral. When the market value of these securities declined, additional securities or cash had to be deposited to maintain this percentage. Because of frequent changes in the market value of the collateral, these accounts had to be monitored very closely.

The primary source of funds for margin lending were secured bank loans. The difference between the two interest rates represented revenue. In addition, firms had the interest-free use of funds provided by the credit balances in the margin customer's account, cash generated in daily operations from checks issued but uncollected, and cash held against securities to be delivered by others. Only retail customers used margin accounts.

MARKET-MAKING AND PRINCIPAL TRANSACTIONS

Whenever a securities firm sold a security that it actually owned, the potential for profit or loss based on fluctuations of market value of the security existed. Securities firms owned securities in order to make markets for OTC transactions or to facilitate block positioning.

OTHER ACTIVITIES

Other revenue earned by securities firms included commissions on commodities transactions, commissions and management advisory fees for mutual fund operations, and income from corporate financial advisory services.

Cost Structure

Expenses for members of the NYSE totalled $6.3 billion in 1977, 94 percent of gross revenue. A summary of expenses of NYSE member firms since 1976 is shown in Exhibit 12–10. The major categories of expense included salaries paid to retail/institutional salespeople, clerical and administrative salaries, occupancy and equipment, communications, promotion, advertising, interest, and other. There had been no substantial changes in the relative importance of each of these categories since 1969–1970, when occupancy and equipment costs had risen as a result of the back-office crisis. Salaries represented over half of total expenses in 1977. Although sales commissions were variable, most other expenses were fixed. Because of shared facilities and overlapping responsibility, it was very difficult to relate categories of expense to revenue. As a result, industry participants had only a general idea of the profitability of different segments of the business. Profit and loss analysis by line of business was further complicated by the belief that different parts of the business were so interdependent that the costs of one were justified by revenues earned elsewhere.

For example, an institutional trading department was considered by some participants an integral part of the underwriting operation and block trading a necessary part of institutional sales.

In general it was believed that retail distribution entailed the greatest expenses for salespeople, clerical and administrative personnel, communications, and occupancy costs. Institutional distribution and market-making, however, required a higher capital investment in inventory. Underwriting required enough capital for the underwriting process itself, but capital was turned over quickly, and underwriting was considered the least capital-intensive part of the business.

Capitalization

Securities firms were highly leveraged. The only limit on leverage was a "net capital requirement" imposed by the NYSE. Minimum net capital for Exchange members was $100,000 in 1977. Net capital could consist of cash, subordinated bank loans, and securities. For purposes of the net capital calculation the value of securities held as equity was reduced substantially from their market value to provide for sudden losses in the market value. Subordinated loans had to have maturity of at least one year. A firm's aggregate indebtedness could never exceed fifteen times net capital.

Before 1950 all member firms of the NYSE were partnerships. Beginning in 1953 securities firms had begun to incorporate, and by 1979 more than half of all NYSE member firms were corporations. This trend was necessitated by the need for both more capital as firms grew larger, and a more permanent form of capital than partnerships could provide. A small number of firms, including Merrill Lynch; Dean Witter; Paine Webber; First Boston; Donaldson, Lufkin, Jenrette; and Bache had gone public in the 1970s. Recent estimates of the capital positions of leading securities firms are contained in Exhibit 12–11.

International Activities

The international operations of U.S. securities firms included international sales of U.S. securities;

international investment banking through which investment bankers assisted their clients in raising capital in the international capital market known as the Euromarket; and the provision of financial services to foreign clients seeking U.S. capital or operating within the United States. Since non-U.S. economies had substantially smaller capital markets or entirely different mechanisms for the provision of investment capital, U.S. securities firms generally did not attempt to provide investment banking services to foreign entities operating within their own countries.

INTERNATIONAL SECURITIES BROKERAGE

As a result of the active trading on organized securities exchanges and the historical strength of the U.S. dollar, the U.S. capital markets were considered to be the most efficient in the world. This set the stage for worldwide interest in investing in U.S. securities. Firms such as White Weld,[5] First Boston, and Kuhn Loeb[6] had opened European retail offices in the mid-1960s.

Foreign owners of U.S. securities were subject to a withholding tax on dividends and interest earned by these securities. This tax varied from zero to 30 percent, depending on the terms of the tax treaty in effect between the United States and the foreign government involved. As a result, very few foreign nationals were willing to buy U.S. debt instruments. However, the potential for capital gains made U.S. equity attractive in spite of the tax. Foreign sale of U.S. equity reflected trends in the U.S. stock market as a whole, increasing substantially in the 1960s, only to fall markedly in the 1970s.

INTERNATIONAL INVESTMENT BANKING

International investment banking involved raising long-term debt capital in the so-called Eurocurrency market as well as arranging for private placements between issuers in one country and investors in another.

Eurocurrency, often called "stateless money," included any currency held outside of its country of origin. Currency left its country of origin when private citizens traveled or emigrated, when govern-

ments spent currency on foreign aid, or when trade deficits existed. The Eurodollar, the original Eurocurrency, was "created" after World War II when U.S. dollars flowed into Europe under the Marshall Plan. In 1970 the total dollar value of all Eurocurrencies was an estimated $65 billion. By 1979 it equaled $500 billion.[7] The largest segment of the Eurocurrency market was the Eurodollar, which accounted for 73 percent of total Eurocurrency volume in 1978, down from 81 percent in 1970. Other significant Eurocurrencies included German marks, Swiss francs, and Japanese yen. Issues designed as investment vehicles for Eurocurrency were called Eurobonds; Eurobonds worth $14 billion were issued in 1978.[8]

The largest issuers in the Euromarket were governments, government agencies, and state-owned enterprises, which together accounted for 48 percent of all Eurobond issues in 1978.[9] Foreign corporations, U.S. corporations, and international organizations accounted for 32 percent, 8 percent, and 11 percent of the remainder. U.S. corporations had been the largest issuers in the Eurobond market when it originated in the mid-1960s. At that time many U.S. corporations were establishing or expanding European subsidiaries, and Euromarket financing was absolutely necessary because the U.S. Government prohibited corporations from investing U.S. dollars abroad. Industry observers suggest that the Eurobond market was actually created by U.S. investment banking firms such as White Weld, Kidder Peabody, Kuhn Loeb, and Morgan Stanley to meet the financing needs of their U.S. clients at the time. The increasing participation of sovereign governments in the Eurobond market was a complex phenomenon that could not be completely explained. Industry observers suggest that in the case of developed countries such as the United Kingdom and Norway, Eurobonds were used to acquire funds for steadily rising deficit spending on social welfare programs and to finance state-owned enterprises. Less-developed nations used the funds to finance purchase of capital goods.

The largest buyers of Eurobond issues were European banks. Swiss banks, in particular, managed

---

[5] Now Merrill Lynch White Weld Capital Market Group.

[6] Now Lehman Brothers, Kuhn Loeb.

[7] *World Financial Markets* (Morgan Guaranty Trust), April 1979.

[8] Ibid.

[9] Ibid.

very large portfolios for clients all over the world and invested heavily in Eurobonds. Other European banks with somewhat smaller portfolios occasionally borrowed funds in the interbank funds market to invest in Eurobonds when the yield on these securities exceeded the cost of interbank borrowing. Government institutions responsible for managing a country's foreign exchange reserves such as a central bank were also large buyers of Eurobonds. At one time central banks had held dollars for this purpose but had converted their dollar reserves to Eurobond holdings as the Eurobond market was developed.

Eurobond financing offered the issuer certain advantages. Eurobonds did not require an elaborate registration process and, as a result, funds could be raised more quickly than in the United States—less than thirty days if necessary. Second, although it was not clear why, Eurobond buyers required fewer protective covenants than their U.S. counterparts. The Eurobond market, in general, tended to offer both issuer and investor greater flexibility than comparable domestic securities. One obvious aspect of this was foreign exchange implications. Through Eurobond issues, a conservative corporate financial officer could acquire funds for foreign investment in the currency to be invested or could, by investing in Eurobonds, match future foreign exchange liabilities with assets. By investing in Eurobonds, an investor (corporate or individual) could hold an especially attractive currency and yet avoid problems such as the withholding tax on dividends or interest earned by foreigners on U.S. securities and similar restrictions on domestic yen issues which made them unattractive to non-Japanese investors.

INTERNATIONAL ACTIVITY WITHIN THE UNITED STATES

The international aspects of investment banking conducted within the United States included raising capital for foreign clients in the U.S. capital markets and financial advisory services for international firms operating, or seeking to operate, within the United States.

Because the United States had the most efficient capital markets in the world, the cost of funds obtained within the United States had historically been the lowest in the world. However, between 1968 and 1974 an Interest Equalization Tax had discouraged foreign borrowers from seeking U.S. capital. The Interest Equalization Tax required that U.S. investors pay a premium on the purchase of securities of non-U.S. issuers. As a result of this premium such securities had to offer a higher interest rate, and this equalized the cost of obtaining funds within the United States with the cost of funds internationally. When the tax was repealed in September 1974, foreign borrowing resumed creating the "Yankee bond" market.

In 1979 issuers of Yankee bonds consisted of extremely credit-worthy governments and government agencies such as the Kingdom of Norway, Australia, and the European Investment Bank. Industry observers believed that access to the Yankee bond market was limited to top-quality credits because institutional investors in the United States were hesitant to purchase these securities. Their reluctance was believed to stem from a lack of familiarity with potential foreign issuers, lack of generally accepted procedures for evaluating this type of investment, and a reluctance on the part of institutional investors to commit themselves to any new type of issue. One final concern related to the potential liquidity of such issues until secondary trading facilities became fully operational. In 1979 the difference in interest rates between Yankee and comparable domestic issues were approximately one-half of 1 percent, down from over 1 percent in 1975. This differential was expected to narrow further, and the volume of Yankee bond issues was expected to increase substantially in the future.

Yankee bond issues had to be registered with the SEC. Issuers of Yankee bonds had to comply with the SEC's public disclosure requirements, recalculating all financial statements according to generally accepted U.S. accounting principles. Because of these requirements, industry experts believed that this market would be used only by government issuers planning to return to the U.S. market for funds repeatedly or international corporations planning to enter the U.S. market.

Competition

In 1979 the securities industry comprised several hundred firms ranging in size from one-person operations offering brokerage and investment management advice, to Merrill Lynch, the largest firm in the industry, which employed more than 20,000 and offered a complete range of investment products to more than 1.6 million customers. Firms in the industry differed in their approach to conducting business, reflecting differences in their historical development, which in some cases dated back to the nineteenth century. On the basis of their historical development it was possible to identify a number of different broad types of firms in the industry.

INVESTMENT BANKING FIRMS

Investment banking firms included such firms as Morgan Stanley; First Boston; Goldman, Sachs; Lehman Brothers, Kuhn Loeb; and Kidder Peabody. At one time investment banking firms dominated the securities industry. Based on extensive and long-standing client relationships, these firms controlled the all-important process of managing new issues. By 1979 most of these firms had expanded their activities to offering a full range of corporate financial services, as well as institutional brokerage and trading and financial advisory services designed for wealthy individuals.

CORPORATE ADVISORY FIRMS

These firms earned income on fees from corporate financial services and did not have trading departments of any substantial size. This group included Dillon Read and Lazard Frères. While these firms had long been investment bankers, it had become increasingly difficult for them to maintain their status within the underwriting community. As a result they seemed to have focused their attention on other aspects of investment banking besides underwriting. The firms were known to have extremely talented corporate finance staffs.

NATIONAL FULL-LINE BROKERAGE FIRMS

These firms had traditionally offered brokerage services to both retail and institutional customers. They included Merrill Lynch, Dean Witter Reynolds, Paine Webber, and E. F. Hutton. This group also seemed to be attempting to broaden and diversify its retail product lines. The largest of the national full-line firms, Merrill Lynch, had begun to use its powerful retail distribution capability to gain entry into investment banking. By 1979 Merrill Lynch was one of the industry's leading underwriters, and Dean Witter Reynolds, E. F. Hutton, and Paine Webber were pursuing similar strategies, though as yet with less success.

INSTITUTIONAL TRADERS

Institutional traders (brokers) had built strategies around their institutional trading capability. One institutional broker, Salomon Brothers, had used its institutional distribution capability to obtain investment banking business in much the same way as retail brokers had used theirs. Salomon was especially strong in competitively bid securities and had gained a significant share of this business in the late 1960s by forging a tightly knit syndicate of aggressive bidders known as the "fearsome foursome." The fearsome foursome included Merrill Lynch, Lehman Brothers, and Blyth & Co. Other leading institutional traders included Donaldson, Lufkin, Jenrette; Weeden & Co.; and Jefferies. Weeden and Jefferies were both third-market dealers.

REGIONAL AND LOCAL FIRMS

Regional and local firms were a very heterogeneous group. The scope of their activities sometimes included investment banking and financial advisory services for small corporations within their territory, as well as securities brokerage. Regional firms often had close ties with national investment banking firms that enabled them to broaden the scope of their services. For example, when a local corporation wished to be listed on a major national exchange, the regional firm would pass this business along to a specific investment banker. In return these firms were invited to participate in selling groups run by the investment banker. Regional firms tended to be active retailers of government securities and OTC stocks. Regional firms had begun to face increasing competition with national firms for regional investment banking business.

SPECIALISTS

The specialist group included firms that acted as specialists on the floor of a securities exchange.

These firms were not permitted to engage in any other brokerage or investment banking activity. Specialists earned income exclusively from commissions on floor brokerage and trading operations.

Commercial Banks

The character of investment banking in the United States was strongly influenced by the fact that the securities industry had historically been insulated from competition from commercial banks. Investment banks were allowed to underwrite and sell securities. Commercial banks were allowed to accept customer deposits and make loans but could not use customer deposits to invest in or underwrite securities other than general obligation government bonds. The distinction between investment banking and commercial banking began with the passage of the Glass-Steagall Act in 1934. This legislation resulted from the belief that the bank failures associated with the Depression had resulted from questionable investments of customers' deposits.

Prohibited from engaging in a broad range of underwriting and financial advisory activities in the United States, the largest U.S. commercial banks had formed international merchant banking subsidiaries. Most of these merchant banking groups were formed in 1970 and were based in London, a major locus of European banking activity. These merchant banking subsidiaries earned fee income for arranging nonbank financing, offering financial advice, and assisting with mergers and acquisitions. Their clients included the international divisions and subsidiaries of U.S.-based corporations, as well as non-U.S. companies.

In 1975 both Chase Manhattan and Citicorp had centralized their worldwide merchant banking activity in New York City, expanded their financial counseling services to domestic customers, and hired former investment bankers to manage their corporate finance departments. The first segment of underwriting to be penetrated by the commercial banks was private placements, where bank involvement was not prohibited by Glass-Steagall. According to *Investment Dealers Digest,* commercial banks handled $1 billion in private placements in 1976, some 5 percent of the total, up from 2 percent since 1974. In addition, in 1979 the largest U.S. commercial banks were reportedly offering advice on mergers and acquisitions. Commercial banks were allowed to participate in the underwriting of municipal, state, and federal general obligation bonds. Approximately one-third of the earnings from the underwriting of general obligation bonds in 1979 was earned by commercial banks.

Legislation that would allow commercial banks to underwrite revenue bonds issued by public agencies was pending in the U.S. Congress in 1979. Security industry groups were lobbying vigorously against the proposed legislation. Although enabling legislation to allow commercial banks to participate in the underwriting of government revenue bonds had thus far failed to win government approval, pressure was mounting to allow banks to compete in this area.

In 1977 New York's Chemical Bank had briefly offered a retail securities brokerage service through its branch banks. Although this experiment was short-lived, it focused attention on the potential use of more than 44,000 branch bank offices as retail outlets for securities. In addition, commercial banks had sophisticated electronic transaction processing systems in place that could be used to process securities transactions.

Competition for International Business

U.S. investment banking firms such as White Weld, Kidder Peabody, Kuhn Loeb, Morgan Stanley, and First Boston had been the original competitors in the Eurobond market. These firms were followed shortly thereafter by Swiss and German banks. Because there was no international version of the Glass-Steagall Act (except in Japan), European banks customarily participated in all phases of financial activity. The German "universal bankers" even held equity in large national corporations and frequently served on the board of directors. Other significant competitors included the investment banking houses[10] of London and Paris and the Japanese. By 1979 most prominent U.S. firms had Eurobond financing capability. Exhibit 12–12 contains *Institutional Investors'* list of the largest international underwriters for 1978, ranked according to the volume of issues managed. The prominence of Japanese securities firms in the list

---

[10] Known in Europe as merchant banks.

reflected a sudden rise in the volume of "samurai bonds," international issues based on yen, which were technically not Eurobonds, although they operated on the same principle.

The conventions for underwriting Eurobonds differed substantially from U.S. practice. Underwriting syndicates were smaller and selling groups did not exist. Six to ten firms would typically underwrite and place an entire issue. Large European banks frequently placed all or part of an issue directly into their own investment portfolios. Firms lacking the ability to commit a large amount of capital to underwrite an issue seldom participated in the underwriting function. Large European firms considered the mechanics of including a large number of firms in an underwriting syndicate too complicated. Underwriters did not attempt to stabilize prices of a new issue, and because of this underwriting Eurobonds entailed somewhat more risk than U.S. underwriting. Smaller firms were reluctant to assume this risk and believed that some large banks were frequently too aggressive in pricing. Conversely, large banks had found upon occasion that smaller firms were unable or unwilling to meet their underwriting commitments when an issue had been unsuccessful. Although precise statistics were not available, it was generally believed that spreads on Eurobond issues were higher than comparable U.S. issues, somewhere in the range of 5 to 6 percent in 1979.

Secondary market trading in Eurobonds was not very well organized. Non-U.S. investors, in general, were not frequent traders, and this was also true of Eurobond investors. Industry observers could not determine whether lack of secondary market trading facilities was the cause or the result of international investors' reluctance to trade actively. This condition had begun to change in 1976, when Salomon Brothers began to make markets in Eurobond issues. Although Salomon was not the first firm to make markets in Eurobond issues, it was the first to promote aggressively its market-making capability. Salomon had publicly committed itself to organizing secondary marketing facilities as part of a drive to achieve prominence in international investment banking. Since 1976 other U.S. firms had increased substantially their commitment to making markets in international issues.

U.S.-based investment banking firms also sup-

plied international clients with corporate financial advisory services. A weakening of the U.S. dollar in the 1970s had brought increased foreign investment in the United States. This investment took one of two forms: formation of U.S. subsidiaries and acquisition of U.S. companies. U.S. securities firms were the initial competitors for this business, but as foreign companies established themselves in the United States, foreign securities firms and banks opened U.S. offices. Once in the United States, these firms began to compete for all types of domestic business. Foreign banks in particular had expanded their U.S. operations substantially. In 1974 sixty foreign banks with $37 billion in assets were operating within the United States. By 1978 there were 122 foreign banks with $90 billion in assets operating within the United States.[11] Although these banks did not accept deposits, they sold certificates of deposit and made commercial loans. Between 1974 and 1978 foreign banks had increased their share of U.S. commercial lending from 10 to 18 percent. These banks obtained their funds from foreign parents who borrowed in the interbank funds market. These same foreign banks, unfettered by Glass-Steagall restrictions, also opened subsidiaries which handled underwriting and securities transactions. Exhibit 12–12 lists leading competitors in the Yankee bond market.

As a result of the alarming increase in foreign presence in the U.S. banking community, the U.S. Congress passed the International Banking Act in September 1978. This act would place foreign banks under the control of the Federal Reserve Board and thereby force them to compete on equal footing with domestic institutions. However, the International Banking Act did not apply to foreign banks already operating within the United States. Prominent Swiss, German, and Japanese banks were exempt from the new legislation because of this provision. In May 1979 Deutsche Bank, the largest German universal bank, opened a New York branch and was exempt from the IBA. Deutsche Bank, with assets of $80 billion in 1979, had applied for permission to open the New York branch before the bill had been passed. Deutsche Bank intended to offer commercial as well as investment banking ser-

[11] *New York Times,* June 22, 1978, Section IV, p. 4.

vices that were handled by a separate subsidiary, Atlantic Securities Corporation.

Consolidation

The total number of NYSE member firms supplying brokerage services to the public had fallen from 476 in 1973 to 371 at the end of 1977.[12] Between 1974 and 1979 the total number of member firms of the NASD (primarily local, regional, and OTC dealers) fell from 3,166 to 2,813. The number of NASD registered reps fell from 201,000 to 181,000 in this same period. Three successive waves of consolidation had occurred in the industry. The years 1968–1972 saw the demise, primarily through acquisition, of fifty-seven NYSE member firms. Sixty more dropped out between the first quarter of 1973 and the first quarter of 1975. Since 1975, despite two relatively prosperous years, the number of NYSE firms dealing with the public declined by forty-five more. The number of firms leaving the industry was considerably greater than those departing from the NYSE. According to one study,[13] 231 firms of some size left the industry between July 1972 and November 1976. Of these 122 merged, while 109 simply disappeared. A number of well-known and highly respected firms had been part of this consolidation, including White Weld (acquired by Merrill Lynch); Mitchell-Hutchens (acquired by Paine Webber); Kuhn Loeb (merged with Lehman Brothers); and Harris Upham (merged with Smith Barney). During this period there were no substantial decreases in the total number of NYSE registered personnel or sales offices.

As a result of these changes, the share of capital and commission revenue of the largest twenty-five firms had increased from 50.9 percent and 40.9 percent of industry totals in 1973 to 64.5 percent and 56.4 percent by 1977. It was generally believed by industry participants that consolidation would continue. Some observers believed that, like the accounting profession, the securities industry would some day be dominated by a very small number of national full-service firms.

[12] This figure excludes Exchange specialists.
[13] H. T. Mortimer, *Who Will Be Left?* (New York: E. F. Hutton, November 1976).

The National Market System

The impetus toward a national market system had come from the Securities Acts Amendment of 1975. The exact form of the national market system was still somewhat vague in 1979. However, the SEC had taken a number of steps toward implementing it. In April 1978, under the sponsorship of the SEC, the NYSE, AMEX, and the regional exchanges formed the Intermarket Trading System, which enabled brokers on one exchange to wire/sell orders directly to any other exchange. In August 1978 a composite quotation system that electronically displayed bid and asked prices for all exchange-listed and OTC stocks came on-stream. It replaced an earlier quotation service that reported only the price at which the security had last been traded. The composite quotation system quickly eliminated any disparities between securities prices on different markets.

In 1979 the mechanisms for the purchase or sale of securities lacked two additional elements that some participants believed would be necessary in a national market: a routing system or message switch procedure that would automatically send orders to the market offering the best price, and a computerized central file that would automatically store instructions to buy or sell securities in the order in which they were received. This final element, designated CLOB for "Consolidated Limit Order Book," was by far the most controversial, because it seemed to threaten current methods of handling block securities transactions. In 1979 the CLOB concept was being tested on the Cincinnati Stock Exchange. The CSE consisted of six brokerage firms, including Merrill Lynch, trading in forty issues. Transactions in the CSE cost an estimated ½¢ per share compared with an average 1¢ per share in the NYSE. Although no one was sure how CLOB would handle block transactions, orders queued and automatically matched by a computer would eliminate third market type transactions where a buyer or seller could be contacted for purposes of negotiation and indications of interest before an actual transaction took place.

As part of its effort to create a national market, the SEC had announced its intention of abolishing the NYSE's Rule 390, which required all transactions in listed securities to take place on the floor of an exchange. The SEC had relented and allowed a deadline for the abolition of Rule 390 to pass on January 1, 1978. Defenders of Rule 390 believed that its abolition would enable large brokers to execute orders in-house and in so doing hasten the trend toward consolidation in the industry. NYSE officials were outspoken in their belief that removal of off-board trading restrictions would be a mortal blow to the NYSE.

These changes in methods for handling securities transactions threatened the very concept on which the exchanges were built, that of an auction market. In an auction market the entire community becomes aware of the level of interest in a particular security, and the role of the securities broker is as agent for the buyer and seller. Some industry observers believed that further changes in the exchange system would turn brokers into dealers and that the dealers rather than the buyers and sellers would determine prices.

EXHIBIT 12-1. *Public and Private Corporate Capital Raised in the United States, 1968–1978 ($ billions)*

Year	Debt	Preferred	Common	Total	Public Financings Portion	Private Placements Portion	Private Placements (percentage of total)
1968				$28	$18.8	$ 9.2	33%
1969				31	22.7	8.3	27
1970	$31	$1	$ 6	38	31.6	6.4	17
1971	34	2	12	48	38.9	9.1	19
1972	30	3	13	46	34.2	11.8	26
1973	24	4	7	35	22.8	12.2	35
1974	37	2	3	42	31.3	10.7	25
1975	50	3	7	60	46.5	13.5	22
1976	53	3	8	64	42.8	21.2	33
1977	50	3	6	62	36.3	25.7	41
1978	45	3	6	54	31.1	22.9	43

SOURCE: *Investment Dealers' Digest, 1969–78.*

EXHIBIT 12-2. *Distribution of 1977 Corporate Securities Offerings by Type of Industry (percent of dollar volume)*

	Manu-facturing	Extractive	Electric Gas & Water	Transpor-tation	Communi-cation[a]	Sales and Consumer Finance	Financial and Real Estate	Commer-cial[b] Other	TOTAL
Nonconvertible bonds	38	4	20	4	9	5	22	8	100
Convertible bonds	75	3	8	8	1	—	3	2	100
Preferred stock	16	—	51	12	6	—	9	6	100
Common stock	9	16	51	1	12	1	8	3	100
Total $ volume	25	5	27	3	9	4	18	7	100

[a] Telephone Utilities issues represent approximately 98% of issues in this category.
[b] Agriculture, construction, wholesale and retail trade and all other non-financial services.

SOURCES: *S.E.C. Statistical Bulletin, February 1979; casewriter's calculations.*

EXHIBIT 12-3. *Sources of Gross Income—NYSE Member Organizations (millions of dollars)*

	1971		1972		1973		1974		1975		1976		1977	
Securities commissions	$2,953	54.9%	$3,210	53.4%	$2,663	55.3%	$2,303	48.9%	$2,949	49.7%	$3,163	45.8%	$2,809	41.7%
Trading and investments	754	14.0%	914	15.2%	430	8.9%	623	13.2%	916	15.4%	1,400	20.3%	1,296	19.3%
Interest on customers' debit balances	355	6.6%	517	8.6%	612	12.7%	604	12.8%	455	7.7%	565	8.2%	754	11.2%
Underwriting	801	14.8%	795	13.2%	420	8.7%	427	9.1%	780	13.2%	853	12.3%	777	11.5%
Mutual fund sales	101	1.9%	83	1.4%	104	2.2%	41	0.9%	36	0.6%	45	0.7%	59	0.9%
Commodity revenues	86	2.2%	119	2.0%	171	3.6%	162	3.4%	176	3.0%	210	3.0%	243	3.6%
Other income:														
Related to securities business	320	6.0%	370	6.2%	416	8.6%	550	11.7%	511	8.6%	530	7.7%	657	9.8%
Unrelated to securities business									105	1.8%	136	2.0%	135	2.0%
Gross income	$5,378	100.0%	$6,008	100.0%	$4,816	100.0%	$4,710	100.0%	$5,927	100.0%	$6,902	100.0%	$6,730	100.0%

SOURCE: *NYSE Fact Book.*

EXHIBIT 12–4. *Changes in Investment Banking Revenue Stream for Sample of Leading Originating Firms, 1973–1977*

Segments	1973	1974	1975	1976	1977
Public underwritings	54.0%	60.2%	65.6%	53.4%	40.2%
Private placements	15.8%	9.2%	8.4%	14.2%	16.8%
Merger, acquisition, and other fees income	16.0%	19.4%	14.2%	18.2%	25.6%
Municipal financing	14.2%	11.2%	11.8%	14.2%	17.4%

NOTES:

1. Base year is 1973. Composite numbers through courtesy of Dillon, Read & Co.; First Boston Corp.; Goldman, Sachs & Co.; Kidder, Peabody & Co.; Morgan Stanley & Co. These aggregate numbers are not weighted by volume of each firm.
2. Assumptions:
   a. Foreign revenues and corporate-related revenues from tax-exempt financings included in totals.
   b. Real-estate revenues excluded.

SOURCE: Samuel L. Hayes, III, "Evolving Competition in Investment Banking," Working Paper HBS 78–47. Graduate School of Business Administration, Harvard University, Division of Research.

EXHIBIT 12-5A. *A Typical Tombstone*

---

*This advertisement is neither an offer to sell nor a solicitation of offers to buy any of these securities.
The offering is made only by the Prospectus.*

NEW ISSUE   April 9, 1979

$100,000,000

Chemical New York Corporation

Floating Rate Notes Due 2004

Interest Rate through October 31, 1979 at 10.90%

Price 100%

plus accrued interest from April 17, 1979, if any

---

*Copies of the Prospectus may be obtained from such of the
underwriters as are registered dealers in securities in this State.*

The First Boston Corporation

Morgan Stanley & Co. Incorporated	Goldman, Sachs & Co.	Lehman Brothers Kuhn Loeb Incorporated	Merrill Lynch White Weld Capital Markets Group Merrill Lynch, Pierce, Fenner & Smith Incorporated	Salomon Brothers
Bache Halsey Stuart Shields Incorporated		Bear, Stearns & Co.	Blyth Eastman Dillon & Co. Incorporated	Dillon, Read & Co. Inc.
Donaldson, Lufkin & Jenrette Securities Corporation		Drexel Burnham Lambert Incorporated	E. F. Hutton & Company Inc.	Kidder, Peabody & Co. Incorporated
Lazard Frères & Co.		Loeb Rhoades, Hornblower & Co.	Paine, Webber, Jackson & Curtis Incorporated	Shearson Hayden Stone Inc.
Smith Barney, Harris Upham & Co. Incorporated		Warburg Paribas Becker A. G. Becker	Wertheim & Co., Inc.	Dean Witter Reynolds Inc.
ABD Securities Corporation		Allen & Company Incorporated	Arnhold and S. Bleichroeder, Inc.	Baring Brothers & Co., Limited
Basle Securities Corporation		Alex. Brown & Sons	Daiwa Securities America Inc.	F. Eberstadt & Co., Inc.
EuroPartners Securities Corporation		Robert Fleming Incorporated	Ladenburg, Thalmann & Co. Inc.	Legg Mason Wood Walker Incorporated
Moseley, Hallgarten, Estabrook & Weeden Inc.			New Court Securities Corporation	The Nikko Securities Co. International, Inc.
Nomura Securities International, Inc.		Oppenheimer & Co., Inc.	Wm. E. Pollock & Co., Inc.	Scandinavian Securities Corporation
M. A. Schapiro & Co., Inc.		Stuart Brothers	Thomson McKinnon Securities Inc.	Tucker, Anthony & R. L. Day, Inc.
Yamaichi International (America), Inc.	Advest, Inc.	American Securities Corporation	A. E. Ames & Co. Incorporated	Bacon, Whipple & Co.
Robert W. Baird & Co. Incorporated	Bateman Eichler, Hill Richards Incorporated		Sanford C. Bernstein & Co., Inc.	Blunt Ellis & Loewi Incorporated
J. C. Bradford & Co.	Butcher & Singer Inc.	The Chicago Corporation	Dain, Kalman & Quail Incorporated	Dominion Securities Inc.
Elkins, Stroud, Suplee & Co.	Fahnestock & Co.	First Albany Corporation	First of Michigan Corporation	Greenshields & Co Inc
Howard, Weil, Labouisse, Friedrichs Incorporated	Interstate Securities Corporation		Janney Montgomery Scott Inc.	Laidlaw Adams & Peck Inc.
McDonald & Company	McLeod Young Weir Incorporated		New Japan Securities International Inc.	The Ohio Company
Piper, Jaffray & Hopwood Incorporated	Prescott, Ball & Turben		Rauscher Pierce Refsnes, Inc.	The Robinson-Humphrey Company, Inc.
Rodman & Renshaw, Inc.	Sutro & Co. Incorporated	Burton J. Vincent, Chesley & Co.	Wheat, First Securities, Inc.	Wood Gundy Incorporated
Birr, Wilson & Co., Inc.	Boettcher & Company	Bruns, Nordeman, Rea & Co.	Doft & Co., Inc.	Freeman Securities Company, Inc.
Gruntal & Co.	Herzfeld & Stern	Jesup & Lamont Securities Co., Inc.	Josephthal & Co. Incorporated	Cyrus J. Lawrence Incorporated
Moore & Schley, Cameron & Co.	Morgan, Olmstead, Kennedy & Gardner Incorporated		Neuberger & Berman	Newhard, Cook & Co. Incorporated
Philips, Appel & Walden, Inc.	Printon, Kane & Co.	Wm. Sword & Co. Incorporated	Daniels & Bell, Inc. Shelby Cullom Davis & Co.	Evans & Co. Incorporated
First Harlem Securities Corporation		Kormendi, Byrd Brothers, Inc.		Nippon Kangyo Kakumaru International, Inc.
Ross Stebbins, Inc.		John J. Ryan & Co.		Sanyo Securities America Inc.

EXHIBIT 12-5B. *Equity Underwriting Syndicate Positions: 1971 Versus 1978*

1971	1978
Special Bracket	*Special Bracket*
Dillon Read	—
First Boston	First Boston
Kuhn Loeb	—
Merrill Lynch	Merrill Lynch
Morgan Stanley	Morgan Stanley
Salomon Brothers	Goldman, Sachs
—	Salomon Brothers
Major Bracket	*Major Bracket*
—	Bache Halsey Shields
Blyth	Blyth Eastman Dillon
—	Dillon Read
—	Donaldson, Lufkin & Jenrette
Drexel	Dresel Burnham Lambert
duPont	—
Eastman Dillon	—
Goldman, Sachs	—
Halsey Stuart	—
Hornblower & Weeks	—
—	E. F. Hutton
Kidder, Peabody	Kidder, Peabody
Lazard Freres	Lazard Freres
Lehman Brothers	Lehman Kuhn Loeb
Loeb Rhoades	Loeb Rhoades-Hornblower & Weeks
Paine Webber	Paine Webber
Smith Barney	Smith Barney Harris Upham
Stone & Webster	—
—	Warburg Paribas Becker
Wertheim	Wertheim
White, Weld	—
Dean Witter	Dean Witter Reynolds
Major Out of Order	*Major Out of Order*
Bache	—
Paribas	—
—	Bear, Stearns
—	L. F. Rothschild
—	Shearson Hayden Stone
	Mezzanine Bracket
	Oppenheimer
	Thomson & McKinnon
Submajor Bracket	*Submajor Bracket*
A. G. Becker	—
CBWL-Hayden, Stone	—
Clark, Dodge	—
Dominick & Dominick	—
Equitable Securities	—
Hall Garten	—
Harris, Upham	—
E. F. Hutton	—
W. E. Hutton	—
Landenburg, Thalman	Ladenburg, Thalman
F. S. Moseley	Moseley-Hallgarten-Estebrook
John Nuveen	—
R. W. Pressprich	—
Reynolds	—
L. F. Rothschild	—
Shearson, Hammill	—
Shields	—
F. S. Smithers	—
Spencer Trask	—
G. H. Walker	—
Walston	—
Wood, Struthers	—

SOURCE: Samuel L. Hayes, "Evolving Competition in Investment Banking."

EXHIBIT 12–6. *The Twenty-five Largest Managing Underwriters in 1977–1978*

Total Corporate Securities

Bonus Credit to Lead Manager					Full Credit to Lead Manager					Full Credit to Each Manager				
1977	1978		$ Volume (millions)	No. of Issues	1977	1978		$ Volume (millions)	No. of Issues	1977	1978		$ Volume (millions)	No. of Issues
1	1	Morgan Stanley	$3,815.9	61	1	1	Morgan Stanley	$7,042.4	58	2	1	Salomon Brothers	$9,955.6	116
3	2	Salomon Brothers	3,295.2	116	2	2	Salomon Brothers	4,672.2	63	1	2	Merrill Lynch White Weld	9,698.3	144
2	3	Merrill Lynch White Weld	3,076.3	144	3	3	Merrill Lynch White Weld	3,162.0	60	4	3	Morgan Stanley	7,423.0	61
5	4	Goldman Sachs	2,912.7	77	5	4	Goldman Sachs	2,818.9	36	5	4	Goldman Sachs	7,157.1	77
4	5	First Boston	1,775.6	79	4	5	First Boston	1,976.9	36	3	5	First Boston	5,984.5	79
6	6	Blyth Eastman Dillon	1,773.8	76	5	6	Blyth Eastman Dillon	1,886.6	31	g	6	Dean Witter Reynolds	5,681.7	75
8	7	Kidder Peabody	1,605.2	85	d	7	Lehman Brothers Kuhn Loeb	1,618.1	29	6[h]	7	Blyth Eastman Dillon	5,593.4	76
8[a]	8	Lehman Brothers Kuhn Loeb	1,585.0	74	7	8	Kidder Peabody	1,370.2	36	h	8	Lehman Brothers Kuhn Loeb	5,238.0	74
b	9	Dean Witter Reynolds	1,122.9	75	14	9	Smith Barney, Harris Upham	926.3	22	9	9	Kidder Peabody	5,212.7	85
12	10	Smith Barney, Harris Upham	1,115.4	52	13	10	Bache Halsey Stuart Shields	713.8	13	14	10	E. F. Hutton	4,282.7	58
17	11	Drexel Burnham Lambert	811.7	57	17	11	Drexel Burnham Lambert	563.0	22	10	11	Smith Barney, Harris Upham	3,950.2	52
13	12	E. F. Hutton	796.7	58	e	12	Dean Witter Reynolds	476.4	15	12	12	Paine Webber	3,807.0	45
15	13	Dillon Read	740.0	34	10	13	Dillon Read	467.0	7	8	13	Bache Halsey Stuart Shields	3,790.4	52
10	14	Bache Halsey Stuart Shields	710.9	52	16	14	Paine Webber	432.3	10	18	14	Drexel Burnham Lambert	3,320.7	57
16	15	Paine Webber	542.9	45	12[f]	15	White Weld	407.0	8	17	15	Dillon Read	3,232.4	34
20	16	Wood Gundy	506.7	10	f	16	Loeb Rhoades Hornblower	361.3	6	–	16	Wood Gundy	2,350.0	10
c	17	Loeb Rhoades Hornblower	423.7	22	15	17	E. F. Hutton	284.3	13	i	17	A. E. Ames	2,000.0	9
11	18	White Weld	419.0	20	19	18	Bear Stearns	229.1	10	18	18	Loeb Rhoades Hornblower	1,653.0	22
–	19	A. E. Ames	394.2	9	21	19	Rothschild, Unterberg, Towbin	105.3	7	11	19	White Weld	1,490.3	20
23	20	Bear Stearns	318.4	23	–	20	Warburg Paribas Becker	75.1	3	19	20	Wertheim	1,229.8	19
22	21	Lazard Freres	212.1	8	–	21	Oppenheimer	60.0	2	25	21	Bear Stearns	1,046.6	23
21	22	Warburg Paribas Becker	188.0	19	20	22	Wertheim	52.4	2	–	22	Donaldson, Lufkin & Jenrette	1,023.6	16
–	23	Wertheim	171.8	19	–	23	Lazard Freres	50.0	1	22	23	Warburg Paribas Becker	936.4	19
–	24	Rothschild, Unterberg, Towbin	144.3	18	–	24	Allen	49.7	4	–	24	Lazard Freres	775.0	8
–	25	Donaldson, Lufkin & Jenrette	144.0	16	24	25	Ohio Co.	48.2	17	–	25	Rothschild, Unterberg, Towbin	518.2	18

[a] 1977 Rankings: Lehman Brothers 7, Kuhn Loeb 14.
[b] 1977 Rankings: Dean Witter 9, Reynolds 24.
[c] 1977 Rankings: Loeb Rhoades 18, Hornblower Weeks 25.
[d] 1977 Rankings: Lehman Brothers 8, Kuhn Loeb 9.
[e] 1977 Rankings: Dean Witter 11, Reynolds –.
[f] 1977 Rankings: Loeb Rhoades 18, Hornblower Weeks 25.
[g] 1977 Rankings: Dean Witter 7, Reynolds 21.
[h] 1977 Rankings: Lehman Brothers 13, Kuhn Loeb 15.
[i] 1977 Rankings: Loeb Rhoades 16, Hornblower Weeks 20.

EXHIBIT 12-6. *(continued)*

Negotiated Debt Offerings

Bonus Credit to Lead Manager

1977	1978		$ Volume (millions)	No. of Issues
1	1	Morgan Stanley	$2,603.3	21
2	2	Goldman Sachs	2,314.2	34
3	3	Salomon Brothers	2,107.0	38
4	4	Merrill Lynch White Weld	1,247.7	39
a	5	Lehman Brothers Kuhn Loeb	852.5	18
5	6	First Boston	818.7	19
6	7	Blyth Eastman Dillon	716.9	10
10	8	Smith Barney, Harris Upham	665.9	12
18	9	Wood Gundy	506.7	10
13	10	Kidder Peabody	460.8	14
24	11	A. E. Ames	394.2	9
21	12	Drexel Burnham Lambert	373.7	14
11	13	Dillon Read	345.0	4
b	14	Dean Witter Reynolds	243.9	8
c	15	Loeb Rhades Hornblower	228.3	3
19	16	Lazard Freres	212.1	8
9	17	White Weld	175.0	4
20	18	Bear Stearns	163.3	7
14	19	McLeod, Young, Weir	112.5	2
16	20	Bache Halsey Stuart Shields	100.8	5
23	21	Paine Webber	83.5	2
17	22	E. F. Hutton	83.3	4
25	23	William Blair	62.5	2
22	24	Warburg Paribas Becker	56.7	2
—	25	Wheat First Securities	44.5	3

Full Credit to Lead Manager

1977	1978		$ Volume (millions)	No. of Issues
1	1	Morgan Stanley	$3,900.0	21
2	2	Salomon Brothers	2,829.7	21
3 d	3	Goldman Sachs	2,500.0	24
5	4	Lehman Brothers Kuhn Loeb	1,085.0	12
11	5	Merrill Lynch White Weld	932.9	12
4	6	Smith Barney, Harris Upham	745.0	9
6	7	First Boston	690.0	9
8	8	Blyth Eastman Dillon	600.0	6
12	9	Kidder Peabody	415.0	8
17	10	Drexel Burnham Lambert	384.5	12
9 e	11	Dillon Read	345.0	4
10	12	Loeb Rhoades Hornblower	295.0	3
16	13	White Weld	200.0	3
21	14	Bear Stearns	180.0	7
19	15	Paine Webber	100.0	1
15	16	Lazard Freres	50.0	1
20	17	E. F. Hutton	45.0	2
14	18	Ohio Co.	40.5	15
—	19	Warburg Paribas Becker	40.0	1
f	20	Dean Witter Reynolds	35.0	1
18	21	Thomson McKinnon Securities	26.0	1
—	22	Bache Halsey Stuart Shields	20.0	1
—	23	Foster & Marshall	13.0	3
—	24	Rothschild, Unterberg, Towbin	12.0	1
—	25	Allen	10.0	1
—		Ziegler Securities	10.0	1

Full Credit to Each Manager

1977	1978		$ Volume (millions)	No. of Issues
1	1	Salomon Brothers	$5,419.7	38
2	2	Morgan Stanley	3,900.0	21
4	3	Merrill Lynch White Weld	3,704.1	39
5	4	Goldman Sachs	3,703.1	34
13	5	Wood Gundy	2,350.0	10
3	6	First Boston	2,040.0	19
18	7	A. E. Ames	2,000.0	9
g	8	Lehman Brothers Kuhn Loeb	1,835.0	18
6	9	Blyth Eastman Dillon	1,101.2	10
h	10	Dean Witter Reynolds	1,051.2	8
11	11	Smith Barney, Harris Upham	980.0	12
17	12	Kidder Peabody	890.0	14
16	13	Lazard Freres	775.0	8
15	14	Bache Halsey Stuart Shields	520.0	5
9	15	McLeod, Young, Weir	450.0	5
—	16	Drexel Burnham Lambert	429.5	2
12	17	White Weld	400.0	14
14	18	Dillon Read	345.0	4
20	19	Paine Webber	301.2	2
i	20	Loeb Rhoades Hornblower	295.0	3
24	21	William Blair	250.0	2
22	22	E. F. Hutton	185.0	4
—	23	Bear Stearns	180.0	7
—	24	Wheat, First Securities	161.0	3
—	25	Den Morske Creditbank	150.0	1
—		Christiania Bank	150.0	1
—		Bergen Bank	150.0	1

[a] 1977 Rankings: Lehman Brothers 7, Kuhn Loeb 8.
[b] 1977 Rankings: Dean Witter 12, Reynolds Securities —.
[c] 1977 Rankings: Loeb Rhoades 15, Hornblower Weeks —.

[d] 1977 Rankings: Lehman Brothers 8, Kuhn Loeb 7.
[e] 1977 Rankings: Loeb Rhoades 13, Hornblower Weeks 24.
[f] 1977 Rankings: Dean Witter 14, Reynolds Securities —.

[g] 1977 Rankings: Lehman Brothers 8, Kuhn Loeb 7.
[h] 1977 Rankings: Dean Witter 10, Reynolds Securities —.
[i] 1977 Rankings: Loeb Rhoades 19, Hornblower Weeks —.

EXHIBIT 12–6. (continued)

Negotiated Equity Offerings

Bonus Credit to Lead Manager

1977	1978		$ Volume (millions)	No. of Issues
2	1	Merrill Lynch White Weld	$1,250.7	55
7	2	Kidder Peabody	762.3	38
1	3	Morgan Stanley	689.9	18
a	4	Dean Witter Reynolds	549.5	37
3	5	First Boston	484.8	21
b	6	Lehman Brothers Kuhn Loeb	368.3	18
5	7	Blyth Eastman Dillon	364.5	23
8	8	E. F. Hutton	267.4	18
9	9	Goldman Sachs	246.4	13
6	10	Salomon Brothers	169.0	14
10	11	Paine Webber	157.3	12
13	12	Bache Halsey Stuart Shields	143.7	8
16	13	Smith Barney, Harris Upham	90.7	9
15	14	White Weld	84.8	3
14	15	Drexel Burnham Lambert	71.4	9
c	16	Loeb Rhoades Hornblower	66.3	3
11	17	Dillon Read	60.7	3
–	18	Rothschild, Unterberg, Towbin	59.7	10
–	19	Allen	39.7	3
–	20	Keffe, Bruyette & Woods	26.5	3
–	21	Eppler, Guerin & Turner	26.1	2
–	22	Wertheim	25.8	2
22	23	Ohio Co.	23.1	4
–	24	Prescott, Ball & Turben	22.9	2
–	25	William Blair	20.1	3

a 1977 Rankings: Dean Witter 4, Reynolds Securities 18.
b 1977 Rankings: Lehman Brothers 11, Kuhn Loeb 19.
c 1977 Rankings: Loeb Rhoades –, Hornblower Weeks –.

Full Credit to Lead Manager

1977	1978		$ Volume (millions)	No. of Issues
2	1	Merrill Lynch White Weld	$1,610.3	35
1	2	Morgan Stanley	911.9	16
5	3	Kidder Peabody	786.1	24
d	4	First Boston	470.1	16
4	5	Lehman Brothers Kuhn Loeb	435.1	14
e	6	Blyth Eastman Dillon	409.6	12
7	7	Dean Witter Reynolds	406.4	13
8	8	Paine Webber	192.3	5
14	9	Goldman Sachs	168.2	6
9	10	Salomon Brothers	132.0	7
8	11	Dillon Read	122.0	3
15	12	Smith Barney, Harris Upham	111.0	9
10	13	E. F. Hutton	94.3	7
11	14	White Weld	75.0	1
f	15	Loeb Rhoades Hornblower	66.3	3
13	16	Drexel Burnham Lambert	51.5	5
20	17	Rothschild, Unterberg, Towbin	43.3	5
–	18	Allen	39.7	3
17	19	Alex, Brown & Sons	26.5	3
–	20	Janney Montgomery Scott	20.0	2
–	21	Donaldson, Lufkin & Jenrette	18.4	3
–	22	Wertheim	17.4	1
–	23	Prescott, Ball & Turben	16.9	1
18	24	Shearson Hayden Stone	16.8	4
18	25	Bache Halsey Stuart Shields	12.5	2

d 1977 Rankings: Lehman Brothers 12, Kuhn Loeb 21.
e 1977 Rankings: Dean Witter 6, Reynolds Securities –.
f 1977 Rankings: Loeb Rhoades –, Hornblower Weeks 16.

Full Credit to Each Manager

1977	1978		$ Volume (millions)	No. of Issues
1	1	Merrill Lynch White Weld	$2,509.1	55
g	2	Dean Witter Reynolds	1,622.8	37
9	3	Kidder Peabody	1,383.5	38
4	4	First Boston	1,101.6	21
2	5	Morgan Stanley	1,092.5	18
6	6	Blyth Eastman Dillon	918.3	23
10	7	E. F. Hutton	908.0	18
h	8	Lehman Brothers Kuhn Loeb	640.5	18
8	9	Bache Halsey Stuart Shields	571.0	8
8	10	Goldman Sachs	526.7	13
7	11	Salomon Brothers	475.7	14
3	12	Paine Webber	429.0	12
11	13	Drexel Burnham Lambert	167.7	9
14	14	Rothschild, Unterberg, Towbin	148.2	10
–	15	Dillon Read	122.0	3
13	16	Smith Barney, Harris Upham	111.0	9
16	17	White Weld	110.7	3
15	18	Deefe, Bruyette & Woods	89.3	3
–	19	Donaldson, Lufkin & Jenrette	78.4	4
–	20	Eppler, Guerin & Turner	78.3	2
–	21	Prescott, Ball & Turben	75.0	2
23	22	Wheat, First Securities	72.9	2
22	23	Warburg Paribas Becker	71.9	2
i	24	Loeb Rhoades Hornblower	66.3	3
–	25	Bear Stearns	64.6	2

g 1977 Rankings: Dean Witter 5, Reynolds Securities 18.
h 1977 Rankings: Lehman Brothers 12, Kuhn Loeb 19.
i 1977 Rankings: Loeb Rhoades –, Hornblower Weeks –.

EXHIBIT 12-6. *(continued)*

Competitive Securities

Bonus Credit to Lead Manager

1977	1978		$ Volume (millions)	No. of Issues
1	1	Salomon Brothers	$969.2	63
2	2	Merrill Lynch White Weld	577.9	50
6	3	Morgan Stanley	522.7	22
3	4	Blyth Eastman Dillon	509.4	39
4	5	First Boston	462.9	38
5	6	Bache Halsey Stuart Shields	458.9	38
7	7	Kidder Peabody	370.3	31
[a]	8	Lehman Brothers Kuhn Loeb	357.5	37
9	9	Paine Webber	352.0	29
11	10	E. F. Hutton	344.5	32
18	11	Dillon Read	334.3	27
[b]	12	Dean Witter Reynolds	324.9	29
13	13	Goldman Sachs	318.1	28
10	14	Smith Barney, Harris Upham	309.1	28
16	15	Drexel Burnham Lambert	296.9	30
8	16	White Weld	133.0	11
[c]	17	Loeb Rhoades Hornblower	129.1	16
—	18	Donaldson, Lufkin & Jenrette	125.2	12
22	19	Warburg Paribas Becker	123.0	15
19	20	Wertheim	111.0	16
24	21	Bear Stearns	83.3	11
21	22	Shearson Hayden Stone	42.8	7
25	23	Rothschild, Unterberg, Towbin	39.3	6
—	24	Weeden	15.0	1
—	25	Stuart Brothers	13.1	2

Full Credit to Lead Manager

1977	1978		$ Volume (millions)	No. of Issues
1	1	Morgan Stanley	$2,230.5	21
3	2	Salomon Brothers	1,660.5	34
4	3	First Boston	803.1	10
6	4	Bache Halsey Stuart Shields	691.8	9
5	5	Blyth Eastman Dillon	621.0	9
2	6	Merrill Lynch White Weld	618.8	13
7	7	Kidder Peabody	150.0	2
11	8	White Weld	106.2	3
10	9	Paine Webber	90.0	2
13[d]	10	Lehman Brothers Kuhn Loeb	88.0	2
14	11	Goldman Sachs	87.2	4
12	12	E. F. Hutton	75.0	2
—	13	Drexel Burnham Lambert	50.0	1
—	14	Warburg Paribas Becker	35.1	2
15[e]	15	Dean Witter Reynolds	35.0	1
9	16	Smith Barney, Harris Upham	11.7	1
—	17	Donaldson, Lufkin & Jenrette	10.0	1
		Edward D. Jones	10.0	1

Full Credit to Each Manager

1977	1978		$ Volume (millions)	No. of Issues
2	1	Salomon Brothers	$4,010.2	63
1	2	Merrill Lynch White Weld	3,435.1	50
3	3	Blyth Eastman Dillon	3,317.9	39
9	4	Paine Webber	3,025.8	29
[f]	5	Dean Witter Reynolds	2,994.3	29
10	6	E. F. Hutton	2,993.7	32
6	7	Kidder Peabody	2,920.1	31
12	8	Goldman Sachs	2,863.9	28
4	9	First Boston	2,829.1	38
7	10	Smith Barney, Harris Upham	2,800.6	28
18	11	Dillon Read	2,765.4	27
[g]	12	Lehman Brothers Kuhn Loeb	2,752.5	37
5	13	Bache Halsey Stuart Shields	2,692.0	38
15	14	Drexel Burnham Lambert	2,646.5	30
13	15	Morgan Stanley	2,430.5	22
[h]	16	Loeb Rhoades Hornblower	1,291.7	16
19	17	Wertheim	1,152.2	16
—	18	Donaldson, Lufkin & Jenrette	945.2	12
8	19	White Weld	926.9	11
23	20	Warburg Paribas Becker	774.5	15
24	21	Bear Stearns	707.5	11
21	22	Shearson Hayden Stone	466.7	7
25	23	Rothschild, Unterberg, Towbin	308.0	6
—	24	Stuart Brothers	115.0	2
—	25	Weeden	75.0	1

[a] 1977 Rankings: Lehman Brothers 14, Kuhn Loeb 17.
[b] 1977 Rankings: Dean Witter 13, Reynolds Securities 23.
[c] 1977 Rankings: Loeb Rhoades 15, Hornblower Weeks 20.
[d] 1977 Rankings: Lehman Brothers —, Kuhn Loeb 8.
[e] 1977 Rankings: Dean Witter 15, Reynolds Securities —.
[f] 1977 Rankings: Dean Witter 11, Reynolds Securities 22.
[g] 1977 Rankings: Lehman Brothers 16, Kuhn Loeb 17.
[h] 1977 Rankings: Loeb Rhoades 14, Hornblower Weeks 20.

EXHIBIT 12-6. *(continued)*

Competitive Debt Offerings

Bonus Credit to Lead Manager

1977	1978		$ Volume (millions)	No. of Issues
1	1	Salomon Brothers	$864.6	52
2	2	Merrill Lynch White Weld	525.3	42
6	3	Morgan Stanley	464.6	17
5	4	Bache Halsey Stuart Shields	440.0	34
4	5	Blyth Eastman Dillon	431.8	30
3	6	First Boston	430.8	34
7	7	Kidder Peabody	317.4	23
[a]	8	Lehman Brothers Kuhn Loeb	315.7	30
18	9	Dillon Read	308.4	22
12	10	E. F. Hutton	306.1	26
9	11	Paine Webber	285.9	20
10	12	Goldman Sachs	269.4	21
11	13	Smith Barney, Harris Upham	267.4	21
[b]	14	Dean Witter Reynolds	266.5	22
15	15	Drexel Burnham Lambert	248.5	23
[c]	16	Loeb Rhoades Hornblower	108.4	11
21	17	Warburg Paribas Becker	107.5	13
8	19	White Weld	107.5	8
19	19	Wertheim	106.4	14
25	20	Donaldson, Lufkin & Jenrette	106.1	10
24	21	Bear Stearns	76.8	10
–	22	Shearson Hayden Stone	38.1	5
22	23	Rothschild, Unterberg, Towbin	36.7	5
–	24	Weeden	15.0	1
–	25	Stuart Brothers	13.1	2

Full Credit to Lead Manager

1977	1978		$ Volume (millions)	No. of Issues
1	1	Morgan Stanley	$1,995.0	16
3	2	Salomon Brothers	1,372.9	29
4	3	First Boston	696.4	9
6	4	Bache Halsey Stuart Shields	691.8	9
2	5	Merrill Lynch White Weld	618.8	13
5	6	Blyth Eastman Dillon	400.0	4
7	7	Kidder Peabody	150.0	2
12	8	White Weld	106.2	3
9	9	Paine Webber	90.0	2
[d]	10	Lehman Brothers Kuhn Loeb	88.0	2
13	11	Goldman Sachs	75.0	3
15	12	E. F. Hutton	75.0	2
10	13	Drexel Burnham Lambert	50.0	1
–	14	Warburg Paribas Becker	35.1	2
[e]	15	Dean Witter Reynolds	35.0	1
–	16	Donaldson, Lufkin & Jenrette	10.0	1
–	–	Edward D. Jones	10.0	1

Full Credit to Each Manager

1977	1978		$ Volume (millions)	No. of Issues
1	1	Salomon Brothers	$3,442.9	52
2	2	Merrill Lynch White Weld	3,031.9	42
3	3	Blyth Eastman Dillon	2,915.0	30
11	4	E. F. Hutton	2,645.0	26
4	5	First Boston	2,636.9	34
18	6	Dillon Read	2,545.0	22
5	7	Bache Halsey Stuart Shields	2,511.9	34
7	8	Kidder Peabody	2,465.0	23
[f]	9	Dean Witter Reynolds	2,443.0	22
9	10	Smith Barney, Harris Upham	2,434.2	21
8	11	Goldman Sachs	2,410.0	21
[g]	12	Lehman Brothers Kuhn Loeb	2,409.1	30
10	13	Paine Webber	2,398.0	20
15	14	Drexel Burnham Lambert	2,225.0	23
13	15	Morgan Stanley	2,195.0	17
[h]	16	Loeb Rhoades Hornblower	1,115.0	11
19	17	Wertheim	1,100.0	14
25	18	Donaldson, Lufkin & Jenrette	788.0	10
6	19	White Weld	671.2	8
22	20	Bear Stearns	655.0	10
21	21	Warburg Paribas Becker	636.3	13
24	22	Shearson Hayden Stone	415.0	5
–	23	Rothschild, Unterberg, Towbin	290.0	5
–	24	Stuart Brothers	115.0	2
–	25	Weeden	75.0	1

[a] 1977 Rankings: Lehman Brothers 14, Kuhn Loeb 16.
[b] 1977 Rankings: Dean Witter 13, Reynolds Securities 23.
[c] 1977 Rankings: Loeb Rhoades 17, Hornblower Weeks 20.
[d] 1977 Rankings: Lehman Brothers –, Kuhn Loeb 8.
[e] 1977 Rankings: Dean Witter 14, Reynolds Securities –.
[f] 1977 Rankings: Dean Witter 12, Reynolds Securities 23.
[g] 1977 Rankings: Lehman Brothers 17, Kuhn Loeb 16.
[h] 1977 Rankings: Loeb Rhoades 14, Hornblower Weeks 20.

EXHIBIT 12-6. *(continued)*

Total Public Finance Issues: General Obligation Bonds and Revenue Bonds

Bonus Credit to Lead Manager

1977	1978	Manager	$ Volume (millions)	No. of Issues
1	1	Goldman Sachs	$1,967.4	98
2	2	Blyth Eastman Dillon	1,211.1	64
6	3	First Boston	1,167.5	45
3	4	Kidder Peabody	1,138.2	68
4	5	Merrill Lynch White Weld	1,125.0	74
9	6	E. F. Hutton	1,096.9	51
5	7	Smith Barney, Harris Upham	1,014.2	44
7	8	Salomon Brothers	1,013.3	45
11	9	Bache Halsey Stuart Shields	582.4	31
12	10	Paine Webber	549.2	38
—[a]	11	Lehman Brothers Kuhn Loeb	425.3	19
14	12	Rothschild, Unterberg, Towbin	395.1	38
21	13	Alex, Brown & Sons	372.2	14
19	14	Wm. R. Hough	357.9	21
—[b]	15	Dean Witter Reynolds	345.2	31
16	16	Butcher & Singer	318.7	41
—[c]	17	Loeb Rhoades Hornblower	312.7	20
10	18	John Nuveen	267.7	23
—	19	Wertheim	258.8	5
—	20	Dain, Kalman & Quail	243.0	20
—	21	Mathews & Wright	233.0	15
—	22	First Kentucky Securities	223.1	4
24	23	Lazard Freres	214.6	10
—	24	Piper, Jaffray & Hopwood	193.3	18
—	25	Baker, Watts	192.0	8

Full Credit to Lead Manager

1977	1978	Manager	$ Volume (millions)	No. of Issues
1	1	Goldman Sachs	$2,655.3	66
5	2	Salomon Brothers	2,143.6	17
2	3	First Boston	1,998.6	25
10	4	Merrill Lynch White Weld	1,387.7	15
3	5	Blyth Eastman Dillon	1,316.1	31
4	6	Smith Barney, Harris Upham	1,279.1	26
7	7	E. F. Hutton	1,243.0	32
6	8	Kidder Peabody	1,133.4	30
9	9	Paine Webber	757.6	18
—[d]	10	Dean Witter Reynolds	737.4	14
14	11	Wm. R. Hough	535.1	16
—[e]	12	Lehman Brothers Kuhn Loeb	490.9	8
15	13	Bache Halsey Stuart Shields	392.5	6
18	14	Alex, Brown & Sons	368.5	9
16	15	Rothschild, Unterberg, Towbin	364.5	22
—	16	Butcher & Singer	362.8	25
—	17	Wertheim	354.9	1
—[f]	18	Loeb Rhoades Hornblower	287.2	7
—	19	Matthews & Wright	278.2	14
23	20	Morgan Guaranty	194.9	2
—	21	Ziegler Securities	187.0	15
11	22	John Nuveen	185.0	9
—	23	American Securities	164.9	9
—	24	Lazard Freres	159.7	5
22	25	Miller & Schroeder	140.4	8

Full Credit to Each Manager

1977	1978	Manager	$ Volume (millions)	No. of Issues
2	1	Goldman Sachs	$7,014.2	98
7	2	Salomon Brothers	5,823.6	45
1	3	Merrill Lynch White Weld	5,809.3	74
3	4	Kidder Peabody	5,196.3	68
6	5	First Boston	4,688.1	45
4	6	Blyth Eastman Dillon	4,582.9	64
8	7	Bache Halsey Stuart Shields	3,778.5	31
5	8	Smith Barney, Harris Upham	3,522.4	44
9	9	E. F. Hutton	2,663.6	51
—[g]	10	Lehman Brothers Kuhn Loeb	2,069.7	19
11	11	Lazard Freres	1,997.2	10
12	12	Paine Webber	1,910.3	38
13	13	Alex, Brown & Sons	1,679.6	14
14	14	Morgan Guaranty	1,620.9	6
—	15	Citicorp	1,596.8	6
—[h]	16	Loeb Rhoades Hornblower	1,554.3	20
—	17	Bank of America	1,429.7	6
19	18	John Nuveen	1,351.0	23
—[i]	19	Dean Witter Reynolds	1,250.2	31
25	20	Dillon Read	1,135.7	6
15	21	Chase Manhattan	1,092.8	4
17	22	Rothschild, Unterberg, Towbin	1,062.2	38
—	23	Dain, Kalman & Quail	1,059.5	20
24	24	Butcher & Singer	920.3	41
—	25	Piper, Jaffray & Hopwood	817.2	18

[a] 1977 Rankings: Lehman Brothers 15, Kuhn Loeb 17.
[b] 1977 Rankings: Dean Witter 18, Reynolds Securities –.
[c] 1977 Rankings: Loeb Rhoades 23, Hornblower Weeks –.
[d] 1977 Rankings: Dean Witter 19, Reynolds Securities –.
[e] 1977 Rankings: Lehman Brothers 12, Kuhn Loeb 20.
[f] 1977 Rankings: Loeb Rhoades 21, Hornblower Weeks –.
[g] 1977 Rankings: Lehman Brothers –, Kuhn Loeb –.
[h] 1977 Rankings: Loeb Rhoades –, Hornblower Weeks –.
[i] 1977 Rankings: Dean Witter 22, Reynolds Securities –.

SOURCE: *Institutional Investor*, March 1979.

EXHIBIT 12-6. *(continued)*

Leading Agents for Private Placements During Full Year 1978 (Giving each manager full credit for any joint placements)

		Firm	Dollar Amt. Managed (000 Omitted)	No. of Issues
a)	1	Salomon Brothers	$2,528,794	92
	2	Goldman, Sachs & Co.	2,476,254	101
	3	First Boston Corp.	2,124,534	45
b)	4	Lehman Brothers Kuhn Loeb Inc.	1,980,956	136
c)	5	Morgan Stanley & Co.	1,966,494	34
	6	Blyth Eastman Dillon & Co.	1,542,456	40
		(including Blyth Eastman Dillon Health Care Funding, Inc.)	184,472	11
		COMBINED TOTAL	1,726,928	51
	7	Kidder, Peabody & Co., Inc.	1,173,665	69
	8	Dillon, Read & Co.	751,671	21
	9	Lazard Freres & Co.	705,000	4
	10	Warburg Paribas Becker Inc.	687,635	55
	11	Smith Barney, Harris Upham & Co.	585,424	50
	12	Paine, Webber, Jackson & Curtis Inc.	546,400	46
	13	Dean Witter Reynolds Inc.	491,311	28
	14	Bache Halsey Stuart Shields Inc.	455,758	26
	15	E. F. Hutton & Co.	283,203	15
	[a]	Merrill Lynch White Weld Capital Markets Group	2,638,037	136
	[b]	White, Weld & Co.	242,440	5
	[b]	Merrill Lynch Pierce Fenner & Smith Inc.	146,922	9

The *Digest* has not included Merrill Lynch; White Weld and Capital Markets Group in the ranking because of the duplication of financing of Merrill Lynch and White Weld prior to their merger.

[a] Totals represent financings of new firms after merger.
[b] Totals represent financings of old firms prior to their merger.

NOT INCLUDED

a) $50,000,000 of short-term notes in one issue with maturity of less than one year. Also reported an additional $134,436,072 of unlisted deals.
b) $41,066,000 of short-term bonds in two issues with maturities of less than one year.
c) $20,000,000 of short-term notes in one issue with maturity of less than one year.

SOURCE: *Investment Dealers Digest*, March 1979.

EXHIBIT 12-7. *Comparative Corporate Finance Staffs for Selected Securities Firms, 1965, 1978*

Firm	*Total Corporate and Municipal Finance Professionals, End of 1965*	*Total Corporate and Municipal Finance Professionals, Beginning of 1978*	*Percentage Increase*
Bache Halsey Stuart	24	42	75
Bear Stearns	10	22	70
Blyth Eastman Dillon	35	122	248
Dillon Read	34	72	55
E. F. Hutton	8	90	1,025
First Boston	25	175	420
Goldman, Sachs	42	156	271
Kidder, Peabody	38	127	181
Merrill Lynch	19	260	1,268
Morgan Stanley	33	135	221
Paine Webber	12	72	475
Salomon Brothers	10[a]	145	1,350
Smith Barney, Harris Upham	36	112	210
Totals for group	319	1,419	345

[a] Author's estimate.

SOURCES: Firms' estimates to author as of January 1978; Samuel L. Hayes, "Evolving Competition in Investment Banking."

EXHIBIT 12-8. *Distribution Capabilities of Securities Firms as of January 1978*

Firm	Number of Domestic Branches	Number of Domestic Retail Salespersons	Number of Domestic Institutional Salespersons	Number of Foreign Branches	Number of Foreign Salespersons
Bache Halsey Stuart	145	1,990	82	15	120
Bear, Stearns	7	220	26	3	12
Blyth Eastman Dillon	39	650	100	3	13
Dean Witter Reynolds	230	3,572	35	12	107
Dillon Read	3	0	66	1	6
Donaldson, Lufkin & Jenrette	6	45	18	3	13
Drexel Burnham Lambert	24	650	50	8	85
E. F. Hutton	191	2,700	100	11	100
First Boston	9	0	211	9	34
Goldman, Sachs	11	———259———			21
Kidder, Peabody	48	750	105	6	38
Lehman Kuhn Loeb	7	175	100	2	10
Loeb Rhoades, Hornblower	150	2,006	111	13	113
Merrill Lynch	308	6,649	560	39	406
Morgan Stanley	2	65	54	3	4
Paine Webber	135	2,080	125	6	27
Salomon Brothers	8	0	91	2	N.A.
Shearson Hayden Stone	116	1,650	50	12	70
Smith Barney	80	1,060	58	5	19
Warburg Paribas Becker	7	110	25	2	25

SOURCES: Firms' estimates except for Salomon Brothers, where statistics are drawn from *Finance Magazine,*
1977, and author's estimates. Samuel Hayes, "The Transformation of Investment Banking,"
Harvard Business Review, January–February 1979.

EXHIBIT 12-9. *Institutional Investors All-American Research Team, 1978*

Ranking			Total Team Positions		First Team		Second Team		Third Team		Runners-up	
1978	1977		1978	1977	1978	1977	1978	1977	1978	1977	1978	1977
1	2[a]	Merrill Lynch	33	22	6	5	9	5	8	6	10	6
2	1	Paine Webber/Mitchell Hutchins	23	23	6	7	2	3	5	3	10	10
3	3	Morgan Stanley	22	21	4	3	7	7	2	3	9	8
4	5	Goldman Sachs	20	17	6	7	5	1	2	3	7	6
5	4	Donaldson, Lufkin & Jenrette	19	20	5	3	2	6	4	5	8	6
6	12	Kidder Peabody	19	11	1	1	1	0	5	4	12	6
7	11	First Boston	19	12	1	0	0	2	5	4	13	6
8	6	Drexel Burnham Lambert	17	17	1	1	2	2	5	4	9	10
9	7	Smith Barney, Harris Upham	17	17	0	0	3	3	5	5	9	9
10	9	Oppenheimer	14	14	0	1	1	2	6	3	7	8
11	17	Blyth Eastman Dillon	10	6	0	0	1	0	2	1	7	5
12	15	Wertheim	10	6	0	0	0	1	3	3	7	2
13	24	Dean Witter Reynolds	9	3	2	2	0	0	2	0	5	1
14	13	C. J. Lawrence	9	9	0	1	3	2	1	2	5	4
15	25	L. F. Rothschild, Unterberg, Towbin	7	3	0	1	0	1	1	0	6	1
16	14	Sanford C. Bernstein	6	6	1	0	3	2	1	4	1	0
17	18	First Manhattan	6	5	0	0	1	1	1	1	4	3
18	18	E. F. Hutton	6	5	0	0	0	1	2	1	4	3
19	21	G. S. Grumman/Cowen	5	4	3	2	0	1	1	1	1	0
20	20[b]	Lehman Brothers Kuhn Loeb	5	5	1	0	0	0	1	0	3	5
	28	Salomon Brothers	5	3	1	1	0	0	1	1	3	1
22	22[c]	Loeb Rhoades Hornblower	4	4	0	1	2	0	0	1	2	2
23	25	Prescott, Ball & Turben	4	3	0	1	1	1	0	0	3	1
24	16	Shearson Hayden Stone	4	6	0	0	0	0	0	2	4	4
25	23	Robertson, Colman, Siebel & Weisel	3	4	1	1	1	0	0	0	1	3
26	25	Rotan Mosle	3	3	1	1	1	1	0	0	1	1
27	28	F. Eberstadt	3	3	1	1	0	0	1	1	1	1

[a]The ranking and totals for 1977 represent those of Merrill Lynch prior to its merger with White Weld.
[b]The ranking and totals for 1977 represent those of Lehman Brothers prior to its merger with Kuhn Loeb.
[c]The ranking and totals for 1977 represent those of Loeb Rhoades prior to its merger with Hornblower Weeks.

SOURCE: *Institutional Investor*, October 1978.

EXHIBIT 12-10. *Expenses of NYSE Member Firms*

	1976		1977		1978
	(millions of $)	%	(millions of $)	%	
Registered representatives compensation	$1,300	19%	$1,300	19%	N
Commissions and fees paid to others	500	7	465	7	O
Clerical and administrative	1,390	20	1,430	21	T
Communication	500	7	530	8	A
					V
Occupancy and equipment	340	5	360	5	A
Promotion	175	3	180	3	I
Interest	700	10	1,000	15	L
Others	1,000	14	1,040	22	A
					B
Total	$5,900	100%	$6,300	100%	L
					E

NOTE: Figures may not add due to rounding.

SOURCE: New York Stock Exchange, *Fact Book,* 1978.

EXHIBIT 12-11. *Capital Positions of Leading Securities Firms, 1972, 1977 ($ millions)*

		Total Capital			Equity Capital	
Rank	Firm	1977	1972	Rank	1977	1972
1	Merrill Lynch & Co. Inc.	646	464	1	646	444
2	Salomon Brothers	192	131	2	162	101
3	The E. F. Hutton Group Inc.	174	82	4	123	60
4	Dean Witter Reynolds Org. Inc.	158	82	3	151	64
5	Bache Group, Inc.	152	124	5	121	104
6	Loeb Rhoades, Hornblower & Co.	120	80	6	98	66
7	Goldman, Sachs & Co.	118	77	7	93	62
8	Paine Webber, Inc.	118	80	9	83	64
9	Blyth Eastman Dillon & Co. Inc.	85	41	13	53	25
10	First Boston, Inc.	84	57	8	84	57
11	Shearson Hayden Stone Inc.	84	30	14	49	22
12	Kidder, Peabody & Co. Inc.	81	46	10	67	41
13	Donaldson, Lufkin & Jenrette	77	64	12	54	58
14	Drexel Burnham Lambert Group	76	42	13	53	25
15	Lehman Brothers Kuhn Loeb Inc.	76	41	15	49	23
16	Warburg Paribas Becker	67	30	16	41	28
17	Morgan Stanley & Co. Inc.	62	20	11	58	15
18	Smith Barney, Harris Upham & Co. Inc.	61	47	20	34	23
19	Thomson McKinnon Inc.	46	29	23	17	10
20	Bear, Stearns & Co.	46	38	18	38	38
21	L. F. Rothschild, Unterberg, Towbin	41	30	21	32	27
22	A. G. Edwards & Sons, Inc.	35	17	19	34	15
23	Inter-Regional Financial Group, Inc.	30	16	22	20	12
24	Oppenheimer & Co. Inc.	29	47	24	12	35
25	Moseley, Hallgarten & Estabrook, Inc.	15	6	25	7	3

SOURCE: *Finance Magazine,* March 1978.

EXHIBIT 12-12.

The Twenty-Five Largest Managers of International Issues 1978[a]	Dollar Volume (millions)	No. of Issues
1 Deutsche Bank	$1,767.5	83
2 Nomura Securities	1,193.7	63
3 Salomon Brothers	1,181.9	42
4 Morgan Stanley	1,137.5	23
5 Union Bank of Switzerland	1,130.7	96
6 Swiss Bank Corp	1,050.9	101
7 Daiwa Securities	970.4	58
8 Westdeutsche Landesbank	889.5	87
9 Yamaichi Securities	881.5	45
10 Nikko Securities	834.1	39
11 Credit Suisse	688.3	41
12 Dresdner Bank	680.9	60
13 Wood Gundy	562.0	18
14 Merrill Lynch White Weld	532.1	45
15 Commerzbank	518.0	47
16 Credit Suisse First Boston	452.7	70
17 Banque Nationale de Paris	446.0	54
18 A. E. Ames	411.8	12
19 First Boston	336.4	28
20 Paribas	330.3	55
21 Goldman, Sachs	267.7	16
22 S. G. Warburg	244.4	41
23 Amro Bank	241.4	32
24 Algemene Bank Nederland	239.3	42
25 Kredietbank Lux	235.8	55

The Twenty-Five Largest Managers of Yankee Bond Issues, 1978	Dollar Volume (millions)	No. of Issues
1 Morgan Stanley	$1,025.0	9
2 Salomon Brothers	1,016.2	19
3 Wood Gundy	506.7	10
4 A. E. Ames	394.2	9
5 Merrill Lynch White Weld	336.3	10
6 Goldman, Sachs	225.7	9
7 First Boston	223.7	8
8 Smith Barney, Harris Upham	181.0	4
9 Lehman Bros. Kuhn Loeb	173.8	6
10 McLeod, Young, Weir	112.5	2
11 Lazard Freres	85.0	4
12 Bache Halsey Stuart Shields	29.2	2
13 Dominion Securities	25.0	1
14 Den Norske Creditbank	18.8	1
15 Christiania Bank	18.8	1
16 Bergen Bank	18.8	1
17 PKbanken	17.9	1
18 Svenska Handelsbanken	17.9	1
19 Scandinavian Sec. Corp.	17.9	1
20 Nomura Securities	17.5	2
21 J. Henry Schroder Wagg	17.5	2
22 Postipankki	14.3	1
23 Union Bank of Finland	14.3	1
24 Scotia Bond Co.	12.5	1
25 Societe Generale	6.3	1

[a]Includes all Euromarket offerings plus all other so-called foreign deals for foreign clients sold primarily within one country in its currency and by a syndicate of that nationality.

SOURCE: *Institutional Investor,* March 1979.

CASE 13

Hospital Affiliates International, Inc., and the Hospital Management Industry

Hospital Affiliates International, Inc. (HAI), was one of the largest companies in the emerging hospital management industry in the United States and the leader in the management contract segment of the industry, with one-third of the total market in 1976. HAI owned twenty-five hospitals in several states and managed fifty other hospitals under contract. Founded only in 1968, HAI had grown from $20.1 million in sales and $859,000 in profits in 1969 to $137 million in sales and $5.3 million in profits by 1976, for an annual compound growth rate of 32 and 30 percent respectively. Exhibits 13–1 and 13–2 present a financial summary of HAI.

Mr. Jack R. Anderson, president and chief executive officer of HAI, anticipated continued vigorous growth for HAI, especially in the contract management segment of the market:

I am confident that over the next five to ten years contract management will become one of the standard alternatives a hospital's board of directors investi-

gates before reaching a decision about the type of management that is best for its institution. When this happens, a market of 2,000 hospitals will be created and I would hope that HAI could keep 25 percent of that market. I would also imagine that HAI will be in businesses that we haven't even thought of yet, maybe ones that don't even exist yet. Hospital management is one of the few remaining cottage industries. The opportunities for a firm that can help promote and manage the change are very great indeed.

However, the contract management market had attracted a number of large and aggressive competitors, such as American Medical International and National Medical Enterprises, resulting in an increased frequency of multiple bids for contracts. In addition, the question of contract renewal was becoming increasingly important as the initial contracts reached maturity. The appropriate responses to these changes were among the issues facing HAI as it looked toward the future.

The Hospital Management Industry

The $56 billion U.S. hospital industry was undergoing change in 1977, spurred in large part by a new force in the industry—the hospital management company. Investor-owned hospitals, or for-profit hospitals owned by investing groups, accounted for a rapidly growing proportion of hospitals. Of the 7,100 hospitals in the United States in 1976, 1,000 were investor-owned, up from 852 in 1966. Large-scale hospital management companies owned 378 of these, and the number was growing. In addition to owning hospitals, hospital management companies managed both investor-owned and voluntary not-for-profit hospitals under contract. A total of approximately 165 hospitals were under management contract in 1976, up from none in 1970.

The thirty-one hospital management companies in 1976 owned from three to as many as seventy hospitals and managed as many as fifty hospitals. The largest management company, Hospital Corporation of America (HCA), had revenues of $392 million in 1975, and revenues for the six largest hospital chains totaled $1.1 billion in 1975. Profit growth in the hospital management industry had been at a rate of 25 percent per year since the industry was created in 1968 (health care spending had grown at an 11.4 percent rate during 1971–1976), and one leading source predicted that hospital management company revenues would grow at 22 percent per year for the next decade. By 1985, therefore, hospital management could be a $20 billion industry, making the industry comparable in size to the defense segment of the aircraft industry today.

History of the Hospital Industry

In 1873 the U.S. Bureau of Education reported 178 hospitals of all types in the United States. By 1909, according to the American Medical Association, there were 4,359 hospitals. During this period the development of surgical procedures and radiology, and the consequent need for antiseptic conditions and specialized equipment, made the hospital indispensable to physicians. Previously, medical care

had been administered in private homes and doctors' offices.

The rapid growth in the need for hospitals resulted in construction of a large number of investor-owned facilities. But as growth in demand for hospital beds moderated in the 1930s, investor-owned hospitals began to decline as voluntary not-for-profit hospitals without any profitability constraints were built. By 1940 the proportion of investor-owned hospitals had dropped to 25 percent. These trends were accelerated by the passage of the Hill-Burton Act in 1946, which enabled communities to obtain federal matching funds for construction of their own nonprofit hospitals. The older independent investor-owned hospitals found themselves short of capital and at a competitive disadvantage, and many either closed down or sold out to their communities. By 1968 only 11 percent of all hospitals were investor-owned.

During the late 1960s, however, the investor-owned segment of the hospital industry revived. Passage of the Medicare and Medicaid legislation in 1965 created renewed investor interest in hospitals and nursing homes. Most important in sparking this was the creation of a large potential government-paid demand, and provisions in the legislation allowing investor-owned hospitals a reasonable return on equity on government-reimbursed services (the figure was currently about 11 percent pretax). Most of the investor-owned hospitals were owned by small groups of physicians or entrepreneurs and were not in a position to capitalize on the new boom. Many were short of capital, inefficiently operated, unable to control the inflationary increases in expenses that occurred during the period, and incapable of dealing effectively with increasingly complex government regulations.

This situation created an opportunity for new firms to enter the industry, and in the next five years more than thirty hospital management companies were organized. The fledgling companies built some new hospitals themselves, but nearly all of their growth came from acquisitions. By 1970 hospital management firms had acquired 246 investor-owned hospitals with 25,135 beds, representing 24 percent and 39 percent of the investor-owned hospitals and beds, respectively. The chains purchased financially troubled but fundamentally sound hospitals, as well as some very profitable hospitals for higher prices. The buoyant stock market of the late 1960s and early 1970s resulted in hospital managment company price-earnings multiples of 30–40, which permitted acquisitions of hospitals for stock and frequent public equity sales.

Hospital management company stock prices collapsed in the general economic recession in 1972, making the acquisition route for growth more difficult. Most hospital management companies shifted their emphasis in two directions. First, they moved increasingly toward construction activities (both of new hospitals and upgrading and expanding existing facilities), which were financed with internal cash flow and unused debt capacity. From 1970 to 1974, for exmple, HCA constructed an average of six hospitals per year, while Humana Inc. built twenty-one hospitals between 1973 and 1975. By 1975, however, industry debt ratios had risen as high as 75 percent of capitalization and construction activity had slowed in the industry. Even if stock prices were to recover, industry observers saw few remaining acquisition opportunities left in the industry, with most of the attractive candidates having already been acquired. Also, according to David Jones, president of Humana (a leading hospital management firm):

> Now we can only replace hospitals rather than build them because we have creamed the fast-growing parts of the country where the need for new hospitals existed. There is an untapped market, but it won't be tappable until hundreds of inefficient nonprofit hospitals being kept alive by government subsidy are allowed to die.[1]

The second major thrust of the management companies was into hospital management contracts, particularly in recent years as financial constraints led firms to seek ways of achieving growth less capital-intensive than ownership. While most of the chains, as well as some outside firms, had signed management contracts starting as early as 1971, Hospital Affiliates International had been the industry leader in management contracts from the beginning. HAI managed fifty hospitals in early 1977, representing approximately one-third of the management contracts then in force.

[1] "Humana's Hopes," *Forbes,* September 1, 1977.

Profile of the Hospital Industry

Hospitals could be characterized in a number of different ways, including ownership, type of patient treated, and teaching or nonteaching. Community hospitals (5,977 in 1975) represented the competitive reference group for the hospital management companies. Community hospitals were acute care general hospitals not owned by the federal government. According to American Hospital Association, 57 percent of all community hospitals (and 70 percent of the beds) were nonprofit "voluntary" hospitals in 1975. A number of these were owned or operated by religious groups. Thirty percent of all community hospitals (22 percent of the beds) were controlled by state and local government, and 13 percent of the hospitals (8 percent of the beds) were investor-owned in 1975 (see Exhibit 13–3).

Geographic concentration of investor-owned hospitals varied considerably. Seventy-two percent of investor-owned hospitals were located in South Atlantic, West South Central, and Pacific regions. California, Texas, Louisiana, and New York accounted for 59 percent of the total, while twenty-nine states had five or fewer investor-owned hospitals. In addition to regional differences in the concentration of investor-owned hospitals there were urban–rural differences. Fifty-six percent of investor-owned hospitals were in metropolitan areas (with 50,000 people or greater), as against 42 percent of nonprofit hospitals.

Industry observers generally agreed that the nation's aggregate supply of beds exceeded the demand for hospital services by as much as 20 percent in 1977. However, in rapidly expanding metropolitan areas such as Houston and Phoenix, shortages of hospital facilities did exist.

The Environment for Hospitals

Hospitals operated in a very complex decision-making environment relative to that of most manufacturing companies (see Exhibit 13–4). Spending for hospital care had increased 14 percent per year between 1965 and 1975, from $13 to $56 billion. The primary stimulus for the rapid growth had been inflation and the passage of Medicare and Medicaid legislation. These federally sponsored health insurance plans enfranchised some 12 million people who previously had not been part of the health care system. In addition, more comprehensive Blue Cross/Blue Shield and private insurance programs plus rising personal income were cited by industry observers as factors encouraging growth.

In 1976 nearly 90 percent of all hospital costs and charges were paid for by so-called third-party payors, with the federal government, Blue Cross/Blue Shield, and private insurance companies providing the majority of such payments. The federal government's share of total hospital expenditures climbed sharply after the advent of Medicare and Medicaid, rising from 37 percent in 1965 to 55 percent in 1975. Since government at all levels, particularly the federal government, was financing an increasing percentage of the national hospital care bill, there was increasing regulation of the hospital industry.

THIRD-PARTY PAYORS

Medicare was a federal program that provided persons aged sixty-five and over and certain disabled persons under sixty-five with hospital and medical insurance benefits. In 1974 Medicare accounted for $8 billion (20 percent) of all hospital expenditures. These benefits included reimbursement for the costs of hospitalization for up to ninety days per incident of illness. In 1976 the Medicare patient paid only the first $104 of hospital costs, and $26 per day after the sixtieth day of hospitalization. Hospitals were reimbursed by the government under a formula by which the government paid all "reasonable" direct and indirect costs of the hospital services that were furnished, including depreciation and interest, in addition to a fixed 11 percent pretax return on equity. Reimbursements were subject to examination and adjustments by federal auditors.

Medicare was a cooperative federal and state medical assistance program, administered by the states, whereby hospital benefits were available to the medically indigent. In 1974 Medicaid accounted for $9 billion (22.5 percent) of all hospital expenditures. While there was only one Medicare program, there were fifty distinct state Medicaid programs,

and the rules, regulations, reporting requirements, and reimbursable costs varied from state to state. Most states paid the hospital a fixed per diem rate based on its reimbursable Medicaid costs as determined by that state program's individual reimbursement formula, rather than at the hospital's standard billing rate. In order to qualify for Medicaid (and Medicare) a hospital had to be licensed under applicable state or local laws and comply on a continuing basis with a number of standards related to safety and the quality of patient care. Other government programs administered by the Defense Department for active service personnel and veterans accounted for $4.6 billion (11 percent) of hospital care expenditure in 1974.

Blue Cross and Blue Shield were private insurance programs that provided subscribers with hospital benefits (Blue Cross) and doctors' services (Blue Shield). In 1974 Blue Cross and Blue Shield accounted for $7.4 billion (18 percent) of hospital expenditures. The program was managed by a network of independent Blue Cross/Blue Shield organizations that varied in their geographic coverage from New York City to multistate regions. Hospitals were paid a negotiated daily (per diem) rate based on their costs as allowable by Blue Cross. The costs allowable by Blue Cross were different from those of Medicare and Medicaid and differed from one regional Blue Cross plan to another. The reimbursement formula most widely used was referred to as "retrospective." In the retrospective formula, a hospital's per diem rate for the upcoming year was based on its most recent fully audited costs. Therefore, the rate for 1977, which was negotiated in late 1976, was based on 1975 costs plus an inflation factor. The inflation factor also varied between regional Blue Cross plans. Blue Shield made payments directly to physicians on a fixed "fee for service" basis.

The final major category of third-party payors was commercial insurance companies. Commercial insurance companies such as Metropolitan Life, Prudential, and Travelers provided health insurance directly to individuals and through group insurance plans of employers. Reimbursement was generally based on the hospital's posted fees. In 1974 commercial insurance companies accounted for $6.3 billion (16 percent) of all hospital expenditures.

TRENDS IN HOSPITAL UTILIZATION

From 1970 to 1975, total admissions to community hospitals had risen about 1.2 percent per year while inpatient days grew at 3 percent because of a rise in the average length of a hospital visit. This was caused primarily by the influx of older and medically indigent patients who often suffered from more serious illnesses, and to the Medicare and Medicaid regulations that paid for certain services only if such services were rendered in a hospital. Reimbursement and admission procedures under Medicare and Medicaid had been modified recently in an attempt to reduce the length of stay per admission.

GOVERNMENT REGULATION OF HOSPITALS

A hospital's operations were subject to myriad local, state, and federal government regulations. Hospitals were inspected periodically by state licensing agencies to determine whether the standards of medical care, equipment, and cleanliness necessary for continued licensing were being met. Hospital construction and expansion were also subject to local zoning and building codes. In most areas construction required the additional approval of local hospital planning authorities, which considered the need for additional facilities as well as the suitability of sites in decisions to approve new hospital construction. The piecemeal regulation of hospitals had become so extensive that in 1974 at least sixteen federal agencies exercised some control over a hospital.

Late in 1974 the U.S. Congress enacted the Social Security Amendments of 1972, which contained numerous provisions that affected the scope of Medicare coverage and the basis for reimbursement of Medicare providers. One critical impact of the legislation was the strengthening of area-wide health planning agencies, called Health Systems Agencies (HSAs). The geographic scope of an areawide health planning agency varied considerably from single cities to multiple-state regions. In general, such planning agencies were established to include areas that, from the government's perspective, should share or at least coordinate health care and hospital services.

Under the law, Medicare reimbursement could be denied for such costs as depreciation, interest, other expenses, and return on equity for capital expenditures that had not received prior approval by a designated state health planning agency, if such expenditures exceeded $100,000, altered bed capacity, or substantially changed the services of a hospital. In response to this provision, an increasing number of states had enacted legislation requiring "certificates of need" as a prior condition to hospital construction, expansion, or introduction of major new services. The Social Security Amendments of 1972 also stipulated that acquisitions of hospitals would require prior approval by the local areawide health planning agencies. The leading investor-owned hospital companies had stated that no adverse effects had been experienced or were anticipated from this provision, but HSAs were becoming increasingly activist in denying planned expansions and promoting lower-cost walk-in clinics and home health care.[2]

An additional feature of the Social Security Amendments of 1972 was an important section providing that admissions of Medicare and Medicaid patients had to be reviewed by an approved Professional Standards Review Organization (PSRO) within one working day following a patient's admission to the hospital, to determine if the admission was necessary. PSROs were also to commence reviewing patient utilization of hospital facilities by July 1, 1978. These provisions were designed to prevent unnecessarily long hospital stays. Though opposition from the medical profession had delayed establishment of the PSROs, industry observers expected implementation of PSROs by 1980.

A second major piece of health care legislation, the National Health Planning and Resources Development Act, was enacted in 1975. While the full effect of the law was still uncertain, it would increase the role of the federal government in such areas as long-range planning of new hospital and clinic construction, control of discretionary hospital expenditures for such items as consultants and new diagnostic equipment, and prior review of any additions or modifications to existing health care facilities.

[2] "Agencies Act to Lower Health Bills by Saying No to Bigger Hospitals," *The Wall Street Journal,* May 5, 1977.

Hospital Operations

A hospital was in the business of providing acute medical services such as surgery, and the diagnostic and therapeutic services necessary to support the needs of the acute care patient.[3] The routine hospital services included room, board, housekeeping, and regular nursing care. Additional services were referred to as "ancillary" and included respiratory therapy, clinical laboratory testing, electrocardiography, ambulance, and emergency room. A hospital's patients were usually divided into inpatient and outpatient categories.

INPATIENTS

Inpatients were persons who had been admitted to the hospital by a physician and were resident in one of the hospital's beds. The hospital's ability to service inpatients was limited by its total number of beds and by the division of its beds between different service groups such as pediatric, obstetrics and gynecology, medical-surgical, and intensive care. A hospital was not permitted to place a medical-surgical patient in a bed certified for another area of the hospital. Consequently, it was not unusual to find one area operating at peak capacity while another was virtually unused. The process of modifying the bed composition was cumbersome, bureaucratic, and lengthy. For example, obstetrics had once been a fully utilized service, but the recent slowing of the birthrate had resulted in an oversupply of obstetric beds. However, some community planning agencies were unwilling to allow the hospital to reduce the number of obstetric beds, perpetuating the oversupply condition.

Hospital charges for inpatients were typically divided into a daily room and board fee and a fixed fee each time an ancillary service was used by the patient. The significance of a hospital's inpatient fee structure for its financial performance was directly related to its mix of patients. If a large percentage of inpatients were covered under any of the cost-based reimbursement programs (Blue Cross, Medicare or Medicaid), the fee set by the hospital had little impact on its revenue-generating ability. This was the

situation many large urban hospitals found themselves in. If a hospital's patient base was primarily self-paying or privately insured, on the other hand, adjustments to the rate structure could produce meaningful changes in revenues and profits. Hospitals were forced to raise their posted fees continually because of a quirk in the Blue Cross reimbursement formula, which in most plans reimbursed the lesser of audited costs or posted charges.

The daily room and board fee included none of the ancillary services and very little of the cost of drugs (usually only aspirin) but did include meals, regular nursing care, and housekeeping services. Daily room and board charges varied substantially from hospital to hospital and even among hospitals within a community. The hospital then charged the patient for every drug dosage, ancillary service, or other hospital services (such as telephone, television, and admissions paperwork) used while in the hospital. The federal and state governments required the hospital to show physical proof that all services charged for had actually been performed in order to qualify for reimbursement, even if reimbursement was on a set fee per diem basis. This meant a separate charge slip for each discrete item in the hospital.

In an attempt to streamline the billing process, many hospitals had adopted the unit packaging concept. All services provided by the hospitals were individually packaged (e.g., every penicillin pill was packaged separately) and charged for. One result of this and reimbursement regulations generally was a virtual explosion of paper flow within the hospital. Industry observers estimated that a hospital processed about twenty unique charges per day per patient. The increased volume of paperwork and the need for more complex and detailed reports to third-party payors had resulted in the rapid growth of computerization in hospitals.

Hospitals often used certain profitable services to offset relatively less profitable ones. For example, an ancillary service such as inhalation therapy was typically quite profitable, because the procedure was easily administered by a technician, the required equipment was inexpensive to buy and had a high patient capacity per day, the therapy required frequent repeat visits by the patient, and the third-party payors allowed a fee of $30 per visit. An ancillary service such as this would be used to offset an

---

[3] There were also long-term facilities, such as mental institutions and tuberculosis hospitals. These are not discussed in this case, though their operations were basically similar.

unprofitable obstetrics ward operating at only 30 percent occupancy, or an open heart surgery unit used once a month.

OUTPATIENTS

Outpatients were persons who used the ancillary services of the hospital without having been admitted. Such patients were usually former inpatients who required additional follow-up treatment in rehabilitation or speech or physical therapy, or patients referred by their private physicians to have laboratory or diagnostic tests performed. The emergency room was also a major source of outpatient visits. Outpatients tended to be more profitable for the hospital than inpatients, because third-party payors reimbursed the hospital for outpatient services on a "fee-for-service" rather than a cost basis.

ORGANIZATION STRUCTURE

Hospitals were usually organized into two separate units divided along functional lines. The *administrator* managed the hospital and performed the scheduling and billing functions, while the *chief of medicine* was responsible for the actual health care delivered by the hospital. At the top of both organizations was the board of directors. Reporting to the administrator was a department head in charge of each ancillary service, with an assistant administrator sometimes adding a third layer of management. However, in most cases the administrator, assistant administrator, controller, and director of nursing were the key administrative officers in the hospital.

The medical organization was composed entirely of physicians, with a physician responsible for each medical service (e.g., cardiology, radiology) provided by the hospital. Physicians also served on the hospital's medical utilization review committee, which was responsible for ensuring that physicians affiliated with the hospital and permitted to admit patients met certain minimum standards of medical practice.[4] The medical side of the hospital was not as structured as the administrative functions because of the operating style of physicians, who

[4] Industry critics argued that these standards were ineffectively low and enforcement very sporadic.

typically viewed themselves as professionally equal. The chief of medicine was the top physician in the hospital and represented the interests of the medical staff to the administrator and board. While the administrator had more direct control over subordinates, the chief of medicine often had more prestige in the hospital's community and had more influence over the board of directors. The dual organization structure in hospitals frequently resulted in internal conflicts over issues such as the quality of care versus the cost of care that had to be resolved by the board.

Hospitals' boards of directors were typically composed of prominent members of the community such as business people, educators, religious leaders, and civic-mined individuals. Board positions were unpaid and usually one of many outside commitments its members had in addition to their primary occupation. Board members generally knew little about the day-to-day operations of the hospital, and the extent of their managerial sophistication varied a great deal by hospital, with larger urban hospitals generally directed by more experienced board members. Board members were more concerned with establishing and maintaining a high quality image in the community than with the detail of hospital operations; they were sensitive to the quality of care delivered by the hospital and complaints by the patients that the hospital was not responsive to their needs.

PERSONNEL AND SERVICES

The largest portion of any hospital's budget was employee salaries and related expenses. Personnel costs represented approximately 50 percent of a hospital's operating budget, with nursing services alone accounting for 35 percent of the total. The remainder of the costs were for supplies, interest, taxes, and maintenance. A typical hospital carried more than 20,000 separate items in its inventory of supplies (including drugs).

Most hospitals did not act in concert with other hospitals when buying supplies or contracting for such services as laundry and equipment maintenance. However, some independent hospitals had begun to pool their resources to achieve economies in purchasing and shared services. In a few instances, independent hospitals had formed nonprofit hospital holding companies to permit significant purchasing cost reductions to be realized, and shared services on the local level were beginning to grow in 1975. Although the process was proceeding slowly, according to the American Hospital Association two-thirds of all hospitals were sharing at least one service in 1976, and government pressure to increase shared services was building.[5]

Hospital Management Contracts

Management contracts were a vehicle through which hospital management companies made their cost-saving, revenue-producing, and purchasing expertise available to independent hospitals. Under the terms of such a contract made with a hospital's board of directors, the management company assumed total responsibility for the hospital's daily operations in exchange for a management fee based on a percent of gross revenues plus an incentive. Most competitors in the industry offered their full range of services only as a single package.

When a management company signed a contract to manage a hospital it *did not* utilize its own personnel to staff the entire hospital, but rather installed from one to a few key managers. While all hospital management firms installed their own administrator to manage the hospital, some firms also brought in their own director of nursing and a financial officer.

The first four to eight months of a management contract represented a turnaround situation, where the management company improved the financial condition of the hospital, reviewed the operations of all the major departments, established quality standards where necessary, and generally streamlined the hospital's operations. These tasks were accomplished either by teams of staff specialists who spent full time consulting with client hospitals or by task forces assembled from the staffs of the management company's owned hospitals. For example, where the task force approach was used the management company would borrow an administrator from one of its owned hospitals, a director of nursing from another, a financial executive from a

[5] Hospitals currently shared such services as laundry, food processing, expensive laboratory and diagnostic equipment and certain medical services, such as obstetrics and gynecology.

third, and an expert in the management of ancillary services from a fourth.

Completely restructuring a hospital's departments and training its personnel could take over a year of intensive effort. As a result, management contracts typically broke even on the fees charged during the first year. Thereafter, industry observers estimated that as much as ½ to ⅔ of the annual fee was profit in 1976. At the end of the term of the contract, the management company faced the requirement that the contract be renewed by the hospital's board.

In addition to installing an administrator and providing the services of staff specialists, a hospital signing a management contract became part of the management company's group purchasing program, often resulting in substantial savings.

Since 1971, HAI, HCA, American Medical International (AMI) and Hyatt Medical Management Services Division (a $30 million hospital management subsidiary of Hyatt Corporation), among others, had signed more than 165 contracts, with an estimated 100 additional contracts under negotiation in 1977. The market for management contracts included investor-owned, voluntary, local, and state hospitals, many of which were beset by rapidly rising costs and confusing government regulations. Industry sources defined the primary potential market for management contracts to encompass all community hospitals with more than 100 beds, which included some 2,000 institutions.

As of 1977 hospital management companies had signed contracts primarily with that segment of these hospitals that were financially troubled, which consisted of approximately 200–300 hospitals, according to industry participants. Hospital financial problems were generally the result of a combination of factors, including poor business procedures in screening patients and billing, poor physician relations, ill-informed trustees, and heavy debt service expenses resulting from past expansion.

The term of a management contract was usually three to five years before renewal, though there was no standard contract in the industry. Fees were generally calculated using a customized formula which took into consideration such factors as the financial results of the managed hospital, improvements in the quality of care delivered, and specific targets for improvements in the operation of the hospital. Average fees ranged from 4 to 8 percent of the annual gross revenues of the hospital, with the percentage falling as the hospital's size increased. More and more contracts were being negotiated as flat fees agreed upon in advance, rather than as percentages of revenue. A typical management contract fee could be calculated by multiplying the fee times the hospital's revenues per occupied bed day. For example, with a percentage rate of 4 percent the revenue per patient day of $150 in a 135-bed hospital that was 70 percent occupied, the annual management fee would be approximately $200,000 per year.

A management firm could achieve some economies in servicing contracts through the clustering of cliet hospitals in one geographic area, allowing more efficient use of regional management and staff specialist time.

Competition in the Hospital Management Industry

At the end of 1975 there were thirty-one hospital management companies, owning or leasing a total of 378 hospitals, representing 51,230 beds. The six leading hospital management firms owned 255 hospitals and managed seventy-nine others for a total of 47,805 beds (see Exhibit 13–5). From 1971 to 1975 the number of beds controlled by these six companies had risen by 24 percent per year, compared to a 2.2 percent growth rate for nongovernment community hospital beds in general.

Competitors in the management contract segment of the industry were becoming more numerous. Competitors for management contracts included not only hospital management companies but hotel management companies (for housekeeping and food management services), consulting firms and certified public accounting firms (which became involved in hospital turnarounds), specialized data processing organizations (which offered payroll and accounts receivable systems), and insurance companies (which sold paperwork management systems, computer systems for billing and accounting, and assistance in maximizing third-party reimbursement). In addition, some former hospital administrators had entered the business by establishing small offices to manage one or a few hospitals. A number of these classes of competition had entered the industry recently, though others had been offering services to hospitals for many years. A final category of competitors were nonprofit groups such as the Lutheran Society and Homes Society, which provided expertise to groups of hospitals who shared the costs.

Bidding for contracts among the hospital management chains was now commonplace, and fees were beginning to fall. Renewals posed a major uncertainty. According to HCA's vice president and treasurer, Sam A. Brooks, Jr.:

> The whole problem of management contracts is that it usually isn't hard to turn a hospital around, and once you do, it is easy to run. Then you have to hustle to prove to the hospital that you can do something for them.

One particularly attractive type of management contract was for development, construction, and then management of a hospital for a foreign country. In 1975 HCA was awarded a seven-year $70 million contract to build and manage Saudi Arabia's new 250-bed King Faisal Specialist Hospital. This was the largest management contract so far awarded.

COMPETITIVE STRATEGIES OF THE LEADING FIRMS

Among the six leading hospital management companies a variety of competitive strategies had been adopted (financial and operating statistics for the leading firms are shown in Exhibits 13–5 and 13–6):

Hospital Corporation of America (HCA). HCA, located in Nashville, Tennessee, was the largest hospital management company in the world. In 1976 HCA owned or leased sixty-eight hospitals containing 14,000 beds. HCA began in 1960 as a single hospital in Nashville but did not begin to expand until 1968, when Jack Masey, founder of the Kentucky Fried Chicken chain, assumed the position of president. From 1968 to 1970 HCA acquired twenty-one hospitals for common stock, the remaining forty-nine hospitals being built by the company from 1968 through 1976. Approximately 50 percent of HCA's hospitals were located in the

Southeastern United States, especially Florida, Tennessee, Texas, and Virginia.

HCA was known in the industry for its special expertise in the design and construction of new hospitals. The thirty-six hospitals constructed since 1970 at a cost of $280 million had been standardized in their design and equipment specifications. This had led to shorter construction times, lower construction costs and interest charges, and a reduction in the time required for a new facility to achieve profitability from one year to five months. HCA attempted to build its hospitals in clusters: a large central facility surrounded by smaller satellite hospitals (usually within a radius of 50 miles). Recently HCA had begun to concentrate on building new hospitals and replacing older out-of-date hospitals with modern ones. Corporate goals were to add six new owned hospitals (900–1,000 new beds) per year over the next five years. The active building program meant that there were a large number of newer hospitals in the HCA system.

Until recently HCA had used management contracts as a means of achieving ownership of a hospital. Typically, HCA would agree to an interim management arrangement while purchase negotiations were being finalized. Therefore, HCA had only ten hospital management contracts at the end of 1975. However, in 1976 HCA had announced the establishment of a separate management contract subsidiary under an HCA vice president who had previously been responsible for the marketing of management contracts. In the last few months of 1976 HCA had announced seven new management contracts, and its targeted goal was to have eighty management contracts, bringing in $15 million in fees by 1983.

HCA still made use of personnel borrowed from its owned hospitals to staff new management contracts. According to industry observers, however, HCA was actively looking to hire its own group of staff specialists dedicated to management contract operations. HCA's initial management contract marketing activities had met with mixed success, but corporate goals were to add up to ten new contracts per year over the next several years.

Recently HCA had become the first hospital management company to succeed in raising long-term debt in the public market. The company sold $33 million of A-rated fifteen-year first mortgage bonds in 1975 and $22 million of common stock in March of 1976.

National Medical Enterprises (NME). NME was the smallest of the six leading competitors with nineteen owned or leased hospitals, 80 percent located in California, which was the company's home base. NME also managed fifteen hospitals under contract in 1976, all of its management contracts having been signed in the previous three years. NME had focused its management contract marketing efforts on nonprofit hospitals, and its goals were to add ten new contracts per year over the next three to five years. NME, the only firm reporting operating income on contracts, reported on operating loss of $818,000 on contract revenues of $3,505,000 in 1976.[6] Despite this, NME claimed it could achieve profit margins of 30–55 percent in the contract management business and expected the recently reorganized division to make a "significant contribution to earnings" in the future.

NME had been active in the management of county hospitals in suburban California communities. Recently the company had begun to develop a team of staff specialists and shift its marketing focus east from its California base. NME typically installed several company employees in a managed hospital.

In addition to hospital ownership and management, NME offered services in hospital design and construction and undertook turnkey hospital development projects. NME also managed respiratory therapy departments for twenty-four hospitals and sold hospital test equipment, hospital supplies, ancillary health services, and industrial and medical gases. These businesses contributed 8 percent of sales and a 3 percent loss after taxes in 1975.

American Medical Interntional (AMI). AMI was the first hospital management company. Founded in California by a bioanalyst in 1956 as a clinical testing laboratory for hospitals, the company purchased two financially troubled customer hospitals.

[6] The contract division contained an undisclosed amount of revenues and expenses as a result of a medical education subsidiary, operating medical buildings, and international development activities. International development costs were $626,000 in 1976, while losses on the medical education subsidiary were reported as $271,000 (Annual Report).

By 1975 AMI owned forty-three hospitals after an aggressive facilities expansion and modernization program, the majority in California and Texas, and had been the first hospital management company to expand internationally, owning hospitals in England and Switzerland. AMI had only seven hospitals under management contracts at the end of 1976, but its corporate goals included "rapid expansion" in that market. The company also considered the international market a significant source of future expansion for its contract business. AMI did *not* have a pool of staff specialists but utilized personnel borrowed from its owned hospitals.

AMI provided other health care services such as inhalation therapy, production and marketing of health education films, medical personnel placement, turnkey development projects, and management of medical laboratories. AMI also offered computerized medical record services for 100 hospitals and had launched a program to offer separate hospital management information systems to investor-owned and nonprofit hospitals. These business activities accounted for 6 percent of AMI's revenues and 24 percent of income before taxes in 1975.

American Medicorp (AMC).   AMC was founded in Philadelphia in 1968 by a young New York investment banker and a Philadelphia lawyer, both of whom had specialized in securing long-term financing for hospitals. Withing two years, AMC had acquired twenty-seven hospitals and nursing homes in California, Florida, and Texas. Seven new hospitals were built between 1970 and 1975. One of the company's hospitals, Sunrise Hospital in Las Vegas, had 486 beds and accounted for more than 10 percent of AMC's pretax income in 1974.

AMC's rapid expansion in the 1968–1972 period led to cost control difficulties. Since then the company had terminated several unprofitable operations, including some hospitals and nursing homes, and reduced its capital expansion budget by 20 percent. AMC had $110 million in goodwill on its balance sheet as of December 1975 and was involved in several legal disputes as to whether a return was to be allowed on that portion of its capital base by third-party payors.

AMC signed seven management contracts in 1975, covering 1,089 beds, and seven more in 1976. According to its annual report, AMC hoped to use the management contract market as a vehicle for future revenue and profit growth. It planned five new management contracts in 1977. AMC was in the process of developing a staff specialist group and implementing an enlarged selling and advertising campaign, and industry observers characterized AMC as an aggressive marketer relative to others in the industry.

Humana.   Founded in California in 1964 as Extendicare, Inc., Humana initially owned and operated extended nursing care facilities for the elderly. The company had grown into the largest extended care provider in the United States by 1967, primarily through acquisition. Humana had also expanded into mobile home parks during this period. In 1969 Extendicare shifted strategic emphasis and began investing its resources in hospital construction. By 1974 the company had fifty-four hospitals and had sold off all of its nonhospital operations (including the extended nursing care facilities and mobile home parks) and changed its name to Humana. By the end of 1976 Humana owned sixty-three hospitals, primarily in Texas, Florida, Alabama, and Tennessee.

Humana's future plans were to concentrate on building new hospitals and expanding existing ones to the extent that funds were available. Humana was the only one of the six leading hospital management companies not active in the contract management business. Mr. David Jones, Humana's chairman of the board, commented on the management contract business in a 1975 interview: "It's like Wall Street—when everybody thinks it's a good idea, it's time to get out."

One industry observer believed that Humana had built the capacity of its owned hospitals in anticipation of demand, which provided ample near-term growth opportunity without new construction. As a result, Humana had only 55 percent occupancy in 1977, as against a national hospital average of 75 percent.

All the major hospital management companies had made significant additions to senior management depth in the 1972–1976 period. This included phasing out of original founders from active management, expanded boards, and increased corporate staffs.

THE SECOND TIER OF COMPETITORS

The second tier of management companies included Hyatt Corporation, Medenco, A. E. Brim & Assoc., Charter Medical, General Health Services, AID, and R. H. Medical. While all the second-tier companies had relatively few owned hospitals, Hyatt, Medenco, and A. E. Brim were quite active companies in management contracts. Exhibit 13–7 shows the number of owned and managed hospitals for the second-tier firms at the end of 1976. Second-tier firms were aggressive bidders and were sometimes willing to reduce the price and length of an initial management contract in order to gain access to a hospital. They did not have teams of staff specialists as of 1976.

Hyatt was considered by many industry observers to be a dangerous competitor because of its affiliation with a large, well-known parent organization, which lent credibility to Hyatt's marketing efforts. Hyatt had been willing to accept one-year trial contracts and to lend money to financially troubled hospitals to facilitate winning contracts. Hyatt was credited with an excellent marketing information network, and it seemed to be able to learn first about many potential management contract situations.

Hyatt, Medenco, and A. E. Brim were all planning stepped-up efforts in management contracts in 1977. Hyatt had made no public projections but was known to be seeking to increase its management contract business. Medenco predicted that it would double its management contract services in 1977, adding up to twelve new managed hospitals. A. E. Brim forecast a doubling of its management contract services within eighteen months.

Future Outlook for the Hospital Industry

A number of important factors promised to affect importantly the shape of the hospital industry in the years ahead.

NATIONAL HEALTH INSURANCE

Although National Health Insurance (NHI) probably would not be enacted by Congress in 1977, industry observers unanimously expected it to become a reality in the next three to five years. The main uncertainty for the investor-owned hospital industry was what form the legislation would take. Although NHI would put hospital purchasing power in the hands of people who were not currently in the health care system, would eliminate bad debts, and would expand the use of currently profitable outpatient facilities, certain versions of the bill would extend the current Medicare reimbursement formula (with its 11 percent before-tax return on equity) to all hospital revenues. That rate of return would hurt the investor-owned hospitals by reducing their ability to borrow in the public market. Another possibility was that all hospitals could be forced to provide the public with more unprofitable services such as emergency centers and maternity and pediatric wards. Finally, if reimbursement rates were negotiated based on industry averages, well-managed concerns could benefit while marginal competitors might be hurt. However, if rate negotiation became a cumbersome, bureaucratic, and political process the entire hospital industry could be reduced to public utility status.

On the other end of the spectrum, Georgia Senator Herman Talmadge had recently introduced a bill in the Senate that would allow investor-owned hospitals a return twice as great as nonprofit hospitals and would penalize high-cost operators and call for more involvement of the private insurance carriers to administer the NHI program. The investor-owned hospital industry was naturally in favor of such legislation.

Industry observers believed that the exact shape the final legislation would take would be a compromise between these extreme points of view. In addition, public opinion would influence that attitude federal legislation took toward the investor-owned hospitals. Historically, the public had viewed profit-making in the hospital sector with mistrust.

An April 1977 initiative by President Jimmy Carter represented a new wrinkle in dealing with the health care problem. The Carter proposal was to limit allowable increases in hospital charges to 9 percent per year and also to establish a national dollar limit on new capital expenditures, to stem the tide of cost increases that had plagued the industry. The proposal had drawn outright opposition from the hospital industry.

EXPANDED HEALTH PLANNING

Industry observers predicted that either under government pressure or by overt legal mandate, hospitals would have to increase the level of coordination among themselves and with all elements of the health care delivery system. Shared services, joint undertakings, consolidations and satellite hospitals were some of the forms this coordination was expected to take. Hospital management companies were enthusiastic about the idea of developing "medical complexes" for communities.

UNIONIZATION

In 1974 Congress amended the National Labor Relations Act to permit unionization of all hospital employees. The amendment had resulted in increased union activity in the health care field, but the number of covered employees was still relatively small.

HEALTH MAINTENANCE ORGANIZATION (HMO)

Industry observers predicted that group purchasers of health services, such as corporations and employee unions, would play an increasing role in structuring the health care industry. Group purchasers had typically paid premiums to insurance companies, who then negotiated with the hospital and physicians. To date, insurance companies had been relatively ineffective in their attempts to control the cost and quality of health care. However, the future could see competitive bidding and standardization of contracts if the group purchasers decided to establish their own health care plans and contract directly with hospital management companies and other health care delivery organizations to provide the desired level of medical services.

The term HMO referred to a variety of prepaid health plans by which a group practice of doctors or a hospital contracted with a given patient population to provide a certain level of health care for a fixed monthly fee. This differed from conventional health insurance in that doctors were paid a flat rate rather than a fee for each procedure performed. The basic concept was to shift the burden of cost control for health services from the patient to an organization that maximized profits by keeping people well and reducing the need for expensive services.

HMOs appeared to hold promise for hospital management companies because they could contract directly with corporations rather than deal with intermediaries such as Blue Cross or Blue Shield. With government sponsorship and encouragement, the number of HMOs was expected to increase. One prediction was that there could be 10,000 HMOs in the United States by 1985. However, such a prediction was highly speculative because government support had been erratic, and many of the early HMOs had failed.

TECHNOLOGY CHANGES

The level of technological sophistication had been increasing at a very rapid rate in the health care industry over the previous decade. Industry observers predicted that the rate of change could continue to accelerate through the late 1980s as an increased demand for the highest quality health care and government money to absorb the increased costs encouraged private enterprise to focus additional research and development resources on the health care industry. A prominent hospital consultant described the situation as follows:

> Five years ago an expensive piece of diagnostic equipment, costing perhaps $500,000, was expected to last at least five and, hopefully, seven years. Today the same type of equipment costs $1,500,000 and will be useful for at most three years. The pressure for change is a combination of the hospital wanting to provide the highest quality care and the physicians being afraid not to. Doctors are very sensitive about their malpractice exposure if they do not have access to the very latest, most advanced, diagnostic and therapeutic equipment.

The Federal Government required, by 1974, that hospitals secure the approval of local planning agencies before buying equipment that cost more than $100,000.

Hospital Affiliates International, Inc.

History

HAI was founded in 1968 by two physicians and two businessmen, Dr. Herbert J. Schulman, Dr. Irwin B. Eskind, his brother Richard J. Eskind, and Baron Coleman. The founders believed that the health care industry was seriously lacking the modern management techniques required to meet the nation's increased demand for high-quality, reasonable-cost, health care. Guaranteeing $2 million of their own capital, they began to build an organization to meet this need. Jack Anderson assumed the position of president soon thereafter, having held high-level financial positions in several large companies before joining HAI.

The original focus of HAI was to acquire or build its own hospitals in rapidly growing regions of the country that needed additional health care facilities. However, in 1971 a unique opportunity propelled HAI seriously into the contract management business. Tulane University's Medical School had performed a financial feasibility study prior to the construction of its new 300-bed teaching hospital and was most disturbed by what it found. The study showed that similar teaching institutions suffered an average operating loss of $2 million per year, which Tulane's administration was not prepared to subsidize. Tulane decided to try to interest professional hospital management companies in bidding on a contract to manage its new facility. While visiting the headquarters of the Hospital Corporation of America (the largest hospital management company, and also based in Nashville), the Tulane representative decided to see HAI as well. HAI had already entered the management contract business with two contracts. After almost seven months of negotiations, Tulane awarded the management contract to HAI in early 1972. Mr. Lanson Hyde, assistant vice president, described the significance of the Tulane agreement:

> When a prestigious, well-respected institution such as Tulane decided to use an outside company to manage its medical center, the entire concept of contract management became legitimized. Tulane was the first nationally known hospital affiliated with a medical school to use an outside management company. The

industry awareness HAI gained by this is what established our reputation in the contract business.

During the next four years, HAI added about nine new hospital management contracts per year, temporarily discontinuing the construction of its owned hospitals in 1974. HAI attempted to turn over management of its owned hospitals to another hospital management company, American Medicorp, in November of 1975, to reduce the degree of leverage in the company and concentrate its efforts in the hospital management contract business. However, the agreement was never completed because of tax difficulties, and as a result HAI decided to remain in the owned-hospital business and to expand its profile in that market by gradually building additional hospitals.

HAI's management contract business achieved another milestone for the industry in 1975, when its first significant number of hospital management agreements (five) came due for renewal. During the year the five agreements were all renewed for a longer period of time than the terms of the original contracts. While no contracts had come up for renewal in 1976, HAI had lost five contracts as a result of terminations. The terminations were the result of several unique situations, which HAI did not believe were representative of its client relationships.[7]

On March 15, 1976, HAI entered into an agreement to manage the Flower and Fifth Avenue Hospital, the teaching hospital for the well-known New York Medical College and, with more than 400 beds, one of the largest hospitals to become associated with a hospital management company. The contract was the first hospital management contract in New York State. In late December 1976, the St. Louis County Hospital awarded a management contract to HAI. St. Louis County Hospital was a 200-bed teaching institution that functioned as a part of the county's Department of Community Health and Medical Care. The contract was HAI's sixteenth of 1976 and its fiftieth overall. In early 1977 HAI was the only hospital management company holding contracts with medical teaching hospitals, St. Louis County and Flower and Fifth being third and fourth in a group including Tulane and Texas Tech.

---

[7] The causes of the terminations will be described below.

Contract Management

HAI was engaged in two business areas, the management of hospitals it owned and the management of other hospitals under contract. HAI provided four basic types of services to hospitals managed under contract. HAI installed a professionally trained hospital administrator who was usually the sole full-time HAI employee at the hospital. In larger hospitals the controller was sometimes an HAI employee as well. In addition, HAI provided the contract hospital with the services of a group of staff management specialists, access to a group purchasing plan, and the ability to utilize a shared hospital management information system.

The administrator was the most visible employee of HAI in contact with the hospital's board. The administrator was responsible for achieving specific health care quality and financial goals agreed to between HAI and the contracting hospital's board of directors and acting as HAI's spokesperson to the community served by the hospital. Most administrators were financially oriented, with master's degrees in Hospital Administration or MBAs.

It was HAI's policy to move an administrator no more than was absolutely necessary, to maintain what management referred to as "administrative continuity" between HAI and the managed hospital. Typically, an administrator would stay at a hospital for two to three years before being promoted to a larger facility, which could be either an owned or a managed hospital. The administrator was augmented by a regional manager, a group vice president, and a senior vice president, who all remained in periodic contact with the contract hospital.

STAFF SPECIALISTS

To help the administrator accomplish the goals of the contract, HAI maintained a group of staff specialists. Exhibit 13-8 lists the areas in which HAI had staff specialists, representing the widest range of all hospital management companies. Mr. Ray Stevenson, senior vice president in charge of HAI's Hospital Management Services Division (HMSD), was particularly proud of the quality of HAI's pro-

fessional staff, a view shared by the other senior managers at HAI.

> Our people are all experienced hospital managers who have risen as high within the traditional hospital management structure as they possibly could. Betty West (vice president in charge of nursing services) had been a director of nursing and an assistant hospital administrator before we found her. HAI has given these people an opportunity to continue to grow professionally that they probably would not have been able to find anywhere else.

The on-site administrator had use of HAI's staff specialists on a regular basis during the initial "intensive care" stage of a management contract and then on a periodic basis throughout the contract's life. Each managed hospital sent a copy of its monthly reports to HAI's headquarters, where they were reviewed and analyzed by the staff specialists. If a specialist identified a potential problem area, then a phone call would be made to the hospital administrator and, if necessary, a site visit would be made. One HAI executive stated, however, that administrators were sometimes reluctant to call Nashville for help because the expense was charged to their budgets and because of the negative connotation they believed it carried for their abilities as administrators.

Two of HAI's key staff specialist groups, described below, were representative of the operations of the staff specialist organization.

Nursing Services. Betty West, vice president, and four staff specialists (all with previous experience as directors of nursing) constituted what she referred to as an "essential" part of HAI's marketing and contract management efforts. The cost control portion of the nursing specialists' task was usually a straightforward application of proven industrial engineering and manpower planning techniques HAI had developed in the hospitals it owned. In addition, HAI worked with the hospital to develop a patient classification system, which permitted a more efficient allocation of nursing services.

In nursing, as with several other areas of hospital operations, HAI implemented a Quality Assurance program, which consisted of a Peer Review program, questionnaires given to both physicians and patients concerned with how the quality of nursing could be improved (the results of the survey were used to establish new goals for the nursing staff) and the linking of administrators' bonuses to the achievement of cost and quality standards. Ms. West commented:

> This is what makes us different from our competition. HAI knows how to measure quality and set quality standards in hospitals. A small hospital could never afford the resources and skills needed to do this, nor have the ability to make comparisons among seventy-five hospitals.

Professional Relations. HAI had a staff specialist department with expertise in physician recruiting and planning, under the direction of Mr. James Smith. Jim Smith was, as he put it, "one of the largest finders and placers of physicians in the world." Mr. Smith reflected on his job:

> This is really a pretty basic business. If you don't have enough doctors to admit patients to your hospital, then you operate below capacity and lose money. My job is to make certain that we will have enough physicians to justify building or operating a hospital. It would cost a hospital about $25,000 per physician to duplicate the kind of service we provide.

Professional relations specialists were assigned regionally, and each could handle twenty to thirty physician requests from client hospitals in a year. Smith believed that the size and service capabilities of his group gave HAI a competitive advantage over other firms in the industry.

Dr. Jae Hill, Director of Staff Services, was the individual directly responsible for the scheduling and management of the staff specialists. Hill described some of the difficulties he faced:

> This is very much like running many professional services organizations. Our people seem to have a two-year life span before their productivity decreases and

they begin to make a conscious effort to find work outside of their assigned specialty.

To put our situation in perspective, we have had a significant turnover within the specialist group in the last four years. Some have left the company while others have taken different positions within HAI. Replacing these people is not an easy affair. We have to find a hybrid individual—one who possesses both a high degree of professional expertise and industry visibility, and a keen business acumen. Being a staff specialist is not like running your area department.

However, HAI preferred not to refer to its staff specialists as consultants. The staff specialist organization had grown substantially since HAI's initial management contracts, in both breadth and depth (see Table 13–1).

GROUP PURCHASING

In addition to gaining the assistance of HAI's purchasing and inventory control staff specialists, a hospital managed under contract became part of HAI's national purchasing program, which encompassed all of HAI's owned and managed hospitals and included most of the items a hospital purchased. The prices offered by a particular supplier were based upon the cumulative purchasing power of the group rather than the individual hospital. Mr. Anderson estimated that the purchasing savings, between 15 and 20 percent of what the hospital had been paying, were equal to up to one-third of HAI's management fees. The group purchasing arrangement required no change in the hospital's purchasing operations. The hospital ordered items in exactly the same manner that they did before joining HAI, and the items were shipped directly to the hospital by the supplier with the discount reflected in the bill.

TABLE 13–1. Numbers of Staff Specialists in Selected Areas

	1971	*1972*	*1973*	*1974*	*1975*	*1976*	*1977*
Nursing services	0	1	1	2[a]	2	4[a]	4[b]
Professional relations	0	1	1	2	4	4	5

[a] One nursing specialist was added late in the year.
[b] Two additional positions were budgeted in 1977.
SOURCE: Casewriter's compilations.

COMPUTERIZED INFORMATION SYSTEM

HAI offered, through McDonnell Douglas's national computer service network, access to a complete hospital billing, accounting, and management information system. The computer package cost a managed hospital 15–20 percent less than the normal price because of HAI's group purchasing power. HAI's staff specialists assumed responsibility for training the hospital staff in the proper use of the system's reports.

The Management Contract Cycle

Management contracts progressed through a series of stages, including the initial contact, management audit, formal bid, early "intensive care" period of turnaround efforts, a "stabilized" period, and, finally renewal negotiations.

Initial Contact. The marketing of new management contracts had been more of an art than a science. One senior executive expressed the belief that when HAI first started in the business advertising and promotion spending would not have done any good, because the market was not ready for it. Therefore, HAI had limited the primary thrust of its marketing program to bidding on contracts once a hospital had made its intentions public. Mr. Anderson described some of the constraints on HAI's marketing effort:

> You must bear in mind the sensitivity of the hospital's current managers to our being called in to review their operation, and the board's reluctance to bring its problems into the open. Even after they have admitted they need help it takes several months to get a contract signed because the board is afraid it's going to relinquish control of the hospital to outsiders. Every sale tends to be unique.

Steven Geringer, the vice president most directly involved in marketing, described HAI's marketing efforts to date:

> About 75 percent of our leads are generated "internally" from our administrators in the field, what we gather from public sources and our reputation as the industry leader. The remaining 25 percent of our leads result from external market development work on our

part. However, the administrators in the field are the key to new leads. They have an amazing information network about which hospitals are in financial trouble or might be looking to change administrators.

HAI also received referrals from influential members of its client hospitals' boards. In addition to actively pursuing leads, HAI participated in seminars, industry conferences, conventions, and public forums, at which management contracts as an alternative to traditional hospital management procedures were discussed. Many of HAI's competitors also participated in such activities. The company also did some very limited advertising in professional journals.

Management Audit. After the initial contact had been made and the hospital's interest in exploring a management contract confirmed, HAI's staff specialists performed a management audit of the prospective client. The audit, which HAI had pioneered, permitted it to gain a thorough understanding of exactly how many person-days of staff specialist time would be needed to complete the requirements of the contract. In addition, the audit became a selling tool. Mr. Stevenson commented on the role of the management audit:

> Of the fifty hospitals presently under contract, only a relatively small percentage were healthy when they signed with us. The rest came to us out of serious need for improved management in their hospital. When we documented, department by department, what could be done by HAI and its bottom line impact, we often hit the hospitals right on the head. I'd say that the audit is a major influence on the hospital board's decision. In addition, it's a way for us to determine if the hospital can possibly pay our fees.

Often the audit revealed truly glaring defects in administration, as described by Mr. Stevenson:

> In one hospital the accounts receivable staff had been told to monitor accounts alphabetically starting at A on the first of each month. Since the staff never made it past the Ls, the last half of the alphabet never got billed. We also often see the hospital with an aging group of physicians. It is not uncommon to see the number of admissions decline as the physician approaches his late 50s or early 60s, and therefore the revenue base of the hospital declines simultaneously.

The Formal Bid. The contract negotiations between HAI and the hospital focused on such issues as scope of services to be provided, the price of the contract and the contract's length. Although some of HAI's competitors were willing to accept one-year contracts, HAI sought to secure a three-year agreement. HAI's "standard" contract typically received extensive customization, which made each one unique. In 1976 HAI was typically one of three companies bidding for the hospital's business, whereas it had frequently been the only bidder in 1972.

HAI offered a single contract management product that provided a complete package of management services to the hospital. HAI did not offer its individual services separately. It charged a premium price that was typically 15–35 percent above that of its closest competitor because of its staff specialists and experience in the contract management business. Management believed that HAI could demand a premium price because it currently offered the best service available in the market place. HAI sought to maintain the industry price levels by purposely not trying to meet the competition. Its fee was generally an annual percentage of revenues or some other measure of hospital activity and was sometimes deferred if the client was in financial difficulty.

"Intensive Care. The "intensive care" phase of the business was the period during which the HAI administrator and staff specialists sought to work a new client into shape, usually in the three to six months immediately following the signing of a new hospital management contract. Mr. Ray Stevenson described the role of his staff in the intensive care phase as follows:

> Usually the hospitals that come to use are in pretty bad shape. We try to balance the need to show the client's board of directors early positive results with our desire to use the situation to begin building a more effective management team in the hospital.

During intensive care, teams of staff specialists worked closely with the administrator and the existing department managers to implement changes in the hospital's operations. During this phase the staff specialists made frequent visits to the hospital.

It was also during this period that HAI's group purchasing and computerized management systems were introduced.

Stabilization. After the most serious operating problems had been resolved, cash flow and profits improved, and the hospital's organization modified, the hospital was classified as being stabilized. The hospital administrator's attention shifted toward developing the managers of the hospital's departments, gradually improving cash flow and profits and expanding the hospital's profile in the community. Staff specialists tended to visit stabilized hospitals less frequently, with the bulk of their attention directed toward newly signed contracts.

Contract Renewal. A typical management contract had a life of two to five years, and the topic of renewal was of great interest to HAI and the industry as a whole. There was general agreement among industry observers that while a hospital would agree to almost anything to avoid the prospect of going bankrupt, the percentage of hospitals that would elect to continue their management contracts was still an unknown. The industry was only five years old, and most of the existing contracts had been signed during the previous two or three years.

To date, HAI had a renewal rate of between 75 and 85 percent, which was in line with the renewal rate for the industry as a whole. HAI's management projected that the renewal rate would decline somewhat as competition increased in the industry. Mr. Geringer, the executive who was closest to the renewal situation, viewed the issue this way:

> At one time we had over 50 percent of the contract management market. Our share has fallen to about 33 percent and we believe it will stabilize at 25 to 30 percent. Our biggest problems have been the five terminations we suffered this year, the confusion caused by the American Medicorp deal, and the fact that we have not been able to institutionalize the sales success of a few key individuals like Ed Stolman.

The five terminations HAI experienced in 1976 had resulted from a combination of people-related problems and events out of HAI's control. In one instance a hospital was sold to another management company after HAI decided not to purchase the hospital itself. In another case, the hospital wanted HAI to put in more of its own money, and in a third, the hospital could not be saved and closed down. In the two other cases HAI had filed suit in U.S. District Court seeking damages from contracts that the company claimed were "wrongfully terminated." In one of these suits HAI's on-site administrator had decided to try and go into business for himself.

HAI was trying to improve the quality of its client base by being more selective in the type of hospital it agreed to manage. Mr. Geringer believed that HAI's competitors were still concerned with the number of contracts they signed rather than their quality.

Stolman viewed HAI's relationship with the hospitals as being long-term in nature:

> Once you are in the hospital and doing your job well, which means providing high-quality patient care at a reasonable cost and helping to make the board more important in the community, then I believe you have an excellent chance of becoming a fixture at the hospital. For example, we have just had our second renewal at Jiles County Hospital.

Competition for Management Contracts

According to Ray Stevenson and other executives, of all the firms in the management contract business only HAI had really "paid its dues." Stevenson commented:

> Our competition has not made the kind of investment in its staff specialists that we have. When we bid for a contract we have a team of experts on hand to satisfy the needs of the client. Our competitors often have to take people from its owned hospitals and assign them to an engagement.

However, Stevenson conceded that contracts had become harder to obtain recently and that competition had forced HAI to reduce its fees by as much as 10 percent over the past two years, though it remained the high bidder. One problem in the contract business was that the hospital boards of directors were not always capable of discerning the difference in quality between HAI and its com-

petitors. However, Stevenson estimated that in 50 percent of the cases it was not the lowest bid that was accepted by the hospital.

Mr. Anderson was actively monitoring the status of HAI's competition:

> There are perhaps three dozen potential competitors in the industry. This number does not include the former hospital administrator who decides to go into business for himself, gets one contract, hires a secretary, and says he is in the hospital management business. About twelve of the firms are active competitors and five are listed on the NYSE. The competition will be able to catch up to us technologically, given enough time and resources. However, we are still the most technologically competent firm in the business. Despite the fact that MCA is not actively involved in the business now, we view them as potentially a very serious competitor.

In late 1976 HAI had added two full-time marketing persons to its staff. The move was prompted in part by the actions of two of the company's more active competitors, Hyatt Corporation with fifteen to twenty management contracts and American Medicorp with fifteen. These firms were characterized by HAI's management as being very aggressive marketing companies with business development staffs larger than HAI's.

Recently, American Medical International (AMI), had begun to offer pieces of its total service to hospitals rather than sell the complete package. Mr. Geringer commented on AMI's action: "When AMI split its product line they hurt the industry. We are not planning to unbundle our basic package and wind up selling nursing services to one client and computer services to another."

International Operations

HAI was currently examining the international market as a source of expansion for its management contract business. The company had one contract in Paris, which it was planning to use as a base for increasing its European operations. HAI was cautious about its business exposure in foreign countries. It planned, for the present, to act as a subcontractor to large U.S.-based multinational corporations such as Abbott Labs.

Owned Hospitals

HAI's twenty-five owned hospitals were located primarily in the Southern half of the United States, especially Texas (thirteen) and Tennessee (seven). While HAI had been in negotiations with American Medicorp, no new hospital construction had been undertaken by the company. After negotiations had been terminated, however, continued expansion of its owned-hospital base was begun. Mr. Anderson expressed the policy of the company: "In the future we will continue to be in both businesses. There are obviously very big differences between owned and managing hospitals. We believe it is important to have a strong position in both."

While new construction projects would be limited by the number of communities that had a real need for new health care facilities, expansion was possible through acquiring existing hospitals. However, any expansion of owned hospitals would take place only in states with reasonable reimbursement formulas. States such as New York were considered to have poor plans and would be avoided, while Texas and Tennessee would continue to be primary expansion areas.

The role of competition in owned hospitals was different from that in managed ones. Mr. Buncher, in charge of owned hospitals, viewed his clients in the following manner:

> Our customer is the physician; the patient largely follows. Of course, we must ensure that the needs of the patient are efficiently and properly provided for at all times, but the main competition is for doctors. It is the physicians who admit patients and it is the patients who generate revenue.

To attract physicians, HAI either built or assisted in the construction of a medical office building adjacent to the hospitals. HAI also tried to have the latest diagnostic and therapeutic equipment available for the physician to use, ensure that all tests were completed and entered in the patient's medical chart on a timely basis, and provide a "more pleasant working environment" for the physician than other hospitals in the service area.

Mr. Buncher believed HAI had an edge in motivating health care professionals because it provided an orderly career path for the administrators, controllers, and nurses who worked for HAI. HAI tried to equal the market salaries for administrators and offer the promise of additional compensation, in the form of a bonus, if the individual's performance exceeded budget. HAI estimated that bonuses could range from an average of 20 percent to a maximum of 50 percent of salary. In addition, administrators were eligible to receive stock options.

Government Relations

HAI viewed the role of government with caution. HAI itself did little lobbying, and no one individual was assigned the task of coordination of the company's lobbying efforts. Lobbying activities included writing letters to representatives and senators in the states where HAI owned or managed hospitals, appearing before legislative committees, and participating in the activities of the Federation of American Hospitals. In certain instances, such as malpractice legislation, HAI lobbied more to prevent bad bills from passing than getting its own views on malpractice reform translated into law.

Within HAI's organization the attitude toward government regulation was a function of the business area the manager was involved in. Previous legislation had been a stimulus for new business in the contract management area. Geringer commented on HAI's experiences:

> I think that regardless of what form a new law takes it will certainly increase the basic complexity of the hospital administrator's and the board's task. Anything that makes this task more difficult will increase the demand for the services of our staff specialists.

The managers in the owned-hospital business did not foresee any specific benefits from new legislation, but they did not perceive it as a threat either. Mr. Buncher expressed his opinion:

> We are managed better than the average hospital in the country. As long as we stay better than average we are O.K., since I expect the law to be targeted to the average hospital's costs. Some people seem a bit frightened by the public utility concept of health care, but certain utilities do very well for their stockholders. Only overt nationalization of hospitals would be a direct threat to us.

Mr. Hilton, the vice president and treasurer, and other executives viewed the specter of National

Health Insurance as one of the fundamental factors influencing HAI's stock price. Pharmaceutical and hospital supply companies sold at multiples of fifteen and twenty-five times earnings, while the hospital management business sold at five to nine times 1976 earnings.

Organization

HAI's organization reflected the two different business areas the company competed in. The two basic line operating groups were the Hospital Management Services Division (HMSD), which managed the hospitals under contract, and the Hospital Operations Department (HOD), which managed the owned hospitals. The staff specialists and management contract marketing group were part of the Hospital Management Corporation (HMC), a wholly owned subsidiary of HAI.

Compensation for HAI's managers, which had historically been above average for the industry, was primarily in the form of salary and bonus. HAI did not provide benefits such as cars, comprehensive insurance programs, and retirement programs, which some of its competitors had recently added to their compensation packages. HAI's salary and bonus levels were currently about average for the industry.

Finance and Control

The finance and control functions were divided between Bob Hilton, treasurer, and Thomas Chaney, controller. HAI's overall corporate financial goals were the reduction of debt in the capital structure, improved control over costs in owned and managed hospitals, and a general improvement in the balance sheet by stressing growth in the management contract portion of the company. Mr. Hilton viewed the latter goals as being somewhat contradictory: "People are sometimes more expensive than bricks and mortar. We have a $5 million annual payroll that I look at as an interest payment on a bond issue. People are an expensive fixed cost."

Mr. Hilton was responsible for establishing and maintaining HAI's liaison with the financial community. He commented on HAI's financial situation:

We are a highly leveraged firm in a highly leveraged industry which makes certain lending institutions nervous. I believe that such leverage is appropriate because we are in a very stable business where declines in revenue, if they occur, are gradual, and most of our costs are reimbursed by third-party payors. In addition, we have excellent liquidity and high depreciation.

Much of Mr. Hilton's time was spent on educating Wall Street and institutions about the hospital management industry and HAI as a company.

Mr. Hilton believed that the availability of future sources of funds would be affected by the industry's ability to convince the banking and investment community that the concept of investor-owned hospitals was sound. In October 1976 HAI sold $12 million of 10 percent senior debentures. This was shortly after Hospital Corporation of America had sold the first issue of straight long-term debt in the industry.

HAI had no formal long-range strategic planning system, although profit forecasting was performed on a regular basis by the firm's senior management.

MALPRACTICE INSURANCE

The problems that all hospitals faced with respect to purchasing adequate malpractice insurance at reasonable rates was a very hot issue in the industry. The rise in both the frequency of medical malpractice suits and the size of dollar awards had resulted in a dramatic increase in malpractice insurance premiums. The hospitals that were hit hardest by the price increases were the large downtown metropolitan hospitals. These institutions typically had the largest percentage of patients subject to cost-based reimbursement and offered many high-risk (from an insurance viewpoint) outpatient and emergency room services. In certain instances when faced with a fivefold to tenfold increase in the size of malpractice premiums, some of these hospitals had decided to operate with no insurance coverage at all.

HAI had pioneered an industry reinsurance program involving several of the leading hospital management companies, which would work to keep premiums down by absorbing a certain portion of the risk within the group. The reinsurance program, started in late 1975, had been most successful thus far and had received wide publicity in trade journals. HAI did not plan to market the medical malpractice program as part of their package of management services because of the different nature of the insurance operation. In the words of one HAI executive, "We are in the hospital not the insurance business."

Future Plans

HAI was committed to remaining in both the owned and managed segments of the hospital industry. However, Mr. Anderson had set different growth targets for the two businesses:

> I hope and expect that our management contract business will grow by about fifteen hospitals per year while we plan to add only two or three new owned hospitals per year. In five years the hospital management business should be 50 percent of profits. It should also account for a substantial portion of our earnings growth, because it's starting from a smaller base.

The decision to remain in both businesses caused what management termed as an "ongoing organizational problem" concerning what type of management structure HAI should adopt. Mr. Anderson expressed his views on the subject:

> The two businesses have very basic differences and require a different skills mix to be managed successfully. For example, we have got to be visible in the contract business while we would prefer to maintain a low profile in the hospitals we own. We could split the two divisions completely, but then we would have to add staff specialists to service our own hospitals. As it is, we now have a hybrid organizational structure, which has been partially regionalized.

While HAI was not planning to offer individual services for the medium- and large-size hospitals, it was investigating the possibility of selling a less intensive management program as a method of penetrating the small hospital market. The institutions had between twenty-five and fifty beds and usually were located in rural communities. Mr. Geringer described HAI's thinking on the matter:

> We would like to sell the small hospital one day per month of line management time for about $20,000-

$50,000 per year of fees. The arrangement could give the small hospital access to the resources at HAI's command. That is something that has been simply out of the question for a hospital that size. We estimate that one line manager could supervise about ten to twelve accounts in a given service area.

HAI was also considering becoming more active in contracts to develop and manage hospitals. Stolman commented:

> In the next several years many hospitals will have to replace their existing facilities. Helping them carry out the development work provides a toehold for a management contract later. However, we plan to limit this to one or two new contracts per year.

DIVERSIFICATION

HAI was examining related new business areas that could offer opportunities for growth in sales and earnings. A list of about fifty businesses was maintained by Mr. Anderson, Mr. Stolman and other senior HAI executives, containing such businesses as housekeeping services, data processing and pure financing businesses such as equipment leasing. Potential new businesses were reviewed periodically with special attention to identifying acquisition candidates in the most promising areas. Each potential diversification move possessed some degree of vertical integration for HAI. Mr. Anderson described the type of business HAI was interested in entering:

> I look for an industry that has definite barriers to entry. The barriers can be either technological or financial or some combination of both. It should also provide above-average sales and profit potential on a long-term basis.

HAI was not planning any immediate acquisition moves. Anderson stated the company's goal as wanting to move into one or two new businesses over the next five years:

> We plan to postpone any vertical integration or diversification decision until the contract market begins to slow down and the role of the government in the health care system has been more clearly defined. However, you must bear in mind that acquisitions are a matter of timing, need, and who is available at what price.

EXHIBIT 13-1. *Summary of Income Statements, Hospital Affiliates International ($ in millions)*

	1976	1975	1974	1973	1972	1971
Net revenues	$137.8	$105.9	$ 68.2	$ 54.8	$ 50.3	$ 38.3
Operating expenses	116.2	89.5	55.4	44.1	40.7	31.3
Depreciation and amortization	5.1	3.6	2.3	1.7	1.6	1.2
Interest expenses	6.1	5.4	3.7	3.0	2.6	1.9
Cost of new facilities	—	(.2)	(.5)	(.6)	(.4)	(.2)
Total expenses	127.4	98.3	60.9	48.2	44.5	34.2
Profit before taxes	10.4	7.6	7.3	6.6	5.8	4.1
Income taxes	5.0	3.4	3.4	3.0	2.6	2.0
Net earnings	5.3	4.2	3.9	3.6	3.2	2.1
Average shares outstanding	2,454,000	2,348,000	2,794,000	2,950,000	2,967,000	2,599,000
Earnings per share (fully diluted)	1.95	1.57	1.34	1.14	.99	.78

SOURCES: Form 10K and annual reports.

EXHIBIT 13-2. *Summary of Balance Sheet, Hospital Affiliates International ($ millions)*

	1976	1975	1974	1973	1972	1971
Assets						
Current						
Cash	7.2	6.9	6.6	6.1	4.8	5.2
Accounts receivable (net)	28.8	25.4	20.9	12.7	10.5	8.8
Supplies, at cost	3.6	3.1	2.4	1.6	1.5	1.5
Prepaid expenses	1.2	.7	.4	.3	.5	.6
Total current assets	40.8	36.1	30.3	20.7	17.3	16.1
Construction funds	—	.1	.6	3.2	4.9	—
Long-term accounts receivable	10.4	9.7	8.1	6.7	2.7	—
	10.4	9.8	8.7	9.9	7.6	—
Property and equipment						
Land	7.5	7.2	6.8	7.3	8.7	8.5
Buildings	38.6	32.7	32.1	28.3	32.6	25.1
Leasehold rights	6.8	6.9	7.2	1.0	.8	.4
Equipment	30.1	26.9	16.1	9.3	8.1	6.2
Construction in progress	.3	.5	1.1	7.3	1.4	1.5
	83.2	74.2	63.3	53.2	51.6	21.7
Accumulated depreciation & amortization	(13.4)	(9.9)	(7.2)	(6.6)	(5.6)	(4.2)
Net property and equipment	69.8	64.3	56.1	46.6	46.0	37.5
Other assets	20.6	21.0	17.6	17.1	17.5	19.4
Total assets	141.7	131.2	112.7	94.3	88.4	73.0
Liabilities						
Current						
Accounts payable	8.8	8.0	7.4	3.1	4.9	3.0
Accrued expenses	4.9	3.5	2.3	1.9	1.4	4.4
Income taxes	3.9	4.4	5.6	4.1	2.0	1.7
Current portion of long-term debt	3.6	3.2	3.1	3.0	2.3	2.2
Total current liabilities	21.2	19.1	18.4	12.1	10.6	11.3
Long-term debt	59.9	54.4	43.9	37.2	35.6	21.8
Deferred income taxes	6.2	5.8	2.7	1.7	1.0	.6
Deferred income	—	1.0	1.0	1.1	—	—
Convertible & subordinated debentures	15.2	16.8	16.9	11.0	12.5	14.1
Total stockholders' equity	39.3	34.1	29.8	31.2	28.7	25.2
Total liabilities	141.7	131.2	112.7	94.3	88.4	73.0

SOURCES: Form 10K and annual reports.

EXHIBIT 13-3. *Classification of U.S. Hospitals in 1975*

	Number of Hospitals	Number of Beds (Thousands)	Number of Beds Per Hospital	Total Assets (Millions)
Nongovernment, not-for-profit hospitals	3,391	650	192	$31,482
State & local government hospitals	1,821	211	116	8,070
Investor-owned hospitals	775	70	90	2,288
Total "community" hospitals	5,977	931	156	$41,840
Federal government hospitals	387	136	351	$ 5,528
Non-federal psychiatric hospitals	543	383	701	4,776
Non-federal tuberculosis hospitals	46	8	174	166
Non-federal long-term general hospitals	221	54	244	1,396
Total "other" (federal government and long-term)	1,197	582	486	$ 9,866
Total: all U.S. hospitals	7,174	1,513	211	$51,706

SOURCES: American Hospital Association, *Hospital Statistics,* 1975 Edition, and casewriter computations.

EXHIBIT 13–4. *Schematic Chart of Health Care Delivery System: Figures for the Year 1971*

SECTORS OF THE HEALTH SYSTEM

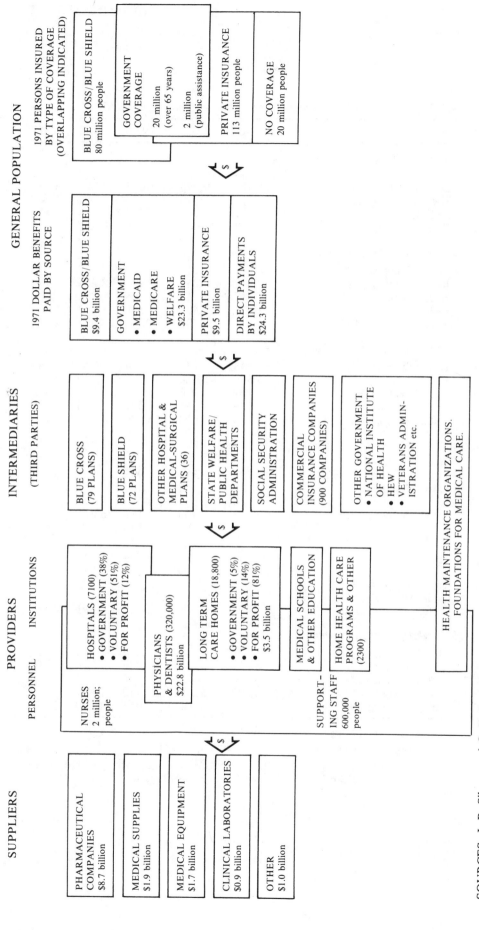

SOURCES: J. B. Silvers and C. K. Prahalad, *Financial Management of Health Care Industries* (Flushing, N. Y.: Spectrum Publications, 1974), p. 270.

EXHIBIT 13-5. *Profile of Leading Hospital Management Companies*

	1976	1975	1974	1973	1972	1971
Hospital Corporation of America						
Hospitals owned	68	62	56	53	46	38
Beds owned	14,000	9,946	8,405	7,764	6,834	4,788
Hospitals managed	17	10	6	4	2	2
Beds managed	2,357	1,702	875	743	470	470
Total beds controlled	16,357	11,648	10,155	9,250	7,774	5,728
National Medical Enterprises						
Hospitals owned	19	18	17	19	18	14
Beds owned	2,549	2,257	2,195	2,337		
Hospitals managed	17	11	8	3	–	
Beds managed	1,481	1,481	848	283	–	–
Total beds controlled	4,030	3,738	3,043	2,620	2,342	1,952
American Medical International						
Hospitals owned	43[a]	43	44	44	44	20
Beds owned	5,500	5,428	4,977	4,930	4,638	2,222
Hospitals managed	7	6	5	–	–	–
Beds managed	936	645	599	–	–	–
Total beds controlled	6,436	6,073	5,576	4,930	4,638	2,222
American Medicorp						
Hospitals owned	35	36	34	33	30	38
Beds owned	7,224	7,314	6,996	6,538	5,544	5,091
Hospitals managed	15	8	1	1	–	–
Beds managed	1,964	1,089	193	73	–	–
Total beds controlled	9,188	8,403	7,189	6,611	5,544	5,091
Humana						
Hospitals owned	63	60	54	47	45	37
Beds owned	8,696	7,796	5,940	4,691	4,168	3,090
Hospitals managed	–	–	–	–	–	–
Beds managed	–	–	–	–	–	–
Total beds controlled	8,696	7,796	5,940	4,691	4,168	3,090
Hospital Affiliates International						
Hospitals owned	25[a]	26	27	23	27	27
Beds owned	3,624	3,445	2,838	1,819	2,102	1,973
Hospitals managed	50	40	26	16	7	2
Beds managed	6,093	5,000	3,120	2,441	571	199
Total beds controlled	9,717	8,445	5,958	4,260	2,673	2,172

[a]Where a company both acquires and sells hospitals in the same year, the number of beds may change while the number of hospitals remains the same.

SOURCES: Annual reports, form 10Ks, and Vince De Paulo, "Status of Proprietary Chains," *Modern Healthcare*, February 1977, p. 38.

EXHIBIT 13-6. *Financial Profile of Leading Competitors ($ in millions)*

	1976	1975	1974	1973	1972	1971
Hospital Corporation of America						
Sales	$506.5	$392.9	$297.7	$223.1	$172.7	$138.2
Profits	27.3	20.9	15.8	12.3	10.4	8.5
Assets	600.0	506.2	415.8	319.7	274.0	207.8
Equity	187.9	143.2	122.3	108.1	91.3	75.7
Return on sales (%)	5	5	5	6	6	6
Return on assets (%)	5	4	4	4	4	4
Return on equity (%)	15	15	13	11	11	11
Current ratio	1.46	1.51	1.51	1.43	1.32	1.83
Long-term debt/stockholders' equity	1.64	2.02	1.78	1.53	1.50	1.37
Average annual price-earnings ratio	8.9	8.8	6.2	12.7	35.0	34.7
National Medical Enterprises						
Sales	$116.1	$ 95.2	$ 74.9	$ 56.7	$ 32.4	$ 26.1
Profits	5.4	4.1	3.5	3.3	2.2	1.8
Assets	183.0	147.8	124.3	115.8	84.5	52.5
Equity	46.6	40.8	37.0	34.4	31.3	28.4
Return on sales (%)	5	4	5	6	7	7
Return on assets (%)	3	3	3	3	3	3
Return on equity (%)	12	10	9	10	7	6
Current ratio	1.65	1.61	1.59	2.13	1.11	1.05
Long-term debt/stockholders' equity	2.11	1.97	1.81	1.89	1.27	0.5
Average annual price-earnings ratio	4.1	3.0	5.2	13.3	22.0	18.0
American Medical International						
Sales	$250.3	$219.3	$170.1	$146.9	$134.4	$113.9
Profits	8.7	5.2	5.2	7.5	7.5	4.8
Assets	311.1	288.5	258.5	207.5	162.1	129.2
Equity	93.0	83.4	79.5	75.7	71.4	61.1
Return on sales (%)	3	2	3	5	6	5
Return on assets (%)	3	2	2	4	5	4
Return on equity (%)	9	6	7	10	11	9
Current ratio	1.82	1.77	1.90	1.83	1.74	1.65
Long-term debt/stockholders' equity	1.66	1.85	1.68	1.30	0.89	0.48
Average annual price-earnings ratio	5.3	5.4	6.9	21.2	34.3	28.0
American Medicorp						
Sales	$335.0	$331.8	$274.7	$213.6	$182.2	$151.2
Profits	15.8	13.0	8.5	3.7	9.9	8.6
Assets	420.0	412.5	390.4	358.1	323.9	283.8
Equity	173.2	166.2	153.3	152.5	148.8	133.1
Return on sales (%)	5	4	3	2	5	6
Return on assets (%)	4	3	2	1	3	3
Return on equity (%)	9	8	6	2	7	6
Current ratio	1.56	1.46	1.61	1.63	1.46	1.12
Long-term debt/stockholders' equity	0.98	1.03	1.14	1.04	0.89	0.80
Average annual price-earnings ratio	4.4	3.8	3.0	15.0	17.8	19.8
Humana						
Sales	$260.7	$195.4	$134.7	$106.7	$ 83.6	$ 64.6
Profits	8.9	6.8	6.1	5.5	4.9	1.9
Assets	340.2	310.9	264.5	199.1	167.3	150.8
Equity	73.8	66.2	59.3	54.2	48.9	39.9
Return on sales (%)	3	3	5	5	6	3
Return on assets (%)	3	2	2	3	3	1
Return on equity (%)	12	10	10	10	10	5
Current ratio	1.41	1.36	1.57	1.78	2.29	1.57
Long-term debt/stockholders' equity	2.77	2.94	2.76	2.18	1.92	2.20
Average annual price-earnings ratio	7.2	5.5	5.5	11.5	23.0	35.9

SOURCES: Form 10Ks, annual reports.

EXHIBIT 13-7. *Owned and Managed Hospitals of Second-Tier Competitors*[a]

	Owned Hospitals	Managed Hospitals
Hyatt	4	22
	(444)	(2,286)
Medenco	13	11
	(1,573)	(1,207)
A. E. Brim	4	19
	(208)	(1,118)
Charter Medical	14	7
	(1,462)	(1,333)
General Health Services	7	1
	(1,271)	(117)
AID	16	—
	(2,583)	
R. H. Medical	4	3
	(661)	(450)
Total	62	63

[a]As of December 31, 1976. Number of beds in parentheses.

SOURCE: Numbers of owned and managed hospitals at the end of 1976 for second-tier companies and their goals for 1977 are taken from a survey conducted by *Modern Healthcare* and reported in the February 1977 issue.

EXHIBIT 13-8. *Staff Specialists*

Accounting	Inhalation therapy
Accreditation	Insurance
Admitting procedures	Labor relations
Ambulatory care	Laboratory operations
Ancillary services	Long-range planning
Budgeting and finance	Maintenance
By-laws	Management engineering
Capital financing	Medical records
Cash flow	Medical staff relations
Certificate of need	Nursing services
Community relations	Personnel
Construction	Pharmacy operations
Credit and collections	Physical therapy
Data processing	Physician recruitment
Dietary services	Purchasing
Education	Quality assurance
Environmental control	Radiology operations
Equipment	Staffing
Financial feasibility	Systems & procedures
Functional programming	Third party reimbursement

PART VI
Strategy Toward Buyers and Suppliers

"Note on supplying the Automobile Industry" describes the relationship between auto parts suppliers and their customers the major automobile companies, a classic example of the challenges of selling to a powerful buyer. The case focuses on determining the implications of structural analysis for the nature of the bargaining relationship between buyers and suppliers. Auto suppliers are confronted with the need to develop competitive strategies that cope with their powerful buyers; at the same time the case provides a close look at the way in which buyers can increase power over their suppliers. This case also provides necessary background for the Bendix Corporation case.

Understanding the bargaining relationship between buyers and suppliers will be important to many other cases in the book.

CASE 14

Note on Supplying the Automobile Industry

The automobile industry was the world's largest industry, dominated by fewer than a dozen major manufacturers. Exhibit 14–1 gives financial and market share data on leading competitors for fiscal 1975. Exhibit 14–2 gives the unit sales of motor vehicles in North America, Europe, and Japan from 1970 to 1975, as well as projected motor vehicle sales for the 1976–1982 time period.

Supplying this industry with component parts was a huge business in and of itself. General Motors (GM) purchases from outside suppliers in 1974 amounted to $16.3 billion, or approximately 52 percent of sales, with purchases of raw materials and components for the product itself amounting to 65 to 75 percent of these purchases.[1] Assuming General Motors' policies were typical (a conservative assumption since General Motors was the most heavily integrated of the world's auto companies) the Big Four U.S. producers purchased ap-

proximately $24 billion in raw materials and components for use directly in their products in 1974.

This case will describe the automotive supply industry, with particular emphasis on the purchasing policies of the major automobile companies. The note will also provide information on the supply of electronic parts as background to Case 15, "Bendix Corporation: Electronic Fuel Injection."

The U.S. Auto Supply Market

The policies of the U.S. auto companies (termed OEMs by auto suppliers) toward outside suppliers were typical of those in many mature and technologically stable industries. Parts were purchased primarily based on price, and OEMs demanded a high level of service from suppliers. The first and foremost prerequisite for an automotive supplier was a track record for reliability. It was a rule of thumb in the industry that a supplier who caused two assembly line closings was generally finished with the OEM involved, because unplanned line

[1] General Motors (A), "Organization of the Procurement Function," Intercollegiate Case Clearinghouse, 9-576-251, 1976, p. 3.

shutdowns cost tens if not hundreds of thousands of dollars per hour. In return for consistent delivery to schedule, a supplier could sometimes receive favorable treatment in the amount of volume awarded, an occurrence more likely at Ford, Chrysler, and AMC than at GM. Reputation for reliability differentiated the major suppliers such as Bendix, Rockwell, TRW, and Eaton from smaller firms. To minimize the risk of supply interruptions, safety stocks of finished components were maintained by both OEMs and suppliers, and stocks of raw materials were maintained by suppliers at OEMs' insistence.

A second critical prerequisite for an automotive supplier was maintaining consistent quality of the components it produced. Failure to maintain quality was the second most common source of supplier termination after delivery problems. Since components came together from all over the country into a highly complex assembly operation, every part was precisely specified at the outset of a contract and rigorously inspected upon delivery. To ensure compliance with specifications and to monitor supplier capabilities, OEMs also rigorously inspected suppliers' plants at the beginning of a contract and periodically thereafter. OEM purchasing teams inspected and analyzed suppliers' facilities, quality control procedures, management quality and depth, stability of raw material sources, and other activities. OEMs also asked for, and received, supplier cost data.

The requirement for reliability and consistent quality by a supplier carried over to OEM sourcing for new items. Suppliers were not considered to be serious contenders for new contract awards (or allowed to participate in OEM preproduction engineering programs) unless they were willing to commit resources to a project. Blue sky concepts and engineers' drawings were not often sufficient to persuade OEMs to begin working with a supplier.

A third critical requirement was that the supplier have the ability to respond to significant variations in volume. In addition to the cyclicality of automobile production, seasonality resulted in peak demands for components in October and a lull in March. Monthly and even weekly revisions in delivery schedules were common with little or no advance notice. A supplier normally built approximately 20 percent extra surge capacity above expected volume in order to meet delivery schedules at peaks.

A final key supplier requirement was to provide a high level of service in all areas. Making product design revisions under intense pressure was one example of expected behavior. Or if a supplier's plant served other end user industries, they were expected to take second priority when automotive demand was particularly heavy.

In return for meeting these requirements, successful suppliers gained access to a very large market. OEMs also commonly funded tooling costs for specialized components, paid their bills promptly, and were known for sticking to their promises. According to a senior auto company purchasing executive: "Suppliers' engineering contributions must be rewarded and manufacturing expertise must be recognized—some suppliers have special knowhow that others do not. It's important to preserve those sources and encourage further progressive efforts." Another said:

> It is our practice to recognize the efforts and cooperation of our vendors, especially where they have worked with [our] engineers on product development. We also give strong consideration to vendor reliability and past performance. Obviously, they also must be in a reasonably price competitive range to remain a viable supplier.

All the OEMs were partially integrated, supplying some of their component needs internally. Some major, critical components (typically engines, transmissions and axles) were known as "captive" and produced exclusively by the OEM; others were subject to OEM make-or-buy decisions. OEMs would backward integrate to produce such a component themselves whenever the economics justified it, and it was not uncommon for a supplier to lose a contract it had held for several years because an OEM found that it could manufacture the component at fractionally lower cost. The capacity utilization of OEM component plants was also a relevant consideration to OEM make-or-buy decisions.

Automobile purchases could be divided into components, modules or subassemblies, and systems (such as brake systems or carburetor systems). OEMs were reluctant to permit a supplier to manufacture a complete *system* for the automobile where it was a high-volume item, except very early in the life cycle of a new innovation. Their purchasing strategy was to break each system used on the vehicle into its component parts, and find two or three firms capable of making each component.[2] The OEM would then assemble the system in-house using these components. OEMs had the internal technical and engineering capabilities to disassemble systems into their component parts and develop specifications for each component. This was used to persuade a supplier to accept a portion of the components business rather than lose it all. The Big Three as a group normally produced approximately 80 percent of complete systems and 50 to 60 percent of the modules or subassemblies going into these systems in-house, using purchased components.

OEMs generally manufactured in-house at least a portion of their requirements for any component that achieved wide acceptance as a basic part of the vehicle. However, they would not normally manufacture 100 percent of their needs of a noncaptive component internally no matter how standard the component was. In a standardized product line such as brakes, OEMs produced a substantial portion of their minimum forecast needs internally, contracted with perhaps two national firms for approximately equal shares of most of the remainder, and used two or three smaller firms to supply the balance and to meet peak demand. In some cases as many as a dozen firms might supply a given OEM. Occasionally new, small suppliers were allowed to bid on established components where multiple sources already existed. For less standard lines and new products, the OEMs often purchased a higher percentage of their component needs from outside suppliers.[3]

The major OEMs varied in the share of standard components they would purchase from outside suppliers, with GM awarding 10 to 15 percent, Ford 40 to 50 percent and Chrysler variable.[4] Exhibit 14–3 gives estimates of the extent of integration by the

big Four U.S. OEMs in 1976, and Exhibit 14–4 gives the estimated sourcing pattern for an example component.

An industry observer commented on the practice of multiple suppliers in automobile company purchasing:

> The auto companies will typically never put a major product into production unless they have at least two or three suppliers for that product, of which at least one is a domestic supplier. This is not a hard and fast law, but it is a rule that they try very hard to employ. The cardinal sin for an auto parts supplier is to close down an assembly line, and the auto companies cannot afford to risk a single supplier having a strike or an equipment failure. Foreign suppliers are avoided if qualified domestic suppliers can be found because of the risks of interrupted supply they entail.

Supply contracts with OEMs were usually for one year, a period that was rarely exceeded. Longer-term contracts usually required approval by the executive committee of the board. Pricing negotiations with OEMs for standard components were notoriously tough, and OEMs aimed to give the supplier a gross margin of 30 percent or less. OEMs had the reputation for being hard bargainers about price, delivery, specifications, and documentation. Potential suppliers sometimes lost contracts because their bid was $.01 per item higher than competitors'. An executive of one supplier of standardized products commented on the situation as it affected his company:

> The OEMs do not acknowledge any long-term relationship with the suppliers but they expect all their suppliers to take very good care of them. By "good care" I mean maintaining an excellent record of meeting delivery schedules (they come down very hard if you are even a little late), meeting specifications exactly even if the difference between specifications and your product is of no significance to the performance of the part, keeping extensive documentation of your manufacturing, testing and quality control procedures and keeping at least a three-week supply of inventory on hand. However, despite all of this they will drag their feet for months before they grant an increase for costs that are outside of your control.

Another executive described the auto companies' negotiating skills:[5]

---

[2] Rarely did a supplier supply all the components of a particular system even as one of several suppliers.

[3] In a few cases, a standard component subject to extremely large economies of scale or very specialized technology might be single sourced.

[4] Chrysler would sometimes purchase 100 percent and sometimes make 100 percent. In some cases Chrysler also purchased a share of its needs without a second source. AMC was by far the least integrated of the major companies.

[5] An example of the nature of the supplier–OEM relationship on prices is Ford's termination of Champion Spark Plug as a

They can and do take apart everything we produce, analyze the separate manufacturing steps it took to complete it, and then cost the product to within a few percentage points of actual cost. They can estimate manufacturing costs to about ± 2 percent, though they have more trouble estimating how fast inventory is turning and how much our investment is. The diversification of our company helps us here.

A supplier's existing business in other component areas was sometimes used as a lever to get the desired terms on some other project. Suppliers were also sometimes played off against one another, especially if they did a significant proportion of their business with the auto companies. An industry participant commented:

> You are truly caught between a rock and a hard place. If you try and push for the best terms possible they hint that your contract on the XYZ product is coming up for renewal soon and one of your competitors has been making inquiries about the upcoming bids. What do you do? Risk incurring their bad will for a few extra pennies per part, or give in? Most of the time they get what they want.

Supplying New Components

Automotive innovations could originate with the supplier or the OEM. Chrysler Corporation, for instance, developed low-cost electronic ignition with no outside participation. Cast camshafts, now used by all OEMs, were developed independently by Campbell, Wyatt, and Cannon foundries.

When attempting technical innovations such as new materials or new types of components, suppliers had to contend with an arduous process of gaining acceptance for their new item. A new item had to undergo several years of testing for reliability before it was accepted. In addition, its introduction sometimes raised difficulties with the OEMs' labor unions, necessitated finding a group of capable suppliers, might require retraining of the dealer service network, and sometimes obsoleted existing manufacturing investment. These factors meant that

supplier. Champion had supplied 100 percent of Ford's needs as well as the aftermarket, and had earned handsome margins. When Champion went public in 1959, Ford became aware of the true profitability of Champion for the first time. By 1961 Ford had acquired Autolite to supply its spark plugs on a captive basis.

change in the automobile industry was evolutionary rather than revolutionary, and some components remained unchanged for decades except for minor changes.

In attempting to compete through technological leadership, suppliers also had to contend with the in-house research and development capabilities of the auto companies themselves. An observer commented:

> The auto companies, especially GM and Ford, have the ability and financial strength to explore all the possible technical alternatives simultaneously. They may not be overly efficient but they certainly get the job done. Our company, while not a small company by any means, just cannot compete in the same fashion. We have to pick and choose how we use our resources to a much greater extent than GM or Ford.
>
> As a result, it is very hard to stay ahead of the auto companies technologically for very long. At best a company might have a year or two breathing space before they catch up to what you are doing. That could be an optimistic figure if they decide to "crash" and put all their resources behind one particular project.

It was generally agreed that greater pricing flexibility existed on new components than on mature items. In addition, while multiple sourcing was a key purchasing policy, OEMs would initially purchase a higher percentage of their component needs from a single outside supplier for new products, especially if the product represented a technological innovation. However, even if a supplier developed a legal monopoly position on a new item through patents, it was understood that the automobile companies would not accept a sole source arrangement for very long. In such circumstances, as well as in those where a supplier had developed an innovative, proprietary product though lacking a patent position, an auto company would guarantee the supplier a share of the business for a three- to five-year period in return for the licensing or sharing of the technology with another source (in some cases with the OEM's own in-house manufacturing division). The major producers varied somewhat in their policies toward new items, with GM tending to bring the manufacture of new items in-house the soonest; Ford usually slower in investing in in-house capacity to take advantage of supplier advances in production techniques; and Chrysler varying its policy depending on the component.

Organization for Purchasing

Suppliers interfaced with five areas within the OEM: engineering, purchasing, design, manufacturing, and top management. Engineering was generally considered by suppliers to be the most critical determinant of success in obtaining a contract, with purchasing second. OEMs had large purchasing and engineering groups charged with the procurement function.

Purchasing at Ford, Chrysler, and AMC was quite centralized for all divisions, while at GM each major division had historically purchased independently with some central coordination. In 1974, however, GM initiated a reorganization in purchasing with the effect of further centralizing and specializing the function. The net effect of the change was corporatewide purchasing of raw materials and "lead division" buying of many components. Buick, for example, sourced braking systems for every GM division.

In-house plants producing components were not immune from the scrutiny of the purchasing organization, as illustrated by the following comments by a GM purchasing official:[6]

> As for allied divisions, we have more battles with them than with outside suppliers. There are no transfer pricing formulas and unlike outside suppliers, they won't give us cost information. We can always threaten to go outside, and that forces the matter to the Central Office Financial staff for arbitration. The CO staff may suggest that the allied division revise its quote. But I won't use quotes from outside suppliers to whip an allied division in line. It's morally wrong unless there's a reasonable possibility I will buy outside. . . .
>
> [I]n most cases allied divisions don't have any outside competition; we are a captive customer. We insist that prices be supported; they refuse to provide cost data; prices are vigorously negotiated. We generally compare prices paid for similar parts last year with this year's quotations and focus our negotiations on the engineering level and component content of each, and the apparent cost differential.

[6] General Motors (A), "Organization of the Procurement Function," Intercollegiate Case Clearinghouse, 9–576–251.

Recent Developments in Purchasing

Two major developments were affecting OEM purchasing in the mid-1970s, particularly at Ford and GM, which had several divisions producing separate lines of automobiles. One has already been mentioned, and that is efforts toward developing more centralized purchasing across divisions to realize economies and assure access to supply. A second development was a trend toward more coordination among product lines, with a view toward increased standardization of components and systems. This trend was reinforcing the OEMs' traditional emphasis in adopting new innovations for the automobile. The goal was to achieve standardization of the component or system across car models, though different divisions of the same company might initially experiment with different approaches to designing a new component or system until one won out. Parts standardization yielded benefits in engineering, in manufacturing, and, particularly, in parts supply and service in the field.

Supplying the Aftermarket

A significant volume of automobile components were sold as replacement parts in the so-called aftermarket. Estimates of aftermarket sales varied widely, but most put sales of replacement parts for automobiles in excess of $6 billion at manufacturers' prices in 1976 excluding tires, batteries, lubricants, and entertainment products. Components varied significantly in the size of aftermarket sales relative to original equipment sales. Frames were essentially never replaced, for example, while spark plugs or brake pads had aftermarket sales well in excess of original equipment sales.[7] There were two basic types of aftermarket components: current and noncurrent. Current components were those still being used in the assembly of new cars, while noncurrent components were used strictly for replacement on cars at least one year old. Since U.S. automotive design had been relatively stable, some

[7] The top ten components in terms of total aftermarket volume were filters, spark plugs, ignition parts, exhaust system parts, brake parts, transmission, shock absorbers, suspension parts, alternators, and gaskets and seals. Frost and Sullivan, *Automotive Aftermarket*, April 1978.

components (particularly in the chassis and drive train) had been current for long periods of time.

Aftermarket components were sold through three basic channels: OEM automobile dealers, independent repair shops, and auto supply retailers. OEMs marketed replacement parts through all three channels and accounted for approximately one-third of aftermarket volume. The balance was supplied by independent suppliers via distributors. For some categories of components, such as body panels, OEM dealer networks enjoyed a 100 percent market share in the aftermarket, as no independent sources existed. For other components, such as tires and shock absorbers, the OEMs' dealers would typically have little share of the replacement market. There was vigorous competition among the aftermarket channels in many components.

For components that were not captive, OEMs obtained replacement parts from automotive suppliers as well as from their in-house manufacturing plants. Where a component was current, OEMs could (and did) lump their own aftermarket needs with needs for new cars. Current components with high aftermarket sales were characterized by very low margins on sales to the OEMs.

U.S. Automotive Suppliers

Approximately 3,000 firms supplied the Big Four OEMs in 1976. Independent auto parts suppliers could be grouped into three categories: a group of large, broad-line companies including Bendix, Rockwell, TRW, Eaton, and Dana; a second tier of medium-sized firms such as Sheller-Globe, Maremont, and Federal Mogul; and a large number of smaller specialist companies. The total sales,

automotive sales, and automotive profitability of the leading firms are shown in Table 14–1. Profiles of these firms are given in Appendix A, with special emphasis on their operations in the electronics area. Exhibit 14–5 gives data on the sales, profitability, and principal product lines of a broader group of automotive suppliers.

Suppliers of Electronic Products

Electronic products widely used in the automobile in 1976 included entertainment products, ignition systems, voltage regulators, and various control devices, with a total value at OEM prices of more than $750 million.

There were three classes of potential competitors in the automobile supply market for electronic products: traditional auto parts suppliers; semiconductor companies; and the in-house divisions of the OEMs themselves.

Traditional Parts Suppliers. Some traditional parts suppliers were active in supplying electronic products, notably Bendix, TRW, Rockwell, Dana, Eaton, and ITT. Many other smaller companies participated in the market as well.

Semiconductor Companies. While they had not traditionally been active in automotive supply, semiconductor companies were also existing and potential competitors in the automotive electronics market, including such companies as Texas Instruments, Fairchild, National Semiconductor, and Motorola. Semiconductor firms produced electronic components, integrated circuits, microprocessors, and electronic sensors, as well as stand-alone

TABLE 14–1. Sales of Leading Automotive Suppliers ($ *millions*)

	1975 Total Sales	Estimated Automotive Sales	% Total	% Automotive Income to Total Operating Income
Bendix	$2,608	$1,333	51%	61%
Eaton	1,558	1,113	71	62
Rockwell	4,943	1,066	22	51
Dana	1,136	1,030	91	N/A[a]
TRW	2,586	1,001	39 +	51

[a] Not available.

SOURCES: Annual reports, Form 10Ks, and casewriter estimates.

electronic products such as calculators and industrial controls. The semiconductor producers had the capability to design and produce electronic circuits for a wide variety of special-purpose and general-purpose applications.

Auto Company In-House Electronics Capabilities. OEMs had assembled many of their own electronics products in the past and supplied an estimated 50 percent of their electronic product needs internally in 1975. All the OEMs were increasing their electronics capabilities in 1976. GM had developed electronics capability through its Delco division, which was able to produce semiconductor devices as well as manufacture hybrid microcircuit assemblies in high volume. It was undoubtedly the most advanced of the three automotive assemblers in electronics capability. Ford and Chrysler were both experienced high-volume assemblers of electronic components as a result of their manufacture of automotive radios. Additional experience was being gained by Ford and Chrysler in electronic ignition systems and voltage regulators, and they were both eventually expected to become capable designers and assemblers of electronic equipment. Both were expected to develop specialized electronic assembly facilities if they were needed, except for production of semiconductors, integrated circuits, and microprocessors, where semiconductor companies were expected to dominate.

The European Auto Supply Market

Automobiles manufactured by the European automobile industry were different in character from those of the United States, reflecting a different set of problems and constraints. While there was yet no legislation dictating standards for emission and gasoline mileage, cars had long been smaller, lighter, more economical, and more performance-oriented than U.S. cars because of the high price of gasoline, historically lower personal incomes, automobile taxation based on engine displacement, and European driving tastes. Components for European automobiles, including mechanical fuel injection and, more recently, electronic controls, were designed to address these differing characteristics.

European automobile manufacturers relied more heavily on outside suppliers than did their U.S. counterparts. As a result, automotive suppliers in Europe were larger relative to OEMs they supplied and played a relatively greater role in technological change. Price levels for components were generally higher. Most of the major U.S. automotive suppliers had European subsidiaries.

The largest European suppliers are listed in Table 14–2, along with an estimate of their automotive sales outside the United States in 1975.

The Japanese Auto Supply Market

Like the European market, Japanese automobile output had different characteristics from that of the United States, reflecting some of the same factors, such as historically high gasoline prices and lower incomes. Recently Japanese emissions legislation had been enacted. Japanese OEMs were growing rapidly and relied heavily on export as well as domestic sales.

Japanese OEMs had relatively low levels of integration, and the Japanese auto supply industry was characterized by close relations between OEM and supplier. OEM and supplier shared the cost of technological improvements, and suppliers pro-

TABLE 14–2. **Largest European Automotive Suppliers** (*millions of dollars*)

	1975 Total Sales	*1975 Estimated Non-U.S. Sales in Automotive*
Robert Bosch	$2,965	$1,720
Lucas	1,330	1,063
Essex (Division of United Technologies)	3,878	750
Bendix	2,600	600

SOURCES: Annual reports, Form 10Ks, and casewriter estimates.

vided high standards of quality and delivery performance that minimized the need for inspection and finished components inventory on the part of OEMs. OEM switching of suppliers was rare, as was OEM backward integration into components that had traditionally been purchased from suppliers.

Suppliers tended to belong to either the "Toyota Family" or the "Nissan Family," identifying the principal OEM to which they supplied components. In some cases OEMs owned equity shares in suppliers or provided other forms of financial assistance. The principal suppliers of electronic products were Nippondenso and Diesel Kiki, who supplied Toyota and Nissan (Datsun) respectively. Toshiba, a major Japanese electrical products manufacturer, was also an important producer of electronic parts for automobiles.

While export sales of Japanese cars in the United States had been increasing, the largest Japanese firms showed little inclination to invest in production facilities in the United States, which some observers ascribed to fear of American labor unions. It was deemed unlikely that the leading Japanese parts suppliers would invest in facilities in the U.S. market unless one of the Japanese automobile producers did. This was unlikely to occur within a five-year time horizon, though few observers were willing to rule it out. Toshiba had been somewhat more aggressive in expansion in the United States, but thus far its involvement remained solely through export.

The Japanese automobile industry was generally regarded as not providing an opportunity for U.S. or European auto supply firms without enormous investments, as Japanese firms exerted a strong hold on the market. The only likely possibility was in licensing of technology.

APPENDIX A
Profiles of Leading Competitors

Robert Bosch Corporation

Robert Bosch was the leading European automotive supplier, headquartered in Stuttgart, West Germany. Bosch was a leader in automotive ignition systems, lighting systems, and more recently fuel injection. It also produced a wide variety of other products, including appliances, radios, television sets, home and industrial power tools, hearing aids, and packaging machines. Fully 70 percent of Bosch's sales had been in the U.S. market in 1914, but expropriations during the two World Wars reduced Bosch's U.S. sales to nearly nothing, despite the fact that foreign sales accounted for approximately 50 percent of Bosch's total sales. The remnants of the old American Bosch operations were now under separate ownership in Ambac Industries, which still used the Bosch name on some of its equipment. Bosch itself had reestablished a foothold in the U.S. market and had a small U.S. subsidiary. Table 14–3 gives a financial profile of Bosch.

Bosch was wholly owned by three descendants of the founder, Robert Bosch, along with a nonprofit, charita-

TABLE 14–3. Bosch Financial Profile (*dollars in millions*)

	1971[a]	1972	1973	1974	1975
Sales:					
Automotive $	942	1,027	1,364	1,615	1,584
Automotive %	55	57	57	55	57
Total sales: $	1,713	1,801	2,393	2,936	2,779
Direct foreign sales %	40	46	52	52	52
Net income	19	36	41	37	52
Depreciation	62	76	101	120	107
Equity	232	406	509	589	603
Assets	785	1,165	1,549	1,841	1,853
Long-term debt	176	193	259	350	316
Capital expenditures	75	75	150	143	115

[a] Translated from DM to U.S. dollars at average annual exchange rates of 3.65, 3.27, 3.20, 2.70, 2.41, and 2.62, respectively for the years 1970–1975.

ble trust carrying the family name. The company was known as one of Germany's most financially sound companies. Bosch had aggressive growth goals and sought to be the dominant world automotive supplier. It had stayed substantially out of the U.S. market (1975 U.S. sales were approximately $100 million), but had recently begun a program of expansion of its U.S. manufacturing capacity coupled with an ambitious acquisition program. It planned to spend $80 million on acquisitions and expansion in the United States in the next several years. Acquisitions would have to be outside the auto parts business because of antitrust considerations.

Bosch prided itself in technological leadership and maintained extensive R&D facilities in almost all aspects of automotive technology. Bosch R&D expenditures since 1970 are shown in Table 14-4.

Bosch was known for producing the highest-quality products and was categorized as a relatively high-cost manufacturer in its markets. It had a beautiful laboratory, office, and production facilities. Observers termed Bosch careful and slow (even ponderous) to get started in new areas, but with great staying power in pursuing them once under way. It had also been termed inflexible in its approaches to problems and management attitude. These characteristics were said to make Bosch somewhat difficult to do business with, and VW and Renault had encouraged companies like TRW and Bendix to increase their European business to provide an alternative to Bosch.

Bosch was the leading producer of mechanical and electronic fuel injection systems in early 1976, having begun volume production in 1967. Active development work was under way at Bosch in all aspects of fuel injection technology. It produced all of its own EFI components, including ECUs, injectors, and oxygen sensors, and had injector manufacturing capacity of 1.8 million units per year, which had been built in the late 1960s. Bosch also produced fuel injection systems for diesel engines. It manufactured the components for diesel injection systems overseas and also in a recently completed U.S. manufacturing facility in Charleston, South Carolina. While its German facilities were not state-of-the-art, Bosch had sent teams of engineers to study Bendix's new injector facility under their cross-licensing agreement.

There were extensive cross-licensing agreements between Bendix and Bosch in many product areas, but all except those involving still outstanding patents were due to expire in 1978.

TRW, Inc.

TRW was a widely diversified firm that operated in the following broad lines of business: electronics and computer-based services; car and truck products; spacecraft and propulsion products; fasteners, tools, and bearings; and energy products and services. TRW produced a wide range of electronic components and systems, such as passive components and semiconductors including large-scale integrated circuits and microprocessors. TRW's corporate strategy was one of selective diversification, and added emphasis was being placed on return on assets employed as a measure of performance in 1975. Under the new emphasis, sales growth would be forgone in favor of higher profitability in some businesses.

TRW produced a wide range of components for cars and trucks, including:

- Valves, valve train parts, piston rings, gray and ductile iron castings, cylinder sleeves
- Steering columns, gears and linkage, suspension components, power steering pumps, manual and power rack and pinion steering gears, truck integral power steering gears, hydraulic motors and components, and hydrostatic steering systems
- Passenger restraint systems, forgings, fasteners, steering wheels, and general components

TRW classified its automotive business into three categories: domestic car and truck products (23 percent of automotive sales), international car and truck products (50 percent) and replacement parts (25 percent). Of domestic car and truck products, 40 percent went into passenger cars and 60 percent into trucks, tractors and other vehicles. Comparable percentages for international car and truck products were 66 and 34 percent respectively. Table 14-5 provides a financial profile of TRW.

TABLE 14-4. Bosch R&D Expenditures Since 1970 (*millions of dollars*)

	1970	1971	1972	1973	1974	1975
R&D Expenditures	$69	$80	$85	$111	$137	$131
% of Worldwide Sales	4.6%	4.7%	4.7%	4.6%	4.7%	4.7%

SOURCE: Annual reports.

TABLE 14–5. TRW Financial Profile (*millions*)

	1975	%	1974	%	1973	%	1972	%
Sales								
Electronics	$ 629	24%	$ 669	27%	$ 538	25%	$ 406	24%
Car & truck components	1,001	39	940	38	862	39	656	38
Other	956	37	377	35	765	36	626	38
Total	2,586	100	2,486	100	2,165	100	1,688	100
International sales	888		802		687		453	
Pretax profits								
Electronics	29	16	44	25	30	19	18	12
Car & truck components	93	50	76	43	87	51	74	51
Total pretax profits	184		176		164		146	
Net profits	86		75		68		59	
Equity	761		694		645		605	
Return on equity								
Assets	1,687		1,698		1,444		1,234	
Depreciation	70		66		57		52	
Capital expenditures	110		128		93		69	

SOURCE: Annual reports.

TRW management had made the following statements about its automotive operations in recent years:

In passenger cars, offsetting in part the decline in demand for large-car components is the surging demand for small-car components. We are fortunate in having anticipated this demand and having made major product and plant investments in the small-car field over the past five years. . . .

Electronics will become increasingly significant in the automotive field. The automotive electronics market is estimated to be $3.5 billion worldwide by 1980. In 1973 TRW established an automotive electronics operation to develop and market a family of electronic sensors and actuators with application in ignition, timing, fuel metering, transmission controls, on-board computers, and emission controls. . . .

We have contributed technical innovations which have made us a major independent supplier to auto manufacturers around the world. TRW breakthroughs include: power rack and pinion steering; forged, heavy-duty pistons; valve alloys; ball joint suspension; positive valve rotation; hydrostatic power steering for off-highway equipment molybdenum-coated.

Rockwell International

Rockwell's specialty in its automotive operations was the manufacture of axles, brakes, and other components for heavy-duty vehicles such as trucks, buses, and trailers and for special-purpose vehicles used off the highway. Rockwell also made universal joints, special gear drives, bumpers, wheel covers, mechanical and suspension springs for passenger cars and light trucks, and plastic components, such as hood and fender assemblies for trucks. Overseas Rockwell made axles, brakes, wheels, springs, and frames. Passenger cars and light trucks accounted for about 21 percent of automotive sales in 1975, while the balance went to heavy trucks and off-road vehicles. Rockwell had recently received a contract to develop microprocessor systems for more efficient automobile engine controls.

Table 14–6 provides a financial profile of Rockwell.

Eaton Corporation

Eaton Corporation operated in the following broad lines of business: vehicle and vehicle components; industrial power transmission systems and components; security products and systems; and other products including controls, fasteners, and aerosol valves. Eaton also produced lift trucks and construction and woodland vehicles. In the vehicle components area, Eaton produced engine valves, hydraulic valve filters, tire valves, leaf springs, piston rings, thermostats, and automotive air conditioning equipment and components for passenger cars and axles, transmissions, and brake assemblies for trucks and off-highway vehicles.

Eaton was considered among the market leaders in engine valves and heavy-duty truck transmissions and drive axles. Of Eaton's total North American sales 33

TABLE 14-6. Rockwell Financial Profile (*millions*)

	1975		1974		1973		1972	
	Sales	Income	Sales	Income	Sales	Income	Sales	Income
Automotive operations (almost entirely automotive components)	$1,066	$ 51.6	$1,004	$ 58.4	$ 883	$ 48.0	$ 697	$ 35.9
Aerospace operations:								
Aircraft (including general aviation)	523	7.3	562	7.2	620	6.8	442	5.2
Space systems & rocket engines	832	34.2	598	21.4	325	10.6	261	6.8
Other	112	3.3	99	2.4	74	2.8	56	.6
Total	1,467	44.8	1,259	31.0	1,019	20.2	759	12.6
Electronic operations:								
Guidance & control, avionics & tele-communication systems & equipment (1)	813	32.9	729	29.3	364	13.8	480	19.9
Calculator products & components	140	(20.3)	169	2.3	84	4.8	24	.4
Total	953	12.6	989	21.6	448	18.6	504	20.3
Utility & industrial operations:								
Utility products	225	21.4	204	12.8	170	12.2	170	13.2
Textile machinery, graphic arts & industrial components	584	(8.0)	651	3.6	551	19.4	467	9.0
Total	809	13.4	855	16.5	721	31.6	637	22.2
Consumer operations:								
Home entertainment & household appliances	503	(22.5)	259	(9.4)				
Power tools	145	1.7	134	2.2	108	7.4	81	4.6
Total	648	(20.8)	393	(7.2)	108	7.4	81	4.6
Grand total	$4,943	$101.6	$4,409	$130.3	$3,179	$125.8	$2,678	$ 95.6
Net income		101.6		130.3		125.8		95.6
Equity		1,126.9		1,095.2		951.7		924.4
Depreciation		115.5		98.3		71.3		65.5
Capital expenditures		169.3		350.1		153.9		119.7

SOURCES: Annual reports and Form 10K.

percent went to the Big Four OEMs, and approximately 50 percent of automotive sales went into passenger cars.

Table 14–7 provides a financial profile of Eaton.

Dana Corporation

In 1975 Dana Corporation operated in the lines of business shown in Table 14–8.

Major automotive product lines were: truck and passenger car frames and other chassis products (16.8 percent of corporate sales); universal joints for trucks, passenger cars, heavy vehicles, aircraft and industrial uses (16.9 percent); gaskets and seals, pistons, piston rings, cylinder sleeves and other engine and chassis parts (17.2 percent); and front and rear axles for light trucks and other vehicles (26.6 percent).

Table 14–9 provides a financial profile of Dana.

TABLE 14–7. Eaton Financial Profile (*millions*)

	1975	1974	1973
Sales:	$1,558.3	$1,760	$1,550
Truck and off-highway vehicle components	472	548	460
Automobile components	357	343	346
Industrial vehicles	215	264	222
Construction & woodland vehicles	69	97	94
Industrial power transmission systems and components	188	191	155
Security products	91	94	82
Other	166	193	191
Pretax income—vehicle components	60	130	121
Pretax income—total	97	173	163
Net income	47.0	89.9	85.9
Equity	698.9	594.3	536.9
Depreciation	47.6	43.3	41.0
Capital expenditures	87.4	98.5	72.1
R&D	26.0	29.9	N/A

TABLE 14–8. Breakdown of Dana Operations

	U.S. & Canada	Worldwide
Light truck original equipment	36%	28%
Service (aftermarket) parts	27	27
Heavy truck original equipment	18	16
Diversified parts and assemblies	11	15
Passenger car original equipment	8	14

TABLE 14–9. Dana Financial Profile (*millions*)

	1975	1974	1973
Sales	$1,136	$1,078	$ 989
Net income	62	61	56
Assets	822	753	635
Equity	431	389	346
Depreciation	33	28	23
Capital investment	49	70	60

EXHIBIT 14-1. *Financial and Market Share Profile of Automobile OEMs, 1975*

	Sales ($ millions)	Net Income ($ millions)	5-Year Average Return on Assets (1971-1975)	U.S. Market Share	Japanese Market Share	German Market Share	French Market Share	Italian Market Share
General Motors	$35,724	$1,253	8.9%	43.8%	0.2%	18.5%	1.8%	3.2%
Ford	24,009	323	5.6	23.2	0.3	13.6	3.4	2.4
Chrysler	11,598	(260)	1.0	11.7	—	2.8	9.0	5.6
AMC	2,282	(35)	2.6	3.7	—	—	—	—
Toyota	8,340	222	7.2	3.7	39.5	0.6	—	—
Volkswagen	7,191	60	-0.3	3.1	0.5	27.3	3.6	3.7
Nissan	5,862	173	3.8	3.9	31.8	0.8	—	—
Fiat	4,298	0	0.4	1.0	—	5.6	4.2	56.8
Renault	4,068	(123)	-1.0	0.1	—	5.8	33.0	6.5
Peugeot	3,647	63	3.5	0.1	—	4.7	37.4	6.3

SOURCES: Annual reports; *Note on the World Auto Industry in Transition,* Intercollegiate Case Clearinghouse, 1981.

EXHIBIT 14-2. *Actual and Forecast Motor Vehicle Production*

(Millions of units)	Actual						Forecasts						
	1970	1971	1972	1973	1974	1975	1976	1977	1978	1979	1980	1981	1982
North America													
Passenger cars:	8.5	8.8	9.6	10.9	9.0	7.6	9.3	10.1	10.1	9.7	9.8	9.8	9.9
Upper limit forecast								10.6	10.6	10.7	10.8	10.8	10.9
Lower limit forecast								8.5	8.1	8.1	8.2	8.2	8.4
% Small cars (up to 111 inches)						40	41	34	42	50	55	58	61
% Intermediate cars (112 to 118 inches)						30	32	35	33	27	25	23	21
% Full-size/luxury cars (over 118 inch)						30	27	31	25	22	20	19	18
Light trucks (up to 16,000 gross weight)	1.8	1.8	2.2	2.9	2.8	2.4	3.1	3.4	3.4	3.3	3.5	3.6	3.8
Medium/heavy trucks	.4	.4	.4	.5	.5	.4	.4	.4	.4	.4	.4	.5	.5
Western Europe													
Passenger cars:													
United Kingdom						1.3	1.3	1.4	1.5	1.5	1.5	1.6	1.6
Germany						2.9	3.5	3.6	3.3	3.4	3.5	3.6	3.7
France[a]						3.0	3.0	3.0	N/A[b]	N/A	N/A	3.4	N/A
Italy						1.3	1.5	1.6	1.7	1.6	2.0	2.0	1.9
Other						1.0	1.1	1.3	N/A	N/A	N/A	N/A	N/A
Total Europe						9.5	10.4	11.9	N/A	N/A	N/A	N/A	N/A
Japan													
Passenger cars						4.6	5.0	5.3	5.7	6.0	6.4	6.7	7.1

[a]By 1980-1982, car weights were expected to be reduced so that the 3,000-pound weight cutoff occurred between the intermediate and full-size care ranges.
[b]Not available.

SOURCES: *Ward's Automotive Yearbook;* Bendix Corporation estimates.

EXHIBIT 14-3. *Estimated Degree of Vertical Integration by North American OEM's in Selected Commodity Groups, 1976*

Product Category, Component	G.M.	Ford	Chrysler	AMC
Body				
Vinyl	E	C	C	E
Cloth	E	Y	E	E
Steel	E	Y	E	E
Stampings	C	C	C	X
Operating hardware	I	Y	E	E
Lamps, switches, instruments	X	X	E	E
Exterior ornamentation	C	Z	E	E
Trim	C	X	C	C
Seats	Y	Z	Z	E
Sealers, weather strip	Y	E	E	E
Glass	E	C	C	E
Convenience items	I	Z	E	E
Interior moldings	N/A	X	E	E
Instrument panel & console	N/A	Z	C	C
Body paint	E	Y	Y	E
Body electrical, other	Y	Z	Y	C
Power Plant				
Base engine				
Block	C	C	C	C
Pistons	C	C	C	C
Rods	C	C	C	C
Heads	C	C	C	C
Intake & exhaust manifolds	C	C	C	C
Cams	E	C	E	E
Crank	C	C	C	C
Valves & valve train comp.	E	Y	E	E
Rings	E	E	E	E
Bearings	N/A	E	E	E
Water pump	C	C	C	C
Carburetor	X	N/A	E	E
Air cleaner	C	C	E	E
Fuel pump	C	N/A	E	E
Ignition system	C	C	C	
Radiator, hoses, etc.	C	X	E	E
Mechanical fan & drive	C	X	E	E
Throttle controls	C	N/A	E	E
Power steering pump	C	Y	E	E
Air pump	C	E	E	E
Engine supports	C	N/A	E	E
Misc. parts & hardware	E	E	E	E
Oil filter	C	E	E	E
Vent & evaporative controls	C	Z	Y	E
Clutch	C	Z	E	E
Torque converter	C	Z	C	E
Final drive				
Prop shaft	C	N/A	C	E
Rear axle	C	Y	C	C
Front axle assy.	C	Y	E	E
Frame structure	E	Y	C	E
Suspension				
Front	C	Y	C	E
Rear	C	Y	Y	E
Shock absorbers	C	X	Z	E

EXHIBIT 14–3. *(continued)*

Product Category, Component	G.M.	Ford	Chrysler	AMC
Steering				
Gear	C	Y	C	E
Linkage	C	Y	E	E
Column	C	Y	X	E
Wheel & horn pad	N/A	N/A	E	E
Attaching parts	Y	Z	E	E
Brakes				
Wheel brakes	C	Z	Z	E
Hubs, drums & discs	C	Z	E	E
Master cylinder	C	Z	C	E
Brake pedal bracket	C	Z	Y	E
Power brake booster	C	Z	E	E
Tubes & hoses	E	E	E	E
Transmission	C	C	C	E
General chassis				
Wheels	C	Z	E	E
Tires	E	E	E	E
Gearshift controls	C	C	E	E
Clutch control	C	C	E	E
Parking brake control	C	C	E	E
Exhaust system	X	Z	E	E
Fuel system	C	X	C	C
Fender shields	C	X	N/A	
Bumpers	C	Y	E	E
Front structure insulators	C	X	C	E
Chassis electrical	X	X	E	C
Tools & jacks	N/A	N/A	E	E
Heat shields	N/A	X	E	E
Chassis indirect materials	E	X	E	E
Electrical assy.	C	X	E	C
Wiring & wiring clips	C	Z	E	E
Heating & air conditioning	C	X	C	E
Restraint systems	Z	E	E	E
Accessory equipment				
Radio	C	C	C	E
Window washer	C	X	E	E
Engine block heater	E	X	E	E
Other	Y	N/A	E	E

C = captive, 100 percent sourced internally.
X = less than 33 percent sourced externally.
Y = 33 to 66 percent sourced externally.
Z = more than 67 percent sourced externally.
E = sourced externally 100 percent.
N/A = not available.

SOURCE: Casewriter estimates from interviews.

EXHIBIT 14-4. *Estimated Sourcing of Seat Belt Systems by North American OEMs, 1972-1973*[a]

| | Customers | | | | | |
Seat Belt Suppliers	G.M.[b]	Ford	Chrysler	AMC	Others	Total
Allied Chemical	38%[c]	43%	—	16%	33%	32%
Firestone Tire	34	42	—	—	17	30
American Safety Equip.	—	15	51	84	17	15
Gateway Industries	7	—	49	—	—	11
Arvin Industries	14	—	—	—	33	8
General Safety Corp.	8	—	—	—	—	4
Total	100%	100%	100%	100%	100%	100%

[a] Estimated total market size (1972 dollars):

1963	$35 million
1967	72 million
1971	145 million
1972	194 million

1972–1980 Growth forecast 20% per year

[b] GM had begun to supply approximately 15 percent of its requirements in-house by 1975–1976.

[c] Market shares are computed on a dollar basis.

EXHIBIT 14-5. *Performance of Selected Medium-Size Automotive Suppliers*

	1975 Sales (Millions)	% Automotive Sales	% Operating Profit in Automotive	4-Year Average Return on Equity (1972-1975)	Product Lines With Particular Strengths	% Automotive Sales to Aftermarket
Arvin Industries	$340.3	73%	95%	8.8%	Exhaust systems	12%
Budd	$794.1	79%	49%	8.7%	Stampings, metal fabrication	Very Low
Champion Spark Plug	$458.2	79%	95%	19.2%	Spark plugs	Very High
Federal-Mogul	$354.2	85%	62%	8.1%	Bearings, seals	47%
Maremont	$292.4	94%	86%	14.0%	Shock absorbers, mufflers	50+%
McCord	$133.2	90%	93%	11.1%	Engine gaskets, soft trim	24%
Monroe Auto Equipment	$155.1	100%	100%	15.4%	Shock absorbers	81%
Purolator	$298.1	39%	22%	18.6%	Filters, radiator and gasoline caps	Very High
Questor	$406.5	42%	1%	5.1%	Exhaust system parts, piston rings, shock absorbers	NA[a]
Raybestos-Manhattan	$210.7	50+%	NA	9.9%	Friction materials	NA
Sealed Power	$141.9	80+%	NA	11.3%	Engine parts	NA
Sheller-Globe	$436.9	59%	59%	12.2%	Soft trim, steering wheels	20%
A.O. Smith	$451.8	77%	127%	4.6%	Frames, stampings	NA

[a]Not Available

SOURCES: *Moody's Industrial Manual*, annual reports, and casewriter interviews.

PART VII
Competitive Strategy in Emerging Industries

The next five cases examine the problems of competing in emerging industries. Emerging industries are characterized by fluid industry structures and much uncertainty about the directions that future industry development will take. Competitive strategy has a particularly large potential impact on performance in such industries, and hence three separate emerging industries are examined in the book.

"Bendix Corporation: Electronic Fuel Injection" describes Bendix's invention and subsequent commercialization of electronic fuel injection systems for automobiles. With its patent expiring, Bendix faces some difficult decisions about how to compete in this fledgling business where sales in the U.S. market are still practically nonexistent.

"The Fiber-Optics Industry" series comprises three cases that successively examine products, technology, markets, competitors, and the strategy of the industry leader (Corning Glass Works) in the emerging fiber-optics industry. This new technology promises to revolutionize communications but represents more potential than actual sales in 1979. A range of scenarios for the future development of the fiber-optics industry must be identified in order to formulate competitive strategy under such uncertain conditions. Based on such an industry analysis, Corning Glass Works must develop a strategy in order to capitalize on its leadership in fiber-optics technology.

"Sierra Log Homes" completes the consideration of emerging industries by describing the situation facing the leader in a small segment of the rapidly growing log homes industry. Sierra is a small, entrepreneurially managed company that faces tough questions about future strategy, given its limited resources. The case also illustrates how the framework for competitive strategy development can be applied to smaller companies.

CASE 15
Bendix Corporation: Electronic Fuel Injection

In early 1976 Douglas Crane, President of Bendix Corporation's Automotive Group, was pondering whether Bendix should go ahead with plans to construct a $10 million manufacturing facility for the production of injectors for electronic fuel injection systems, another step in Bendix's entry into the electronic engine controls business. It was raining as he reviewed the progress of the entry to date:

> Bendix's entry into the electronic engine controls business has so far contributed to three executives losing their jobs and badly hurt another man's career. Now we are at the threshold of embarking on another step that in many ways is more difficult than the ones we have taken before, and which further commits us to this market before it really even exists.

The proposed injector manufacturing facility was another piece of the electronic fuel injection puzzle that had begun many years previously in the Automotive Group. Bendix Corporation had a large stake in the automotive business, with automotive accounting for more than 50 percent of Bendix's sales in 1975 and Bendix holding a position as the largest independent supplier of motor vehicle components in North America. Electronic fuel injection was thought to have the potential of becoming a billion-dollar total market, up from almost nothing in 1975, and success in the business could mean substantial new sales and profit growth for Bendix's oldest and largest business group. However, the puzzle leading to success in electronic fuel injection was not yet complete.

Background

Bendix was incorporated in the early 1900s in South Bend, Indiana, to serve the growing automobile manufacturing industry with starter motors, brake linings, air filters, and other products for the original equipment market. In the 1920s Bendix relocated to its present headquarters near Detroit, Michigan, and expanded its line of automobile products to include brake system hardware, brake linings, fuel pumps, fuel filters, air filters, and related products for use in automobile, trucks, tractors, and other vehicles.

By early 1976, Bendix served four basic markets: automotive (52 percent of sales); aerospace and electronics (26 percent of sales); shelter and housing (14 percent of sales); and industrial and energy group (8 percent of sales). Bendix had been referred to as one of the best managed companies in the United States. From fiscal 1970 to fiscal 1975 sales increased from $1.7 billion to $2.6 billion for a compound annual increase of 10 percent while profits increased at a compound rate of 22 percent per year.[1] This performance was achieved despite a severe recession in 1974 and 1975, price controls in the early 1970s, and a generally high rate of inflation during most of the period. Many observers ascribed a part of Bendix's above-average performance through difficult times to its chief executive officer, W. Michael Blumenthal, who had come to Bendix in 1968 and become President in 1970. It was under Mr. Blumenthal's leadership that Bendix expanded into its four basic businesses to achieve balanced growth through involvement in countercyclical business areas. Exhibits 15-1 and 15-2 summarize Bendix's financial performance.

Bendix was organized into five operating units—Automotive; the Fram Corporation (wholly owned by Bendix); Aerospace; Industrial Energy; and International—each headed by a group president. The first four were product-oriented groups, while the International Group sold the range of Bendix products overseas. Group presidents reported to an Office of the Chief Executive (OCE), which included Blumenthal and three executive vice presidents. Each group was divided into business units headed by group vice presidents and further divided into divisions under division general managers.

The Bendix Automotive Business

The Automotive Group and the Fram Corporation sold separate product lines to the original equipment market (OEM) and aftermarket in North America, primarily the United States and Canada. Automotive sales to foreign markets were the responsibility of the International Group, which was divided on a country basis. The North American portion of Bendix's $1.3 billion world-wide automotive business in 1975 represented about $700 million. Bendix's automotive operations served the car, light truck, heavy truck, and "off-the-road" construction equipment segments of the automotive market. The car segment was the largest, accounting for more than 75 percent of Bendix's sales, while the off-the-road segment had experienced the most rapid growth during the early 1970s.

The Automotive Group produced a wide variety of products, including drum and disk brakes, brake linings and other friction materials, vacuum and hydraulic power brakes for both cars and trucks, air brake compressors, wheel and master brake cylinders, actuating controls for trucks and tractor trailers, power steering assemblies, valves, starter drives, air pumps, carburetors, fuel pumps, and several electronic metering and control systems.[2] The Fram Corporation produced filters, air cleaner assemblies, fans, and windshield wiper arms and blades. Fram also produced spark plugs and vacuum and mechanical controls under the Autolite brand name after purchasing the Autolite Division from the Ford Motor Company in late 1973.

Bendix's automotive products were sold both to manufacturers of original equipment (OEMs) and to wholesale distributors for sale in the replacement market or "aftermarket." On a worldwide basis, sales to OEMs accounted for about two-thirds of automotives sales, with the replacement business making up the remainder. In the North American market sales in the replacement market were slightly more important. OEM sales were made to a rather limited number of customers, with only six companies—General Motors, Ford, Chrysler, AMC, Peugeot, and Renault—accounting for about 40 percent of Bendix's worldwide automotive sales (or 60 percent of OEM sales).

The Automotive Group's strategy had been to attempt to become a major supplier (typically a market share of 25 percent) in each of its product areas, and Bendix was the largest independent parts supplier to the North American market in early 1976. It had developed an excellent reputation as a technologically advanced and reliable supplier of parts for the industry. Bendix sought to remain at

---

[1] Bendix operated on a fiscal year ending September 30.

[2] The metering and control systems were not electronically sophisticated.

the leading edge of automotive technology, encompassing new products, new materials, new engine configurations, and new personal transportation modes should they appear. The Automotive Group's goals were to expand its penetration both in North America and abroad to become a world leader in the automotive industry. In addition, it sought to expand its penetration in the aftermarket.

The Automotive Group competed with a wide range of competitors, including several comparably large auto parts suppliers—TRW, Rockwell International, Eaton, and Dana—a group of second tier firms such as Midland Ross and Sheller-Globe; a large number of small regional companies; and the in-house component manufacturing divisions of the major auto companies themselves. Overseas Bendix competed with a similar array of firms, with major international competitors including Robert Bosch, Lucas Industries, ITT Teves, Ferodo, Mintex, several Japanese firms, and the overseas units of TRW and Rockwell. Bosch was perhaps Bendix's most significant overseas competitor and was in a number of overlapping product areas with Bendix. A companion case, *Note on Supplying the Automobile Industry* (Case 14), describes the automotive parts business and gives profiles of some of the leading competitors.

History of Bendix's Involvement in Electronic Fuel Injection

In 1951 Robert Sutton, a Bendix engineer working in an aerospace division whom one manager referred to as "an airplane buff," devised a system that would permit airplanes to fly upside down. At the time it was not possible for airplanes to fly upside down for extended periods, because their engines used gravity to feed gasoline into the cylinders. If exactly the right amount of gasoline could be force-fed directly into the cylinder through an injector, the problem would be solved. After some tinkering, a workable electronic fuel injection system was developed based on then state-of-the-art electronics technology—the vacuum tube.

Bendix patented the idea in 1951 at a cost of $500, but very little was subsequently done with the invention with respect to aircraft because of the delicacy and unreliability of vacuum tube technology. A number of engineers in the automotive area saw an application for electronic fuel injection in automobiles, but this proved not to be feasible since the cost of fuel injection was high relative to existing carburetor systems, and vacuum tubes were unable to operate in the difficult internal environment of the internal combustion engine.[3] One Bendix manager recalled the situation at the time: "We were very pleased with ourselves. We ran around, showed everybody our invention, went to all the trade shows, did a lot of talking; everyone was very impressed and thought it had a great future, except nobody placed any orders."

The new invention sat on the shelf for approximately ten years. One or two individuals, working primarily on their own time, tinkered with the project. Despite the lack of activity, Bendix had been awarded a broad, "ironclad" patent on the idea, covering all aspects of shooting combustable material into a cylinder for burning. The patent effectively meant that no one else could manufacture any kind of fuel injection system without Bendix's permission.

In the early 1960s responsibility for the project was officially transferred from the aerospace division to the carburetor division in Elmira, New York. The transfer was effected because management believed that the automotive industry presented a larger potential market for the product than aerospace, and Elmira's general manager, Jack Campbell, was a strong believer in the potential of the idea. Campbell saw electronic fuel injection as a concept involving Bendix in the frontier of fuel management technology, and he assigned several engineers to work on the project despite the lack of formal research and development budget for it. This work was to set the stage for the transformation of the long-orphaned project into a full-fledged business opportunity.

The Electronic Fuel Injection System

Electronic Fuel Injection (EFI) performed the same role in the internal combustion engine as the tradi-

[3] The internal combustion engine was known as a very "hostile" environment for electronics, with fumes, vibration, and heat levels of 200° Fahrenheit.

tional carburetor. The primary function of both was to mix air and fuel in the correct proportions for the most economical fuel consumption consistent with the desired performance characteristics of the automobile, and then feed the mixture into the cylinders for burning.[4] The carburetor, a mechanical device for introducing fuel into the engine, controlled flow of fuel through detecting the flow of air through a tube called the Venturi, except during transient conditions such as starting a cold engine and acceleration, when accessory devices supplied a fuel mixture with a higher gasoline-to-air ratio. Carburetor systems cost in the range of $55 to $75 in early 1976.

An EFI system, on the other hand, used sophisticated electronic circuitry to determine the best fuel/air mixture. An EFI system cost approximately $250 to $300 in 1976 and consisted of the following components as illustrated in Exhibit 15-3.

• *Electronic control unit* (ECU), the electronic "brain" of the system. The ECU's job was to continuously evaluate such external data as altitude, temperature, humidity, and engine parameters such as driving speed, the level of oxygen in the exhaust gases, and engine temperature to determine the optimal air-to-fuel mixture. Early ECUs consisted of a combination of analog and digital electronic circuitry, though ECUs were expected soon to become all digital and to incorporate microprocessors as part of their circuitry.

• *Injectors* were precision electrical spray nozzles, which released an exact quantity of fuel into the cylinder for ignition. In 1976 EFI systems had one injector per cylinder.

• *Sensors and actuators* either fed data to the ECU or carried out the ECU's instructions. Sensors were used for such tasks as measuring the temperature of the engine coolant, the amount of oxygen in the exhaust, and the position of the throttle. Early EFI systems did not have oxygen sensors, but these were expected to be added in the near future. Actuators were used to adjust fuel pressure, manipulate the engine's idle speed, etc. Technically, the injector was an actuator, though it was usually treated separately.

The two other EFI components were similar to those used by carburetor systems:

Fuel pump— the pump performed exactly the same function that it did in a conventional carburetor system, forcing the fuel from the fuel tank to the injector.

Throttle Body— the device which regulates the amount of air ingested by the engine. This component was not exactly the same as in a conventional carburetor system, but it was similar and not very complex to produce.

The operation of an EFI system was different from that of the conventional carburetor. EFI was self-regulating and would automatically adjust the air-fuel mixture to an optimal level and remain in "tune" regardless of the driving habits of the owner, length of the trip, terrain, or state of wear of the vehicle.[5] A conventionally carbureted vehicle could be adjusted for only one state of operation—for example, a carburetor adjusted efficiently at sea level would often appear sluggish at higher elevations because of the difference in oxygen levels.

This difference resulted in a number of improvements in engine performance with EFI. First, the engine would start up quickly and perform smoothly under almost any weather conditions. Test cars had been subjected to sustained conditions of extreme heat and cold and a wide variety of humidity conditions and then started without difficulty. Second, EFI needed little or no adjustment by a mechanic and was subject to very little wear as it was used. Third, EFI was able to sense how efficiently the engine was using gasoline and adjust the fuel mixture accordingly. This was done through use of an oxygen sensor to measure the oxygen content in the engine exhaust, adjusting the fuel mixture to achieve the optimal state where no oxygen was left in the exhaust gases. EFI's ability to continuously monitor such variables as exhaust oxygen content meant that EFI was able significantly to reduce emissions of nitrous oxide (NOx). The carburetor could correct the fuel mixture based on only one parameter—air flow—and even this would often fall out of adjustment. Thus, EFI could significantly reduce engine emissions by precisely

---

[4] An automobile's performance was measured by the vehicle's ability to accelerate to cruising speed, pass other cars on the highway, and to respond to the driver's commands.

[5] Such a system was referred to as being a "closed loop system."

controlling the air-fuel mixture while maintaining drivability of the vehicle. Precise control of the air-fuel mixture was necessary in order to realize the emissions conversion capabilities of a three-way catalyst. This newer catalyst was effective in reducing the level of nitrous oxides emitted, as well as reducing the emitted hydrocarbons and carbon monoxide. A conventional mechanical carburetor could not keep the air-fuel mixture within a narrow enough range to utilize the benefits of a three-way catalyst and could not maintain the drivability of an emission-controlled engine.

An intermediate system between EFI and conventional carburetors was mechanical fuel injection, sometimes called continuous injection. Continuous injection utilized injectors to shoot the fuel directly but computed the correct air-fuel mixture through conventional mechanical means using a vane deflected by inlet air-flow. Mechanical fuel injection offered some performance advantages over the carburetor, but it was subject to wear, could get out of adjustment, was quite difficult to adjust properly, and was less self-correcting for differences in climate, terrain, and driving conditions. Mechanical fuel injection systems and electronic fuel injection systems cost about the same in early 1976, though the cost of electronic systems was expected to fall in relative terms.

The Bosch Licensing Agreement

From 1951 until 1967, despite Campbell's belief in the product, Bendix's fuel injection system had gained very limited acceptance and was used only on some expensive European passenger cars and on special high-performance racing machines. The few systems in use had been mechanically rather than electronically controlled, and no company had any extensive expertise in high-volume manufacturing of fuel injection system components. Bendix, the world patent holder, had not invested in any in-house manufacturing capability at all and was licensing its patent to the few firms that were using injectors.

In early 1967 the name of the game changed when Robert Bosch Corporation approached Bendix to negotiate a license agreement under which it could manufacture fuel injection systems on a large-scale.

Bosch had obtained a contract from the Volkswagen Corporation (VW), a major West German producer of automobiles, to supply a fuel injection system for its 1968 models. VW wanted a fuel injection system to achieve greater horsepower and improved engine performance on its small cars without increasing engine displacement, which in Europe was the basis on which automobiles were taxed.

VW's decision to use fuel injection rather than the conventional carburetor system represented a major innovation in the automotive industry. Carburetor technology was very well known and had been in use, in some form, from the earliest days of mass-produced automobiles. The last real innovations in automobile technology had been the introduction of the automatic transmission in the late 1940s and, more recently, disk brakes in the mid-1960s. Therefore, VW's move was certain to attract much attention in trade press and the industry in general. VW's decision was in part possible because of the configuration of the European automobile industry, which differed in some respects from that of the United States. European auto manufacturers were smaller than the major U.S. companies and relied heavily on independent companies for their parts needs—firms such as VW tended to be less vertically integrated than the major U.S. automakers. This allowed European producers to implement changes in their manufacturing processes faster than their U.S. counterparts, which had many billions of dollars invested in specialized plant, equipment, and tools.

Bosch was planning to use both electronic and mechanical fuel injection systems rather than solely EFI because of the expense of the still cumbersome electronic components, the need to bring the system into production very rapidly, and Bosch's special expertise in mechanically controlled devices. While mechanical systems did not have the electronic circuitry allowing continual adjustment for changes in external and internal factors, however, Bosch still needed Bendix's permission to manufacture a mechanical system.

Bendix granted Bosch a license in late 1967, and Bosch constructed its ECU and injector manufacturing facilities in 1968. The agreement netted Bendix a royalty fee for each system produced by Bosch and placed certain restrictions on where and to whom Bosch could make and sell its systems. Bendix could not make EFI for sale in Bosch's markets until the expiration of the agreement in 1978, and the agreement also gave both Bendix and Bosch the right to share in technological developments and visit each other's facilities. However, some at Bendix, notably Jack Campbell, were disturbed that one of Bendix's most active and capable competitors should be capitalizing on a Bendix innovation.

Indeed, as a result of the licensing agreement Bosch had capitalized very nicely on fuel injection systems in the European car market by 1976. Bosch's system did well because the car's weight, economy, and performance requirements were substantially more important in Europe than in the United States. In addition to taxation based on the size of the engine, gasoline had been selling at two to three times U.S. prices in Europe for some time. By the mid-1970s Bosch supplied mechanical fuel injection systems to nearly all of the major European OEMs and sold electronic fuel injection systems as well to VW, BMW, and Porsche. It was estimated that Bosch had sold approximately 3 million mechanical and electronic systems by 1976, with an average of approximately five injectors per system.

In the early 1970s Bosch licensed (with Bendix's permission) a major Japanese auto parts manufacturer, Diesel Kiki, to manufacture EFI for Japanese automobile manufacturers. Bosch and Bendix jointly licensed another Japanese manufacturer, Nippondenso, shortly thereafter. Diesel Kiki was part of the Nissan Group (Datsun), and Nippondenso was part of Toyota. Bosch provided assistance in constructing injector and ECU manufacturing facilities, which were completed in 1973 using the latest available technology. Both firms had produced in excess of 50,000 electronic fuel injection systems in 1975, and this number was expected to grow.

External Changes in the U.S. Market

Fuel injection had languished in the U.S. despite these strides in Europe and Japan. However, as Bendix's deal with Bosch was being signed, external changes were occuring that would have a significant impact on the feasibility of the electronic fuel injection system for automobiles in the United States.

Antipollution Regulations

In the late 1960s the public began to show mounting concern for the quality of its environment, one highly visible component of which was the cleanliness of the air. The first concrete steps taken by government toward air pollution control were in California, in response to growing public fears about the heavy smog in the Los Angeles basin. The automobile was identified as a major source of Los Angeles's air pollution and that in urban population centers generally, and in 1970 California passed the first automobile pollution control law, which specified the maximum permissible amounts of engine pollutants that could leave the exhaust.

The impact of the California regulations was to force the auto companies to engineer two versions of their product, one for the California market and one for the United States in general. To meet the new standards auto companies relied on essentially "off-the-shelf" technology that they had been experimenting with for several years, consisting of refinements to the carburetor, the addition of an exhaust gas recirculation valve to the engine, and addition of an air pump to force extra air into the exhaust manifold, thereby improving the cleanliness of the exhaust. The effect of these changes was to make automobiles more expensive and more difficult to adjust by other than a well-trained mechanic, and to downgrade their performance. The initial emissions-controlled cars were harder to start in hot or cold weather, underpowered when going up hills and accelerating onto highways, and less efficient in their use of gasoline.

By the presidential elections of 1972, air pollution had become one of the most significant topics of national debate, and national legislation in the form of the Clear Air Act was passed in 1972 over the strenuous objections of the automobile industry. The act extended the existing California regulations nationwide and went on to reduce maximum permissible pollution levels in steps toward final target levels that were scheduled to be required on 1978 model cars (see Exhibit 15–4). Stiff penalties were provided for failing to meet the standards. The first real test for the automobile industry was to come in late 1976, when the designs for 1978 models would be frozen to permit retooling. While interim 1976 and 1977 standards could be met with relatively little difficulty, the act stipulated major reductions in all major classifications of engine pollutants in 1978. There were major uncertainties in early 1976 about whether the strict 1978 standards would be upheld by Congress or delayed.

The Arab Oil Embargo

Shortly after the Clean Air Act, another event shook the industry—the 1973 Arab oil embargo. The resulting gas shortages and higher gasoline prices turned the American public's attention toward the more fuel-efficient foreign cars, whose share had grown to account for 20 percent of the U.S. auto market by 1976. The concern for fuel economy was reinforced by the federal government, which passed the Energy Policy and Conservation Act in December 1975. The act mandated minimum miles per gallon averages for each auto company's fleet of cars. The mileage standards were scheduled to increase from 18 miles per gallon for 1978 models to 27.5 miles per gallon for 1985 (see Exhibit 15–4). The auto companies' overall averages on 1976 models were less than 14 miles per gallon. In addition, several industry observers were concerned that this legislation could become the same kind of highly political topic that pollution standards had been, with mileage standards and implementation time frames just as easily changed as the pollution maximums had been.

What made these new pollution and mileage standards even more vexing to the industry was their effect on automobile performance, and the fact that they were in part contradictory. The public's conception of a good automobile did not include hard starting, sluggish acceleration, and frequent engine adjustments. Further, reducing air pollution to meet the pollution standards meant sacrifices in fuel economy and vice versa, unless new technologies could be employed. However, the dual requirements of improved mileage and reduced pollution had to be dealt with by the automakers and dealt with very quickly indeed.

The Electronics Revolution

The late 1960s and early 1970s were also a time of great change for the electronics industry. The vacuum tube had given way to the transistor, the integrated circuit, and by 1974 to the microprocessor, and technological change in electronic circuitry showed few signs of abating. The technological development meant several things to the future of electronic fuel injection and electronic control of the engine generally. First, it substantially lowered the price of the system itself, because the new components could perform many times the number of operations per dollar cost than could the older components, and electronic component prices were expected to continue declining. Another major improvement was in the reliability of electronic devices. The new components had no moving parts to wear out, gave off almost no heat of their own, and were very small, which made them relatively easy to shield from the engine's vibration. In addition, the service and repair of an electronic control unit was made easier since entire ECU modules could be removed and new ones replaced in a matter of minutes. Finally, the advances in electronics technology had increased the range of the ECU in providing the best balance between fuel economy, emissions, and performance through continuous adjustment of the mixture of fuel and air. The newest generation of components, the microprocessor, could respond to a wider range of variables than ever before and monitor these variables more frequently.

Electronic Engine Control

Until recently EFI had been viewed as a distinct business in and of itself, but the advent of the microprocessor caused Bendix and others in the industry to widen their view from EFI to the broader area called "electronic engine controls." The process by which the fuel mixture was fed into the cylinders was but one process the microprocessor could control and manage. Douglas Crane, Bendix Automotive Group president, expressed his opinion about the place of EFI in the future engine controls business:

There are really three separate games going on in electronic engine control. The first is the EFI itself which regulates the flow of fuel into the engine. The second concerns the timing of the spark ignition which provides the energy to burn the fuel. The last deals with managing the exhaust gas recirculation flow, a common technique for decreasing the level of NOx emissions.

All three affect gas mileage and engine emissions, and control over all three engine functions will clearly be necessary if the automakers are to possibly meet the 1985 mileage/emissions standards being contemplated by the federal government.

One approach being investigated was the use of a central micro-computer to manage all engine functions. Dr. John Weil, Bendix's chief of research and development, commented on another view of how future electronic control systems might develop:

> We can forsee a system of micro-computers designed to control different aspects of the car's performance, which, while not linked together through a main computer, would function by sharing information. For example, one computer system could control the engine; another computer system could control the brakes; a third could control the passenger's environment. All would communicate with each other, yet each would be able to operate independently. It's not difficult to imagine that within ten years all mechanical functions on a car would be controlled electronically as the price of electronic components decreases and the need for reliability and efficiency increases.

Proponents of the single "on-board" computer approach cited lower costs, greater accuracy in the control process and easier maintenance in the field. Proponents of the multiple system approach, on the other hand, argued that redundant systems provided an extra margin of safety in the event of a failure, would be easier to implement since each system could be tested and refined independently, and would increase the overall flexibility in the system to respond to additional electronic control needs in the future. This flexibility caused some to judge the multiple system approach to be actually less expensive over the long run.

Douglas Crane commented on possible industry direction over the next several years as it sought to deal with statutory requirements that were not yet finalized:

All the major companies have very active electronic engine management R&D programs. You will see every car make use of a different approach to try and solve the problem, particularly in view of the uncertainty over future emission standards. In fact, I would not be at all surprised to see different divisions of General Motors go down separate paths. Some will move to an all electronic system as far as they can while others will try to graft electronics on to the carburetor to protect their sizable investment in plant, equipment and tooling.

For example, Chrysler made a lot out of its "lean burn" engine—which is really just a form of electronic spark control—but the problem is much broader than just spark control alone. Ford's electronic engine control (EEC) system is another development effort aimed at centralized microcomputer management of the engine.

Experimentation in approaches to electronic control had already begun in the industry. Stand-alone subsystems in electronic ignition timing and control of exhaust gases had been announced by Ford and Chrysler, while electronic subsystems for fuel cutoff and transmission shift scheduling were expected to be introduced.

For the long term, to meet the very rigorous 1985 federal mileage and pollution requirements some observers foresaw the possibility of more fundamental changes in the automobile engine. Crane commented:

> For the last 2 or 3 miles per gallon it might be necessary to have to go to improved diesels or some other technology than we have today. The diesel engine gets 25 percent better mileage, but it is hard starting, noisy, gives off exhaust odors and cost $250–$500 more than gasoline engines. In addition, diesels have a tough time with the NOx standards. The Senate/House compromise version of the pollution bill has raised the NOx minimums, which many believe was done to allow diesels a chance.

European producers already offered diesel models, though they had gained only limited acceptance in the United States and several American manufacturers planned experiments with diesel options on their cars. However, even the most bullish forecasts gave diesel only a 10–20 percent market penetration by 1985, with only 50,000–100,000 units annually through 1980.

The Seville Contract

The Bosch licensing agreement coupled with these environmental changes caused Jack Campbell and his group to be even more determined to find some way to capitalize on Bendix's invention of the fuel injection concept. However, while Bosch was working with VW to perfect its fuel injection system, Bendix was maintaining a very conservative attitude toward new investment in EFI. Bendix's corporate posture was to restrict new investment in research and development and specialized plant and equipment for EFI to the level of its licensing fees from Bosch. One manager commented on the company's treatment of EFI:

> We didn't honestly believe that something as different as EFI was practical in the U.S. auto market. In addition, the people directly responsible for automotive operations were wary of becoming involved in a new technology, especially one that included electronics as a primary component. No one was willing to kill the concept, given what Bosch was doing with it in Europe, but no one was willing to back it as an investment, either. Therefore, EFI languished for several years.

Bendix did try to extend the basic patent with new breakthroughs and modifications to the existing system, but these efforts were not particularly successful, and the basic EFI patent was due to expire in 1978.

Campbell decided the best way to break into the U.S. auto market with EFI was to begin with the most expensive cars. His reasoning was that EFI was still substantially more expensive than conventional carburetors (then $500 versus $55) despite the dramatic cost reductions due to improved technology. On the top-of-the-line Cadillacs, Lincoln Continentals, and Chrysler Imperials (all of which sold for more than $10,000), however, the added cost of EFI would be a small item, and the auto companies might be interested in the operational advantages of the system as a marketing device.

Campbell chose to start with the Lincoln-Mercury Division of Ford, because his Bendix division was already doing business with Ford in car radios, air pumps, and other products. In the spring of 1971 Campbell was able to interest Ford in trying the EFI on the Continental Mark IV but was unable to obtain clearance from Automotive Group management to commit funds to the project. Campbell commented on the situation as it existed within Bendix:

> Each week we had a new dog and pony show. Every time I wanted to do something the people above me wanted to monitor it. Every time I wanted to spend money they wanted to slow it down. I spent more time selling inside the company than outside the company. They were afraid of what would happen if we became heavily involved with Ford or General Motors. I don't believe that I would have had that much trouble getting the product started if they would have left me alone and let me get the job done.

Automotive Group top management, all of whom had been with Bendix for many years and risen through the ranks in engineering/manufacturing or accounting, were skeptical of a story they had heard before. EFI had been discussed for more than ten years and never amounted to anything, and Jack Campbell was telling his story once again. They finally agreed to develop a system with Ford, but on the condition that Ford pay for the entire $3 million to $4 million in estimated up-front development cost. Other companies had approached Ford without making such demands, and Ford decided to conduct its development effort without Bendix. Ford began working on electronic engine control with Motorola, Essex, Toshiba, and Ford's own Electrical and Electronics Division.

The Cadillac Division of General Motors presented Campbell's next market opportunity. In the early 1970s Cadillac had decided to produce a new smaller eight-cylinder luxury car called the Seville. It was to be positioned in the auto market to compete with Mercedes Benz, which had been making inroads into Cadillac's traditional market. The Seville was to be the first of a new line of small luxury cars within the Cadillac Division. Bob Lund, then the general manager of the Cadillac Division, saw EFI as providing Seville with excellent performance and start-up qualities with only a marginal increase in the overall cost of the car (which was approximately $13,000 fully equipped). Taking the initiative, Lund approached Campbell directly to arrange a meeting at Cadillac's headquarters. Lund had met Campbell previously and was aware that Campbell was anxious to obtain a contract for the EFI and that he had been negotiating with Ford for some time.

The meeting went exceedingly well from Campbell's perspective. Lund had already made up his mind about the desirability of EFI as standard equipment on the Seville and was anxious to get Bendix moving. Lund agreed to pay for all of Bendix's start-up cost on a dollar-for-dollar basis, give Bendix a five-year contract with guaranteed production volumes, and make the contract profitable for Bendix to undertake. In return, Bendix would agree to full and open sharing of their technology and patents with Cadillac. However, securing management approval proved to be more difficult than Campbell anticipated.

Management of Bendix's Automotive Group remained skeptical about start-up ventures and new technologies, particularly this one. They were reluctant to sell the idea to top corporate management and did not believe that Bendix could successfully complete an electronically related venture that involved a brand new product line and might involve a new manufacturing facility and a new manufacturing process. In an effort to break the bottleneck, Campbell arranged a meeting between Lund and Blumenthal. Lund was eager to get the EFI project started in time to meet the Seville's production schedule, which anticipated getting out the new car in record time for an entirely new model. If the agreement could not be reached then, Cadillac would have to rely on a conventional carburetor system to avoid holding up the production schedule. Lund agreed to give Bendix a five-year contract for 100 percent of the Seville's production volume, or the first 300,000 systems Cadillac bought, whichever was greater. However, just before the contract was to be signed Blumenthal demurred; he wanted to deal directly with GM's president.

Blumenthal was aware that a division of GM could be overruled by the corporate office when it came to contract and pricing negotiations with outside suppliers and wanted to be absolutely certain that GM's top management was firmly behind Cadillac's decision to use EFI. After some discussion Lund agreed to the request and referred the matter to Edward Cole, GM's president. Shortly thereafter Bendix got the terms it requested and the contract

was signed in December 1973; however, Blumenthal was still somewhat apprehensive about dealing with G.M. Only one division of a U.S. car manufacturer had made a tangible commitment to EFI, and one Bendix manager commented that after the contract was finally signed Blumenthal remarked, "G.M. will get us before this is all over."

Meeting the Seville EFI Contract

After signing the agreement with General Motors, Bendix faced the task of beginning to supply Cadillac with an expected 60,000 EFI systems per year within eighteen months despite the lack of any in-house manufacturing capability, a legacy of the conservative investment policy followed with respect to the new product. Bendix also lacked substantial experience in high-volume manufacturing this type of sophisticated electronic component, since most of Bendix's electronics manufacturing had been in the aerospace divisions with small lot sizes, and in comparatively low-complexity car radios.

Since Bendix did not have time to build an injector plant of its own, which required a lead time of two years, it had anticipated buying the injectors it needed from Bosch under a cross-licensing arrangement. However, Bosch found that it did not have enough excess capacity to meet all of Bendix's requirements and was unwilling to build another injector plant without a long-term contract from Bendix. Bendix decided instead to buy a portion of its needs from Bosch and purchase the rest from Nippondenso and Diesel Kiki, Bendix's and Bosch's Japanese licensees of EFI. Jack Campbell, given responsibility for the project, also hurriedly sought other subcontractors who could supply other EFI components, since normal lead times for ordering manufacturing equipment were eighteen to twenty-four months. Satisfactory sources for the various sensors, actuators, and other EFI components were secured.

ECU Manufacturing

While most of the EFI components were to be subcontracted, it was decided that Bendix would manufacture ECUs itself at its former radio plant in

Newport News, Virginia, now producing air pumps for Ford. This plant had considerable excess space, which made it an attractive location for the new Seville business, and since radios and the ECU were both electronic in nature it was hoped that some synergy might be present. For a company already involved in high-volume electronic manufacturing, ECU capacity could be put on line in six to nine months as an addition to an existing facility and required little specialized equipment that was not used in other forms of electronics manufacturing. For Bendix, without such experience, an investment of about 2 million dollars would be required, primarily for sophisticated electronic test equipment that an established firm in electronics manufacturing would have. Bendix planned to purchase electronic components from outside suppliers and already had the capability to design its own circuits and produce its own etched circuit boards internally.

Bendix management chose Robert Hoge to manage launching ECU production in Newport News. Hoge recalled his surprise at getting the assignment:

> I was managing a brake products plant in Canada, doing very well. My background as an electronics engineer and an MIT fellow graduate led my superiors to come to me and urge me to take this new position. Although neither I nor anyone else on my proposed team knew very much about electronics manufacturing, they were persuasive and I felt a sense of obligation to give it a try.

In practice, the manufacture of radios, a well-known and relatively unsophisticated technology, could not be compared with the care and precision needed to produce the ECU. The ECU was a very complex component that required highly trained personnel and a dust- and fume-free manufacturing environment. Like most electronic assemblies, there was a significant learning curve involved in ECU manufacturing, particularly on the first 75,000 units.

The Newport News plant proved a less than ideal home for the new venture. Since no electronics production had taken place in the plant for more than two years the best electrical engineers and manufacturing specialists had left. Current air pump manufacturing was a noisy and dirty operation, which was to go on side by side with ECU production. Hoge found little cooperation from the Newport News plant manager, who seemed more concerned with the air pump business than with the ECU start-up and did little to help Hoge get established and provide staff support. An inadequate budget had been allocated by this plant manager for refacilitizing the ECU portion of the plant, and some of the needed expensive electronic test equipment went unpurchased. Borrowed staff from Bendix's aerospace operations were utilized.

To complicate matters even further, no one at Bendix had ever produced an ECU for EFI, and the original specifications for the component were not based on real production experience and proved to be infeasible. Hoge reflected on what happened at the time:

> The project quickly started going bad. We were missing deadlines, equipment was not being delivered on time; my people were giving estimates for time and dollars that I had no way of evaluating properly. Therefore, I committed myself and our group to making deliveries and meeting production schedules which were basically impossible to do. The pressure from the Cadillac Division to fulfill our contract was very high. Cadillac needed these components as part of their scheduled and highly publicized start-up production of the Seville, and Bendix had encouraged Cadillac not to develop an alternate carburetor system for the Seville. If we could not fulfill our obligation we could have a very difficult time with the rest of our G.M. business. So there was tremendous pressure, both from within Bendix Corporation and from General Motors, to do something about the project. Unfortunately, I was the something they did something about.

A management shakeup resulted in Hoge's being relieved. But the pressure extended further, and the president of the Automotive Group asked to be demoted and reassigned to the brake products business. The request was accepted and other early retirements followed—top management's feelings about Bendix's inability to manage a start-up in a high-technology manufacturing process had unfortunately been reinforced.

Faced with a management vacuum in automotive, Blumenthal recruited Douglas Crane to be the group president for Automotive in May 1975. Crane had been group vice president in charge of worldwide industrial operations at AMF, and previously senior group vice president in charge of aerospace, automotive, and recreational vehicle parts production and steel fabrication at the Wickes Corporation. Crane quickly became personally involved in the management of the project:

> When I arrived I asked to have all our microprocessor experts meet in my office. A little later *he* walked in, though it did not seem funny at the time. I went to see Blumenthal and told him that we had a very serious problem. He told me to do *whatever* was necessary to solve the problem.
>
> I assumed direct control of the Newport News plant and for all practical purposes was the Group VP as well as the Group President. I recruited several good electronics people from companies like General Electric, Texas Instruments, and Rockwell, and tripled the size of our engineering department in a year. I also brought in some manufacturing talent with experience in electronics manufacturing and recruited Charles Flannagan, who was head of Texas Instruments' electronic controls group, to manage the EFI business.
>
> Some of the problems were a function of the old management's attitude toward the ECU project. The idea of spending $1 million on a piece of electronic test equipment would send them into shock.

Crane recalled the final weeks before the first deliveries of ECU's were due: "We had thirty or forty engineers down there with soldering guns making ECUs, and we were flying them to Cadillac in Jetstars. I didn't quite get to the soldering gun stage myself, but almost."

Bendix met its delivery schedule to Cadillac, and by early 1976 the ECU manufacturing process was operating smoothly, though it was currently undergoing modifications to accept newer microprocessors as the "brain" of the system. The ECU had already been redesigned several times since the original versions produced as a result of technological progress.

Sensors and Actuators

Each Bendix EFI system required a variety of sensors and actuators. Most sensors and actuators were relatively low-cost items ($1–$10), and many involved no special technological difficulties, though there was more than one technological approach to performing the sensing function in some cases.

However, manifold pressure sensors and oxygen sensors, both important to the developing technology in EFI, were technologically sophisticated, especially oxygen sensors, whose technology was termed a "black art." Oxygen sensors were similar to spark plugs in both appearance and manufacturing technology. Participation in the spark plug business was almost a necessity for entry into oxygen sensors, and as much as 85 percent of the manufacturing equipment was common.

Initially, Bendix purchased its sensors and actuators from outside suppliers, primarily Bosch. However, Bendix had plans to add the capability to produce them internally through the Autoline division, making Bendix the only source of oxygen sensors besides Bosch, which had been making them for some time.[6] Bendix was also planning to manufacture temperature and manifold pressure sensors inside, through incremental investments in existing manufacturing facilities. The time and investment requirements for beginning production of all these devices were significantly less than that for injectors.

The Proposed Injector Plant

By early 1976 the Seville was selling very well, and the electronic fuel injection system was thought to be contributing to this, which raised the question of what Bendix's next step in EFI should be. The immediate decision facing Bendix was whether or not to build its own injector manufacturing facility. Bendix was currently purchasing injectors from its licensees—Bosch, Nippondenso and Diesel Kiki—at a cost penalty of $1 to $2 per injector because of the need to import them from abroad.

Injector manufacturing was a very capital-intensive process utilizing high-precision, high-volume turning and grinding equipment. Walter Schauer, the Bendix manager in charge of planning for the facility, described injector manufacturing technology:

---

[6] The chief U.S. manufacturers of spark plugs were Autolite, Champion, and the AC division of General Motors. Both Champion and AC were working on the development of oxygen sensors.

On a scale of one to ten, this is definitely a ten-level technology. To give you an idea of the reliability of the product, if a car engine is designed to travel 150,000 miles before breaking down, the electronic fuel injection system will have gone through 150 million cycles by the end of that time. In addition, fuel flow tolerances of less than 1 percent to 1.5 percent are required for the system to operate efficiently. Even slight pressure fluctuations can cause fuel flow problems, which will result in poor performance.

There are several very critical grinding operations which require tolerances of 1 to 1.5 microns. This kind of grinding operation is done by perhaps five companies in the entire world, and only a dozen companies manufacture equipment that can possibly do the job. This equipment has been undergoing improvements in the last decade in its ability to meet these tolerances at high volumes.

Labor content in the injector manufacturing process was relatively small, though there was significant labor content in final assembly and testing. This led to a learning curve for injector manufacturing, which was expected to flatten after the production of 500,000 to 1,000,000 units. The minimum efficient size of an injector facility was approximately 1 million units per year, requiring an investment of $8 million to $10 million and a two-year lead time from go-ahead to production. An additional comparable increment of capacity could be added to an existing injector facility for approximately one-half the original investment with eighteen months' lead time.

The technology for manufacturing injectors had undergone very close scrutiny by Bendix for an extended period. In December 1974 Bendix made a detailed study of Bosch's manufacturing process, which it was allowed to do under its licensing agreements, that formed the basis for Bendix's own manufacturing feasibility study. Schauer had also recently spent several months in Germany studying Bosch's manufacturing process. Bendix's planned facility would incorporate improvements in equipment that had occurred since Bosch's facility was constructed. Bendix's proposed facility was to have an annual capacity of 1.2 million units.

Exhibit 15–5 gives Bendix's financial projections for the proposed injector manufacturing business, as well as financial projections for the other major components of the EFI system.

The Market for Electronic Fuel Injection in 1976

The rate of development of the market for electronic fuel injection remained uncertain in 1976. The auto companies, except for Cadillac-Seville, had been carrying on work in EFI and electronic engine controls on a reserve basis. However, GM, Ford and Chrysler were accelerating their in-house research programs involved in electronic closed-loop systems, and all had announced the intention of beginning internal manufacture of electronic control units for automobiles. Both Ford and GM were already involved in electronics manufacturing and envisioned additional applications for the ECU on the automobile.

The development of EFI was dependent on the cost of the system relative to the conventional carburetor, on the ability of the auto manufacturers to improve their existing carburetor and ignition systems, and on the government's actions with respect to future mileage and emissions legislation. From 1974 to 1976 the auto companies had been able to do surprising things with their carburetor systems. Carburetor precision had been improved by the addition of electronic subsystems that modulated the air/fuel ratio and by mechanical improvements. An industry participant commented on the companies' achievements:

> When you consider that the auto companies probably have between $5 billion and $8 billion invested in plant and tooling for the manufacture of carburetors, it is no surprise that they are pulling out all the stops they can in R&D to prolong the life of the carburetor. However, the modifications also make the carburetor systems more expensive and more complex to adjust and repair. It's still unclear how far they can take carburetor technology.

The cost of carburetors had been inching up with these improvements, and Bendix estimated that the cost of carburetors would rise to the $86-to-$90 range by 1981. Bendix management believed that the auto companies would pay a premium for non-carburetor fuel controls if they provided a benefit in meeting emissions and fuel economy standards, the premium depending on the size of the car. It was estimated that the cost of electronic fuel injection systems would have to fall to approximately $100 to achieve meaningful market penetration of the small car (less than 111-inch wheel base) market, $150 for the medium car (112-inch to 118-inch) market and $200 for the full-size car market.[7]

Bendix expected that technological change and increases in production volume would bring down the cost of EFI. Exhibit 15–6 gives Bendix's projections of EFI costs, which Bendix management estimated to have an uncertainty of ± 15 percent. Expected major reductions in the cost of the ECU were expected in line with rapid technological progress in electronics that was decreasing the cost per function. Another significant part of the cost reduction in EFI was to come from a decrease in the number of injectors used in the system, as discussed by Dr. Weil:

> At this point we're using an eight-injector system, working toward what could be a two-injector system for eight-cylinder engines and a one-injector system for four-cylinder engines. If we can reduce the number of injectors needed from eight to two or from four to one, we will substantially reduce the cost of the system as a whole. There will be certain performance tradeoffs that have to be made as a result, but it will definitely bring the cost of our system more in line with the cost of a conventional carburetor system.

As Bendix contemplated building an injector manufacturing facility, improvements in injector design were already on the drawing boards. Bendix management estimated that improvements in injector design might ultimately require investments of several million dollars in retooling costs for injector manufacturing, though they would not require complete re-equipping of an injector plant.

Diesel Fuel Injection System

Fuel injection systems for diesel engines had been in use for some time and were produced by a number of U.S. and foreign companies. While diesel systems were quite different from gasoline systems, there were some commonalties that might affect the

development of both. The diesel fuel injection market is briefly profiled in Appendix A.

Legislative Uncertainties

In 1976, the year in which car designs had to be finalized for the 1978 models, the auto companies and Congress were involved in a heated public debate about the ability of the industry to meet the 1978 emissions standards. While emissions standards for 1976 and 1977 had been met, the companies were arguing that meeting the 1978 standards was impossible with existing technology. The federal government was insisting just as vehemently that it could be done with the best technology available. Meeting the 1978 standards in the short run required three-way catalysts and electronic engine controls, and Bendix believed that if the 1978 standards were maintained electronic fuel injection would be nearly mandatory for all cars over 3,000 pounds (112-inch wheel base or higher). However, if the standards were relaxed for one to three years, the consensus of industry predictions, then carburetor systems could continue to be used during that period or longer. Douglas Crane commented on the situation:

> The auto companies really can't meet the standards given the currently available and implementable technology. I'm fairly certain that the government is going to alter the legislation to whatever Detroit's best effort really is. Clearly, they are not going to shut down the auto industry, and that is exactly what would happen if they tried to enforce the 1978 standards right now.

Over the longer run, the need for electronic fuel injection would be influenced by the rate at which government standards were enforced and the ability of the industry to adopt alternative solutions to the dual mileage/emissions problem. With respect to the mileage standards, most industry executives agreed that fleet averages of 22–24 m.p.g. could be achieved with already known methods, primarily reducing the size of the car and engine. After all, European cars had achieved high gasoline mileages for many years. However, unless the industry went to all cars less than 3,000 pounds (or in the present compact range), electronic engine controls in-

---

[7]EFI would eventually have an aftermarket, primarily for replacement injectors. Given system reliability, however, this market could take as long as five years to develop, and its size was extremely uncertain without actual field experience.

cluding EFI would be needed on the larger cars over 3,000 pounds to meet the 26 to 27.5 m.p.g. standards for fleet averages combined with the tougher 1978 emission standards. Fleets with nearly all cars less than 3,000 pounds would signal the end of the American family car with capacity for more than four passengers, and it appeared that neither the federal government nor the public was prepared to accept this outcome. Bendix had estimated, however, that 58 percent of North American cars would be small cars weighing less than 3,000 pounds by 1981, up from 40 percent in 1975. For cars of less than 3,000 pounds, technological advances might allow the meeting of statutory requirements with-

out EFI, though EFI would improve performance and drivability.

The shape of government emissions standards remained uncertain. In early 1976 it was increasingly evident that Congress would reaffirm the original statutory levels for hydrocarbon (HC) and carbon monoxide (CO), but might back off from the stringent nitrous oxide (NOx) standards in the 1.0–2.0 grams per mile. Industry observers were predicting that final NOx standards in the 1.0–2.0 grams per mile range were now likely to go into effect around 1982. NOx levels at 2.0 grams per mile or below would require sophisticated engine controls if fuel economy and drivability were also to be attained.

EXHIBIT 15-1. *Bendix Condensed Income Statement (millions of dollars)*

	1975[a]	1974	1973	1972	1971	1970
Sales:						
Automotive	$1,333.0	$1,254.8	$1,077.4	$ 839.2	$ 764.4	$ 718.1
Aerospace	715.2	630.8	608.7	570.8	552.0	638.6
Shelter	330.4	383.1	377.0	214.7	169.1	148.4
Industrial/energy	246.7	226.0	169.7	154.1	111.0	150.3
Other	(17.7)	(13.8)	(3.3)	(9.9)	16.3	24.7
Total sales	$2,607.6	$2,480.9	$2,229.5	$1,768.9	$1,612.8	$1,680.1
Income before interest & tax:						
Automotive	117.2	123.8	125.9	97.7	73.6	66.3
Aerospace	48.6	34.8	20.5	31.8	29.3	23.3
Shelter	5.3	18.1	20.7	13.3	7.5	5.4
Industrial/energy	34.8	25.1	5.1	1.9	(3.5)	5.7
Total profit before interest & tax	$ 205.9	$ 201.8	$ 172.2	$ 144.7	$ 106.9	$ 100.7
Cost of sales	2,053.3	1,952.3	1,771.7	1,378.7	1,271.7	1,171.8
Selling, general & administrative	315.6	291.2	255.2	216.6	200.3	176.1
Depreciation & amortization	49.3	51.6	49.0	45.6	44.2	32.1
Interest	42.8	45.0	30.1	23.4	24.1	20.6
Other	22.5	16.3	5.6	4.3	3.7	0.9
Net income after taxes	$ 79.8	$ 75.8	$ 69.3	$ 56.0	$ 42.1	$ 32.3

[a]Bendix's fiscal year ended September 30.

SOURCES: Form 10Ks and annual reports.

EXHIBIT 15-2.   *Bendix Condensed Balance Sheet (millions of dollars)*

	1975	*1974*	*1973*	*1972*	*1971*	*1970*
Assets						
Cash & securities	$ 71.2	$ 46.2	$ 44.3	$ 35.1	$ 50.7	$ 57.7
Receivables	392.7	361.9	340.3	289.8	261.9	275.2
Inventories	537.9	574.4	487.9	421.2	423.6	409.2
Other	17.9	17.2	19.4	17.3	14.7	16.8
Total current assets	1,019.7	997.7	891.9	763.4	750.9	758.9
Property, plant & equipment	423.0	445.5	418.2	380.5	355.6	324.2
Investments	28.5	29.6	28.5	27.8	21.3	19.5
Goodwill	87.4	94.6	78.1	53.3	54.2	50.9
Other	9.0	9.7	10.3	10.2	17.3	14.7
Total assets	$1,567.6	$1,579.1	$1,427.0	$1,235.2	$1,199.3	$1,168.2
Liabilities						
Notes payable	$ 90.5	$ 181.5	$ 133.6	$ 105.0	$ 147.3	$ 118.1
Accounts payable	221.6	217.5	173.0	116.8	103.4	97.3
Accruals & other	193.7	178.5	158.7	144.0	113.7	115.7
Total current liabilities	$ 505.8	$ 577.5	$ 465.3	$ 365.8	$ 369.8	$ 331.1
Long-term debt	285.8	235.0	248.7	195.7	185.0	189.2
Deferred taxes	19.4	26.8	24.2	19.2	21.5	19.4
Minority interest	25.0	58.3	53.2	50.2	48.8	72.7
Stockholders' equity	731.6	681.5	635.6	604.3	574.2	555.8
Total liabilities	$1,567.6	$1,579.1	$1,427.0	$1,235.2	$1,119.3	$1,168.2

SOURCE: Annual reports.

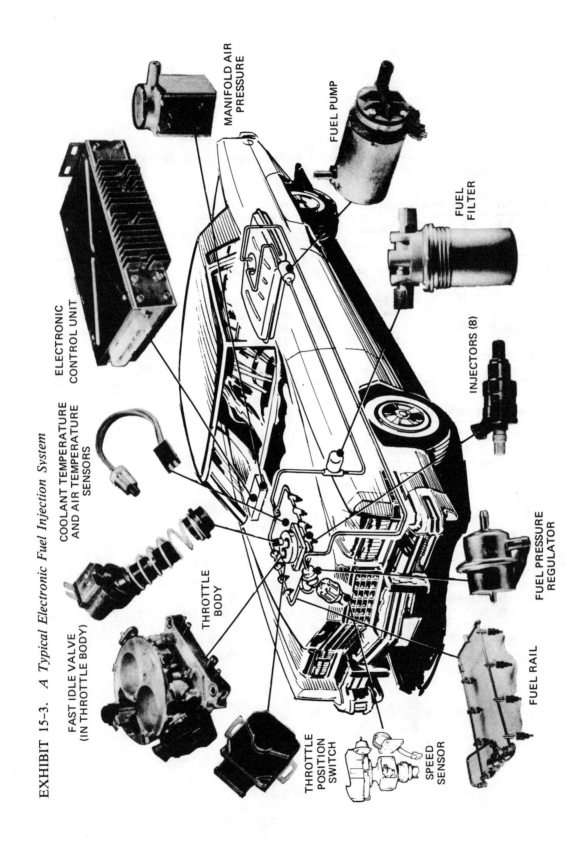

EXHIBIT 15-3. A Typical Electronic Fuel Injection System

MANIFOLD AIR PRESSURE

FUEL PUMP

FUEL FILTER

ELECTRONIC CONTROL UNIT

COOLANT TEMPERATURE AND AIR TEMPERATURE SENSORS

INJECTORS (8)

FAST IDLE VALVE (IN THROTTLE BODY)

THROTTLE BODY

FUEL PRESSURE REGULATOR

THROTTLE POSITION SWITCH

SPEED SENSOR

FUEL RAIL

EXHIBIT 15-4. *Existing and Proposed Statutory Requirements for Automobile Emission and Fuel Economy*

A. Emissions Maximums[a] (*grams of pollutant per mile*)

Model Year	Statutory Authority	Hydrocarbons (HC)	Carbon Monoxide (CO)	Nitrous Oxide (NOx)
Effective for 1976	Federal	1.5	15.0	3.1
	California	.9	9.0	2.0
Effective for 1977	Federal	1.5	15.0	2.0
	California	.41	9.0	1.5
Statutory for 1978	Federal	.41	3.4	0.4
	California	.41	3.4	0.4
Senate/House compromise proposal for 1981	Federal	.41	3.4	1.0

B. Fuel Economy Standards[b]

Model Year	Minimum Fleet Average Miles per Gallon
1978	18
1979	19
1980	20
1981	21.5
1982	23.0
1983	24.5
1984	26.0
1985	27.5[c]

[a] Statutory requirements under the Muskie Bill, enacted in 1974.
[b] Statutory requirements under the Energy Policy and Conservation Act of 1975.
[c] Under the act the Secretary of Transportation was given discretion to reduce the 1985 requirements to 26.0 miles per gallon, or effectively extend the 1984 requirements indefinitely.

SOURCE: Company documents.

EXHIBIT 15-5. *Bendix Financial Projections for Electronic Fuel Injection ($ 000)*

	1975 Estimated Actual	1976	1977	1978	1979	1980	1981
ECU							
Net sales	$ 4,115	$ 8,407	$10,268	$17,282	$29,806	$ 50,934	$ 59,624
Gross profit	(1,446)[d]	1,956	1,756	4,615	8,177	11,344	14,274
% of sales	(35.14)%	23.2%	17.1%	26.7%	27.4%	22.3%	23.9%
Profit before tax	(2,671)	(2,299)	(3,478)	(1,214)	1,631	3,515	5,694
% of sales	(64.91)%	(27.3)%	(33.9)%	(7.0)%	5.5%	6.9%	9.5%
Investment base	4,157	5,450	6,836	6,518	8,157	12,028	13,444
ROI %[a]	(31.95)%	(19.8)%	(23.6)%	(7.6)%	12.5%	17.3%	24.1%
Approximate number of units[b]	50,000	65,000	90,000	150,000	500,000	750,000	800,000
Injectors							
Net sales			$8,070	$13,667	$17,111	$ 28,907	$ 31,680
Gross profit			2,173	8,689	8,396	7,256	8,237
% of sales			26.9%	63.5%	49.1%	25.1%	26.0%
Profit before tax		$ (306)	(1,914)	5,347	4,550	2,371	2,830
% of sales			(23.7)%	39.1%	26.6%	8.2%	8.9%
Investment base		1,150	7,663	10,244	10,882	20,734	30,790
ROI %[a]			(10.9)%	29.2%	23.8%	8.0%	6.9%
Approximate number of units		520,000	720,000	1,600,000	2,800,000	5,300,000	5,600,000
Sensors							
Net sales			$ 1,129	$ 2,013	$ 9,218	$ 22,646	$ 26,058
Gross profit			205	704	2,828	6,733	6,963
% of sales			18.2%	34.9%	34.4%	29.7%	26.7%
Profit before tax			(2,881)	(2,511)	564	3,170	3,127
% of sales			(255.2)%	(124.7)%	6.9%	14.0%	12.0%
Investment base			535	1,682	4,175	7,608	7,098
ROI %[a]			(278.0)%	(75.6)%	8.2%	23.7%	25.0%
Approximate number of units		185,000	270,000	1,320,000	4,100,000	11,800,000	13,000,000
EFI mechanical hardware[c]							
Net sales	$ 9,817	$13,681	$ 6,900	$ 9,797	$ 754	$ 1,008	$ 1,202
Gross profit	3,410	2,378	1,789	1,026	203	336	401
% of sales	34.74%	17.4%	25.9%	10.4%	26.9%	33.3%	33.3%
Profit before tax	(369)	(1,480)	152	(757)	141	284	344
% of sales	(3.76)%	(10.8)%	2.2%	(7.7)%	18.7%	28.2%	28.6%
Investment base	6,667	4,141	1,975	1,012	183	210	231
ROI %[a]	(.47)%	(16.5)%	6.1%	(36.7)%	42.1%	72.3%	79.2%
Total EFI							
Net sales	$13,932	$22,088	$26,367	$42,759	$55,889	$102,495	$118,564
Gross profit	1,964	4,334	5,923	15,034	19,604	25,669	29,875
% of sales	14.10%	19.62%	22.46%	35.16%	35.08%	25.0%	25.2%
Profit before tax	(2,986)	(4,085)	(8,121)	865	6,886	9,340	11,995
% of sales	(21.43)%	(18.49)%	(30.80)%	2.02%	12.32%	9.1%	10.1%
Investment base	10,824	10,741	17.009	19,456	23,397	40,580	51,563
ROI %[a]	(12.3)%	(17.7)%	(22.7)%	4.4%	17.4%	14.0%	14.2%

[a]Bendix computed ROI by adding back to profit before taxes an assessed corporate capital charge equal to 4 percent of the investment base. Then corporate taxes (48 percent) are subtracted to yield profit after taxes. Profit after tax divided by the investment base equals ROI.
[b]Bendix planned to sell ECUs for other uses besides fuel control. The figures given are unit sales for fuel control.
[c]Includes sensors and injectors in 1975 and 1976.
[d]Parentheses indicate a loss.

SOURCES: Company documents and casewriter compilations. Certain figures have been altered, though the integrity of the figures has been preserved.

EXHIBIT 15–6. *Project Costs to Automobile Company of an Eight-Injector Electronic Fuel Injection System*

	1976	1979	1981
Throttle body	$ 16.58	$ 16.83	$ 15.45
Fast idle valve	8.06	1.70	1.70
Fuel pressure regulator	5.38	2.00	2.00
Eight fuel injectors	98.65	61.50	51.50
Fuel filter	1.50	.35	.35
Fuel rails	19.06	17.00	15.00
Coolant temp. sensor	3.93	2.10	2.00
Air temp. sensor	3.97	2.10	2.00
Throttle position sensor	6.39	4.00	3.00
Fuel pump	36.37	27.00	24.50
ECU	127.96	75.00	56.00
Total	$327.85	$209.58	$183.50

SOURCES: Bendix Corporation projections and case-writer computations.

APPENDIX A
Diesel Engine Fuel Injection

Fuel injection systems had been developed for diesel engines, the engine increasingly installed in trucks, heavy equipment, and to a limited degree automobiles. Fuel injection systems for diesel and gasoline engines were different in a number of respects. Diesel engines were ignited by creating high pressure on the fuel-air mixture, and not by a timed spark. This meant that cylinder pressures were much higher in diesel engines, as was the delivery pressure of fuel from the fuel injectors. In addition, diesel injectors were not actuated directly by electronic circuitry but rather by a mechanical "governor."

Despite these differences, the basic technology and manufacturing process for diesel injectors were similar to those of injectors for gasoline engines. It was estimated by industry sources that a firm already producing in one area could halve the time it took to get into the other compared to a completely new entrant, and that approximately half of the production equipment was common to the manufacturing processes for gasoline and diesel injectors.

The producers of diesel injection systems in the United States were AMBAC Industries, the Hartford Division of Stanadyne, Robert Bosch, and many of the major diesel engine manufacturers, including General Motors' Diesel Equipment Division. Overseas the major competitors were Bosch, Cav-Lucas, Diesel Kiki, and Nippondenso. In 1974 Bosch began construction of a plant in Charleston, South Carolina, to produce diesel injec-

tion equipment for sale in the North American market. Bosch was acknowledged as the world leader in diesel injection.

AMBAC Industries

AMBAC was a leading producer of diesel injection equipment in its American Bosch Division. A financial profile of AMBAC is shown in Table 15–1.

This American Bosch Division (Springfield, Massachusetts) manufactured [diesel] fuel injection systems (pumps, nozzle holders and spray nozzles) and diesel engine accessories, such as pumps and governors. In addition to giving technical and engineering assistance to various manufacturers, this division designed and adapted fuel injection equipment to the special needs of particular engines. The division had specialized in the manufacture of a multiplunger pump for heavy-duty trucks and a single plunger pump for farm and construction equipment and for medium and light trucks.

American Bosch had a research laboratory for research and development work on fuel handling systems for various kinds of engines. The division was at present engaged in the development and testing of advanced fuel injection systems for substantially im-

TABLE 15-1.   AMBAC Industries Financial Profile (*millions of dollars*)

	1975	1974	1973	1972
Sales	$187.9	$181.2	$164.0	$143.5
Sales in diesel & fluid power products	55.8	55.2	43.8	36.2
Net profit after taxes	9.4	8.1	7.4	4.4
Depreciation	4.9	4.7	4.5	5.1
Equity	74.7	67.7	61.2	56.1
Assets	146.7	159.0	148.4	138.4
Long-term debt	41.9	59.1	58.9	57.2
Capital expenditures	4.7	6.1	5.7	2.7
Return on equity	12.6%	12.0%	12.1%	7.8%

proving fuel economy and meeting future emission levels. It received another research and development contract from Ford Motor Company and was continuing development of a gasoline fuel injection system for the Ford PROCO (programmed combustion) engine. [from 1975 Form 10K]

Lucas Industries

Lucas was also a leading producer of diesel injection equipment, primarily in Europe. A financial profile of Lucas is shown in Table 15-2.

Lucas Industries was a leading world manufacturer of electric, hydraulic, and mechanical equipment used by internal combustion, diesel, and gas turbine engines; road and rail vehicles; ships; and aircraft, in addition to manufacturing a wide range of industrial products.

Lucas was perhaps the largest supplier of diesel injection equipment in Europe and was aggressively expanding its position:

In France an important event was our acquisition of a controlling interest in our previously associated company Roto-Diesel . . . we expect strong growth in the future as a result of the increasing use of diesel engines. . . . In Spain we have merged all our interests in the manufacture of diesel fuel injection equipment with Condiesel SA in which we now have a 47% shareholding. . . . We are also proceeding with our arrangements to establish the manufacture of diesel fuel injection equipment in Japan . . .

The large increase in the cost of oil has led to more attention being paid to the fuel used per passenger

TABLE 15-2.   Lucas Industries Financial Profile (*millions of pounds*)

	1975	%	1974	%	1973	1972
Sales						
Vehicle equipment	455.7	80.0	355.9	78.6		
Aircraft equipment	70.9	12.4	60.9	13.4		
Industrial products	43.5	7.6	35.9	8.0		
Total sales	570.2	100.0	452.8	100.0	399.2	339.8
Operating Earnings						
Vehicle equipment	35.1	91.1	16.9	10.0		
Aircraft equipment	.9	2.2	1.2	6.3		
Industrial products	2.6	6.7	0.9	4.7		
Total operating earnings	38.5	100.0	19.0	100.0		
Geographic distribution of sales:						
% U.K.	60		63			
% Other Europe	19		14			
% North and South America	8		8			
Net profit after taxes	16.3		9.3		16.9	13.2
Equity	200.9		189.2		186.0	163.3
Assets	432.8		383.8			
Long-term debt	46.6		44.5		44.8	43.1
Return on equity	8.1		4.9		9.1	8.1

mile and this has meant that much of our earlier work on engine management is now coming to fruition. The growth in the demand for diesel engines fully justifies the major efforts we have undertaken to maintain our lead to this field. . . . The research and development work on electronic systems continues to be very important. We are particularly concerned with improving the inherent reliability of these systems which are used to an increasing extent in the fields of engine management, wheel slide protection, alternators, etc. [Lucas Annual Report]

Stanadyne, Inc.

Stanadyne was a diversified firm that produced diesel injection equipment in its Hartford Division. A financial profile of Stanadyne is shown in Table 15–3.

Stanadyne, Inc., Products

Consumer Products:
   plumbing products
   fasteners & sawblades
Ferrous materials
Industrial products:
   valve train products
   contract components and assemblies

The Hartford Division manufactured and sold diesel fuel injection pumps under the Roosa Master trade name, nozzles under the Pencil Nozzle trade name, filters under the Master Filter trade name and air starters under the Start Master trade name to diesel engine manufacturers primarily for use in agricultural machinery, roadbuilding equipment, generator sets, on-the-road vehicles and trucks, and marine and stationary engines.

The Company announced in January of 1976 that it had received a letter of intent from one of the major automobile manufacturers to purchase the Company's diesel fuel injection equipment for use on an eight cylinder diesel engine under development for light trucks and passenger cars. [Form 10K].

Essex Group

Essex was a division of United Technologies. Its products were broadly classed as electric current carrying and controlling devices, and included insulated building wire, magnet wire, automotive electrical wire harnesses, and associated electromechanical devices. Seventy-five percent of Essex's sales come from the electric utility, telephone, automotive, appliance, and construction markets. Essex sold to more than 20,000 customers primarily throughout the United States. To a *limited* extent it also manufactured and sold in certain foreign countries. A financial profile of Essex is given in Table 15–4.

TABLE 15–3.   Stanadyne, Inc. Financial Profile (*dollars in millions*)

	1975	1974	1973	1972	1971
Sales	$188.7	$233.1	$201.2	$155.5	$131
% Plumbing Products	26	21	27	25	21
% Fasteners and Saw Blades	11	17	13	13	15
% Cold Drawn Steel (Hartford Div)	21	23	20	19	14
% Diesel Fuel Injection Equip.	17	16	14	15	14
% Automotive Valve Train Pots.	13	11	13	14	15
% Contract Precision Components	12	12	13	14	21
	100	100	100	100	100
Net income	$ 9.1	$ 13.2	$ 10.7	$ 7.9	$ 6.2
Depreciation	4.2	4.5	4.0	3.6	3.5
Equity	74.6	69.9	61.0	56.3	52.4
Assets	95.0	96.5	90.7	73.2	66.6
Long-term debt	.3	.3	1.6	—	—
Capital expenditure	4.8	7.1	5.5	3.8	2.7
Long-term debt/equity	0.004	0.004	0.03	—	—
P/E	7	4	6	16	13
Percent Contribution to Pre-tax Income					
Consumer products	38%	44%	46%	48%	
Ferrous materials	26%	24%	16%	13%	
Industrial products	36%	32%	38%	39%	

TABLE 15–4.   Essex Group Financial Profile (Division of United Technologies)[a] (*dollars in millions*)

	1975	1974	1973	1972	1971
Total sales	$766	$934	$845	$696	$596
% Wire products	56.4	63.1	59.8	57.0	56.1
% Electrical switches and control devices	22.0	18.0	20.5	22.0	21.2
% Metal and plastic fabricated parts	7.9	7.5	7.8	9.5	10.4
% Other	9.2	7.0	7.2	6.5	6.7
% Motor carrier	4.5	4.4	4.7	5.0	5.6
	100.0%	100.0%	100.0%	100.0%	100.0%
% Sales to Ford Motor Co.	22.9	19.9	21.2	21.5	20.7
% Sales to Chrysler Corp.	8.2	6.8	7.8	7.2	7.0
Net income	$ 42.3	$ 40.4	$ 40.4	$ 37.1	$ 30.7
Depreciation	15.9	16.1	13.6	11.9	11.3
Equity	342	334	277	250	225
Assets	474	500	465	446	409
Long-term debt	10	15	108	112	116
Capital expenditure	20.0	34.1	34.7	16.2	15.3
Long term debt/equity	0.3	0.04	0.39	0.45	0.52
Average P/E	—	—	6	13	13

[a]Essex Group became a wholly owned subsidiary of United Technologies on 2/5/74.
SOURCE: Annual reports and Form 10Ks.

CASE 16
The Fiber-Optics Industry in 1978: Products, Technology, and Markets

From smoke signals to semaphores, man has attempted to harness light for communication. In 1880 Alexander Graham Bell demonstrated that speech could be transmitted on a beam of light. By 1978 scientists had developed techniques for transmitting light through glass fibers smaller than a human hair, and a revolutionary new industry had been born. Fiber optics promised major improvements in performance compared to conventional communication systems in which electric signals were transmitted over copper wire, a technology contained in literally hundreds of products. Exhibit 16–1 illustrates the two transmission techniques. Although industry sales were less than $30 million in 1978, fiber optics was one of the most talked about technological developments in industry in the 1970s. Dozens, possibly hundreds, of firms were either already industry participants or waited and watched from the sidelines ready to enter.

This case will describe the products, technology, and markets for fiber optics, as well as provide an overview of its history to date. Subsequent cases will describe the competitors in the fiber-optics in-

dustry as well as the impact of fiber optics on related industries such as wire and cable, connectors, and electronics.

The reader should keep in mind, in interpreting this data, that even the participants in this new industry were themselves uncertain of where technological developments would eventually lead, and there were no experts to advise them. There were also as many predictions of future markets, manufacturing technology and competitive scenarios as there were industry participants and observers. Information about the industry was constantly changing in light of the evolving technology and competitive situation, and the material in these cases can only be a snapshot blurred by the rapid movement of its subject.

Fiber-Optic Systems

Alexander Graham Bell's experiments in 1880 led to the development of the "photophone," in which a narrow beam of sunlight was focused onto a thin mirror and directed toward a light detector. The sound waves of human speech near the mirror caused it to vibrate, and the resulting variations in energy reaching the detector were reconverted into sound waves through the reverse process. The photophone was never viable commercially, but it demonstrated the technical feasibility of light-wave communications.

Three types of light-wave communication systems had been seriously explored in the 1970s: atmospheric, light-pipe and fiber-optic. All the systems consisted of a light source, carrier, and receiver. In the atmospheric system, a laser beam sent light energy through the air to a remote receiver, much like microwave systems, which transmitted high-frequency radio signals over the air. Unlike microwave systems, however, atmospheric light wave systems were severely affected by adverse weather conditions and thus impractical. Light-pipe systems were based on the transmission of light through a vacuum tube where gas "lenses" refocused the light at intervals. Light-pipe systems were technologically feasible but prohibitively expensive.

By far the most promising approach to light-wave communication was the fiber-optic system, where a laser or light-emitting diode (LED) source directed light into a glass or plastic fiber. Light was transmitted efficiently through the fiber because of some unique properties of optical quality fibers and was received and converted into an electrical signal by a semiconductor receiver. Because of the very low cost of glass and plastic as raw materials and the prodigious information-carrying capacity of light, fiber-optics systems appeared to have vast potential for commercial application. Although high-loss optical fibers had been used for many years in illumination and image transmission, technological advances in the early 1970s had led to the development of low-loss fibers, which made light wave communications systems possible.

The Configuration and Properties of Fiber-Optic Systems

Fiber-optic systems fitted into the broad category of "communication" systems, which had the distinguishing function of transmitting information over a distance, whether it be voices, pictures, data, or machine instructions. All communications systems required a signal source, a technology for carrying the signal over distance, a means of modulating or imprinting a pattern on the signal that could be meaningfully interpreted when it was received, and a receiver for the signal. Usually the information itself had to be converted from its original form into a signal that could be assimilated into the system, and reconverted back to its original form at the receiving end. In 1978 nearly all communication systems relied on the use of electrical signals sent over copper wire or waves beamed through the atmosphere.

In fiber-optic systems the signal was light. It was transmitted through fibers in a manner governed by the technology of optical physics. The unique components of a fiber-optic system were the light source, the optical fiber, the cable encapsulating the fiber, the light detector, and the connectors and couplers needed to assemble the pieces of the system. The light signal was modulated or imprinted with information using existing electronic equipment. Exhibit 16–2 is a diagram of a fiber-optic system. In 1978 a number of different technologies existed for each of the important components of fiber-optic systems, which introduced tradeoffs in system design between information-carrying capacity, the distance over which this information could be carried, reliability, and cost.

Light Sources

Fiber-optic light sources had to meet a number of requirements that were related to the quality of the light emitted. To understand these requirements, it is necessary to discuss briefly some of the relevant properties of light. Light consists of energy which varies in intensity as it travels over distance. Because of this variation, light is said to travel in waves as illustrated in Figure 16–1.[1]

Light waves can be characterized by their *wavelength* and *frequency*. Wavelength refers to the distance within which variations in intensity are

---

[1] The speed of light varied with the nature of the material through which it was being transmitted and also varied slightly depending on its wavelength and frequency. The significance of these facts for fiber-optic systems will be described below.

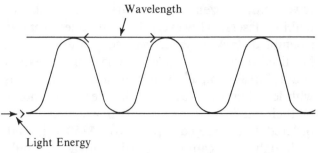

Wavelength

Light Energy

FIGURE 16-1. **Light Waves**

repeated. It is measured in nanometers (nm), a billionth of a meter. Frequency describes the number of times per second that this variation occurs. When referring to other forms of energy that travels in waves, frequency is normally measured in "hertz," or cycles per second. When referring to light waves, frequency is measured in nanoseconds (ns, a billionth of a second). The shorter the wavelength of the light, the higher its frequency. Relative to other forms of energy that travel in waves, such as audible sound and radio energy, light waves have a very high frequency. As a result, light has a very high *"bandwidth,"* which is the extent of the range of frequencies over which an information system can function. The highest usable frequency determines the upper limit of bandwidth. High bandwidth can be equated with high information capacity.

Light waves travel in beams, series of roughly parallel waves of light, each of which has a different wavelength. Since light of different wavelengths travels at slightly different speeds, a beam of light will spread or disperse as it travels. This phenomenon is termed *material dispersion*. The extent to which material dispersion occurs depends on the range of frequencies contained within the beam of light. This range is called the beam's *spectral width* and is measured in angstroms, or one hundred millionths of a meter. The narrower the spectral width, the less material dispersion.

A fiber-optic light source had to emit light that could be absorbed efficiently by the optical fiber. In order for this to happen, the light had to be emitted in a narrow beam to minimize energy loss when entering the fiber, and have a wavelength between 800–900 nm and 1,000–1,100 nm. The light source also had to emit light with high frequency. The frequency of the light emitted by the source deter-

mined the rate at which the signal could be modulated and the amount of information it could carry. Light sources also had to have very high intensity to maximize the distance the light could travel through the fiber. Reliability, dependability, and low cost were other desirable characteristics of light sources.

Only two kinds of light sources, both based on semiconductor technology, emitted the type of light appropriate for fiber-optics: the light-emitting diode (LED) and the semiconductor diode laser. LEDs used in fiber-optics were refined versions of those found in the visual display units of pocket calculators. A small well was etched into the face of an ordinary LED to produce a narrow beam of light roughly comparable in size to an optical fiber.

The semiconductor diode laser, no bigger than a grain of salt, consisted of several layers of semiconductor material, which emitted light when a small electrical charge caused the material to give off energy in the form of photons. The photons were amplified within the laser and emerged as a beam of light with very high intensity and extremely narrow spectral width.

LEDs were a more dependable source of light than lasers, that is, LEDs would emit light at a predictable frequency and were less sensitive to fluctuations in their power source and to changes in temperature and humidity. LEDs also had a longer lifetime—up to 100,000 hours. Although lasers were very delicate, they had some fundamental advantages as fiber-optic light sources: they emitted a high-frequency beam of light of high intensity. In addition, the spectral width of laser light was typically 20 angstroms. The LEDs used for lightwave communications had a spectral width of 350 angstroms. As a result, when laser sources were used, there was less material dispersion, and laser light could be used more efficiently. This efficiency was achieved in two ways. Because there was less material dispersion, more laser light entered directly into the fiber, as shown in Figure 16-2.

Fiber   Fiber

LED   Laser

FIGURE 16-2. **Material Dispersion of LED and Laser Compared**

Second, signals were sent from a source in the form of a burst of light called a pulse. Each pulse represented a bit of information. Because the light pulse consisted of light that spread out as a result of material dispersion, the pulse also spread out as it traveled through the system. This was termed *pulse dispersion.* When pulses spread to the point where they became indistinguishable, they lost their information-carrying value, and the modulation rate had to be slowed down to allow for pulse dispersion. However, because a laser light pulse had a narrower spectral width, there was less pulse dispersion, as illustrated in Figure 16-3. Because there was less dispersion, laser pulses could be sent at a faster rate than LED pulses, increasing the information-carrying capacity of the system.

The LEDs used in fiber optics were modifications of those developed in the 1960s for the semiconductor industry for commercial uses such as visual display devices in computers, calculators, and digital watches. LEDs were readily available. Depending on their quality and the quantity in which they were purchased, LEDs ranged in price from $10 to $550. The price of LEDs was expected to drop below $5 for less complex versions and below $10 for high-quality versions within five years as a result of volume production.

Laser technology was changing rapidly in 1978. Most lasers were used in developmental work, and lasers had not been readily available until 1978, when several companies began to produce them specifically for the fiber-optic applications. Recent advances in laser production technology had resulted in a new generation of lasers with greatly increased lifetimes—up to 100,000 hours in some cases—and more reliable and predictable performance characteristics. Because semiconductor lasers had to be made from precisely aligned layers of semiconductor materials, production was a very delicate process considered to be something of an art. One industry observer believed that there were fewer than a dozen people in the world capable of making lasers. However, because one properly assembled stack of semiconductor materials could be sliced into thousands of tiny lasers, one expert could fill a company's production requirements with less than three days' work a year. Depending on their quality and the quantity in which they were ordered, lasers ranged in price from $150 to $1,000. Although significant technological advances would be necessary, some observers believed that laser production would be automated, and with automation, expected the price to fall to $10. A more realistic estimate was that prices would fall to $50 by 1983. Exhibit 16-3 illustrates typical performance characteristics for LED and laser sources in 1978.

Optical Fibers

In order to understand fiber optics, it is necessary to understand how light behaves when it travels through matter. Materials through which light will travel can be classified by their *index of refraction,* which is the ratio of the speed of light in a vacuum to its speed in the particular material. Light rays of the same frequency travel through different materials at different speeds. Because of this, a light ray bends as it passes from one transparent medium to another through a phenomenon known as *refraction.* When a light ray passes from a medium with a lower refractive index to one with a higher refractive index, the ray is bent. However, light will not pass from a medium with a high refractive index to one with a lower refractive index. Instead it will be reflected back into the original medium.

In fiber-optic systems, light is directed into a fiber consisting of one transparent material (called the *core*) surrounded by another material with a lower index of refraction (called the *cladding*). As a result, the light will stay within the fiber and be reflected back and forth along the interface of the two materials through the length of the fiber as shown in Figure 16-4.

The practical application of light's capacity to travel through transparent fibers was historically limited by the prohibitive losses in intensity that occurred as the light traveled through the fiber. The weakening of the light signal as it travels is termed *attenuation* and is measured in decibels of intensity

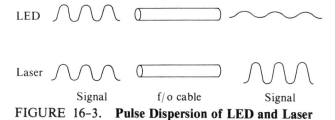

FIGURE 16-3. **Pulse Dispersion of LED and Laser**

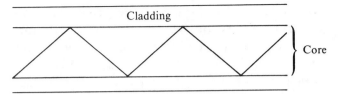

FIGURE 16-4.

Signal

Fiber

Signal

FIGURE 16-6.

per kilometer (db/km). Such losses were primarily due to impurities in the fiber material, variations in the diameter of the core, and imperfect alignment of the core/cladding interface with the central axis of the core. It was only after fibers had been developed in which attenuation losses were reduced to 20 db/km that telecommunications applications of fiber optics became possible. It had taken major advances in materials and fiber manufacturing technology to make this possible.

Dispersion of light as it traveled through a fiber was a second technological obstacle that had to be overcome in developing practical fiber-optic systems. As explained earlier, dispersion occurred because light consisted of a range of wavelengths that traveled at different speeds, and light signals had a natural tendency to spread out as they traveled. This pulse dispersion was exaggerated by additional dispersion, which occurred within the fiber. Dispersion within the optical fiber came about because light that entered parallel to the central axis of a fiber had to travel a shorter distance through the fiber than light that entered at an angle and bounced from side to side as it traveled down the fiber channel as shown in Figure 16-5. This form of dispersion was called *modal dispersion*. In the earliest optical fibers, known as *step-index* fibers, the core had one refractive index and the cladding another. Modal dispersion in step-index fibers limited their information-carrying capacity, and attempts to reduce this dispersion had led to the development of two other types of fibers known as *graded-index* and *single-mode* fibers.

In graded-index fibers, the index of refraction gradually decreased with distance from center of the core. Because of this, the light rays that deviated

from the core's central axis traveled faster than those that did not. This reduced dispersion, as illustrated in Figure 16-6. Graded-index fibers were much more difficult to manufacture than step-index fibers. They could be used with LED sources for short to medium distance applications but required laser sources for long-distance applications.

Because of the many paths over which the light traveled through the core, both step and graded-index fibers were classified as multimode fibers. *Single-mode* fibers, a very new technology in 1978, had a very small core. A very narrow beam of light could pass through the core with a minimum of pulse dispersion as illustrated in Figure 16-7. Because of this property, single-mode fibers offered extremely high information-carrying capacity. Single-mode fibers had such high information-carrying capacity that they required highly sophisticated laser sources and very sensitive detectors to achieve this information-carrying potential. Such components had not been fully developed, and this, coupled with the difficulty of manufacturing single-mode fibers, had meant that they were not available for commercial use in 1978. However, industry observers believed that major fiber producers were devoting extensive R&D effort toward the single-mode fiber. Some industry observers were outspoken in their belief that single-mode fibers were destined to become the dominant fiber technology, but there was much disagreement on this issue.

Fiber Production

Optical fibers were made from high-quality glass or plastic. Fiber-optic technology required that these materials be highly purified—this was indicated by the fact that in fiber production, impurities were

Signal in

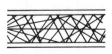

Fiber

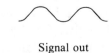

Signal out

FIGURE 16-5.

Signal in

Core   Cladding

Signal out

FIGURE 16-7.

measured in parts per billion. The properties of the raw materials themselves, as well as the production process used, determined the performance characteristics of the fiber. In general, plastic fibers had higher loss rates and were the least expensive to purchase. One company, E. I. du Pont de Nemours, made only plastic fiber and had not revealed its production process. In 1978 most fiber was made from glass.

The important performance parameters of fiber were bandwidth, attenuation, core diameter, numerical aperture, and usable length. The bandwidth of a fiber determined the rate at which signals could be sent through it. The fiber's bandwidth was a function of modal dispersion within the fiber. Bandwidth was measured in hertz, or cycles per second, and each cycle could contain two bits of information.[2] Bandwidth varied from one megahertz (one million cycles/second) in high-loss fiber to almost ten gigahertz (ten billion cycles/second) in the most sophisticated fibers. As noted earlier, attenuation determined the distance over which the fiber could carry a signal, with lower attenuation increasing the distance. Optical fibers suitable for use in communications application could be classified into two categories based on attenuation losses: high-loss and low-loss fiber. High-loss fiber had attenuation losses ranging from 50 to 500 db/km and could be used in short- to intermediate-distance applications involving distances of less than one kilometer. Attenuation losses in low-loss fiber were less than 50 db/km and because of this low-loss fiber could be used for long-distance applications.

Core diameter, measured in microns (one thousandth of a millimeter), affected the efficiency with which the fiber could be coupled and the ease with which it could be handled. Fibers with small core diameters could carry signals over a great distance, but they required laser light sources. In addition, small fibers were very difficult to work with.

The numerical aperture of a fiber was a measure of the degree to which it could absorb light. Numerical aperture was calculated as a function of a maximum angle to the central axis at which light could be traveling and still enter the fiber—the

higher the numerical aperture, the greater the light-gathering ability of the fiber. Fibers with low numerical aperture had to be used with laser light sources, which emitted very focused beams. Exhibit 16-4 indicates the range of performance characteristics of the fibers commercially available in 1977 (latest date for which information is available).

A variety of processes could be used to manufacture glass fiber in 1978, though none had really been used for large-scale production. The processes differed in refractive index profiles and attenuation rates that could be achieved. All the processes required highly purified raw materials, and many of the ingredients used in fiber production were highly toxic and required special handling. Because of the high purity required, production had to take place in what was called a "clean room environment," where air filtration systems and work procedures were specially designed to reduce contaminants in the air. Some of the processes were batch-type operations, which required preparation of a glass mixture called a "preform," which was subsequently made into fibers by various drawing methods. Preform manufacture was similar to the manufacture of other high-quality optical products such as lenses. A few of the processes could be designed to be continuous.

The leading fiber production techniques in use in 1978 were (1) multiple fiber drawing; (2) rod and tube; (3) double crucible; (4) stratified melt; and (5) vapor phase oxidation. These processes are illustrated in Exhibit 16-5.

In the multiple fiber drawing process, as many as 1,000 glass preforms were heated and drawn simultaneously to produce a low-cost step-index fiber. Fibers produced using this method were high-loss fibers. In the rod and tube technique, glass preforms consisting of rods and hollow tubes of different refractive indices were produced. The rod was inserted into the tube, which had the lower refractive index. When fed into a furnace, the rod and tube melted together to form a single unit, which was then drawn into fiber. This process produced a step-index fiber of moderate loss rate.

The double crucible production technique utilized purified glass contained in separate crucibles. The glass for the core was placed in an inner crucible and the glass for the cladding in the outer cruci-

---

[2] The peaks and troughs in the energy variation of the light wave could each be used to carry information.

ble. The openings of both crucibles converged at the bottom, and when the crucibles were heated, molten glass flowed out the bottom and formed a single fiber. This process could be run continuously. When properly executed, the double crucible method produced high-quality graded-index fiber. However, the refractive index profile could not be controlled precisely, and the double crucible method sometimes presented quality control problems for demanding fiber applications.

In the stratified melt process, molten cladding material was floated on top of molten core material in a crucible. A preform could be drawn upward from the double-layered melt. By continually feeding the crucible with core and cladding raw material, it was possible to make this a continous process. The stratified melt method produced step-index fiber.

The most sophisticated approach to fiber production in 1978 was the vapor phase oxidation technique (VPO). In a VPO process called chemical vapor deposition (CVD), glass in highly heated gaseous form was passed through a hollow quartz tube, which was heated with a torch. The heating caused the gaseous glass to deposit on the inside of the tube. Layer upon layer of core could be built up in this way, and its index of refraction gradually and precisely increased. After sufficient material was deposited within the tube to produce a fiber of the desired refractive index, the tube was collapsed to a single fiber by further heating. The CVD process was by far the most time-consuming fiber production process. The hollow tubes had to be less than 10 inches long or they collapsed under heat. It took between two and five hours to complete the vapor deposition process for a 10-inch tube of less than ½ inch diameter. This tube could be reheated and drawn to create a "graded-index" fiber more than a mile long.

In a modified version of the CVD, vapor was deposited on the outside of a solid rod to create the cladding. In the modified CVD process, larger preforms could be used and the cladding could be deposited more rapidly. However, when vapor was deposited on the outside of the rod, some condensation occurred, and this increased attenuation. Because the VPO process could be so precisely controlled and eliminated the need for molten glass,

which picked up impurities, the CVD process produced the lowest-loss fibers available in 1978—1 db/km.[3] Corning Glass Works held 200 process and materials patents on the CVD processes and had sued International Telephone and Telegraph (ITT) for allegedly violating these patents.

A number of other fiber production processes were still in an experimental stage. In one, a preform was rotated under a laser beam, which intersected the preform at right angles. The laser created a core by heating the inner 60–80 percent of the preform, thereby increasing its index of refraction. Two professors at Catholic University in Washington, D.C., had developed another process in which impurities were removed from glass through an ion-exchange process to produce a very low-loss fiber. Finally, there were rumors that one unidentified company was developing a low-loss fiber in which the core was liquid.

No matter what the production process, the final step in fiber production was pulling the fiber around a large rotating drum, which moved horizontally during winding so that successive turns of fiber did not overlap. Drawing rates of up to 30 feet per second were possible in 1978; this was the drawing rate for copper wire. After drawing, all fibers needed to be coated to protect the surface from chemical attacks and mechanical damage, which would result in signal loss. Some fibers were coated during the fiber drawing process, while other coating processes included dipping, extrusion, and spray coating. The coating was usually plastic.

FIBER PRODUCTION COSTS

Fiber production costs were not easily available in 1978, even to industry participants. All estimates were at best approximate, because full-scale production had not yet begun. Table 16–1 contains one industry observer's estimate of the variable costs in the CVD and the stratified melt process for 100,000 kilometers of fiber. The capital equipment for fiber production at this rate, according to this same source, was believed to be $2.6 million for CVD, $1.3 million for double crucible, and $1 million for

---

[3] Laboratory, not commercial, production.

TABLE 16–1.   Optical Fiber Production Costs in 1978
(dollars per kilometer)

	CVD	Stratified Melt
Raw materials	.25	.15
Coating	.10	.10
Labor and overhead	6.85	6.85
Energy	.35	.45
Maintenance	1.50	.90
Other	1.45	1.35
Total cost (at 100% yield)	10.50	9.80

SOURCE: H. Elion and C. Elion, *Fiber Optics* (New York: Decker, 1978).

stratified melt. When asked to elaborate on the assumptions behind the above figures, the author cited above could reveal only that they were based on "full-scale production" of 100,000 km/year. If full-scale production was not necessary, a company could purchase equipment to make a CVD preform for $50,000, heating equipment for $50,000, and additional fiber drawing and handling equipment for $100,000. Similarly, a single set of equipment for the double crucible process cost $250,000 for the crucible and heating equipment and $100,000 for fiber drawing and handling equipment. Because of the sensitive nature of the information, it was difficult, if not impossible, to verify these figures.

Fiber production costs were expected to decline. Corning Glass Works, believed to be the industry's largest producer of glass fiber, had led the entire industry in projecting publicly that the price of fiber would eventually reach 15¢ per meter.

Optical Cables

In order to be usable in fiber-optic systems, the very fragile optical fibers had to be packaged into cables. Cabling provided strength and protection from environmental hazards such as moisture, abrasion, high temperatures, and breakage. Cabling also protected the fiber from bending—when the fiber was bent at too great an angle, the signal could be lost.

The cabling process was a continuous process involving the wrapping of successive layers of plastic, steel, or aluminum materials around the optical fibers as illustrated in Exhibit 16–6. As was the case with conventional copper cable, the wrapping, and the precise cable configuration varied depending on

the need to protect the fibers, which in turn depended on the application. When several optical fibers were incorporated into a cable, they were frequently twisted around a central passive fiber, which served to strengthen the cable. Alternately, strands of Kelvar® (a high-strength du Pont plastic) or steel could be incorporated into the cable for the same purpose.

The technology for optical cabling was essentially the same as that for cabling copper and required the same equipment. A cabling line cost $250,000. Because of its fragility, however, optical fiber had to be handled more carefully during the cabling process than did copper.

In November 1978 low-loss fiber optic cable cost $2 to $3 per meter and high-loss cable cost $1 to $2 per meter. One industry participant's breakdown of these costs is shown in Table 16–2.

According to the same source, optical cable costs would eventually reach 20¢ per meter for low-loss cable and 10¢ per meter for high-loss cable. The cost of fiber would eventually represent 50 percent of total cable cost. Other industry participants agreed with these estimates.

Optical cables were available in two configurations: cables containing one or more discrete fibers, and cables containing so-called "fiber bundles." In discrete fiber cables, each fiber was shielded and was a path for a signal. Fiber bundles were produced by heating as many as 1,000 preforms in a drawing furnace. These fibers fused to form a single optical path, which was used with a single light source. Because it consisted of many fibers, the bundle could still carry a signal if a few fibers broke. As a result, fiber bundles were the most common and least costly optical cable available in 1978.

Fiber bundles were an outgrowth of "short-fiber" technology and were made by the same proc-

TABLE 16–2.   Components of Fiber-Optic Cable Costs

	Low-loss Optical	High-loss Optical
Fiber	50%	35%
Cabling process	20%	30%
Cabling material	10%	10%
Kelvar	5%	10%
Testing	15%	15%

SOURCE: Bart Bielawski, "Seicor Optical Cables," in *Electronic News*, November 13, 1978.

ess used to make optical fibers used for illumination. Most industry observers believed that as single fiber production technology improved, fiber bundles would become obsolete.

Light Detectors

The detector in a fiber-optic system converted the optical signal into an electrical signal that was compatible with conventional equipment and communication networks. A good signal detector had to respond well to light at the peak intensity wavelength of the light source and fiber combination used (800–900 nm, 1,000–1,100 nm). It also had to operate with low interference and have high reliability, a long operating life, and small size.

Two types of semiconductor detectors could be used in fiber-optic systems in 1978: the PIN photodiode and the avalanche photodiode. The PIN[4] photodiode was the simpler of the two, and had been available commercially for many years for use in other electronic applications. The PIN photodiode had its peak sensitivity to light signals at 800–900 nm in wavelength and could be used with LED light sources and medium- to high-loss fiber. It ranged in price from $20 to $60 in 1978. The avalanche photodiode was somewhat more complex than the PIN photodiode in that it consisted of more layers of silicon material. The extra layers provided a built-in amplification process that enhanced the electrical signal that was produced when light hit the detector. The avalanche diode, which had been developed specifically for fiber-optical applications, had less interference, was efficient across a wider spectrum of light frequencies, and had a faster response time to signals than the PIN photodiode. The avalanche photodiode was most appropriate for use in fiber-optic systems operating in the 800–900 nm wavelength. However, in 1978 the avalanche photodiode was expensive to produce, not very reliable, and not widely available. They ranged in price from $60 to $350. For systems

---

[4] PIN refers to the silicon layers in the sandwich of which the photodiode consisted. In this sandwich, a neutral layer of silicon lay between a positive (deficient in electrons) and a negative layer (having a surplus of electrons) of silicon. When the photons of light hit the negative layer as they passed through the sandwich, this created an electrical charge.

operating at wavelengths above 1,000 nm, experimental devices had to be used.

A great deal of developmental work was under way on detectors in 1978 and had been for several years. The previously available semiconductor detectors had had peak sensitivities at wavelengths of 600 nm; work on fiber-optic applications had resulted in the development of detectors operating in the 800–900 nm range and above. To take advantage of the greater capacity of laser light sources, developmental work was being done on avalanche photodiode, which could function with wavelengths at the 1,000+ nm range. Because the pace of technological change was so rapid, there was considerable uncertainty about future developments in detector technology. It was assumed by many that detector prices would follow what industry participants referred to as "the silicon curves," which meant that prices would fall 20 percent each time cumulative volume doubled. Because only very small amounts of relatively inexpensive raw materials were required, some industry observers believed that all detectors would eventually cost less than $10.

Connectors, Couplers, and Splicing Techniques

The separate parts of a fiber-optic system described above were each designed to maximize signal efficiency, the length signals could be transmitted, and the total information-carrying capacity of the system. However, a final and critical task in designing fiber-optic systems was connecting the separate parts of the system together. Where two optical fibers were to be joined, for example, the ends of the hair-thin fibers had to be aligned precisely but, to avoid damage to the fibers, could not touch. The fragility of some of the components, the small size of the optical fiber, and the precise tolerances necessary for efficient signal transmissions required specifically designed "linking" mechanisms for fiber-optic systems. The linking mechanisms were connectors, couplers, and splices.

Splices permanently joined two fibers, while connectors joined one fiber to another fiber but were not permanent. Couplers were a form of connector used to join fiber-optic systems containing several optical pathways and multiple light sources and/or detectors. Couplers, connectors, and splices had similar performance requirements. They had to minimize light loss, meet the strength, lifetime, and environmental parameters of the system as a whole, and be easy to install.

Connectors. Connectors consisted of mated pairs. They had to be designed to hold the fiber securely without damaging it and to align the fiber precisely when joined. In 1978 commercially available connectors had insertion losses (losses due to the connection) ranging from 1.0 to 2.5 db.

Fiber-optic connector technology had been drawn from electronic connector technology. Although the first fiber-optic connectors were modified versions of conventional connectors, more specialized and efficient designs had become available in 1978. Their cost ranged from $3 per mated pair for high-loss connectors to $250 per mated pair for low-loss connectors. No radical changes in fiber-optic connector technology were expected, but the average price per mated pair was expected to fall from an average of $50 in 1978 to $3.50 in 1987.

Couplers. Any fiber-optic system involving more than one signal and detector required a coupler to allow a signal from a single source to travel to a number of detectors. Couplers could be made by fusing fibers with heat. A signal directed into the fused section was weakened but continued to travel through all the fibers that had been fused. Couplers in which mirrors were used to send the light signal off into one or more attached fibers had been developed in 1978. All couplers had to be fabricated under controlled conditions and then attached to fibers by means of fiber-optic connectors. Couplers were available on a limited commercial basis in 1978. However, because sales were limited, accurate price data were not available.

The need for couplers would increase as applications involving multiple sources and detectors were developed. For this reason, a great deal of developmental work was being done to improve coupler design and efficiency. In addition, industry participants were developing optical switches capable of routing optical signals through a complex fiber network.

Integrated Optics

Some industry participants, such as Bell Labs, Texas Instruments, and Hewlett-Packard, were believed to be working on the development of an integrated optical circuit (IOC). Much like the electronic integrated circuit, an integrated optical circuit consisted of a source, fiber, and detector unit mounted on a tiny silicon chip. When available, the IOC would be able to perform all the functions of a conventional integrated circuit. In communications systems using fiber optics, the IOC would eliminate the need to convert from optical to electronic signal transmission. Although it seemed to be a real possibility, the technological problems that remained to be solved led industry observers to believe the IOC would probably not be available until the late 1980s.

Fiber-Optic Data Links

Late in 1978 a number of companies had begun to offer preassembled fiber-optic data links. These links were complete fiber-optic communications systems designed to accept electrical input data and deliver it as electrical output some distance away. The systems consisted of LED or laser light sources, glass or plastic cable, PIN or avalanche photodiode detectors, and ancillary equipment. Since the cable usually had to be attached to the source and detector units, connectors were also supplied. Optical data links were available in lengths up to two kilometers and ranged in price from $188 to $2,000. The prominent suppliers of links included Galileo Electro Optics, ITT, 3M, Valtec, and Hewlett-Packard. TI and H–P used fiber purchased from Galileo, Valtec, and du Pont.

Markets for Fiber Optics[5]

The capabilities of a fiber-optic system depended on the properties of the components from which it was built, and there were a number of tradeoffs to be

[5] The contents of this section are based on interviews with industry observers, participants, and customers and commercially available market reports, including *Fiber Optic Communications in the United States* (International Resource Development, August 1977).

made in systems design involving such parameters as information carrying capacity, distance over which the system could operate, cost, reliability, durability, and commercial availability in 1978. In general, however, fiber-optic systems could be said to have a number of advantages over conventional communications systems:

Bandwidth. Because the frequency of light waves was higher than that of electrical signals, the modulation rate (the rate at which information could be superimposed on an optical signal) was also higher. Table 16–3 shows the total information-carrying capacity of various communication links. The large information capacity of fiber-optics systems could be used either for extremely high rates of data transmission or for complex types of data transmission (i.e., simultaneous voice, video, and data signals).

Freedom from Electromagnetic Interference (EMI). Because they did not use electricity for signal transmission, fiber-optic systems could not be distorted by electromagnetic interference. Conversely, signals passing through optical fibers did not contribute to interference in other systems. As a result, fiber-optic systems could function freely in environments where other electrical systems were in use. When copper cable was used in such environments, conduits had to be built or shielding had to be placed on the cable at a cost of $3–$5/meter.

Security. Because optical fiber did not carry or radiate electromagnetic signals, fiber-optic systems could not be tapped.

Small Size and Light Weight. The use of optical cables offered substantial size and weight advantages over conventional cabling with equivalent communication capability. Depending on application, weight could be reduced by a factor of ten to a factor of one hundred.

Ability to Withstand Severe Environmental Conditions. Glass fibers could reportedly withstand temperatures of up to 800° C for up to thirty minutes without damage, in contrast to copper cable, which could withstand temperatures only up to 300° C. Plastic fibers were not so resistant to heat. In addition, optical fibers were more resistant to corrosion than copper, and they were expected to be less sensitive to moisture.

Safety. Fiber-optic materials could not produce sparks and could not catch fire.

Cost. In 1978 fiber-optic communications systems were more expensive than conventional ones, but nearly all observers expected fiber optics eventually to have a cost advantage over conventional copper wire and cable. Reliable estimates were difficult to obtain because of the confidential nature of the data, and meaningful comparison was difficult because most applications were still highly experimental. Also, since volume production of fiber-optic components had not begun, industry participants could only hypothesize about the extent of the potential cost advantage. Most of the optimism about the relative cost effectiveness of fiber optics stemmed from the fact that glass was already a much cheaper raw material than copper, and cop-

TABLE 16–3. Information-Carrying Capacity of Selected Communications Systems

	Twisted Pair Wire	Coaxial Cable	Radio	TV	Micro-Wave	Fiber Optics
Usable bandwidth (Hz)[a]	$.5 \times 10^3 - 5 \times 10^3$	$5 \times 10^3 - 2 \times 10^8$	4.2×10^3	4.2×10^6	4.2×10^7	4.2×10^{11}
Number of usable voice channels[b]	0–1	$0 - 10^4$	1.0	10^3	10^4	10^8
Number of usable video channels[c]	0	0–10	0	1	10	10^5

[a] The frequency of the signal source determined the nominal frequency. Inefficiencies within the system resulted in a usable bandwidth that was somewhat less than normal frequency.
[b] Voice channels required 4.2×10^3 Hz per channel.
[c] Video channels required 4.2×10^6 Hz per channel.
SOURCE: Industry analyst's estimates.

per prices were expected to increase. Someday fiber-optic systems would be cheaper than conventional systems mainly because of their increased information-carrying capacity.

One way to look at the potential size of the market for fiber-optics was to examine the market for wire and cable communications. Because of differences in information-carrying capacity, it was difficult to compare the cost of fiber-optic cable with conventional copper cable. The size of a copper cable depended on its application. Information-carrying capacity increased as size increased, and price increased accordingly. In 1978 twisted pair wire copper cable, the most common type of cable, cost 3¢/meter pair. A "typical" twisted pair cable contained fifty to several thousand pairs. Another widely used cable, coaxial cable, ranged in price from 37¢ to $12.00/meter. Industry sources indicate that copper represented 30 percent of total cable cost, with other materials and labor/overhead accounting for an additional 30 percent and 60 percent of total cost, respectively.

The telecommunications wire and cable market could be measured in pounds, billions of conductor feet (BCF), and dollars. As reported by the U.S. Department of Commerce, an estimated 930 million pounds of copper was used for telecommunications wire and cable in 1977. At an average price of 65¢ a pound, the copper was worth $600 million. In 1977, according to figures compiled at ATT and the U.S. Independent Telephone Association, 385 BCF of copper cable had been used for telecommunications. ATT had spent $1,950 million and the independent telcos, $590 million on cable. This figure included labor, which represented an estimated 25 percent of total cost. Total expenditure by ATT and the independents on equipment associated with signal transmission other than wire and cable had been an estimated $500 million in 1977.

Estimated cable sales to other markets are contained in Table 16-4. Coaxial cable was sold to the CATV and computer industries. Flat wire was sold exclusively to the computer industry, while hook-up wire, multiconductor shielded wire, and multiconductor unshielded wire were sold to many different industries. U.S. consumption of equipment for use in sending electronic signals, exclusive of telecommunications, was estimated to be $1.2 billion in

TABLE 16-4. Non-Telecommunications Wire and Cable Sales *(millions of dollars)*

	1977	1978
Coaxial cable	$140	$155
Flat cable	124	133
Hook-up wire	97	105
Multiconductor, shielded (twisted pair wire)	64	60
Multiconductor, unshielded (twisted pair wire)	37	38
Total	$462	$491

SOURCE: *Electronics Magazine,* January 4, 1979.

1978 and was expected to grow at a rate of 9 percent per annum through 1985, according to fiber-optic industry observers. As illustrated in Exhibit 16-7, estimates of the potential size of the fiber-optic market varied somewhat.

Another approach to determining the market for fiber optics was to examine the particular end uses where fiber optics might have an application. All observers seemed to believe that fiber optics had potential applications in the following markets: telecommunications, computers, cable television, military communications, industrial control, and a number of special markets including aircraft, aerospace, automobiles, and nuclear power stations.[6] Exhibit 16-8 contains typical market forecasts.

Telecommunications

Telecommunications applications were generally considered to be the largest potential market for fiber optics. The telecommunications industry consisted of two sectors: the telecommunications common carriers who provided telecommunications services, and the telecommunications equipment industry, which sold hardware to these common carriers. Telephone service revenue had totaled $46.3 billion in 1978. The Bell System was the dominant common carrier in the U.S., consisting of twenty-one operating companies, and had accounted for approximately 85 percent of telecom-

[6]The data on market sizes and anticipated growth reported in the following sections were compiled from Census Bureau data, *Standard & Poor's Industry Surveys,* published sources, and field interviews.

munications service revenue in 1978. More than half of the remaining 15 percent was attributable to General Telephone and Electronics (GTE), and the rest to United Telecom, Central Telephone, and some 1,500 smaller "independent" telephone companies, some with only a few dozen telephones. Independents, not affiliated with the Bell System, were strongest in the Southwest. Because cost-effective telephone service required that any given area be part of a single telephone network, each of the common carriers had a monopoly in its service area. The most important function of the common carriers was to maintain uninterrupted telephone service, and regulatory bodies to which these companies were responsible reacted adversely to poor performance in this area. For this reason ATT required all new equipment have less than two hours of down time per year.

Telecommunications common carriers served two very different customer groups: residential and business customers. The residential customer used the telephone only for voice communications and required a single line to which extensions were attached. The business customer required voice and possibly data communications facilities. In addition, the business customer used the telephone system for intracompany communications, often between separate geographic locations. The larger business customer required a private switching center (PBX) to route this internal traffic. The *Fortune* 500 companies have accounted for 62 percent of the toll, or long-distance, telephone service revenues earned by the telecommunications common carriers in 1978.

Figure 16–8 shows the configuration of a typical telephone system, as well as the types of communications wire and cable connecting the various components of the system. Telephone service in-

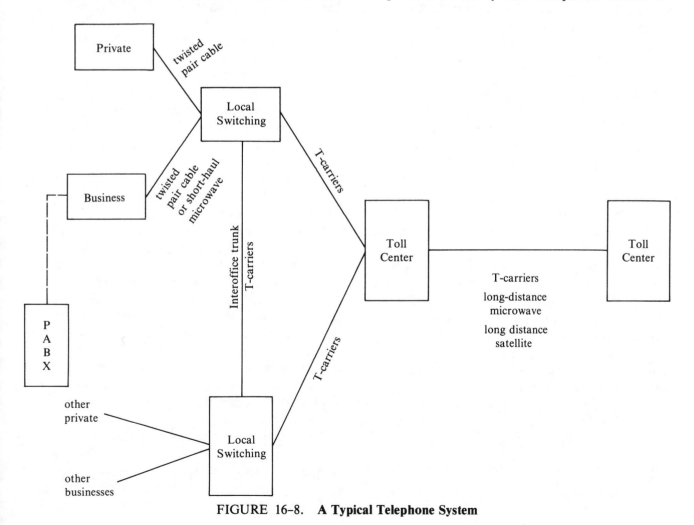

FIGURE 16–8. **A Typical Telephone System**

volved providing private or business customers access to each other through a complex switching network. The first level of the hierarchy of the telephone network was local switching, where two customers within close geographic proximity (5 to 7 miles) were connected to each other through one switching center. Customers within the same metropolitan area but not in close proximity were connected by the second level of switching, through an "interoffice trunk." Interoffice trunks connected the local switching centers. There were approximately 6,000 local switching centers in the United States. A third level of the hierarchy connected customers in different metropolitan areas. This occurred through "toll centers," which were connected to all the local switching centers.[7]

As shown in Figure 16–8, components of the network could be connected with a variety of different types of communication devices, including twisted pair copper wire, coaxial cable, short-haul microwave systems, long-haul microwave systems, and satellites. Twisted pair copper wire was nearly always used for wiring the customer's premises and connecting the customer to the local switching center, both low-volume applications. Interoffice trunks were the most heavily used part of the telephone network. Interoffice trunks also primarily utilized twisted pair copper wire bundled in a variety of forms known as "T-carriers." T-carriers were electronic digital transmission systems specifically designed to increase capacity. They could contain several thousand copper twisted wire pairs. The T–1 system, introduced by Bell in 1962, could provide twenty-four separate voice circuits. T–2 and T–3 systems were introduced in 1975. The T–4 carrier, a coaxial cable, was introduced by Bell in 1976 and provided 4,032 voice circuits. T-carrier cable, which had accounted for almost all of the capacity growth in metropolitan areas since its introduction, has an annual growth rate of 20 percent. T-carriers were also used to connect local switching centers to toll centers.

Coaxial cable was one of the several long-distance transmission systems for connecting toll centers. Long distance systems using coaxial cable

were designated the L-systems. Like twisted pair wire, coaxial cable was made of copper. Coaxial cable was designed to transmit signals at a higher frequency than ordinary twisted pair copper cables. This greatly increased the information-carrying capacity of coaxial cable relative to twisted pair cable, as was shown in the data presented earlier. Coaxial cable had a capacity of up to 10,800 voice circuits per coaxial conductor. Because several coaxial conductors were contained in each "L" system cable, the capacity was substantially greater, up to 108,000 voice circuits per cable in the L–5.

Microwave systems, another form of long-distance transmission, were radio relay networks wherein signals were sent through the air between antennas spaced up to 25 miles apart. In order for microwave systems to work, the radio signal had to be aimed directly at the receiver; any obstruction such as a tall building or a hill resulted in signal loss. Microwave relays had the capability of transmitting data, television, and voice signals. Short-haul microwave systems could be used for local transmission. Each microwave system required an antenna, receiver, and electronic transmission equipment at an estimated cost of $500,000. At the receiving end of a microwave system, high-capacity copper cable was currently being used to transmit the signal to its final destination. The Bell System's long-distance microwave network handled 70 percent of the interstate telephone traffic in the United States in 1978. The newest technology for long-distance signal transmission was satellite transmission. Satellites, which orbited in a fixed position in space, were used as relays to transmit signals between two earth stations spaced thousands of miles apart. Although satellites cost several million dollars to "install," three satellites orbiting in space could service hundreds of earth stations all over the globe. An earth station consisting of a receiver and electronic equipment cost from $300,000 to $1,000,000, depending on its size. Earth stations required high-capacity cable to complete the signal transmission. ATT's satellites handled 5 percent of U.S. interstate telephone traffic in 1978.

The provision of telecommunications services was a regulated industry in the United States as it was, more or less, throughout the world. However, recent changes in telecommunications regulations had increased competition in the U.S. industry in

---

[7] The Bell System handled the switching between the local switching centers of all its operating subsidiaries as well as among all the independent telephone companies in order to provide nationwide service.

several key areas. The Carterfone decision in 1968 had exposed ATT to competition in the so-called interconnect business. This referred to the sale of equipment to residential or business customers, which was then "interconnected" to the telephone service network. This market included residential telephones and PBX (Private Branch Exchange) switching equipment for business customers with multiple telephones. In addition, ATT faced increasing competition for intercity communications from the "specialized common carriers." Using either satellite or microwave circuits, these companies offered both short-haul and long-distance service in voice, data communication, and facsimile transfer, in direct competition with Bell.[8] New companies such as MCI Communications and Satellite Business Systems,[9] as well as major telephone equipment suppliers such as ITT and Northern Telecom (see below) were competing with Bell for some very lucrative segments of the telecommunications business. Particularly important was competition in data transmission, where companies moved tremendous volumes of data from point to point. This area had yielded substantial revenues to Bell, because companies had leased telephone lines in order to transmit data. Revenues from data communication in 1978 had been $2.9 billion, 6 percent of total telecommunication service revenue, and most of this had been earned by ATT. Data transmission, the fastest growing segment of the industry in 1978, was believed to be growing at an annual rate of 15 to 20 percent. By 1980 70 percent of all U.S. companies would be connected for data communication through specialized or common carriers. The growing importance of data transmission was bringing Bell into direct competition with IBM as well as the other specialized carriers.

The basic telephone market was a mature market in the United States in 1978, with approximately 95 percent of all U.S. households having telephones. The total number of telephones served by the in-

dustry was growing at an annual rate of 4 to 5 percent, largely reflecting population increases. Common carrier revenues had risen from $40.6 billion to $46.3 billion in 1978, a 14 percent increase. The additional 9 percent growth over the growth in telephones had come from increased sales and increased service to the existing customer base. This had been the pattern since 1972. The telephone service companies had spent an estimated $14 billion on construction in 1978, of which ATT had spent $12 billion. Of this, 49 percent had been spent on new capacity, an expenditure that reflected constantly changing demographic patterns in the United States. The remaining 51 percent had been spent on modernization and replacement. ATT depreciated its equipment over a twenty-year period, and all telephone equipment had to meet this lifetime requirement.

The telecommunications equipment part of the industry manufactured telephone equipment for use by the telecommunications common carriers. Total shipments of the telephone and telegraph equipment had equalled $6.3 billion in 1978 according to the U.S. Census Bureau. Telecommunications equipment sales had grown at a rate of 6 percent annually and were expected to continue to grow at this rate through the early 1980s. Total sales of equipment in 1975 are shown in Table 16–5. Besides Western Electric, other major telephone equipment manufacturers were GTE, ITT, Stromberg Carlson, Northern Telecommunications, and ICI. These companies competed as second suppliers for the Bell System, as suppliers to the independent telecommunications companies, and in the interconnect segment of the market, where they could

---

[8] By law the Bell System could offer only regulated communication service. It was unclear whether data and video services were regulated communications as defined by the Communications Act of 1934. However, this law was being rewritten in 1978.

[9] Satellite Business Systems was a consortium of Aetna Life & Casualty, Comsat General Corp., and IBM, which had received FCC authorization to provide satellite communication service in February 1977.

TABLE 16–5. Sales of Telecommunications Equipment

Telephone switching and switchboard equipment	$1.83 billion
PBX equipment	.15 billion
Other telephone and telegraphy apparatus[a]	3.10 billion
Total	$4.99 billion

[a] This category was believed to include cable and associated equipment.
SOURCE: U.S. Census of Manufactures. Figures for more recent years were not available.

sell directly to the business or residential end user.[10] Competition in the telephone equipment industry was vigorous.

In addition, in 1978 the U.S. Congress was rewriting the Communications Act of 1934 and was considering legislation requiring Western Electric to separate from the Bell System and compete as an independent company. Criticism of its relationship with Western Electric had caused Bell to increase somewhat the use of independently manufactured equipment.

Technological change had influenced the nature of telecommunications equipment. The telephone industry was gradually replacing the electromechanical switching equipment in its local exchanges with the electronic equipment. This equipment was smaller, less expensive to produce, and more efficient than existing equipment. This new electronic equipment sent signals in digital rather than analog form, the earliest transmission technology. Analog transmission duplicated human speech with continuously changing frequencies, which represented the continuously changing original signal. For digital transmission, the original voice signal, which was analog in form, was converted into a discrete series of binary bits representing the original variations in frequency. Digital signals could be sent faster and with less interference than analog. All data communications were digital in form. Although the technology had been available for well over ten years, ATT had replaced only 23 percent of its switching equipment with electronic digital equipment, and conversion to digital would continue to be very gradual.

The existence of cheap, more complex electronic devices had also increased the use of high-speed multiplexing. Multiplexing increased the capacity of existing communications cable by enabling one communication channel to carry several signals simultaneously. Because voice communication required relatively low transmission rates, high frequency transmission facilities could accommodate several voice signals by sandwiching the signals in sequential form and sending them to separate receivers. Alternately, voice signals could be interspersed in data transmission. Although both analog and digital signals could be multiplexed,

multiplexing digital signals was simpler, more efficient, and cheaper.

A major item supplied to the telecommunications industry was wire and cable. Annual shipments of telephone communications cable (twisted pair copper wire and coaxial cable) were notoriously cyclical, as shown in Table 16–6. Although independents accounted for 15 percent of industry sales, because of the relative importance of short-haul communications in their business mix they purchased a disproportionately large share of cable. The major suppliers of telephone cable, other than Western Electric, were: Anaconda Telecommunications, Brand Rex Co., Essex Electrical Wire and Cable, General Cable, Okonite Co., Superior Cable, and Phelps Dodge.

Fiber Optics and Telecommunications

Although some observers suggested that fiber optics could eventually replace all conventional copper telecommunications cable, the lack of integrated optical circuits and optical switching devices in 1978 limited fiber optics to applications where fiber-optic systems could be plugged into the system via electro-optic interfaces. In spite of this, fiber-optic technology seemed to have enormous potential. The increased capacity could be used to provide increased capacity for voice communications or to meet the heavy information content of video and data communications. Its small size was an important consideration in the twenty-five largest metropolitan areas, where space in underground conduits was severely limited. In addition, because of their low attenuation, fiber-optic systems could operate over longer distances than conventional cables and required fewer repeaters.[11]

TABLE 16–6. **Shipments of Communications Cable** *(billions of dollars)*

1973	1974	1975	1976	1977	1978
1.7	2.0	1.5	2.1	2.6	2.9[a]

[a] Estimated.
SOURCE: U.S. Department of Commerce.

---

[10] These companies competed in international markets as well.

[11] In order to send signals over long distances, repeaters were used for signal regeneration. Conventional repeaters cost

This not only reduced equipment costs but in metropolitan areas also resulted in significant savings in the cost of acquiring space to house repeaters.

Immunity to EMI and radio frequency interference would greatly reduce "cross-talk" where parties could overhear conversations carried on adjacent wires. Because of this, optical fibers could be packed more densely than copper wire. Immunity to interference also eliminated the need for electrically grounding the system, isolating power sources from cable, and shielding the cable. These all resulted in systemwide cost savings in using fiber optics.

In general, fiber optics became more cost competitive with conventional systems as the distance served by the link increased.[12] However, the compelling need for increased capacity in interoffice switching led many observers to believe that the earliest telecommunication application would be in short-haul systems. Fiber-optic systems worked best when signal transmission was in digital form.

By 1978 field trials designed to determine whether fiber-optic systems could work under actual operating conditions had been conducted. The tests were designed to determine whether adequate repairs and splices could be made to fiber-optic systems in the field; whether fiber-optic cables could stand the rigors of installation and harsh environmental conditions, typical of telecommunications applications; whether the systems could meet the high reliability standards of the telephone companies; and whether the systems could be maintained by existing telephone service personnel. In 1978 Bell, GTE, and ITT all had operational fiber-optic telephone links. As a result of a year-long trial of an interoffice link in Chicago, ATT announced that it was completely satisfied with the performance of this new technology. By the end of 1978 both GTE and ATT had begun to advertise

---

$4.16/voice circuit, typically contained 4,000 circuits and were contained in boxes measuring $9 \times 6 \times 6$ feet. Fiber-optic repeaters combined detector and source in a single unit. These repeaters could be placed at intervals up to 15 miles, some three to five times greater than repeaters for conventional systems. Some 90 percent of all metropolitan switching centers were built within 7 km of each other and would not require fiber-optic repeaters.

[12] This was generally true of all fiber-optic applications.

fiber optics as a significant new technological breakthrough.

Video Communications

In cable television (CATV) the TV signal normally sent through the atmosphere was fed directly into a subscriber's television set by cable. A CATV firm erected a master antenna and transmitted the signals to subscribers via coaxial cable. CATV was first introduced in areas where broadcast TV signals were too weak for ordinary TV receivers, but it had spread to metropolitan areas. Subscribers paid an installation fee of $10–$15, and a monthly charge of $5–$10. In 1977 there were nearly 3,600 CATV systems serving 12 million subscribers in the United States, which represented approximately 17 percent of the available U.S. market.[13] While subscriber growth was expected to be 7 to 10 percent through the 1980s, new cable systems would only grow at a rate of 2 to 3 percent. However, some observers believed that once cable TV obtained a 30 percent market share, a rapid growth would begin. This had been the case with color TV. Recent growth in the industry had led some observers to believe that explosive growth was close at hand. In Canada, CATV systems served 60 percent of the market. Canadian cable television companies rebroadcast U.S. television signals.

CATV systems consisted of three basic components: the reception station, the head end, and a distribution system. TV signals were received by antennas placed on towers and then passed by coaxial cable to the head end facility, where the electrical signal was amplified before distribution. Coaxial cable was also used to carry signals from the head end to the population center, usually a distance of 3 to 4 miles. These coaxial cables, called "supertrunk," because of their high information-carrying capacity, cost $3 per meter. Feeder lines branched off the distribution cables, and drop wires connected the feeder lines to a terminal on subscriber's premises. The terminals were then connected to the subscriber's TV.

According to the National Cable Television Association, revenue growth in the U.S. CATV in-

---

[13] *Television Fact Book,* 1977.

dustry would be approximately 18 percent yearly through 1980, from a base of $770 million in 1977.[14] The six largest CATV operators based on the number of subscribers were TelePrompter; Telecommunications, Inc.; Warner Cable Corp.; American TV and Communications Corp.; Cox Cable Communications; and Viacom International. Revenues of the top six ranged from TelePrompter's $101.8 million in 1976 to Cox Cable's $29.3 million. Hundreds of smaller companies also offered CATV service. Each company served from one to many geographic areas, and only one company was franchised in any given area.

In addition to regular subscriber service, CATV operators were contemplating expansion into other broadband service areas that included pay TV, high-speed data transmission, facsimile, electronic mail, picture telephone, education, business conferencing, traffic control, parking control, and electronic funds transfer in 1978. While pay TV was being offered in 1978, these other applications were still in the pilot project stage. The estimated market for CATV equipment was as shown in Table 16–7.

Fiber optics were believed to have advantages for CATV because of its expanded data-carrying capacity and the potential cost advantage. The first fiber-optic applications were expected to be in coaxial trunk lines, but industry observers agreed that fiber optics could someday replace all CATV cable. In 1978 several fiber-optic experiments in CATV systems were operational. In New York, TelePrompter was using an 800-foot fiber-optic link to carry TV signals from microwave equipment on the roof of a high-rise building to head end equipment thirty floors below. The cable was a step-index fiber made by Belden Corporation, with an attenuation loss of 10 db/km. Rediffusion, Ltd., a British cable

television company, had been operating a 4,700 foot fiber-optic CATV link since March 1976. The system utilized a Corning step-index fiber in a cable produced by BICC Telecommunication Cables, Ltd., with an attenuation loss of 12.6 db/km to connect antenna and head end equipment. Beginning in February 1977, a five-subscriber two-way CATV system using optical fibers was being tested in Japan. The project was financed by the Japanese Ministry of International Trade and Industry (MITI). A second MITI project involving a 300-subscriber field test was begun in February 1978 and would cost $17 million. Actual test operation would begin in 1979. In 1978 Harris Corporation installed an 8.5-km cable TV transmission line in London, Ontario, for a consortium of Canadian cable television companies. Also in 1978, two fiber-optic cable TV systems capable of providing interactive voice, video, and data services were installed for the State of Kentucky. Times-Fiber Communications, a major supplier of conventional coaxial cable to the CATV industry and also involved in fiber optics, installed the systems.

Closed circuit television (CCTV) represented another potential market for fiber optics. CCTV involved the direct connection of a TV camera to a television screen. It had specialized applications including traffic surveillance, security services, business meetings, visual monitoring of control panels and meters, educational programming, and live sports events. CCTV equipment was identical to CATV equipment, although cheaper equipment and smaller-capacity cabling could be used in most CCTV installations. According to the U.S. Department of Commerce, CCTV equipment sales were $10 million.[15] In 1978 General Cable Corp. had in-

[14] Ibid.

[15] U.S. Department of Commerce, Current Industrial Reports, 1977.

TABLE 16–7. CATV Equipment Sales by Year (millions of dollars)

Year	Studio and Headend Equipment	Transmission Lines[a]	Converters[b]	Feeder Lines & Drop Wire	Total
1976	$8.4	$25.0	$21.6	$27.7	$ 82.7
1977	8.6	25.3	26.3	29.3	89.5
1978	10.8	26.0	43.0	35.0	114.0

[a] Coaxial trunk lines, antenna to headend, headend to population center.
[b] Electrical equipment used at the headend to amplify electronic signals.
SOURCE: Electronics Magazine, January 1978.

stalled a fiber-optic CCTV system for the Union Pacific Railroad.

Computers

In 1977 the computer industry was a $14.4 billion industry that was growing at an annual rate of 12 percent.[16] Computer systems consisted of a central processing unit (CPU), which performed the computing function, and peripheral equipment, which was used to enter, store, display, and retrieve information from the central processor. Three separate categories of computing equipment existed: mainframe computers, minicomputers, and microprocessors (or microcomputers). Mainframe computers generally had the greatest computing capability and the highest cost. However, the fastest-growing segment of the computer industry was in the smaller minicomputers, with sales growth expected to exceed 30 percent annually throughout the 1970s. The low price of minicomputers coupled with their rapidly increasing computing power had fueled this growth. Microprocessors, the newest computing technology, were the ultimate in miniaturization and consisted of a single integrated circuit, which could function as the central processing unit of a computer. Microprocessors were gaining market share in the two large traditional markets for minicomputers: industrial process control and data communications. The price/performance characteristics of all three computer market segments were beginning to converge as mainframe prices dropped,[17] and both minicomputers and microprocessors were developed with broader ranges of computing capability. The entire industry was engaged in increasingly fierce price competition in 1978, with many firms crossing the boundaries of their traditional market segments. This industry was also characterized by rapid technological change. Every competitor wanted to be or appear to be on the cutting edge of new technology. The only constraints on change was the time it took to design, engineer, and produce entirely new computer models. In the case of large mainframes this "design

---

[16] Standard & Poor's.

[17] In April 1977 IBM dropped the price of its system 370 mainframe computers by 30 percent.

lag" was three to five years, for minis it was approximately two years. Computer customers required extremely reliable equipment. Once installed, computers were generally maintained by the vendors' field service personnel. All equipment had to be relatively easily and quickly repaired when failure occurred. Excessive down time could cause customers to switch to a competitor's equipment.

The computer industry was dominated by IBM, which held an estimated market share of 70 percent. Long the leader in mainframe computers, IBM had recently moved into the minicomputer market. IBM was considered to be the most conservative company in the industry in adopting new technologies. However, this in no way detracted from IBM's position as industry leader. Other significant competitors included Sperry Univac, Control Data, Honeywell, and Burroughs in mainframes; Digital Equipment, Data General, Hewlett-Packard, Honeywell, and Prime in minicomputers; and Texas Instruments, Intel, and Data General in microprocessors. The capital investment required to offer a broad line of computers, particularly mainframe computers, constituted a substantial barrier to entry. However, several electronic companies with capability in new integrated circuit and microprocessor technology had recently entered the market, including Texas Instruments.

The market for mainframe computers was believed to be nearly saturated in 1978. Normal customer upgrading was believed to foretell a continued 6 percent annual increase in sales. Faster growth depended on reaching new markets, with the most fertile territory being companies with sales of less than $25 million, and on developing new applications. The largest gains were expected to come from the growing acceptance of distributed data processing (DDP), which combined minicomputers at a local site (called an intelligent peripheral) with a central mainframe computer. As was the case in telecommunications, another important source of revenue growth would come from expanding the range of services provided to the existing customer base.

The performance characteristics of fiber optics that interested computer manufacturers most were its increased data-carrying capacity and its immunity to EMI. The computer central processing unit could process data faster than data could be transmitted to the rest of the system. Improved transmission rates in computers ranged from sixteen to twenty-five megabits per second—which fiber-optics data transmission rates could easily triple. Computer systems were also extremely sensitive to EMI. A fluorescent light bulb could introduce errors or "noise" into the system. As a result, computing rates frequently had to be slowed to compensate for noise, and cabling had to be shielded from EMI at an estimated cost of $5 per meter in addition to the cost of the cable itself. The average price of the cable used in computer application was 78¢ a meter.

Fiber optics could potentially replace all of the copper wire currently in use. Cables represented somewhat less than 3 percent of total cost to the end user of a medium-size computer system and less than 1 percent of the cost of large systems. Computer wire and cable could be divided into four categories: interfaces among central processors, interfaces among computer peripherals, connecting computers to peripherals, and internal wiring.[18]

Connecting Central Processors. Of the 100,000 central processors shipped in the United States annually, about 6,000 required interconnection with other central processors. Central processors typically processed information at the rate of 56 megabits per second, and very high capacity cable was required for CPU interconnection. It cost an estimated $2.00 a meter and required up to three days of labor to connect. Based on an estimated average distance of 155 meters between computers, cable requirements equaled more than 900 kilometers annually. If the cost of the cable were to decrease, furthermore, the distance between processors could increase. In addition, any time central processors changed location, new cabling was necessary.

Connecting Peripherals. The market for computer peripherals was growing at 28 percent a year. In 1977 more than 400,000 terminals were shipped, including display terminals, printers, terminals system controllers, and special-purpose terminals, and more than half of these required interconnection. This application required a data rate of less

[18] Data from *Kessler Marketing Intelligence,* October 1978.

than ten megabits a second, and coaxial cable, which cost 33–38¢/meter in 1978, could be used. The amount of cabling necessary in this application was determined by the distances involved. Because these distances could vary substantially, it was difficult to estimate the total cable required for this application.

Connecting Central Processor to Peripheral. In 1978 the average distance from computer to peripheral was 25 meters, and distances extended up to 2 kilometers in some applications. Cable performance requirements were similar to peripheral-to-peripheral applications. In 1977 the total cable requirements for computer to peripheral links was estimated at 6 million meters. Since this type of equipment was moved frequently, there was a substantial retrofit market. Distributed data processing systems changed the nature of the cable requirement somewhat. Although the distances involved were not reduced, DDP systems used data buses or data highways to connect the so-called intelligent peripheral to the mainframe. Rather than being connected directly to the mainframe, each peripheral was connected to a high-capacity data bus, which carried information from several peripherals to the main frame. Data buses would need to have a data handling capacity of 50 megabits per second.

Internal Wiring. Each of the 500,000 peripherals and computers sold each year contained copper wire, which could be replaced by optical fiber. Though there were no available estimates of the amount of wire in each unit, it was known that any given connections involved were less than 3 meters. Replacement of the internal wiring with optical fiber would greatly increase system data-handling capability. However, in 1978 the cost of fiber-optic light sources, detectors, and connectors was considered too high to justify use of fiber optics for internal wiring.

In 1978 almost all major computer companies were investigating fiber optics, although they were extremely reluctant to disclose the nature and extent of their activities. The greatest interest seemed to be focused on CPU to peripheral links and interconnecting CPUs. Interfacing peripherals was also being investigated, as were data bus applications, but the lack of fully adequate fiber-optic coupling devices and switching mechanisms made the latter application appear to be somewhat more remote. In its investigation of fiber optics, IBM was known to have tested optical cable from all of the major suppliers and had worked on the problem of developing appropriate connectors. As early as 1975 IBM had tested a fiber-optic system which interconnected subassemblies within a computer, operating at the rate of 25 megabits per second. In 1978 IBM remained noncommittal about when and where fiber optics would be used in their computers. In 1978 Sperry Univac had demonstrated a system connecting terminals in the Houston City Library with the municipal fire department. The fiber-optic link was 1.6 km long and operated at a rate of 2,400 bits per second (.00024 megabits).

The Military Market

A number of unique properties of fiber-optic systems had long attracted the interest of the military: immunity to electromagnetic interference; immunity to the effects of radiation; security from interception; small size; and light weight. The Army, Air Force, and Navy were all working on fiber-optic applications. The principal military applications in 1978 were in the internal wiring of weapons systems in aircraft, helicopters, ships, and submarines. Fiber optics was also being investigated for data transmission to and from satellite ground stations and for data transmission on the battlefield.

In 1977 the Department of Defense had established a Tri-Services Committee to coordinate fiber-optics development activities and prevent duplication of designs and systems. All three services and the Department of Defense had worked closely with industry participants (primarily ITT, Valtec, and Corning) on developmental work. The first government contracts had been let in 1974, and the U.S. Army had been instrumental in the development of a rugged fiber-optic cable. In 1978 numerous tests of fiber optics were being conducted by the military.

The Department of Defense's budget totaled $112 billion in 1977. Defense spending was a matter of political concern, which reflected presidential and congressional input, and as a result could vary

from year to year. The total DOD budget in 1975 and 1976 had been $88 and $98 billion, respectively. Of the total 1977 budget some $10.8 billion had been allocated for R&D, and some 35 percent of this was estimated to have been spent on electronics. According to the observers estimates, 5 percent of this budget had been spent on communications systems for which fiber optics could potentially be substituted. A number of large military contracts had been made with producers of fiber-optic equipment for developmental work in the $300,000 to $500,000 range.

Industrial Controls

The industrial controls industry consisted of equipment sold to the process industries (called process controls) and equipment (called discrete controls) that governed the operation of separate machines. The industrial process control manufacturers served the process industries such as petroleum, chemicals, food processing, cement, and others. Industrial process controls adjusted flows, mix, temperature, and other variables of the production process and collected data on these activities in one central control room. Discrete controls governed the functioning of individual machines and could be set to command the machine to do specific tasks: turn on/off, drill, cut, fold in a specified sequence, and so on. Discrete controls could be centralized in one control facility but as of 1978 generally were not.

Industry sales were over $6 billion in 1978 and were cyclical, reflecting fluctuations in the economic cycle. The main competitors in this market included Foxboro Instruments and Fisher & Porter in process controls and Honeywell in discrete controls. Westinghouse, General Electric, and Babcock & Wilcox were other well-known participants. These companies treated the industrial controls market as consisting of specialized segments determined by the different industries they served and were typically quite decentralized.

By 1978 electronic controls had begun to replace electromechanical control systems. Computerized control systems were available, and the development of the microprocessor had increased the rate of conversion to computerized systems. Whatever the technology, copper cable was used for signal transmission. Because data rates of less than one megabit were required, conventional copper wiring was adequate for most applications. However, because of the electromagnetic interference that characterized the typical industrial environment, copper cable had to be armored or placed inside conduits at a cost of $3–$5 per meter.

When used in industrial control applications, fiber-optic systems would eliminate the need for protective shielding. Because fiber-optic systems never generate sparks, their use would also eliminate the risk of fire or explosion. A number of competitors in this industry were believed to be investigating fiber optics.

Other Markets

In 1978 the range of potential applications for fiber optics was expanding rapidly. There were a large number of applications where fiber optics had one or more specific performance features that made it very attractive. One market was in nuclear and electrical power plants, where optical fiber's freedom from EMI, improved security and the fiber's absolute protection from sparking resulted in greatly increased safety. One nuclear power plant would require approximately 200 miles of communications cable. According to the National Energy Commission, seventy nuclear power plants were under construction in 1978. There were hundreds of electric utility plants in the United States. Although the rate of growth in capacity additions had slowed somewhat since 1970, electric utility companies had spent $13.8 billion in the construction and repair of power generation facilities in 1977. In 1978 Westinghouse and Babcock & Wilcox were testing short-distance fiber-optics systems in electric utility plants.

Another use for fiber optics was the transmission of geological data when drilling oil wells. EMI was a major problem in use of conventional cable for this application. As of 1978 some 650 oil drilling units were in operation, each requiring some 26,000 feet of very rugged cable.

Fiber optics could also replace conventional cable in gasoline pumps, because of the need to protect against fires. There were 5 million gasoline pumps in the United States, each requiring approximately 5 feet of cable. The main supplier of gas pumps, Exxon-owned Gilbraco, had begun to convert to fiber optics in 1977.

The automobile industry already consumed more than $2 million worth of fiber optics, primarily in dashboard illumination. This was almost all high-loss fiber, but as more electronic devices were introduced the potential automotive uses for fiber optics would increase.

Small size, low weight, and freedom from EMI and sparking made fiber optics attractive to the military and commercial aircraft manufacturers. Use of fiber optics could eliminate the need for $500 worth of circuit breakers in a typical aircraft, which had been necessary because of possible EMI. Aircraft operating costs would be reduced an estimated $2,000 over the lifetime of an aircraft, for each pound of its weight that could be reduced. Copper wiring ranged from 200 to 400 pounds in a typical aircraft, whereas fiber-optic systems weighed one-tenth those of copper. Finally, a malfunction in the communications system of a bomber resulting from spark or EMI could cause the bomber to fire its bombs inadvertently. In 1978 Boeing, McDonnell-Douglas, Northrup, and Hughes were all known to be investigating fiber optics.

Historical Overview

In their earliest form, high-loss optical fibers were used to transmit images from and to illuminate otherwise inaccessible locations. Earliest uses included medical instruments such as bronchoscopes and colonoscopes, in which fibers were used to examine organs in the body. Optical fibers were also used for automobile dashboard illumination, in test equipment, and for directional signs for airport runways. These early fibers had losses in the range of 1,000 to 1,500 db/km, low enough to carry light but too high to transmit a meaningful signal very far. They could be used with almost any light source, including high-intensity light bulbs. The earliest producers of fiber were mainly optical companies engaged in the making of lenses and other high-quality glass. These included Corning Glass Works, American Optical Corporation, the Electro-Optics Division of Bendix Corporation, Mosaic Fabrications, a division of Bausch & Lomb (a maker of medical equipment), and Valtec, Inc. Plastic fiber made by E. I. du Pont was used for dashboard illumination in automobiles. Well over 100 companies produced high-loss fibers as part of diversified glass-making operations.

The invention of the laser at Bell Labs in 1960 stimulated interest in the development of a low-loss fiber that could take advantage of lightwaves' high information-carrying capacity. Learning about technological breakthroughs, the British Post Office, operators of the British telephone system, made known its serious interest in using optical fibers for telecommunications. Bell Labs and the British Post Office reportedly approached Corning Glass Works to inquire about the feasibility of developing a fiber capable of transmitting 1 percent of a light signal over a distance of one kilometer. This was equivalent to a loss of 20 decibels per kilometer. At this level of loss, light could travel without amplification equipment as far in an optical fiber as conventional signals did over copper wire.

In 1970 Corning announced that it had reached the 20 db/km goal. The Corning fibers were produced using a chemical vapor deposition technique called doped deposited silica (DDS), which Corning later patented. In May 1974, using a variation of the DDS method, Bell Labs reported development of fibers with losses as low as 1.2 db/km at 1,060 nm wavelength. These reductions in signal losses below 20 db/km increased the distance light could travel from the original goal of 1 kilometer to 10 or 15 kilometers.

In June 1974 Corning announced the first commercially available fiber-optic cable, with an attenuation loss of 30 db/km. Quantity orders were priced at $25.00 a meter. The cable was designed to be used with a light source and detector package that could be purchased from Texas Instruments for $1,000. In May 1975 Corning announced the availability of "Corguide," an optical cable that contained six individual optical fibers with an attenuation loss of 20 db/km. The cable was priced at $13.50 a meter. In February 1976 Corning began selling fibers with losses of 6–10 db/km for $1 a meter. The earliest fiber-optic connectors, modifications of existing electronic connectors, were developed by Corning with the cooperation of Deutsch, a connector manufacturer. Although the constantly changing dimensions of fiber-optic cable caused connector manufacturers to claim that they were unable to offer low-loss fiber-optic connectors, by 1978 low-loss connectors were commercially available.

By 1978 field trials of fiber-optic systems had begun. The emerging fiber-optics industry consisted of a large number of companies. ITT, Corning, and Bell had established themselves as majors and were continuing their developmental work. In 1978 ITT, with four different divisions within the company working on fiber-optics, manufactured optical fibers, cable, sources, detectors, and connectors. ITT was using a CVD process for fiber production and had been sued by Corning for patent infringement. Bell Labs and Western Electric had, between them, capability to produce complete fiber-optic systems on a small scale. Western was believed to have pilot fiber and cable production capacity. Corning was producing both fiber and cable in the industry's first full-scale fiber production in North Carolina. Siecor Optical Cables, a joint venture between Corning and the German electronics company Siemens, was formed in December 1977. Siecor offered cables as well as splicing and terminating equipment and some light sources and detectors. Of the three original developers of low-loss fiber, only Corning publicized its activities widely.

A number of the companies that had been producing optical fiber for high-loss applications had expanded into low- to medium-loss fiber production by 1978, including former units of Bausch & Lomb, Mosaic Fabrications and Valtec. A number of new fiber-optics companies were formed in 1977 and 1978, many of them seeded with former employees of Bell Labs and other fiber-optic producers.

A number of established companies in other industries has also begun to offer fiber-optic products, including Belden Cable, General Cable, and 3M in optical cables (using purchased fibers), and Hewlett-Packard, Texas Instruments, Motorola, RCA, and Harris in light sources and detectors. Other than fiber producers, however, no company could be described as having made a large commitment to the industry by 1978.

A sense of excitement mingled with confusion characterized the industry in 1978. The products, the companies participating in the industry, and the seriousness of their commitment were extremely difficult to determine. Rumors of new entrants and new product breakthroughs circulated constantly. New product announcements and reports of mergers, expansions, and personnel additions filled the newly created fiber-optics sections of periodicals such as *Electronics News* and *Laser Focus*. Industry participants, hungry for information, attended numerous conferences at which exhibitors displayed new products, speakers discussed the latest developments in fiber-optics technology, and attendees swapped business cards and made noncommittal statements about their interest in fiber optics. Seminars and "working sessions" designed to educate engineers about the fundamentals of fiber-optic systems design were held under the sponsorship of prominent engineering associations such as the Institute of Electrical and Electronic Engineers.

In 1978 total industry sales were estimated to have been less than $30 million, up from $5 million in 1975. Industry participants claimed that the only people making money in the industry were consultants and conference organizers. Three or four professional market research firms published reports on fiber optics, and although each new report contained very little new, up-to-date information, they were scrutinized carefully by industry participants fearful lest they overlook a single potentially relevant fact.

Although the United States seemed to have world leadership in fiber-optic technology in 1978, there was also substantial international activity. In Japan, under the direction of MITI, companies such as Nippon Electric, Nippon Sheet Glass, and Sumitomo Electric had developed fiber-optic capability. The Japanese field trials of an interactive cable TV project called the Hi-Ovis Project had attracted worldwide attention and involved thirty-four private corporations. In its first foreign fiber-optic venture, Nippon Electric and Sumitomo had supplied a 9-kilometer optical telephone trunk link for Disney World in Florida in July 1978. In Canada Federal Communication Commissioner Jeanne Sauvé had announced that the Canadian government would back Canadian industry's effort to develop world-class capability in fiber optics. In 1978 Canada already had a full range of fiber-optics capability. Prominent Canadian companies in fiber optics included Northern Telecom, Bell Northern Research, and Canada Wire and Cable Company. In England, the ITT subsidiary Standard Telecommunications Labs had both optical fiber and cable capability and had installed a field system for the British Post Office. Other British participants in fiber optics included: British Broadcasting Corp., which was investigating fiber optics in cable TV; Plessey, a British telecommunications equipment supplier that supplied optical fiber; and Rank Optics, a former "short fiber" manufacturer that now supplied a medium-loss fiber. Other European companies involved in fiber optics included Thompson-CSF, a French telecommunications equipment supplier; Siemens of Germany; and Philips of the Netherlands. Many of the European telecommunications equipment suppliers had signed joint development agreements with Corning in 1974.

EXHIBIT 16-1.   *A Fiber Optic Cable Compared to a Twisted Pair Copper Cable of Equivalent Capacity*

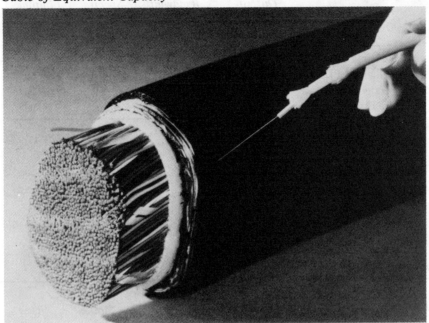

Corning Photo 468.77   Copper Cable/Optical Waveguide
SOURCE: Corning Glass Works.

EXHIBIT 16-2.   *A Typical Fiber-Optic Communication System*

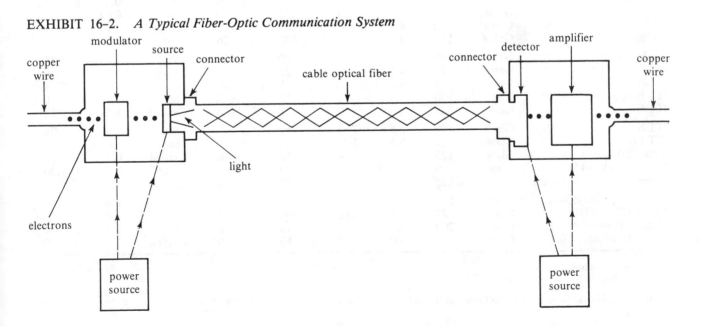

EXHIBIT 16-3. *Comparison of Light Source Types*

Light Source Types	Output Power Range (mw)[a]	Bandwidth Range (mbps)[b]	Spectral Width (Angst.)	Lifetime Average (hours)
Large area LED	1–7	10–40	350	6×10^4
Small area LED	0.5–1.5	20–200	330	5×10^4
CW laser diode	3–40	30–900	20	4×10^4
Pulsed laser diode	100–400	0.1	20	3×10^4

[a] A measure of light intensity.
[b] Megabits per second.

SOURCE: H. Elion and C. Elion, *Fiber Optics in Communication Systems* (New York: Decker, 1978).

EXHIBIT 16-4. *Parameters of Some Typical Commercial Optical Fibers and Cables*

Manufacturer and Fiber ID Number	Fiber Material	Fiber Diam. (um)[a]	Cable Diam. (um)	No. of Fibers	Fiber Atten. (db/km)	Tensile Strength (kg)	Index Profile	Max. Length (km)	Numerical Aperture
Bell North. BNR–7–1–A	Glass	100	—	1	10	30	Graded	0.5	.22
Bell North. BNR–7–2–A	Glass	100	—	1	10	30	Step	0.5	.20
Bell North. BNR–7–2–B	Glass	100	—	2	10	90	Graded	0.5	.22
Corning 1028	Glass	125	—	1	6	10	Step	10.0	.18
Corning 1152–3	Glass	125	—	1	10	10	Graded	10.0	.20
Corning 1156–7	Glass	125	5.0	7	6	10	Graded	10.0	1.6
Corning Corguide	Glass	125	5.0	7	20	200	Step	1.0	1.8
Dupont PFX–S120R	Glass	600	2.4	1	50	80	Step	1.0	—
Dupont PFX–P740	Plastic	375	—	7	470	11	Step	1.0	—
Dupont PFX–P140R	Plastic	400	—	1	470	40	Step	1.0	—
Dupont PFX–P240R	Plastic	400	—	2	470	90	Step	1.0	—
Fiber Optic Q1–1–10	Glass	125	—	1	20	10	Step	0.01	.25
Fiber Optic Q1–7–5	Glass	125	—	1–7	50	30	Step	0.01	.25
Galileo 2000	Galite[b]	70	4.2	210	400	26	Step	1.0	.66
Galileo 3000	Galite	110	4.2	1–19	100	26	Step	1.0	.48
Galileo 4000	Galite	200	4.2	1–19	30	26	Step	1.0	.40
Galileo 5000	Galite	125	4.2	1–19	20	26	Step	1.0	.20
General Cable AT	Glass	125	26.0	30	5	400	Graded	1.0	.21
ITT PS–05–10	Glass	500	—	1	10	150	Step	1.5	.30
ITT GG–0205	Glass	125	—	1	5	150	Graded	1.5	.25
ITT S1	Glass	500	2.5	1	10	45	Step	1.0	.28
ITT LD	Glass	500	2.5	7–19	10	100	Step	1.0	.28
Siecor SIL–K4–15–10K	Glass	125	6.5	4	10	50	Graded	0.2	.20
Siedor SIL–K4–15–30K	Glass	140	6.5	4	30	50	Step	0.2	.20
Times Fiber GP10–SAIO	Glass	125	8.5	10	10	50	Step	1.0	—
Times Fiber SAI–55–90	Glass	125	—	1	7	50	Step	1.0	.16
Valtec HHV–RT03–45	Glass	75	5.3	180	400	50	Step	1.0	—
Valtec LH–PC05–07	Glass	200	3.2	7	40	10	Step	1.0	—
Valtec MHV–MG05001	Glass	125	4.0	1	10	10	Graded	2.0	.20

[a] Units are microns.
[b] Plastic fiber.

SOURCE: Manufacturers' product sales literature, 1977. (For further and latest data, contact manufacturers.)

EXHIBIT 16-5. *Fiber Production Processes*

Stratified Melt Process

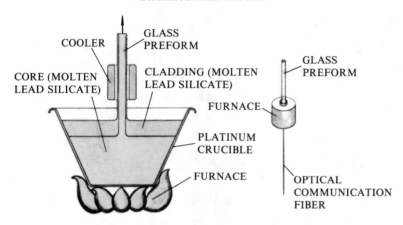

Optimum core/clad interface control with clean room capability to prevent material contamination

Multiple Fiber Drawing Process

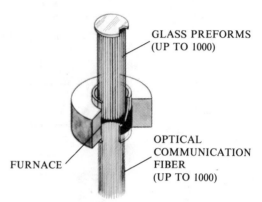

Most efficient glass fiber drawing procedure

Vapor Oxidation Process

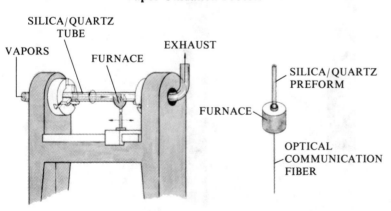

Single Precision Drawing Process

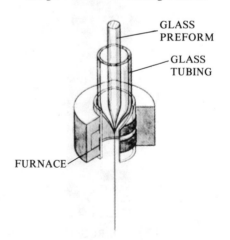

EXHIBIT 16-6.   *A Typical Fiber-Optic Cable Configuration*

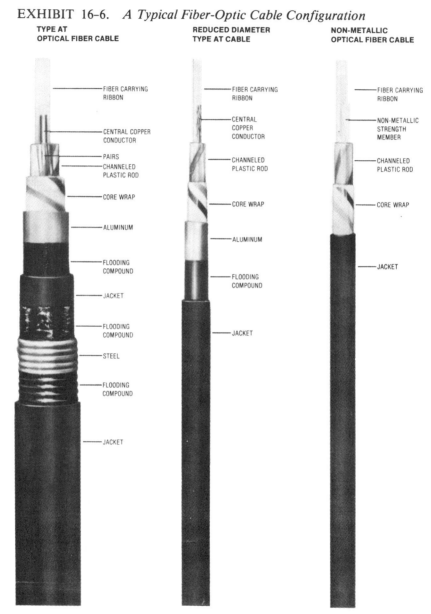

SOURCE: General Cable Corporation, 1978, reproduced from advertisement.

EXHIBIT 16-7.   *A Summary of Market Projections for the North American Fiber-Optic Systems Market (constant 1978 dollars in billions)*

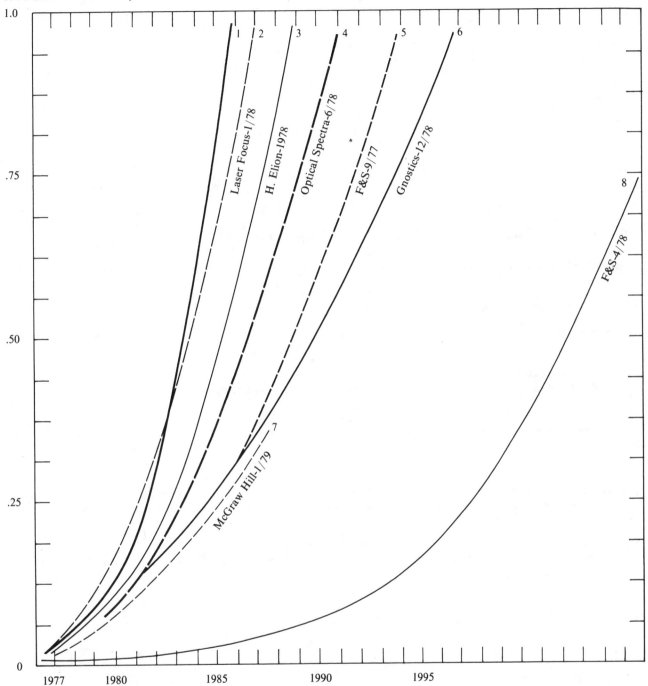

1. International Resources Development, *Fiber Optic Communication in the United States,* August 1977.
2. *Laser Focus Magazine,* January 1978.
3. Elion and Elion, *Fiber Optics in Communication Systems.*
4. *Optical Spectra Magazine,* June 1978.
5. Frost and Sullivan, Report No. 415, September 1977.
6. Gnostic Concepts, December 1978.
7. *Electronic News,* January 1979.
8. Frost and Sullivan, Report No. 549, April 1978.

EXHIBIT 16-8. *Estimated Market for Fiber-Optic Communication Systems, 1987[a]*

A. Estimated Expenditures on Fiber Optics (*dollars in millions*)

Commercial telecommunications	$350.0
CCTV and broadcast TV	3.0
Data communications	2.0
Computer applications	75.0
Other	
(industrial, office equipment,	
instrumentation	15.0
Military and aerospace	100.0
Total	$545.0

SOURCE: Frost and Sullivan Report No. 415.

B. Estimated Expenditures on Fiber Optics (*dollars in millions*)

Telephone	$ 620.0
CATV	40.0
CCTV	15.0
Interconnection of CPUs	24.0
Computer to Peripheral	257.0
Industrial and Commercial Use	
(non-computer)	69.0
Military	86.0
Total	$1,111.0

SOURCE: International Resources and Development, *Fiber-Optic Communications in the U.S.*, August 1977.

[a] The text of each of these market surveys described the headings used for these projections in more detail. However, because of the ambiguous nature of the classifications used, it was not possible to compare these two forecasts directly.

CASE 17
The Fiber-Optics Industry in 1978: Competition

In 1978 the possibility of large-scale applications of optical fibers had created a flurry of activity in companies with the capacity to produce fiber-optic systems or components. Potential customers and competitors stood by, surveying a scene of rapidly changing dimensions as participants readied themselves to compete according to their perceptions of how the game ahead would be played and won. Manufacturers of conventional communications products watched closely and began to evaluate an appropriate response. Industry sales had risen rapidly, as shown in Exhibit 17–1, and the stakes to be won or lost in this game began to appear increasingly large.

This case will describe the business and competitive developments that occurred as the industry began to emerge in the 1970s. In addition, each of the North American producers of optical fiber for use in communications is profiled. Information on fiber-optic products, technology, and potential markets is given in Case 16, "The Fiber-Optics Industry in 1978: Products, Technology, and Markets." More detailed information on Corning Glass

Works' activities in the industry is given in Case 18, "The Fiber-Optics Industry in 1978: Corning Glass Works."

Historical Development

Before technological developments in the early 1970s made their use in communications applications possible, optical fibers had been contained in a number of products, where they were used to transmit heretofore unobservable images or illuminate otherwise inaccessible locations. John Tyndall had demonstrated the principle of light transmission through a transparent medium in the nineteenth century. In Tyndall's demonstration a light was shone into a water-filled barrel with several holes in its side. When the room was darkened, the flowing water carried light as it ran out the holes in the barrel. However, it was not until the early 1950s that a process for the production of strong, flexible glass fibers was developed and the principle applied. These early fibers, made of glass or plastic, had transmission losses in the range of 1,000 to 1,500 db/km, low enough to allow them to transmit light but too high to carry a meaningful signal. Applications for these fibers, called "short-fiber" applications because the distances involved were typically less than one meter, included industrial and consumer products.

The chief industrial application of fiber optics was in automobiles, where optical fibers were used to illuminate the instrument panel, thereby eliminating several bulbs that would otherwise be located in inaccessible places under the dashboard. Fibers were also used for face-plates in cathode ray tubes, in inspection equipment used to examine otherwise hidden areas, and in highway and airport signs, where the fibers could be used to spell out directional information without glare and without requiring electrical connections. Optical fibers were also used in medical examining instruments such as endoscopes, bronchoscopes, and colonoscopes. The main consumer applications for optical fibers were decorative lamps and Christmas tree ornaments. In decorative lamps a group of fiber optic filaments radiated from a central light source to create a "fireworks" effect.

In 1973, before sales in communications applications began to have a measurable impact, total industry sales in fiber optics were estimated to be $4 million, with industrial and consumer use each accounting for one-half. In 1973 glass fiber cost less to produce than plastic. However, the ends of glass fibers had to be polished, which made glass fiber more expensive to work with than plastic fiber, which could be cut with a razor and did not require polishing. Glass was used only in applications where it had an obvious advantage over plastics, such as the ability to withstand high temperatures. For example, glass fibers had to be used in medical equipment that needed to be sterilized. Plastic fibers accounted for an estimated 60 percent of total fiber sales in 1973.

There were two major producers of optical fiber in the early 1970s: Corning Glass Works and du Pont. Corning made a high-loss, step-index glass fiber. Du Pont made a high-loss plastic fiber, which was sold primarily to the automobile industry. The du Pont fiber, called Crofon, was an acrylic fiber clad with polyethylene plastic that sold for 5¢ a foot in 1973. Other producers of early high-loss fiber included the Electro Optics Division of Bendix Corporation; the Electro Fiberoptics Division of Valtec Corp., a division of American Optical (a producer of high-quality glass lenses and instruments); and a division of Bausch & Lomb, a manufacturer of medical equipment and ophthalmic products.

Early Developments in Communications Applications

The invention of the laser at Bell Labs in May 1960 had stimulated interest in finding a way to take advantage of lightwaves' high potential capacity for carrying information. Vitally interested in cultivating communications applications of the laser, Bell Labs scientists had developed several light-based communications systems. One of Bell's early schemes was a light waveguide system, which sent laser beams through a long metal pipe filled with inert gas to keep out moisture. At intervals along the pipe, lenses refocused the beam, and mirrors were used to deflect the beam around bends in the pipe. This system worked but proved to be too expensive for practical use.

In 1966 K. C. Kao and G. A. Hockman of Standard Communications Labs, a British subsidiary of International Telephone and Telegraph, published a research paper that described why the authors believed that glass or plastic fiber could be used to transmit data at optical frequencies. In theory they proved that the light loss in glass fibers need only amount to a few decibels per kilometer. Motivated by Kao's and Hockman's research, the British Post Office, operators of the British telephone system, indicated their serious interest in using optical fibers for telecommunications and approached Bell Labs. Together Bell Labs and the BPO reportedly approached Corning Glass Works, requesting Corning's opinion about the possibility of developing a glass fiber capable of transmitting 1 percent of a light signal over the distance of one kilometer—equivalent to a loss of 20 decibels per kilometer. At this level of loss, light could travel without amplification equipment as far in an optical fiber as conventional signals did over copper wire, a distance that varied from 1 to 3 miles depending on the capacity of a specific copper wire. In the mid-1960s scientists in research laboratories at each of these organizations, drawn together by their mutual interest in optical fibers, began to cooperate on fiber development on a more informal basis. Information was shared, and each lab verified experiments of the others.

In 1967 scientists at Nippon Electronic and Nippon Sheet Glass, working independently of Corning and Bell, announced that they had developed a step-index optical fiber 1 meter long that had losses equivalent to 3,000 db/km. This was the first step-index optical fiber. In 1970 Corning Glass made the historic announcement of laboratory development of a step-index fiber with a loss of 20 db/km; the initial goal had been achieved! By May 1972 Corning could produce a fiber with an attenuation loss of less than 4 db/km.

In 1971, as part of an ongoing research effort in semiconductor technology, C. A. Burrus of Bell Labs developed a variation on the semiconductor LED photodiode design that made it more efficient for use with optical fibers. This photodiode, called the Burrus photodiode, produced a more powerful light than an ordinary LED and eventually became the most commonly used light source for fiber-optic applications.

In June 1974 Corning began to sell a fiber-optic cable consisting of nineteen separate step-index fibers. Designated B-19, the cable had an attenuation of 30 db/dm. It was available in lengths up to 500 meters and cost $25/meter for orders of 5 kilometers and over, and $57/meter for orders of less than 5 kilometers. The fibers in the cable could be used with an LED source and avalanche photodiode detector produced by Texas Instruments. The source and detector were sold together and cost $1,000. These components could be assembled into a system operating at a wavelength of 820 nm.

In 1975 a number of companies began to offer fiber-optic products, and although industry sales in communications applications were estimated to have been less than $5 million, the new technology began to attract the attention of the investment community as well as the scientific and engineering communities. However, many of the developments that contributed to the formation of this industry were not significant enough on an individual basis to have been documented in detail. In general, it is known that Corning and Bell were joined by a number of other companies by 1975. These included

Harris Corporation, General Telephone and Electronic (GTE), and International Telephone and Telegraph (ITT), the last having presumably been at work on fiber optics since Kao's paper was published in 1966. Valtec Corp. and Galileo Electro-Optics Corp., two of the smaller companies that had been producing optical fiber for short-fiber applications, also began to produce medium to low-loss fiber in 1975. Because these companies were privately held at the time, very little information on their activities was available. It was known that Galileo Electro-Optics Corp. was incorporated in 1973 and had acquired the Mosaic Fabrications and the Electro-Optics Divisions of Bendix Corporation. Bendix management made no comment on the action. However, the sale resulted in an extraordinary charge to 1973 income. As stated in the notes to 1973 Bendix annual report, "1973 earnings reflect an extraordinary charge of $.6 million after tax on income of $.1 million resulting from the sales of five minor operating units and of equity in three foreign affiliates."

By 1975 a number of electronics companies had begun to be involved in the development of sources and detectors. Considered the technological leader in source and connector technology, RCA had three groups at work on fiber-optic devices, one in Montreal, one in Lancaster, Pennsylvania, and one in Sarnoff Labs, RCA's main research facility in New Jersey. RCA's products were used by Bell Labs in their own development work. Texas Instruments also had a small research program under way and was marketing PIN and Avalanche photodiodes.

In May 1975 the newly created Telecommunications Products Department of Corning Glass began to sell a low-loss fiber-optic cable under the brand name Corguide. Corguide contained six separate fibers, each of which had an attenuation of twenty decibels/km at a wavelength of 820 nm. The cable was sold for $13.50 a meter. High-strength material was incorporated into the cable design, making Corguide the first optical cable sturdy enough for outdoor use. Corguide cables containing differing numbers of fibers offering a range of bandwidths and attenuation levels were introduced shortly thereafter.

In May 1975 Laser Diode Labs (LDL), a newly formed company, became the first company in the industry to sell semiconductor diode lasers on a commercial basis. These lasers, which sold for $200–$300, had a guaranteed lifetime of 500–1,000 hours. Other LDL products included LEDs for fiber optics, conventional LEDs, and gallium arsenide crystal, the material of which LEDs and lasers were made. LDL sold crystal to other manufacturers of semiconductor devices. LDL was considered a technological leader in fiber-optic light sources.

In 1975 two former researchers at Bell Labs, Dr. Franklin W. Dabby and Dr. Ronald B. Chessler, formed Fiber Communications, Inc., to produce low-loss optical fibers. The two founders had worked on development of a vapor phase oxidation process patented by Bell and the new company produced fiber believed to be made using the VPO process. Irving Kahn, former president of Tele-Prompter, was believed to have been one of the venture's early backers.

In May 1975 Galileo Electro-Optics acquired the fiber-optics facilities of Bausch & Lomb. Also in May 1975, two leading connector companies entered the fiber-optics industry in full force. Amphenol RF, a division of Bunker Ramo, which had been supplying connectors for optical cable made by Galileo Electro-Optics, announced that it was prepared to deliver connectors to satisfy any fiber-optic cable requirement. These connectors, modified versions of standard copper cable connectors, could be delivered within six weeks. The Cannon Connector Division of ITT announced that it could supply customized devices for fiber-optic uses for delivery within four months. In August 1975 Corning revealed that it had been working with the Electronic Components Division of Deutsch Co., a connector manufacturer, on the development of a fiber-optic connector that would have losses significantly less than other available connectors, somewhere in the range of 0.3 db per connector. These connectors were to be available on a commercial basis by the end of 1975.[1]

The Defense Department played but a minor role in funding basic research in fiber-optics. In 1975 the Pentagon spent only an estimated $5 million in this area. Most of these funds were spent on a triservice development project testing off-the-shelf fiber-optics components for use in aircraft wiring. In January the Army signed an $80,000 contract with

Corning to develop a fiber-optic cable rugged enough for battlefield use. In July 1975 the Air Force awarded a $1.6 million contract to IBM for a fiber-optic wired navigation and weapons control system for the A–7 jet fighter.

Herbert Elion of Arthur D. Little estimated that approximately $100 million was spent by industry participants on basic research on fiber-optics technology in 1975, a figure he believed would double in 1976.[2] Lee Davenport, president of GTE Labs, indicated that at GTE fiber optics had grown into "a major development project" and that GTE would begin field tests of fiber-optic systems in 1976.[3] It was believed that scientists at Bell Labs considered all of the major technological problems relating to fiber-optics solved and were ready to promote the technology as the "fundamental transmission method for the Bell System."[4]

In 1976 a number of companies seemed to be gearing up for volume production of fiber-optic products. In February Corning began to sell uncabled optical fiber. Fiber prices ranged from $10.50 a meter for small quantities of high-quality graded index fiber down to $1 a meter for thousand-meter orders of high-loss step-index fiber. In April 1976 three other companies announced the commercial availability of standardized optical cable. Du Pont introduced a cable called PFX, which contained seven plastic optical fibers, with an attenuation loss of 470 db/km. The du Pont cable had the advantage of being extremely easy to work with, and it could be used with readily available electronic components. The fiber could simply be pushed into connectors that were available from Amphenol and AMP, and trimmed with a razor blade as necessary. ITT began to sell a standardized line of general-purpose cables made with plastic-clad glass fiber. The cables offered by ITT included lightweight and heavy duty versions and ranged in attenuation from 8 db/km to 50 db/km. Prices ranged from $6 to $15 per meter. The ITT fibers were made by a vapor phase oxidation process. Also in April 1976, Fiber Communications, a company organized in 1975 by two former Bell Labs scientists instrumental in the development of the vapor phase oxidation fiber

[1] Electronics, August 21, 1975, p. 29.

[2] Business Week, September 1, 1975.
[3] Ibid.
[4] Ibid.

production process, began to sell an optical cable called Fiberguide. The cable contained a single all-glass fiber with an attenuation ranging from 25 db/km to 40 db/km at a cost that ranged from $3 to $15 a meter.

In July 1976 Corning brought a suit against ITT alleging patent violation in fiber production.

Valtec Corp. acquired Laser Diode Labs, a manufacturer of fiber-optic light sources, at a cost of $550,000 in 1976. The Electronic Industries Association created a committee to develop standards for fiber-optic connectors in October 1976.

In 1976 fiber-optic technology was sufficiently advanced to support a number of field trials of fiber-optic communications. What was described as "the world's first operational optical fiber communications link" was installed in Dorset, England, in February 1976.[5] The system was assembled with cables, terminals, and connectors developed by ITT's British subsidiary Standard Telecommunications Laboratories. It connected the video-display unit and the central processing unit of a computer owned by the Dorset police department. It had a capacity of ten megabits per second and carried information over a distance of several hundred yards.

In March 1976 Rediffusion Ltd., a British cable television company, installed a 1.4-km fiber-optic trunk line for test purposes in Hastings, England. The system used a fiber-optic cable that had been fabricated by BICC Telecommunication Cables Ltd., a British wire and cable producer, using Corning fiber. Other components were supplied by Plessy Ltd., a British manufacturer of electronics equipment and a major supplier of telecommunications equipment to the British Post Office. In New York, TelePrompter Manhattan Cable Television Corp., the largest cable television operating company in the United States, installed an 800-foot fiber-optic link, which carried signals from microwave equipment on the roof of its corporate headquarters to receiving equipment thirty-four floors below. The signals were then sent to subscribers over existing conventional coaxial cable. The optical cable was assembled by Belden Wire and Cable Corporation with fibers supplied by Fiber Communications.

In 1976 ATT tested a fiber-optic communication system under simulated operating conditions at a Western Electric facility near Atlanta, Georgia. The system, which carried signals at a rate of 44.7 megabits/second, covered a total distance of 10.9 kilometers. The system tested two types of cable, one manufactured by Western Electric and the other by Corning. Bell Labs supplied all other equipment, and Bell labs personnel worked closely with the staff of Western Electric in installing and maintaining the system. The objective of the trial was to determine how well the fiber-optic link interfaced with conventional communication equipment and whether or not the fiber-optic cable could withstand the rigors of an operating environment. Speaking at a public demonstration of the system, George C. Dacey, vice president, Transportation Systems, Bell Labs, commented: "It is possible that in the early 1980s there will be substantial Bell System use of this technology. . . . However, special applications that take advantage of the unique properties of optical fibers . . . . could occur earlier."[6]

In February 1977 the U.S. Army announced that by the mid-1980s it would be replacing copper wire with optical fiber in its tactical communications systems. The Army revealed that it had existing contracts for various projects in optical communications with Corning, ITT Electro-Optical Products Division, ITT Cannon Connector Division, GTE-Sylvania, RCA, and Valtec's Laser Diode Labs. This announcement began what observers considered a major U.S. military commitment to fiber-optic technology. A substantial increase in government contracts followed the initial Army announcement.

In May 1977 General Telephone & Electronics began a year-long field trial of optical equipment carrying actual phone calls over a 5.6-mile stretch between a long-distance switching center in Long Beach, California, and a local exchange in Artesia, California. The system transmitted at a rate of 1.544 megabits/second, a rate comparable to that of conventional local exchange links used by all telephone companies. The system operated at an 815-nm wavelength using LED light sources and Avalanche photodiodes as receivers. The optical cable, developed by General Cable Corp., used six

[5] *Laser Focus*, February 1976.

[6] *Electronics*, July 22, 1976, p. 44.

graded-index optical fibers supplied by Corning. The system was designed and developed by GTE Laboratories located in Waltham, Massachusetts. Based on the results of the field test, Lee L. Davenport, President of GTE Labs, commented that he expected GTE to use optical transmission systems on a permanent basis in the early 1980s on trunk routes linking switching centers in metropolitan areas.[7] In August GTE installed a second system in Hawaii.

On May 11, 1977, ATT began operation of an optical communication system in downtown Chicago. The system carried voice and video signals between two telephone central offices 1 mile apart, and voice and data signals between a central office and a large business customer's location one-half mile away. The system used LED and laser light sources interchangeably, and a cable consisting of eight ribbons each containing twelve step-index glass fibers. The components, connectors, and cables were designed and manufactured by Bell Labs and Western Electric. Problems of installation were handled cooperatively by Bell Labs, Western Electric, and Illinois Bell engineers. The system used components and repeaters that had been tested at the Atlanta experiment. The Chicago test would determine whether the optical communication system could withstand the rigors of actual operating conditions, and if the practical problems of installing and maintaining inherently fragile optical communication systems in congested metropolitan areas could be solved.

Finally, Valtec Corp. and CommScope,[8] a cable manufacturer, installed an interoffice link for the Central Telephone and Utilities Corporation, an independent telecommunications operating company. The 2.6-km link was located in Las Vegas, Nevada, and was inaugurated at the December Convention of the U.S. Independent Telephone Association. It was used to handle telephone traffic in the MGM Grand Hotel, where the convention was being held. In England, an optical telecommunication system was installed north of London by Standard Telephone and Cables, Limited, for the British phone system.

A series of further competitive developments occurred during 1977. In February 1977 Fiber Communications, Inc., merged with Times Wire and Cable, a producer of conventional cable that was a subsidiary of Insilco Company. The new company's assets totaled $20 million to $25 million. Insilco retained 51 percent of the newly formed company's stock. The company would emphasize optical cable for cable television applications. In September 1977 Galileo Electro-Optics Corp. acquired the wire and cable business of the Revere Corporation of America for an undisclosed sum. The wire and cable business had an estimated $3 million in sales. Revere Corporation had been a subsidiary of Neptune International, a manufacturer of measuring equipment and waste treatment systems.

In April 1977 Canada Wire and Cable Company acquired 13 percent of Valtec Corp. outstanding stock, in a deal said to be worth $1 million. The agreement with Canada Wire and Cable included an option to purchase 100,000 additional shares, which was valid until 1978. Canada Wire, a subsidiary of Noranda Mines, a natural resource company with sales of $1.4 billion, was the largest producer of power wire and cable in Canada. In December 1977 Valtec acquired CommScope Company, a conventional telecommunications cable company with sales of $14.3 million in 1976. In discussing the CommScope acquisition, Valtec's Godbey described it as giving the company nearly total vertical integration; the only element missing was in-house detector capability.[9] Godbey said he himself believed that vertical integration would be necessary to compete in optical communications: "I envision the next five years in the optical communications business as a period for complete turnkey systems. The customer doesn't want to get involved in the disciplines of lasers, couplings, fibers. . . . He [or she] will say, 'I have an interface here and an interface there. Give me a system that can go from A to B.' "[10] In addition, Valtec had issued an industrial revenue bond for $750,000 in 1977 to add 30,000 square feet of fiber production capacity. These would double existing production capacity.

In June 1977 General Optronics Corporation was

---

[7] *Electronics*, May 12, 1977, p. 34.

[8] CommScope had been purchased by its employees in 1976 from Superior Continental Corporation, an independent telephone equipment supplier.

[9] "Valtec's Big Push in Optical Communications," *Optical Spectra*, March 1976.

[10] *Ibid.*

established to manufacture diode lasers for optical communications. The chairman of the new company was Irving B. Kahn, a director of Times-Fiber Communications and the president was C. J. Wang, formerly of Hewlett-Packard, the developer of the double heterostructure gallium-arsenide laser. The senior production engineer of the new company was Robert E. Albano, formerly of Laser Diode Labs.

Northern Telecom, Ltd., the manufacturing subsidiary of Bell Northern, Canada's chief telephone operating company, formally became a factor in optical fibers on September 16, 1977, with the announcement of the formation of a new Optical Systems Division. This marked the culmination of four years of research conducted jointly by Northern Telecom and Bell Northern Research Laboratories, a research subsidiary owned by Northern Telecom and Bell Canada. The new division was to occupy space in a 1-million-square-foot cable plant operated by Northern Telecom Canada, Ltd. at Lachine. Starting with only a handful of experts, the division had as its ultimate objective to develop, manufacture, and market fiber-optic systems for sale in Canada and the United States.

In December 1977 Corning Glass Works announced that it would convert half of a 77,000-square-foot facility in Wilmington, N.C., to full-scale production of optical fibers, which Corning officially called "optical waveguides." Scheduled for completion in September 1978, the new plant would be capable of producing ten times more optical fiber than Corning's 6,000-square-foot pilot plant in Erwin, New York. At the time of the announcement, Leroy Wilson, head of the Electronic Products Division of Corning, stated that Corning expected optical waveguide production to become a "significant" business.[11]

Also in December 1977, Corning Glass and Siemens A.G., a West German electronics and telecommunications equipment company, formed Siecor Optical Cables, Inc. Siecor's product line included optical fibers from Corning and cabling and components from Siemens. Siecor's cables were manufactured in West Germany using Corning fibers. Manufacturing operations would be moved to the United States when justified by demand. Siecor also offered splicing, testing, and installation equipment.

The U.S. National Committee of the International Electrotechnical Commission, an affiliate of the National Standards Institute, met in Moscow in June 1977 to set standards for fiber-optics used in telecommunications equipment. These included standards for physical and electrical characteristics of fiber-optic cables, light and signal parameters, and splicing and coupling techniques.

In 1978 a great deal of attention was focused on the fiber-optics industry. Periodicals such as *Electronics, Laser Focus,* and *Electronic News* began to cover industry developments extensively. News included reports of new products, new applications, corporate developments, and the results of an ever increasing number of field trials. GTE, ATT, and ITT began to advertise fiber optics as a dramatic new technological breakthrough in which they were playing a major role. These advertisements appeared on television as well as in the popular periodicals such as *Time* and *Newsweek*.

In January 1978 a new company, Electro-Optic Devices Corporation, was formed to design and manufacture connectors, couplers, and terminating devices for fiber-optic links. Times-Fiber would be the principal customer. Irving B. Kahn, a director and stockholder of Times-Fiber, also held a large portion of Electro-Optic Devices' stock.

In February 1978 Canada Wire and Cable announced the formation of a fiber-optics subsidiary, Canstar Communications. Canstar had two operating divisions: systems and products. The systems division could design, assemble, and install fiber-optic communication systems. The products division manufactured optical fibers[12] and cables. A preproduction facility had been established early in 1977. Canada Wire had previously been involved in several fiber-optic system tests in electrical power stations. Early in 1978, Corning Glass and Canstar signed a supply agreement for delivery of up to 20,000 kilometers of Corning fiber over the next two years. Canstar would use Corning fiber until its own fiber production process became competitive. Canstar would also be contracting out some cable

[11] *Laser Focus,* December 1977.

[12] In 1974, Canada Wire had acquired exclusive license to a low-loss optical fiber process developed by two professors at Catholic University.

production. Canstar indicated that the fiber and cable would be used in projected Canadian optical communications turnkey systems installations.

In March 1978 three former Valtec employees established FiberOptics Technology Corporation. The company planned to supply low- to medium-attenuation fibers, cables, and assemblies. Fiber-Optics Technology would also supply fiber-drawing machinery at a cost of $100,000.

In March 1978 Canada's principal telephone company, Bell Canada, announced that it was testing a fiber-optic link between two of its switching centers in Montreal. The experimental link was installed jointly with Northern Telecom. The fibers were fabricated at Bell-Northern, and the cable was produced by Northern Telecom. Other Canadian field tests during 1978 included an 8.8-km link to transmit cable TV signals installed by Harris Corporation and a 5.1-km phone line for the Alberta Government Telephone System, also designed and installed by Harris. Harris's previous fiber-optic systems work had been for the military.

Speaking at a computer and telecommunications conference in April 1978, R. J. Allio, President of the Canstar Communications Division of Canada Wire and Cable, predicted that five or six computer companies would begin to use fiber-optic data links within a year. His prediction was based on dealings with a number of U.S. computer companies that were testing Canstar cable. In June 1978 Valtec Corp. announced plans for a public offering of 400,000 shares of common stock.

In June 1978 the fiber-optics subcommittee of the International Electrotechnical Commission met to ratify nine proposed standards for fiber-optics product definitions, performance requirements and test procedures. The proposals did not include specifications for the size, dimensions, or physical characteristics of fiber-optic components. The proposed standards were based on U.S. standards being developed by the Electronic Industries Association's committee on fiber-optics standards. The EIA subcommittee included representatives from Corning, Hughes Aircraft, IBM, Belden Wire and Cable, and Amphenol, to name but a few.

In July 1978 a conference on fiber-optics was held in Boston, reportedly the first conference and trade show devoted exclusively to fiber optics. Some industry participants chose this opportunity to in-troduce new products. Siecor demonstrated a new optical cable splicing machine. A new line of low-loss fiber was introduced by Optelcon, Inc., a recently established fiber maker. Both Valtec and Dolan-Jenner Industries, a small fiber-optics company, introduced fiber-optic links for short-distance, high-volume applications. A fiber made in France by Quartz & Silice, a French glass manufacturer, was shown by its new American subsidiary, Quartz Products Corporation. Companies using optical fiber, in cable manufacture, with attenuation losses as low as 5 db/km, included 3M Company and Belden Cable Corp. The 3M Company introduced a 30-meter data link that used a flat optical cable, the first flat optical cable to be offered as a standard commercial product. Flat cable, in which the conducting strands lay side by side, was used for certain computer applications. The fiber used in this cable was supplied by five outside vendors.

In July 1978 the Belden Corporation announced the formation of a new group within the company to produce fiber-optics products that would introduce a line of optical cable using fibers supplied by Quartz Products and Corning. Belden made metal wire and cable products for the electronic, automotive, electrical, and consumer markets.

In July Motorola, Inc., began to sell semiconductor sources and detectors for fiber-optic applications in the $2–$3 price range. The initial offerings were adaptations of existing products and could be used only for very low bandwidth, short-distance systems. The products were designed to fit into fiber connectors available from AMP. Prices were kept low to encourage engineers to experiment with the new technology. Applications would be in low bandwidth areas such as industrial process control. Management indicated that the company might look at integrating optical components into complete transmitters and receivers for high data rates. To do so Motorola would have to develop more sophisticated fiber-optic devices.[13]

A new optical fiber company, Fiberguide Industries, was formed in July 1978 by two former members of the Bell Labs staff. The company would produce glass and plastic fibers and some specialized fiber-optic devices.

Also in July 1978, Charles H. Elmendorf, assis-

_____
[13] *Laser Focus,* July 1978.

tant vice president of ATT, announced that "our experience (with the Chicago system) has convinced us that a lightwave system should be one of our transmission options for heavy volume routes between telephone switching offices."[14] The Bell System planned to place its first optical link in regular telephone service before 1981.

Fiber-Optics Industry Participants

As Exhibit 17–2 illustrates, well over one hundred companies could be considered industry participants, measured by having at least one product touted as an entry in fiber-optics. However, attention focused on a relatively small number of companies belonging to one of four groups that seemed to industry observers to be of special significance to future industry development. The first group included the producers of low-loss optical fiber. Only six U.S. companies offered fibers with an attenuation of under 20 db/km in early 1979: Corning Glass Works, Fiber Optic Cable Corporation, Galileo Electro-Optics, International Telephone and Telegraph (ITT), TimesFiber, and Valtec. All but Fiber Optic Cable Corporation, a newly formed and almost completely unknown company, are described below. Corning is profiled in a companion case.[15] Financial profiles of these firms are presented in Exhibit 17–3. Three non-U.S. organizations also sold low-loss fibers: Northern Telecom of Canada (profiled below); Quartz & Silice, a French glass manufacturer; and Schott, a West German glass manufacturer.

A second group of significant industry participants were electronics companies. In this group were Hewlett-Packard (H–P), Texas Instruments, RCA, Rockwell, Motorola, Fairchild, and Honeywell. Each of these companies marketed either sources, detectors, modulators, or power sources for fiber-optic applications. Both H–P and TI marketed fiber-optic data links using purchased optical cable. H–P had been among the first in the industry to market such a device and had one of the best links available in 1979. Both H–P and TI had excellent reputations in semiconductor technology,

and industry observers and participants speculated widely about their level of interest in and commitment to fiber-optic technology. TI engineers had participated in a number of fiber-optics technical conferences, but company spokesmen were evasive about the nature of the work being done at TI.

A third group comprised the conventional wire and cable companies, including Anaconda, Belden, Brand Rex, General Cable, Okanite, Phelps Dodge, and Superior Cable, to name but a few. It was known that a number of these companies were seriously considering manufacture and sale of optical cables. General Cable had been involved in the industry for several years and marketed a line of optical cable made with Corning fiber. General Cable made telecommunications cable and produced most of the cable required by General Telephone and Electronics, of which it had once been a subsidiary. General Cable had participated in several major fiber-optic field trials. Belden Cable supplied a diversified line of cable for telephone, computer, power, and other use. In 1979 Belden offered an optical cable made from fiber purchased from Quartz Products, the U.S. subsidiary of Quartz & Silice.

A fourth group of companies consisted of potential entrants. Rumors circulated constantly within the industry that certain well-known companies were about to enter. Any large conglomerate was a possible candidate in the eyes of some observers. A group within Exxon Enterprises, a subsidiary of Exxon Corporation located at Elmsford, New York, was known to be developing photodetectors for fiber-optic applications. Although very little was known about the venture, this rumor lent credibility to the belief that powerful new competitors could have a dramatic impact on industry development.

THE BELL SYSTEM (ATT)

More than one hundred years old, the Bell System comprised twenty-three operating companies, Western Electric, its manufacturing subsidiary, and Bell Telephone Laboratories, a research unit owned jointly by ATT and Western Electric. ATT dominated the U.S. telecommunications service market. ATT reported income of $4 billion on sales of $30.4 billion for the first three quarters of 1978. This was earned by providing telecommunications service.

[14] *Ibid.*
[15] See Case 18.

Western Electric earned $490 million on sales of $8.1 billion in 1977 through the sales of equipment for telecommunications. Ninety-six percent of Western's sales were to Bell's operating companies, 1.5 percent were to the U.S. Government, and the remaining 2.5 percent were to other customers. Western Electric supplied a full line of telecommunications equipment and was the largest producer of such equipment in the world. Western Electric also acted as the centralized purchasing agent for equipment purchased by Bell's operating companies to supplement the Western line or more often to provide alternative sources. Outside purchases totaled more than $1 billion in 1978.

Since ATT had been forced to divest itself of its international operations in the 1920s, Western had served only the U.S. telecommunications market, the largest in the world. However, in 1977 Western had resumed international activities when the company won a contract to install a microwave relay system for the Saudi Arabian telecommunications network. Company spokesmen had indicated that they hoped to expand international activities in the future.

Bell Labs employed more than 17,000 people in basic and applied research in telecommunications, including 2,000 Ph.D.s Bell Labs' research budget had totaled $902 million in 1978 and was allocated as shown in Table 17–1. Bell scientists had made important discoveries in the physical sciences and mathematics. Significant contributions had been made in the development of vacuum tubes, transistors, integrated circuits, lasers, and digital electronics, to name but a few areas. Bell Labs assigned

TABLE 17–1. Bell Labs Expenditures by Technical Area

	%
Switching systems	19.9
Defense systems	2.7
Business information systems	12.1
Research and patents	12.3
Electronics technology	17.2
Computer technical design	1.7
Network planning and customer service	16.3
Transmission systems	16.6
	100%

Source: Bell Labs, "Facts About Bell Laboratories."

15 percent of its staff to laboratories located at seven Western Electric manufacturing facilities.

Western Electric, Bell Labs, and operating company personnel had worked together on the largest and most recent of ATT's fiber-optics projects. In this and earlier tests of fiber-optic systems, ATT had used components and fiber developed and manufactured internally. These tests had also included experimentation with equipment manufactured by other industry participants, most notably Corning fiber, Bell Northern Research light sources, and detectors from RCA.

Western Electric had pilot fiber and optical cable production at the Western Electric facility in Atlanta, Georgia. Although the company did not reveal its production processes, it was believed to utilize a vapor phase oxidation process to produce a low-loss graded-index glass fiber. Industry observers estimated Western's optical cable production at 500 km in 1975, 1,500 km in 1976, and 3,000 in 1977.

E. I. du PONT de NEMOURS

Du Pont had 1977 sales of $9.4 billion and participated in four lines of business: chemicals (18 percent of sales), plastics (23 percent), specialty products (27 percent), and fibers (33 percent). Du Pont sold basic commodity-type chemicals, resins, coatings, adhesives, plastic wrap, and fabric for use in apparel, carpeting, and industrial applications. Specialty products included metal and glass materials used in electronic components and equipment for the manufacture of printed circuit boards. In 1972 du Pont had acquired Berg Electronics, a producer of electronic connectors. Although many of du Pont's products were commodities, a large number were proprietary products, including "Kelvar" a high-strength material used as a strengthening element in conventional as well as fiber-optic cable construction. Du Pont emphasized the role of research and development in the success of the company. Perhaps the best-known products developed and at one time patented by du Pont were nylon and orlon synthetic fabrics. The company was known to be extremely secretive about its operations.

In addition to Crofon, a very high-loss fiber which du Pont had manufactured, cabled, and sold to the automobile industry for dashboard illumination since 1965, du Pont manufactured a line of medium- to high-loss fiber-optic cable called the PFX series. PFX cables offered either an all-plastic fiber with an attenuation loss of 400 db/km or a plastic-clad lower-loss fiber with an attenuation of 60 db/km. The high-loss fiber cable could be used in applications involving distances up to 50 meters. The medium-loss cable could be used for distances up to several hundred meters.

Du Pont fibers had large numerical apertures and could be used with inexpensive light sources and detectors. They could be connected easily, and du Pont's fiber-optic cables were extremely rugged. They could be walked on and even run over by trucks without injury. Dr. Kenneth Kamm of du Pont's new business development staff commented that "many [computer manufacturers] plan to use plastic fibers in their first optical data links because of ease of field service and durability."[16] He also indicated that du Pont was not planning to manufacture low-loss fiber and cables.

GALILEO ELECTRO-OPTICS CORP.

Galileo Electro-Optics was a privately held company, founded in 1973. Sales in 1977 were believed to have been $15 million, up from $6.5 million in 1975. Galileo's products could be grouped into three categories: electrical and electronic components, fiber-optic products, and electrical wire and cable. Products for short-fiber applications, such as faceplates and image intensifiers, were believed to account for a significant portion of Galileo's sales. Electrical and electronic components included fiber-optic sources, detectors, and auxiliary equipment for fiber-optic systems. These were made at a facility in Wanamassa, New Jersey, but no additional information on this activity was available.

Galileo's fiber-optics activities were located at a 135,000-square-foot facility in Sturbridge, Massachusetts, also company headquarters. The company produced six different types of fiber: two low-loss, two medium-loss, and two high-loss fibers under the name Galite. High-loss fibers were made from plastic. A different production process was used in making each different type of fiber. These production processes included multiple fiber drawing, rod and tube, stratified melt, a laser drawing process, and vapor phase oxidation. The company was active in the marketing of high-loss fiber-bundles. In 1978 the company had introduced Galite 6,000, a low-loss graded-index fiber made by a vapor phase oxidation process. Galileo had full systems capability; that is, the company manufactured all parts of a fiber-optic system except connectors. Galileo also manufactured short-fiber products at the Sturbridge facility.

After its acquisition in June 1977 the Revere cabling facility was redesignated the Optical and Electronic Cable Division. This division would continue to produce insulated and specialty copper cable in addition to optical cables made from Galite fiber.

Dr. Raymond E. Jaeger directed Galileo's research and development, assisted by a staff of some fifty engineers. Dr. Jaeger was formerly a research manager in fiber optics for Bell Telephone Labs.

Galileo had not participated in any major field trials. The company concentrated its effort in the sale of high- to medium-loss cable and fiber-optic data links.

INTERNATIONAL TELEPHONE AND TELEGRAPH (ITT)

ITT, the largest supplier of telecommunications equipment in the international (non-U.S.) market, had been created in 1925 when ATT was forced to divest its international operations. In 1977 ITT had earned $562 million on total sales of $13,146 million in five lines of business, which included Telecommunications and Electronics (28 percent of sales); Engineered Products (26 percent), Consumer Products (19 percent), Natural Resources (6 percent), and Insurance and Finance (21 percent). Sixty percent of total sales were international. ITT had a strong position in the European telecommunications market, with European sales accounting for two-thirds of ITT's telecommunications business.

ITT's activity in telecommunications included sale of telecommunications equipment (23 percent of total corporate sales), operation of telecommunications systems (1 percent), and defense and avionics (4 percent). Telecommunications equipment included the full range of equipment for in-

[16] "How Du Pont Faces the Fiber-Optics Future," *Optical Spectra*, April 1977.

stalling and maintaining telephone systems as well as interconnect equipment. In 1977, with the acquisition of North Electric, ITT began to compete in the U.S. telecommunications equipment market. In addition, ITT had installed advanced electronic switching systems for South Korea and Nigeria to help these nations develop modern telecommunications systems.

ITT's telecommunications system operations provided international telegraph, telex, telephone, and other communications service by submarine cable, satellite, and radio. Defense and avionics activities (4 percent of total corporate sales) included the manufacture, sale, installation, maintenance, and operation of military telecommunications and electronics equipment, primarily for the U.S. Government.

ITT's Electro-Optic Products Division in Roanoke, Virginia, coordinated companywide activities in fiber optics. Eleven units within the company were involved in fiber optics as either manufacturers or consumers. The Roanoke facility produced fiber, cables, sources, and detectors. The ITT–Cannon Electric Division in Santa Ana, California, was considered by some industry observers to be the best fiber-optic connector supplier in the industry. Separate ITT divisions had cooperated on field trials and government contracts in the installation of complete systems.

ITT was very secretive about its activities in fiber optics. With the exception of Charles Kao, who had moved to Roanoke headquarters, no one from ITT participated in industry conferences or trade shows. It was known that ITT was producing medium- to low-loss fiber using primarily a chemical vapor deposition process.

NORTHERN TELECOM, LTD.

Northern Telecom, a subsidiary of Bell Canada, was the largest supplier of telecommunications equipment in Canada, with an estimated 75 percent market share and second only to Western Electric in North America. Northern manufactured a full range of telecommunications products, computer-related equipment, and selected electronic components. These products were sold to Bell Canada, the largest Canadian telecommunications service company, independent telephone companies in the United States, government-controlled telephone operating companies abroad, and private buyers of interconnect equipment. In 1971 Northern had established a U.S. subsidiary, Northern Telecom, Inc., which was aggressively pursuing sales in the U.S. market. Canadian sales had declined from 72 percent of total sales in 1971 to 60 percent in 1978. U.S. sales had risen from 4 to 22 percent of total sales in the same time period.

Northern and Bell Canada jointly owned Bell Northern Research (BNR) which was believed to have the most extensive R&D facilities and budget (an estimated $75 million in 1978) of all Canadian corporations. BNR was known to have devoted considerable effort to developing digital communications equipment and was fully committed to applying technological developments in this area to products for private customers. As a result, Northern, using equipment designed by BNR, was a technological leader in the telephone interconnect market. In addition, Bell Northern had signed a licensing agreement with Western Electric Company, which allowed the company to use all patents issued on Western Electric inventions as well as any patents subsequently issued on inventions made prior to that date (including fiber-optics) prior to June 30, 1980.

The Optical Systems Division of Northern Telecom manufactured, on a limited scale, three low-loss optical fibers. The production process was believed to be vapor phase oxidation. The division also manufactured lasers, LEDs, detectors, connectors, splices, and data links. Some industry observers considered the LEDs developed for use in fiber-optic systems by BNR, and manufactured by Northern, to be the best available in 1978.

TIMES–FIBER COMMUNICATIONS, INC.,/ GENERAL OPTRONICS/ ELECTRO-OPTICS DEVICES

Times-Fiber was formed in 1977 by the merger of an Insilco subsidiary, Times Wire and Cable, with Fiber Communications, Inc. Times Wire, established in 1945 and a leading supplier of coaxial cable to the CATV industry, was believed to have a market share of 50 percent in coaxial cable for CATV use. Fiber Communications, Inc., founded by two former Bell Labs scientists, produced low-loss, graded-index optical fiber. Insilco, a conglomerate known to give its subsidiaries almost total independence in running their own operations, owned 51 percent of Times-Fiber. The rest of the stock was privately held. One well-known stockholder and director was Irving B. Kahn, former president of TelePrompTer. Interlocking ownership tied Times-Fiber to two other recently formed companies: General Optronics, which produced lasers and LEDs, and Electro-Optics Devices Corporation, a manufacturer of fiber-optic connectors, couplers, and beam splitters. It was known that Times-Fiber also owned a portion of General Optronics stock. Irving Kahn was chairman of both companies and was also believed to be a large stockholder.

Times-Fiber's 1977 sales were estimated at $25 million on assets of $21 million, including a net worth of $14.7 million. Total company employment was about 500 persons. In 1978 Times-Fiber had manufacturing facilities in Phoenix, Arizona; Hayeville, North Carolina; Chatham, Virginia; and Meriden and Wallingford, Connecticut. Only the Connecticut plants produced optical fiber and cable, with the other plants producing copper wire and cable. Times-Fiber sold its conventional products through commissioned salespeople and manufacturers' representatives who were located in forty-four offices in twenty-six states.

Time's fiber-optic products were low-loss optical fiber and cable, including step- and graded-index glass fibers with attenuation losses of 10 db/km. Times-Fiber did not reveal its fiber production processes. It was believed that an outside vapor phase oxidation process was used for loss graded-index fiber production. Times-Fiber had a license agreement with Western Electric, which gave the company access to fiber production technology developed by Dr. Chessler and Dr. Dabby while at Bell Labs. Dr. Chessler and Dr. Dabby headed Times-Fiber's research and development staff of approximately a dozen people.

General Optronics was located in Plainfield, New Jersey. Company president was C. J. Wang, formerly of Hewlett-Packard. The research staff included a former researcher of Laser Diode Labs. The company produced high-quality diode lasers and LEDs. General Optronics had publicly announced plans to automate the laser production process. Although complete automation seemed somewhat remote, the company had apparently succeeded in automating parts of the process.

Electro-Optic Devices had its headquarters in New York City and a 5,000-square-foot manufacturing facility in Wallingford, Connecticut. Management had announced that it would direct much of its R&D effort to designing fiber-optic systems for Master Antenna Television (MATV) and for security applications in multiple-dwelling units. In MATV systems each television within a building was connected to a rooftop antenna by coaxial or fiber-optic cable to receive either broadcast or CATV signals.

VALTEC

With sales of $30.9 million in 1977, Valtec Corp. was a publicly held, vertically integrated manufacturer of fiber-optic products. In addition to a full line of products for fiber-optic communications applications, Valtec manufactured fiber-optic signs, fiber-optic lamps, and precision optical products. According to the 1977 annual report, commercial and industrial applications represented 80 percent of total corporate sales, while government and consumer sales accounted for an additional 8 and 12 percent of total sales, respectively. According to this same source, communications products (believed to include fiber-optic signs) represented 61 percent of total sales and electro-optics the remaining 39 percent.

Valtec was founded in 1967 as the Electro Fiberoptics Corporation by Valtec's president, James Godbey, who had died unexpectedly in 1979. The original company had $200,000 in equity capital and a staff of five. The company had acquired a precision optical components and coatings manufacturer, The Valpey Corporation, in 1972, and changed its name to Valtec. In 1977 Theodore S. Valpey, Jr. was company chairman.

In 1979 the company had its headquarters in West Boylston, Massachusetts, and employed approximately 650 people at facilities located in West Boylston, Massachusetts; Waltham, Massachusetts; Holliston, Massachusetts; Metuchen, New Jersey; Catawba, North Carolina; and Costa Mesa, California. Valtec's fiber-optics products included fiber and cable, sources, and auxiliary electronic equipment as well as short-fiber products.

Valtec manufactured high-, medium- and low-loss optical fibers. Valtec offered step- and graded-index glass fibers with attenuation losses as low as 10 db/km. Total production for fiber in 1978 was believed to be 5,000 km. Valtec had entered into a licensing agreement with Western Electric in mid-1976 that permitted Valtec to use Bell System patents for production of fiber, cable, and associated equipment, and Valtec was believed to use a vapor phase oxidation process for low-loss fiber production. Rod and tube was used for medium- and high-loss fiber production.

Valtec offered three low- and medium-loss cable varieties in 1977: heavy-duty for demanding field environments, medium for intrabuilding and vehicular communications systems, and light-duty cable for laboratory use. Valtec's unit, CommScope, was manufacturing fiber-optic as well as conventional cable in its Catawba plant in 1979, and Valtec was expected to discontinue cabling operations at the West Boylston plant. Valtec's Laser Diode Labs unit supplied fiber-optic sources for use by Valtec in the manufacture of data links. LDL also sold light sources, LEDs and lasers to other industry participants. LDL had, however, sharply curtailed sales of the gallium arsenide crystal.

EXHIBIT 17-1. *Fiber-Optic Industry Sales (millions of $)*

	High-Loss Fiber Sales	*Fiber for Communications*	*Fiber Optic Systems for Communications (Including Labor and All Materials Except Fiber)*	*Total*
1975	5	1	4	10
1976	5.7	2	6	13.75
1977	6	5	11	22
1978	7	6	24	37

SOURCE: Estimates by industry participants.

EXHIBIT 17-2. *Manufacturers of Fiber-Optic Products*

Optical Fibers and Cables (includes international)

AEG-Telefunken	Hitachi Cable
American Optical	ITT
Anaconda Wire & Cable	Keystone Optical Fibers
Bell-Northern	Klinger
Belden	Mitsubishi Rayon
BICC	Nippon Electric Company
Cables de Lyon	Optics Research
Canada Wire and Cable	Pilkington Brothers
Corning Glass	Pirelli Industries
Dainichi Nippon Cables	Poly-Optics
Dolan-Jenner Industries	Quartz Products
Du Pont	Quartz & Silice
Dyonics	Rank Precision Industries
Fiber Optic Cable	Schott
Fort	Siecor
Fujikura Cable Works	Siemens
Furukawa Electric	Sumitomo
Galileo Electro-Optics	Thomson Brandt
General Cable	Times Fiber Communication
	Valtec

Fiber Optic Connectors or Splices

AMP	Hellerman-Deutsch
Aio Sansho	ITT
Bell-Northern	Meret
Bunker Ramo	NEC
Deutsch	Opto Micron Industries
Electro-Fiberoptics	Sealectro
Fujitsu	Spectronics
Furukawa Electric	Thomas & Betts Corp.
	Thomson & CSF

LED or Laser Light Sources

AEG-Telefunken	Monsanto
Bell-Northern	National Semiconductor
Fairchild Semiconductor	NEC
Fujitsu	Philips
Galileo	Plessey
General Optronics	RCA
Hewlett Packard	Sepetronics
Hitachi	Tektronics
ITT	Texas Instruments
Laser Diode Laboratories	Thomson & CSF
Meret	Times Fiber Communications
	Valtec

PIN or APD Photodetectors

AEG-Telefunken	Hughes Aircraft
American Electronics Laboratories	Infrared Industries
ASEA-HAFO	ITT
Bell-Northern	Meret
Bell & Howell	Motorola Semiconductor
Centronic	NEC
Devar	Nuclear Equipment Corporation
EG&G	Optoelectronics
Electro-Nuclear Laboratories	Philips
EMI Electronics	Plessey
Fairchild Semiconductor	Quadri
Ferranti	Quantrad

EXHIBIT 17-2. *(continued)*

PIN or APD Photodetectors

Fort	Raytheon
Fujitsu	RCA
Galileo	Spectronics
General Electric	Texas Instruments
General Instrument	Thomason & CSF
Hewlett Packard	Twentieth Century Electronics
	United Detector Technology

SOURCE: Manufacturer's product sales literature.

EXHIBIT 17-3. *Financial Profiles of American Producers of Low-loss Optical Fiber*
($ in millions)

	Total Sales		Net Income	Total Assets	D/E	R&D Expenditures
Corning Glass Works						
1974	1,051		48	987	.17	38
1975	939		31	921	.18	42
1976	1,026		84	1,027	.34	49
1977	1,120		92	1,081	.36	55
1978	1,252		82	1,211	.17	55
E. I. du Pont de Nemours						
1974	6,910		404	5,980.3	.17	344
1975	7,222		272	6,425.0	.18	336
1976	3,861		459	7,017.8	.23	353
1977	9,435		545	7,430.6	.23	367
1978[a]	7,904		567	7,980	.20	NA
Galileo Electro-Optics Corp. E[b]						
1974	4.5		NA[c]	3.7	NA	NA
1975	6.5		NA	4.4	2	NA
1976	NA		NA	NA	NA	NA
1977	15.		NA	NA	NA	NA
1978	NA		NA	NA	NA	NA
International Telephone and Telegraph						
1974	11,154		451	10,697	.48	452
1975	11,368		398	10,408	.51	483
1976	11,764		489	11,070	.50	525
1977	13,146		562	12,286	.46	608
1978[a]	10,562		472	13,702	.29	NA
Northern Telecom (Canada)		*U.S. Sales*				
1974	970.7	90	53.8	568	.36	44.1
1975	1,018.4	93	67.5	590	.20	49.1
1976	1,112.0	112	77.1	706	.14	61.5
1977	1,268.6	210	85.3	811	.11	68.5
1978	1,425	310E[b]	NA	NA	NA	NA
Times Fiber Communications E						
1974	NA		NA	NA	NA	NA
1975	NA		NA	NA	NA	NA
1976	NA		NA	NA	NA	NA
1977	25		NA	21	.30	NA
1978	NA		NA	NA	NA	NA
Valtec						
1974	6.8		.134	NA	.58	NA
1975	6.6		.158	NA	.48	NA
1976	15.8		.688	NA	.70	.213
1977	30.9		1.3	17	.52	.383
1978	NA		NA	NA	NA	NA
Western Electric						
1974	7,382		315	5,240	.30	394
1975	6,590		107	5,000	.28	413
1976	6,931		217	5,178	.20	391
1977	8,135		490	5,876	.19	440
1978[a]	NA		NA	NA	NA	NA

[a] Three quarters only.
[b] E = Estimate.
[c] NA = Not available.

CASE 18
The Fiber-Optics Industry in 1978: Corning Glass Works

Corning Glass Works had been a pioneer in fiber-optics and was a leading participant in the emerging fiber optics industry in 1978. This case describes Corning as a company, the history of Corning's activity in fiber optics, and its position in fiber optics in 1978. Background information on fiber-optics products, technology, markets, and competition is given in Cases 16 and 17.

Corporate Profile

Corning Glass Works was the leading producer of products from glass and related materials in the United States, having produced glass products since 1851. Armory Houghton, Jr., Corning's chairman, was the fifth generation of his family to head the company. The Houghton family still owned 16 percent of the stock of the company; the remaining 84 percent was publicly traded on the New York Stock Exchange.

In 1978 Corning produced a wide variety of products from glass, glass-ceramics, and corollary technologies. Consumer products (26.6 percent of sales in 1977) included tableware and housewares made from heat-resistant glass and glass-ceramic compositions. Housewares were marketed under the brand names Corning Ware, Corelle, and Pyrex. Consumer durable good components (30 percent of 1977 sales) were sold to other manufacturers for use in the manufacture of such products as television tubes and lighting products such as light bulbs, fluorescent lights, and automobile headlights. Capital goods components (20 percent of 1977 sales) were sold to other manufacturers for use in products linked to capital investment spending. Corning products included chemical process systems, electronic products, and optical waveguides. Optical waveguides was Corning's name for fiber optics. Health and science products (20 percent of 1977 sales) included medical instruments, diagnostic testing systems, laboratory equipment, and optical and opthalmic products.

Corning also owned partial interest in three non-consolidated U.S. corporations: a 50 percent interest in Dow Corning Corporation, a manufacturer of silicones; a 50 percent interest in Pittsburg Corning, a manufacturer of glass blocks for architectural use; and a 25.2 percent interest in Owen's Corning Fiberglass, a leading manufacturer of fiberglass products, primarily used for insulation. International sales, including exports, equaled 20 percent of total Corning sales in 1977. Principal international manufacturing subsidiaries were located in France and the United Kingdom. Corning's international activities were frequently joint ventures.

Only once had Corning significantly departed from its traditional lines of business. In 1962 the company acquired Signetics, a manufacturer of integrated circuits. In 1975, after thirteen years of trying to compete in the electronics industry, Corning sold the subsidiary at a pretax loss of $9.5 million.

Most of Corning's products were the result of extensive research and development by the company. In 1978 approximately $55 million was spent on basic research, development, and engineering, with more than 1,300 people employed in the research function. Corning's expertise in glass technology was renowned, and the company was frequently asked by potential customers to develop glass products for specialized applications.

Corning's stock was being traded at ten times earnings in 1978, compared to as much as forty-eight times earnings in the early 1970s. A major reason was that sales of glass for television picture tubes, which had accounted for nearly one-half of all sales and three-quarters of total profit in the 1960s and early 1970s, was less than 10 percent of sales in 1978. Japanese penetration of the U.S. TV market had hurt Corning by diminishing the shares of U.S. TV producers. As the company's financial results had lost some of their luster, Corning's top management was placing great emphasis on building a broader earnings base and was anxious to restore Corning's image as a high-technology company. Fiber optics had been selected as a top priority development in the company and as perhaps the single most promising opportunity Corning faced.

A financial profile of Corning is shown in Exhibit 18–1.

Historical Activities in Fiber Optics

Corning had been involved in fiber optics from the very early days of the industry. It had been approached by Bell Labs and the British Post Office, soon after Kao's and Hockman's 1966 research, to see if Corning could develop a fiber with attenuation of only 20 db/kilometer. Corning began working actively on fiber-optics research, in cooperation with scientists at Bell Labs. Corning had signed a cross-licensing agreement with Bell Labs in the mid-1960s in order to obtain needed technology for the troubled Signetics subsidiary, and the agreement gave Bell access to Corning's fiber-optics patents.

In 1967 scientists at Nippon Electric and Nippon Sheet Glass, working independently of Corning and Bell, announced that they had developed a step-index optical fiber 1 meter long, which had losses equivalent to 30 db/km. This was the first step-index optical fiber. But in 1970 Corning made the historic announcement of laboratory development of a step-index fiber with a loss of 20 db/km, achieving the initial goal. A laboratory group led by Dr. Robert D. Mauer had succeeded in eliminating the impurities in the high-silica optical quality glass used as the raw material and found a way to combine core and cladding while retaining these purity levels. Using Corning's broad glass production know-how, Mauer's group developed a technique for drawing a glass preform into an optical fiber without destroying its delicate structure. Further advances in the production of step-index fibers resulted in dramatic decreases in attenuation losses. By May 1972 Corning could produce a fiber with an attenuation loss of less than 4 db/km.

In 1974 Corning signed joint development agreements covering fiber optics with telecommunications equipment (including wire and cable) manufacturers in England, France, Italy, Germany, and Japan. In Germany, Corning and Siemens formed Siecor, a joint venture to produce optical cables. By June of 1974 Corning began to sell a fiber-optic cable consisting of nineteen separate step-index fibers with an attenuation of 30 db/km. It was available in lengths up to 500 meters and cost $25 per meter for orders of 5 kilometers and over, and $57 per meter for orders of less than 5 kilometers.

The fibers in the cable could be used with an LED source and avalanche photodiode detector produced by Texas Instruments. The source and detector were sold together and cost $1,000.

In May 1975 the newly created Telecommunications Products Department of Corning Glass began to sell a low-loss fiber-optic cable under the brand name Corguide. Corguide contained six separate fibers, each of which had an attenuation of 20 db/km at a wavelength of 820 nm. The cable was sold for $13.50 a meter. High-strength material was incorporated into the cable design, making Corguide the first optical cable sturdy enough for outdoor use. Corguide cables containing different numbers of fibers offering a range of bandwidths and attenuation levels were introduced shortly thereafter.

In August 1975 Corning revealed that it has been working with the Electronic Components Division of Deutsch Co., a connector manufacturer, on the development of a fiber-optic connector that would have losses significantly less than other available connectors, somewhere in the range of 0.3 db per connector. These connectors were to be available on a commercial basis by the end of 1975.[1]

In February 1976 Corning began to sell optical fiber separately, while previously it had sold only cabled fiber. Six types of fiber were made available, each with different attenuation and bandwidth characteristics. Two were step-index fibers and four were graded-index fibers made by Corning's patented doped-deposited-silica process. Prices ranged from $10.50 a meter for small quantities of high-quality fiber to $1 a meter for kilometer-size quantities of higher-loss, low bandwidth step-index fiber. David B. Stout, supervisor of administrative services at the Telecommunications Products department at Corning, commented: "We now have the experience to produce our fibers commercially."[2] He also indicated that Corning had decided to begin the sale of fibers at that time because of the progress that had been made on the production of other optical components.

On July 14, 1976, Corning brought a suit against ITT alleging patent violation in fiber production. Also in 1976 Corning announced the formation of

Siecor, a joint venture with the West German firm Siemens A.G. The joint venture was to produce certain fiber-optic products in the United States and abroad.

In December 1977 Corning announced that it would convert half a 77,000-square-foot facility in Wilmington, N.C., to full-scale production of optical fibers. Scheduled for completion in September 1978, the new plant would be capable of producing ten times more optical fiber than Corning's 6,000-square-foot pilot plant in Erwin, New York. Prior to 1977 optical fiber production had taken place in Corning's research laboratory. At the time of the announcement, Leroy Wilson, head of the Electronic Products Division of Corning, stated that Corning expected optical waveguide production to become a "significant" business.[3]

Also in December 1977, Corning Glass and Siemens formed Siecor Optical Cables, Inc. Siecor's product line was cable made from optical fibers from Corning. Siecor's cables were manufactured in West Germany using Corning fibers, but manufacturing operations would be moved to the United States when justified by demand. Siecor also sold splicing, testing, and installation equipment as part of its installation service. Siemens produced all other fiber-optic components, including light sources, detectors, and connectors, and these were sold directly to customers. Siemens also had the capability to design complete systems.

Situation in 1978

By 1978 Corning offered a line of twenty types of optical fiber with attenuation ranging from 3 to 10 db/km. For orders of more than 100 km, prices ranged from $0.65 a meter for a fiber with an attenuation of 10 db/km to $3.10 per meter for a fiber with an attenuation level of 3 db/km. Corning used the inside and outside vapor phase oxidation processes to produce its fibers.

Corning sold fiber direct to customers in uncabled form. Cabled optical fiber ("Corguide") was sold by Siecor Optical Cable, Inc. Corning had made strong commitments to all its fiber customers, including other cable manufacturers, that it would

[1] *Electronics,* August 21, 1975, p. 29.
[2] *Electronics,* February 19, 1976.

[3] *Laser Focus,* December 1977.

sell fiber on equal terms to all comers, including Siecor.

Corning at one time had led the fiber-optics industry in connector technology and had once had state-of-the-art capability in sources and detectors. While Siecor still led the industry in the development of field detectors. While Siecor still led the industry in the development of field splicing techniques and splicing equipment, by 1979 technological initiative and leadership in light sources, detectors, and connectors had passed to other industry participants.

In 1979 Corning had commenced what company spokesmen termed "full-scale" production of optical fiber at a new plant in Wilmington, N.C. Capacity was in the "tens of thousands of kilometers." Industry observers believed that Corning had sold approximately 1,200 km of fiber-optic cable in 1978.

There were two Siecor facilities: Siecor Gmbh, a West German facility established in 1974, and Siecor Optical Cables, a U.S. facility located not far from Corning headquarters and established in December 1977. Siecor marketed Corguide cables as well as a line of Siecor cables made with Corning fiber.

Siemens

Siemens, Siecor's German parent, was one of the largest publicly held companies in Germany, with 1977 sales of $11.9 billion. Siemen's business consisted of the following: components (5 percent of corporate sales), data systems (15 percent), power engineering (31 percent), electrical installations including power cable and wire (11 percent), medical engineering (10 percent), telecommunications equipment, including wire and cable (22 percent), and other (6 percent). Siemens' product line included mainframe computers, electronic data processing equipment, microprocessors, integrated circuits, and semiconductor devices.

Siemens was a major supplier of telecommunications equipment to the German Post Office, operator of the German telephone service. Siemens also had substantial export sales of telecommunications equipment. Over half of Siemen's total sales were outside of West Germany, and Siemens ranked second to ITT in sales of telecommunications equipment outside the United States. The company had begun to test a fiber-optic trunk link between two local switching offices in Berlin in 1978.

EXHIBIT 18-1. *Summary of Financial Results, Corning Glass Works*

Consolidated Statements of Income	1978	1977	1976	1975	1974	1973
Net sales	$1,251,728	$1,119,630	$1,025,905	$938,959	$1,050,962	$945,785
Cost of sales	849,710	762,424	701,647	708,455	797,528	656,746
Gross Margin	402,018	357,206	324,258	230,504	253,434	289,039
Selling, general and administrative expenses	217,874	187,756	166,773	151,819	160,925	146,300
Research and development expenses	63,570	54,812	48,857	42,285	37,628	35,172
	281,444	242,568	215,630	194,104	198,553	181,472
Income from Operations	120,574	114,638	108,628	36,400	54,881	107,567
Royalty, interest and dividend income	27,061	20,572	18,038	11,317	15,272	19,066
Interest expense	(18,312)	(18,465)	(19,704)	(21,802)	(19,571)	(15,193)
Other income (deductions), net	8,195	7,611	3,745	(5,211)	(1,611)	(7,542)
Income before taxes on income	137,518	124,356	110,707	20,704	48,971	103,898
Taxes on income	60,531	53,201	51,874	7,723	19,182	50,076
Income before minority interest and equity earnings	76,987	71,155	58,833	12,981	29,789	53,822
Minority interest in (earnings) loss of subsidiaries	(1,566)	(1,174)	(595)	2,617	1,832	(1,258)
Equity in earnings of associated companies	28,942	22,102	25,475	15,539	16,504	17,818
Net Income	$ 104,363	$ 92,083	$ 83,713	$ 31,137	$ 48,125	$ 70,382
Per Share of Common Stock						
Net income	$5.89	$5.20	$4.74	$1.76	$2.73	$4.00
Dividends	$1.73	$1.56	$1.50	$1.40	$1.40	$1.40
Average shares outstanding (thousands)	17,732	17,696	17,648	17,635	17,601	17,573
Consolidated Statements of Financial Condition						
Working capital	$ 376,763	$ 342,387	$ 296,240	$243,294	$ 222,349	$233,491
Investments	188,886	164,361	146,203	124,517	110,852	91,252
Plant and equipment, at cost (net)	402,242	360,664	346,445	358,884	403,582	336,602
Goodwill and other assets	18,562	16,991	19,843	23,689	35,318	24,746
	986,453	884,403	808,731	750,384	772,101	686,091
Loans payable beyond one year	163,398	158,767	167,175	172,686	183,029	120,316
Other liabilities and deferred credits	81,338	59,196	41,049	35,384	53,322	54,769
Stockholders' equity	$ 741,717	$ 666,440	$ 600,509	$542,314	$ 535,750	$511,006
Additions to plant and equipment	$ 103,232	$ 69,600	$ 48,742	$ 62,072	$ 136,596	$119,213
Depreciation and amortization	$ 57,428	$ 50,923	$ 52,493	$ 54,916	$ 54,430	$ 44,642
Dividends paid	$ 30,690	$ 27,622	$ 26,492	$ 24,705	$ 24,672	$ 24,623
Current earnings retained in the business	$ 73,673	$ 64,461	$ 57,221	$ 6,432	$ 23,453	$ 45,759
Number of stockholders at last dividend date	15,583	16,164	16,059	16,472	16,321	14,654
Owens-Corning Fiberglas Corporation earnings:						
Total	$ 24,760	$ 24,051	$ 15,054	$ 7,624	$ 5,194	$ 9,080
Per share	$1.40	$1.36	$ .85	$ .43	$ .30	$ .52

NOTE: Dollars in thousands, except per share amounts.

CASE 19
Sierra Log Homes, Inc.

Sierra Log Homes was the leading producer of authentic handcrafted homes and other authentic log structures in 1977 and a participant in the emerging log home industry. Spurred by the "back to nature" movement, the desire to own a unique home, and the superior insulating and cost qualities of logs as a construction material, the log home industry had been growing at the rate of more 50 percent per year since 1970, reaching an estimated $150 million in sales in 1976. While most log homes were "milled," or machine made, Sierra was unique in its ability to handcraft authentic log homes on a large scale using traditional methods. Many companies, primarily milled-log home producers, had entered the fledgling industry, and new competitors seemed to be entering the industry daily. In this context Sierra faced the challenge of adapting to its rapidly changing industry environment.

The Log Home Industry

Log homes had been built in the United States for more than 200 years, and pioneer log cabins had always held a special place in the American heritage. After a long period of dormancy, however, the log home was perhaps the fastest-growing new form of housing construction in 1977. While data on this embryonic (reborn) industry was hard to come by, industry sources estimated that the industry had been growing at the rate of 50 to 100 percent per year since 1970. This rapid growth had attracted literally hundreds of new companies, and more than 900 companies were estimated to produce some form of log home in 1977. The industry was characterized by a wide variety of product, operating philosophies, and problems.

Types of Log Homes

There were two basic types of log homes. Ninety-five percent of the log homes being produced were *milled-log homes,* structures constructed of logs that had been machined by a milling operation, thereby allowing the logs to fit together exactly. There were a wide variety of approaches used in making milled-log homes, ranging from squaring off two or more sides of each log so that they lay flat on top of each other, to elaborate tongue-in-groove arrangements for stacking the logs. There were also a number of approaches to joining the ends of the logs and placing insulation between them. Products of different companies also differed in whether they used hand-peeled or machine-peeled logs, and whether or not interior log walls were machined to be flat or left round. Exhibit 19-1 shows the most common milled-log construction techniques, and a photograph of a typical milled-log home.

The purpose of the milling operation was to convert irregular, round logs into a regular, exactly dimensioned building that could be easily assembled and would yield a flat inside wall if desired. Milled-log homes were assembled from log sections of 8 to 12 feet in length, and most milled-log homes came in precut kit form. The great majority of producers sold kits in a variety of standard floor plans, though a few would produce a custom kit to customer specifications. Kits included log walls at a minimum, and many included floor and roof structures, windows, doors, and other house components. The kits were relatively easy to assemble and could be assembled either by the owner or by a contractor on the owner's foundation. Similarly, owners could finish their own homes or contract for the finishing operation.

While the overwhelming majority of firms in the log home industry produced milled-log homes, a handful of companies constructed *"authentic"* *log homes* in the original, handcrafted style of the pioneers. Less than 5 percent of the log homes produced in 1977 were authentic log homes. In the authentic log home, whole round logs in up to 40-foot lengths were notched at the ends and assembled by hand. The spaces between the unmachined and irregular logs was filled with insulating material and some form of sealing or "chinking" material. Chinking usually took the form of a white or gray cement composition, though sometimes small wood slats were utilized. Because of the lack of machine milling, no two authentic log homes were ever exactly alike. Authentic log home producers either built the home on the customer's homesite or constructed the log structure of the home on the manufacturer's premises. In the latter case, the building was carefully marked, disassembled and shipped to the customer's site, where it could be quickly reassembled on the owner's foundation. As with milled-log homes, finishing operations could be done by the customer or contracted out. While most authentic log homes

were currently being custom-made to customer specifications, most authentic log home manufacturers had a variety of standard designs from which the customer could choose. Exhibit 19-2 shows the construction techniques used in authentic home manufacture as well as a photograph of a Sierra authentic log home.

The Properties of the Log Home

The log home obviously had some unique aesthetic qualities as a form of home construction. Logs had a number of other desirable properties as a construction medium as well, though the properties of milled and authentic log structures were somewhat different. Logs had excellent insulating qualities, and a log building was very inexpensive to heat and cool. With 6- to 12-inch thicknesses of solid wood, the authentic log home had up to six times the insulating value of a conventional frame structure, and many instances of dramatically low heating bills had been reported.[1] The milled-log home, since some of its surfaces had been machined, offered somewhat less of an advantage than the authentic structure, which used whole, round logs. In addition to their insulating advantages, all forms of log homes required almost no maintenance. The logs were impregnated with preservative materials and required little or no refinishing (a favorite industry quip was, "Sure you have to refinish these homes, once every 200 years.") Authentic log structures were also characterized by structural strength and had excellent seismic (earthquake) properties.

Finally, although comparisons were hazardous, log homes were at least comparable and probably less expensive to construct than conventional homes. Costs depended critically on the manner in which the home was finished and what was included in the standard of comparison (e.g., land, plumbing and heating systems, etc.). But after proper adjustment for such factors, most industry sources pegged the log home at 10 to 25 percent less expensive than the conventionally built home since solid logs replaced exterior siding, framing, insulation, and finished interior walls. In addition, because it was relatively easy many owners could and did par-

---

[1] One recent report cited figures of less than $25 per month.

ticipate in the erection and finishing of their log home themselves.

Against these advantages lay some problems, which resulted from the newness of the log home as a common form of home construction. First, the quality of log homes, particularly milled-log homes, was erratic as a result of the many new and small firms in this sometimes cottage industry. Imprecise joining, warping, and cracking sometimes occurred. Some producers' homes were poorly designed, and some had been known to furnish incomplete kits and provide little or no support after the home was sold. A second problem was that architects were unfamiliar with logs and their properties, and most companies building log homes had to provide assistance to the customers' architect or provide architectural services themselves.

Another problem was that the engineering properties of logs were only beginning to be documented and understood. Local building codes had made no provision for logs, and the local building authorities had virtually no standards to go by either in their previous training or in available construction data sources. As a result, the early log homes built in any particular area sometimes faced the prospect of an extended process of convincing local building authorities of the structural integrity of log buildings, and educating them about the properties of logs.[2] This sometimes required special engineering calculations, since organizations like the International Conference of Building Officials (ICBO) had not yet published recommendations on construction standards for log structures. If a substandard quality log building was among the first erected in an area, this could effectively block further sales of log homes without great effort. Once the first new successful log buildings had been constructed in an area, on the other hand, difficulties with building authorities were typically no longer faced.

Since milled-log homes were made from 8- to 16-foot log sections while authentic homes used up to 40-foot logs, the two forms of log homes were structurally quite different. Each had to surmount the problems of building department approval,

though if one form of log home got approval it was sometimes helpful to the other. However, the few firms making authentic log homes had found that in some cases a previous approval of a milled-log home in an area might hurt them in gaining approval for their homes (or require unnecessary and costly modifications) if the local building authority tried to apply the same standards.

There were a number of national and regional building code approval organizations, including ICBO, Building Officials and Code Advisors (BOCA), and the Southern Building Conference (SBC). These organizations issued approvals for housing manufacturers' products, which favorably influenced local building authorities. Some of the larger log home companies had sought and gained approval by one or more of these organizations. However, local building codes took precedence over national or regional codes, so area by area approval still had to be gained. In many local areas as well as nationally, building codes were becoming more stringent, and government regulation of housing was increasing. Some movement was beginning toward a single uniformly stringent national building code.

Energy use had become a problem as well. There was controversy about the insulating qualities of milled-log buildings that related in part to the lack of testing that had been done. The Farmers Home Administration, which set standards for construction of farm structures, had recently proposed insulation standards which threatened milled-log producers. Log home producers claimed that these standards were unfair and based on testing methods inappropriate for log homes. The efforts of a recently formed group of milled-log manufacturers were being mobilized to oppose the standards.

The Demand for Log Homes

Log homes were a part of the multibillion-dollar housing industry. Table 19–1 presents statistics on the number and value of private single family units started in selected years. The average cost of conventional housing had risen dramatically, from $27,500 in 1972 to $45,000 in 1976 according to the *Census of Housing.*

While reliable numbers were extremely difficult

---

[2] One article reported that it had taken a full eighteen months to persuade a building department in New Jersey to approve a log home, though this long a period was a rarity. ''The House You Build Yourself at a Price You Can Afford'', *Family Circle,* May 1976.

TABLE 19-1.   Number and Value of Private Single Family Units Started in Selected Years

	1976	1975	1974	1973	1972	1968	1963
Private single family units started[a]	1,163,400	892,800	888,100	1,132,000	1,309,000	899,400	1,012,400
Value of the home:[b] Under							
$25,000	N/A	10%	14%	23%	40%		
$25,000–$34,999	N/A	26%	34%	36%	32%		
$35,000 and over	N/A	65%	53%	42%	28%		

NOTES: N/A = not available; figures may not add due to rounding.
SOURCES: [a] U.S. Department of Commerce, Bureau of the Census, Construction Reports, *Housing Starts,* March 1977.
[b] U.S. Department of Housing and Urban Development, *1975 Statistical Yearbook,* Table 49.

to get, one thing was certain—demand for log homes was booming. It was estimated that 10,000 log structures had been built in the United States in 1977, and one source predicted 15,000 to 18,000 would be built in 1978.[3] The reasons given ranged from the "back to nature" movement and the spirit engendered by the American Bicentennial to even more intangible factors. In the words of one commentator:

Ask anyone who has built and lives in a log cabin, "why?" and chances are good he'll answer, "It has always been my dream." There's something about such a lifestyle that makes people feel a great independence of spirit. For many it's part of a drive toward self-sufficiency and a wish to have something positive and personal to say about how they live. The heart knows that the mind can't explain.[4]

Another observer noted:

Log houses seem to satisfy some intrinsic human need to live with wood and to feel truly at home. [This log home buyer]'s attitude is not uncommon. After a disappointing decade in which a lot of people lost their trust in such institutions as presidents, politics, the sanity of the system, and the soundness of the dollar, many seem to be shaping a lesser faith around getting back to basics. Along with homemade bread, compost heaps, and wood stoves, log houses have lately emerged as one of the important symbols of this new mystique.[5]

Log home buyers spoke in terms such as "a retreat from today's plastic society" and "a wonderful

feeling of substance" in describing their reasons for purchasing log homes. Log homes were a nonstandard home that departed from what others were doing architecturally, and people wanted to be different. Log homes also fitted with the movement to live in the country and small towns and get out of the major urban areas. While economy and practicality were sometimes mentioned as reasons for purchasing log homes, they rarely seemed to be the primary motivation. Closely related to this was a trend toward people constructing or playing a part in constructing their own homes.[6]

While in the 1960s and early 1970s most log homes had been purchased as second or vacation homes, by 1977 the majority of log homes were being purchased as primary dwellings. Some log home companies reported that 80 to 90 percent of their homes went to the primary market.[7] Market studies by log home companies had found that log home buyers spanned all income levels and social strata, including professional persons building $70,000-and-up homes as well as individuals from all backgrounds who did a substantial amount of the work constructing the home themselves. Log homes seemed to appeal to a particular kind of customer seeking the aesthetic properties of logs, and log home companies did not view themselves as competing with conventional housing. Commercial uses of log structures were just beginning, and motels, restaurants, lodges, churches, offices, and stores had been built from logs. Many observers expected the commercial market to grow as logs became a more common building medium, par-

[3] Casewriter conversation with editor, *1978 Log Home Guide for Builders and Buyers,* Muir Publishing Co., Ontario, 1977.
[4] "Log Cabin Renaissance Is Going on Now in the Northwest," *Sunset,* October 1976, p. 74.
[5] "A Log House You Build from a Kit," *Country Journal,* 1976.

[6] *Wall Street Journal,* September 1, 1976.
[7] "Lincoln Log Kits, Once Just Kid Stuff, Now Occupy Adults," *Wall Street Journal,* July 24, 1975.

ticularly in resort areas, though problems with building authorities were more acute since commercial building codes were more stringent.

Interest in log homes had long been high in New England states, the Northwest, and the Rocky Mountain states such as Montana, Idaho, Utah, and Colorado. However, by the 1970s log homes had been built in most if not all states. Demand was strong all over the United States, with the current demand growth strongest in the Northwest, Midwest, Virginia, West Virginia, and North Carolina. Sales to California, initially a growing area, had tapered off considerably because of particularly difficult problems with building codes.

Purchasing a log home was a major purchase decision for the buyer, and buyers usually engaged in extensive information gathering in their purchase decision. Though buyers varied in the purchasing behavior, the typical buyer wrote to a large number of companies requesting product literature, visited a number of finished homes, and talked actively with as many as fifteen companies. While almost all buyers were aware of the availability of the milled-log home, many did not know about the authentic log home since it was produced by relatively few companies and not available in all areas.

Buyers of log homes had a bewildering variety of companies, kit packages, and custom building options to choose from in 1977. There was little standardization in the offerings of firms in the industry, and this extended all the way from the basic construction technique of the home to what was included in a kit (e.g., windows, doors, roofing material, etc.). What was included in a kit even varied for different models offered by the same company in some cases. This confusion made product and price comparisons very difficult on a product that was already inherently complex. Also, buyers often placed great emphasis on the initial kit price and did not look carefully at the cost of finishing the building.[8] Misleading impressions about price had not been helped by the profusion of magazine and newspaper articles about log homes, which had stressed the low price of log home kits.

Buyer confusion was heightened by the very names that log home companies had adopted. Company names such as Real Log Homes, Authentic Log Homes, and Rocky Mountain Log Homes connoted a log home made in the pioneer style, yet all three were milled-log home producers.

The Log Home Production Process

Producing milled-log homes and authentic log homes involved quite different production processes.

MILLED-LOG HOMES

Milled-log homes were produced with relatively simple milling and cutting operations on sawmill and woodmilling equipment. The cost of acquiring minimally acceptable equipment was modest, and a small firm could enter the business for as little as $5,000. As a result, milled-log home production was a cottage industry with many firms producing on a very small scale. Leading milled-log producers had invested substantially more in larger-scale manufacturing facilities, however.

The largest plants in the industry were highly automated; they used computerized woodmilling equipment custom-designed and manufactured for milled-log producers by machinery firms.[9] In addition, some leading firms made a portion of their own special purpose equipment in-house. The milling, grooving, notching, and other operations performed in milled-log production were relatively simple. The chief manufacturing problem was developing the capability to produce rapidly the fifteen to twenty different configurations of milled-logs that were the components of kits.

The largest plants in the industry had the capacity to produce 500–1,000 standard homes per year and represented a total investment of $750,000 to $1,000,000. Because of transport costs for finished houses and the need for ready access to raw materials, the leading milled-log producers had constructed decentralized plants in various population centers. The leading producers foresaw some modest increase in plant sizes and automation, but

---

[8] The cost of a finished home usually ranged form two to four times the cost of the price of the kit. *1978 Log Home Guide for Builders and Buyers.*

[9] In addition, at least one milled-log home company advertised custom equipment it had designed for its own facilities for sale to other log home producers.

all agreed that there were few economies of scale in milled-log production.

Labor content in the process was small for the large producers. It was estimated that as few as twenty to thirty unskilled and low-skilled employees could produce 500 or more milled-log homes per year. Training of production employees required several weeks. Most milled-log companies used mechanically peeled logs as raw material, peeling with readily available machinery. The milled-log company produced pre-cut 8- to 16-foot milled-log sections, packaged the appropriate components into kits, and bundled and palletized them for shipping.

AUTHENTIC LOG HOMES

Authentic log homes were entirely handcrafted, and the production process was very labor-intensive. A construction crew laid out the building from blueprints, selected the logs, and hand cut and notched the logs to erect the building. The process required considerable skill in workmanship and in selecting logs to minimize the effect of their natural taper on the aesthetic qualities of the structure. The logwork of the building was constructed in its entirety, including the log components of roof structures, porches, garages, and so on. Then the logs were carefully numbered and disassembled for shipping. Since authentic log homes used logs of up to 40 feet in length, it was necessary to use mechanical means to lift the logs in the assembly process and to disassemble the building for shipping. Firms used specially adapted loaders or tractors for this task, in addition to small cranes. Large-capacity log loaders were used to move logs from inventory to the building site. In addition to this equipment, the only tools used in construction were chain saws, power chisels and various measuring and marking devices.

The authentic log home producers made use of hand-peeled logs.

Raw Materials

A log home required from fifty to several hundred logs in its construction, with an average of approximately 200. All authentic log home producers and some milled-log producers used lodgepole pine, a variety of pine tree that grows very tall and straight with few branches except for a tuft of branches near the top. Lodgepole pine was also desirable because of its relatively small amount of taper, which reduced waste in the milling operation or greatly simplified authentic log home construction. Lodgepole pine grew in relatively few places in the United States, because it required elevations of 6,000 feet.

While all authentic log home producers preferred lodgepole pine, they could sometimes use spruce or white pine if it was growing about 6,000-foot elevations, which caused the tree to grow very tall and without much taper. However, since milled-log homes utilized much shorter spans and ran the logs through a sawmill, the height, taper, and straightness of the tree were much less important to milled-log producers. Milled-log companies used plantation pine, white pine, spruce, cedar, and Douglas fir in addition to lodgepole pine.

It was important that the logs used in constructing both milled and authentic log homes be thoroughly dry to prevent warping, which could open up cracks in milled-log walls, cause difficulties with chinking, and introduce structural problems. Most log home companies preferred to use so-called standing dead timber, or trees that had been killed by a forest fire or by disease and had dried "on the stump" for several years. If these were not available, then the logs needed to be stockpiled and dried for four to eighteen months. Log home companies typically held enough logs for three to six months' production in inventory. Some milled-log companies had used live (or "green") lumber in buildings without aging, and this had led to quality problems.

Assuring a steady supply of standing dead houselogs had proved difficult for many log home companies. The use of timber for house logs was a new phenomenon, created by needs of the log home industry. Standing dead timber had previously been almost worthless because it was unusable by conventional sawmills. The newness of the use was reflected in a lack of experience by timber owners and logging companies in dealing with house logs. The usual measurement criteria for timber (board feet) did not even apply to house logs, for example.

In many cases timber stands were mixtures of standing dead house logs and green timber used by conventional sawmills, and it had been extremely difficult to get timber owners and logging companies to sell or log just the house logs. House logs volumes were not as great as log volumes required by sawmills, nor were house logs commanding prices as high as green timber. They had to be carefully selected to meet specifications, while green timber for sawmills did not. For all these reasons, both the U.S. Forest Service and private timber owners (e.g., railroads, large sawmills) had not been fully cooperative in selling house logs to log home companies. The problems were most acute for authentic log home producers, who were more selective in their log requirements than milled-log companies.[10]

Yet the demand for house logs had been growing rapidly, fueled by the growth of the log home industry. The Forest Service and other timber owners were beginning to recognize the value of house logs. This and active bidding by log home producers had driven up the price of standing dead logs in recent years. The cost of uncut logs "on-the-stump" ranged from 5¢ to $6.00 per log in 1977, the upper part of the range reflecting recent price increases. In addition to bidding up prices, the many new log home producers had been a part of the availability problem themselves. Small fledgling companies sometimes had not paid their bills or had not been able to handle the log volumes promised to loggers. This had caused disillusioned loggers to abandon further involvement with house logs altogether.

Milled-log companies using green timber faced log supply problems as well, and raw materials were a problem for the entire industry. Green timber users faced competition from large lumber companies, and supplies were tight and prices rising. Several of the leading milled-log producers had employees looking for log supplies on a full-time basis.

Log home companies, with rare exceptions, did not own timber themselves, nor did they log it. They contracted with independent loggers to log and deliver the trees. Loggers either harvested logs from timber stands they already controlled or bid on new timber sales containing house logs. A timber sale could be bought with a relatively modest up-front guarantee, the bulk of the cost being paid as the timber was harvested. While there were large logging companies, some of which controlled appropriate timber resources, most log companies were forced to resort to one of the many relatively small independent loggers to harvest logs in the small quantities and specialized locations characterizing their needs.[11] These small, independent loggers were not always reliable in meeting delivery schedules. In addition, weather problems plagued the logging industry, with snow, mud, or fire danger sometimes preventing any logging activity at all for several months.

Logging was a capital-intensive business, with an investment of $600,000 required for even a small-scale logging operation, not including maintenance facilities for the equipment, which broke down frequently under logging conditions. The cost of logging a house log ranged from $4.00 ot $8.00 per log, while the cost of transporting it to a manufacturing site was on the order of $6.00 per log for timber located a day's drive away or less. Therefore, the total cost of logs delivered to a log home producer's manufacturing location ranged from $12.00 to $18.00 per log. The total cost of a green log was in approximately the same range.

Shipping

Most log home companies used independent trucking companies to ship disassembled buildings or kits to the customer's building site, generally on flatbed trailers. The cost of shipping a log home was approximately $1.00 per loaded mile for each trailer or part of a trailer used, though the cost declined to about $.75 per mile for distances over 1,000 miles. A larger log home sometimes required more than one trailer, and the shipping costs had to be increased proportionally. Milled-log homes were easier to ship than authentic homes because they

---

[10] In addition to great selectivity, authentic log home companies required 40-foot logs, longer than the typical 33-foot length of logs that conventional logging companies dealt with. This required modifications in logging and hauling procedures.

[11] Most large loggers were also unofficially affiliated with the large sawmills.

used shorter, standardized log sections and could be readily bundled and palletized.

Financing

As with most home purchases, buyers generally required financing in building log homes. Conventional home financing institutions had had to be persuaded to lend money for log home construction. National institutions guaranteeing home financing, such as the Federal Housing Administration (FHA) and Veterans Administration (VA), had only recently approved a handful of loan guarantees for log homes, while the Federal Land Bank[12] had not yet been willing to guarantee financing for log homes at all, though the matter was under review. Local saving and loan institutions and commercial banks, the mainstay of housing construction financing, had been skeptical about lending for log home construction in many areas. While the situation was improving, many would not lend at all, while others would only lend 50 percent of the value of the house rather than the usual 70 to 80 percent. The profusion of milled-log home companies, some manufacturing low-quality products and not meeting delivery dates on time (or in some cases at all), had led to bad experiences for some banks and made them even more wary of lending for log home construction. Log homes were not eligible for government housing subsidy programs.

Dealers and Marketing

Most log home companies sold their products through networks of independent (licensed or franchised) dealers. Dealers engaged in local marketing activities worked with customers in selling the houses, helped in arranging financing, and in some cases also contracted to erect and finish the home—in other cases the customer had to make arrangements with a contractor or otherwise arrange to erect and finish the home. The leading log home companies had extensive dealer networks of as many as 100 dealers or more and sold to dealers at a discount off the list price of the home. Dealers in

12 An agency like the FHA, which guaranteed loans for ranch and farm construction.

the industry were a mixed bag of individuals, ranging from high school shop teachers to real estate brokers to contractors. No particular set of skills was deemed necessary by log home companies except basic business skills, though construction experience was helpful. Dealers generally had to invest in a model home as qualification for becoming a dealer, which in many cases they lived in. The leading log home companies had full-time personnel interacting with dealers and produced dealer training manuals, dealer newsletters, and so forth.

Manufacturers usually sold their products at list prices. The customer was generally required to make a 40 to 50 percent down payment before the house was produced, with the balance due on delivery. The larger log home companies were beginning to advertise, in some cases heavily. Advertising was primarily in specialized magazines such as *Better Homes* and *Yankee,* though some had experimented with national magazines like *Time* as well as limited use of TV spots. Dealers engaged in local advertising, with some log home companies participating on a cooperative basis.

Some of the leading companies were beginning to offer warranties on the products.

Competition

Competition in the log home industry could be divided into four categories: milled-log producers, authentic log producers, independent commercial builders, and the enthusiasts who sought to build their own homes from scratch. The first two categories were manufacturers of the log structures only, while independent builders and enthusiasts constructed complete log homes on the homesite.

MILLED-LOG COMPETITORS

Manufacturing precut cabins dated back to the 1920s, and a company named Ward Cabins was credited with developing the original idea over a long period of time extending into the early 1960s. However, until the late 1960s the production volume of milled-log buildings amounted to only a trickle. As the demand for log homes grew in the late 1960s and early 1970s, a flood of new firms entered the industry. By 1977 it was estimated that 900 or more companies were producing milled-log homes, many of which were extremely small firms producing a few buildings per year. Nearly all companies were growing rapidly, according to industry sources.[13] Ex-loggers were a source of entrants into the industry, particularly small-scale entrants, and many of the companies had also produced other types of homes.

Milled-log companies were located near sources of trees and were concentrated in New England, the Midwest, North Carolina, and Western states. Exhibit 19–3 lists some of the leading firms, along with available data on their product lines, distributor organizations, and manufacturing approaches. While the leading firms produced products of adequate quality, which had been professionally designed, engineered, and approved by the major code approval agencies, some of the smaller firms did not, and erratic quality was a problem in the industry. The smaller firms also did not always participate in required government programs like Workmens Compensation and OSHA.

The great majority of milled-log companies produced kits. As was noted earlier, their milling and joining techniques varied widely, as did the items that were included in the kit. Depending on what was included, the finished home could cost between two and four times the cost of the basic kit. A result of these differences was a great deal of confusion in the market, as claims and counterclaims were made about costs and quality. Most milled-log companies produced kits in a variety of models, with some firms offering fifty or more different designs and sizes. While milled-log products differed in quality, no milled-log producer had a product that was not or could not be readily copied by other firms. The larger firms tended to have more extensive and professional portfolios of designs and models, however.

While data on individual companies was difficult to come by, and only tentative efforts had begun to form an industry association, some estimates of industry sales were available, as shown in Table 19–2.

Of the many milled-log producers, there were perhaps fifty firms that produced more than thirty homes per year. The acknowledged industry leader

[13] *1978 Log Home Guide,* p. 41.

TABLE 19–2. Estimated Milled-Log Industry Sales *(millions of dollars)*

Year	Sales
1971	$ 12
1974	60
1975	110
1976	150

SOURCES: *Moneysworth,* January 31, 1977; *Chicago Daily News,* Sunday Supplement, February 15, 1976.

was Real Log Homes.[14] Real Log Homes manufactured milled-log homes in four large plants located in Vermont, North Carolina, Montana, and Arkansas. Two more plants were reportedly under construction. Each plant was automated and could produce 500 or more homes per year, and all plants were reportedly producing at or near capacity in 1977. Company spokesman pegged output at "Quite a few more than 2,000 homes per year." Real Log also produced windows, doors and some other components in three plants located near three of its milled-log home plants.

At an average kit price of approximately $8,000 to $18,000 (including windows, roofing material, and so on), Real Log sales were probably in the $20 million to 35 million range, and the company had been growing rapidly. While no known log home producer was a public company, Real Log's profits were said to be good, and visits to its facilities supported this impression. Real Log produced a wide variety of models through a national network of "over 100" dealers, according to a company spokesman, and sold homes either direct at list price or to its distributors at a 17 percent discount. Real Log was the only log home company whose products had been approved by both the FHA and VA as well as the four major building code approval agencies (ICBO, BOCA, UBA, and SBC). Real Log advertised extensively in national and regional magazines such as *Sunset, Southern Living, Better Homes,* and *Time.* It tended to reduce advertising once a new plant became established, however, relying on word of mouth and its dealer network.

[14] Real Log Homes was technically part of a holding company called Traditional Living. Besides manufacturing log homes themselves, Traditional Living was engaged in manufacturing "post and beam" homes and made windows, doors, and other mill work components for use in its homes.

Real Log had been the standard of comparison for many in the industry. An industry executive commented on how competitors viewed Real Log:

> Competitors look to Real Log for moves, and for data. They look to Real Log to see how it is doing things. Real Log went Code a few years back. Now others are all going Code. Real Log changes prices. Others change prices. Real Log introduces new models, others introduce new models. . . . Some companies use Xeroxs of Real Log's catalogs and plans.

Another of the leading milled-log producers, New England Log Homes (NELHI) in Hamden, Connecticut, was an offshoot of Real Log. Vito Vizziello, President of NELHI, had been a Real Log dealer and decided to go into business for himself. Vizziello reportedly made use of Real Log plans and designs as well as copied its production methods. Real Log had successfully sued Vizziello, but the court settlement left NELHI in business, and NELHI was growing rapidly.

NELHI had two large plants in operation, with capacities of 500 homes per year or more, and was planning an additional facility. It had reported that it was producing at the rate of 800 homes per year and that 1977 sales would be in the $5 million to $10 million range.[15] 1978 sales were expected to be double 1977 levels. NELHI reported that it had "almost 100" franchised dealers and planned additions to its dealer network. It advertised more aggressively than Real Log Homes, using magazines and some experimentation with TV. NELHI advertising expenditures were reported by company spokesman as in excess of $150,000 annually and spokesmen had termed profits as "excellent." NELHI had secured approval from some but not all of the major financing and approval agencies and was seeking further approvals.

The other leading milled-log producers followed generally similar policies to Real Log and NELHI, involving dealer networks, advertising, and so forth (see Exhibit 19-3). By and large their dealer networks were not as extensive nor their plants as large and automated as the industry leaders. As of 1977 there were only a few other multiplant firms, though most firms were growing aggressively and

reporting major increases in sales in the 30 to 100 percent per year range.

AUTHENTIC LOG HOME COMPANIES

The authentic log home segment of the industry had far fewer firms than the milled-log segment, and in 1977 there were only a handful of firms producing authentic log structures. The leader in the authentic segment was Sierra Log Homes, located in Glacier, Wyoming. Sierra had begun production of authentic homes on a large scale in 1973, the first such firm in the industry. Sierra's success had spawned a number of competitors; all other competitors in the authentic log segment were in some way spinoffs of Sierra. The two most firmly established of these competitors, Rustic Log Homes and Big Valley Log Homes, were located within five miles of Sierra in western Wyoming, one on either side of Sierra's log lot on Wyoming Highway 93. Rustic Log Homes was started in early 1974 by an ex-partner in Sierra, and Big Valley Log Homes was started in May of 1976 by an ex-Sierra distributor. Two other firms had been started by ex-Sierra distributors, and two others were started by ex-Sierra construction crew members.

Authentic log home producers concentrated on the production of custom homes, though each offered a number of standard models the customer could order. Sierra had twelve models, Rustic Log Homes offered six, and Big Valley Log offered the same models as Sierra did. All three producers were developing independent distributors, though Sierra appeared to have much wider distribution than the other two firms. None of the authentic log home producers had done extensive advertising, but Sierra's distributor network had advertised in their respective local areas.

None of the authentic log home producers were publicly held, and thus information on their sales could not be completely verified. However, Rustic Log Homes produced an estimated twenty-five buildings in 1976 and thirty buildings in 1977, while Big Valley Log Homes had produced approximately six or seven in 1976 and ten in 1977. Rustic Log Home employees had reportedly participated in erecting twenty of these buildings on customers' homesites. The other authentic producers had produced fewer than ten buildings each in 1977. Sierra

---

[15] "NELHI: Hand Peeled and Proud Of It," in *1978 Log Home Guide For Builders and Buyers;* casewriter interviews.

Log Homes had produced more than 100 buildings in 1976 and approximately 175 buildings in 1977. Not all authentic log home companies produced products of equal quality, with Sierra the quality leader.

INDEPENDENT COMMERCIAL BUILDERS

Although they did not manufacture log buildings on a large scale, there were other entities that participated in the log home industry. A few specialized building contractors had constructed custom log homes from scratch, including the logwork and finishing. True Log Building (Jonesport, Maine), Pacific Log Homes (British Columbia, Canada), and Lodgepole Construction (Missoula, Montana) were firms engaged in such work. None of these efforts had been on a large scale, and production ranged from one to four buildings per year.

ENTHUSIASTS

Another class of participants in the industry were individuals who wanted to build their own log homes from scratch. A recent happening was the formation of pioneer-style homebuilding groups, who built log houses on a small scale as a semi-hobby. These developments were being reinforced by an increasing amount of information being disseminated about log home construction. "How-To" books, making log building look simple, were appearing. Universities, community colleges, forestry schools, and private individuals were offering courses about building with logs.[16] This information was in part complementary to the purchase of log kits or premanufactured log shells, as well as directed to those individuals wanting to build a complete home.

Sierra Log Homes, Inc.

History of the Company

In 1972, after quenching his wanderlust with a year of traveling throughout the world as a principal in a

---

[16] "The Log Cabin Renaissance", *Sunset,* October 1976. There were at least two large scale schools of log building: B. Allan Mackie School of Log Building (British Columbia) and Bar E. Ranch School for Log Home Building (Redland, Washington). *1978 Log Home Guide.*

firm he co-founded while a student at the Harvard Business School, Cameron Bach was seeking an opportunity to get involved in a business that promised to take advantage of the movement toward leisure and the outdoors that had swept the United States. He had read an article predicting the demise of a dying craft—the art of constructing houses out of logs using the traditional, handcraft methods. While log cabins had been common in eighteenth- and nineteenth-century America, the art of building them was rapidly disappearing and had been preserved only in the minds of a few aging oldtimers.

After looking around, Carmeron Bach discovered only one person building authentic log homes who was not in retirement, a transplanted Wyoming rancher named Vince Raymond living in Lakeview, Washington. Raymond had been building one to three log houses a year for more than ten years but had few managerial aspirations, and the business had not grown. In 1972 Raymond had formed a partnership with another person, Rob Johnson, to provide an infusion of management talent into the business. The partnership was in grave financial difficulty when Cameron Bach met the two partners, and the company had shrunk to two employees. Operating on his belief in the potential of the business, Cameron Bach and the two partners jointly incorporated a new company, Sierra Log Homes, with Cameron Bach investing $3,000 of his own capital. Bach set out to develop the skills to allow the construction of authentic log homes on a large scale.

The first years of Sierra's existence were devoted to developing a way to systematize the building of custom, handcrafted log houses, keeping the company going financially, and sorting out the management problems that developed. The idea of handcrafting the log structure of the home in a central location and then dismantling and shipping it to the owner's site proved to be the breakthrough that made large-scale production possible. Trial and error led to the transference of the skills to construct log homes from Raymond to crews of Sierra employees. Specialized equipment and tools were developed to aid the handcrafting process. By late 1972 Sierra was producing one and a half authentic log homes per month and shipping them exclusively to customers in Washington. It was the only known producer of such products in the United States.

Financing the growing business did not prove to be an easy task. An initial SBA loan secured by Bach funded early growth, but repeated financial crises characterized the early years. By early 1973 other problems had cropped up. The three initial partners could not all coexist in the business, and Rob Johnson left the company, taking over a Sierra distributorship in Wyoming.

Sierra was also faced with other difficulties. While customer enthusiasm for the product was high from the beginning, there were difficulties in persuading local building authorities to approve authentic log construction despite its greater strength, and in finding financial institutions to finance log homes. Painstaking selling efforts and special engineering calculations conceived by the company slowly won more and more local areas over.

Sierra had purchased some land in Wyoming early in 1972, anticipating the need eventually to relocate to gain greater access to raw materials. In mid-1973 Vince Raymond was pressing to move to the Wyoming location—Raymond was from Wyoming. Cameron Bach agreed reluctantly with the timing of the move, in view of the financial stringency of the company's situation, and Raymond moved to Glacier, Wyoming, to establish the new location. Severe difficulties were quickly experienced, however. The Wyoming operation became overextended, and losses and $400,000 in debt incurred by Raymond threatened the entire company. With the survival of the company at stake, Cameron Bach agreed to assume the debt Raymond had incurred in return for becoming sole owner of the company, Raymond having stated a desire to retire. The Lakeview, Washington, operation was left to a small group of Washington employees, and Sierra consolidated its operations in Glacier, Wyoming. With a plentiful supply of labor and access to logs, Glacier had remained Sierra's sole manufacturing location.

Vince Raymond was not long out of the picture, however. By early 1974 he had started a competing firm nearby in Wyoming (Rustic Log Homes), and had talked Sierra's number one distributor into switching companies. Within eighteen months the distributor had parted with Rustic Log Homes due to quality and delivery difficulties with Raymond's

new company and had formed his own authentic log home company. This company spawned another competitor when one of its distributors left. Raymond found new distributors and remained as one of Sierra's direct competitors in 1977. So did the group of Sierra employees at the old Washington location.

Between 1974 and 1977, finally under Cameron Bach's sole control, Sierra rebuilt financial strength, expanded its network of independent distributors, and made continuous advances in its ability to produce log structures of numerous varieties and sizes. Improvements in equipment were made, often improvised versions of commercially available general purpose equipment—Sierra was too small to command special purpose applications from tool and equipment suppliers. An experienced former builder, Ollie Lunde, was hired to be construction superintendent. Understanding of the design and structural properties of log building accumulated. By 1977, after weathering the downturn in construction activity in 1975 and 1976, Sierra was by far the largest producer of authentic handcrafted log structures. Its success attracted more imitators, however, and in 1976 Rob Johnson gave up his Sierra distributorship in Wyoming to form a competing company, Big Valley Log Homes. An ex-Sierra employee also helped set up another authentic log home company in Montana, for a consulting fee of $5,000. Despite this, with its debt completely repaid, distributor network building, and customer inquiries coming in at a rapid pace, Sierra had established itself as the industry leader.

Products

Sierra was the first and largest producer of authentic log structures, handcrafted at the company's location in Glacier, Wyoming. Sierra's log structures ranged from small cabins to luxury homes selling for $500,000, million-dollar condominium projects, and lodges constructed from logs. Cameron Bach commented on product policy: "We constantly focus on our objective to produce the highest quality product on the market along with meeting any promises made to customers and distributors. Many of our competitors, I am happy to state, do not share the same objectives.''

The company constructed the log walls, the log roof structure, and, in some cases, log floor beams, log porches, and interior log staircases for the home (all called the "log work") on its log lot in Glacier. The logs were then marked and disassembled and loaded onto one or more flatbed trailers to be trucked to the location where the house was to be constructed. Upon arrival, the log work was reassembled on the customer's property by one of Sierra's independent distributors. Finishing the home was the customer's responsibility, and the customer could contract with a Sierra distributor or some other firm to accomplish these tasks—Sierra's formal responsibility stopped when the log work was shipped.

Most of Sierra's homes and other log structures were produced to customer specifications. Working either through an architect closely affiliated with Sierra who was familiar with the properties of logs, or through an independent architect who consulted with Sierra's staff, the customer produced a set of blueprints for the home. Since the size of logs varied, handcrafted methods did not always allow exact replication of plans, and log architecture was new to many customers and architects, there was nearly always a process of adjusting the plans as the building was actually constructed. These decisions were made by the construction crew and construction superintendent, with the customer consulted in extreme cases. Sierra's custom-built log structures varied widely in manufacturing complexity.

In addition to its custom building activities, Sierra had twelve standard home designs that could be built from specifications, ranging in size from one- to four-bedroom models in a variety of styles.[17] The customer choosing a standard design dispensed with the need for architect involvement. In some cases customers chose relatively slight modifications to standard designs, which required little architectural work but a redrawn set of blueprints. Approximately 10 percent of the log structures pro-

duced by Sierra in 1977 were standard designs, 25 percent were modified standard designs, and 65 percent were custom built.

Cameron Bach cited many advantages of the handcrafted log homes over milled-log homes:

> Our homes are handcrafted, and their aesthetic qualities cannot be matched by the machine made, dimensioned milled-log homes. The Sierra product looks better, has better insulating qualities, needs no paneling or insulation on the interior, is structurally stronger, requires less maintenance, and is quieter inside. And all this for comparable cost. We can also build most anything out of logs, while our competitors offer only a limited number of models.

> While the milled-log companies point to the chinking on our homes as a source of problems, we think that the chinking is superior in appearance and we have never had difficulty with the chinking when it has been properly installed.

Customers

Sierra sold its log structures to customers located all across the United States with the exception of the Eastern Seaboard, with concentration in the Western states. Unlike most milled-log producers, the majority of Sierra's customers were upper-income business and professional persons, and about 65 percent of Sierra's homes had a finished cost in excess of $70,000, although Sierra sold homes of all sizes to all income levels. Commercial structures accounted for approximately 15 percent of Sierra's dollar sales, including lodges, restaurants, condominiums, offices, and stores. The balance of Sierra's sales were for homes. While the great majority of the houses Sierra sold in its early years were second homes, approximately 90 percent of Sierra's homes were primary homes in 1976, and only 10 percent were second or vacation homes.

Marketing

Sierra had never engaged in extensive marketing of its product and had never spent a dollar in advertising. The product sold largely by word of mouth, with nearly every completed home leading to addi-

---

[17] Sierra had been forced into developing its standard designs by a 1975 article in the *Wall Street Journal,* mentioning Sierra's name and implying that all log home companies had portfolios of standard designs. In response to more than 3,000 inquiries for portfolios, Sierra decided it had better have one.

tional sales in its area. The priority of the company thus far had been in producing a high-quality product and meeting customer requirements on schedule, and not on rapid volume expansion.

As a result of word of mouth and numerous articles in newspapers and magazines, Sierra received a large and snowballing number of inquiries about its products from all over the United States. It received approximately 200 letters per week, of which approximately 30 percent requested a portfolio of log home designs, which was sold for $3.00.[18] When a customer was located in the service area of a Sierra distributor, he was referred to the distributor for further information. For the substantial number of letters Sierra received from outside its existing distributor service area, it merely sent its brochure and product literature upon request. In addition to inquiries, twenty to thirty people a day visited the Sierra office or log lot in the summer months. Many of these had driven by the log lot, and the sight of the houses under construction had stimulated them to stop. Many had also been to Sierra's two nearby competitors' log lots, and competitors encouraged customers to visit Sierra to learn about the product, but then allow them to match or better Sierra's price quotations.

Customers (and potential distributors) visiting the Sierra location were greeted by one of Sierra's two office sales personnel, invited to view the pictures and brochures Sierra had available, and often given a tour of the log lot. Interested customers were directed to finished Sierra homes in the area and in some cases were given tours of these homes by the Sierra staff. Sierra was in the process of building a large authentic log construction office on its log lot, where potential customers could view the product firsthand as well as see the log lot in operation without the need for a tour. The log office was half finished in 1977, and priorities had been shifted to meeting the demand for orders, which was increasing Sierra's delivery time to more than three months. Sierra had not developed extensive construction manuals or elaborate brochures, though

these were characteristic of many of the larger milled-log producers.

Distribution

Sierra sold its product through thirty-nine independent distributors, located in nineteen states and Canada (one distributor). The distributor network was relatively new, with only two or three distributors having been with the company for more than three years. No single distributor accounted for a substantial share of Sierra's business. Sierra looked for distributors who had direct experience in the construction industry, since the distributor always arranged for erecting the log structure and usually aided the customer in finishing the home. Most distributors were contractors, who contracted with customers for the complete erection and finishing process as well as sold the customer the log work. However, some distributors were not directly in the construction industry but had developed relationships with subcontractors who completed the log house. No formula for selecting distributors had been discovered, and there was some distributor turnover. Distributors were allotted a territory in which they were the exclusive sellers of Sierra.

Erecting and particularly finishing a log house raised some unique problems that a conventional house did not, and a distributor-contractor had to go through a period of learning how to work with logs. Both Sierra management and distributors agreed, however, that a competent contractor could learn to work with logs relatively quickly after one or two experiences. When a distributor constructed his initial home, Sierra management consulted with the construction crew on technical matters such as chinking methods, window and door installation, finishing the logs, and so on. Often a Sierra employee would accompany the first house a distributor ordered and aid in its erection (though not in finishing). Sierra attempted to visit distributors periodically, but this occurred only on an intermittent and informal basis.

Sierra's distributors were responsible for working with local building authorities to ensure that building codes were met and building inspectors were educated on the properties of log structures.

---

[18] The elapsed time between Sierra's sending a portfolio to a potential customer and an order from that customer could be quite long. For example, Sierra had recently shipped a home to Mobile, Alabama, to a buyer who had requested a portfolio two years earlier.

Substantial effort and time were often required to introduce log homes into a new area. Distributors also helped the customer develop financing sources and were responsible for all customer contact, including billing and customer inquiries.

Distributors also took the lead in promoting the Sierra product through advertising. Some distributors had engaged in advertising, but after the startup phase they usually relied extensively on word of mouth to sell the product. Sierra provided brochures, portfolios, and other promotional material at cost. While it provided assistance to distributors, Sierra required each distributor to finish one log structure as a qualification for obtaining a distributorship. This reflected management's view that a completed Sierra log home was the best selling tool for the product. Distributors had found that a Sierra home could be immediately placed on the market and sell for far more than the cost of constructing it.

Most distributors had contacted Sierra upon learning of Sierra's products through magazine or newspaper stories or word of mouth. Sierra continued to receive regular inquiries from potential distributors at the rate of three or four a week but was not seeking to expand its distributor network aggressively in the next twelve months. The emphasis was on developing the existing network of distributors, many of whom had finished only a small number of log structures.

Cameron Bach commented on the distributors:

Our distributors are our interface with the customer. We are not in the construction business, but our distributors are, since they actually erect and often finish the house. With our help, they deal with the hassles of permits, inspectors, and local situations that are so common in the construction industry. We stress the independence of our distributors, and we do not allow our distributors to use the name Sierra in the name of their companies.

Pricing

Sierra sold the logwork to distributors at a distributor price, which ranged from $8,000 to $25,000. Distributors applied a markup to this price when preparing an estimate for the customer. Sierra did not specify retail prices to the distributors, and distributor markups varied. Sierra sold direct to customers not in a distributor's territory and had a published retail price list it gave to inquiring customers outside distributors' territories. Sierra had raised its prices in early 1977 in response to cost increases. In the purchase of a Sierra home, one-third of the cost of the logwork was due when an order was placed, one-third when the construction of the logwork reached the "top of the walls," and the balance at the time of shipment. Customers sometimes attempted to purchase the logwork direct from Sierra to avoid dealing through a distributor. It was Sierra's firm policy not to sell logwork direct in an area that had a distributor.

Raw Material Supply

Sierra's principle raw material was logs, and obtaining a steady supply of logs had been a continuing problem since the company began large-scale production of homes. Each Sierra home required an average of 150 to 300 logs, from 7 to 12 inches in diameter at the tip. Sierra made exclusive use of standing dead timber, most of which had been killed by forest fires or disease. Sierra had contracted with independent loggers to harvest the logs and deliver them to the log lot in Glacier. Working with loggers had been a challenge, according to Bach:

Today's performance was typical. One logger didn't come in because he was helping his neighbor's mother-in-law move. Another didn't make any deliveries because he is out hunting. And a third called and said he is no longer going to bring in house logs because his wife overdrew his checking account and his log skidder is being repossessed.

On several occasions, production of homes had had to stop because of the unreliability of log supply, and employees had to be used on tasks other than producing houses. Sierra was experiencing increasing competition for logs from other log home producers, both authentic and milled. In 1977 Sierra had tried to build a stockpile of logs to serve as a buffer against these uncertainties and was also considering backward vertical integration into logging to help alleviate the supply problems.

Production

Sierra had pioneered large-scale construction of authentic or handcrafted log structures, and it was the leader in authentic log construction technology. The production of Sierra's homes was characterized by the juxtaposition of handcrafting and artful use of special purpose equipment. The basic unit of production was the construction crew, consisting of a crew leader and two crew members. The three-person crew size was the result of a great deal of experimentation over Sierra's history. The three-person crew was responsible for constructing the logwork for the log structure in its entirety, and the crew was a self-sufficient unit with personnel able to operate all the equipment necessary to construct the structure as well as accomplish all the handcrafting. The crew selected the logs, constructed the home, and loaded the marked logwork onto the truck for shipping. In emergency situations another crew member might be assigned to a building to speed construction time. In mid-1977 there were twelve construction crews. The company's order backlog had increased to three months and had been as high as six months. Indications were that orders from existing distributors were accelerating.

The construction operation was a handcraft one, supported by special purpose machinery, all of which had been developed by Sierra. The construction crew selected the logs based on their length and size relative to the stage of the building. Log selection was an art, since logs were tapered, and offsetting sizes had to be selected to mold a level and symmetrical building of the specified type. Specially adapted tractors were used to move the very heavy logs from place to place. The notching of the logs to fit together and produce a symmetrical structure of the desired shape was the most intricate operation, making use of specially designed scribing tools and specially adapted power chisels. Investment in equipment was in the hundreds of thousands of dollars. A typical 1,000-square-foot log home required approximately two and a half weeks to construct by an experienced three-man crew, down from twelve to fourteen weeks in 1972. The cost of the typical log structure was approximately 30 percent direct labor, 30 percent logs, and 40 percent overhead and profit.

The construction crew was a highly skilled unit, and training a new crew member to achieve full productivity required three to six months. It took six months more for a crew member to be qualified to be a crew leader. However, a new third crew member could be added to an experienced crew with little loss in output, since the experienced men took up the slack. Building authentic log homes was different from other construction work, and even experienced construction workers had to start from scratch in the training program. Construction workers were paid on a straight hourly basis, and their wages were well above the standard for the area and were increased with frequent raises. The typical construction worker had some college education. Construction crew members occasionally left the company, particularly during winter periods in the past, when there had been few orders and thus no work for periods of time. Crew members leaving the company, as well as those let go, were readily hired by Sierra's competitors. That had occurred six times in the past two years.

Construction crews reported to three foremen, who supervised four crews in 1977. The foremen reported to Ollie Lunde, the construction superintendent. Lunde was paid a salary plus a commission on every home that was shipped from the log yard.

The construction crews were supported by a log grader and sorter; a corps of peelers, who hand-peeled the bark off the logs; a maintenance department, which maintained the trucks, loaders, chain saws, and other equipment; equipment operators for log unloading, transporting, and crane operation; a sawmill operator; and general yard hands for dispensing materials and cleanup. When logs were unloaded at the log lot in Glacier, the first step was grading and sorting them by size. Then they were transported to peeling racks for peeling. Using long two-handled knives, the bark was hand-peeled from the logs giving them a distinct, handcrafted appearance. Peelers were paid a piece rate per log peeled, adjusted for the logs' size. Peeling was backbreaking work and served as an excellent recruiting ground for construction crew members. All members of construction crews had begun as peelers and had proved themselves and been given a chance at construction. Peelers were supervised by Sierra's peeling foreman, Matt Randall.

Peeled logs were selected by construction crews for use in buildings. A sawmill was used to produce flat sides on logs used for roof structures and floors. Once completed, a building was loaded on a flatbed trailer by the construction crew and crane operator. Sierra made exclusive use of an independent trucking company to haul its log structures to customer locations all over the United States. Sierra had a fully equipped maintenance faculty to ensure timely repair of construction machinery. Maintenance was the responsibility of a maintenance foreman and an assistant in 1977. The number of support personnel was approximately equal to the number of construction crew members in 1977.

While Sierra employed no formal R&D program in 1977, there were continual efforts to improve the product and production methods. Cameron Bach commented:

> We have periodically revised our log lot layout, construction techniques, and our equipment since we first started the company, and continue to do so. This has improved our production efficiency dramatically. We need to support some testing which will definitively establish the durability of our chinking, and the properties of log structures in general.

Organization and Finance

Sierra had a small management group, consisting of Cameron Bach; Bob Molloy, who coordinated the architectural work, priced buildings, interfaced with distributors, and was responsible for architectural problems in the construction process; Ollie Lunde, the production superintendent; the three construction foremen; and Matt Randall, the peeling foreman, who was also in charge of log procurement. Cameron Bach provided overall supervision and performed the finance function as well as becoming involved in all other aspects of the business in a policy-making and systems development capacity. Exhibit 19-4 shows the Sierra organization structure.

Sierra was the largest employer in its county. Its employees were drawn primarily from ranching, logging, and construction, and for many Sierra was

the first real company they had worked for. There was an adequate supply of hourly labor available to Sierra in 1977, though finding managerial talent had always been a difficult task. Given Sierra's size, Cameron Bach was continually asked to become involved in local government and social activities but had thus far resisted such invitations.

As of 1977 Sierra had eliminated all its debt, and Cameron Bach hoped to avoid further borrowing to finance growth. In view of Sierra's payment terms for its log homes, the company had almost no accounts receivable. Its primary working capital investment was in logs, though the company had not maintained extensive log inventories. Sierra's pretax profit margins were in excess of 20 percent in 1976.

Cameron Bach had been a Certified Public Accountant before he received an MBA from the Harvard Business School. He had joined Sierra after a year as a consultant overseas. Bach drove a jeep and the company's Ford Granada, and no one at Sierra including Bach had ever been seen wearing a necktie. Sierra maintained a modest office in Glacier's small downtown, a short distance from the log lot.

Competition

Sierra's most direct competitors were Rustic Log Homes and Big Valley Log Homes, located on either side of Sierra's log lot. It was nearly impossible for a customer to come to visit Sierra without passing one of the competitors' log lots. Many customers visited Rustic and Big Valley in addition to visiting Sierra, and Sierra's competitors often sent potential customers to listen to Sierra's salespersons and receive Sierra's price list as part of their own selling efforts. Cameron Bach commented on the competitive situation:

> We have our biggest problems with competitors in the local market, and when people come to Wyoming to look at our homes. Our competitors sell direct to these people, while we quote our retail prices to protect our distributors. If a customer received a low price quote from us and then went to one of our distributors who might give him a higher quote, we would create a lot of problems. We have another problem in that our customers cannot always see the better quality and

structural integrity of our homes as compared to the competitors'.

Rustic and Big Valley followed nearly identical pricing and payment structures to those of Sierra. In addition, both companies utilized three-person crews, similar production techniques, and nearly identical tools and equipment. Many employees at the two firms had been at Sierra. Cameron Bach remarked:

When we make a change in our production technology, it doesn't take long for Rustic and Big Valley to pick it up. Customers also tell me that they see Sierra brochures and plans openly displayed at our competitors, and a lot of their sales literature and standard home designs are very similar, if not identical, to ours. I remember once a few years back I decided to have color coded hard hats, red ones for peelers and yellow ones for the construction crews. Several days later Rustic's peelers had red hats and their crews yellow hats. I sometimes wonder what would happen if I lined up our employees in a straight line and marched them off a 3,000-foot cliff. I am sure that the next day my competitors would do the same thing, because if Sierra does it, it must be good for business.

While Rustic's prices were comparable to those of Sierra, Big Valley had followed a strategy of quoting very low prices, as much as 15 to 20 percent lower than Sierra's retail prices depending on whether the base was Sierra's pre-1977 prices or its recently raised prices. Big Valley's retail prices were very near the old prices at which Sierra sold to its distributors.

Cameron Bach reflected on recent competitive developments:

I lost at least five or six orders to competitors last year because I could not promise delivery soon enough. Sierra is realistic when quoting a delivery date, and our honesty sometimes costs us. In many instances our competitors cannot meet a delivery date, but will take the order anyway.

I have also had a couple potential distributors who first came to us but decided to sign with my competitors because we were either already covered in a market area, or were not planning immediate expansion.

Competition with milled-log homes was less direct but also important. Nearly all buyers compared the Sierra home to milled-log homes. While Sierra had been the only log home producer in the area when it came, by 1977 there were over more than twenty milled-log producers in Sierra's immediate area. Several milled-log producers were located very close to Sierra's log lot, and Real Log Homes had a plant in Missoula, Montana.

Milled-log producers competed with Sierra by citing lower prices, the "irregular" dimensions of the authentic log home, and potential problems with chinking falling out or cracking. All three claims were debatable, in the researcher's opinion, but nevertheless claims and counterclaims flowed freely in the industry.

Recent Developments

In 1977 the log supply problem had become acute, and a substantial number of lost orders and distributor grumbling had resulted from the inability to produce. In addition, a fire at the company's sawmill had been a setback and there had been a theft of some construction crew equipment. While thousands of dollars of tractors, chain saws, and other equipment had been left, exactly the equipment and tools to set up four construction crews had been taken, right down to the $2.00 chisels. Despite this, orders remained very strong and the backlog was lengthening rapidly, and Sierra looked forward to continued growth as its supply constraints eased.

EXHIBIT 19–1. *Milled-Log Home Construction Techniques*

I. Log Joining Procedures

FULL ROUND
(most common)

**VARIATION ON FULL
ROUND**

**3 SIDES
SQUARE**

**2 SIDES
SQUARE**

II. Milled-Log Corner Section

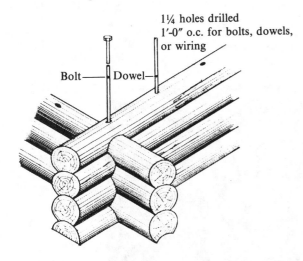

1¼ holes drilled
1'-0" o.c. for bolts, dowels,
or wiring

Bolt —— Dowel —

Locking Corner

III. Typical Milled-Log Home

III. A Sierra Authentic Log Home

EXHIBIT 19-2. *Authentic Log Home Construction Techniques*
I. Wall Construction Methods

Hand notched corners

Chinking

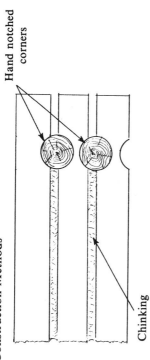

II. Hand Peeling Process and Partially Completed Building

EXHIBIT 19-3. *Leading Milled-Log Home Companies*

Company	Location	Date Founded[a]	No. of Models	No. of Dealers	No. of Known Plants	Logs Hand-peeled	Logs Machine-peeled
1. Airlock[b]	Las Vegas, N. M.	1955	55	2	1		✓
2. Alta Industries	Halcottsville, New York	*	20	–	1		✓
3. Andrew, L. C.	South Windham, Maine	1916	15	40	1	✓	✓
4. Authentic Log	Laramie, Wyoming	1973	30	50+	1		✓
5. Boyne Falls Log	Boyne Falls, Michigan	1945	A.C.	11	1	✓	
6. Building Logs	Gunnison, Colorado	1945	many	12	1	✓	✓
7. Chisum Industries	Grand Island, Nebraska	1975	A.C.	31	1[c]		✓
8. Classic Log	Lac La Biche, Alberta	1977	7	1	1		✓
9. Colorado Log	Englewood, Colorado	1972	22	11	1	✓	✓
10. Crockett	West Chesterfield, New Hampshire	1974	many	6	1	✓	✓
11. Green Mountain	Chester, Vermont	1972	A.C.	only direct sales	1	✓	
12. Justus	Tacoma, Washington	1954	several	28	1	✓	✓
13. Lodge Log	Boise, Idaho	1975	9	204	1		✓
14. National Log[b]	Thompson Falls, Montana	1944	55	7	1		✓
15. New England Log	Hamden, Connecticut	1970	30+	70	2[c]	✓	
16. Northern Products	Bangor, Maine	1968	13	–	1		✓
17. Pioneer Log	Newport, New Hampshire	1962	several	18	1		✓
18. R & L Log	Guilford, New York	1970	11	6	1	✓	
19. Rocky Mountain Log	Hamilton, Montana	1969	10	several	1		✓
20. Sylvan Products	Port Orchard, Washington	1959	5	*	1		✓
21. Vermont Log	Hartland, Vermont	1963	many	90	4		✓
22. Youngstrom Log	Blackfoot, Idaho	1962	19	15	2		✓

NOTES: "–" denotes that no information was available, and not an entry of zero. A.C. = All homes custom built.

[a] In most cases, significant activities had begun only recently for these firms, with activities before 1970 on an extremely small scale.

[b] Airlock and National Log were part of the same company.

[c] Another plant had been announced.

SOURCES: *1978 Log Home Guide* and casewriter research.

EXHIBIT 19–4. *Organization Chart*

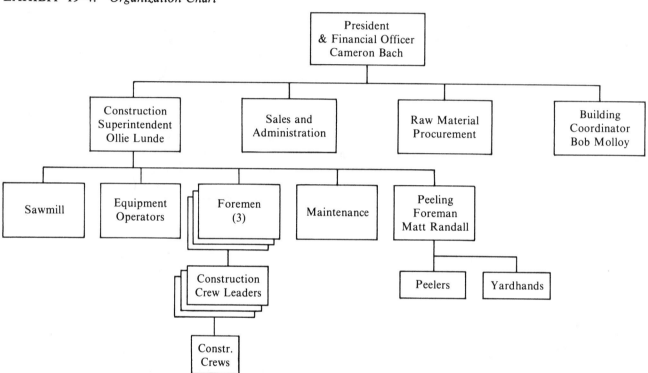

SOURCE: Casewriter interviews.

PART VIII
Declining Industries and Divestment

The next three cases focus on the related questions of declining industries and divestment. ''The Receiving Tube Industry in 1966'' and ''The Baby Food Industry in 1965'' consider two industries just as they are about to enter a protracted period of shrinking sales. The nature of competition in the period of decline ahead must be assessed, and the implications of this analysis for the strategies of the various industry participants takes on central priority if the firms are to recover any of their investments during the hard times ahead.

The ''EG&G, Inc.'' series shifts attention from the consideration of options in declining industries to the close-up examination of a divestment decision. EG&G has a sick division, described in the case, that is a candidate for divestment. Management must decide how to proceed, mindful of the economic and organizational issues involved.

The Receiving Tube Industry in 1966

A receiving tube was an active electronic component capable of detecting, modifying, and amplifying electrical signals. It was used as a key component in radios, television receivers, communications equipment, audio amplifiers, and many other electronic products. Receiving tubes had been the first electronic components and had been the basis on which the modern electronics industry had been built. However, in 1966 receiving tubes competed with transistors (invented in 1947) and integrated circuits (invented in 1958) for use in electronic devices.

Demand for receiving tubes had reached a second "peak" in 1966, with booming color television set sales providing the major impetus. 282,677,000 receiving tubes were consumed for original equipment (OEM) applications, while 123,272,000 tubes were consumed for replacement purposes, with a total dollar value of $301 million. However, even as the receiving tube industry enjoyed this demand there were substantial doubts about its continued viability in the face of new generations of electronic components.

The Product

In a receiving tube a metal filament or "cathode" was heated by electric current and emitted a stream of negative electrons, which jumped across a vacuum to the positively charged anode or plate. The receiving tube was sometimes called a "vacuum tube" because of this vacuum. A grid or wire screen between the filament and plate controlled the flow of electrons by varying the negative charge on the grid, which repelled or allowed to pass the negatively charged electrons. Tubes had connecting pins for plugging them into "sockets" in the electronic device to be powered, and each variety of tube had its own unique socket.

By 1966 the technology of receiving tubes was quite mature. While firms such as RCA held patents on some general-purpose receiving tube designs, competitors could easily design around these patents and create a tube whose performance was equivalent. Receiving tube manufacturers "cross-engineered" the tube designs of their competitors in order to have tubes that would be interchangeable.

As a result, receiving tubes of competing manufacturers were essentially identical, though there were some specialized applications where proprietary technology remained. Receiving tube technology developed by RCA had also been licensed to foreign electronics firms that had subsequently competed against the U.S. industry.

Markets

Receiving tubes were sold to a variety of markets, including OEMs, government, franchised independent dealers, other tube manufacturers, and private label sellers. Each of these markets had somewhat differing characteristics, and receiving tube manufacturers utilized strategies of careful market segmentation.

The OEM Market. Receiving tubes were used by manufacturers of television sets, radios, audio components, instrumentation, and many other electronic products. Tubes were specially designed to meet the needs of OEM customers of significant size and were manufactured to order in large volumes. As a result the inventory requirements for serving the OEM market were small. Television sets, and to a lesser extent radio receivers, represented the primary markets for tubes in 1966. Both industries were relatively concentrated. RCA held approximately 35 percent of the TV set market in 1966, followed by Zenith at 20 percent, Motorola at 10 percent, GE at around 10 percent, and GTE Sylvania and Westinghouse with less than 10 percent each. Markets for tubes in audio components, instrumentation, and other applications were more fragmented and often required higher-technology, more specialized tubes.

The receiving tube had a low unit cost and represented a relatively small proportion of the total value of the products in which it was a component, but its integrity was crucial to the operation of these products. Since quality was critical, extensive inspection and testing characterized tube manufacturing. Price competition in receiving tubes had not been severe until the market entry of Japanese tube producers in the late 1950s.

Manufacturers sold to OEMs through their own sales forces, offering engineering assistance, special test data, and extensive service. The tube manufacturers with the best reputations commanded a slight price premium. Many large OEM users of receiving tubes manufactured a significant proportion of their needs internally, particularly the major television set producers. In addition, tube manufacturers sometimes purchased tubes from each other and from foreign firms to fill out their lines in the case of low volume or especially costly or proprietary tubes.

The Replacement Market. Replacement tubes for repairing electronic products were another important market for receiving tubes. There was a propensity to replace burned-out tubes with tubes of the same manufacturer, if available, which created strong competition among receiving tube producers to be designed into customers' sockets in the OEM market. Because of the proliferation of tube varieties for different OEMs, tube manufacturers often had in excess of 1,000 different varieties of tubes in inventory. Manufacturer investment in inventory to serve the replacement market was substantial in view of the need to provide good service and to stock these many varieties.

Replacement tubes were sold through a number of channels. Most were sold through either independent or company-owned distributors to the thousands of dealer-affiliated and independent repair shops for electronic products. These same outlets often sold other products or components made by the receiving tube manufacturers. Brand name and quality reputation as an electronics producer were critical in the independent service market, and there was substantial advertising of tubes both to servicepersons and to distributors.

Independent distributors were franchised and typically carried one major receiving tube line and a secondary line to hedge against stockouts.[1] Receiving tube manufacturers employed sales forces to sell to their distributors and cultivated them with discounts off list prices, bonuses, trips, and favorable credit terms. Manufacturers often financed significant portions of the distributor inventory of their tubes in the form of accounts receivable.

[1] They also typically carried other electronic and electrical components, including those manufactured by receiving tube manufacturers.

There were two other markets for replacement tubes. One was tubes sold to OEMs who had their own service organizations, such as Zenith. Tube manufacturer brand name was less important in this market than in the independent servicing market, and many OEMs like Zenith purchased U.S.-made or Japanese private label tubes for sale under their own brand name in order to lower costs. The other market for replacement tubes was to private brand sellers of electronic products who had their own service organizations, such as Sears and Montgomery Ward. These buyers also purchased private label tubes carrying their own brand, frequently sourced from the Japanese. The market for private brand replacement tubes was known as the private brand replacement market.

Governmental and Industrial. A limited quantity of receiving tubes was sold to government and industrial users for specialized applications such as communications equipment, process control equipment, weapons, and the like. These applications often required higher-technology and/or higher-fidelity tubes than so-called entertainment grade tubes sold in the mass markets, and many of them relied on properties of tubes that would be very difficult to duplicate with semiconductor technology.

Historical demand for receiving tubes is shown in Exhibit 20–1. The early 1960s had been a period of rapid growth for receiving tubes because of the geometric growth in the use of tubes in color television receivers. Radio receivers, the main user of receiving tubes in the 1950s, had typically contained five tubes or less. A black-and-white television set contained nine or ten receiving tubes, however, and a typical color television receiver used twenty-three tubes in 1962. As color television designs had evolved, sixteen or seventeen receiving tubes per set were common in 1966.

Foreign Competition

Japanese companies had entered the U.S. receiving tube market in the late 1950s with a strategy of very low prices. Imports of Japanese tubes had grown rapidly, as shown in Table 20–1.

Japanese manufacturers had concentrated primarily on the high-volume OEM and private brand replacement markets and on the technologically simple varieties of tubes. There had initially been resistance to Japanese tubes due to lingering resentments from World War II, but as U.S. receiving tube prices rose and Japanese tubes improved in quality, Japanese penetration began to occur. Japanese tubes were sold at discounts of up to 20 percent of the prices of domestically made tubes, and Japanese manufacturers provided little customer support or engineering assistance. They typically reverse-engineered domestic manufacturers' tubes. Japanese penetration of the independent service replacement market had been small because of a lack of distribution and dealer relationships.

Receiving Tube Manufacturing

The production process for making receiving tubes was relatively simple, though requiring high precision. The main steps from beginning to end included (a) fabrication of raw materials; (b) placing these components on structural jigs, which held the materials in relative proximity to each other; (c) welding these pieces onto a base; and (d) sealing the assembly in an evacuated glass envelope.

Many receiving tube manufacturers drew their own wires and produced their own cathodes, which were the rods that heated up in the receiving tube. Some plants also wrapped grids and manually positioned them for welding operations, while others

TABLE 20–1. Imported Receiving Tubes Consumed in U.S. Consumer Electronics Products *(in millions)*

	1960	*1961*	*1962*	*1963*	*1964*	*1965*	*1966*
Japanese receiving tube unit shipments	16.3	20.3	27.3	36.4	31.1	46.1	48.5
Value of Japanese receiving tube shipments	$4.5	$5.4	$7.3	$9.2	$8.1	$11.6	$13.3

SOURCE: Census of Manufacturers.

shipped components to offshore plants for assembly and welding operations. Some companies carried out the entire manufacturing process offshore.

The most critical assembly operation in tube manufacturing was the spraying of the cathode, a wire-wrapped nickel or other metallic rod. The cathode was sprayed with a special electron-generating coating. The cathode spraying operation required precise tolerances and quality control. It determined the quality of the rest of the tube. The "cage" of the receiving tube was assembled by placing the wire grids and wire-wrapped cathodes onto mica bases, where they were welded into place. The glass envelope was shaped from glass tubes (usually purchased from Corning Glass Works) and was mounted and sealed. Gases were then evacuated from the sealed chamber.

Most of the fabricating operations for receiving tubes were labor-intensive, though final assembly was done by machine. Quality control and meticulous testing were the keys to the consistent quality, and skilled labor was necessary for portions of the manufacturing process. The labor force for most receiving tube manufacturers had been in place for many years. Direct and indirect labor were the chief elements of cost in tube manufacturing, comprising approximately 40 percent of total costs. Materials costs were second in size. A substantial amount of testing and measuring equipment was also required as part of the manufacturing process for quality control.

Receiving tubes were assembled inside factories that were clean and dustless to avoid any contaminating particles that could result in a malfunction. Plants frequently had work surfaces covered with tiles or parqueted hardwood. The tube assembly operation was carefully supervised in these "clean" surroundings, but even then some technical difficulties occasionally occurred in the production process. Though manufacturing receiving tubes was relatively standardized, there was a certain element of "black magic" involved in producing tubes. There could be a run of defective tubes for unaccountable reasons, and this meant that extensive inspections were necessary.

Receiving tube manufacturing shared few if any operations with the production of other electronic components or devices, and equipment for fabrication, assembly, and testing of receiving tubes was highly specialized. Each variety of receiving tube that was produced required a separate set-up on the assembly line. Economies could be enjoyed by producing long runs of various tube types, and the set-up costs typically necessitated runs of at least 10,000 units of a given type of receiving tube for break-even. Since some tube designs broke even at such a high volume, tube-makers often sold to each other to round out their product lines. The savings involved in an offshore plant or a "feeder" facility could be substantial in receiving tube production, given the high labor content.

By the mid-1950s most producers of receiving tubes were producing them on automated assembly lines. An efficient facility cost a minimum of $12 million in plant and equipment, and manufacturing receving tubes also required significant investments in automation that had been, and continued to be, made by major producers. Economies of scale had increased significantly in the late 1950s and 1960s.

A Historical Overview of the Receiving Tube Industry

Thomas A. Edison first noticed in 1880 that a small metal plate or wire placed at the base of an evacuated glass-enveloped lamp became electrically charged when the filament within the bulb was heated to incandescence. By the 1920s there were more than 150 manufacturers of nearly 300 brands of receiving tubes, who sold them to 150 to 200 manufacturers of radio sets. The largest radio manufacturers were RCA, General Electric, Philco-Lansdale, Atwater-Kent, Majestic, Emerson Electric, and Crosley. The receiving tube producers included many "Ma and Pa" operations as well as some larger firms, including Sylvania, Ken-Rad (later General Electric), National Union Electric, Raytheon, Westinghouse Electric, Arcturus, Hytron Electric (CBS), Philco-Lansdale, Johnsonberg Tube Company, Tun-Sol Electronics, and RCA.

Consumption of receiving tubes in radios had plateaued by World War II; radio had become a mature product. However, postwar television production needed even more receiving tubes. Thus the receiving tube industry thrived as television was commercialized.

After World War II, under the reconstruction

policies of the U.S. government, receiving tube manufacturers gave their technology to the defeated war powers. As a result of this technology transfer, Japanese industry had developed to the point that exports to the U.S. market became a significant factor by the late 1950s. Raytheon had sold its technology and some of its manufacturing assets to Nippon Electric Company (NEC) in 1963. This enabled a Japanese producer to make the technological leap in matching the quality of U.S. tube producers. After NEC had done so, other Japanese tube manufacturers learned how to produce American tube varieties. By 1966 rising Japanese competition had caused tube prices to drop 40 percent since pre-Japanese times.

SUBSTITUTE TECHNOLOGY

In 1948 two American Telephone and Telegraph employees at Bell Laboratories discovered the transistor effect and subsequently described it in a research paper. Texas Instruments was among the first companies to try to commercialize the transistor, the first generation of semiconductors. Semiconductor or "solid state" technology had inherent advantages over the receiving tube for most applications, including greater reliability, longer life, and ultimately lower cost.

In military markets and other markets where extreme reliability and performance were crucial, solid state technology was adopted while it was still quite costly. Receiving tube use peaked in 1955, as transistors replaced receiving tubes in high-technology applications. In entertainment markets, cost was a primary consideration, so penetration of solid state devices was much slower.

In 1956, the year after the historical peak in receiving tube consumption, some transistor manufacturers had predicted that half the TV sockets using tubes would be lost to transistors by 1961. Engineers at major TV producers like Zenith, Philco, Magnavox, Emerson, and the RCA Television Set Division recognized that solid state was inevitable once cost and reliability improved but had predicted at this time that tubes would be in some use for ten to fifteen years longer. By 1966 solid state technology had not been commercialized as quickly as had been expected by many observers, and a fully solid state TV was not yet commercially

feasible. However, in 1966 TV manufacturers were in the process of converting to a solid state TV chassis.

The first firms to manufacture solid state components included Texas Instruments, Transitron Electric Corp., and Hughes Aircraft. These were among the top five producers of semiconductor devices in 1957, and none had produced receiving tubes. However, the producers of receiving tubes had entered into manufacture of solid state components by 1966. The production techniques involved in making transistors and other semiconductors were completely different from those required in receiving tubes, though semiconductors were sold through the same basic distribution channels as receiving tubes.

Despite the advent of solid state technology, in 1966 demand for receiving tubes for color television had grown to a level that required the remaining receiving tube manufacturers' plant capacity to operate on a seven-day, multiple-shift basis in order to meet the demand. Although capacity was strained, no firms had invested in new plant facilities. The shortfall was absorbed by imported tubes.

Competition in 1966

As a result of import competition, the pretelevision plateau in tube demand, and increasing automation, by 1966 there were only four major U.S. receiving tube manufacturers: General Electric, RCA, GTE-Sylvania, and Westinghouse. Three of these companies controlled 80 percent of the U.S. receiving tube sales in 1966: RCA had 34 percent of the market, GTE-Sylvania 30 percent, and GE 16 percent. Raytheon, Hytron (CBS), Philco, and Tung-Sol, which had previously produced both television sets and tubes, had discontinued both products. Of these only Raytheon and Philco continued to merchandise replacement tubes under their brand for their receivers, purchased from other tube-makers.[2] North American Phillips and particularly Raytheon sold replacement tubes for use in repairing other manufacturers' sets as well as their own.

---

[2] Philco had sold its tube making assets to GTE-Sylvania.

Firms such as Sears, Zenith, Motorola, Admiral, and Magnavox purchased and sold private branded tubes for their in-house repair operations. Imported receiving tubes competed with the domestic tubes for OEM applications and for some private brand replacement applications. Major Japanese firms exporting tubes to the United States in 1966 included Matsushita, Hitachi, Toshiba, NEC, and Mitsubishi.

The chief domestic competitors in receiving tubes in 1966 are profiled below. Exhibit 20–2 summarizes their financial performance.

RCA Corporation. The RCA Corporation had pioneered the development of radio, black-and-white television, and color television and was considered by some observers to be the epitome of an electronics company. RCA was engaged in the manufacture of consumer products; commercial, military, and space apparatus; and computers and data processing systems in 1966. RCA also operated television and radio broadcasting stations and a television and radio network, and supplied programming for broadcasting. RCA had other operations in book publishing, truck rental and leasing, and construction equipment; it operated an extensive distribution and servicing network for its products. RCA was organized into twenty-one subsidiaries and an international division and had corporate sales of $2,549 million in 1966. As a corporate strategy, RCA tended to invest in technologically based new businesses. It had many investment opportunities in 1966.

The RCA Receiving Tubes Division manufactured receiving tubes as well as semiconductors for consumer products, computers, and computer memories. RCA was heavily forward-integrated. RCA Corporation consumed receiving tubes internally in its television and radio receivers, public address systems, transmitters, and aerospace products. Several military products produced by RCA Corporation also used its own specially designed receiving tubes. RCA held many patents on its general-purpose receiving tube designs and derived considerable income from licensed receiving tube technology overseas. RCA helped to set up receiving tube factories in other countries and collected royalties on their productive outputs, even if it was subsequently exported to the United States.

RCA domestic receiving tubes had been historically manufactured at four plants: Harrison and Woodbridge, New Jersey; Cincinnati, Ohio; and Indianapolis, Indiana. The Harrison plant was the site of the original RCA facility. RCA also produced receiving tubes in plants in Mexico and Brazil, although the output of these plants was usually consumed domestically in their respective locations. RCA had no offshore plants for production of domestically marketed receiving tubes.

RCA had closed its Indianapolis receiving tube plant in about 1960, deploying the labor force to other RCA operations nearby. This decision was being severely criticized in 1966 as demand for tubes had increased rapidly in the color television OEM market. In 1966 RCA produced tubes in facilities most observers believed to be less automated than its competitors. The three remaining receiving tube plants in 1966 were relatively old. RCA had made few apparent investments in receiving tube manufacturing in the 1960s, and its production technology was more labor-intensive than that of other tube producers.

RCA's strong position in the receiving tube market stemmed in part from the reliability of its products and its high level of service, as well in part from its strong position in the TV set market. RCA had invested substantial resources in product development and quality control. RCA's quality reputation was buttressed by research facilities that were unparalleled in the television receiver industry. RCA engineers had helped Corning Glass to perfect the glass envelopes used in making receiving tubes and television picture tubes. RCA worked with receiving tube customers such as Magnavox, Admiral, Philco, Muntz, and Emerson to produce high-quality television receivers.

RCA had created the "Nuvistor," a compact metal and ceramic tube, as a partial response to the transistor. Although the Nuvistor had been adopted in several RCA commercial applications and in some of RCA's military applications, the Nuvistor was not widely used because it had not proved to be a lower-cost product than the transistor.

RCA maintained strategically placed inventory reserves so that customers received quality components as needed for their plants to avoid production delays. This allowed OEM customers to hold minimal inventories of tubes while RCA bore the cost of inventory. In addition to warehouse services provided to OEM customers, RCA also helped to establish and finance independent electronics distributors who frequently carried only the RCA product line. Approximately 80 percent of RCA's sales of receiving tubes in the replacement market were sold through independent distributors, with much of the rest sold through the captive RCA Distributing Corporation. RCA was very active in using promotional devices to stimulate the marketing of its receiving tubes in the replacement market. RCA had introduced a trip program for its distributors in 1961.

General Electric Company. General Electric was the largest manufacturer of electrical equipment in the United States in 1966. It was engaged in the development, manufacture, and sale of equipment, supplies, and appliances for the generation, transmission, control, and use of electrical power. General Electric's electrical products ranged from lamps, household applicances, X-ray equipment, and industrial apparatus to complete utility power plants. General Electric was organized into six groups: Aerospace and Defense Group; Components and Construction Group; Consumer Products Group; Electrical Utility Group; Industrial and Information Group; and the International Group. Corporate sales were $7,177 million in 1966, broken down as follows: industrial components and materials, 33 percent; consumer goods, 27 percent; heavy capital goods; 22 percent; and defense products departments, 18 percent. Receiving tubes were part of the Components Group.

General Electric had once been the second largest receiving tube producer, but it ranked third in 1966. General Electric had acquired the Kentucky Radio Company (Ken-Rad) in 1944 in order to enter the receiving tube business and had been one of the last major electronics companies to do so. It produced a relatively narrow line of tubes (more than 900 tubes). At one time it had produced metallic tubes (like RCA's Nuvistors) but had discontinued that product line because of uneconomic sales volumes.

General Electric was forward-integrated as well, producing television receivers, radios, and a variety of other products that used receiving tubes. General Electric consumer electronics products were sold through common independent and company-owned distribution channels and supported by an in-house service organization. General Electric also produced semiconductors and supported several research laboratories in electronic products.

Tubes were produced in domestic plants located in Ownesboro, Kentucky, and Tell City, Indiana, in 1966. General Electric also operated an offshore plant in Singapore, which enjoyed very low labor costs but required lead times for shipping, processing, and repackaging even using airlift transportation. In Singapore, receiving tube components were mounted, soldered, and shipped to Owensboro, where they were sealed. Special tubes, low-volume tubes, and unique jobs were produced in their entirety in General Electric's domestic receiving tube plants. While General Electric's plants were relatively old, GE had invested in developing cost-saving operations and equipment.

General Electric produced some proprietary tubes, which it sold to the other manufacturers, and also bought tubes from other manufacturers to fill out its line. In addition to purchasing tubes from RCA, GTE Sylvania, and other domestic tube producers, General Electric purchased the tubes of foreign producers as well.

General Electric was strong in the replacement market and was the first receiving tube manufacturer to introduce trips as premiums for distributors in 1960. It had built a strong system of independent distributors as its channel for merchandising tubes to the replacement market.

General Electric had strict financial performance goals, and the Tube Products Department maintained a policy of never undercutting competitors, although it would meet price cuts if they occurred. Moreover, on several occasions General Electric initiated increases in receiving tube prices.

General Telephone and Electronics Corporation (GTE-Sylvania). General Telephone and Electronics Corporation (GTE) was a holding company that controlled more than thirty domestic operating telephone companies and subsidiaries engaged in manufacturing: radio, television, and electronics products; communications and industrial control equipment; data transmission and processing hardware; and specialized military and industrial communications equipment. Consolidated corporate sales in 1966 were $1,401 million.

GTE manufactured receiving tubes in its subsidiary, Sylvania Electric Products, Inc. (GTE-Sylvania), which GTE had acquired in 1959. GTE-Sylvania had sales of $454 million in 1959 and was one of the largest manufacturers of electronic tubes, photoflash lamps, and fluorescent and incandescent lamps. GTE-Sylvania also manufactured television and radio sets, semiconductor products, and cameras. It was a participant in national defense projects and was among the leading producers of traveling wave tubes, high-power tubes, klystrons, and other industrial and military-grade receiving tubes in addition to entertainment-grade tubes. In addition to its U.S. business, GTE-Sylvania sold receiving tubes worldwide—to Canada, parts of Europe, and Latin America.

GTE-Sylvania had been one of the first large tube manufacturers. As Nilco Lamp company, it had produced receiving tubes for radio receivers. GTE-Sylvania had also done extensive research with the U.S. military to develop "fuze" tubes for ordinance and subminiature tubes, such as lock-ins and guided missile receiving tubes. Its very wide product line included government, industrial, military, and entertainment-grade receiving tubes.

GTE-Sylvania pursued an aggressive differentiation strategy to serve the two principal receiving tube markets—OEM and replacement—maintaining two separate sales forces. As a special service to OEM customers, GTE-Sylvania offered customized engineering services. GTE-Sylvania's engineering staff would design products to suit a customer's requirements or it would cross-design (reverse engineer) the receiving tubes manufactured by competitors to enable its customers to have a second source.

The replacement market sales force dealt with the more than 700 electronics distributors who carried GTE-Sylvania's receiving tubes. The replacement market sales force was given pricing discretion and used promotions—trips, prizes, and incentive plans—to motivate its dealers to sell Sylvania components, though not to the degree that its competitors did. GTE-Sylvania also helped its distributors financially. Both GTE sales forces also sold semiconductors.

GTE-Sylvania was forward-integrated into television production and also produced a narrow line of other consumer products—radio receivers and stereophonic phonographs. GTE-Sylvania was one of two television producers that had held out against using Japanese tubes (the other was Zenith Radio, whose receiving tubes were supplied by GTE-Sylvania). GTE-Sylvania's semiconductor division produced transistors and integrated circuits. GTE-Sylvania maintained separate research laboratories for its entertainment products, electronics systems, parts, and semiconductor divisions.

GTE Sylvania produced receiving tubes in dedicated plants located in Altoona, Emporium, and Williamsport, Pennsylvania, and Burlington, Iowa. It also had a preassembly plant in Juarez, Mexico. GTE had invested heavily in automated tube assembly facilities from 1962 through 1966. GTE-Sylvania manufactured many of the components that went into its receiving tubes. It refined its own mica disks, drew its own wires, wound its own grids, sprayed its own cathodes, and at one time had made the glass envelopes for tubes. It also sold many of the tube components it produced to other tube makers.

Westinghouse Electric Corporation. Westinghouse was engaged in the manufacture and sale of electrical apparatus and appliances for the generation, transmission, utilization, and control of electricity and in the manufacture and sale of steam and gas turbines and associated equipment. Westinghouse's products were highly diversified and included practically all electrical and related mechanical equipment required by electric power companies, electrified railroads, and the Navy and marine industry, as well as some equipment for the aviation industry. In addition to these heavy industrial products, Westinghouse produced household appliances, including radios and televisions, and operated radio and television stations. The electronics (as opposed to electrical) related business of Westinghouse represented approximately 10 percent of corporate sales. Corporate sales in 1966 were $2,581 million.

Westinghouse produced a relatively small quantity of receiving tubes in its Electronics Tube Division, which were primarily sold internally to the unit that produced Westinghouse television receivers. Westinghouse produced receiving tubes only for consumer products. In addition to supplying its own internal needs for receiving tubes, Westinghouse sold receiving tubes to some small competitors, which manufactured television or radio receivers and did not have the in-house capacity to manufacture receiving tubes. Westinghouse's receiving tube plant was located in Bath, New York, and had not been modernized. Lamp production operations were also active in that plant in 1966.

Raytheon Company. The Raytheon Company engineered, manufactured, and sold electrical and electronic equipment in 1966. An important part of its business was devoted to design, development, and production of the Navy's guided "Sparrow III" missile and the Army's "Hawk" missile systems. Among its many products, Raytheon also manufactured electronic tubes, including klystrons and other power tubes; industrial and military-grade receiving tubes; germanium semiconductor devices; silicon transistors; and many other electronic components. Corporate sales in 1966 were $709 million. Raytheon had acquired a television receiver firm, Belmont Radio, in 1945 but had divested the television receiver business in 1956 and sold its assets to Admiral Corporation. Raytheon had never been successful in the OEM entertainment business.

Raytheon receiving tube operations had been located in Newton, North Windham, and Quincy, Massachusetts. In December 1963 Raytheon announced that it would close the North Windham entertainment-grade tube plant, consolidating these tube operations and those of the Quincy tube plant into the plant at Newton, Massachusetts. Raytheon continued to produce industrial and military-grade tube varieties. Soon afterward, Raytheon divested its entertainment-grade receiving tubes production facilities altogether. When it divested its entertainment-grade receiving tubes, Raytheon sold its tube-making equipment in Europe.

Raytheon contracted with Nippon Electric of Japan to supply it with receiving tubes, which Raytheon merchandised to the replacement market under the Raytheon name. Raytheon tubes were available only in the most popular, higher-volume models and were sold at a modest discount to tubes of the other U.S. manufacturers but at prices above those of Japanese firms. Raytheon's distributors carried Raytheon's tubes as a second line, in addition to some other tube manufacturers' full lines.

EXHIBIT 20-1.   *Manufacturers' Sales of Receiving Tubes by End Use (000 omitted)*

Year	Original Equip. Mfgrs.	Replacement or Renewal	Export	Government	Total	Dollar Value	Average Unit Price
1939	65,284	25,375	7,841	NA[a]	98,500	$27,985	$.28
1940	72,249	28,994	7,233	NA	108,476	27,610	.25
1941	92,031	33,782	10,025	NA	135,838	47,500	.35
1942	64,640	36,495	6,612	NA	107,747	43,000	.40
1943	54,507	19,637	3,106	32,828	110,078	51,000	.46
1944	60,207	20,899	4,552	43,405	129,063	62,140	.48
1945	57,235	40,462	4,995	36,786	139,478	68,500	.49
1946	129,637	65,228	9,991	361	205,217	101,000	.49
1947	131,987	43,530	23,184	833	199,534	107,000	.54
1948	146,162	47,056	10,687	815	204,720	112,000	.55
1949	147,298	39,696	10,073	1,686	198,753	119,000	.60
1950	301,483	69,325	10,768	1,385	382,961	250,000	.65
1951	247,855	94,597	24,483	8,754	375,644	261,000	.69
1952	241,406	83,843	13,935	29,335	368,519	259,116	.70
1953	293,601	112,785	20,614	10,091	437,091	303,675	.69
1954	246,729	115,358	15,922	7,080	385,089	275,999	.72
1955	288,810	150,718	24,442	15,832	479,802	358,110	.75
1956	262,898	166,558	25,397	9,333	464,186	374,186	.81
1957	240,708	184,493	23,378	7,845	456,424	384,402	.84
1958	191,832	167,805	24,597	13,132	397,366	341,929	.86
1959	227,669	170,729	19,969	14,569	432,936	368,872	.85
1960	200,362	161,092	21,375	10,226	393,055	331,742	.84
1961	118,176	150,249	22,245	14,336	375,006	311,098	.83
1962	190,140	134,390	19,804	16,905	361,239	301,525	.83
1963	233,668	133,016	16,958	11,902	395,544	297,000	.75
1964	212,010	125,006	20,430	10,642	368,088	272,000	.74
1965	232,921	130,325	17,198	16,108	396,552	282,000	.76
1966	282,677	123,273	19,335	17,595	442,879	301,000	.68

[a]Not available.

SOURCE: *Electronics Marketing Handbook.*

EXHIBIT 20-2. *Corporatewide Financial Performance of Receiving Tube Competitors in 1966 (in millions)*

	1966	1965	1964	1963	1962	1961
General Electric						
Sales	$7,177.3	$6,213.6	$4,941.4	$4,918.7	$4,792.7	$4,456.8
Profits	338.9	355.1	237.3	270.6	265.8	242.1
Return on sales	.05	.06	.05	.06	.06	.05
Total assets	4,789.2	4,260.4	3,090.4	2,986.4	2,819.5	2,677.4
Shareholders' equity	2,149.2	2,067.0	1,888.0	1,816.8	1,694.9	1,576.1
Return on equity	.16	.17	.13	.15	.16	.15
GTE-Sylvania						
Sales	807.6	639.9	551.8	473.2	431.8	418.2
Profits	42.5	19.5	14.9	12.2	8.5	4.6
Return on sales	.05	.03	.03	.03	.02	.01
Total assets	458.4	354.1	328.5	304.6	303.8	310.8
Shareholders' equity	202.2	176.8	169.3	164.4	162.2	161.6
Return on equity	.21	.11	.09	.07	.05	.03
RCA						
Sales	2,548.8	2,042.0	1,797.9	1,779.1	1,742.7	1,537.9
Profits	132.4	101.2	93.9	66.0	58.5	35.5
Return on sales	.05	.05	.05	.04	.03	.02
Total assets	1,471.6	1,269.4	1,131.7	1,129.5	1,058.9	943.7
Shareholders' equity	692.9	593.0	523.4	530.8	489.4	449.2
Return on equity	.19	.17	.18	.12	.12	.08
Westinghouse Electric						
Sales	2,581.4	2,389.9	2,271.2	2,127.3	1,954.5	1,913.8
Profits	119.7	106.9	76.7	47.8	57.1	45.4
Return on sales	.05	.04	.03	.02	.03	.02
Total assets	1,951.6	1,711.5	1,606.6	1,542.6	1,516.5	1,531.8
Shareholders' equity	1,103.1	1,037.9	983.9	969.2	970.9	971.3
Return on equity	.11	.10	.08	.05	.06	.05
Raytheon						
Sales	709.0	487.8	454.1	488.9	580.7	562.9
Profits	18.4	11.0	8.2	.09	9.6	6.9
Return on sales	.026	.023	.018	.00	.02	.01
Total assets	382.0	273.7	235.7	234.7	256.6	252.6
Shareholders' equity	161.0	125.8	109.1	108.4	109.1	99.6
Return on equity	.11	.08	.07	.00	.09	.07

SOURCE: Annual reports.

The Baby Foods Industry in 1965

Baby foods were commercially processed formulas or special foods strained to a very fine consistency to be fed to infants. Baby foods were consumed primarily by children from birth to the age of approximately two years. The number of new births had reached a peak in 1957, and baby food manufacturers had publicly estimated a 16 percent increase in births by the mid-1960s. Instead, births had declined 12 percent from the 1957 peak by 1965, resulting in excess capacity in the industry.

The Product

Baby foods were mixed, chopped, strained, or puréed dairy products, fruits, vegetables, or meats processed for consumption primarily by infants. The principal types of baby foods included (a) juices and soups; (b) precooked cereals; (c) strained and chopped vegetables and meats; (d) fruits; (e) desserts; (f) junior cookies and teething biscuits; (g) egg yolks; and (h) meat base and milk formulas. These types of baby food could be grouped into three categories: (a) formulas, manufactured mostly by subsidiaries of drug companies; (b) infant foods; and (c) junior formulations of infant foods.

"Junior foods" were more coarsely ground in texture than infant foods. Each category was consumed by babies, progressively, as they matured and their diets became more varied.

Formulas, juices, and cereals were the first products eaten by a child. Canned baby foods were consumed by babies between the ages of two months and eighteen months. Commonly, physicians recommended that the child add fruits and vegetables to its diet in the second month, meats during the third and fourth months. Chopped junior foods were introduced to the child's diet in the ninth or tenth month. As soon as the baby could consume solid foods with ease, baby foods were no longer included in its diet. Therefore, demand for baby foods was a function of births and of the proportion of babies being fed commercially prepared baby foods. Consumption of baby foods had been growing slightly faster than the rate of population growth, because a growing proportion of babies were being fed commercially prepared baby foods.

Baby foods could be somewhat physically differentiated on the basis of quality of raw materials used, flavors, and packaging. Thanks to strict sanitation requirements in production facilities, all baby food brands were equally free from contamination. Most brands of baby food also offered the same flavors and a wide assortment of products. However, perceived product differentiation in baby foods seemed to transcend physical differences; mothers seemed to believe that there were differences between brands of baby food and were loyal to their brands. Extensive promotional outlays were used to differentiate baby foods and ensure that they received wide grocery store shelf space.

Commercially prepared baby food products were close to being necessities for infants' feeding in 1965. Some mothers prepared homemade baby foods, and the development of food-processing home appliances (blenders, food grinders) had made the preparation of home-cooked baby foods somewhat easier. However, less than 5 percent of babies were fed with homemade baby foods in 1965.

Births had reached their absolute peak in 1957, when 4.3 million babies had been born. By 1965 the number of births had fallen to 3.76 million babies. Consumption of canned baby foods in 1960 had amounted to 872.8 million pounds, or approximately $233 million at manufacturers' prices ($266 million at retail). Approximately 42 percent of this volume was made up of fruits processed for baby foods ($98 million); 29 percent was meat products ($68 million); 17 percent vegetables ($40 million); 12 percent custards and puddings ($28 million). Sales of baby cereals accounted for another $23 million. Exhibit 21-1 shows the shipments of canned baby food over time. In 1965 an average jar of baby food cost 14¢.

In 1958 the marketing department of Gerber Products had forecast that births would increase from the 1957 peak of 4.3 million to 4.4 million by 1965 and predicted a 16 percent compound growth rate in births from 1965 to 1970. This optimism regarding future growth in births was widespread in the baby food industry, despite some uncertainties held by demographic forecasters outside the industry. New plants and warehouses were being built on the basis of such forecasts in the mid-1960s.

Markets

While the ultimate consumer of baby foods was the infant, the purchaser was usually its mother. The principal outlet for baby foods was the grocery store, which accounted for 90 percent of baby food sales. Convenience stores also sold some baby foods. Originally, baby foods had been sold through drugstores as a high-margin medicinal product. By 1965, however, baby foods were by and large a lower-margin, higher-turnover grocery store item. Grocery stores carried only a limited number of baby food lines, making shelf space competition crucial.

In addition to branded sales through grocery stores, there was a private label market for baby food. Private label brands represented approximately 5 percent of the total U.S. market. There was also an institutional market (e.g., hospitals and nurseries), which purchased some of its requirements either from the major branded baby food producers or from companies that specialized in private brands. Because institutions were strongly interested in low prices, private label brands were quite successful in some institutions. Other institutions preferred branded baby foods because of the quality of care they connoted.

Different brands of baby food had tended to be favored in various parts of the country, and not all baby food manufacturers merchandised their products in all geographic markets. Beech-Nut baby food was most intensively distributed in New England and was also sold on the West Coast, with little or no representation in the Midwestern markets. Swift had its strongest position in the Midwest. By contrast, Gerber and Heinz sold to the entire United States.

Marketing

The two most important factors that seemed to motivate purchases of a particular brand of baby foods were brand awareness and the shelf space devoted to the brand. Baby food companies were selling mothers reliability and nutritional expertise. Some brand names had become synonymous with high-quality care for babies, and baby food producers spent considerable sums to develop and retain their image of reliability. Although the baby food companies had spent considerable sums to differentiate their products, demand was still somewhat price-sensitive. Gerber brand baby foods could sell for a penny or so more at retail than other brands (an 11 percent premium), but price differentials beyond this could shift customer purchases to other brands.

The number of sidings (shelf space) devoted to a particular baby food brand was related to but did not necessarily reflect fully that brand's share of the market. For example, although Gerber Products had held a 62 percent market share in baby food sales in 1962, a shelf space study conducted that year found the following shelf space allocations in a typical baby foods display: Swift & Company received 3 percent of the shelf space; Clapp 16 percent; Heinz 18 percent; Beech-Nut 21 percent; and Gerber 36 percent. By 1965, however, the declining number of births and hence baby food sales volumes had been clearly noticed by grocers. As the demand decreased, grocers began to carry only one or two branded baby food lines. Since Gerber was best known in the United States, it was usually one of those brands, and pressure on the smaller producers had intensified.

In the early 1960s, when births had been near their peak, grocery stores had used baby foods as traffic-building sale items. However, as volumes decreased grocers were demanding wholesale price reductions, rebates, discounts, and off-invoice inducements to carry a particular brand, and these were widespread in 1965. Grocers also received promotional displays, coupon deals, and other merchandising aids. The retail price of baby foods had gone up as grocers stopped passing on their discounts to customers in 1965.

There was a high degree of product turnover in baby foods. Gerber estimated, for example, that 40 percent of its 1965 sales volume had been in products introduced in the previous ten years. It was believed to be necessary to introduce improved versions of baby foods as well as completely new flavors on a regular basis to maintain consumer confidence. Firms engaged in significant R&D to create new varieties of baby foods.

ADVERTISING AND PROMOTION

Baby food companies used direct consumer communications to move their baby foods off the grocers' shelves. The principal promotional tools used were direct home mailings, hospital samples, and advertising.[1] Advertising emphasized the nutri-

tional quality of the brand as well as the brand name. Exhibit 21-2 shows the total media expenditures on baby foods for several years, ending in 1965. In 1960 Gerber had spent $3,771,000 on media advertising, or about 3 percent of its sales. Gerber's total advertising and sales promotion expenditures amounted to 6.8 percent of its sales. In the same year Swift spent $620,000 on media advertising, or 5.5 percent of Swift's baby food sales, and its advertising and sales promotion expenditures amounted to 15 percent of its baby food sales.[2]

SALES AND DISTRIBUTION

Baby foods were sold to grocery stores either through wholesalers or direct via a manufacturer sales force and "detail men." Baby food detail men went into grocery stores to check inventory, to take orders, and to place the baby foods on the shelves for sale to the customers.

Leading firms also had medical detail sales representatives who called on obstetricians and also visited maternity and pediatric wards of hospitals as well as pediatricians to establish the nutritional value of their firms' baby foods. Doctors' recommendations were also sought by baby food companies in order to sell their particular brand. Free samples were usually distributed to convince mothers of the reliability of a particular brand.

Physical distribution of baby foods occurred through regional warehouses and also direct from plants in areas near the plants.

Manufacturing

The assets to process baby foods were (a) the physical plant and warehouses; (b) general purpose stainless steel food processing machinery, such as grinders and pressure-cooking equipment; (c) specialized food-processing machines associated with a particular raw material, such as pear coring machines; and (d) some specialized equipment (e.g., strainers) used only in the preparation of

---

[1] Gerber Products used a direct home mailing program emphasizing nutritional advice concerning the feeding and care of infants and of free samples. As the infant matured through each stage of the baby food feeding cycle, Gerber sent a sample of the appropriate food, instructions concerning how to use it, and coupons to buy more Gerber baby foods.

[2] In 1960 Beech-Nut Foods had spent $3,142,000 on media advertising; H. J. Heinz spent $2,004,000, and Clapp spent $214,000.

foods of the consistency of baby foods, or to automate a particular operation such as stacking or sterilizing the small containers characteristic of baby foods.

In order to produce baby foods, the raw materials—fruits, vegetables, and proteins—were cleaned, inspected, cut or eviscerated, and cooked. Dry ingredients were weighed, inspected, and blended before cooking. Vacuum steam cooking processes were used to preserve vitamins and minerals. Containers were then filled and shipped. Many inspections were interspersed between each stage, and production was highly automated. Several hundred thousand cartons of baby food could be processed in a week, with speeds varying depending upon which flavor or type of baby food was being produced. Manufacturing costs reduction programs were common. Special purpose high-speed machines were being created for the unique needs of the baby food processors.

Quality control was crucial in baby food production. The third shift of every baby food plant was devoted to steam cleaning the stainless steel machinery. Cans and jars had to be date-coded to ensure that they did not exceed their shelf lives. The average inventory replacement cycle for baby foods was over a year—largely because some crops were available only once a year.

Capital requirements in the industry could be estimated from historical outlays on facilities by industry participants. In 1947 the Beech-Nut baby foods plant in California had cost approximately $6 million, including warehouses and equipment. Gerber constructed a North Carolina baby food plant in 1958 for $4 million and a plant plus warehouse in 1964 for $10 million. Although the cost of a complete baby foods production complex was relatively high, the cost of adding an incremental production line within a general purpose food-processing complex was considerably less expensive. There did not seem to be significant economies of scale in production. The more than 100 different varieties were produced several times per year by the major firms.

Suppliers

The fruits, vegetables, meats, and cereals used to produce baby foods were supplied by farmers, farm marketing cooperatives, and meat packers. Crops were seasonal, and baby food packers scheduled their production to accommodate the harvest dates of the various crops they used. Since most foods were perishable, there were limits to the length of time produce could be stored. There was no substantial differences between a particular grade of these raw materials in a particular geographic region. Baby food firms were essentially price takers in the market for raw materials, and suppliers were fragmented.

Although several of the baby food companies had considered backward integration in 1957, only H. J. Heinz owned and operated farms, which supplied some of its raw material needs in 1965. The other baby food packers contracted for crops on a yearly basis with farmers in regions where good crop conditions were present. Some companies developed their own seed and distributed it to their growers. Field men employed by the baby food firms supervised the care and progress of contract farms.

A Historical Overview of the Baby Foods Industry

In 1900 babies had been fed farina and other cereal preparations also eaten by adults. The first cereal expressly for babies was "Pablum," introduced in 1915. The first canned foods produced especially for babies were sold through drugstores as medical prescriptions. Several origins have been suggested for the canned baby foods industry. According to one source, the industry had its beginning in 1921 when Harold A. Clapp, a Rochester, New York, restaurant owner, prepared a formula of beef both, vegetables, and cereals reduced to a purée to feed his ailing baby daughter. Clapp's product was soon merchandised through drugstores for 30¢ to 40¢ per can.

In 1928 Dan Gerber, whose father owned a Fremont, Michigan, vegetable and fruit packing plant, conceived of the idea of volume processing of vegetables for babies that could be merchandised inexpensively in grocery stores like adult food products. Increased competition from Gerber's products forced Clapp to begin selling his baby foods through grocery stores, and their price was reduced to 14 or 15 cents per can. Beech-Nut and Heinz began producing baby food after Gerber. In 1947 Swift pioneered processed meat products especially for babies. Gerber quickly followed Swift's lead by signing a co-packing agreement with Armour & Company, another meat-packing firm. Heinz introduced baby meat products in 1952, and Beech-Nut began co-packing baby meats with Hormel & Company in 1955. The introduction of baby meat products was a significant product innovation, the most recent such innovation in the industry.

While these firms were competing in the baby food industry in 1965, there had been some unsuccessful entrants into the baby foods business. The Hygeia Company of Buffalo entered the baby food business in 1930, selling its products through the drug trade. After two or three years Hygeia had left the industry, having been unable to mount the necessary marketing effort. Stokely-Van Camp had entered the market in the 1930s and distributed its baby foods in a few areas but had withdrawn from the market by early 1947.

Libby, McNeil also had entered the baby food business in the mid 1930s and offered a complete line of baby food fruits, vegetables, vegetable-meat combinations, and juices on a national basis for several years. While Libby had done quite well through World War II, it began to slip badly in 1947. By the mid-1950s Libby had only two or three markets where it had a significant share, and its share was only 2 to 3 percent in those markets. Libby discontinued its baby food line in 1960. Campbell Soup had attempted to market four or five varieties of baby soup in the late 1940s but had failed to establish itself in the business. In 1959 General Foods had test-marketed a limited line of baby foods under the Birds-Eye label. It then launched a substantial advertising and promotional campaign and moved out of its test market. However, Birds-Eye baby foods were withdrawn two years after introduction when the operation did not prove profitable.

Since 1955 infant cereals had accounted for about 10 percent of the baby food industry, excluding juices and formulas. Mead Johnson was first to enter the cereals market in 1915 with its "Pablum" cereal. In 1956 Mead Johnson's "Pablum" cereal had held about 50 percent of the market, and Gerber's infant cereals about 25 percent. By 1962

these market shares had been reversed: Mead Johnson had 21 percent of the cereals market, and Gerber had 50 percent.

Competition

Six major companies produced baby foods or cereals in 1965. The sales of the three leading baby food producers comprised approximately 91 percent of industry sales in 1965, as shown in Exhibit 21-3. The three leading baby food companies all merchandised a full line of baby fruits, vegetables, meats, desserts, juices and cereals. The competitors were not equally represented in all parts of the United States. Gerber had approximately 70 percent of the West and Southwest. Heinz and Clapp shared the remaining 30 percent in the West, with Swift and Beech-Nut only minor factors.

The main competitors are profiled below, with Exhibit 21-4 summarizing their corporate wide financial performance:

Gerber Products. Though it was a regular food packer for a time after it invented baby food in 1928, from 1943 to 1960 baby food had been Gerber's only business, and in 1965 babies were Gerber's only business. By 1965 Gerber Products also owned Knoll & Company (which produced vinyl baby pants and bibs) and Kapart (which produced stretch outer garments for infants). These were a minor portion of Gerber Products' 1965 sales volume of $194.0 million but represented a Gerber strategy of garnering "more bucks per baby." Gerber's sales were primarily domestic, with only 10 percent coming from foreign operations.

Gerber Products had been the industry leader in baby foods since its 1928 decision to sell baby foods in grocery stores. Its cherub-faced corporate trademark was synonymous with babies, and Gerber had a reputation for high quality. Every year some 3 million mothers received samples of Gerber cereals through the mails soon after the birth of their children. Later they received strained food samples when the infants were old enough to consume them. Gerber also supported its products by sponsoring television shows, by advertising in magazines, and through cooperative promotional programs with hospitals and obstetricians.

Gerber Products offered the widest line of baby foods in the industry. It produced many flavors and consistencies of fruits, vegetables, meats, juices and soups, precooked cereals, desserts, cookies and teething biscuits, egg yolks, and infant formulas. Gerber devoted considerable attention to developing new products for babies to appeal to mothers' desires for improved products. During 1964 Gerber had dedicated a new research facility in Fremont, Michigan, at corporate headquarters. The research lab developed new baby foods and methods of packing them. In 1964 almost 40 percent of Gerber Products' sales volume had come from products it had developed in its labs in the previous decade.

In the infant formula market, Gerber had also tried to capture a significant market share with its Modilac® product. Gerber's efforts to become the leading full-line baby food company—from formula to toddler meals—were not fully successful, however, because Gerber's sales of formula never achieved a critical volume. Consumers seemed to expect a formula producer to be affiliated with a pharmaceutical laboratory.

Because Gerber Products was so dedicated to the production of baby foods, its plants were the most specialized in the industry. Gerber produced baby foods in plants located in Fremont, Michigan (built in 1928); Oakland, California (1943); Rochester, New York (1950); Asheville, North Carolina (1959); and Fort Smith, Arkansas (1965). Gerber also had several international licensees (in Australia, France, Germany, Italy, Japan, Philippines, South Africa, and the United Kingdom), and subsidiaries in Canada (1950), Costa Rica (1958), and Mexico (1959).

The plant locations also served as warehouses, and Gerber had 100 percent distribution through supermarkets and other large food stores using a sales force of 1,200. Gerber was particularly well-positioned to service the South, Southwest, and Western regions. Gerber purchased fruits and vegetables from farmers in the several regions where its plants were located. Some Gerber foods—particularly its meats and fruit juices—were produced under contract for Gerber by nearby food processors and by meat-packing plants.

In 1958, the year after the peak number of births

(4.3 million) Gerber had forecast 4.2 million births in 1960; 4.4 million in 1965; 5.1 million in 1970; and 5.8 million in 1975. The new Asheville and Fort Smith plants reflected this long-range forecast.

Beech-Nut Foods. In 1965 Beech-Nut Packing Company was a part of Beech-Nut Life Savers, Inc., which manufactured chewing gum, candy coated gum, cough drops, chocolate products, fresh baked pies, coffee, tea, mints, fruit drops, paper cartons, cosmetics, toiletries, and baby foods. Corporate sales were $206 million in 1965.

Beech-Nut Packing Company had merged with Life-Savers in 1952, and prior to the merger sales had been $83.5 million with a return on sales of 3 percent. In 1965 Beech-Nut Foods contributed 30 percent of corporate sales and 35 percent to 40 percent of corporate income.

Beech-Nut Foods offered a line of baby food products that was nearly as wide as Gerber's. In addition to offering a wide line of products, Beech-Nut had also attempted to lead the industry through research and development in baby nutrition, through the introduction of new products, and through the continued upgrading of existing products. In 1965 Beech-Nut was attempting to increase its share of the U.S. market. Beech-Nut had scarcely touched the growing opportunities for export sales, foreign licensees, and foreign subsidiaries in 1965.

Beech-Nut distributed its baby foods in the same manner as did Gerber Products, though it did not have distribution in all parts of the nation. Beech-Nut operated baby food plants in the following locations: Canajoharie, New York (1899); San Jose, California (1947); and Rochester, New York (1955). Beech-Nut Foods had also purchased a plant site at Three Rivers, Michigan (1953), for possible expansion of baby food facilities. In 1965 *Barrons* reported that Beech-Nut was planning to build a baby foods plant in Michigan in anticipation of the next baby boom.

Beech-Nut was not vertically integrated. Like Gerber, it processed produce purchased from farmers. Its baby meat products were packed for it under contract by Hormel & Company.

H.J.Heinz Company. The H. J. Heinz Company was a widely diversified, vertically integrated food processor in 1965. Its principal products included soups, ketchups and other tomato products, pickles, vinegar, baked beans, spaghetti condiments, individual plate lunches, baby foods, tuna fish, pet foods, and many other food products. The many different types of foods produced by Heinz and its subsidiaries were sold under the "Heinz" label and the trademark "57 Varieties." H. J. Heinz also sold tuna and fish products under the name "Starkist" and pet foods under the name "9 Lives." Heinz operated eleven plants and numerous raw materials receiving stations and warehouses. Most of these properties were leased.

Corporate sales of H. J. Heinz Company were $519.6 million in 1965, of which 46 percent were international. U.S. baby food sales represented about 10 percent of the sales of the Heinz U.S.A. food division.

Heinz was the largest baby food company worldwide, but it had achieved its greatest successes in the baby foods business abroad. Heinz had 80 percent of world sales of baby food. Its subsidiaries— Plasmon (Europe), Alimentos Heinz C.A. (Venezuela), and H. J. Heinz Company of Australia Ltd.—had achieved rapid growth and market dominance, which Heinz U.S.A. could not duplicate in its home market. Heinz was an innovator in baby foods worldwide but not in the United States. When Alimentos Heinz C.A. (or Plasmon) developed a new baby food product, it was tested in markets where Heinz was the leading baby food brand. Then, if it was successful there the innovation might be introduced in the United States.

Heinz offered 185 varieties of infant fruits, vegetables, meats, cereals, and other preparations overseas, but only 115 varieties in the U.S. market. In the United States Heinz competed on price when necessary to hold its desired market share. Brand loyalty to Gerber was not so strong that one cent or more differential could not entice some mothers to purchase Heinz baby foods instead. Generally, its price strategy gave Heinz baby foods an image of somewhat lower quality than Gerber's.

Heinz had a baby food sales force, and three U.S. plants were dedicated to processing Heinz baby foods, located in Pittsburgh and Chambersburg, Pennsylvania, and Tracy, California. Heinz baby foods were distributed through the logistical system used for other Heinz food products. Some of its products were produced for it by co-packers and were sold under the Heinz label.

Swift & Company. Swift was the largest meat-packer in the world in 1965. It was engaged in meatpacking and producing related food lines throughout the United States and to some extent abroad, through forty-six packing houses. Principal products were meats and meat products; poultry; butter, cheese, margarine, and ice cream; eggs; hides, skins, wool, and leather; cottonseed products; soybeans, peanut oils, peanut butter, cooking oils, and other vegetable compounds; phosphate rock; plant food, livestock and poultry feed, and pet foods; and industrial chemicals, among other products. Consolidated Swift & Company sales in 1965 were $2.75 billion. Its products were distributed through an extensive company logistics system.

Swift & Company was a very specialized producer of baby foods. It manufactured only baby meats, egg yolk dinners, and other high-protein baby foods. Swift had been forced to follow a narrow-line product strategy by the provisions of a consent decree in the 1920 antitrust suit against the five major meat-packaging firms. The suit precluded packers from expanding into other food products.

Swift baby meats were produced at three meatpacking plant locations in St. Louis, Missouri; St. Paul, Minnesota; and Fort Worth, Texas. These plants were also engaged in other types of packing operations, including pet foods.

Swift research chemists had developed baby meats in 1946 to take up slack in underutilized meat packing plants. Swift's sales force had promoted the new product successfully as a specialized high-protein supplement to satisfy the special nutritional needs of infants relatively late in the baby's feeding cycle. Sales of Swift baby meats had peaked in 1954, eight years after their introduction. The subsequent decline was due in part to the fact that Swift's initial success had been imitated by others in the baby foods business, who had added meats to their already wide lines of fruits, vegetables, juices, and cereals for babies.

Later, in an effort to make better use of its assets, Swift co-packed high-protein meats for other baby food companies who did not themselves produce a line of baby meats. Swift packed meat for babies under the "Beech-Nut" and "Topco" labels, as well for other private label accounts. The volume of meats packed for Beech-Nut and Topco represented 30 percent of the baby meat volume produced in the Swift plants in 1965.

The St. Louis plant producing baby meats and other products was being closed down in 1965, and there was excess capacity in both the Fort Worth and St. Paul plants. This slack enabled these plants to produce the baby meat products formerly packed at St. Louis.

Mead, Johnson & Company. Mead, Johnson manufactured more than 185 consumer products, including nutritional products for infants and all ages, and pharmaceuticals and contraceptives sold mainly by prescription. Mead, Johnson also produced Metrecal® for weight reduction in the nonprescription market. Its corporate sales in 1965 were $22.9 million.

Mead, Johnson offered a very narrow line of baby foods consisting of three items. It produced Pablum®, a precooked cereal for infants: "Bib" juices; and Enfamil®, an infant formula. Mead, Johnson had gotten its start as a company with Pablum® cereal in 1915. Pablum® cereals, "Bib" juices, Enfamil® infant formula and other special-purpose nutritional products of Mead, Johnson were marketed through grocery stores by the Edward Dalton Division.

Although sales of Enfamil® had risen 16 percent in 1965 and had made inroads into competitors' market shares of the $100 million infant formula market, sales of Pablum® and "Bib" juices had recorded declining sales volumes in 1965. Pablum® cereals and "Bib" juices were priced competitively with the products of Beech-Nut, Heinz, and Gerber, although Heinz may have been slightly less expensive at retail. "Bib" and Pablum® were nevertheless losing share. Mead, Johnson's share had

eroded more than 20 percentage points since 1955, thanks largely to Gerber. But Enfamil® had become second in infant formula sales to Abbot Laboratories (who produced Similac®). Profits for Mead, Johnson's Pablum® and "Bib" juices were holding stable in 1965 as sales volume waned, largely because promotional expenditures supporting these products had been reduced.

Abbott Laboratories. Abbott Laboratories was a leading domestic producer of pharmaceuticals, hospital products, medicinal chemicals, antibiotics, bulk intravenous solutions, and vitamin products. Abbott Laboratories also manufactured and distributed chemicals for agriculture and industry. Its corporate sales in 1965 were $236.8.

Abbott Laboratories' subsidiary, Ross Laboratories (which had been acquired in 1964) produced Similac®, a nondairy (hence hypoallergenic) infant nutritional formula for the baby food market. Ross Laboratories was located in Columbus, Ohio, with plants in Sturgis, Michigan, and Mitchel, South Dakota. The company also produced "Pream" a nondairy coffee creamer, and other products. Pediatric products contributed approximately 17 percent of Abbott Laboratories' total corporate sales in 1965.

Abbott Laboratories specialized in infant formulas within the baby food market. Although Abbott Labs rarely advertised its formula, Similac® was the leading product of that type sold in the United States. Abbott Labs used the same "medical detail" sales force to persuade doctors to recommend Similac® to new mothers as it used to sell doctors on the use of Abbott Laboratories' intravenous solutions and other products. The medical sales force added credibility to the formula's claims of nutritional value, and doctors' recommendations to mothers to use the formula had greatly increased the product's credibility with mothers.

EXHIBIT 21-1. *Manufacturers' and Retailers' Shipments of Canned Baby Foods (millions of dollars)*

	1947	1954	1958	1963	1964	1965
Canned baby foods (not including baby meats)	$ 71.1	$148.7	$185.2	$230.8	$232.3	$245.6
Baby meats	4.9	17.5	17.9	21.9	24.4	23.0
Total estimated manufacturers' sales of canned baby foods	76.0	116.2	203.1	252.7	256.7	268.6
Total retail sales of canned baby foods	107.0	N/A	251.7	288.5	298.0	306.5
Estimated retail margins on baby foods	41%	N/A	24%	14%	16%	14%

SOURCE: Census of Manufacturers.

EXHIBIT 21-2. *National Media Advertising Expenditures of Baby Foods Producers (thousands of dollars)*

	1965	1964	1963	1962	1961
Beech-Nut Foods					
Foods	$427.1	$432.1	$111.0	$ 52.3	$ 97.4
Juices	–	–	–	291.6	12.3
Cereals	–	–	–	13.1	12.3
H. J. Heinz U.S.A.					
Baby foods	–	93.7	333.5	759.1	1114.6
Swift & Company					
(Meats only)	11.2	36.0	114.2	–	167.8
Mead, Johnson & Company					
Formula	22.4	2.0	5.5	–	268.0
Pablum	–	39.4	–	–	–
Abbot Laboratories					
Formula	–	–	–	–	–
Gerber Products					
Foods	1975.7	2793.4	2468.9	1680.6	1401.7
Juices	–	–	–	–	–
Formula	33.8	6.9	–	4.8	6.1

SOURCE: *Leading National Advertisers.*

EXHIBIT 21-3. *Estimated Competitors' Market Shares in Baby Foods*

Canned baby foods and cereals

Gerber Products	52%
Beech-Nut Foods	20%
H. J. Heinz	18%[a]
Swift & Company	2%
Mead, Johnson & Company	3%
Clapp	1%
Other, private brands	4%

Infant formulas

Abbot Laboratories	25%
Mead, Johnson & Company	10%
Gerber Products	2%
Many other, small firms whose market shares were less than 1% each.	

[a] H. J. Heinz co-packed baby foods for Topco, as well as sold under its own brand. Topco is a retail purchasing cooperative for approximately thirty-two independent, noncompeting food chains. Topco bought its products from the baby food manufacturers and sold them under the Topco label.

EXHIBIT 21-4. *Overall Corporate Performance of Baby Food Manufacturers*[a] *(in millions)*

	1965	1964	1963	1962	1961
Gerber Products					
Sales	$ 194.0	$ 178.3	$ 170.8	$ 153.5	$ 138.8
Profits	14.4	11.8	10.8	9.4	8.1
Return on sales	.07	.07	.06	.06	.06
Total assets	101.8	90.3	84.3	76.6	69.7
Shareholders' equity	77.4	69.4	63.2	57.1	51.9
Return on equity	.19	.17	.17	.16	.16
Beech-Nut Foods					
Sales	206.2	186.6	167.0	159.8	137.7
Profits	16.2	14.7	12.8	11.6	10.3
Return on sales	.08	.08	.08	.07	.07
Total assets	136.6	112.0	104.9	96.5	95.7
Shareholders' equity	101.0	92.7	85.4	79.2	73.4
Return on equity	.16	.16	.15	.15	.14
H. J. Heinz					
Sales	519.6	488.2	464.2	375.8	366.0
Profits	16.7	14.5	12.4	14.2	13.1
Return on sales	.03	.03	.03	.04	.04
Total assets	383.1	369.8	336.3	285.1	272.2
Shareholders' equity	204.7	193.7	184.9	159.0	147.1
Return on equity	.08	.07	.07	.09	.09
Swift & Company					
Sales	2,751.0	2,610.1	2,473.5	2,494.6	2,489.0
Profits	16.4	25.1	17.1	16.3	(0.7)
Return on sales	.005	.01	.007	.007	(.003)
Total assets	634.2	640.8	609.6	593.4	587.3
Shareholders' equity	415.8	411.5	394.9	387.4	380.5
Return on equity	.04	.06	.04	.04	(.001)
Mead, Johnson					
Sales	112.9	95.8	92.3	108.8	130.4
Profits	5.9	4.1	4.3	4.4	9.6
Return on sales	.05	.04	.05	.04	.07
Total assets	89.1	81.7	56.9	55.9	73.4
Shareholders' equity	61.2	57.5	69.7	69.5	54.7
Return on equity	.10	.07	.06	.06	.18
Abbott Labs					
Sales	236.8	212.6	158.6	144.1	129.9
Profits	24.7	22.6	17.7	14.8	12.0
Return on sales	.10	.11	.11	.10	.09
Total assets	233.7	209.4	178.9	163.5	144.5
Shareholders' equity	162.7	151.6	123.0	113.0	104.6
Return on equity	.15	.15	.14	.13	.11

[a]These figures are for total corporate entities. Financial results in baby food only were not disclosed.

CASE 22
EG&G, Inc. (A)

In 1974 EG&G was enjoying success as the manufacturer and marketer of a wide variety of technically oriented products. EG&G's operations were international in scope, and the financial community had recently sized up EG&G's performance very favorably.

> EG&G has reported successively higher quarterly sales and earnings comparisons with year-earlier results throughout the current economic recession. We believe that its energy technology related activities, successful acquisition, and strong financial management capabilities are chiefly responsible for its excellent earnings performance. . . . EG&G is uniquely associated with energy research and development and has a reputation for providing the highest quality products and services in its specialized field. [Merrill, Lynch, *Institutional Report*]

Exhibits 22-1 and 22-2 give EG&G's financial history and recent balance sheets and income statements.

Background

In the course of America's development of nuclear energy, one of the more formidable problem-solving groups around was a trio of MIT professors named Edgerton, Germeshausen, and Grier. The three worked so well together that in 1947 they decided to form a company, whose name bore their initials, which would serve as a prime contractor to the Atomic Energy Commission and other government agencies in furnishing a variety of scientific and technical services in the electronic and nucleonic fields. From the beginning the company was technically oriented, putting the emphasis on invention and entrepreneurship. During the 1950s revenue came primarily from government contracts. However, under the impetus of Bernard O'Keefe, one of the original employees, EG&G at that time took its first tentative steps toward diversification into the commercial market, attempting at the same time to become more "hardware" than purely service oriented.

The 1960s was a period of success for high technology firms, and the government continued its heavy demand for EG&G's services. EG&G went public in the early 1960s and enjoyed a great reception, with P/E's as high as 100. In 1965 Bernard O'Keefe was made president. About the same time, the environment in which the company operated also began to change. Technology for technology's sake was becoming less sacrosanct, and the federal government began to shift its support from space programs into Viet Nam. O'Keefe decided it was time to take major diversification steps with the equity money then available in order to broaden the still relatively narrow focus of the firm's business. About twenty technically oriented companies were acquired during this period, which more than doubled the business areas in which EG&G was involved. During this period the management systems used throughout EG&G were financial accounting procedures, which sometimes lacked consistency between business areas, and a periodic companywide forecast of sales and profits. Some of the more commercially oriented divisions were using an early planning system. Until 1969 EG&G returned outstanding financial results, with consistent eps growth of 15+ percent and return on stockholders' equity of 15+ percent.

The year 1969 brought a number of traumas to EG&G. For the first and only time during its existence the company lost money (see Exhibit 22–1) because of large cost overruns on a fixed-price government contract. In addition, the stock market was no longer enamoured of high-technology companies and thus EG&G's stock price, not to mention the value of senior management's accumulated equity holdings, took a nosedive. Several managers referred to this experience as their first realization that EG&G could make mistakes.

Following this experience, which one senior manager referred to as "an identity crisis," control became a popular goal at EG&G. Bernard O'Keefe, in particular, put great stress on planning and the ability to predict problems. He believed that management needed access to information on which to base decisions about which business units to keep in the company and which ones to spin off. The company began to pay attention to limiting the amount of resources tied up in accounts receivable and inventory. EG&G, which had always valued the innovative engineer, began to demand increased management skill as well.

O'Keefe also saw the need for planning throughout the company. The early long-range planning system had been developed internally over the preceding eight years and used primarily in commercially oriented divisions was modified in order to make it uniform and applicable to all divisions.

O'Keefe hired an outsider, Dean Freed, experienced in the use of planning, to take over the operational management of the business. At the same time he hired outside consultants, Arthur D. Little and some academics from the Boston area, to evaluate the company's planning system. Having been reassured that the system was a valid and consistent one, he encouraged operating managers to cooperate with the head of planning, George Gage, in implementing the system throughout the company.

During the next two to three years, Freed and Gage worked with the operating managers to implement the system. George Gage said,

> When the planning system was being developed much of my time was spent working on the system itself. Subsequently as the system began to mature and stabilize my time was increasingly spent on selling and applying the system throughout the company. Our experience indicates that about two years are required from the time a system is first introduced in an organization to the time when that organization is producing good plans.

EG&G in 1974

Although EG&G did sell off some of the acquisitions it had made in the 1960s after the loss in 1969, it still produced a wide variety of products and services. By 1974 EG&G provided scientific and technically oriented products, custom equipment, systems and related or specialized services to government and industrial customers. Its products and services were classified into six business areas: components for industrial equipment, scientific instruments, environmental testing systems and services, biomedical services, high-technology systems and services for the federal government, and Energy Research and Development Administration support.

Corporate goals were explicitly stated by top management in the Planning Manual developed by George Gage:

> EG&G is a company dedicated to develop and prosper from the commercial, industrial, and government application of technological products and services. Since technological progress and its market acceptance are not always predictable, the company strategy is to diversify its resources into a number of market areas,

a variety of products and services, and a judicious blend of mature and emerging industries. Organizationally this translates into a number of self-sufficient divisional profit centers, grouped by market compatibility, with corporate emphasis on performance measurement, planning, and resource allocation. The corporation is thus uniquely qualified to identify and exploit opportunities in products and services for a variety of markets from mature as well as emerging technologies. . . .

The long-term growth goal we have chosen is an appreciation in earnings per share of 15% per year while maintaining a minimum annual return of 15% on our stockholders' equity. These goals will require performance considerably above average, but are reasonable and achievable with above-average effort.

EG&G tried to meet these goals by participating in a large number of high-technology industrial and government markets. Typically EG&G was, or was striving to be, a leader in its market segments.

The Company Milieu

EG&G's corporate headquarters was in an industrial development in Bedford, Massachusetts, near Route 128. The area contained a great number of other technical firms, and at any given lunch hour a visitor would see groups of employees jogging around the buildings or playing frisbee. EG&G's head office, built in the 1960s, had simple decorations, which attempted to alleviate the cinder-block walls.

The company's senior management was in Bedford (see Exhibit 22-3 for an organization chart). The president, Bernard J. "Barney" O'Keefe, was a jovial extroverted man involved in many projects outside the company, such as organizing private business in Massachusetts to fund a Chicago consulting firm's study of the management of the State of Massachusetts. He was on the board of directors of eleven companies.

Dean Freed, executive vice president in charge of directing all of the corporation's operating divisions as subsidiaries, had an office next to O'Keefe's. He had a direct, efficient manner, which quickly revealed a very thorough grasp of all that went on in the company. He had joined EG&G in 1970, after having worked as a vice president responsible for

three divisions at Bunker Ramo and holding executive management positions at TRW, Inc., in manufacturing and marketing. He had received a B.S. in mechanical engineering from Swarthmore College and an M.S. from Purdue University. His office was decorated with aerial photographs, and two large battered briefcases were always kept nearby. In describing Freed a colleague said:

> Dean is really a superior manager. He's like a teacher. He knows how to improve an inventory system or marketing program. When he's dealing with other managers he is completely straightforward. He likes people to argue back at him and never bears a grudge against them the next day if they do.

George Gage was vice president in charge of planning at EG&G and also had an office among the top executives at Bedford. He had joined EG&G in 1962 with the mission "to develop and implement a meaningful planning system to support long-term goals" and had recently been made a vice president. When Dean Freed joined the firm, Gage switched from reporting to O'Keefe to reporting directly to Freed. Gage had two assistants. Otherwise, Freed and Gage had no staff support.

Many of EG&G's managers were rarely at Bedford since the company's businesses were so geographically dispersed. The company had operations in twenty states and sixteen foreign countries. The majority of employees at EG&G had similar backgrounds. When asked about the type of person who worked at EG&G, George Gage said, "Oh, of course, we're all engineers."

Critical to the management process to EG&G was the monthly management meeting. It was held at corporate headquarters in Bedford. The meeting was chaired by O'Keefe and comprised Freed, the seven group vice presidents, and the senior staff. There was a prescribed agenda which typically consisted of announcements, operations review, investments, acquisitions, and general discussion. O'Keefe used the announcements segment to inform the committee of new ideas he had gained in his travels around the country. A participant described the meeting as the "chief communication vehicle at EG&G."

An important committee within EG&G was the Business Development Committee, which was composed of O'Keefe, Mr. Germeshausen (the retired chairman), Mr. White (vice president and treasurer), Mr. Wallace (a group vice president), Gage, and Freed. Mr. O'Keefe and Mr. Germeshausen did not attend all meetings. The main function of this committee was to review the five-year plans of the company's divisions. The reviews took place once a year at the divisional headquarters.

The Planning Process

The planning process at EG&G was divided into two parts: the Five-Year Plan and the Profit Plan. The principal activities related to the two segments took place at different times of the year. The Five-Year Plan focused on strategy setting. The Profit Plan was a financially oriented plan covering a twelve-month period. Both were described in the EG&G Planning Manual, which was provided to all managers in both a desk copy and a portable form.

In reflecting on his impression of the planning system, Dean Freed said:

> It is a great advantage for division managers to be given a framework of analysis, a way to test ideas. Basically, we want planning to test whether the things which a division manager wants to do with his assets are *consistent* with the strategy and competitive position of that particular division. In fact, I'd say going through our planning process and getting to fully understand all its implications is a magnificent business school.

Corporate Structure and the Planning Process

The lowest level at which EG&G required strategic planning was the "business element." This was defined as a "business system which involves a single product line or a particular service capability being supplied to satisfy the needs of a single market segment." George Gage brought the idea of business elements to EG&G when he joined the company in 1962. During the intervening years the idea grew from use only in the commercial products division to corporatewide acceptance.

Top management believed that good definition of business elements was important because business elements were homogeneous products or services in a single market segment, and thereby particularly well suited for analysis and forecasting. As

one manager put it, "In many of our businesses EG&G has concentrated on specialized segments which business element managers are able to totally understand. The key is to describe the right battlefield, define the right business element."

EG&G had 101 separate business elements with total sales of $163 million, each the responsibility of a business element manager. These ranged in size from more than $5 million in sales for the largest business element to twenty-three business elements with less than $500,000 annual sales. In the last two years, EG&G had added twenty-five new business elements (sixteen through acquisition and nine through internal development), divested four, and discontinued four others.

Above the business element level were twenty-seven divisions, each directed by a division manager. The division manager had responsibility for the delineation of business elements in the division and for their profit and loss and return on investment. Division managers were also responsible for developing strategies for their divisions as a whole, as well as being expected to be intimately involved in the development of the strategies of each individual business element within the division.

Divisions were grouped under seven group vice presidents. These individuals were responsible for the performance of a number of divisions or one particularly large division. They also were part of the corporate administration. One group vice president described his job as "an extension of Dean Freed." Therefore, the group vice presidents were closely involved in the development of strategy while at the same time were responsible for aiding top management in evaluating strategic plans.

In 1974 top management published the Planning Manual in a permanent form. Previously, a new planning manual and directions had been prepared every year incorporating the changes that had taken place. Management now felt that the system was sufficiently mature and did not expect any large changes in the future.

The Five-Year Planning Procedure

The first half of each year was dedicated to developing the company's Five-Year Plan. Exhibit 22–4 presents a graphic representation of the system as well as a timetable for the different steps involved. Basically, the Business Development Committee provided the group vice presidents with planning guidelines, which they in turn modified and cascaded down through division managers to the business elements. Then the business element, division, and group managers created their own detailed five-year plans. There was a review by the Business Development Committee of the plans. Finally, the consolidated Corporate Plan was reviewed by the board of directors.

1. PLANNING GUIDELINES

The first step of the five-year planning process took place in January of each year. After reviewing the previous five-year plans George Gage wrote a preliminary draft of Planning Guidelines for the group vice presidents. This draft was submitted to the members of the Business Development Committee, who modified it. In Gage's opinion it was Freed who had the main input into the final contents of the Planning Guidelines. These guidelines were on one-page forms and contained both quantitative and qualitative goals for the groups.

Once the guidelines were received the group vice presidents began the cascading process, which would eventually create guidelines for each business element based on the corporate guidelines modified by intervening levels of management. Top management expected to have its planning guidelines modified and Gage described the procedure as an "opportunity to get all the ground rules and assumptions sorted out before the managers began the Five-Year Plan."

Soon after the Planning Guidelines were received, the Business Development Committee sent out a notice of the date on which each division would be reviewed. Accompanying this notice were any modifications in the planning procedure for that year and occasionally instructions to aid the uniformity of calculation such as foreign currency exchange rates.

The corporate planning staff did not provide the business element managers with any forecasts or environmental assumptions. Freed was skeptical about long-range economic forecasts: "After about one year's time I'd just as soon use astrology." Business element managers were expected to do

their own environmental assessments appropriate for their units. "After all," said George Gage, "inflation is good for some of our businesses and bad for others. We don't want to provide our managers with pronouncements which will keep them from analyzing their own situations."

2. FIVE-YEAR PLAN—
THE BUSINESS ELEMENTS

After receiving the division manager's Planning Guidelines, business element managers set to work developing the information for Form K, the "Long-Range Plan, Business Element Summary" (see Exhibit 22-5). This was the only form devoted to strategy itself. The Planning Manual described Form K as follows:

The purpose of Form K is to provide a convenient one-page summary of its major strategic factors, a succinct statement of the business strategy, and a forecast of performance expected. The use of Form K greatly facilitates communication and discussion regarding the business element.

Once a business element manager was satisfied with the overall strategy of the element, there were several other forms to be completed in order to express the strategy in financial terms. The first was Form L, "The Business Element Operating Statement" (see Exhibit 22-6). This was an income statement that isolated certain expense items; the form also required actual results for previous years to be compared with those forecast. Investment also had its own forms with which the business element manager had to contend. Form C, the "Investment Data" form (see Exhibit 22-7), focused attention on the balance sheet and cash ratios.

3. FIVE-YEAR PLAN—THE DIVISION

Division managers were also responsible for a strategic Five-Year Plan. First, they worked with their business element managers in order to perfect the individual plans. After the division managers were satisfied with these individual plans, they were required to develop Five-Year Plans for their divisions as a whole. Each consisted of (I) Divisional Goals, (II) Divisional Strategy, and (III) Divisional Summaries.

Divisional strategy was to discuss the direction

and emphasis for the division as a whole and provide a summary statement of the Form K for each existing business element and a summary statement of the strategy for any new business development and/or acquisition. The Divisional Summaries were provided on forms similar to the ones completed by the business elements.

4. FIVE-YEAR PLAN—GROUPS

Once the business elements and divisions completed their plans, the group vice presidents consolidated them. Their job, more than the other two levels, consisted mainly in summing the results of their subordinates. They needed to verify consistency and worked with any of their managers whose plans did not meet expectations. Also, if the overall financial results were inadequate when compared with the expectations of the planning guidelines previously negotiated, the group vice president would work on improvements both in terms of existing operations and in developing new business ideas. At times group vice presidents became aware of a weak plan among their elements. Although they would do their best to improve that plan, they might well inform the Business Development Committee about the problem in advance of the reviews.

5. CORPORATE REVIEW

Prior to the corporate review, the Business Development Committee received and reviewed copies of the Five-Year Plan as submitted. The reviews themselves took place at the divisions' own headquarters. Each review considered all the business elements for which the division manager was responsible. Each division was represented by four or five people, including the division manager, his principal managers (including the controller), and possibly a divisional staff assistant. Depending on the preferences of the division manager involved and the need to explain a recent change that might be affecting a particular market, there was sometimes a brief presentation. One division manager said he used this presentation as an opportunity to give some visibility to an impressive manager in his division.

The question and answer period that followed was the heart of the review, however. Heated arguments could and often did take place during these. As one group vice president said:

> The Business Development Committee is sometimes wrong, and specifically, sometimes Dean Freed is wrong. His strength is his ability to comprehend the masses of details which make up the operations of this company. But he tends to get fixated on one little point which doesn't fit or bothers him in some way.

Another perspective on Freed at review meetings:

> He's a very involved manager. He likes to understand all the facts of the business. And sometimes the operating managers know better than he does. I guess if you had to fault him, it would be that he overmanages. Of course, that's easy to say about anyone until something goes wrong, . . . and that doesn't happen very often around here.

The result of the question and answer period was either approval of the plan as presented or a consensus to do the plan again along the lines suggested by the Business Development Committee. Every year there were three or four significant revisions of the twenty-seven divisional plans presented.

The Five-Year Plan was not directly linked with a manager's compensation. It did come into consideration when a manager was being considered for advancement. Although EG&G had a personnel department, it was Dean Freed and the group vice presidents who made decisions about managers advancing to the division level.

A couple of division managers had been removed for not being able to come to grips with the planning expectations at EG&G. Dean Freed reflected on the seriousness with which the inability to plan strategically was viewed:

> It is a serious problem if a division manager has one business element whose Five-Year Plan is not rigorous and consistent. If succeeding Five-Year Plans exhibited the same problems, that division manager's career is in trouble. After all, if it's easy for me to see the fallacy of the strategy in the time I spend studying the plan, why didn't the manager?

When the committee was at a location evaluating a plan, it started by trying to understand the market involved, as described in Form K. From an understanding of the market, the committee then tried to evaluate whether the strategy was consistent with that market. Freed said, "If a business element has had 5 percent of a market and forecasted that it would have 30 percent of the market in five years, they need a more creative strategy than 'trying harder.'" Once the Business Development Committee approved a business element and division plan, the division and business element managers were finished with the formal preparation of the Five-Year Plan for that year.

Although the planning process involved a great deal of time and effort on the part of EG&G managers, they seemed to appreciate the information it provided. One division manager said:

> It really takes a lot of work to complete the requirements but once you learn the system with the aid of George Gage it becomes an extremely useful management aid. All the other managers have the same frame of reference so it makes communication easier. It's important to be forced to take a long look at what you're trying to do rather than constantly dealing with the day to day problems. Without the requirement I know I would postpone it in favor of the operating problems at hand. Beyond that, it is a great reference during the year with which to judge your progress.

6. CONSOLIDATION AND PRESENTATION TO THE BOARD

After careful review of the divisional Five-Year Plans, Gage and Freed were chiefly responsible for producing the forecasts of sales and earnings on which corporatewide planning was based. Bernard O'Keefe used these forecasts as part of his presentation to the board of directors of the consolidated Five-Year Plans. Top management expected financial results to vary from forecast because of unforeseen and uncontrollable events, but EG&G had an excellent record in forecasting the performance of its ongoing businesses. The board had never rejected a corporate Five-Year Plan but did offer suggestions, such as an adjustment in the procedure for treating inflation, which were used in planning the following year.

The Profit Plan (the One-Year Plan)

The annual Profit Plan was prepared in the fall of the year in the context of the Five-Year Plan. Business element managers, division managers, and

group vice presidents were all required to prepare yearly Profit Plans. It was the ability of the managers to meet the yearly Profit Plan that was tied directly to a manager's compensation. If managers met their Profit Plans they received a bonus. If they did better than their plan, they received a higher bonus, but lower than if they had accurately forecasted the superior performance. At the division level approximately 10–20 percent of a manager's salary was variable, depending on performance versus plan. Just how the allocation was made varied among divisions, depending on the nature of the risk involved and the amount of flexibility available to the manager.

The Profit Plan was the basis for operations management and control of the business in the next twelve-month period. Like the Five-Year Plan, the One-Year Plan was reviewed by a group of senior corporate executives. In this case it consisted of Freed, Gage, Jack Dolan (the corporate controller), and the applicable group executive. The coordination of business strategy and financial control was achieved through these meetings and the One-Year Plan.

The Monthly Management Meeting

Each month at the management meeting, group vice presidents had to present their divisions' monthly financial reports, which consisted of bookings, sales, operating profit, and operating capital. Each group vice president had the opportunity to fill in the narrative behind the cold financial results, and acquisitions and future acquisition candidates were also discussed as well as any new business ideas. Participants felt that the informality of this meeting led to a high degree of candor.

At approximately the same time as the management meetings were held, Dean Freed met individually with each group vice president in order to review the financial results of the divisions. During the meeting the two discussed anything of interest which was happening in the division. Freed explained:

> During these meetings I insist on discussing strategic issues. I am just not interested in the operating problems of the divisions. They can solve them better than

I can. What I want to hear about is new ideas, staffing requirements, and potential problems.

Divisions and groups prepared monthly financial results, which they were able to use in judging their performances. Although the division managers had complete discretion in the management of their divisions, many of them employed a monthly meeting format, analogous to the corporate one, in order to meet with their business element managers and discuss problems or new ideas in light of the data contained in the financial results.

Planning and Innovative Strategy for the Corporation

George Gage commented on the interaction of planning and innovation:

> Our planning system does an effective job of controlling and measuring our base operations. It even provides our managers with uniform methods of evaluating new business development. However, eliciting bright new ideas is beyond the scope of our system. Naturally in a firm like ours innovation and new business development are vital. At the very least, I hope the planning system doesn't stifle new ideas.

The compilation of element and division five-year plans identified needs of the corporation relative to its goals but did not generate innovative ideas. Many ideas for new business directions came from the business element level. There seemed to be a corporatewide belief in the ability of all managers to provide a creative input. For example, the divisional Five-Year Plan asked for new business development ideas as the third section of its "strategy" requirement. One senior manager said, "There aren't many cases where the headquarters has been the source of creativity in terms of new products."

Top management, particularly Bernard O'Keefe and Dean Freed, did address the problem of corporatewide strategy. They held meetings from time to time specifically addressing the overall strategy of the company. In years past EG&G had held retreat meetings in hopes that a new physical surrounding might elicit new perspectives. They were abandoned as not useful. Dean Freed felt that EG&G had less of a problem than some single product, single market companies in maintaining an unbiased perspective on the corporation's future. "Heterogeneity is a great aid in avoiding irrational, emotional attachments to a particular strategy," he said.

While recognizing the benefits of planning, not the least of which was a comparable basis for defending requests for capital, several managers expressed concern about continuing innovation. One group vice president said, "Really good ideas are thought of in unorthodox ways, and planning imposes an orthodox system." He went on to speculate about the possible disincentives imposed on creativity by such an exhaustive planning system. "Innovative ideas can be successfully subjected to planning, but there's always a risk of their being stifled."

EXHIBIT 22-1. *EG&G Financial Highlights (as reported)*

	Sales As Reported (000)	Net Income (Loss) (000)	Income (Loss) Per Share	Assets (000)	Shareowners' Equity (000)	Common Shares Outstanding
1965	$ 51,441	$1,542	.51	$12,884	$ 8,176	3,008,552
1966	64,655	2,012	.59	16,331	10,148	3,439,978
1967	88,728	2,948	.71	35,173	16,448	4,190,136
1968	111,628	3,619	.78	50,327	24,800	4,554,264
1969	119,989	(2,175)	(.49)	57,542	22,536	4,612,569
1970	112,925	1,009	.20	52,546	23,084	5,717,712
1971	111,745	2,437	.51	52,914	25,113	5,746,773
1972	125,387	3,393	.65	64,580	32,063	5,765,551
1973	137,841	4,519	.81	69,943	37,516	5,776,044
1974	162,949	5,716	.97	77,084	44,079	5,781,898

SOURCE: Annual reports.

EXHIBIT 22-2. *EG&G Balance Sheets (recast)*

	1974	1973
Assets		
Cash	$ 1,656,000	$ 2,277,000
Short-term investments, at cost which approximates market	8,362,000	8,170,000
Accounts Receivable	24,733,000	22,089,000
Contracts in process	1,863,000	1,619,000
Inventories	20,316,000	14,340,000
Prepaid Federal income taxes	—	803,000
Other current assets	800,000	474,000
Total Current Assets	$ 57,730,000	$ 49,772,000
Property, Plant and Equipment		
Land	$ 964,000	$ 776,000
Buildings and leasehold improvements	12,318,000	11,332,000
Machinery and equipment	22,723,000	22,002,000
	$ 36,005,000	$ 34,110,000
Less — Accumulated depreciation	20,817,000	19,873,000
Net Property, Plant and Equipment	$ 15,118,000	$ 14,237,000
Investments	$ 3,134,000	$ 4,637,000
Other Assets	$ 1,032,000	$ 1,144,000
	$ 77,084,000	$ 69,790,000
Liabilities		
Notes payable and current maturities of Long Term debt	$ 1,108,000	$ 1,606,000
Accounts payable	8,311,000	7,591,000
Accrued expenses	8,118,000	7,906,000
Accrued taxes	5,138,000	4,003,000
	$ 22,675,000	$ 21,106,000
Long Term Debt		
3½% Convertible, subordinated debentures	$ 6,241,000	$ 6,241,000
Other, less current maturities	3,395,000	3,113,000
	$ 9,636,000	$ 9,354,000
Deferred Federal Income Taxes	$ 694,000	$ 323,000
Shareowners' Investment		
Preferred stock	$ 22,000	$ 22,000
Common stock	5,792,000	5,783,000
Capital in excess of par value	6,469,000	6,399,000
Retained earnings	31,836,000	26,827,000
	$ 44,119,000	$ 39,031,000
Less — Cost of shares held in treasury	40,000	24,000
Total shareowners investment	$ 44,079,000	$ 39,007,000
	$ 77,084,000	$ 69,790,000

EXHIBIT 22-2. *(continued). EG&G Consolidated Statements of Income*

	1974	1973
Net Sales and Contract Revenues	$ 162,949,000	$ 143,997,000
Costs and Expenses		
Cost of Sales	$ 126,336,000	$ 113,125,000
Selling, general and administrative expenses	25,675,000	23,136,000
	$ 152,011,000	$ 136,261,000
	$ 10,938,000	$ 7,736,000
Net Fee from Operating Contract	1,233,000	1,176,000
Income from Operations	$ 12,171,000	$ 8,912,000
Equity in income of investments	310,000	319,000
Interest expense	(796,000)	(778,000)
Other income (expense), net	(267,000)	(227,000)
Income Before Income Taxes	$ 11,418,000	$ 8,680,000
Provision for Federal and foreign income taxes	5,702,000	3,846,000
Net Income	$ 5,716,000	$ 4,834,000
Earnings Per Share	$ 0.97	$ 0.82

EXHIBIT 22-3. *Organization Chart*

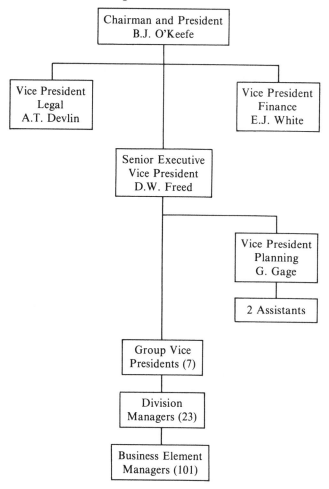

EXHIBIT 22–4. *Five-Year Planning Process*

January — Vice president planning and executive vice president review past performance and write new planning guidelines. Send to group vice presidents.

↓

February — Group vice presidents assess and modify guidelines and set guidelines for divisions.

↓

March — Division managers receive planning guidelines which they amend and send on to business element managers.

↓

Business element managers complete financial forms, which result from Form K strategies.

↓

April — Division managers work with the business element managers to perfect their plans.

↓

Group vice presidents work with their divisions on their plans.

↓

May — Final review meetings are held at division headquarters.

↓

June — Corporate consolidation of all results.

↓

Presentation to the board of directors.

EXHIBIT 22–5. *Business Element Summary: Form K*

LONG-RANGE PLAN: BUSINESS ELEMENT SUMMARY

1. Product and/or Service	2. Customers	3. End Use

4. Direct Competitors / Sales this Market Last Year (CY) / Market Share	5. Competitive Advantages	6. Competitive Disadvantages

Total Direct Market $ _____ K 100%

7. Market Alternatives (Competing Techniques)	9. Summary of Strategy		

TYPE: Build, Hold, Harvest, Withdraw, Explore

DIRECTION: Base, Market Seg., Output Diff., Market Devel., Output Devel.

POSTURE: Leader, Me-Too, Performance, Value, Price, Economy, Prestige, Quality

8. Factors Affecting Future Market Growth

10. History/Forecast										
Market										
Share of Market, %										
Sales										
Operating Profit, % to Sales										

Date _____

Form K (Rev. 1)   (Sub Element)   (Business Element)   (Division)

EXHIBIT 22–6. *Business Element Operating Statement: Form L*

BUSINESS ELEMENT OPERATION STATEMENT

Operating Statement $K	CYª									
Market										
Share of Market, %										
Bookings										
Sales										
Cost of Sales										
Gross Margin										
Gross Margin, % to Sales										
R&D										
Selling Expense										
Local G&A										
Group G&A										
Corporate G&A										
Operating Profit										
Operating Profit, % to Sales										

SALES DETAIL

	By Type of Contract	By Geography	By Source of Funds	

CY ___ Sales Mix	Cost Plus $____K
	  Fee $____K
	Fixed Price
	Standard
	  Price $____K
	TOTAL $____K
		USA $____K
		W. Europe $____K
		Rest of
		  World $____K
		
		TOTAL $____K
			Defense $____K
			Other $____K
			  Gov't.
			Non-
			  gov't. $____K
			SUBTOTAL $____K
				(Business Element)
				
				(Division)

Date _____

ªCY = calendar year.

EXHIBIT 22–7. *Investment Data: Form C*

INVESTMENT DATA

Investment Detail $K	CY								
1. Accounts Receivable 2. Contracts-in Process 3. Inventories 4.									
5. Accounts Payable 6. Accrued (Prepaid) Expenses									
7. Operating Capital 1+2+3-5-6									
8. Assigned Fixed Assets at Cost 9. Accum. Depreciation, Assigned Assets									
10. Assigned Net Fixed Assets 8-9									
11. Allocated Fixed Assets at Cost 12. Accum. Depreciation, Allocated Assets									
13. Allocated Net Fixed Assets 11-12									
14. Net Other Assets (Liabilities)									
15. NET INVESTMENT 7+10+13+14									
16. Long-Term Lease Commitments									
17. TOTAL INVESTMENT 15+16									

CASH FLOW

	CY								
18. 0.5 x Operating Profit (when negative, use as 1.0 x operating profit) 19. Depreciation and Amortization 20. Other Sources (Uses)									
21. Increase (Decrease) in Operating Capital 22. Capital Additions									
23. NET CASH FLOW 18+19+20-21-22									

SUMMARY

	CY								
24. Sales									
25. RONI 26. ROTI									
27. Operating Profit, % to Sales 28. Operating Capital, % to Sales 29. Net investment, % to Sales									
30. Accounts Receivable, DSO 31. Inventory Turnover									

Date _____   _____   _____
                                                    (Business Element)   (Division)

CASE 23
EG&G, Inc. (B)

In May 1974 Dean Freed, executive vice president of EG&G, wondered what he would do at the review meeting for the Electro-Mechanical Division (EMD) scheduled for the following week. The division's previous year's results were disappointing, but division management expressed in their recently submitted 1974 five-year plan the belief that the situation could be turned around.

Background

In the 1960s EG&G developed a new technology involving ceramic to metal seals. Management felt there was a good opportunity to exploit the new technology in connectors for electric cables. When two types of cables needed to be joined, connectors were clamped onto each end, and these were fastened using mechanisms of varying complexity. The higher the frequency or voltage to be transferred, the more complex was the required connector. Depending on their complexity, connectors could cost from a nickel to five dollars or more. Higher-technology, higher-priced connectors were manufactured in the United States, while low-cost con-

nectors were increasingly being manufactured abroad.

EG&G had a specific application for their new connector in the defense work they were then doing for the U.S. government's Sandia missile program. The high-technology connector was able to eliminate radio interference, which affected the guidance of missiles in enemy territory. In order to be able to take advantage of the expected demand in the Sandia missile program, EG&G began to look for the best way to gain knowledge of the market and to develop the manufacturing capability necessary to produce this new connector.

The Strode Company, a small firm located in Franklin, Massachusetts, was brought to EG&G's attention. Strode, a manufacturer of standard technology connectors, had not been particularly successful and was known to be available for sale. EG&G's management felt that the fixed costs of Strode's operation could be supported by EG&G's proprietary defense business. To this base EG&G's management hoped to enter other specialty markets in which their technological advantage could be exploited. In this way EG&G planned to avoid Strode's competitive disadvantages in competing head to head with commodity producers who could manufacture connectors at lower costs because they produced and sold much greater standard volumes. However, the addition of specialty work to Strode's line would require the hiring of more engineers to do the designing and more highly skilled workers to produce the more varied products. EG&G acquired Strode in 1969, and it became the Electro-Mechanical Division, with all operations continuing in its existing facilities.

Strode's base businesses consisted of miniature coaxial cable connectors for microwave applications and radio frequency (RF) applications. Coaxiacal cables were composed of a tube of electrically conducting material surrounding a central conductor held in place by insulators. They were used to transmit signals of high frequency. About one-half of Strode's sales was in standardized connectors; the other half was in connectors for specialty applications.

The manufacturing process was straightforward and required only general purpose machinery, though highly skilled machinists were necessary for some operations. Even experienced machinists, who were themselves in short supply, required about three months of training before they were competent to produce the new EG&G connector.

EMD was at a great cost disadvantage in the sale of standardized parts in comparison with its chief competitor, Amphenol Corporation, which controlled 25 percent or more of the market. Strode's specialized work had greater profit potential, but this had not yet been realized because of problems with cost control and a small potential market. In an attempt to cover fixed costs, Strode produced standardized connectors in order to keep manufacturing at capacity despite the very low margins on these standardized items.

Freed remembered how Jim Sheets, the division manager, had been a driving force behind acquiring EMD. Sheets had been with EG&G for fifteen years and had had an outstanding record of achievement. As the manager of a highly successful business element, he had brought in a remarkable 10 percent of the corporation's profit in one year. Therefore, when Sheets began promoting the idea of a new division to exploit the ceramic to metal seal technology, Freed felt he had to be taken seriously. Sheets was familiar with the technology since it had

been developed in his previous division. He had proved himself as a business element manager and had earned, by part-time study, his MBA in 1968. There had been a general consensus among management that promoting Jim Sheets to division manager was a fitting reward for one of the company's outstanding young executives. EMD was placed in the Technical Products group under the direction of group VP Joe Giuffrida. The group consisted of six other divisions and thirty-seven other business elements.

It was not long after its founding that EMD ran into its first problems. By early 1970 it became clear to the management of EMD that the defense market for connectors that EG&G had planned on would not develop because of defense budget cuts. The Business Development Committee, group management, and the management of EMD jointly searched for other markets in which their new technology might be applicable and profitable. It was decided to explore the possibility of selling the high-quality connector as a component to the cable television industry.

Cable Television

Cable television was a system for carrying television signals by wire rather than transmitting them through the air. It produced better reception and, in some cases, more channels. The wire used was a coaxial cable that could carry many different channels simultaneously. A typical cable system consisted of a television antenna placed in a location with good reception such as a high hill. The signal was then fed by cable to a "head end" which amplified the signal for the system's distribution cables, comprising "trunk" cables, which extended from the head end; "feeder" cables, which were along individual streets; and "drop" cables, which went into subscribers' homes. (See Exhibit 23–1.) EMD proposed to capitalize on the growth in this market by providing connectors between trunk and feed line distribution cables. The connector market was primarily a new rather than replacement market. Each connector was designed to have a longer life than the system in which it was placed.

Jim Sheets realized that there was no one in

EG&G who was knowledgeable enough about the cable television industry to manage such a business element. Therefore, in a departure from usual EG&G procedure of advancement from within, an outside talent search was made in order to find a suitable business element manager. The search produced Mike Killion, who had a considerable track record as a marketer in the cable television industry, having worked in sales for Jerrold, the leading cable television equipment producer. Killion was no longer with Jerrold and was working in sales at an electronics firm in Lawrence, Massachusetts. Killion expressed an interest in returning to the CATV business. He was impressed with EG&G's product and its prospects in the industry and was able to communicate his enthusiasm and experience to Sheets and Giuffrida, who decided to hire him after a joint interview.

Having hired Killion, EMD management looked forward with excitement to its participation in the CATV industry. In the past fifteen years cable television had grown at a compound annual rate of better than 20 percent. By 1970 cable television reached 7 percent of American households, and the industry had grown to a total of $500 million in annual revenue. Killion conducted extensive surveys and research in order to discover what qualities in connectors were valued by CATV builders so that EG&G's product would have distinctive features separating it from competitors.

The Rand Corporation, in a 1971 study of the cable television industry, predicted high growth for cable over the next two decades. (See Exhibit 23–2.) *Barron's* said in 1971, "past success is dwarfed by future potential in the cable television industry" and predicted a total CATV market of $2.4 billion by 1980. One of the changes that led *Barron's* to predict such high growth was particularly interesting to EG&G. Before 1972 CATV was not allowed in major metropolitan areas by the Federal Communications Commission. By mid-1971 the FCC's new chairman, Dean Burch, let it be known that cable television would be allowed in cities. EG&G's connector had the distinguishing characteristic of being the best cable connector on the market for eliminating interference. This was a greater problem in urban than rural areas, and therefore EMD felt its product had a distinct advantage in the growth era ahead.

In the 1972 Five-Year-Plan, EMD expressed its strategy as one of improving margins in the base connector business by emphasizing specialty rather than standard products and by improving manufacturing techniques. EMD had reduced dependence on government contracts and wanted to maintain more than 50 percent of their income in the commercial rather than the government sector.

The 1972 plan went on to be more specific about the EMD's strategy for commercial business:

> The commercial business segment of the division business will include some share of the nonmilitary communications and instrument microwave markets. The major emphasis, however, will be directed at specific and concerted entry into the newly energized CATV connector market. The business in two facets, equipment manufacturers and cable distribution operators, has the proper size and growth potential to limit competition in number and size, but still be an attractive opportunity for the division.

Freed recalled that the move into CATV was seen as an entrance into a young, dynamic market with important future growth potential. See Exhibit 23–3 for the unusually detailed strategy statement that EMD submitted in the 1972 Five-Year-Plan. Freed also reviewed the planning forms that EMD had completed in 1972. Two of these of particular interest to him are included in Exhibit 23–4: the Business Element Strategy (Form K) for the CATV element and the Division Operating Statement (Form B).

He also reviewed the Form Ks for the two other business elements in the division, "Special Seal and Microwave Devices," and "the RF Connectors," both of which showed serious problems in 1972. The special seal and microwave devices were being sold mainly to Sandia as a method of eliminating radio interference. However, this limited the business element to one customer, the federal government, whose funds for and interest in such technology were being curtailed. The "Summary of Strategy" emphasized the need for "new product or new market activity." The RF connector also had serious problems. EG&G had a small market share, 7 percent, and ranked seventh in the market. Although EG&G had the advantage of a reputation for quality in the field, there was not enough demand for that quality to cover the fixed costs of the operation. EG&G was at a cost disadvantage to the larger producers when it came to standardized parts. EMD's "Summary of Strategy" discussed the need to develop better "linear programming techniques for production control, regulate operation and business mix to optimize profit margin and growth." Sales to government contractors made up 94 percent of the RF connectors' sales.

At the first review session of a Five-Year Plan for the new CATV business element, Freed recalled, Mike Killion had put on an impressive performance. He demonstrated a full grasp of the relationships among main actors within the cable television industry. He explained how the critical factor in selling connectors was the manufacturer's relationship with the distributors. CATV system installers were usually independent local contractors. They purchased their supplies from distributors who were organized in a number of layers. A key success factor for a producer of CATV equipment was to establish a good relationship with a national distributor who in turn had contacts in all regions. Killion had conducted conversations with a number of major distributors and had reported that they all perceived the unique advantages of EG&G's connector and looked forward to selling it. Killion developed sales forecasts for the connector, designed a sales brochure, established sales representatives around the country, and helped work on engineering problems. In fact, Killion's performance was so impressive that the Business Development Committee selected the CATV connector business element as one of its top five growth prospects for the 1972–1977 period.

In the 1973 plan, the division once again submitted its optimistic projections about the opportunities for CATV:

> The Electro-Mechanical Division strategy relates to a vigorous "build" role with special emphasis on the commercial business opportunity which is now posed by accelerated growth in the cable television industry. The market situation seems unique in terms of timing, demand, relative competitive weakness and close relation of expertise and facilities necessary to produce connectors for CATV and the microwave business.

The division also returned improved financial results in 1972. (See Exhibit 23–5.)

Because of its poor financial performance, the Business Development Committee at EG&G studied the RF connector business of the Electro-Mechanical Division in February 1973. The committee, with the assent of EMD management, decided that the RF connectors had to be phased out, since the product seemed to lack any real profit potential. It was felt that the CATV business would take up the slack. The Business Development Committee stated in its 1973 Planning Guidelines, "The RF connector business element should go to 'Harvest' strategy, phasing down as CATV builds."

There were encouraging signs as 1973 proceeded. One of the objectives that the CATV element planned to achieve was to give the Gilbert Company, the number one supplier of connectors to the CATV market, some strong competition. Mike Killion was very optimistic about EG&G's ability to gain on Gilbert. Gilbert was having difficulty getting proper financing from its parent company, and Gilbert's main strength, its relationships with its distributors, also seemed to be deteriorating. When Killion was able to establish an exclusive distribution arrangement with Anixter/Pruzan, who had previously been the distributor for Gilbert, the division felt it was advancing according to plan. Anixter/Pruzan's initial order was for $300,000 worth of connectors at a time when EMD was carrying no inventory, and EMD's previous orders had been about one-tenth of that size. Also, improvements in manufacturing were enhancing the quality of the product.

Some of the interim financial results returned in 1973 were disappointing, however. Freed noticed that the CATV element was not making the sales or returning the profit that had been expected. Freed had also read that urban installation of cable systems was turning out to be more costly than expected, but he was not sure what impact this would have on the connector business. Financing was becoming increasingly hard to come by and expensive, and a recession had slowed economic growth. This squeeze caused those involved in CATV construction who had limited access to capital to buy their equipment from low-cost suppliers. Price cutting began to take place among suppliers of CATV components. Freed knew EMD could not compete for long on price, but he felt it was difficult to judge the danger of price cutting since EG&G's other high-quality products had tended to be immune to price cutting. When questioned about the financial results, Jim Sheets showed concern over them but insisted that headquarters was acting impatiently. Mike Killion continued to be extremely optimistic about the future of EG&G in the CATV connector market. He said at the Profit Plan review in 1973:

> All the clients I talk to say we have the best connector in the industry. After all, we just signed on with Anixter/Pruzan. Give us a chance to get that operation going. Gilbert is crumbling and we are going to be the ones to take up the slack. We are now suffering from a cyclical problem of distribution but it should be straightened out in nine months to a year. The quality which we build into our connector is very desirable in this business but at times the higher price will temporarily cut into our sales volume.

Joe Giuffrida, the group vice president, was sympathetic to the arguments of his two managers and felt they should be given more time to prove themselves.

It was in this context that Freed received the results of 1973 and the next Five-Year Plan from EMD. The financial results for 1973 were disappointing. (See Exhibit 23–6.) Instead of making $100,000 in the CATV market, the division lost $98,000 in 1973.

When Freed reviewed the Form Ks for the two government-oriented connector business elements he saw a deteriorating situation. The Form K for the "Special Hardware" connector forecast a decrease in its already small sales and listed no market alternatives. It had the disadvantage of being more expensive than competitors' products and thus saw little hope of expanding out of the specialty market, which while profitable was just too small. The RF connector had slipped from 7 percent of the market to 3 percent and now was ranked tenth in terms of market share among the competitors. Freed also noted that lack of modern equipment was still a problem and that manufacturing costs in RF connectors were high relative to competitors'. He was encouraged by the element's forecast growth in sales and slight improvement in forecast earnings, although he was not sure if the Strategy Summary for RF Connectors could support such optimism:

> Continue responsive effort to build selective share of near standard connector business. Expand scope of coverage to increase marketing emphasis on individual OEM accounts served by the largest of the small competitors, nationwide. Concentrate on profitable near standard business opportunities and new client conversion list—exploiting long term former customer relationships and organizational flexibility to provide responsive customer service and cost effective product. [Form K, 1974.]

However, CATV was the business element from which future growth was planned, and Freed wanted to review their Form K (Exhibit 23–7) at length. He also reviewed Form C (Exhibit 23–8), which highlighted the investment EG&G had in the entire EMD.

Freed tried to order his thoughts about the upcoming meeting with the EMD. EMD was not performing up to the level of EG&G's goals, and he knew Giuffrida made it a policy to distribute the financial results of all his business elements at the monthly meetings held by his group. On the other hand, Sheets and Killion had warned from the beginning that the CATV connector would take a number of years to become established. In the past EG&G had financed promising products, such as a component for the Xerox copier, for six years before they became profitable.

EXHIBIT 23-1. *Diagram of Cable System*

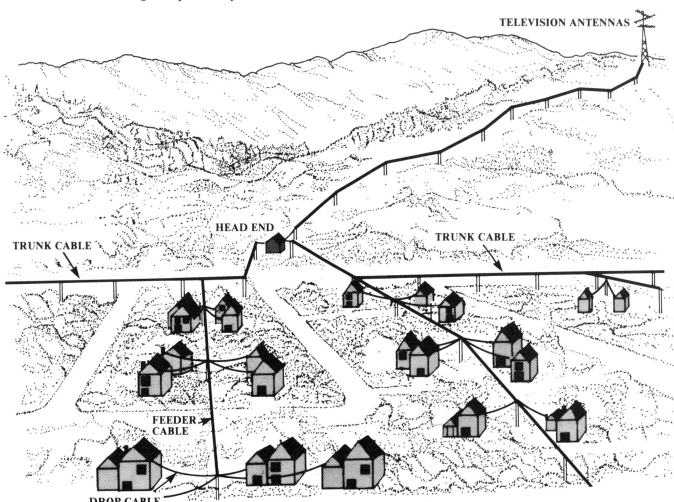

Conventional one-way cable system serving residential subscribers

SOURCE: The Rand Corporation.

EXHIBIT 23-2. *Growth of Cable Television*

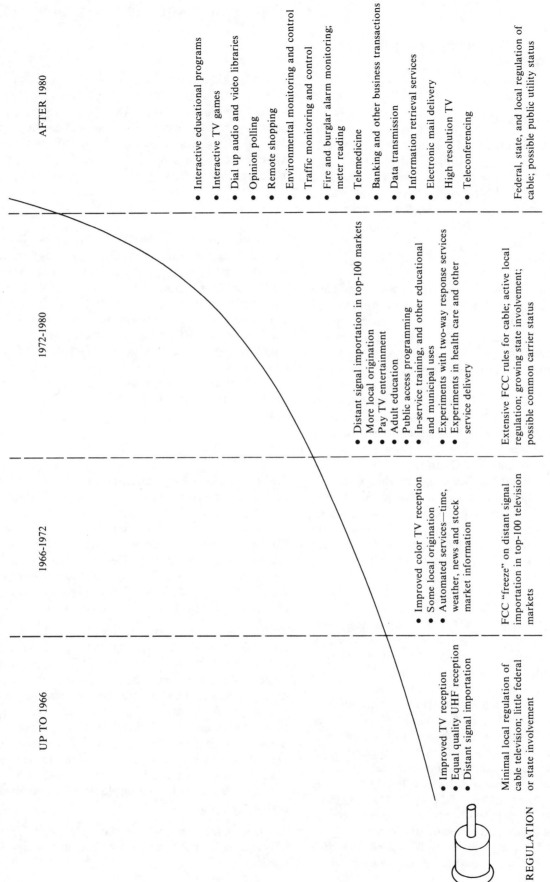

	UP TO 1966	1966-1972	1972-1980	AFTER 1980
	• Improved TV reception • Equal quality UHF reception • Distant signal importation	• Improved color TV reception • Some local origination • Automated services—time, weather, news and stock market information	• Distant signal importation in top-100 markets • More local origination • Pay TV entertainment • Adult education • Public access programming • In-service training, and other educational and municipal uses • Experiments with two-way response services • Experiments in health care and other service delivery	• Interactive educational programs • Interactive TV games • Dial up audio and video libraries • Opinion polling • Remote shopping • Environmental monitoring and control • Traffic monitoring and control • Fire and burglar alarm monitoring; meter reading • Telemedicine • Banking and other business transactions • Data transmission • Information retrieval services • Electronic mail delivery • High resolution TV • Teleconferencing
REGULATION	Minimal local regulation of cable television; little federal or state involvement	FCC "freeze" on distant signal importation in top-100 television markets	Extensive FCC rules for cable; active local regulation; growing state involvement; possible common carrier status	Federal, state, and local regulation of cable; possible public utility status

Potential growth of cable television services

SOURCE: The Rand Corporation.

439

EXHIBIT 23-3. *EMD Strategy for Entry into the CATV Connector Industry, April 1972*

CATV Connector

1. STRATEGIC ROLE

The strategic role of the CATV connector business element is to provide (1) divisional growth, (2) better balance between government and commercial funding sources in the Electro-Mechanical Division marketing mix, and (3) entrance into a young, dynamic market with important future growth potential.

2. STRATEGY

It is a major Division goal to establish a significant (30%), and ultimately leading market position in the specific area of outdoor connectors for aluminum sheath trunk and feed line distribution cable, capitalizing on the impending new growth predicted for the purely commercial CATV market. It will not be practical to establish the degree (%) nor the timing for success until we are 2 or 3 years into the program. The necessary market penetration will be obtained by (1) exploiting an existing, unstable management situation of the present industry leader (Gilbert Electronics, a Transitron subsidiary), (2) exploiting existing EG&G-Startronics expertise in connector design and high volume, reproducible manufacture, (3) concentration of prime sales efforts among the top 50 multi-construction contractors, and (4) taking advantage of 17 years of personal contact and sales experience with many of the key principals among the largest MSO's and equipment manufacturers.

3. MARKET

Newly revised (March 31, 1972) FCC regulations governing the reuse, through cable distribution, of television signals in high density population areas (top 100 markets) have motivated a formerly dormant cable television equipment and construction industry to substantially increased activity. The resulting market for outdoor connectors estimated at $4 million level in 1971 is expected to reach the $8 million level by 1976. The new FCC regulations for the high density markets require 2-way capability. Because of these factors, in addition to the pure entertainment facet of cable distribution networks, the potential for use as a special purpose two-way communication link between subscribers and vendor/service organizations should realize a sustained high rate of new construction for the industry well beyond the time period of this business plan. Indeed, the industry which originally called itself Community Antenna Television, outgrew that small town image of itself and became Cable Television and now, with the local program organization and the exciting new two-way facilities, considers itself in the broadband communications business. At present only about 8% of the 60 million TV homes in the USA are connected to a CATV system.

4. CUSTOMER GROUPS

The Cable Television customer groups can be viewed in the following segments: (1) Multiple Systems Operators (TelePrompTer); (2) Equipment Manufacturers (Jerrold); (3) Construction Contractors (Burnup & Sims); (4) Single system operators and (5) Distributors (Anixter-Pruzan). The current business plan is to concentrate on the 50 largest Multiple System Operator (MSO), 12 largest Equipment Manufacturer (OEM) and 20 Construction Contractor organizations for new/replacement business as appropriate. In the initial stages, all sales effort will be from the business element manager.

5. COMPETITION

The weather-proof, radiation-proof aluminum connectors used in overhead and underground CATV distribution services are within the current technical and production capabilities of the Electro-Mechanical Division. Current suppliers are Gilbert-Transitron (58% of the market) and a number of smaller firms with comparably smaller market shares. These include Craftsman-Magnavox (11%), LRC(11%), Communication Dynamics (9%), ITT Gremar Canada (6%), and others (5%).

The Gilbert-Transitron relationship is strained and unstable. The founder, Gilbert, who until recently directly controlled the operations of the company is no longer on the scene. Transitron is not noted for management prowess nor stability. Magnavox Craftsman and Communication Dynamics are not solely dedicated to the outdoor connector market as this is only a portion of their overall business. ITT Gremar (Canada) is hampered in the U.S. market by duties and customs-clearance problems resulting in slower response. LRC is a very small company in a remote location with limited expertise and resources.

The timing for immediate market entry seems particularly appropriate. A line of 5 types in each of 4 cable sizes is adequate.

SOURCE: Company records.

EXHIBIT 23-4. *1972 Form K: CATV Business Element*

Long-Range Plan: Business Element Summary[a]

1. Product and/or Service

CATV weather proof connectors for outdoor service in overhead and underground distribution installations.

2. Customers

Multiple Systems Operators (50 largest)
Distribution Equipment Mfrs. (12–16 largest)
Construction Contractors (20 major)

3. End Use

CATV distribution cable interconnection devices for entertainment and broadband communications.

4.

Direct Competitors	CY71 Sales This Market	Market Share
Gilbert (Transitron)	2500	58
Craftsman (Magnavox)	500	11
LRC	500	11
ITT Gremar (Canada)	250	6
Communications Dynamics	400	9
Others	150	5

Note: Figures refer to noncaptive market. Jerrold & Vikoa (OEM's) make selected types for systems use.

Total direct market $ 4300   K   100%

5. Competitive Advantages

Connector manufacturing expertise.
Management stability.
Dominant competitor in management difficulty
Other Suppliers small/distant
Financial and technical resources for potential expansion.

6. Competitive Disadvantages

Lack of image and tangible experience in CATV market segments
Significant portion of components supplied in-house by equipment OEMS.

7. Factors Affecting Future Market Growth

Freedom from FCC restraints for entertainment rebroadcast.
Deployment and utilization of two way, multi-channel cable networks for non-entertainment uses.

Avg. Market Growth Rate, Next 5 years 15%/yr

8. Competing Techniques

Microwave relay links (Theta Comm) for municipal areas
Satellite communications

9. CY71 Sales Mix By

AEC & DOD	_____ % CPFF	_____ %
Other Gov't	_____ % Fixed Price	_____ %
Commercial	100 % Std. Prod.	100 %
Foreign	_____ % Serv.	_____ %
Total	100 % Total	100 %

10. Summary of Strategy — Establish a significant market position in the CATV connector business. Exploiting the following aspects:

1. New market growth for CATV as a result of FCC revision of rebroadcast regulations.
2. Unstable management position of industry leader, Gilbert, as part of Transitron and in the absence of the founder.
3. EG&G expertise in connector design and reproducible manufacture.

Date   May 1972   CATV Connector Business Element

Form K(72)   Electro–Mechanical Division

[a] Form K varied slightly in its format from 1972 to 1974.

EXHIBIT 23–4. *(continued)*. EMD Form B: Operating Statement 1972

CY72–76 Plan: Operating Statement

OPERATING STATEMENT $000	ACTUAL						FORECAST			
	CY67	CY68	CY69	CY70	CY71	CY72	CY73	CY74	CY75	CY76
Sales	70	252	2340	1710	1765	2000	2625	3200	3900	4800
Cost of Sales	66	240	2111	1652	1523	1549	1957	2263	2738	3362
Gross Margin	4	12	229	58	242	451	668	937	1162	1438
Gross Margin, % to Sales	6	5	10	3	14	23	25	29	30	30
R&D	—	—	—	—	—	—	15	40	60	60
Selling Expense			142	143	127	150	208	268	325	452
G&A (Non-Corporate)	*	*	*	*	103	109	143	170	228	270
Other Income (Expense)					(6)	(17)	(23)	(28)	(35)	(45)
Corporate G&A	*	*	*	*	45	50	74	91	114	136
Operating Profit, B.T.	4	12	87	(85)	(39)	125	205	340	400	475
Operating Profit, % to Sales	6	5	4			6	8	11	10	10

*included in Cost of Sales

SALES/OPERATING PROFIT BT BY BUSINESS ELEMENT

	CY67	CY68	CY69	CY70	CY71	CY72	CY73	CY74	CY75	CY76
Sp. Seal & Microwave Devices	70/4	252/12	328/21	392/17	416/42	350/32	375/42	400/53	435/58	475/66
RF Connector			2012/66	1318/((102))	1349/(81)	1650/93	1900/113	2000/130	2000/162	2000/167
CATV Connector						–/–	350/50	800/157	1465/180	2325/242
Total Sales Operating Profit	70/4	252/12	2340/87	1710/(85)	1765/(39)	2000/125	2625/205	3200/340	3900/400	4800/475

Date ___May 1972___

Form B(72)

Electro-Mechanical Division

EXHIBIT 23-5. *EMD Form B: Operating Statement 1973*

CY73–77 Plan: Operating Statement

OPERATING STATEMENT $000	ACTUAL				FORECAST				
	CY69	CY70	CY71	CY72	CY73	CY74	CY75	CY76	CY77
Sales	2340	1710	1765	1887	2480	3150	4000	5100	6050
Cost of Sales	2111	1652	1523	1471	1840	2310	2870	3720	4420
Gross Margin	229	58	242	416	640	840	1130	1380	1630
Gross Margin, % to Sales	10	3	14	22	26	27	28	27	27
R&D	—	—	—	—	—	—	—	—	—
Selling Expense	142	143	127	135	219	300	430	520	585
G&A (Non-Corporate)	*	*	103	106	117	155	182	210	265
Other Income (Expense)	—	—	(6)	10	36	25	40	50	60
Corporate G&A	*	*	45	40	68	80	98	115	145
Operating Profit, BT	87	(85)	(39)	125	205	280	380	485	575
Operating Profit, % to Sales	4	(5)	(2)	7	8	9	10	10	10
SALES/OPERATING PROFIT BT BY BUSINESS ELEMENT									
CATV Connector	—/—	—/—	—/—	—/—	600/100	1200/150	2000/300	2800/300	3600/375
RF Connector	2012/21	1318/(102)	1349/(81)	1508/72	600/65	1750/100	1900/135	2150/160	2300/175
Sp. Seal & Microwave Devices	328/21	392/17	416/42	379/53	280/40	200/20	100/20	150/25	150/25
Total Sales/Operating profit	2340/87	1710/(85)	1765/(39)	1887/125	2480/205	3150/280	4000/380	5100/485	6050/575

Date   April 1973

Form B(73)

Electro-Mechanical Division

EXHIBIT 23-6. *EMD Form B: Operating Statement*

CY 74–78 Plan: Operating Statement

OPERATING STATEMENT	ACTUAL RESULTS				FORECASTS				
	CY70	CY71	CY72	CY73	CY74	CY75	CY76	CY77	CY78
Bookings			2025	1769	2300	2800	3225	4000	4800
Backlogs		441	579	491	541	641	746	911	1061
Sales	1710	1765	1887	1857	2250	2700	3120	3835	4650
Cost of Sales	1652	1523	1471	1646	1750	2050	2340	2850	3455
Gross Margin	58	242	416	211	500	650	780	935	1195
Gross Margin, % of Sales	3	14	22	11	22	24	25	26	26
R&D	–	–	–	–	–	–	–	–	–
Selling Expense	143	127	135	192	210	255	285	340	400
G&A (Non-corporate)		103	106	105	115	130	140	165	190
Corporate G&A		45	40	52	55	70	80	100	120
Other (income) expense / Under (over) applied Overhead		(6)	(10)	(18)	(20)	(20)	(25)	(35)	(40)
Operating Profit	(85)	(39)	125	(156)	100	175	250	345	445
Operating Profit, % of Sales	–	–	7	–	4	7	8	9	10
SALES/OPERATING PROFIT BY BUSINESS ELEMENT									
RF	1318/(102)	1349/(81)	1508/72	1240/(85)	1650/88	1800/110	2100/160	2500/200	2900/255
Special	392/17	416/42	379/53	259/27	250/22	150/15	120/10	135/15	150/15
CATV				358/(98)	350/(10)	750/50	900/80	1200/130	1600/175
Total Sales/Operating Profit	1710/(85)	1765/(39)	1887/125	1857/(156)	2250/100	2700/175	3120/250	3835/345	4650/445

CY 73 Sales Mix				
	AEC Cont.	$ — K	USA	$ 1857 K
CY 73	Other CPFF	$ 200 K	W. Europe	$ — K
Sales	Fixed Price	$ 59 K	Rest of	
Mix	Std. Price	$ 1598 K	World	$ — K
	Total	$ 1857 K	Total	$ 1857 K

USA Sales Only

AEC	$	K
DOD	$ 1499	K
Other Gov't	$ —	K
Non-Gov't	$ 358	K
Sub-Total	$ 1857	K

Intercorporate

CY 73 ___   Sales = S ___ K

ELECTRO-MECHANICAL
(Division)

Date ___ April 1974 ___

Form B (Rev 1)

444

EXHIBIT 23–7. *1974 Form K: CATV Business Element*

Long-Range Plan: Business Element Summary		

1. Product and/or Service

CATV aluminum sheath cable connectors and adaptors

2. Customers

Cable television manufacturers and service organizations.

Distributors	24%
OEM	17%
Multiple System Operators	42%
Small System Operators	17%

3. End Use

Cable Network distribution connectors
— Cable to cable splice
— Amplifier or tap to cable
— Terminators
— Adaptors

4. Direct Competitors

	Sales CY 73	Market Share
Gilbert	1525	36%
LRC	1000	24%
EG&G	360	9%
Coral	300	7%
Cambridge	250	6%
Tidal	250	6%
ITT	200	5%
Pyramid	50	1%
Others	250	5%
Total direct Market	$4185K	100%

5. Competitive Advantages

— Superior product for areas and applications sensitive to radio frequency interference.
— Dominant competitor (Gilbert) unstable.

6. Competitive Disadvantages

— Premium price
— Emerging competitor (LRC) with cost effective product
— Anixter-Pruzan distributor liaison temporarily ineffective.

7. Market Alternatives (Competing Techniques)

Conventional television reception.

8. Factors Affecting Future Market Growth

— MSO access to investment funds
— Federal regulatory rulings
— State and local franchise practices
— Inflation related subscriber rate hikes.
— Potential for 2-way consumer services.

9. Summary of Strategy

— Explore short-term viability of CATV business
— Appraise Anixter-Prusan distributor potential
— Expand and improve distributor sales network selectively in key geographic areas of the United States.
— Continue to cultivate OEM liaisons through direct sales effort.
— Expand product line to provide adequate but lower price product for more general use in non-RFI and turnkey applications.

10. History/Forecast

	CY72	CY73	CY74	CY75	CY76	CY77	CY78
Market Compound Growth 24%/Yr.		4185	4500	5400	7000	9200	12100
Share of Market			9	8	14	13	13	13
Sales			358	350	750	900	1200	1600
Operating Profit, % to Sales			(3)	(3)	7	9	11	11

Date April 1974	CATV	ELECTRO-MECHANICAL
Form K	(business element)	(division)

EXHIBIT 23–8. *EMD Form C: 1974 Investment Information*

Investment Detail	SK	Actual				CY74 Estim.	Forecast			
		CY70	CY71	CY72	CY73		CY75	CY76	CY77	CY78
1. Accounts Receivable			396	424	518	525	580	640	780	950
2. Contracts-in-Process				6	19	10	5	5	5	5
3. Inventories			542	493	709	630	700	755	830	900
4. Other			2	2	3	5	5	5	5	5
5. Accounts Payable			73	117	247	120	140	160	190	230
6. Accrued (prepaid) Expenses			75	165	137	140	170	195	210	260
7. Operating Capital	1+2+3+4-5-6		792	643	865	910	980	1050	1220	1370
8. Assigned Fixed Assets at Cost			678	715	712	742	782	832	832	942
9. Accum. Depreciation			342	428	430	480	530	585	845	710
10. Assigned Net Fixed Assets	8-9		336	287	282	262	252	247	237	232
11. Allocated Fixed Assets at Cost										
12. Accum. Depreciation										
13. Allocated Net Fixed Assets	11-12									
14. Net Other Assets				7	2	2	—			
15. NET INVESTMENT	7-13-18-14		1128	937	1149	1174	1232	1297	1457	1602
16. Long-Term Lease Commitments										
17. TOTAL INVESTMENT	15-19		1128	937	1149	1174	1232	1297	1457	1602

PART IX
Global Industries

The final section of the book is a three-case series on the world television receiver industry. This series of cases focuses on the reasons why industries become global and the problems of competing on a coordinated global basis. The television industry series also provides a summary vehicle, pulling together many of the concepts explored in earlier cases in the book.

"The U.S. Television Set Market: Prewar to 1970" examines the U.S. television set market from its inception after World War II until 1970, by which time the industry had become mature. RCA's strategy for pioneering the industry can be closely examined, as can the process by which the industry has been evolving. "The U.S. Television Set Market: 1970–1980" describes the process by which the television set industry became global, largely through the efforts of Japanese companies. The case allows an evaluation of the strategies of the various players in contributing to this outcome.

The last case, "The Television Set Industry: Europe, Japan, and Newly Industrializing Countries" describes the structure and competitive situation in the other major markets for television sets around the world besides the United States. Armed with an in-depth worldwide perspective, all firms must consider the strategic options facing them. Japanese, American, and European firms all face difficult challenges in an increasingly mature business. Coalitions or alliances among firms in different countries are increasingly being considered as a strategic option.

CASE 24
The U.S. Television Set Market, Prewar to 1970

Television had emerged from a dream in the laboratory as far back as the 1880s to a prominent element in American life by 1970. The U.S. television set industry was born, for practical purposes, right after World War II. It had grown by 1970 into a major industry, having gone through booms in black-and-white and later color sets. From a peak of 140 manufacturers, less than a dozen significant ones remained.

This case describes the U.S. television set industry from its genesis to 1970. After reviewing the early history of TV, the case summarizes the structure of the industry from 1947 to 1960 and profiles of the major competitors in 1960. The balance of the case describes industry developments and significant competitive moves chronologically over the 1960 to 1969 period. Exhibit 24–1 gives financial data on major competitors, and Exhibit 24–2 gives data on TV set demand from 1946 to 1969.

Early Developments in TV

The initial development of TV occurred in a number of countries. From the early all-mechanical systems first proposed in 1884, TV gradually evolved into an all-electronic system by the end of the 1930s. World War I halted much of the work on television. After the War it was resumed, notably in the labs of J. L. Baird in England and C. F. Jenkins and General Electric Company (GE) in the United States. Baird gave the first demonstration television in 1926 by electrically transmitting moving pictures in half-tones. The picture was flickering and crude, and displayed on a dim receiver only a few inches high. In the United States, GE began daily tests over the experimental TV station WXAD in 1928, and RCA began similar tests in 1931 in New York. David Sarnoff, president of RCA, predicted that within five years TV would become "as much a part of our life" as radio.

It was realized, though, that the early TV systems were limited in their sensitivity. Good-quality pictures on a reasonably sized screen would require 300 lines in the picture, and this would require electronic systems. By 1932, however, RCA had demonstrated all-electronic TV. Developments thereafter were rapid in Europe, the United States, and Japan, resulting in improved picture quality.

449

In the United States the principal developmental work was done by RCA. Experimental transmissions occurred with ever increasing frequency. By 1939 NBC had started a regular TV broadcasting service, and a number of manufacturers had introduced small quantities of TV sets in the market. World War II, however, put an end to the further commercialization of TV. At the outbreak of the war it was estimated that some 10,000 sets had been sold to the public.

Broadcasting and Standardization

It was realized early that the widespread acceptance of commercial TV would require nationwide standards for transmission and receivers. As early as 1929 the Radio Manufacturers Association (RMA) set up a committee on TV for the purpose of coordinating and guiding the experimental TV work going on. By 1936 a set of TV standards (with 441 lines per picture) had been proposed and a report submitted to the FCC. NBC began telecasting experimental programs in 1939 without any formal approval of the standards by the FCC. In the latter part of 1939 the FCC authorized limited commercial sponsorship of such transmissions and announced that it would hold hearings on standards in January 1940.

During the hearings several sectors of the industry voiced strong opposition to the 441-line standard, urging that a higher picture quality could be achieved with more lines. The FCC then announced that commercialization would not be permitted until the industry agreed on one standard. To do so the RMA set up the National Television System Committee, comprising technical experts from all the involved companies. The NTSC submitted its compromise recommendation of a 525-line standard to the FCC in March 1940. The FCC officially adopted the needed standard in May 1941.

WNBT, New York (NBC), became the first commercial TV station, offering fourteen hours a week of programming. By the end of 1941 there were six commercial stations in operation. However, telecasting was halted by World War II in April 1942.

In 1944 and 1945 the FCC held new hearings to reexamine the frequency allocation to TV broadcasting and to allocate stations geographically. Most important members of the industry, including

RCA (which owned NBC), Philco, and DuMont, wanted TV to get off to a fast postwar start in the very high frequency (VHF) band of the frequency spectrum. However, an opposition group emerged, led by CBS, Zenith, and Cowles Broadcasting. This group, pushing a new CBS color TV system (to be discussed later), wanted TV to be assigned to a much higher frequency band—the UHF (ultra high frequency) band. However, power tubes and transmitters for dependable UHF service were yet to be developed. CBS and its allies argued that these problems, though difficult, could be solved with one or two years of industry effort. The RCA camp countered that if the United States waited for engineering perfection, TV would never get off the ground. The CBS group accused RCA of trying to freeze TV in that part of the spectrum where its patents, investment, and control were dominant. The RCA group countered that the others were afraid that TV would cannibalize radio. The RCA group won out in the end.

The initial FCC plan allocated part of the lower end of the TV spectrum to certain emergency services. In terms of geographical separation the FCC originally provided for spacing stations using the same channel about 200 miles apart and stations using adjacent channels 85 miles. Under industry pressure the FCC finally settled on co-channel separations of 150 miles and adjacent channel separations of 75 miles.

It became apparent in 1947 that sharing TV channels with emergency services did not work because of interference. The UHF advocates used new FCC hearings to reiterate that commercial TV in the crowded VHF band was not a good idea. By 1948 there were thirty-six TV stations on the air and about seventy under construction. Interference between nearby stations proved to be serious. On September 30, 1948, the FCC declared a freeze on the licensing of any new TV stations in order to have time to consider the frequency allocation problem and also the problems posed by color TV.

The freeze lasted for three and a half years, prolonged by the Korean War. In the intervening period the FCC held extensive hearings on lifting the freeze and on the color TV issue. The new frequency allocations provided for 500 stations in the VHF band and 1,400 stations in the UHF band. The VHF stations were quickly built, and some UHF stations were built too. By the middle of 1954, 90 percent of the country had TV coverage.

The U.S. TV Set Industry, 1946–1959

TV sets were first reintroduced after the war in the autumn of 1946. Manufacturers made optimistic predictions about future sales. The postwar economy was a period of rapid growth, with tremendous pent-up demand for consumer durables. Economic growth continued strongly through 1959 with only temporary lulls and some material shortages during the Korean War years beginning in 1950.

By 1949 demand for TVs was running at a level two years ahead of even the most optimistic forecasts that had been made in 1946. Demand peaked in 1950, continued roughly level through 1955, and declined modestly through the late 1950s. The composition of TV set demand changed. Replacement sales of TVs tended to be console models, while the increasing number of second sets being purchased in the late 1950s were largely portables. By 1959 the black and white TV market was thought by most to be mature, reaching slightly over 85 percent of households with at least one set.

Numerous improvements were made in black-and-white TV during its first thirteen years. The quality of the picture continually improved. Early round 10 inch picture tubes were replaced by 12½-inch screens in 1949, and 17-inch and 21-inch rectangular screens in the early 1950s after Corning Glass Works' breakthroughs in bulb-making technology. The 21-inch screen became standard on console models for the remainder of the 1950s.

The popularity of portables grew rapidly in the mid-1950s. GE introduced a very successful 14-inch portable in 1956 that sold 250,000 units in six months, propelling GE into the number two spot for a year or so. RCA, Admiral, and Emerson rushed to respond with portables of their own. Portables with 17-inch screens soon became the standard and became more compact as a result of the new 110° deflection angle picture tube bulbs that had been developed by Corning. In 1960 Corning introduced two new bulb sizes, 19-inches and 23-inches, with more rectangular, sharper cornered screens. These were expected to replace the 17-inch and 21-inch tubes as standards.

DISTRIBUTION

Most TV set manufacturers sold to distributors (a mix of independent distributors and factory-owned branches), who in turn sold to retailers. The main exceptions were Sears, which was a retailer that also manufactured (through Warwick), and Magnavox, which sold directly to a small number of retailers. In the early years TVs were sold through outlets as diverse as beauty parlors, hardware stores, gas stations, and dry cleaners. By 1959, however, the distribution channels for TVs paralleled very closely those for major appliances.

Independent TV distributors had territorial exclusivity and generally sold only one brand. Some manufacturers, notably GE, had established factory-owned branches in some areas. Distributors set the price at which TVs were sold to retailers. Competition among distributors had increased in the 1950s, and some distributors had dropped TV sets. Manufacturers had also sought to strengthen distributor networks by dropping weak distributors and attempting to attract the strongest distributor in an area.

Many manufacturers published a "suggested list price" for retailers, but this practice was waning. Distributors had made some efforts to curtail the discounting of TV sets that had broken out in the late 1950s, but this had not proved particularly successful.

There were 50,000–60,000 retailers of TV sets in 1960, distributed as shown in Table 24–1. The number of retailers had gone through two peaks, one in 1951 and another in 1954. Retailers carried an average of four or five brands of TVs, though some carried a single brand. Generally the single-brand outlets were small stores in small communities. Manufacturer pricing structures encouraged retailers to "sell up" the customer to higher-price models. By the late 1950s TVs were in-

TABLE 24–1. TV Set Retailers

Furniture stores	14,370
Household appliance stores	10,620
Radio and TV stores	10,710
Department and other general merchandise stores	5,700
Other	15,720
Total	57,120

creasingly being sold in large discount stores and national chains, whose aggressive pricing was putting pressure on the small TV-appliance store. Manufacturers were beginning to sell to these high-volume channels directly.

During the early days of TV, TV owners and prospective customers were extremely concerned with service. After 1955 set reliability improved considerably, mainly because of reduced failures in the picture tube. For example, an RCA service contract dropped in price from $100 in 1950 to $69.95 in 1955. Service was performed by factory-owned and -operated service companies, the service departments of independent distributors, "authorized" independent service repairmen, service departments of single-brand dealers, independent servicemen who also sold sets, and independent servicemen who did not sell sets. RCA was the only large firm that operated its own service company over the entire market it served. Warranty service was performed by the distributor or factory service organization. Most service outside warranty was performed by small independent servicemen. Servicemen often played an important role in the purchase decision, as consumers would often ask for advice regarding the quality of a particular brand.

The nature of advertising of TV sets had changed during the brief history of the industry. The original emphasis was on informing customers about the nature of TV programs and picture quality. This shifted to stress the enjoyment and educational benefits of TV programs in general. By 1959 advertising was competitive, trying to persuade consumers to buy one brand of TV set over others. Manufacturers advertised nationally, while retailers advertised locally, assisted with cooperative funds from the manufacturer, which represented approximately 30 percent of manufacturer's ad budgets.

MANUFACTURING

A TV receiver consisted of a metal *chassis* on which most of the components were mounted, a *tuner* to select the channel one wanted to watch, electronic *circuitry* to process the signal, a *picture tube* to display the picture, and a *cabinet* to house all these elements. Sets were assembled in a rather complex operation that was set up on assembly lines.

The original working electronic components in TV circuits were vacuum tubes. Some companies had started replacing some or all of the vacuum tubes with transistors by the late 1950s, though initially transistors were more expensive. Most of the major companies had also started using printed circuit boards in the mid-1950s. These boards had wiring printed on them in the form of a thin conducting layer. Components would be cheaply inserted into these boards, and all the components soldered at once. At least one company, Admiral, had tried using automated insertion of components onto printed circuit boards. It had had only modest success because of the complexity of TV circuits, and hand insertion remained the method used industrywide in 1959.

Production cost for an average set was approximately 66 percent of manufacturer's selling price in 1960 and was broken down into materials (75 percent), labor (10 percent), and overhead (15 percent). The picture tube and cabinet were major cost items. Marketing was close to 10 percent of sales, and federal excise tax 9 percent of sales. An investment of approximately $5 million was necessary for an efficient assembly facility that could produce 1 million black-and-white sets per year.

Picture tubes consisted of a glass bulb that was combined with a phosphor and an electron gun. Glass-making was highly capital-intensive, and all manufacturers pruchased glass bulbs from Corning and Owens Illinois. The phosphor was deposited in a layer on the inner front surface of the bulb to form the luminescent TV screen and covered with a thin layer of aluminum to increase the contrast and brilliance of the picture. The electron gun was inserted into the neck of the bulb and sealed. A vacuum was then created in the bulb, and a heavy plate of glass was laminated onto the front surface of the screen for safety.

Picture tube assembly was automated and less labor-intensive than set manufacturing. An investment of $4 million was required for an efficient black-and-white picture tube plant that produced 1.2 million units per year. Picture tube manufacturing costs were significantly elevated if the plant was not running near full capacity.

COMPETITION

Most of the firms that entered TV set manufacturing had been radio manufacturers before the war. Numerous firms rushed to make TVs after 1947, and the number of firms reached a peak of 140 in 1950. By 1950 there was overproduction, and the resulting rivalry caused many of smaller, financially weak assemblers to withdraw. Competition remained keen through 1956, when there was another exodus of manufacturers, many of whom were large, well capitalized firms: CBS-Columbia, Du-Mont, and Stewart-Warner. Most of the losers in this wave were firms that had not been in the radio or appliance businesses previously and had found it difficult to establish distribution networks.

By 1959 there were thirty-five firms producing TV sets, and the bulk of industry sales were accounted for by RCA, Zenith, GE, Admiral, Motorola, Philco, Magnavox, Sears, and Sylvania. Market shares for this period can only be estimated (see Table 24-2).

Picture tube manufacturers had gone through a similar process of attrition. By the end of 1959 there were only nine picture tube manufacturers left, six of whom were integrated into TV set manufacturing.

THE DEVELOPMENT OF COLOR TV

The development of color TV hinged on two issues—mechanical versus all-electronic systems, and noncompatible versus compatible systems. Mechanical color TV systems involved a rotating disk, while electronic systems had no moving parts. Noncompatible systems did not allow existing black-and-white receivers to view the color broadcast even in black and white, while compatible systems did.

While development work on color had begun earlier, the first practical color TV was a mechanical system tested in 1928. In 1940 CBS demonstrated its "field sequential" mechanical color TV system. At the end of the war the only system in any reasonable

state of development was still CBS's system. In 1946 CBS petitioned the FCC to adopt its system, asking that the FCC set aside twelve MHz channels in the UHF frequency region (black-and-white channels required six MHz of channel width). CBS's system was strongly attacked by RCA. In the middle of the FCC hearings RCA unveiled its own all-electronic color system. RCA agreed to propose tentative color standards in eighteen months. The net result of the hearings was that the CBS proposal was rejected.

During 1948 RCA and others began trying to improve the electronic color system. Breakthroughs were achieved by employing red, green, and blue dots on the face of the picture tube screen. Meanwhile, CBS demonstrated an improved version of its system, though it was not compatible, and its pictures still lacked the definition of high-quality black-and-white pictures.

As a result of the CBS progress, the FCC announced that it would hold hearings on color TV standards in the fall. The FCC's announcement plunged RCA researchers into what many believe was the most intense, high-pressure industrial research activity ever undertaken in peacetime. In October RCA stunned the industry by demonstrating, for the first time, an all-electronic, compatible color TV system. The system was still in the lab, and no field tests had been made, but RCA stated that the color problem was solved. Hearings began the following month. CBS insisted that it would begin commercial broadcasting immediately, if authorized. Manufacturers of CBS's demonstration sets testified that the color receivers for the system could be manufactured for only slightly more than current black-and-white sets.

In October 1950 the FCC approved the CBS system, ruling that its adoption was in the public in-

TABLE 24-2.   Market Shares of Leading TV Set Producers

1948		1949		1956		1959	
Company	Share	Company	Share	Company	Share	Company	Share
RCA	43%	RCA	20%	RCA		Zenith	18%
Philco	17%	Admiral	11%	⌈Admiral		RCA	
⌈Admiral[a]		GE	8%	GE		GE	12%
GE	2%	Philco	7%	Philco		⌈Admiral	
⌊Others		⌈Motorola		⌊Motorola		Philco	
		⌊Zenith		Zenith	6%	Motorola	
						⌊Sears	

[a]Firms grouped together had similar shares, but exact figures cannot be determined.

terest. The FCC's decision dismayed many in the industry, who pleaded for more time to perfect the all-electronic compatible system. RCA took the matter all the way up to the Supreme Court, which in May 1951 ruled that the FCC had the right to make such a decision.

In June 1951 CBS began color transmissions and even made a few TV sets. But the Korean War forced CBS to terminate its operations. Also in June, the industry set up a second National Television System Committee (NTSC) to arrive at a color system. For the next two years the NTSC was involved in extensive engineering work involving eighty companies. By 1953 the NTSC had achieved a compatible, all-electronic system, and CBS yielded. In Decemeber 1953 the FCC accepted the NTSC color standards. RCA held many of the patents on which the NTSC system was based.

The Justice Department began investigating RCA in 1954, alleging that it was using its patent position in radio and TV to restrict trade. In 1958 RCA signed a consent decree that made all its patents more freely and cheaply available, including those on color TV.

Immediately after the FCC decision to adopt the NTSC color standards, a number of manufacturers rushed into the market with great expectations.[1] Color sets sold from between $500 and $1,000, compared to $200 for black-and-white sets. Color set assembly was somewhat more complex than that of black-and-white sets because it involved more than three times as many components. Predictions of color set sales made in December 1953 called for annual output of 1 million units by 1955.

A number of major companies held back from color, among them GE, CBS, and Zenith. One reason was that many in the industry were waiting for the development of a new, less expensive color picture tube. RCA's 21-inch round shadow-mask tube was the early standard, with a number of other tubes being seriously studied. The leading alternative, the chromatron tube, was being developed by Chromatic Television Laboratories, 50 percent owned by Paramount Pictures.

[1] Some manufacturers, like Admiral, felt that this initial surge of expectations cut into the sales of large-screen black-and-white consoles in 1954 as consumers held off in favor of color. By 1955–1956 this was no longer true when it was realized that good color was still in the future.

RCA was the only company that had spent the millions of dollars necessary to tool up for mass production of color tubes by 1959. Having spent more than $10 million on picture tube research alone, RCA felt that the shadow-mask was the most feasible of all the contenders. Many observers regarded the color picture tube as the most complex and difficult consumer good ever to be manufactured. Color tubes had three electron guns, one for each primary color, and required intricate deposition of a million tiny colored phosphor dots on the screen. The shadow-mask had to be precisely aligned with the dots. Color tube production required a minimum investment of $10 million or more for an efficient scale facility. Small-screen and large-screen tubes had to be produced on different production lines, while tubes with similar screen sizes could be produced on the same line.

Unfortunately, sales of color TV proved to be dismal. Only 20,000 or so color TVs were bought by consumers in 1955. High cost, poor and dim picture quality, and lack of color programming were the key reasons. Soon thereafter all the companies making color TV withdrew from the market except RCA and Packard-Bell, a small West Coast company. Of the two networks broadcasting some programs in color, CBS ceased doing so, leaving NBC alone. By 1959 there were but twenty-five local TV stations actively broadcasting color out of some 500 nationwide.

Profiles of Selected TV Producers in 1960

RCA. RCA was established after World War I at the behest of the U.S. government in order to ensure the nation a home-based capability in international wireless communication; this had been handled during the war by the U.S. branch of the British-owned Marconi company. The U.S. assets of Marconi were taken over by GE, Westinghouse, and AT&T and renamed Radio Corporation of America. RCA began selling radio receivers in 1922. In 1926 it formed NBC, which began operating two national radio networks: the Red and the Blue. The Blue network had to be divested under new FCC rules in 1943 and was sold; it became the ABC network. The phonograph and record industries were entered in 1929. In the 1930s the Justice Department forced the divestiture of RCA so that it became an independent company.

RCA had been experimenting with TV in its labs since 1925. It was centrally involved in every phase of TV (studio equipment, broadcasting, receivers) from the very beginning. For the first three postwar years, RCA supplied most picture tubes used in the industry. RCA Victor TV sets were made available to the public in September 1947. RCA held the leading market share until 1959, when it was overtaken by Zenith. Part of RCA's dominance during the 1947–1959 period is explained by the fact that most independent servicemen had been trained through RCA institutes. However, the antipathy that the RCA Service Company created with the independent servicemen was blamed for RCA's loss of the number one position in black-and-white.

RCA introduced color TV with great fanfare in 1954, publicly expecting sales to reach 350,000 units the following year. Actually only 25,000 to 30,000 color sets were sold in the first two years. Sales crept along to the end of the decade. RCA continued vigorously to push color TV, however. NBC aggressively added color programming, at a loss. RCA Service Company held clinics all across the country to train servicemen to repair color sets. RCA engaged in extensive dealer promotions, demonstrations and point-of-sale gimmicks. RCA also made private label color TVs for those few firms that wanted to sell them. By 1960, after six years of promotion, only an estimated 600,000 color sets were in use. RCA had invested $130 million in development and production of color TV, including color picture tube facilities at Lancaster, Pennsylvania, where it also made black-and-white picture tubes. (The comparable figure for RCA's investment in black-and-white television was $50 million.)

RCA's rise had been guided by General David Sarnoff, whose foresight was cited as the reason for the commercialization of radio, black-and-white TV, and color TV. One of Sarnoff's policies was to invest heavily in R&D, and then license the patents to other companies; licensing was a corporate function that reported directly to him. General Sarnoff did not believe in direct foreign investment, preferring to license foreign companies. In the early 1950s he had developed close ties with leading firms in the Japanese radio and TV industry and had licensed them in both radio and TV technology. In

the mid-1950s RCA's nearly 12,000 radio and TV patents yielded royalty revenues of $12 million to $13 million annually.

Zenith. Zenith sold radio and TV sets, radio-phonograph combinations, record players, and hearing aids. Unlike other TV set makers, Zenith was almost purely a consumer electronics company, having stayed away from defense contracting as a matter of policy.

After World War II Zenith wanted TV to be in the UHF frequency spectrum and to be viewer-supported (i.e., pay TV). As a result it was a year late in getting into the TV set market, which it entered by acquiring the patents of the Farnsworth Corporation (one of the early innovators in TV) in 1948. That same year Zenith acquired the Rauland Corporation, a manufacturer of TV picture tubes.

Zenith's rise to the number one position began after the boom in the TV market came to an abrupt end in the mid-1950s. Panic selling caused prices to fall, and this induced many manufacturers to sacrifice quality by using cheaper components and ignoring styling. The adverse public reaction caused inventories to pile up, and prices fell further.

Zenith took advantage of this situation. It had always had a reputation for quality; in 1956 it raised its advertising budget by 20 percent and introduced a new line of "decorator" cabinets. The company's fetish for quality caused it not to adopt the printed circuit technology that other firms were converting to.[2] While it cost more to hand-wire and hand-solder all connections, Zenith stressed that such practices resulted in greater operating dependability. Hand-wiring was also preferred by servicemen, who were still unfamiliar with printed circuits. This, coupled with the fact that Zenith's chassis was designed for easy accessibility, won the company the support of the independent servicemen.

In 1956 Zenith ranked sixth in the TV set market, with sales of 460,000 sets. By 1959 Zenith was first, producing more than 1 million sets annually. In addition, its retail prices averaged $3 more than the industry average on table and portable models, and $10 more on consoles. Zenith's Space Command remote control systems, costing $60 extra, was on 25

---

[2] Zenith had a bad first experience with printed circuits in their early days when they still curled and cracked under the heat of set operation.

percent of the Zenith sets sold in 1960. This success had caused a $7.5 million expansion program to be launched in 1959. That year Zenith had also become involved with an experimental pay-TV system.

Admiral. Admiral was primarily engaged in producing radios, TVs, phonograph combinations, record changers, and household appliances such as refrigerators, electric ranges, air conditioners, and related products. It also made electronic products for defense purposes. Appliances and TVs were produced in a number of foreign countries.

Admiral had been involved in radio since 1934. It entered the TV business in late 1947 and became one of the top three producers in 1949, manufacturing more than 400,000 sets. Its strength was inexpensive radio-TV-phonograph combinations. The company produced slightly fewer than 1 million sets in 1950, and by the end of that year had the capacity of 5,000 sets per day. During these years Admiral was one of the heaviest advertisers in the TV industry, spending more than $9 million in 1959. Distribution was handled through eighty-four distributors in the United States and 34,000 dealers.

Admiral was active in introducing printed circuits and automation in 1955. In 1958 it introduced a compact remote control unit, which it claimed helped it attain the number one position in portables during 1959. This development became entangled in a patent infringement suit with Zenith.

Admiral began making color TV sets in 1954 in very small quantities. It ceased doing so in 1957 but reentered in 1959.

General Electric. GE was the largest manufacturer of electrical equipment in the United States, engaged in the development, manufacture, and sale of products for the generation, transmission, utilization, and control of electrical power. Products ranged from lamps, household appliances, x-ray equipment, and industrial apparatus to complete utility power plants.

In 1956 GE made a bid to become one of the top two TV manufacturers by aggressively pricing its new portable set. Observers believed that this attempt was soon abandoned because of low margins.

Magnavox. Magnavox manufactured black-and-white TVs, stereo-high fidelity systems, communi-

cations systems, lightweight airborne radar, antisubmarine warfare equipment, and other products. In 1959 Magnavox sales were about $30 million in TV, $30 million in stereo systems, and $30 million in government and industrial products.

Magnavox concentrated on high-quality, high-price sets. Its emphasis was on 24-inch TVs, which represented approximately 40 percent of its TV sales. In 1958 Magnavox had introduced its first TV-stereo-high fidelity combination, which proved so popular that a full line of combinations was introduced in 1959, ranging in price from $399 to $650. Magnavox had no entry in the portable TV market until late 1959, when it introduced a 17-inch set. Magnavox had extensive cabinet and woodworking facilities and prided itself on its fine furniture cabinets.

Magnavox utilized a unique distribution system, selling direct to about 1,500 dealers with about 2,000 stores. Magnavox claimed it was the only major product line in the industry that was fair-traded in all states with appropriate laws, and generally achieved price integrity in all other states. Many dealers sold Magnavox exclusively. Magnovox outlets did not cover the entire country, but the company was planning to expand its network.

Motorola. Motorola was primarily engaged in the manufacture and sale of home and portable radios, TV sets, and phonographs. It also manufactured semiconductors, automobile radios, two-way communication systems, and microwave and telemetering systems and did substantial military development and production work.

Motorola was founded as a radio manufacturer and entered military electronics in World War II. It entered the black-and-white TV industry in 1947 and the semiconductor business in 1952. Color TV manufacture was commenced in 1954 but dropped shortly afterward.

National Video Corp. National Video commenced business in 1949 as a manufacturer of picture tubes for black-and-white TV manufacturers. By 1959 it had a three-shift capacity of 1,250,000 tubes annually. It purchased its glass bulbs from Corning and Owens Illinois and made its own electron guns.

National Video was the third largest picture tube

manufacturer in the United States and the largest independent, producing about 12.5 percent of total output. In 1959, 95 percent of its tubes were sold on an OEM basis to set manufacturers, and 5 percent went to the replacement market and for export. Approximately 85 percent of total sales were accounted for by six manufacturers (Admiral, Motorola, Muntz, Setchell-Carlson, Travler Radio Corp., and Warwick).

Philco. Philco manufactured TVs, radios, radio-TV-phonograph combinations, refrigerators, air conditioners, electric ranges, and home laundry equipment. The company produced components, including picture tubes, vacuum tubes, and transistors, as well as microwave communications systems, radar equipment, missiles, and computers.

Philco had been heavily involved in radio from the early days of the medium and in 1948 claimed to be the world's largest home radio producer. Philco had engaged in TV research since 1928 and was an original entrant after World War II. Philco was an innovator in TV, especially early in the industry's development. In the 1947–1955 period Philco focused on large-screen (24 inch) models, claiming to have the largest market share of this segment. The company introduced 14-inch and 17-inch portables in 1956. Its strong position in transistors allowed it to introduce the world's first battery-operated transistor TV in 1959. Philco introduced color receivers in 1955 but withdrew in 1957. U.S. distribution was handled through 102 distributors and more than 20,000 franchised dealers. The company was active internationally through sixteen licensees and six subsidiaries and international divisions.

GTE-Sylvania. Sylvania was one of the largest manufacturers of electronic tubes, photoflash lamps, and fluorescent and incandescent lamps. It also manufactured radios and TV sets, semiconductors, and cameras. The company was acquired by GTE, which was a regulated telephone company, in 1959.

Sylvania was one of the three most highly integrated manufacturers of TV sets and was a leading supplier of black-and-white picture tubes to other firms. Sylvania's chemical and metallurgical division produced phosphors used in the picture tubes, and Sylvania also produced many of its own TV and tube parts and components.

Since 1948 Sylvania had a minority interest in Thorn Electrical Industries Ltd., the largest independent manufacturer of lighting products and TV sets in the United Kingdom. Sylvania also had subsidiaries and joint ventures all over the world, primarily engaged in lighting products. Its Canadian and Mexican subsidiaries also made radios and TVs.

The U.S. TV Set Industry, 1960

INDUSTRY DEVELOPMENTS

During 1960 NBC greatly expanded its color broadcasting. An observer commented:

> About all that is holding back an enormous increase in available color programs, in fact, is the attitude of NBC's two big network rivals. The Columbia Broadcasting System, reluctant to give any aid and comfort to RCA and unwilling to undertake the expense of colorcasts for the small audience of color set owners, envisioned more advancement of its color schedule, which so far in the 1959 to 1960 season had totaled 6 hours. . . . the American Broadcasting Company had yet to try its first color show.[3]

New wide angle 19-inch and 23-inch black-and-white TV receivers replaced the old 17-inch and 21-inch models as the industry's most popular screen sizes during 1960. In the latter half of the year there was a downturn in black-and-white sales, while sales of color sets increased sharply.

RCA, the only color tube manufacturer, was selling the color tube to set manufacturers for $85, compared with $25 for a monochrome tube. The maintenance fee for a contract covering installation of a color set and unlimited service for a year was $70, considerably less than the $140 that it had been earlier. The drop was attributed to improvements in color set quality and reliability. RCA's cheapest color set retailed for $495 in 1960. RCA publicly stated that even if output were boosted to 500,000 sets a year this would reduce set price by only $50 to $75. RCA chairman, David Sarnoff, insisted, "There is nothing on the horizon which promises significantly lower priced or better color TV."

[3] *Wall Street Journal,* March 17, 1960.

The Paramount color picture tube was the only radically different tube technology that appeared to be near commercial production. Employing a single electron gun, it was believed that the Paramount tube could be produced at least as cheaply as the three-gun RCA color tube. In addition the chassis required was easier to manufacture and was estimated to cost about $50 less. A Paramount vice president said, "We'll have a finished set to sell this year, although we haven't decided to make it ourselves or license it."

Interest in manufacturing color sets increased in 1960. Emerson Radio, having abandoned color in 1959, resumed production in the fall. "Color sets are the coming thing" conceded Benjamin Abrams, president of Emerson, in explaining his decision to get back into the business. "We want to be in the market, even though we know we'll lose money for a couple of more years." At least five other TV manufacturers approached RCA about buying its color picture tube for sets they were planning to assemble.

GE, Westinghouse, and Sylvania were continuing research on color TV but were letting RCA bear the brunt of the promotional effort while they awaited a real deluge of public demand. The vice president and general manager of Westinghouse's Consumer Products Group, Chris Witting, said, "It just has not reached the point where it is worthwhile for us to make color sets." Other black-and-white TV producers that sat it out, at least through 1960, were Zenith, Motorola, Travler Radio Corp., and Philco. RCA continued to build tubes for the three existing color TV competitors.

Thompson Starrett Co., Inc., expected to start importing a Japanese chassis for 21-inch color TV sets, to be priced cheaper than the cheapest American-made set. Several Japanese firms were considering direct sale of color sets in the United States, even though color broadcasting in Japan was still in the test stage. The Japanese manufacturers who stated intentions to produce the color sets included Toshiba, Sony, and Matsushita. All except Sony was licensed to use RCA's picture tube patents.[4] An RCA spokesman said:

[4] Sony sought to develop its own tube based on the Paramount patent.

It may seem strange that RCA would agree to license Japanese firms which may become its direct competitors in the world market. But RCA, which also has licensed Japanese firms to use some of its radio patents, sees nothing strange about such transactions. It is now and has been RCA's policy to license responsible companies here and abroad to use RCA's patent rights on reasonable terms.

RCA. RCA substantially converted its black-and-white line to the new 19-inch and 23-inch picture sizes. RCA color TV sales increased markedly. Commenting on the industry RCA noted, "The year marked color's arrival as a more than $100,000,000 business including home receivers, tubes, video tapes, cameras, and other equipment servicing the local independent broadcaster."

RCA was the top color producer by a wide margin. RCA reportedly accounted for at least 80 percent of the total volume (95 percent by other accounts). After years of investing in developing and promoting color, RCA broke into the black in late 1959. Its color picture tube operations had also reportedly started making money in late 1959 or early 1960. In 1960, according to management, profits ran to "seven figures."

RCA executives felt certain that the time was ripe to overcome consumer resistance to the current high prices of color sets by stepped-up promotion. RCA introduced a device in dealers' showrooms that would split a color screen in half, showing color on one side and black and white on the other. A heavy RCA magazine advertising campaign, featuring Perry Como in color, alerted readers: "Look what's happened to color TV since you last saw it!" And some 500 school, church, club, and social groups sat through a free movie entitled "The Wonderful World of Color," produced by RCA for more than $50,000. While RCA denied that big factory price cuts were likely on color sets, price cuts were being made by many of its dealers under the guise of trade-ins. Some dealers were then offering as much as $200 for old monochrome sets toward the price of a new color receiver.

Zenith. Zenith produced and sold more than 1 million TV receivers in 1960 for the second consecutive year. While industry black-and-white sales declined substantially from 1959, Zenith's declined only slightly, thereby strengthening Zenith's number one position in the industry. In explaining Zenith's success, a non-Zenith industry executive said: "The answer must be that Zenith sticks to the making and selling of TV sets and other home entertainment products almost exclusively. Other producers go more and more into the more expensive fields in electronics like computers."

The Zenith line consisted of thirty-five TV receivers and five TV-stereo combinations. These included fine furniture pieces as well as slim portables.

Admiral. Admiral registered the first operating loss in its history in 1960. "Abnormally high costs and charges stemming from extraordinary development problems on government contracts and from the commercial electronics division together with unprofitable appliance manufacturing and marketing operations exceeded $5,000,000 during the year." However, according to Admiral there was increasing interest in black-and-white TV-radio-phonograph combinations and in color TV. Admiral began using the new wide-angle 19-inch and 23-inch tubes in its black-and-white line. Admiral had reentered the color market in August 1959 with a new line having suggested retail prices ranging from $595 to $895. According to Ross Siragusa, Jr., vice president of the Electronics Division, the move had proved profitable at every level—factory, wholesale, and retail.

During 1961 it was planned that the radio and stereo production would be moved from Chicago to the huge electronics facility at Harvard, Illinois. That move would permit the shipment of mixed carloads and truckloads of TV receivers, radios, and stereos for the first time, thus reducing transportation costs.

Magnavox. Magnavox reported record sales and earnings in TV in 1960.

Motorola. Motorola's consumer products sales volume decreased. Reasons cited were the economy and the highly competitive condition that prevailed in the TV industry caused by some manufacturers pricing TV sets unreasonably low, ostensibly to make room for the newly introduced 19-inch and 23-inch models. Motorola refrained from this unwarranted price-cutting. Instead, the company chose to reduce inventories in an orderly manner as an aid to distributors and dealers as well. Motorola's sets emphasized quality and styling, and the average Motorola factory TV selling price was 11 percent higher than the industry as a whole in 1960. Motorola had associated itself with Drexel Furniture Company and Heritage Furniture, Inc., in the design of cabinetry. Motorola introduced a new series in 19-inch slimline console TVs in 1960 with five models in three basic designs. Motorola also introduced the first large-screen (19-inch) transistorized portable TV in 1960 that could be played on regular house line voltage or on a self-contained energy cell. The introduction of the new set marked the beginning of a gradual evolution by Motorola from vacuum tubes to transistors.

Philco. Generally, 1960 was a bad year for Philco consumer durable goods business, including TV sets. In the portable market Philco continued to secure a substantial market share with its 17-inch and 19-inch models. In 1960 Philco began to push its "cool chassis," designed to improve reliability. For the first time in industry history, Philco began offering a ninety-day warranty on all parts and labor.

General Electric. GE's sales of radio and TV receivers continued strong until late in the year. Emphasis in the TV division continued to be on improving service. GE introduced an electronic entertainment center combining radio, TV, and stereo phonograph.

GTE-Sylvania. GTE-Sylvania began production of a 19-inch bonded shield picture tube, with a glass safety panel bonded directly to a face plate, resulting in sharper, clearer pictures. GTE-Sylvania introduced the industry's first square-screen 19-inch receivers with bonded shield tubes. The squared screen showed more of the available picture. A year earlier GTE-Sylvania had marketed the first 23-inch set with the same tube.

The U.S. TV Set Industry, 1961

Black-and-white TV recovered much slower from the general recession than other items. As a result of the sharp production cutbacks beginning in August 1960, inventory positions throughout the industry were low. Consequently, TV set prices were much firmer than they had been throughout most of 1960. Wide-angle 19-inch and 23-inch receivers now accounted for 85 percent of the industry's sales.

While more than twenty-four manufacturers made TV sets in 1961, six of them—Zenith, RCA, Philco, Admiral, Motorola, and General Electric—accounted for more than 70 percent of the total. Other sizable manufacturers were Magnavox, GTE-Sylvania, Westinghouse, and Emerson. Farther down the list in volume were Packard-Bell, the Olympic Division of Siegler Corp., and Muntz TV.

Some observers were expecting booming sales in 1962 as replacement demand in TV increased because more than half the sets in use were made in 1956 or earlier. Several competitors were successful at raising their share of the total TV dollar volume by inducing customers to upgrade their purchases.

Portables were becoming increasingly important, and by the end of the year portable TV set prices tumbled as manufacturers fought for sales. Motorola had begun shipping a 19-inch portable to retail at $139.95, which was $30 less than its previous lowest-price model. Admiral, Westinghouse, and others entered with new sets in the same price range. Price-cutting in early 1961 had been restricted to bottom-of-the-line portables, but executives worried that it could spread to other models as well. The pressure for lower costs occasioned by price-cutting caused some firms to make greater use of cheaper foreign components. Other firms simplified circuitry and left out built-in antennas.

Sony introduced an 8-inch battery operated, fully transistorized black-and-white portable, retailing for $280 in the U.S. market. Public reaction to the new Sony set was characterized by *Television Digest* as "Cute—but too expensive." Sony indicated that it sold about 8,000 of those sets in the United States in 1961.

COLOR TV

A number of producers were predicting that 1961 or 1962 would mark the long-heralded breakthrough in color. A number of manufacturers announced greatly increased color set sales, including Magnavox, RCA, and Admiral. An editorial comment early in the year explained color's problems:

> In many ways, color TV is trying to retrace growth patterns of black and white TV. It got its start in two of the places that cradled black and white—bars and high-income homes. And, like black and white, color faces a "which comes first" problem—advertising and programming, or the sale of enough sets to receive color. But black and white had an important advantage: the nearest thing to it was the radio. Color had to prove that it was worth the difference over black and white.[5]

More color broadcasting was helping sales. NBC was planning to double its color broadcasting hours. In addition, local color programming was being increased in the three largest markets for color TV sets (Chicago, Los Angeles, and New York) and in many other cities. CBS had only a sporadic color schedule, and ABC still none at all.

While RCA did a small volume in color portables, selling for $495, its main color model (and those of other manufacturers) retailed for around $600, which was triple the average industry price for black-and-white. In a surprise move in June, however, Motorola announced the development of a new 23-inch rectangular color picture tube, which was 5-inches shorter, front to back, than the 21-inch round RCA color tube then on the market. The Motorola tube would cost approximately the same as RCA's. At the time of the announcement Motorola was one of the major holdouts from color TV, having characterized the upsurge in interest in color TV as "an overpublicized, marketing flurry."

In February 1961 Zenith announced its entry into the color TV market, the result of the expenditure of several millions of dollars of research over a period of eight years aimed at improving the performance and reliability of color receivers. The new Zenith sets had a three-gun shadow-mask picture tube with increased brightness, and the service-saving horizontal chassis design and hand-wired circuits characteristic of Zenith black-and-white sets. Zenith said that one motive in reentering color was to keep dealers happy. Color TV was a high-priced

---

[5] *Business Week*, March 11, 1961.

item offering a considerable promotion allowance and dealer margins.

Announcing Zenith's entry in the color TV market, president Joseph Wright said: "Not long ago we said we weren't ready, but things have changed since then. We've been working for a good long time on a receiver that met our standards for good performance and reliability and now we think we've got that receiver." RCA's response to Zenith's entry into the color market was given by president John Burns: "We welcome the entry of Zenith into the color TV field." The other major color holdout, GE, changed its tune and started making color TVs in 1961 as well.

Zenith's and GE's entries brought the list of manufacturers making color TV to RCA, Zenith, GE, Admiral, Emerson-DuMont, Magnavox, Philco, Olympic, and Packard-Bell. Sylvania entered at the end of 1961 and said it would make its own picture tubes. In 1961 aggregate color sales were estimated to run possibly as high as 200,000 units. Zenith's entry was considered a major breakthrough, because many dealers were reluctant to handle color TV as long as the largest TV producer avoided it. New companies in the color TV market also increased advertising and publicity in 1961, boosting industrywide sales.

RCA. RCA black-and-white TV set sales were led by a large increase in 17-inch and 19-inch portables. RCA claimed to have expanded its share of the total TV set market. RCA claimed that sales of color sets in November 1961 spurted ahead of black and white for the first time since RCA introduced color in 1954. In March 1961 RCA announced that it had developed a new, brighter color picture tube, to be used by RCA and Zenith.

Zenith. Zenith black-and-white TV sets continued to incorporate hand-wired chassis and other previous features. Zenith successfully sued Admiral over its Space Command and circuit patents. Zenith also initiated suits against Motorola and Hazeltine on these patents. As stated above, Zenith entered the color TV set market in 1961, emphasizing hand-wiring, no printed circuit boards, and "no production shortcuts" on its color sets.

Zenith started production of TV components and devices in a new 100,000-square-foot plant in Paris, Illinois. Plans were finalized for a 700,000-square-foot facility to house warehousing, manufacturing, and administrative facilities next to Zenith's Chicago main plant.

Admiral. Admiral reported improved earnings, attributed to "centralization of all consumer electronics production at Harvard, Illinois, continued emphasis on achieving more efficient operations with reduction of overhead costs and a trend to increase sales of merchandise at the middle and top end of the TV, stereo, and appliance lines." Sales of TV, radio, and stereo increased during the year. In August 1961 Admiral introduced the first black-and-white TV set with wide-angle 27-inch picture tubes. Admiral's color TV volume continued to increase during the year.

General Electric. GE's new TV line included a line of educational sets, including a TV-audio center specifically designed for classroom use. Also introduced were specialized receivers for hotel/motel installation.

Magnavox. Magnavox gained market share in black-and-white sets because of an improved tuning system. Magnavox stressed black-and-white sets with large picture tubes. While Magnavox sold color sets, it did not intend to expand market development and promotion until color TV sets were improved. Its color TV chassis and tubes were purchased from outside.

During the year Magnavox acquired a 200,000-square-foot furniture factory to supplement its existing high fidelity and TV cabinet facilities. Cabinets had been in short supply. Magnavox also leased a woodworking facility to produce lumber for its cabinet facilities.

Motorola. Motorola's share of black-and-white TV sets improved during the year. For the third consecutive year, Motorola won the Mahogany Association "Grand Award" for outstanding furniture craftsmanship. Late in the year it introduced a 19-inch portable, selling for $139.98, which was about $20 below competitors', and announced a 23-inch model to be priced at $169.95.

Philco. On December 11, 1961, Philco was acquired by the Ford Motor Corporation. The board of directors of the new Philco Corporation elected Charles E. Beck, president and chief executive officer. Mr. Beck was Ford's director of business planning prior to his new position with Philco.

GTE-Sylvania. Sylvania's total sales and earnings declined, principally because of lower sales of home electronic products and components. The 1962 TV set line was wider than any previous Sylvania line and incorporated new technical improvements such as a new Flexi-Core™ transformer-powered chassis and a multifunction remote tuning system. Sylvania also developed a new phosphor to improve substantially the brightness of its picture tubes.

The U.S. TV Set Industry, 1962

It was estimated that 60 percent of all black-and-white sales would be replacement sets. Another 18 percent were expected to come from the growing second-set market, mostly portables. Portables offered lower dollar profits to manufacturers.

In 1962 Motorola stole a march on the industry with its inexpensive 19-inch large-screen black-and-white portable. Competitors complained about cheap, stripped-down sets. Toward the end of the year the trend toward large-screen portables was reversed when GE, Philco, and Delmonico introduced lightweight portables with 16-inch screens. Zenith planned a 16-inch portable for 1963, but Admiral and RCA were holding back to see what reception the new size got.

In 1962 most informed estimates were that color set volume topped 435,000 sets, which was more than double the number sold in 1961. For 1963, moreover, the figure was projected as high as 700,000. An RCA spokesman stated that if the supply of tubes, which RCA alone made, had not been limited, more than 500,000 sets would have been sold. The impressive showing of color sets in 1962 was attributed in large part to the changed consumer attitude toward color. The change apparently stemmed from more reliable, trouble-free color receivers, relatively low cost service contracts, and an improved picture tube that was 50 percent brighter than earlier models. NBC increased its color broadcasting, and ABC and CBS both began color telecasting.

RCA. In 1962 RCA sold more than 1,000,000 TV sets, and the dollar volume in TV sets exceeded the previous high attained in 1950. The demand for color TV receivers pushed RCA's production facilities to the limit, even with the rise in picture tube output that was achieved through a $10,000,000 investment to expand production lines at Marion, Indiana, and Lancaster, Pennsylvania. RCA had hoped to come out with a 90° rectangular color tube that was 5 inches shorter during the year. However, late in 1962 it was announced that because of an inability to achieve desired quality it was holding off introducing the 90° tube for the next nine to fifteen months. RCA black-and-white TV set sales were also strong, and RCA had a strong position in the portable market.

Zenith. Zenith sold more than 1 million black and white sets for the fourth successive year, with the biggest seller a 19-inch portable. Color set production in 1962 was approximately 90,000 up from 25,000 in 1961. Zenith began color TV tube production on a pilot basis, with full production scheduled by mid-1963.

Admiral. Admiral reported notable gains in TV sets and combinations. Its sales of color TV more than doubled over 1961. With the completion of expanded TV facilities at Harvard, Illinois, Admiral's production capacity for color receivers reached 100,000 units per year. Compact 23-inch black-and-white TV sets, including the industry's first portable 23-inch models, were introduced. Early in 1963 Admiral planned to introduce its first lightweight 16-inch black-and-white portables, the only ones marketed with wireless remote control. Admiral noted that there was continued pressure on profits in TV sets due to the "exceptionally keen competition in the industry."

General Electric. GE reported improved TV set sales over 1961. It introduced a new 22-pound Escort black-and-white portable set, which reportedly received excellent acceptance. GE gained a strong percentage of sales of TV receivers for hotel/motel installations.

Magnavox. Despite reporting increased sales in black-and-white sets, Magnavox's market share was declining. Portables and table models accounted for approximately 60 percent of industry sales but only 25 percent of Magnavox sales, which were concentrated in over-23-inch sets, where it sold more than the rest of the industry combined. Magnavox announced plans to launch lower-priced ($129) portables in the spring of 1963. In color sets, Magnavox announced a doubling of sales and more aggressive sales and advertising.

During the year Magnavox announced plans for the construction of a $5 million, 500,000-square-foot facility in Greenville, Tennessee, to produce color and black-and-white sets. Scheduled for June 1963 completion, the plant was to be "completely automated."

Motorola. Motorola prepared to reenter the color TV market in mid-1963. In black and white, it stressed its collection of sets with fine furniture styling. Motorola's success with its large-screen portables helped it add 3,000 dealers, and it began to talk of moving from the fifth spot in total unit sales to the third spot.

National Video. Profits of National Video were squeezed by upward pressure on costs and competitive pressure on selling prices. Two major competitors making black-and-white tubes withdrew during the year, with the initial effect of lowering prices as the remaining tube manufacturers competed for customers of the exited firms. National Video became the only remaining independent picture tube manufacturer in 1962.

National Video was testing a rectangular color picture tube in collaboration with Motorola. It reported that color picture tubes cost approximately five times as much as black-and-white tubes in 1963.

Philco. Philco carried on an intensive program of appraisal and product realignment in 1962. The Philco Consumer Products Division was reorganized along functional rather than product lines. On January 3, 1963, Philco and RCA agreed without payment of damages by either to withdraw their claims against each other in a complicated antitrust and patent litigation that had been pending since 1957. At the same time the two companies entered an agreement under which each granted to the other various patent licenses in the radio, TV, transistor, and data-processing field. Under this agreement RCA paid Philco $9,000,000.

GTE-Sylvania. Sylvania reported an increasing market share in TV. Its 19-inch portable black-and-white TV set was rated number one by an independent survey organization. In several especially competitive markets, Sylvania instituted a direct factory-to-dealer marketing program, leading to improved sales. Black-and-white picture tube production was consolidated in one location, and the production of color TV picture tubes was planned to begin in 1963.

The U.S. TV Set Industry, 1963

Black-and-white TV sales were higher in spite of a sharp increase in color TV sales. Very small screen sets were growing in popularity, with screens ranging from 4½ to 11 inches, measured diagonally, and weighing from 8 to 15 pounds, compared to about 40 pounds for the standard models. Many of the small sets were highly transistorized.

For the first time since RCA began pushing color TV in 1954, every major set maker had or was entering the field. Instead of contracting for the production of color chassis, as most manufacturers had been doing, by the year's end virtually every company was making its own. In early 1963 RCA estimated that the market could absorb 750,000 to 1 million color TV sets that year. Most other companies were less optimistic, with the average guess ranging from 500,000 to 600,000 sets. There was still lingering skepticism regarding the actual potential of color TV. Monochrome sets, comparable to color sets (presumably 21-inch models), were selling for an average price of $200. Some TV executives argued that until color was brought down to within $100 of that range, it would not command a mass market.

Price-cutting began to appear in color TV. In June Admiral announced a 21-inch set for $399.95, and GE replied with a lesser cut to $450. RCA's lowest-priced set stayed firm at $495. At the laboratories of Paramount Pictures Corp., work was continuing on its Chromatron picture tube. The only Paramount licensee was Sony Corporation, which was trying to develop a Chromatron in a tube size that could be used in a portable set.

RCA. RCA's home instruments business in 1963 produced the best sales and earnings for consumer products in the company's history. Color TV was largely responsible, especially in the profit performance. RCA's output of color receivers in 1962 was believed to have approximated 280,000 sets, which represented about 65 percent of the market. W. Walters Watts, a group executive vice president, stated, "We used to just try to sell color TV. Now we're selling RCA Victor color TV." While RCA continued to produce color sets on contract for others in 1963, it gave notice that starting in 1964 all of its capacity would be needed for its own output.

A sixth color TV receiver assembly line was opened during the year at RCA's Bloomington, Indiana, set manufacturing plant. Also, a substantial increase in the output of picture tubes was achieved with the completion of new facilities at the Marion, Indiana, and Lancaster, Pennsylvania, tube plants. Despite this, RCA had informed set makers that color tube shipments would be on an allocation basis.

Zenith. Zenith's black-and-white sales reached an all-time high. However, color sets made the greatest contribution to increased sales volume, and output was estimated at 200,000 units. Zenith offered a wide variety of color set styles, including a budget-priced table model color TV. It stressed its commitment not to use printed circuit boards.

Quantity production of 21-inch round color picture tubes began in the second half of 1963 at the new $20 million Knox Avenue plant. By December the production rate was more than 10,000 per month. Zenith had indicated that it would offer tubes to other set makers.

Admiral. Admiral introduced a new lightweight 11-inch personal black-and-white portable TV soon after GE's May introduction (see below). It soon found a ready market as the second or even third set in the home, and the set was in short supply at year end. Sales of Admiral's line of seven black-and-white TV models increased during the year. Ad-

miral produced three color TV models, all using the 21-inch round tube. Backed by heavy advertising, color sales were more than 50 percent ahead of the previous year. According to management, Admiral had capacity to build in excess of 100,000 color sets in 1963 and expected to sell this entire output.

Admiral noted concern about the availability of color tubes. While the company had no production facilities for color TV tubes, the situation was being carefully considered by the board.

General Electric. In May 1963 GE introduced a line of 11-inch black-and-white sets weighing just 13 pounds and listing from $99.95 up. This aided GE TV sales in rising to the highest total ever achieved. GE produced approximately ten color set models during the year.

Magnavox. Magnavox claimed the widest selection of black-and-white sets in the industry. Color TV sales were up 30 percent, but during the fourth quarter inability to get color picture tubes forced shortening of the line to only a few top-priced models. Magnavox began producing its own color chassis in the spring of 1963.

In marketing, Magnavox stressed its direct distribution and retail price maintenance. Its $5 million Greenville, Tennessee, TV plant went into operation in August 1963. Magnavox had no plans to produce color tubes. Magnavox announced in early January 1964 its intention to become a private labeler, with Montgomery Ward the primary customer.

Motorola. Motorola reported consumer product sales equal to 1962, but earnings decreased as a result of heavy expenditures for the development of a new color TV picture tube and the initiation of production at National Video. In 1963 Motorola announced that it had reentered color set production. Its 1964 line of color TV sets included eight models ranging from $650 to $1,650 that featured the 23-inch 92° rectangular tube that Motorola developed two years earlier and that National Video was producing exclusively for Motorola. The line also included three sets ranging from $449.95 to $529.95 using RCA's 21-inch, 70° round tube. According to executive vice president Taylor, Motorola's square tube design was "offered to every tube manufacturer but we had no takers."

Motorola forecast that it would have "tens of thousands of the sets in customer's homes by the end of the year." However, it and National Video had problems with producing the 23-inch rectangular tube. The delay led to reluctance of dealers to buy other Motorola consumer products until they received delivery of the much wanted rectangular tube color sets.

National Video. Unit deliveries of black-and-white picture tubes declined 6 percent. Sales were affected adversely by an increase in the demand for smaller picture tubes. Production of 23-inch rectangular color picture tubes commenced during the year but ran into difficulties.

Philco. Philco continued to realign its commercial activities in 1963. In the spring of 1963 Philco began to assemble color TVs in its own plant. It planned to boost its color business by 300 to 400 percent.

GTE-Sylvania. Sylvania began making its own color TV sets in 1963. Until then its color sets had been built by Packard-Bell. Sylvania began the production of color TV picture tubes in 1963 and expected to increase its output substantially in 1964. It was making the 21-inch round color tube. Research programs in color TV, including investigation of new phosphors to improve the clarity and brightness of the TV picture, were expanded substantially.

Japanese Firms. Many of the small-screen (12-inch and below) black-and-white sets being sold in the United States were made in Japan. This size range had not proved popular when U.S. manufacturers first introduced it in the mid-1950s but seemed to be catching on in 1963. Japanese imports increased rapidly. In Japan, demand for black-and-white sets had peaked in 1962 at slightly more than 4 million sets and had declined slightly in 1963.

The penetration of the Japanese in the U.S. market had begun in the latter half of the 1950s with the pocket transistor radio. The first transistor radio had been produced by a U.S. company, but it was the Japanese that made it a real commerical success. Japanese companies had developed the small speaker and small varicon tuning capacitor that allowed miniaturization of the sets.

Japanese transistor radios were first imported into the United States by a group of general merchandise (e.g., cigarette lighters, toys) importers working through Japanese trading companies. In 1959 the Japanese held their first serious electronics show in the United States.

As the quality and low cost of these Japanese products became increasingly evident, Motorola began sourcing Japanese transistor radios on an OEM basis. Other U.S. companies like RCA, GE, Admiral, and finally Zenith too gradually added Japanese products to their lines.

Black-and-white TVs from Japan had begun trickling into the United States in late 1960, when Sony began selling its novel, battery-operated transistorized micro-TV. Matsushita entered on Sony's heels. In 1962 three companies were involved, and in 1963 there were ten. The majority of Japanese sets were sold under retailer's private labels or under U.S. manufacturers' labels. Sony was the only Japanese company that sold exclusively under its own label, following an exclusive distribution strategy through a few large and reputable stores. Sony products were expensive, provided high dealer margins, and were not discounted. Sony also handled its own distribution almost from the very beginning.

In 1963 a few color chassis made by Victor Company of Japan (a semiautonomous subsidiary of Matsushita) were imported by the Delmonico Division of Thompson Starrett Co. These were fitted with round 21-inch U.S. color tubes and sold at prices comparable to U.S. models. The volume, however, was negligible.

The U.S. TV Set Industry, 1964

The black-and-white market was becoming mainly a replacement market, and sales were primarily portables and table models. This benefited GE particularly, because GE had long specialized in these lines, including micro-TVs. RCA and Zenith had also benefited because they produced a reasonably full line. In 1964 RCA, GE, and Zenith had somewhere between 50 and 55 percent of the black-and-white market, up from 45 percent in 1963. GE introduced the first completely transistorized black-and-white portable TV made in the United States, a 9-inch model.

The growing demand for color TV continued in 1964. In January demand for the RCA color tubes was exceeding production. It was understood that RCA retained at least 50 percent of its tube output for its own use. RCA was selling color picture tubes to more than twenty-four other set producers (including GE, Motorola, and Magnavox, which said that it could not get enough tubes from RCA), up from fifteen a year earlier. Admiral said it received all of the tubes it needed, because "we were one of the first companies to do tube business with RCA, and RCA is allocating tubes to people it has been doing business with the longest." Industry sources felt that 1.5 million sets could have been sold if tubes had been available.

RCA dropped prices on color sets by $130 to $150 on its 1964 models, catching most of the industry by surprise. Edward Taylor, executive vice president of Motorola, said, "we're shocked—we don't regard this as a proper position for the industry leader." The president of another set maker said, "Holy cats! They've knocked the gravy off the industry just as it got started. We had figured that we could have two good years more before the real price shaving got going." When manufacturers revealed their new lines shortly thereafter, major producers like Zenith and Motorola also cut their prices. Magnavox did not. Retail price-cutting in color sets had been prevalent well before the manufacturer price cuts, and color TV was being handled more and more by discount stores.

RCA did not cut its price on color tubes, where trade sources estimated that RCA made a profit of between $35 and $45 each. Magnavox and Motorola asserted that RCA was overcharging the industry for its 21-inch round tube. They were shortly joined by Admiral, which held that RCA in the past few years had made significant cost reductions in its manufacturing of the 21-inch round color tubes, but the prices of these tubes had remained essentially the same over the past ten years ($98.50).

RCA. RCA black-and-white unit sales increased 12 percent over the 1963 figure, and share increased despite the competition of lower-price small-screen receivers. RCA's color TV sales in 1964 equaled in dollar terms the combined total of all other RCA home instruments. The division's overall color TV business increased 20 percent. This included a 40 percent rise in RCA brand color set dollar sales during the year. In the fourth quarter in new slimmer 25-inch color set was introduced with a new rectangular tube made by RCA. Preparations were also made in 1964 for introducing a 19-inch rectangular tube color receiver during 1965.[6]

Zenith. Combined factory sales of Zenith black-and-white and color TV receivers during the year exceeded 1.75 million units, establishing a new sales record for the industry. Zenith introduced the first handcrafted 12-inch personal black-and-white portable set. In mid-1964 Zenith claimed it had 30 percent of the color market compared to RCA's 50 percent. By the end of the year a very large percentage of Zenith's color TVs were equipped with its own color tubes. Color tube capacity was increased, and production of a 25-inch rectangular color tube was begun late in the year. Further facilities expansion in tubes was planned.

Admiral. Admiral announced its decision to produce its own color picture tubes in August 1964. In trade interviews Admiral said that RCA's pricing policy was chiefly responsible for the decision. Admiral said that it would spend about $12 million to start color TV tube production at its Chicago plant. Admiral was planning to have facilities to produce 19-inch and 25-inch rectangular tubes and 21-inch round tubes. Initial capacity was to be 30,000 tubes a month, but capacity might be doubled by the end of 1966. Admiral "might sell some to foreign set producers" but the company hadn't any plans to sell color TV tubes to other U.S. set makers.

In December Admiral became the first manufacturer to offer a complete choice of color TV screen sizes, 21, 23, and 25 inches. The 23-inch and 25-inch models featured the newest type of rectangular picture tubes. In black-and-white, portable TV volume climbed sharply. Admiral's TV production facilities were pressed all year. The board of directors approved an expansion program for 1965 to increase production by 25 percent. New capacity of the plant was to be 1.3 million TV receivers.

[6] RCA's previous color tubes had been the round, 21-inch varieties.

General Electric. GE introduced a 9-inch transistorized, battery-operated black-and-white TV set costing $159.95. The 11-inch portables introduced in 1963 contributed strongly to 1964 TV sales. In color TV, GE was emphasizing reliable performance through ten-day home trials in many locations. Its color line was expanded in the fall.

Magnavox. Color TV was Magnavox's most significant growth product. The company did not immediately cut prices in response to RCA's price cut. A Magnavox spokesman noted at the time that the company's business was mostly in the upper end of the price spectrum, and that better selling rather than lower prices was needed. Sales of color TVs exceeded production capacity. Magnavox introduced a 12-inch portable black-and-white set made for it by Nippon Electric Company of Japan. Magnavox also acquired Kent-Coffey Manufacturing Company in North Carolina, a manufacturer of high-quality furniture, to supply TV cabinetry.

Motorola. Motorola achieved record sales in consumer products, led by color TV. The new 23-inch rectangular tube developed with National Video came on stream and moved the company from virtually no position in color TV early in the year to a position among the top four in color TV by year's end. Motorola reduced color TV prices during the year to meet price cuts. In January 1965 Motorola announced plans to enter the business of producing rectangular color TV tubes by 1966 as a second source to National Video. In black-and-white, Motorola introduced a new 12-inch portable set.

National Video Corp. Acceptance of the 23-inch rectangular tube was termed excellent. All tubes were going to Motorola. National Video was working on 25-inch rectangular tubes that it hoped to put in production by 1965.

Philco. Philco began pilot production of 21-inch round color picture tubes at Lansdale, Pennsylvania. Full-scale output was expected to begin in the first quarter of 1965.

GTE-Sylvania. Sylvania pioneered the development of a rare earth phosphor allowing true red rendition, solving a major technical problem in the in-

dustry. Prior to this, manufacturers had to "deaden" the blue and green colors to balance the weak performance of the existing red phosphor.[7] In addition to a substantial increase in the production of color TV tubes, a new Color Bright 85 tube based on the new phosphor, which provided a picture 40 percent brighter than previous tubes, was placed in production. Sylvania also began producing 25-inch rectangular color tubes late in the year.

Total sales of Sylvania entertainment electronic products increased. Color TVs using the new Sylvania color Bright 85 picture tube were introduced in June and met with instant approval. Late in 1964 the company introduced its first 25-inch color sets with rectangular picture tubes, supplementing the 21-inch round tube models.

Japanese Firms. Mr. Siragusa of Admiral had noted early in the year that Japanese firms were aggressively invading the U.S. TV market and probably would sell 600,000 of the estimated 9 million sets to be sold in the United States in 1964. He noted that American manufacturers might be able to slow the trend down if they manufactured more 9-, 11-, and 16-inch sets, where the Japanese were doing well. Actual Japanese imports were 710,000, and practically all 16-inch and below black-and-white sets. Demand for black-and-white sets in Japan had continued to slide in 1964.

Around this time the Japanese manufacturers began taking control of their U.S. distribution. The Japan External Trade Relations Organization (JETRO) in New York, a division of MITI, prepared exhaustive studies on all aspects of doing business in the United States. These studies were provided to the Japanese manufacturing firms. The firms set up liaison/assistance offices that worked in parallel with the local importers; there were then expanded into complete sales offices, and importer contracts were not renewed.

The year 1964 was when the first Japanese color TVs began arriving in the United States, though sales of color TVs in Japan were negligible. The responsibility for this rested with Sears Roebuck & Company. Sears had first approached RCA and then Zenith, asking them to produce private label

[7] RCA too began using this phosphor soon thereafter, according to the press.

color TV sets. After neither would agree to it Sears went to Japan, where it provided Toshiba with color TV designs from Warwick (which Sears controlled). Toshiba used these as a base from which it made its own modifications. Sears taught Toshiba how to style its sets to attract the U.S. consumer. In the fall Sears introduced a 16-inch color set made by Toshiba that retailed for $300, which was $69 less than the price of the Warwick-made set that Sears had been selling until then.

The U.S. TV Set Industry, 1965

Black-and-white sales were at a record high, with increasing emphasis on replacement, second, and third sets. For the first time color set dollar sales exceeded black-and-white sales, and some manufacturers (notably Zenith and Magnavox) raised prices slightly on color sets. All color tube plants were operating virtually around the clock, but color tubes were still in short supply.

At year end waiting lists were common for American-made color sets. Demand was expected to continue strong, and by 1970 color set sales were predicted to be 7 million units a year or higher. Rectangular picture tubes made a major impact in 1965, available primarily on higher-priced models. Profit margins for manufacturers of color picture tubes were estimated at 35 percent by one source. Market shares are shown in Exhibit 24–3.

RCA. RCA's color sets produced the highest profit of all product lines. One-third of RCA's corporate profit increase from 1960 to 1965 was attributed to color TV. RCA's color set production facilities operated at full capacity throughout the year. Industry estimates placed RCA's unit market share at between 35 and 40 percent of the color market. A 19-inch, 90° rectangular picture tube was put into production as a companion to the 25-inch model already moving off assembly lines. Plans were announced to introduce a 15-inch rectangular color tube in the first quarter of 1966. The RCA 21-inch round color picture tube, which had been the industry standard for the past decade, was to be phased out.

In June RCA announced a $50 million program designed to more than double RCA's color set capacity by mid-1967 and to double picture tube output by mid-1968. Later in the year the magnitude of the planned expansion had been increased to $86 million. Industry estimates placed RCA's 1965 color tube output at approximately 1.4 million units. In early May RCA had been forced to return to rationing its 21-inch color tubes to other set makers. RCA said it had to reestablish an allocation system to avoid curtailing its own set production.

In Canada RCA's subsidiary company, RCA Company, Ltd., announced plans for a $25 million color picture tube plant in Ontario designed to produce rectangular tubes at an annual rate of more than 300,000 by mid-1967. Canadian broadcasters were scheduled to start color transmission by October 1, 1966.

Zenith. Zenith produced more than 2 million black-and-white and color sets in 1965, including 1.5 million black-and-white sets. Color tube production in the fourth quarter was at a rate of nearly 1 million units a year. Industry estimates gave Zenith 20 percent of the color set market. In 1965 Zenith completed the third major expansion of its color TV tube production facilities. In December the company announced the beginning of the fourth expansion, a $17 million color picture tube facility program that, with the addition of the second color tube plant, would take color tube capacity to nearly 2 million units by early 1967.

Admiral. Admiral color set sales increased more than 200 percent in 1965, largely consoles with 23-inch and 25-inch rectangular tubes in compact, handcrafted wood cabinets. In black-and-white TV increased sales were stimulated by the introduction of new 9-, and 12-, and 17-inch rectangular flat-faced screen sizes "pioneered" by Admiral. Admiral expanded its role as a major national advertiser with heavy investment during the year.

Admiral constructed a $12 million, 120,000-square-foot facility for making color picture tubes. The first 25-inch color tubes were produced on schedule in mid-September. Admiral planned to boost annual capacity to 600,000 tubes by the end of September 1966. During 1965 Admiral also initiated expansion of TV set assembly facilities.

General Electric. GE announced in May 1965 that it would begin making color picture tubes in 1966. It began with small 10-inch tubes using a new "in-line'' arrangement of the electron guns. These tubes went into GE's new line of Porta-Color TVs which sold for $250. GE's color TV line also included 25-inch sets.

Magnavox. Magnavox's 1964 color TV sales were $80 million, versus $35 million in 1964, and were limited by color tube shortages. Magnavox expected to have enough tubes in 1966 to double production over 1965. Magnavox sold a disproportionate share of higher-priced, high-quality units and had the highest average price in the industry. It continued to expand wood TV cabinet facilities.

Motorola. Motorola reported explosive demand for its 23-inch rectangular tube color TV set line, fully recovering the previous years' outlays on development. It was estimated that Motorola ranked number three in the industry, with a 10 to 12 percent share by some estimates. Production had been limited by color tube availability. Motorola's own $8 million color tube plant was expected to begin production in 1966, to reduce external sourcing to one-half of total needs. In 1965 Motorola became the world's largest manufacturer of semiconductors.

National Video Corp. National Video reported dramatic improvements in sales and earnings due to industrywide acceptance of its 23-inch rectangular color tube. Motorola, as well as Admiral, Magnavox, GE, and Westinghouse, signed long-term contracts to purchase color tubes. In black-and-white tubes, management was concerned about increasing emphasis on less profitable smaller tube sizes.

Philco. A new $20 million color TV tube manufacturing plant was under construction in Lansdale, Pennsylvania, and was to have an ultimate production capacity of 500,000 tubes annually. Production of 21-inch round color tubes and 19-inch rectangular color tubes was to continue at existing Philco facilities until the new plant was in operation.

GTE-Sylvania. Sylvania consumer electronics products set new records in 1965 due to color TV sets. In December Sylvania entered the small-screen portable TV market with the introduction of a fully transistorized black-and-white set. Construction of

a second color picture tube manufacturing facility began in August. Total manufacturing capacity would approach 2 million color picture tubes annually. Sylvania supplied tubes to seventeen of the country's twenty-one color TV set manufacturers.

Preparing for the anticipated large-scale expansion of the international TV market, production began in Venezuela and Trinidad, and TV manufacturing companies were acquired in Spain and Costa Rica, the latter serving Latin America. Plans were also completed for construction of a color TV picture tube plant in Canada.

Other U.S. Companies. Westinghouse announced that it would begin making color tubes in 1966 for its own purposes and for other set makers.

Japanese Firms. While demand was off sharply in Japan in 1965, Japanese firms sold nearly 1 million black-and-white sets in the United States, most of which were 16-inches and under. Nearly 60 percent of the sets were sold under U.S. brand names like Philco, Magnavox, Emerson, Olympic, and Arvin. About 300,000 were sold under Japanese brand names—nearly all of these were small screen transitorized sets. Sony had four models (9, 5, and two 4 inches) and accounted for 200,000 of the brand name sets. The remaining brand name sets were mostly Panasonic. U.S. producers were concentrating on the 12-inch size, and competition between them and the Japanese were fierce. In the larger sizes, where unit demand was large and precision required in manufacturing was only modest, the Japanese felt disadvantaged.

In color TV, Sears took on Hayakawa (Sharp) as a second source. Sears's success with private labeling was causing other large U.S. retail chains like J. C. Penney, Montgomery Ward, and W. T. Grant to also consider this course of action.

The U.S. TV Set Industry, 1966

Total sales of black-and-white sets declined, while those of small-screen portables increased. In color TV the high level of sales that began in August 1965 continued into 1966. With demand running far ahead of supply, there was a critical shortage of picture tubes as well as of other components like copper and cabinets. Labor was also in short supply.

1966 also saw demand begin shifting toward smaller 18-inch and 20-inch color sets.

Supply was expected to continue to lag behind demand in 1967. Some observers expected 1967 to be a 10 million set year. In September some major manufacturers raised prices by an average of 3 percent on color TVs citing the various shortages as a reason. The move was initiated by Motorola and Zenith, then followed by RCA and Admiral. In the last quarter, however, color TV sales growth slowed below expectations, causing some companies to lay off part of their work forces in December. Tight money and higher interest rates were blamed.

RCA. RCA home entertainment product sales exceeded their 1965 figure by 33 percent, and projections pointed to more than $1 billion in 1967. During the year RCA pioneered the use of integrated circuitry in TV receivers. It was concentrating its efforts on color TV at the expense of black and white and was nearing completion of its massive expansion program in color receivers and tubes.

Zenith. Zenith's black-and-white sales were flat, but color sales increased more than 80 percent in dollar terms from 1965. Zenith introduced a new Automatic Fine Tuning system and a new line of fine wood cabinetry. Early in 1967 Zenith broke ground for a $10 million color and black-and-white TV set facility in Springfield, Missouri.

Admiral. Admiral credited color TV with making a major contribution to the fact that Admiral had its second highest profits and highest sales in its history. The color tube division became profitable in April 1966. Admiral's factory sales of black-and-white TV went up, and Admiral increased its share of the market.

A new subsidiary, Admiral Overseas, was established to manufacture electronic components and finished products in Taiwan for export to the United States, an 83,000-square-foot plant near Taipei to be completed in May 1967. The Color Picture Tube Division began another expansion in the fall to raise annual production to 900,000 picture tubes.

General Electric. GE reported that Porta-Color TV (using the small GE tube) and other black-and-white portable TVs had experienced fast growth in 1966. Sales of large-screen color TVs had been limited by a shortage of tubes. New color tube facilities in Syracuse, New York, were scheduled to begin production by the year's end. GE was working on applying integrated circuits to TVs. Overseas, GE acquired Kube GmbH, a West German company that was among Europe's largest TV manufacturers.

Magnavox. Sales of Magnavox color sets increased 120 percent over 1965. Magnavox offered more than thirty color TV models. In black-and-white the trend to smaller sets hurt Magnavox's large-screen consoles and combinations.

Motorola. Motorola's color TV sales were up substantially from 1965. Black-and-white sales increased, while the industry decreased. Motorola moved to increased utilization of solid-state technology in black and white. Several black-and-white models were completely solid-state except for a voltage rectifier tube. The new color TV picture tube plant in Franklin Park, Illinois, started production in February, and by year's end was producing at a profit. Black-and-white production was transferred to a recently expanded facility, and Franklin Park was devoted almost entirely to color set production.

National Video Corp.. National discontinued black-and-white tube production in November, and the majority of the facilities were converted to color tube production. Two new tube sizes were introduced, a 19-inch and a 25-inch. A 21-inch tube was to be introduced later that year.

Philco. It was disclosed that Philco's color TV tube plant in Lansdale, Pennsylvania, ultimately would have an annual capacity of 600,000 tubes. In 1966 production of microcircuits, transistors, electronic components, and subassemblies, as well as some finished products, was begun in Taiwan.

GTE-Sylvania. Sylvania's 1967 color TV incorporated an improved picture tube with greater brightness. The new color TV plant in Smithfield, North Carolina, began production in September, and a major addition was planned for 1967. Overseas, Sylvania began TV production in Jamaica, expanded its TV picture tube plant in Mexico, and began construction of a TV picture tube plant in Venezuela. It also expanded TV, radio, and stereo set production in Spain and Trinidad.

Japanese Firms. Japanese sales of black-and-white sets continued to be strong. Color sales were still relatively small. While color set production had increased rapidly in Japan, reaching 500,000 in 1966, only Matsushita had announced plans to increase marketing efforts in the United States. Matsushita, like Sony, sold a significant percentage of its black-and-white sets under its own brand name. It now planned to expand its line of consumer products in the United States from 70 to 100 different items and to double its advertising budget while greatly adding to its retail outlets.

Meanwhile, a number of U.S. retail chains signed on Japanese manufacturers to produce private label color TVs. For example, Montgomery Ward took on Hayakawa (Sharp), while J. C. Penney took on Matsushita to make Penncrest label. Later, Sears forced Hayakawa to choose between being a second source for Sears and a first source for Ward. Hayakawa chose Ward, and so Sears took on Sanyo as a second source. Many smaller U.S. chains also started sourcing private label sets from Japan. Japanese color sets were not superior technologically but enjoyed lower manufacturer cost primarily due to cheaper labor.

1966 also saw the tentative introduction into the United States of a few 19-inch color TVs under Japanese brand names such as Toshiba, Hitachi, and Panasonic (Matsushita).

The U.S. TV Set Indusry, 1967

Total sales of black-and-white TVs fell, with growing emphasis on portables. RCA, Sylvania, and Westinghouse increased black-and-white tube prices.[8] The withdrawal of National Video from black-and-white picture tubes to concentrate on

color tubes was apparently straining the capacity of the remaining manufacturers.

A sharp slowdown in the rate of industry color TV sales began in the fourth quarter of 1966 and continued throughout 1967. The lower level of sales resulted in an inventory buildup and price-cutting. Color tube prices fell as well. By midyear large layoffs were widespread. For 1968 most analysts were projecting an increase to 7.5 million sets. A great deal of stress was placed on the fact that color penetration was only 17 percent of households.

The year also marked a dramatic shift in the demand mix for color TVs toward table and portable models. This heightened the inventory problem, since the consoles that manufacturers had in stock were not what consumers wanted. Analysts expected the 1968 mix to be 50-50, versus nearly 80 percent consoles in 1965. Best estimates were that manufacturers made 15 to 20 percent margins on consoles but only 5 percent on table models. In the short run, price-cutting was beginning to occur.

RCA. Noting that only 25 percent of the nation's households then owned color TV receivers, RCA concluded that the growth potential of the market was still impressive despite the slowdown in 1967. RCA said it was taking steps to expand its penetration into the medium price and second set markets, including compact furniture consolettes and the industry's first 14-inch color portable receiver.[9] The portable was an immediate success.

Zenith. Zenith color TV unit sales (up over 30 percent) of substantially more than 1 million sets exceeded black-and-white unit sales for the first time. Automatic tuning was added to more color models, and Zenith introduced a new high-performance, handcrafted chassis in its color TVs. It broadened its color line to include a 14-inch diagonal portable. Early in the year Zenith had stated that the industry's biggest seller would still be the 25-inch color TV console priced from $550 to $700 a set. Zenith attributed its success to its traditional emphasis on high-price consoles. In black-and-white, new rectangular screen portables were offered in

---

[8] Effective January 1, picture tube sizes came under a new federal regulation, under which, generally speaking, an old tube of a given number of inches in size was now called a diagonal tube of one inch less in size.

[9] This set, introduced in April, was priced at $329.95. Until then the company's lowest-priced color set was a 19-inch model listed at $399.

12-, 16-, 19-, and 21-inch diagonal picture sizes with great success.

Admiral. Admiral reported disappointing, unprofitable operations in color TV in 1967, caused primarily by the sharp slowdown in the growth rate of industry color TV sales and the resulting inventory buildup. Cost-cutting efforts were initiated. Admiral introduced a number of new color sets at below $500, boosting the number of such sets in its line from six (at year end 1966) to eighteen. Production difficulties had delayed the changeover of Admiral color tube production to the 18-inch and 20-inch sizes. In black-and-white, Admiral experienced a decline in sales. Admiral was developing a hybrid[10] design but had not introduced such sets as of 1967.

General Electric. GE reported that its sales of both black-and-white and color TV had been adversely affected by industrywide trends. In March GE became the first company to crack the $200 price level with two new 11-inch color sets. Plans included the introduction of a 14-inch color portable to supplement the existing 10-inch Porta-Color sets. GE made all its 10-inch color tubes itself, and began a pilot introduction line for manufacturing large-screen color TV picture tubes in Syracuse, New York.

Internationally, GE's major drive in 1967 was to coordinate further the operations of its varied offshore affiliates. Porta-Color TV sets manufactured in Italy, for example, were added to the line of color receivers marketed by Kuba GmbH, the West German affiliate.

Magnavox. Magnavox's sales were below expectations in 1967. More than 75 percent of its sales were in big-picture, high-profit-margin TV sets and combinations. Magnavox black-and-white volume declined, but less than the industry. Magnavox continued to diversify in furniture during the year.

Motorola. Motorola's color TV sales were considerably below forecast, and inventories became excessive. Significant losses were registered in the consumer products division in 1967. In the fourth quarter Motorola introduced America's first all-transistorized (except for rectifier tube) color TV, with a modular chassis promoted as "the works in the drawer" concept. Motorola called the new line "Quasar," which was available only in nine selected markets. Motorola black-and-white TV sales were strong.

National Video Corp.. As color set sales slumped, National Video's existing long-term supply contracts were no longer considered realistic. Accordingly, customers were offered substantial modifications in the terms. National Video moved to modify equipment to produce other tube sizes besides its sole 23-inch variety.

Philco. Philco's market share increased in both color and black-and-white TV. During the year Philco incorporated integrated circuits in some color TV sets. The new color TV facility at Lansdale was completed as well. Philco began producing TV sets in Italy for European markets. In addition, Latin America's first color TV production facility was opened by a Philco subsidiary in Mexico. In Brazil, Philco captured nearly one-third of the TV market.

GTE-Sylvania. Sylvania introduced its largest color TV line in history in 1967, emphasizing fine cabinetry, extensive use of transistors, some integrated circuits in some models, and a new remote control device. Sales of color picture tubes to other manufacturers fell. Sylvania's tubes emphasized its updated Color Bright™ tube with new phosphors that made it twice as bright as the 1964 tube. Sylvania claimed to have the lead in tube brightness.

Japanese Firms. Japanese color TV imports were nearly 350,000 units, most of which were private label sets and small-screen portables. Total production of color sets in Japan reached 1.3 million.

While the breakdown of RCA's royalty revenues was a closely guarded secret, the 1967 *Television Digest* reported that RCA and the Electronics Industries Association of Japan had extended for five years the patent-licensing arrangement then in force. Under this RCA received royalties from Japanese manufacturers on a per-product basis—0.45

---

[10] Hybrid sets had vacuum tubes as well as solid-state components like transistors.

percent of factory value for each AM radio, 0.9 percent for FM, 1.75 percent for black-and-white TV, and 2 percent for color TV. In contrast, most U.S. licensees paid on a per-patent per-use basis.

The U.S. TV Set Industry, 1968

The market for black-and-white sets was surprisingly strong, contrary to the decrease everyone was forecasting early in the year. In color TV, sales increased to more than 5.8 million units and surpassed black-and-white in volume for the first time. Color portables continued to increase in importance, but average factory prices held close to the $362 figure for 1967. This was attributed to selected price increases by some producers, as well as the higher prices commanded by the increasing number of hybrid (partly transistorized) color TVs in the market. The trend toward increased use of solid state devices was expected to accelerate in 1969 and was expected to keep prices up. The feeling in the trade was that Zenith would introduce its first solid-state color set, a move that meant an end to the advertising them of "handcrafted sets."[11] Color tube prices dropped somewhat, and there was no tube shortage.

RCA. RCA reported that once again color TV had been pivotal in leading it to the best year in its history in consumer products. Following the success of its 14-inch portable color TV receiver, RCA pioneered an 18-inch model in 1968 that combined portability with a screen dimension large enough for family viewing. In 1968 RCA also introduced the first solid-state color set. RCA's share of the black-and-white market increased in 1968 and it was stressing small portable sets.

Zenith. Zenith's color TV sales increased at a rate twice as great as the rest of the industry, as did its black-and-white sales. Zenith introduced several new hybrid chassis and was the first color TV manufacturer to successfully apply an integrated circuit as the demodulator of a color receiver. Zenith also introduced two new tuning systems. Zenith introduced a new portable 16-inch color TV

[11] *Barrons,* October 28, 1968.

to complement the 14-inch set introduced earlier. Zenith continued its attempts to diversify its electronics business but remained almost solely in consumer electronics.

Admiral. Admiral introduced a 16-inch portable color TV and a lightweight 12-inch model early in 1969. Both used color tubes designed exclusively by Admiral. As a result, Admiral claimed that it offered the public the widest range of picture sizes in the industry, from a 12-inch portable to a 23-inch console. All portable color sets featured hybrid chassis. Big-screen color TV still represented by far the largest percentage (60 percent) of Admiral sales. Admiral's 1969 black-and-white line was highlighted by the extensive use of solid-state devices in many sets.

The Color Tube Division produced five different tube sizes in 1968, incurring significant start-up costs on the new portable tube sizes (12-inch and 16-inch). Early in 1968 Admiral announced a three-year standard replacement guarantee on its color tubes, contrasted to the one-year industry standard.

General Electric. GE's TV sales showed a major improvement over 1967, with color TV realizing its best sales year. GE was equipped by 1968 to manufacture virtually all of its own picture tubes.

Magnavox. Magnavox's volume increase in color TV was three times the industry increase, and Magnavox claimed it was one of the three top producers. *Forbes* ranked Magnavox number one in the electrical products category on the basis of both current and sustained (five-year) profitability. Magnavox offered more than forty color TV models and twenty combination models. It planned to introduce a smaller-screen color set in 1969. Magnvox's marketing system of selling directly to a limited number of outstanding dealers was stressed as one of the company's great strengths.

Motorola. Motorola's Quasar line of solid-state color sets was launched nationally in September. Quasar led a recovery of Motorola color TV sales. Otherwise the color TV line was shrunk. A majority of the 20-inch and 23-inch color tubes used in 1968 were supplied by Motorola's own plant. Motorola also sold some 20-inch tubes to other manufacturers.

Philco. Sales of Philco TVs increased during 1968. Early in 1969 Philco launched an aggressive merchandising program for its consumer products including extensive use of network TV, newspaper, and national magazine advertising to illustrate product advances.

GTE-Sylvania. Sylvania offered sixty-three color TV models in 18-, 20-, and 23-inch sets and a new 14-inch portable size. All models used its bright picture tube. The new larger-screen-size sets (20 and 23 inches) featured a new chassis with two-thirds solid-state devices. Production of 12-inch black-and-white TV sets began at Sylvania's new Hong Kong subsidiary.

Westinghouse. In December Westinghouse announced that it would sharply curtail its sale of TV sets and stereo phonographs. Production and marketing of console TV and stereo units would be stopped altogether. Westinghouse planned to continue marketing portable TV sets sourced from Japan. Industry sources were inclined to view the Westinghouse move as a partial retreat from the hotly competitive TV and stereo market, where, they suggested, the company had not fared especially well. Westinghouse's share of the TV market was estimated by sources at less than 3 percent.

Japanese Firms. Sony introduced an improved new color picture tube, the Trinitron, in 1968 after an aborted effort with Paramount's Chromatron tube some years earlier.

The U.S. TV Set Industry, 1969

Government efforts to cool the economy and slow down inflation resulted in an extremely tight money situation, and with it lower sales of consumer durables. Fourth-quarter sales of color sets were sharply lower, and industry volume for the year was approximately 5.5 million units, the first dip in sales since color entered the mass market in 1962. A major factor affecting all domestic manufacturers was increased imports of sets produced abroad. There

was also a shift in consumer demand from the upper to the less profitable lower end of the price line. By year end, there were twenty U.S. TV manufacturers, down from forty-three in 1963. (See Exhibit 24–3 for market shares.)

RCA. Quoting independent surveys, RCA claimed leadership in color TV sales to the consumer for the sixteenth consecutive year. In 1969 RCA introduced the Hi-Lite 70 Transvista Series, which featured a brighter picture. It also introduced a color set with a remote control tuner that used computer logic for silent, instantaneous channel selection. For the third consecutive year RCA introduced a new size of portable, namely a 16-inch model. RCA began constructing a $19 million glass plant for color TV picture tubes at Circleville, Ohio, thus becoming the only picture tube maker in the United States that was vertically integrated into glass.[12] RCA stated that it increased its market share of U.S.-produced black-and-white receivers.

Despite the positive statements, though, RCA's share of the color TV market was slipping. Its sets had begun to receive poor quality ratings from various groups, and Zenith's sets were consistently being rated higher. Many observers partly blamed RCA's computer entry for diverting a major share of R&D resources from every other product in the company.

RCA had made significant diversification moves in the late 1960s through acquisitions of Hertz and Random House.

Zenith. Zenith's color TV share increased. It introduced a Chromacolor color TV picture tube (in 23-inch size) in June 1969. The new patented tube offered enhanced sharpness and contrast. The Chromacolor system also incorporated Zenith's fine tuning system and a hybrid chassis. Zenith said it was in the process of finalizing plans for overseas manufacturing operations to protect its position in consumer electronics.

Admiral. Admiral reported decreased color TV sales. It acquired Cortron Industries, Inc., which was the TV receiver, console stereo, and wood cabinet manufacturing subsidiary of Montgomery

---

[12] The only other color tube makers that were integrated into glass were Philips of Holland and Sony and NEC of Japan.

Ward. Cortron was to be operated as a wholly-owned subsidiary and was to continue to supply Montgomery Ward under a long-term contract.

Admiral offered thirty-seven color TV receivers in five different screen sizes. The company had by now begun making portable color TV chassis in its Taiwan plant. A new 100 percent brighter Solar Color picture tube was introduced in a variety of big-screen models in December. In black-and-white TV, eight different picture tube sizes were available in twenty-nine models, including a new solid-state 9-inch TV with an optional battery pack.

General Electric. GE began importing a small black-and-white portable set to replace the 9-inch set it had been assembling from foreign plants. On the international front, GE sold its West German TV subsidiary, Kuba GmbH, to AEG-Telefunken in a $13.9 million stock deal.

Magnavox. Magnavox offered a wide range of color TV models, with the industry's widest selection of screen sizes. It introduced Total Automatic Color, combining automatic tint control with automatic fine tuning. This important innovation was well received in the market.

Motorola. Motorola increased its share of color TV sales in the over-$600 retail price range. It introduced its Quasar II (partial solid-state) line in lower-priced console and table models designed to compete in the color market's fastest growing segment. Work was accelerated on the development of Quasar portables for 1970. The Quasar system of replaceable solid-state minicircuits was instituted on two important black-and-white TV screen sizes. Major cost improvement measures were begun to standardize chassis and parts. It was decided to consolidate domestic facilities by phasing out the Elgin, Illinois, plant. Construction was begun on a plant in Taiwan to meet foreign competition.

National Video Corp. National Video went bankrupt on February 26, 1969.

Philco. Philco increased its entries in the portable TV field. It introduced eight new 14-, 16-, and 18-inch color sets; five black-and-white sets; and Hi-Bright Magicolor picture tubes, which were significantly brighter than previous Philco tubes. Financial results were depressed. Philco's Italian subsidiary broke ground for an electronic plant to manufacture color TV sets and to expand its black-and-white TV capacity for sale in European markets.

GTE-Sylvania. Sylvania's 1970 color TV line extended its hybrid chassis to its 18-inch models. While industry sales were lower than 1968, Sylvania's were higher. Three new color picture tubes were introduced, utilizing newly developed phosphors providing increased brightness and greater contrast. Sylvania reported unusually intense price competition in color picture tubes, because of industry overcapacity and leveling off of color set demand.

Westinghouse. Westinghouse ceased manufacturing color TVs in 1969. It continued selling color picture tubes on the open market, made at its facilities in Elmira, New York.

Japanese Firms. Japanese color TV imports to the United States were 880,000 units. Imports from Japan bore an 8 percent duty and shipping and insurance costs of approximately 10 percent of the F.O.B. Japan price. In Japan, Hitachi became the first company in the world to convert its entire color TV line to 100 percent solid-state design.

The major motivation was energy conservation, since 100 percent solid-state sets used less than half the power of equivalent vacuum tube sets. MITI had helped by sponsoring separate studies at different companies into the applications of solid-state technology to various aspects of color TV design. These studies were then circulated among all participating companies, to either use or not use as they wished.

EXHIBIT 24-1. Financial Performance of Selected TV Set Competitors, 1960–1969 (dollars in millions)

	1960	1961	1962	1963	1964	1965	1966	1967	1968	1969
Admiral										
Sales	$187.9	$192.1	$201.5	$216.1	$238.0	$306.4	$414.6	$308.9	$377.0	$354.4
Depreciation	4.7	4.2	4.0	4.4	4.9	5.9	7.9	9.2	8.3	7.3
Net income	(1.7)	2.9	2.0	3.0	4.0	6.5	10.0	(3.7)	0.5	1.5
Return on sales (%)	1.3%	1.4%	0.3%	1.3%	1.7%	2.1%	2.4%	(0.99)%	0.13%	0.42%
Return on equity (%)	(2.8)%	4.6%	3.1%	4.6%	5.8%	8.6%	12.1%	(4.5)%	6.0%	1.8%
Marketable securities	—	—	—	—	—	—	—	—	—	—
Debt to total capital	7.9	5.1	17.8	16.1	21.8	19.4	18.9	29.7	28.9	26.4
Capital expenditures	1.8	1.5	2.3	2.1	1.8	11.8	16.4	18.4	6.1	6.0
Dividend payout	—	—	—	—	—	—	.19	(.34)	—	—
General Electric										
Sales	$4197.5	$4456.8	$4792.7	$4888.0	$4941.4	$6213.5	$7177.3	$7741.2	$8381.6	$8448.0
Depreciation	116.0	117.9	127.1	127.7	129.3	188.4	233.6	280.4	300.1	351.3
Net income	200.1	242.1	265.8	270.6	237.3	355.1	339.0	361.4	357.1	278.0
Return on sales (%)	4.8%	5.4%	5.6%	5.5%	4.8%	5.7%	4.7%	4.7%	4.3%	3.3%
Return on equity (%)	13.5%	15.4%	15.7%	14.9%	12.6%	17.2%	15.8%	15.9%	14.7%	11.5%
Marketable securities	325.5	205.0	263.9	237.8	369.4	353.4	100.3	96.8	87.7	127.7
Debt to total capital	14.0	12.5	11.4	9.9	9.1	13.4	17.7	23.1	23.1	21.0
Capital expenditures	136.9	145.2	125.4	111.9	130.0	332.9	484.9	561.7	514.7	530.6
Dividend payout	.88	.73	.67	.68	.83	.61	.69	.65	.66	.85
GTE-Sylvania										
Sales	$431.2	$418.2	$431.8	$473.2	$551.8	$640.0	$807.6	$822.9	$842.6	$814.1
Depreciation	11.0	11.4	12.0	11.8	11.7	18.4	22.0	30.3	32.0	32.7
Net income	12.7	4.6	8.5	12.2	14.9	19.5	42.5	39.2	27.5	33.7
Return on sales (%)	2.9%	1.1%	2.0%	2.6%	2.7%	3.1%	5.3%	4.8%	3.3%	4.1%
Return on equity (%)	7.6%	2.8%	5.3%	7.4%	8.8%	11.0%	21.0%	14.8%	10.0%	10.2%
Marketable securities	NA	NA	NA	NA	NA	NA	NA	NA	NA	NA
Debt to total capital	32.3	32.2	31.3	30.2	28.6	26.3	22.9	29.5	26.9	15.9
Capital expenditures	NA	NA	NA	NA	14.4	12.0	19.0	12.7	18.0	18.0
Dividend payout	.76	2.2	.94	.82	.67	.61	.45	.32	.50	.65
Magnavox										
Sales	$124.9	$140.8	$201.9	$174.5	$227.2	$333.3	$455.7	$464.3	$562.9	$539.8
Depreciation	1.8	1.8	2.3	2.9	4.0	5.2	6.0	7.4	8.4	9.6
Net income	6.5	9.0	12.6	11.3	13.8	23.0	34.7	32.8	42.3	39.8
Return on sales (%)	5.2%	6.4%	6.3%	6.5%	6.1%	6.9%	7.6%	7.3%	7.5%	7.2%
Return on equity (%)	44.6%	23.3%	26.5%	21.4%	22.9%	28.4%	33.0%	26.3%	25.9%	21.3%
Marketable securities	33.5	—	—	10.0	8.2	25.6	13.4	17.3	7.0	25.2
Debt to total capital	1.5	0.1	3.9	4.6	5.9	6.6	20.5	6.1	15.2	13.4
Capital expenditures	3.6	3.9	—	—	—	—	2.0	—	16.6	5.5
Dividend payout	.33	.33	.35	.49	.48	.32	.34	.38	.37	.50

EXHIBIT 24-1. *(continued)*

	1960	1961	1962	1963	1964	1965	1966	1967	1968	1969
Motorola										
Sales	$ 299.1	$ 298.2	$ 346.9	$ 377.9	$ 419.1	$ 517.0	$ 682.4	$ 630.0	$ 775.1	$ 873.2
Depreciation	6.4	7.2	9.5	10.2	11.4	12.7	17.9	22.7	25.8	28.3
Net income	12.6	9.5	13.2	12.9	20.7	31.8	33.0	18.8	28.3	33.8
Return on sales (%)	4.2%	3.2%	3.8%	3.4%	4.9%	6.2%	4.8%	3.0%	3.7%	3.9%
Return on equity (%)	13.0%	9.3%	11.8%	10.7%	15.0%	19.3%	17.1%	9.1%	11.8%	10.4%
Marketable securities	NA	NA	11.8	4.8	7.0	21.1	5.8	0.6	26.3	19.7
Debt to total capital	.21	.31	.28	.26	.23	18.8	25.7	24.0	28.8	21.9
Capital expenditures	17.5	11.6	16.3	24.0	13.0	28.3	63.8	33.8	36.3	51.4
Dividend payout	.30	.42	.31	.31	.22	.19	.19	.33	.22	.19
Packard-Bell										
Sales	$ 44.0	$ 31.9	$ 49.7	$ 49.4	$ 40.0	$ 34.2	$ 45.4	$ 54.9	$ 806.7[a]	$1295.0
Depreciation	0.57	0.58	0.62	0.67	0.56	5.91	7.86	9.17	8.27	7.26
Net income	0.21	(9.5)	(1.4)	1.21	1.87	0.30	1.05	1.30	40.7	60.1
Return on sales (%)	0.47%	(29.8)%	(2.9)%	2.46%	4.71%	0.89%	2.3%	2.4%	5.0%	4.6%
Return on equity (%)	1.84%	(143.6)%	(8.47)%	95.1%	63.6%	7.2%	16.1%	14.1%	14.0%	14.7%
Marketable securities	—	—	—	—	—	NA	NA	NA	NA	7.0
Debt to total capital	12.5	43.5	69.6	90.3	62.2	60.0	42.8	38.7	33.0	29.1
Capital expenditures	0.97	(0.06)	(0.2)	(0.55)	(0.5)	(0.8)	0.43	0.21	NA	109.9
Dividend payout	1.94	(0.01)	—	—	—	—	—	—	0.05	0.09
Philco/Ford										
Sales	$ 400.6	$6709.4[b]	$8089.6	$8742.5	$9670.8	$11,536.8	$12,240.0	$10,515.7	$14,075.1	$14,755.6
Depreciation	6.5	21.1	22.8	23.3	24.2	26.7	30.8	34.5	36.6	38.5
Net income	2.3	409.6	480.7	488.5	505.6	703.0	621.0	84.1	626.6	546.5
Return on sales (%)	0.57%	0.10%	5.94%	5.59%	5.23%	6.09%	5.07%	0.80%	4.45%	3.70%
Return on equity (%)	2.09%	13.64%	14.69%	13.69%	13.08%	16.54%	13.39%	1.79%	13.14%	10.75%
Marketable securities	—	765.0	819.1	907.6	740.7	900.2	518.3	30.3	821.6	445.1
Debt to total capital	28.7	7.99	6.38	5.31	5.37	6.17	6.27	6.72	6.46	5.51
Capital expenditures	6.3	52.6	43.2	140.1	307.3	432.5	419.3	404.5	121.0	146.3
Dividend payout	.16	.40	.41	.41	.44	.33	.43	3.12	.42	.48
RCA										
Sales	$1486.2	$1537.9	$1742.7	$1779.1	$1797.0	$2042.0	$2548.8	$3014.1	$3106.2	$3187.9
Depreciation	27.1	34.1	41.0	46.5	51.1	62.4	72.5	151.0	170.4	181.5
Net income	35.1	35.5	58.5	66.0	93.9	101.2	132.4	147.5	154.0	151.3
Return on sales (%)	2.36%	2.31%	2.95%	3.71%	4.59%	4.95%	5.19%	4.90%	4.96%	4.74%
Return on equity (%)	8.11%	7.91%	10.53%	12.44%	15.76%	17.06%	19.11%	17.36%	16.56%	14.78%
Marketable securities	3.3	21.5	108.9	249.7	233.8	253.6	28.9	45.7	129.6	61.4
Debt to total capital	25.99	34.38	34.28	32.47	32.75	30.05	27.55	33.23	34.09	31.18
Capital expenditures	59.2	56.3	55.0	60.0	84.9	101.4	197.7	186.2	189.5	176.2
Dividend payout	.53	.57	.34	.44	.62	.38	.36	.37	.44	.45

EXHIBIT 24-1. (continued)

	1960	1961	1962	1963	1964	1965	1966	1967	1968	1969
Zenith										
Sales	$ 254.1	$ 274.2	$ 312.2	$ 349.8	$ 349.8	$ 392.0	$ 470.5	$ 625.0	$ 653.9	$ 705.4
Depreciation	1.7	1.8	2.3	3.8	5.0	5.1	6.8	9.5	10.2	12.0
Net income	15.2	18.0	19.6	20.9	24.3	33.6	43.5	41.0	47.3	39.6
Return on sales (%)	6.0%	6.6%	6.3%	6.0%	6.2%	7.1%	7.0%	6.3%	6.7%	5.8%
Return on equity (%)	17.3%	18.3%	18.1%	17.4%	18.4%	22.7%	25.9%	22.1%	22.7%	17.6%
Marketable securities	33.5	26.6	26.7	28.4	37.0	44.9	33.7	54.2	92.1	85.1
Debt to total capital	—	—	—	—	—	—	—	—	—	—
Capital expenditures	4.2	2.1	9.6	12.3	4.2	10.9	20.4	18.0	13.4	21.6
Dividend payout	.51	.50	.55	.59	.59	.56	.58	.62	.56	.67

[a] Acquired by Teledyne. Post-1967 results are given for Teledyne.
[b] Acquired by Ford Motor Company, December 1961. Post-1960 results are given for Ford.

SOURCE: Annual reports.

EXHIBIT 24-2. *The Composition of Television Set Demand, 1946–1969*

	1946	1947	1948	1949	1950	1951	1952	1953	1954	1955	1956	1957
Factory production and imports												
Black-and-white (units M)[a]	.01	.18	.97	2.97	7.36	5.31	6.19	6.87	7.41	7.74	7.35	6.39
Color (units M)	—	—	—	—	—	—	—	—	.01	.02	.10	.09
Black-and-white (dollars M)	$ 1.0	$ 50.0	$226.0	$574.0	$1397.0	$944.0	$1064.0	$1170.0	$1040.0	$1068.0	$ 934.0	$ 831.0
Color (dollars M)	$ —	$ —	$ —	$ —	$ —	$ —	$ —	$ —	$ 2.0	$ 10.0	$ 46.0	$ 37.0
Black-and-white market by type												
Table and portable (units M)	—	.12	.65	1.79	2.94	2.28	2.84	3.22	4.25	4.44	4.75	3.85
Console (units M)	—	.04	.18	.99	3.77	2.77	3.04	3.76	2.89	3.08	2.53	2.39
Combinations (units M)	—	.03	.15	.22	.76	.33	.22	.24	.21	.24	.11	.16
Color market by type												
Table and portable (units M)	—	—	—	—	—	—	—	—	NA	NA	NA	NA
Console (units M)	—	—	—	—	—	—	—	—	NA	NA	NA	NA
Combinations (units M)	—	—	—	—	—	—	—	—	NA	NA	NA	NA
Replacement market												
Black-and-white (% of unit sales)	—	—	—	—	—	—	35.0%	26.0%	40.0%	39.0%	52.0%	59.0%
Color (% of unit sales)	—	—	—	—	—	—	—	—	NA	NA	NA	NA
Imports (units M)												
Black-and-white total	—	—	—	—	—	—	—	—	—	—	—	—
Black-and-white from Japan	—	—	—	—	—	—	—	—	—	—	—	—
Color total	—	—	—	—	—	—	—	—	—	—	—	—
Color from Japan	—	—	—	—	—	—	—	—	—	—	—	—
Imports by distributors and dealers												
Black-and-white (units M)	NA	NA	NA	NA	NA	NA	NA	NA	NA	NA	NA	NA
Color (units M)	NA	NA	NA	NA	NA	NA	NA	NA	NA	NA	NA	NA
Private label sets sold												
Black-and-white (U.S.-made) (units M)	—	—	—	—	—	—	—	—	—	—	—	—
Black-and-white (imported)	—	—	—	—	—	—	—	—	—	—	—	—
Color (U.S.-made)	—	—	—	—	—	—	—	—	—	—	—	—
Color (imported)	—	—	—	—	—	—	—	—	—	—	—	—
Total TV stations on the air	6	12	16	51	98	107	108	126	356	422	459	494
Saturation (% of households)												
Black-and-white first set	—	.04	.4	2.3	9.0	23.5	34.2	44.7	55.7	64.5	71.8	78.4
Black-and-white second set	—	—	—	—	—	—	—	—	—	2.1	3.3	5.0
Color first set	—	—	—	—	—	—	—	—	—	.01	.04	0.2
Color second set	—	—	—	—	—	—	—	—	—	—	.01	.01

EXHIBIT 24-2. (continued)

	1958	1959	1960	1961	1962	1963	1964	1965	1966	1967	1968	1969
Factory production and imports												
Black-and-white (units M)	5.05	6.28	5.71	6.17	6.70	7.24	8.36	8.75	7.70	6.00	7.00	7.12
Color (units M)	.08	.09	.12	.15	.44	.75	1.40	2.69	5.01	5.56	6.22	6.19
Black-and-white (dollars M)	$686.0	$806.0	$750.1	$757.5	$851.0	$841.0	$896.0	$910.0	$756.0	$555.0	$591.0	$554.0
Color (dollars M)	$34.0	$37.0	$47.0	$56.0	$154.0	$258.0	$488.0	$959.0	$1861.0	$2015.0	$2086.0	$2031.0
Black-and-white market by type												
Table and portable (units M)	2.72	3.61	3.28	3.80	4.56	4.99	6.65	7.32	6.40	5.38	6.39	6.66
Console (units M)	2.07	2.57	2.21	2.14	1.84	1.96	1.64	1.32	1.05	0.59	0.59	0.44
Combinations (units M)	.13	.17	.22	.23	.30	.31	.21	.11	.04	.03	.02	.02
Color market by type												
Table and portable (units M)	NA	NA	NA	NA	NA	NA	.16	.32	1.13	2.15	3.15	3.66
Console (units M)	NA	NA	NA	NA	NA	NA	1.18	2.09	3.79	3.56	3.27	3.01
Combinations (units M)	NA	NA	NA	NA	NA	NA	.12	.24	.40	.40	.23	.20
Replacement market												
Black-and-white (% of unit sales)	65.0%	70.0%	69.0%	75.0%	69.0%	69.0%	65.0%	65.0%	65.0%	56.0%	65.0%	63.0%
Color (% of unit sales)	NA	NA	NA	NA	NA	NA	NA	NA	.20%	.13%	.10%	.13%
Imports (units M)												
Black-and-white total	—	—	.02	.02	.16	.45	.71	1.05	1.31	1.29	2.04	3.12
Black-and-white from Japan	—	—	.02	.02	.16	.45	.71	1.05	1.23	1.22	1.64	2.21
Color total	—	—	NA	NA	NA	NA	NA	NA	.21	.32	.67	.91
Color from Japan	—	—	NA	NA	NA	NA	NA	NA	.21	.31	.66	.88
Imports by distributors and dealers												
Black-and-white (units M)	NA	NA	.01	.01	.14	.22	.33	.34	.30	.71	1.22	1.93
Color (units M)	NA	NA	NA	NA	NA	NA	NA	NA	NA	NA	.24	.45
Private label sets sold												
Black-and-white (U.S.-made) (units M)	—	—	—	—	—	—	—	—	.61	.38	.30	.20
Black-and-white (imported)	—	—	—	—	—	—	—	—	.76	.67	.94	1.25
Color (U.S.-made)	—	—	—	—	—	—	—	—	.39	.35	.37	.37
Color (imported)	—	—	—	—	—	—	—	—	.19	.26	.41	.51
Total TV stations on the air	523	545	559	579	603	625	649	668	699	737	785	837
Saturation (% of households)												
Black-and-white first set	82.9	85.4	86.5	88.0	88.9	89.6	89.4	87.7	84.0	78.3	71.7	64.6
Black-and-white second set	7.3	8.9	11.3	12.6	13.8	15.7	18.0	20.2	23.1	27.0	30.2	33.4
Color first set	.4	.5	.6	.8	1.1	1.7	2.9	4.9	9.0	15.3	22.9	30.4
Color second set	.01	.01	.01	.02	.02	.02	.03	.07	.2	.5	.9	1.5

[a]M = millions.

SOURCES: U.S. Bureau of the Census, *Merchandising, TV Factbook*, U.S. ITC.

EXHIBIT 24-3. *Market Share Estimates*

	1965	*1966*	*1967*	*1968*	*1969*
Black-and-white TV market share					
Zenith	NA[a]	NA	NA	22.0	22.0
RCA	NA	NA	NA	17.0	17.0
General Electric	NA	NA	NA	11.0	12.5
Sears	NA	NA	NA	8.25	9.5
Admiral	NA	NA	NA	8.0	7.0
Motorola	NA	NA	NA	6.5	6.0
Philco/Ford	NA	NA	NA	6.0	6.0
Magnavox	NA	NA	NA	4.5	5.25
Color TV market share					
RCA	34	33	32	30.0	27.5
Zenith	22	21	21	20.0	21.0
Magnavox	6	6	8	9.0	10.0
Sears	7	7	7	6.0	7.0
Motorola	9	10	6.5	7.0	6.0
Admiral	8	9	7	6.5	5.5
General Electric	NA	NA	7	5.25	5.5
Philco/Ford	2	3	NA	4.0	3–5.5
Sylvania (Subsidiary of GTE)	5	5	NA	NA	3–5.0
Color picture tube production (thousands of units)					
RCA	1,450	2,300	NA	NA	NA
Sylvania (Subsidiary of GTE)	500	1,150	NA	NA	NA
Zenith	450	1,100	NA	NA	NA
Motorola	50	250	NA	NA	NA
Admiral	—	250	NA	NA	NA
Philco	—	100	NA	NA	NA
National Video	—	1,250	NA	NA	NA
Total	2,850	6,400			

[a]NA = not available.

SOURCES: Color and black-and-white TV market share estimates for 1968 and 1969
from *Television Digest*. Years refer to model years (July to June). 1967 color
TV market share figures from *Barrons*, October 28, 1968. 1965 and 1966
figures for color TV market share from *Finance*, January 1966. Color TV
market shares are shares of production.

CASE 25
The U.S. Television Set Market, 1970–1979

The decade of the 1970s saw dramatic shifts in the structure of the U.S. TV set industry. As industry demand matured, the roster of U.S. participants changed and foreign imports and later foreign direct investment in the United States permanently changed the industry landscape. Fundamental changes occurred in product and process technologies. All the while, legal skirmishing between domestic and foreign firms added a new dimension to industry rivalry.

This case describes the progress of the industry over the 1970 to 1979 time period. The bulk of the case is chronological, discussing important industry events and competitor behavior each year through the period. The case concludes with an overview of product and process changes in TV sets, a summary of the shifts in manufacturing strategy that occurred, and an update on recent legal developments. Exhibit 25-1 presents summary financial information for competitors over the period. Exhibit 25-2 gives the composition of TV set demand, and Exhibit 25-3 shows the distribution of demand by type of retail outlet. Exhibit 25-4 presents market shares of major competitors, and Exhibit 25-5 shows the penetration of imports. Background information on early industry history is contained in Case 24.

1970

Black-and-white TV sales were down 3 percent from the previous year, despite the recession. Color TV registered a decrease of 13 percent. Sales of portable color TV (19 inches and under) increased. 1970 also witnessed the introduction of three new sizes of color picture tubes—19, 21, and 25 inches. The 25-inch size was a hit.

On January 1 RCA cut prices on color picture tubes 12 to 16 percent, depending on size and competitive situation. This brought down the going price for a 23-inch tube—the largest seller—to about $80. A little over two years earlier the same tube cost $130. In April Motorola withdrew from color picture tube production and disposed of its equipment. Industry sources said that the exit of

482

National Video (February 1969) and Motorola together reduced capacity by about 1.5 million units. Industry tube capacity was still thought to be more than 10 million units. At the height of the drive to expand capacity, the industry had planned to turn out more than 12 million color tubes, according to a spokesman for Sylvania.[1]

RCA. RCA maintained its sales leadership in color TV for the seventeenth consecutive year. RCA expected the industry to turn around in 1971. In July it introduced an 18-inch color TV using a 110° tube, which was about 4 inches shorter than 90° tubes. In addition, about 75% of RCA's circuitry was solid-state and contained in eleven plug-in modules. The solid-state sets carried a one-year warranty, as opposed to the ninety-day warranty on older models. Suggested list price was under $450.

RCA acknowledged that it made color and black-and-white TV parts in a Mexican border facility. Also, electron guns for color TV picture tubes were being assembled at the RCA electronics component plant in Juncos, Puerto Rico. Sales of RCA picture tubes declined in 1970. After reappraising domestic requirements and recognizing total industry over-capacity, the company announced plans to discontinue color TV tube manufacture at Lancaster, Pennsylvania, and consolidate color tube operations at Scranton, Pennsylvania, and Marion, Indiana. Results were more promising abroad. Sales of color TV tubes to Europe were up sharply in 1970, as were sales of picture tubes manufactured in RCA's Canadian plant. In April an RCA executive vice president heading electronic component operations had said that he did not consider current "idle" capacity to be "excess" capacity. "In the next year or two we will be using it."[2]

Zenith. Zenith's color and black-and-white TV set sales declined 18 percent and 10 percent respectively, from 1969, less than the industry. Zenith's increase in share was attributed to the new Chromacolor tube as well as to Zenith styling, remote control, and automatic tuning. The number of Chromacolor screen sizes was increased. In black-and-white TV Zenith continued to maintain the number one position in the industry. Zenith exited black-and-white picture tube manufacture during the year.

Joseph S. Wright, chairman of Zenith, said he was confident enough about the sales outlook that Zenith was not looking for color picture tube contracts outside to keep its lines going. "We buy a few tubes and we sell a few but we don't intend to become a component supplier to the industry."[3] Zenith was constructing a major manufacturing facility in Taiwan to produce black-and-white TV sets and electronic components. Another plant was being constructed in Matamoros, Mexico, for the manufacture of color tube components. A producer of radio and TV cabinets was acquired. Research facilities were also expanded to allow broader work on lasers, electro-optics, microwave tubes, and home video recording. Zenith Research won an award for its basic scientific research in 1970.

Zenith petitioned the U.S. Treasury to impose countervailing duties on Japanese color TV imports.

Admiral. Admiral's consumer operations were unprofitable. The new color TV line was highlighted by 25-inch models, most of which featured the new solar-color system with the black matrix picture tube, and hybrid circuitry. New 25-inch color-stereo combination sets were introduced. Sales of hybrid portable color TV sets (19 inches and under) increased.

In February National Union Electric, which in 1965 acquired control of Emerson Television and Radio, agreed to let Admiral take over the manufacture of Emerson and DuMont-label color and black-and-white sets, along with other home entertainment products such as radios, phonographs, and tape recorders. However, NUE would continue to handle design, engineering, and marketing. This contract, along with the Cortron acquisition from the previous year, made private labeling a significant business for Admiral and made Admiral the fourth largest color TV maker after RCA, Zenith, and Magnavox.

General Electric. GE's service network was bolstered by tying more closely together servicing

---

[1] *Wall Street Journal,* April 20, 1970.

[2] *Ibid.*

[3] *Ibid.*

dealers, independent servicing agencies, and the eighty-seven factory service branches. GE, reacting to Motorola's exit from color tubes, said that it produced picture tubes only for its own use and would continue production because "we ought to be able to make them for less than we can buy them," according to I. L. Griffin, vice president and general manager of the TV division.[4] GE exited from black-and-white picture tube manufacture.

Magnavox. Magnavox claimed it maintained the number three industry position in sales dollars, though it was forced to reduce its work force by 13 percent. It complained of disruptive pricing due to domestic competition, inventory problems, and Japanese dumping. Magnavox said it would not discount. Its color line included the industry's widest selection of screen sizes, furniture styles, finishes, and color. Magnavox acquired 40 percent of Construcciones Electronics, S.A., in Mexico, which manufactured consumer electronic products for the Mexican market, including TVs.

Magnavox's rise to first place in console stereo and third place in color TV was a major industry success story and was believed to have resulted largely from its distinctive franchising system; the company had about 2,600 dealers that handled its products exclusively. In 1970 the FTC filed a complaint alleging that Magnavox fixed retail prices for dealers and used coercive practices to assure that dealers did not discount sets.

Motorola. Motorola's consumer electronics business incurred a loss, estimated by analysts at $3.3 million on sales of $175 million. Color TV sales had been driven below 1969 levels; blamed were the economy and liquidation of color set inventories at attractive prices by certain competitors. Several new Quasar II and Quasar portable color sets were introduced, some with the lowest manufacturer's suggested retail prices ever on modular sets. Motorola also introduced "Insta-Matic" automatic fine tuning.

In April Motorola announced the closing of its Franklin Park, Illinois, color picture tube facility.[5] The equipment was sold to GTE-International for one of its overseas color picture tube plants. The closure resulted in an extraordinary nonrecurring expense of $1.4 million (11¢/share).

Commenting on the move, Motorola said, "We got into color tube production a bit reluctantly. Then as color set sales increased we asked ourselves if we wouldn't look silly if we couldn't get all the tubes we needed. So we went into production ourselves. So did a lot of others. But the color boom never did materialize as we expected and we all went in too far and too fast. We obviously weren't confronted with any tube shortage."[6] Because of the need to make a variety of sizes of tubes, Motorola found it difficult to keep production of any one tube size high enough to be profitable.

Philco. Philco claimed to have improved its U.S. market share in most of its consumer product lines in 1970, including color and black-and-white TV sets. It said that it had made substantial reductions in fixed costs. Philco also reported that its color tube production was up substantially from the previous year because of a contract to supply another set maker.

GTE-Sylvania. Sylvania's new line included new 25-inch console sets. The line contained some models with completely solid-state chassis, electronic tuning, and an improved picture tube. Sylvania reported that its sales declined less than the industry's. A new Color Bright® 85 Black Mask picture tube was introduced, providing greater brightness and more contrast using new phosphors developed by Sylvania. The tube was sold to other TV manufacturers as well as for Sylvania's own 1971 line. Sylvania's outside sales of picture tubes were down. Sylvania ranked behind both RCA and Zenith in color tube output but considered itself first as a supplier to the industry at large.

Overseas, the SABA GmbH subsidiary increased its sales of all products. GTE International acquired Hopt Electronic GmbH, one of West Germany's largest producers of tuners for radios and TVs, and acquired Empire S.A., a Brazilian producer of TVs, radios, and stereo phonographs.

Japanese Firms. All major Japanese firms followed Hitachi's lead of a year earlier and converted

---

[4] *Ibid.*

[5] By one estimate, the capacity of this plant was 750,000 tubes per year. *New York Times,* October 28, 1973.

[6] *Wall Street Journal,* April 20, 1970.

completely to 100 percent solid-state models. U.S. consumers were by now completely sold on the idea of solid-state; their immensely favorable reaction to the Japanese sets surprised all the U.S. manufacturers. At that time Motorola was the only U.S. manufacturer with a completely solid-state set.

Legal Action. The U.S. Treasury Department ruled in 1970 that Japanese sets were being dumped in the United States. The Treasury imposed a 9 percent bond requirement on sets against possible duty requirements. The case was sent to the U.S. Tariff Commission to see if the dumping had injured U.S. firms. Meanwhile, Zenith had petitioned the Treasury again asking countervailing duties on Japanese imports. It claimed that Japanese manufacturers were receiving subsidies from their government.

1971

Sales were aided by the decline in interest rates and reached 7.1 million units. After poor results in 1970, in 1971 most producers enjoyed improved margins. Virtually all had launched austerity programs in 1970. There was an increased use of solid-state chassis among U.S. manufacturers. Most notable was the RCA XL-100 series of 100 percent solid-state sets carrying a one-year warranty. Solid-state models helped arrest the slide of average factory prices, which were around $332 per unit early in 1971.

President Nixon imposed a 10 percent temporary surcharge on imports and also took actions that led to an upward valuation of the Yen of 8.3 percent by year's end. The two actions came to be known as "Nixon Shock" in Japan. The effects of Nixon Shock on the cost structure of imports from Japan is shown in Exhibit 25–6.

RCA. Color TV, still the leading RCA consumer business, made a recovery in 1971. RCA held onto market share leadership. RCA introduced the XL-100 series, the industry's broadest line of 100 percent solid-state large-screen color sets. The chassis were made with a number of solid-state ceramic circuit modules—a technology that only RCA seemed to pursue. The XL-100 series carried a full one-year guarantee, versus ninety days on earlier sets. Other product innovations for 1971 included low-cost remote control, coupled with an all-electronic tuner.

Domestic TV manufacturing was consolidated in a single facility at Bloomington, Indiana, with the closing of the company's Memphis, Tennessee, plant. The new RCA glass plant came on stream, making only high volume 19-inch and 25-inch color glass funnels and panels. RCA exited black-and-white picture tube manufacturing, converting its Marion plant to color picture tube production (Marion had made black-and-white picture tubes since 1949). Internationally, in Britain a 49 percent joint venture with Thorn was in the start-up phase of color picture tube production. In France, RCA entered into a 49 percent joint venture with Thomson to manufacture color picture tubes. In Taiwan RCA was constructing a plant to make black-and-white picture tubes in collaboration with Chung-Hwa, a local interest.

RCA withdrew from the computer business, taking an after-tax writeoff of $250 million.

Zenith. Zenith maintained its lead in black-and-white sets but suffered some erosion in color set market share, in part because it did not respond quickly to widespread second-quarter price reductions that it had expected to be temporary. Zenith reported increasing emphasis in new models on solid-state modules and circuitry and introduced a new 16-inch portable line of Chromacolor sets. Near year end Zenith reevaluated its entire color product line and went on a crash program to bring out a new line of 23-inch solid-state receivers one year ahead of planned 1973 introduction, in response to RCA's successful introduction of XL-100 sets.

In order to reduce manufacturing costs, color TV picture tube manufacturing at the Knox Avenue plant in Chicago was terminated. All color TV picture tube production was now concentrated in Zenith's Melrose Park facility. Zenith's Taiwan factory began making small black-and-white sets to augment production at Plant No. 1 in Chicago.

During 1971 Zenith acquired a majority interest in the Movado-Zenith-Mondia Holding Company, a Swiss firm with a strong position in the watch market in Europe and elsewhere in the world. Zenith continued to explore the video recording and playback field. Research efforts were trimmed and redirected more closely to Zenith's existing consumer products.

Admiral. As a result of cost-cutting and consolidation, Admiral showed a profit in 1971 compared to the loss in the previous year. The new Admiral color TV line included a series with 80 percent solid-state chassis. Admiral was planning to introduce in 1972 a new, all-solid-state black-and-white TV receiver, as well as a new modular chassis color TV composed of nine individual modules. In May 1971 Admiral discontinued color tube production and sold its manufacturing equipment to RCA. It had been producing approximately 900,000 color tubes annually.[7] Color tube manufacturing operations had contributed materially to the 1970 losses.

General Electric. GE reported improved color TV sales. It introduced an improved color picture tube using more brilliant phosphors. New production facilities were commenced in Singapore for black-and-white TVs in order to stay competitive.

Magnavox. Magnavox stressed that all its color TV receivers were manufactured in the United States, despite the growing industry trend to overseas assembly or purchase. Whereas consoles declined as a percentage of total industry color set sales, Magnavox's corresponding percentage increased. Recognizing the increasing importance of table and portable models, Magnavox introduced new models in these areas. It also began using black matrix color tubes.

Magnavox signed a consent decree with the FTC in June agreeing not to enforce price maintenance in free-trade states. The order barred Magnavox from preventing the dealer form handling competing lines and from requiring the dealer to carry a full line. Early in 1972 Magnavox completed a new plant in Nogales, Mexico, to produce components and small black and white TVs previously purchased overseas.

Motorola. Motorola reported sales up to 70 percent versus the domestic industry's 28 percent, and this and a cost reduction program resulted in signifi-

---

[7] *Financial World,* March 15, 1972.

---

cant profits. Quasar advertising spending was maintained at high levels. Black-and-white set sales were ahead of 1970 as well. A major management reshuffling occurred throughout the entire company.

The production rate of Quasar sets doubled from the 1970 level. TV production lines were installed in Quincy, Illinois, to supplement Franklin Park, Illinois, assembly facilities. Motorola's Taiwan assembly plant began delivering small-screen black-and-white sets.

Philco. Philco had an operating profit in 1971 and also achieved record sales of component stereo systems, refrigerators and color TV sets in the U.S., up 44, 25, and 12 percent respectively, from 1970 levels. Philco introduced color TV sets with black matrix picture tubes. In Brazil, Zuckor-Ford maintained its position as the country's leading manufacturer of TV sets. Late in 1971 Philco's 25-inch color TV sets also began to be produced in Brazil, where color TV broadcasting was scheduled to begin in March 1972.

GTE-Sylvania. Sales of color TVs and color tubes were ahead of the previous year. Sylvania's 1971 line included the first 17-inch set manufactured by the domestic industry. Sylvania also introduced a series of large screen TVs and TV-stereo combinations using the Color Bright 100® picture tubes. Sylvania developed a new 100° deflection angle color picture tube, capable of reducing cabinet depth by 4½ inches. International earnings from color TV and color tube sales were down due to lowered prices and increased costs in West Germany and the rest of Europe.

Japanese Firms. A number of observers foresaw a long-range erosion of TV profit margins because of rising Japanese imports. In March the import total in 1971 was expected to advance around 3 percent to 950,000 color units. The figure was actually 1,281,000, with the Japanese accounting for 1,191,000. Currency revaluations, however, were expected to reduce Japanese competitiveness.

Legal Actions. In 1971 the Tariff Commission ruled that Japanese dumping was injurious to U.S. competitors. The Treasury began the process of assessing what duties on Japanese sets should be.

1972

Sales of color TV sets were more than 8,000,000 in the United States for the first time. Strong demand was attributed to increasing penetration of households, improved picture quality, rapid cable TV growth, and low prices due to competition. The trend to solid-state continued. Notably, Zenith introduced its first 100 percent solid-state TV in a 25-inch console model.

A major development was the large-scale arrival of in-line color picture tubes. In conventional tubes electron beams were shot out of three separate guns arranged in a triangular fashion. In the in-line system the three beams were mechanically arranged in a line and fired generally from a single gun. In-line tubes were more reliable, more compact, needed fewer adjustments and were $3 to $5 cheaper to produce. It was believed that the in-line system would become the industry standard on screen sizes 19 inches and below.

Along with changed electron guns, companies were beginning to use different types of masks. The basic shadow-mask consisted of holes, with the phosphor and dots on the screen arranged in triangular groups of threes. Sony's Trinitron, introduced in 1968, used a vertical aperature grill with vertical phosphor stripes on the screen. The vertical grill blocked fewer electrons, letting more hit the screen and thus producing a brighter picture.

Toshiba had begun using vertical phosphor stripes on the screen in conjunction with a mask that had vertical slots punched in it. This was almost as good as Sony's aperature grill. RCA had begun using the slot-mask/vertical phosphor stripe system as well in 1972 with its in-line tube. GE also adopted this system during the year. Most other companies soon followed suit.

RCA. Use of the XL–100 solid-state chassis was increased in RCA models. The growing world market for color TV kept picture tube production at near capacity levels at RCA plants not only in the United States and Canada but also in Europe, where RCA had a joint venture with local manufacturers. During 1972 RCA introduced a new precision in-line color picture tube. It also began production of a new wide-angle color picture tube for the European market. A significant increase in capacity was achieved during the year by the new color glass plant in Circleville, Ohio. RCA also began constructing an addition to its color picture tube plant in Scranton, Pennsylvania, scheduled for completion in February 1973.

Zenith. Zenith introduced its first all solid-state color chassis in June 1972, one year ahead of the original planned introduction date (only in 25-inch sets). It announced a new one-year parts and labor warranty on the 100 percent solid-state models. Concurrently it gave up its "handcrafted" advertising theme. A third generation Super Chromacolor picture tube was introduced in most screen sizes (16, 19, and 25 inches). Zenith also introduced a new, lower priced 16-inch portable and a low-priced 19-inch table model. Zenith's black-and-white TV sales continued to lead the industry for the thirteenth consecutive year.

In 1972 Zenith became the only company to attempt plantwide automation in the United States. The much publicized move involved the installation of $7 million worth of automatic-insertion machines and associated equipment, including computers. At the same time Melrose Park color tube production capacity was doubled through investment in new equipment and a reengineering of production techniques, and was operating at capacity. In September Zenith ran a TV commercial featuring Zenith workers discussing the fact that Zenith did not accept the myth that the American worker could not match the quality of overseas workmanships.

Commenting on why Zenith had not aggressively attacked overseas markets, a Zenith executive stated:

> It's hard to explain why a decision is made *not* to do something. There are a number of reasons behind it—including innate cautiousness. For one, we've always had our hands full with U.S. demand and we've always tended to stick with what appeared to be the biggest payoff and what we knew how to do best. For example, an additional two market share points in the Los Angeles area alone represents more sales volume than there is in most foreign markets. Also, we didn't feel we could compete with the local companies in those markets unless we were willing to sacrifice some of our margin, and we were unwilling to do that. We are basically a U.S. company and likely to stay that way.

Admiral. Admiral attributed the increase in its color TV sales in 1972 to special feature color TVs. In 1972 Admiral introduced four 25-inch color TV models featuring built-in eight-track tape cartridge players. Admiral said that the new year would see the introduction of a 100 percent solid-state chassis by Admiral. The company introduced an extended five-year warranty on color picture tubes, up from three years. In order to increase overall capacity and meet the projected sales volume for 1973, the company expanded its Taiwan plant and altered the layout of the Harvard, Illinois, plant.

General Electric. GE reported a boom year for color TV in 1972, with its sales increasing ahead of the industry's. It introduced 100 percent solid-state Porta-Color 16-inch sets.

Magnavox. In the second quarter Magnavox introduced its first 100 percent solid-state color set, with a large screen and modular chassis. However, it explained the delay in introduction of 100 percent solid-state portables (Magnavox already had 85 percent solid-state hybrids) by revealing that the company planned to introduce truly innovative portable units using super-bright in-line color tubes that would not be available until 1973. Magnavox pioneered the video game market by introducing Odyssey brand TV games that plugged into any 18- or 25-inch TV set. These were the first games using TV screens as displays.

Motorola. Motorola color TV sales increased about 40 percent. Console sales remained above industry averages, despite an industry trend to portables. Prices were increased slightly on many models. A new 14-inch Quasar portable was introduced. Black-and-white sales climbed 40 percent versus 8 percent for the industry. Major expansion programs were in progress at the Toronto color TV assembly plant, the Taiwan plant, and the Quincy, Illinois, facility.

Philco. A new line of Philcomatic III color TV sets were introduced in 1972 featuring a 100 percent solid-state chassis with plug-in modules for easier servicing. Increased color TV sales were reported. Philco announced plans to phase out the Philadelphia TV assembly plant within the next two years

and to consolidate U.S. TV operations in a three-plant complex in Lansdale, Pennsylvania. In São Paolo, Brazil, Philco began building a plant to make color TV circuit boards. The TV plant was fully automated and used computer-controlled insertion machines. These plants were made possible by a deal that Ford had negotiated with the Brazilian government whereby Philco could offset the extremely high import duties on components with credits from the export of assembled circuit boards.

GTE-Sylvania. Sylvania's new color TV line was still heavily weighted toward 24-inch consoles. The use of black matrix tubes was expanded, but the use of solid-state chassis remained limited. Sylvania reported that the market for color tubes was strong. Overseas sales were generally up substantially.

Japanese Firms. Imports from Japan dipped, affected by the upward revaluation of the yen. Sony began to build a color TV assembly plant in San Diego, California.

Legal Action. Magnavox petitioned the Treasury for countervailing duties against Japanese imports. The Treasury did not act.

1973

Color TV production was the highest ever. With imports nearly flat, the gain all went to domestic manufacturers. Profits, however, were not strong. Though the use of solid-state had been increasing over the past few years, all firms seemed to jump on the bandwagon in 1973. An RCA executive estimated that industry sales in 1973 were 54 percent hybrid and 46 percent solid-state.

Philco sold its color picture tube plant in Lansdale, Pennsylvania, to Zenith. That left five U.S. tube manufacturers out of ten several years earlier—RCA (33 percent), Sylvania (30 percent), Zenith (20 percent), GE, and Westinghouse (both much smaller shares). The tube manufacturers were all expanding capacity. An RCA spokesman projected that tube sales would increase from 7.9 million in 1973 to 9.1 million in 1977 and 1978.

A Westinghouse spokesman noted that capacity of about 14 million tubes in 1969 had been reduced to a little under 10 million by 1973. He projected a supply/demand balance in tubes, as did Zenith. A Sony Corporation of America spokesman said, however, that "like most companies, TV companies have a tendency to overbuild. If they need 10% more capacity for next year, they build 50% figuring that they'll need that much five years down the road."

RCA. RCA lost market share leadership in color TV for the first time despite the fact that it sold more color TV sets than in any other year in its history, spearheaded by its XL–100 solid-state line and a broadened line of portables. RCA blamed the decline in profit on TV and audio products on the fact that "prices in this highly competitive environment did not keep pace with rapidly rising costs of labor and materials." In January 1974 RCA announced its intention to increase prices on virtually all TV models. A new management group in consumer electronics drew up plans for a major restructuring of RCA's product line. As a first step, RCA decided to phase out its ceramic thick-film modules introduced in 1971. Integrated circuit technology had progressed faster than expected and obsoleted the thick-film technology.

RCA registered a moderate worldwide gain in sales of picture tubes to other set manufacturers and distributors. RCA's four U.S. picture tube manufacturing plants operated on a six-day week for most of the year. Production capacity was increased at Marion, Indiana. An investment of $16.8 million was made in the Lancaster, Pennsylvania, plant and a 40,000-square-foot addition to the glass-making facility in Circleville, Ohio, was under construction at year end. Expansions of color TV facilities were also made in the United Kingdom, France, and Brazil.

Zenith. Zenith color TV share was the highest in history in 1973, and for the first time it wrested the number one position from RCA. However, margins were down. Zenith stressed the new Chromacolor II system incorporating 100 percent solid-state and electronic tuning. In black-and-white, Zenith led the industry for the fifteenth consecutive year.

A $68 million domestic expansion program was initiated, which would add 2.2 million square feet to the company's manufacturing and engineering fa-

cilities in the United States. Zenith acquired a 405,000-square-foot color picture tube plant in Lansdale, Pennsylvania, from Philco Corporation. The acquisition provided Zenith with its second color picture tube manufacturing facility. As part of the deal, Philco agreed to purchase its color picture tube requirements from Zenith for two years. A $30 million investment would raise capacity at Lansdale from approximately 600,000 to 1.1 million tubes annually. When the Lansdale expansion and modernization were completed, Zenith would be able to produce more than 3 million color picture tubes annually. As a further step in Zenith's program to manufacture many of its own components, the company expanded its Matamoros, Mexico, facility. The operation, which produced electron guns for color TV picture tubes, would also house assembly lines for the manufacture of TV tuners.

Admiral. After negotiations in 1973 on April 1, 1974, Admiral Corporation merged with Rockwell International Corporation.

General Electric. GE's color TV sales increased, but TV was not in the "strong performer" category.

Magnavox. The Consumer Electronics Group registered a loss, though the fourth quarter was profitable. Magnavox introduced a new color TV line in May 1973, backed by aggressive advertising, with 90 percent of the models 100 percent solid-state. New in-line negative (black) matrix color picture tubes were added into both 17-inch and 19-inch portable and table models. All Magnavox's 25-inch models (consoles) used the Super Bright black matrix tubes. Magnavox stressed its extensive reliability testing on all its solid-state sets.

In 1973 Magnavox offered frequent price promotions thoughout the year to work down hybrid set inventories. Efforts were made at components standardization across lines. As a result of major cost improvement programs launched in 1973, facilities were consolidated and three plants were closed or scheduled to be closed.

Motorola. Motorola's color TV sales were ahead of 1972, but growth was below the industry's. The Consumer Products Division showed a loss due to lower than expected volume, cost increases, and a shift toward less profitable portable and small-screen sets in both black-and-white and color. The continuing shift away from consoles toward portable sets had had a particularly severe effect on Motorola who was traditionally strong in large-screen and console sets. Motorola's price rise in late 1972 was not generally followed, and a reduction in advertising had also hurt sales. Black-and-white sales increased 20 percent.

In late 1973 it was reported that Motorola was planning to penetrate the Japanese color TV market with its Quasar line of solid-state sets in the 22-inch and 25-inch sizes. Aiwa Co., Ltd., a leading Japanese consumer electronics concern, was to act as Motorola's agent in Japan. Motorola expected to capture about 1 percent of the Japanese market (approximately 60,000 sets, factory value $14 million) in two to three years.

Philco.   The color circuit board plant in São Paolo began functioning and circuit boards were sent to the United States for final assembly. However, during the three-month period July to September, every IC that Philco bought from its supplier, Motorola, was defective, and the defects were not discovered until after assembly. Thus every color TV made during that period had to have its circuit boards replaced. The cost of this finally convinced Ford management to dispose of the TV business. As a first step, the color TV tube manufacturing plant in Lansdale, Pennsylvania, was sold to Zenith. The plant had a capacity of 600,000 tubes a year; it actually produced 400,000.

GTE-Sylvania.   Sylvania introduced self-adjusting GT-Matic™ solid-state color sets in 13-, 19-, 21- and 25-inch screen sizes. Sylvania announced a 20 percent expansion of capacity (from three assembly lines to four) at Smithfield, North Carolina, in January 1973, citing anticipated increases in color TV and audio unit demand. Color picture tube capacity was expanded at the Ottawa, Ohio, tube plant. Sylvania claimed to be the nation's largest TV picture tube producer.

Westinghouse.   Commenting on picture tube operations, a Westinghouse spokesman said: "We're making many more tubes now than when we were in

the set business. Today we serve practically every set maker and we feel they buy from us because they'd rather spend money to buy the most expensive part of their sets from someone other than a competitor."[8]

Japanese Firms.   Japanese imports into the United States decreased slightly. Sony began constructing a Trinitron color picture tube plant near its San Diego color TV set assembly plant, at a cost in excess of $10 million.

Legal Action.   Matsushita filed a challenge against the Treasury's ruling of dumping. The Supreme Court refused to review the issue in 1973.

1974

Sales of black-and-white TV declined by a little over 1 million units. One analyst said, "People buying second sets still buy color. Black and white has been relegated to a third or fourth set. It's rapidly being wiped out."[9] Color TV shipments by U.S. producers were 7.8 million units, compared to 9.3 million sets the year before. Widespread layoffs and plant closings had managed to bring the production rate below the sales rate by year end. For 1975 the general feeling was that color TV shipments would about match the 1974 level, although some companies were looking for a slight improvement.

Late in 1973 RCA had tried to instigate a price increase but was forced to roll back its prices when competitors refused to follow. Costs, however, continued to rise. Caught in a squeeze, the industry as a whole sustained a $31 million net operating loss on TV in 1974. GE said it was profitable in color TV, but most observers believed that profit was inconsequential, if it existed at all. Some observers thought that even RCA was losing money on color TV. By the end of the year the major companies seemed to be on record in favor of a price increase.

During the year Teledyne-Packard-Bell discontinued TV operations, and Rockwell consummated the takeover of Admiral. Philco sold its TV business to GTE and a cabinet plant to Zenith. Motorola

[8]*New York Times,* October 28, 1973.
[9]*Wall Street Journal,* March 2, 1974.

sold its TV business to Matsushita, and Magnavox was acquired by North American Philips. Commenting on the mergers, Roy Pollack, vice president and general manager of RCA's Consumer Electronics Division, offered this opinion: "I think some of the acquisitions weren't thought out well. I sure wouldn't make the prediction that all of them will jell. I've got to believe that ½ of them won't stick."[10]

John Nevin of Zenith said:

> Historically there has never been any correlation between the financial willingness of the parent and the ability of the subsidiary to lose its shirt in TV. On the other hand you can make the case and I am inclined more to this position that Matsushita and Philips didn't buy shares in the American market to demonstrate that they can lose their shirt.[11]

RCA.   RCA's unit sales of color sets declined by 13 percent from 1973. Describing the TV situation in 1974 RCA stated "the color TV industry suffered a double impact: the sharp decline in sales and the continuing profit margin squeeze between inflated costs and fiercely competitive prices." The restructuring of RCA's consumer electronics operations began to be felt in 1974. In the spring RCA became the first full-line U.S. manufacturer to devote its color TV production exclusively to 100 percent solid-state receivers designed to maintain the highest standard of performance and reliability. Although this decision knowingly risked price competition from lower-cost hybrid models, it accelerated the industry trend to the solid-state standard and put RCA in a strengthened position to meet future demand for state-of-the-art sets. The company also achieved significant production economies by streamlining its color line to thirty-one models, employing fewer basic chassis designs.[12] According to observers, RCA first began to compete strongly on the basis of price during 1974.

---

[10] *Wall Street Journal,* December 4, 1974.

[11] *Ibid.*

[12] RCA discontinued production of 14-inch and 18-inch screen sizes in June, so that its 1974 line consisted of only 15-, 17-, 19-, 21- and 25-inch sizes. A spokesman commented: "The message of the marketplace has been loud and clear. People are fed up with the overwhelming amount of screen sizes and chassis. Production costs have surged with the varied product mix." Later RCA dispensed with the 21-inch size as well.

RCA's tube operations were affected by the sharply reduced worldwide demand for color TV picture tubes. On the technology front, in the European market the precision in-line color TV picture tube concept was expanded to include large screen sizes with 110° deflection. Initial production of the new tubes was planned for early 1975 in Scranton, Pennsylvania, with subsequent production by RCA ventures in Italy, England, and France.

RCA announced that its recently introduced line of radios, phonographs, and tape recorders would be its last; they accounted for only 5 percent of consumer electronics sales and had lost their profitability.

Zenith.   Zenith's color set share improved slightly though its sales declined, mitigated by strength in furniture console models. Profits were severely depressed. Commenting on the future, John Nevin, president of Zenith said:

> Zenith will struggle to be more profitable next year. Obviously we have a considerable task. I think the problem next year is going to be more rising labor costs than rising material costs. . . . We haven't been successful in recent years in recovering costs in the price of products. I'm hopeful this may start to happen next year. But I use the word "hopeful" rather than the word "expect."[13]

Zenith was the black-and-white leader for the sixteenth consecutive year, though it lost share slightly due to shortages of small-screen models. A major Manufacturing and Material Division reorganization was initiated in 1974. In December 1974 Zenith announced that the Lansdale, Pennsylvania, color picture tube plant, which it had acquired from Philco in July 1973 and in which it had made a substantial investment, was being closed indefinitely. The plant was to be kept ready to produce Chromacolor picture tubes of varying sizes if needed.

On September 20, 1974, Zenith filed an action in the United States District Court in Philadelphia against twenty major Japanese TV and electronics manufacturers[14] and their Japanese and U.S. sales subsidiaries, and Motorola, Inc., alleging violations

---

[13] *Wall Street Journal,* December 4, 1974.

[14] The manufacturers named were Matsushita, Sony, Toshiba, Hitachi, Sanyo, Sharp, and Mitsubishi.

of U.S. antitrust laws and the U.S. antidumping law of 1916. In the complaint, Zenith sought injunctive relief in excess of $300 million to be trebled as provided by law. The complaint alleged that the Japanese defendants organized to develop and employ their joint economic power to launch "a predatory invasion and seizure of the U.S. market in each consumer electronic product category." The complaint further alleged that this conspiracy consisted of a "concerted scheme" to fix and maintain high prices in the Japanese home market and to fix and maintain artificially low prices for consumer electronics products exported to the United States.

Admiral. After the merger, consumer products were expected to account for about 15 percent of Rockwell's total sales. In 1974 the Admiral group was unprofitable, resulting from a generally depressed industry, higher material costs that could not be recovered with increased prices, and costs associated with the start-up of new production facilities. In 1974 Admiral had a 100 percent solid-state color TV set in the 25-inch size using a super-solar color tube. It carried a five-year picture tube protection plan and a one-year free parts and labor warranty. Portable sets were offered with screen sizes ranging from 9 to 22 inches.

A Rockwell task force with representatives from the Home Entertainment Division, the Collins Radio Group (acquired in 1973), and the Micro Electronics Group was at work developing plans to strengthen home entertainment products technologically for both the short and the long term.

General Electric. GE disclosed severe pressure on TV margins because of material cost increases and announced a new line of (solid-state) TV receivers with "outstanding reliability." On prospects for 1974, Donald Perry, vice president and general manager of GE's Home Entertainment business, said, "Retailers are cutting down on inventories and being plagued by a cash squeeze, but the public confidence is still there. I don't think people look at a TV set any more as a luxury item. It's gotten down to being an essential . . . prices are going to have to go up about 5 to 10 percent for GE and (we hope) this will offset cost increases."

Magnavox. North American Philips, a subsidiary of Philips of Holland, purchased via a tender offer 84 percent of the total outstanding stock of Magnavox. Advantages to Magnavox were cited as access to R&D. The Magnavox CEO, Robert H. Platt, resigned from the company and was replaced by Pieter C. Vink, president and CEO of North American Philips.

The Magnavox Consumer Electronics Group suffered a severe drop in sales and reported a loss of more than $40 million on sales of approximately $250 million. Losses for the group were expected to continue into 1975, though at a lower level. Among other things, this was blamed on a large portion of industry sales in smaller sets or "specially priced" sets. In December Magnavox introduced a unique 25-inch color TV that combined the convenience of remote control with electronic tuning that enabled the user to tune to any one of eighty-two VHF and UHF channels instantly. The Nogales, Mexico, black-and-white TV and components plant was closed, and production was shifted elsewhere. The Nogales closing made Magnavox the only major domestic TV producer without an offshore TV plant.

Motorola. On May 28, 1974, Motorola sold its U.S. and Canadian TV manufacturing facilities (Quasar line) to Matsushita Electric Industrial Co. of Japan. This marked its exit from the color TV business. In December it exited from black-and-white TV manufacturing as well by selling its Taiwan facility to Oak Industries Inc. (of Crystal Lake, Illinois). TV production was to be terminated, and Oak was to close the Hong Kong plant and shift the equipment to Taiwan, where it would make tuners and tuner components.

When the sale to Matsushita was proposed, Zenith called it a "flagrant violation of antitrust laws" and Magnavox called it "illegal" (Magnavox was acquired later that year by North American Philips). The Justice Department made Motorola put off the sale for one month and seek other qualified buyers. Zenith offered to negotiate on the purchase of the facilities but was unwilling to acquire the Quasar brand name, inventories, or TV distributorships owned by Motorola. Motorola finally sold out to Matsushita, not being able to find an alternate. In any case, Motorola had made it clear that sale or no sale, it was not going to continue in the TV business.

Philco. Philco sold its home entertainment products business in the United States and Canada, including certain of the rights to the Philco name, to GTE-Sylvania. In January 1975 the cabinet-making facility in Watsontown, Pennsylvania, was sold to Zenith. In February 1975 GTE-Sylvania, Inc., purchased Philco Taiwan Corp., a Philco-Ford subsidiary that manufactured black-and-white TV sets in Taiwan.

GTE-Sylvania. Sylvania's domestic sales and earnings in TV sets and tubes were adversely affected by industry conditions. Sylvania introduced the second generation of its self-adjusting color TV sets, utilizing the G-Matic II chassis. Also introduced was a new Dark-Lite high contrast color tube, used in the majority of G-Matic II color TV sets. Sylvania said it was "one of the nation's top two producers of TV picture tubes" and produced the industry's largest variety of picture tubes. Several new tubes were introduced in Europe. Commenting on the Philco purchases, Sylvania said that it planned to continue production of black-and-white sets in Philco's 167,000-square-foot Taiwan plant.

Japanese Firms. Imports declined in 1974. Matsushita acquired the TV business of Motorola for approximately book value and immediately embarked on a $15 million program to upgrade production technology at Motorola's Franklin Park plant, including automatic insertion and other automation. Productivity began to improve dramatically.

Legal Actions. In 1974 the Treasury exempted Sony from any dumping charge. Sony had always denied it had violated the law. In September 1974 Zenith filed the antitrust suit in Philadelphia against several Japanese manufacturers and their subsidiaries, as described above.

In 1974 the Tariff Act of 1930 was changed by the Trade Act of 1974. As a result, the U.S. Tariff Commission was renamed the International Trade Commission (ITC), and numerous procedural

changes were made in the handling of trade issues. Among these was a requirement for the Treasury to act within a specified period on dumping petitions it received. The Trade Act of 1974 was signed into law on January 4, 1975.

1975

The worldwide economic slump caused by the 1973 oil price hike continued into 1975, though the situation began improving in the second half of the year. TV was one of the last consumer products to recover, and sales for the year of both color and black-and-white TV were below 1974 levels. Sharpened competition, much of which was attributed to RCA, put downward pressure on prices.

RCA. To start the writeup for the year, Robert W. Sarnoff, son of David Sarnoff, resigned as chairman of the board and as a director. In the third quarter of the year RCA launched its automatic Color Trak system in a select group of RCA XL–100 sets. The Color Trak system was designed not only for state-of-the-art performance but for efficient manufacture with six modules versus the twelve in the XL–100 chassis. Black-and-white TV shared in the product improvement with the introduction of RCA's first total product line change in twenty-eight years. The line consisted of seven models based on two chassis, compared with the previous fifteen models and eleven chassis. During the year RCA began moving some color chassis assembly operations to Juarez, Mexico.

In England the color tube plant jointly owned by RCA (49 percent) and Thorn Electrical Industries Ltd. operated at half its capacity because of a severe recession, higher value-added taxes, and heavy pricing pressure from imported tubes. As a result, it was announced early in 1976 that the plant would be closed. The closing of the Thorn color tube joint venture and a Harrison, New Jersey, vacuum tube plant resulted in a $20 million pretax loss charged against 1975 earnings. Despite the depressed U.S. and international market for color tubes, RCA increased its share of this market and continued its product improvement with the introduction of a high-contrast phosphor tube featured in the Color Trak system.

Zenith. Zenith sales dropped only 6.5 percent in units, and its color TV market share increased. The marketing effort of Zenith was most successful in the premium priced console TV market. Zenith console sales increased by 2.6 percent. Zenith introduced a new remote control electronic tuning system, more integrated circuits in its sets, and new series of portable 13-inch color TVs. In black-and-white, Zenith maintained leadership and introduced sixteen new solid-state models. Major rearrangements were accomplished in manufacturing facilities throughout the United States. Efficiency improvements were registered in both set assembly and tube manufacture. Zenith stated it was able to recover cost increases through price increases for the first time in three years.

Admiral (Rockwell). The Admiral Group of Rockwell's consumer operations lost money during the year. Despite the losses, Rockwell management felt that changes made in the Admiral Group had considerably strengthened it and the prospects for the long term were much improved. At fiscal year end the Admiral Group was restructured. However, internal friction arose from the fact that new solid-state designs by Rockwell engineers, with experience in the defense and aerospace business, were incompatible with the needs of the fiercely competitive color TV market.

General Electric. GE reported disappointing sales in color TV. It stressed its strength in smaller sets and portables, which were favored by existing sales trends. The 1975 color line emphasized changeover to 100 percent solid-state models, with only one hybrid unit (a 10-inch model). Prices were increased on the 1975 line, 6 percent on color and 5.5 percent on black-and-white. The service network for GE and Hotpoint appliances and TV was further expanded, despite the recession.

Magnavox (North American Philips). North American Philips acquired the remaining 16 percent of Magnavox shares. Magnavox's Consumer Electronics operations were again unprofitable but began operating at a profit in the final quarter.

Magnavox claimed an increased market share in color TV, especially in the higher-priced console segment. Advertising was expanded. The new color TV "Star System" introduced in 1974 was extended from the initial 25-inch models to 19-inch models as well. In May 1975, Magnavox suspended purchasing 25-inch color tubes from Westinghouse because of defects. It began initial steps in preparation for mass production of the video disk player in the United States. The Odyssey line of video games was expanded.

GTE-Sylvania. Sylvania color TV set and tube sales were down. Severe price competition depressed profits. All of Sylvania's 1975 models featured completely solid-state chassis. Most sets had the G-Matic self-adjusting feature, first introduced by Sylvania to the industry in 1973. Sylvania claimed to be the second largest domestic producer of TV picture tubes. Sylvania began producing Philco brand TVs in August 1975, which were different from Sylvania models (lower technology). The Philco brand sets were meant to compete with Sears, K-Mart, and other private label products. Sylvania maintained two separate sales organizations for the two different labels. Internationally, new sets were introduced in Germany and Canada. The Brazilian operations were terminated by a fire.

Japanese Firms. Though total imports were down slightly, Japanese imports rose. Sanyo, Hitachi, Toshiba, and some others began introducing color TVs priced 15 percent or more below comparable U.S. brands. As a result, Sears, Montgomery Ward, and other mass merchants began shifting private label business away from U.S. manufacturers. Consequently, the Japanese share of portable color TV private label business began rising from the 25 percent level of early 1975.[15] Matsushita revamped the Quasar line by reducing the number of circuit models per chassis.

Legal Actions. A Federal District Court struck down the part of Zenith's antitrust complaint against Japanese firms relating to the Robinson-Patman Act. Zenith pressed on with its other claims.

[15] *Business Week,* September 20, 1976.

1976

Color TV sales recovered, but more slowly than expected. The benefit to U.S. producers was marginal, since the increase was mostly accounted for by Japanese imports. Many U.S. manufacturers cut back production. With material costs having risen 5 to 10 percent per year over the past few years and with severe pricing pressure on TV sets pushing down picture tube prices, the picture tube manufacturers were unhappy. The 25-inch color tubes that sold for about $86 in 1974 were now selling for about $78. Furthermore, the industry was operating well below capacity. In November Westinghouse, the last independent color tube maker, decided to exit from the business. It said that over the past eighteen months it had "lost millions of dollars" in its Entertainment Tube Division. In 1976 it had not been able to improve its position domestically because of increased imports, while on the export front it was experiencing increased freight and duty costs in Europe. The color tube equipment from Westinghouse's plant was eventually sold to Sony for its San Diego plant.

RCA. RCA's new Color Trak sets accounted for 42 percent of RCA's total dollar sales in color TV and contributed to the year's increase of some $40 on the average retail price paid for an RCA console receiver and a $20 increase for the average portable and table model. Profits increased significantly in both sets and tubes. RCA was able to respond to the increased import competition by reducing prices on its 19-inch models early in the second half. RCA said that it essentially maintained its share of the U.S. color TV market despite sharply increased Japanese sales. The company did not join in efforts by others in the TV industry to seek import quotas or other restrictions on the imported sets. Support of free trade had been a longstanding RCA policy, reinforced through the years by the company's stake in international licensing.

RCA's picture tube operations moved from a loss to a profit position thanks to sales gains from the growing overseas market and rigorous cost reductions. Fully half of RCA's picture tube production, including that of its foreign subsidiaries and affiliates, went into sets manufactured abroad. New plant expansions were planned for 1977 in Mexico and Brazil. RCA entered into a $71 million long-term technology transfer contract with the government of Poland that included the installation of color TV picture tube manufacturing facilities in Poland, with a capacity of 600,000 tubes per year, to be operational in the first half of 1979. Corning Glass Works received a simultaneous but independent contract to supply the glass technology on a turnkey basis.

Zenith. Zenith's color TV sales were up, but share declined slightly. Profits were up somewhat because of lower manufacturing costs—prices were not increased. Zenith introduced a number of new features in 1976 and continued to show particular strength in the market for large-screen console color TV receivers. Zenith's console sales were a substantial contributor to its financial performance during 1976.

Zenith's black-and-white share declined slightly, though it maintained its eighteenth consecutive year of industry leadership. It lowered prices late in the year to meet competition. In February 1976 Zenith announced it had developed an entirely new high-performance in-line picture tube in collaboration with Corning Glass Works. The tube was brighter and cheaper to manufacture. Zenith, with this tube, was perhaps the last manufacturer to go to a slotted mask tube. Zenith hoped to license it to other manufacturers. However, Sylvania decided not to take out a license on the new Zenith/Corning tube, because the larger dimensions of the new glass envelope would cause problems with cabinet costs and styling.

Zenith planned to convert all existing color TV models to a new X-chassis design by 1978, involving a higher proportion of automatic insertion circuit boards. In 1976 about $13 million was invested in machinery and equipment to support new TV models and components, of which $6 million was for production equipment to support the new color picture tube.

Admiral (Rockwell). The Admiral Group had greater losses in fiscal 1976, due primarily to intensified foreign competition, decline in demand in home appliances, and the foreign currency translation losses. Two new high-performance color TV chassis were introduced. The new ERA II set was modular in design and featured the first 100 percent modular interconnect system.

General Electric. GE color TV sales improved. GE introduced a system that automatically adjusted a set's color rendition using a VIR (vertical interval reference) system, which read a special color and tint reference signal broadcast with many programs. It claimed this feature boosted color console sales above 1975 levels.

Magnavox (North American Philips). Magnavox's Consumer Electronics operations were profitable for the year. Color TV unit sales increased, and share held steady. In black-and-white, Magnavox introduced new 9-inch and 12-inch models with plug-in and battery-powered capability, strengthening its position in "a shrinking, but still important, unit market."

GTE-Sylvania. The consumer electronics business was unprofitable because of both U.S. TV losses and European TV losses. GTE reorganized, creating a new Consumer Products Group. Sylvania remained the second largest domestic producer of TV picture tubes and an important supplier of picture tubes and other components in Europe and Latin America. Difficulties were experienced by Sylvania's TV set operations in Europe, primarily because of depressed prices in Germany.

Japanese Firms. Imports of color TV climbed sharply, reaching 40 percent of total sales in the third quarter. Part of this increase represented private label sets substituting for the decline in Warwick's private label shipments to Sears. Sanyo acquired Warwick's TV manufacturing operations during the year. Sony purchased most of Westinghouse's color picture tube equipment, shipping it to its San Diego facility.

Some observers believed that the gains made by the Japanese were based on sound business reasons, namely strong channels of mass distribution and a low cost position. The latter was attributed to extensive modularization in design and a high degree of production automation. John Nevin of Zenith did not share this view. Pointing to Matsushita's 1974 acquisition of Motorola's TV business and to the (then) proposed purchase of Warwick Electronics

by Sanyo, he said: "They certainly aren't buying up U.S. manufacturers because they go along with this voodoo that the Japanese are the only efficient TV manufacturers and that the rest of us are a bunch of clowns."[16]

Legal Actions. In January 1976 the Treasury ruled on Zenith's countervailing duty petition, holding that no subsidies by the Japanese government existed. Zenith appealed to the U.S. Customs Court. Also in January GTE-Sylvania asked the ITC to investigate "unfair methods of competition and unfair acts" engaged in by five Japanese manufacturers. Later in the year the ITC was petitioned by a newly formed labor-management coalition calling itself COMPACT (Committee to Preserve American Color Television), asking for import relief. COMPACT comprised suppliers to the TV industry, including Sprague Electric, Corning, and Owens Illinois, and a small TV set manufacturer, Wells-Gardner. None of the large TV set manufacturers joined COMPACT. Commenting on the situation, *Business Week* noted: "Waging the toughest pricing battle the industry has seen the Japanese have tripled their share of the huge U.S. TV market, and panicky U.S. manufacturers and labor unions want action to halt the import tide." The action of COMPACT drew strong criticism from the administration, Justice Department, State Department, and FTC.

In September 1975 Matsushita filed an antitrust suit against Zenith. It charged Zenith with violations of the Sherman Act and the Robinson-Patman Act, alleging that Zenith conspired to restrain trade in color and black-and-white TVs and that Zenith practiced price favoritism with certain key customers. Matsushita asked treble damages.

1977

Black-and-white sales increased somewhat while color sales recovered strongly. However, prices remained under pressure from strong competition. RCA introduced its 1977 models at distributor prices as much as $15 below their Zenith counterparts. RCA also had aggressive trade-in programs

[16] *Ibid.*

that gave buyers $40 to $100 credits on their old color sets. Zenith cut prices in January, followed by further cuts in February and more cuts in the summer on its new models. A GTE spokesman commented on Zenith's actions: "It's the most unusual happening—the industry leader doing this—in my experience. And, of course, it makes it rougher on us. They're buying share of market—but at tremendous expense."

RCA. RCA claimed it was the most profitable American manufacturer of TV sets. RCA share and profits increased despite $20 million in additional costs from new labor contracts. Color TV costs were reduced by design of a new "Xtended Life" chassis and the installation of new and improved automatic test equipment. RCA's color picture tube facilities were hard pressed to keep up with demand in the United States, Europe, and Latin America. New equipment was installed in Marion, Indiana, to be used for an improved line of color tubes as part of the conversion of RCA color receivers to the energy saving "Xtended Life" series. RCA planned to invest $50 million over the next several years to enhance its position as a worldwide supplier of color picture tubes.

Zenith. Zenith maintained its leadership position in both color and black-and-white TV sales, although market shares for both declined slightly. Zenith made a significant gain in its share of the color TV console market. New product programs in the smaller-screen portable area were developed for mid-and late-1978 introduction. Zenith stressed features on its color sets and sold at prices equal to or higher than competitors. Zenith had planned to introduce its horizontal X-chassis TV set in the fall of 1977. Zenith suddenly postponed the program because of cost problems in manufacturing the 19-inch and 25-inch versions.

In September Zenith announced that the 8 to 10 percent manufacturing cost savings initially prediced for the 100° glass envelope for tubes developed with Corning had not been achieved, and that the program was therefore being discontinued. During 1977 Zenith wrote down the inactive color TV tube facility in Lansdale, Pennsylvania, reducing 1977 profits by $12.2 million. It "was no longer required to meet the company's foreseeable future

requirements." In late 1977 Zenith decided to move a major part of its operations offshore, laying off 25 percent of its work force. While final assembly would remain in the United States, the effect of transferring color TV module and chassis operations to lower labor cost areas was expected to reduce Zenith's costs by from $10 to $15 per color TV receiver produced. As part of the overhead reduction program, in September Zenith decided to discontinue basic research, laying off 100 people. Only product development was to be continued.

General Electric. GE color TV set sales improved and market share increased. GE introduced a new remote control system using an infrared (instead of the conventional ultrasonic) signal. It received an Emmy Award for the first application of the vertical interval reference (VIR) signal system to TV receivers.

In December GE and Hitachi Ltd. of Japan announced plans for the formation of a new jointly owned company, General Television of America, Inc., for the engineering, manufacturing, and marketing of GE, Hitachi, and private label brand TV sets and for the manufacture of color TV picture tubes for other color TV manufacturers. Under the proposed agreement, the new company would combine GE and Hitachi technologies and would utilize the facilities and personnel of GE's current TV business. The combination was expected to make GE's business more profitable by realizing higher volumes of production. GE and Hitachi each would own 50 percent of the shares of the new company, establishment of which was contingent upon necessary corporate and government approvals.

Magnavox (North American Philips). Magnavox color TV sales and earnings increased, as did market share. The portable color TV line led the gains, and two 19-inch models were introduced. Consumer acceptance of Touch Tune receivers was high. Magnavox said it was investing in automated equipment and new circuitry design to reduce cost while increasing performance of its sets and fully expected to remain competitive.

GTE-Sylvania. Sylvania's loss in consumer electronics was substantially less than the previous year, thanks largely to European sales. The 1978 line featured an advanced electronic tuner system and a series of color Supersets with the highest level of performance and reliability ever in a Sylvania set. Sylvania's West German subsidiary substantially increased share.

Japanese Firms. Mitsubishi opened a plant in California to assemble complete color TV kits in early 1977 but closed it after the Orderly Marketing Agreement (discussed below) included kits in the import quota. The plant was reopened in early 1978 with parts sourced from both the United States and Japan. In late 1977 Toshiba decided to build a $6 million color TV assembly plant in Lebanon, Tennessee. Hitachi and GE announced the establishment of a joint venture in 1977 as well.

Legal Actions. The ITC, ruling on COMPACT's petition for import relief, found that the domestic TV industry was being injured as a result of increased imports. It recommended that Japanese color TV imports for the next five years be subjected to higher tariffs. To head this off, the administration negotiated a voluntary Orderly Marketing Agreement (OMA) with Japan. Under the terms of the OMA, Japanese imports of color TVs were restricted to 1.56 million complete sets and .19 million incomplete sets per year for a three-year period ending June 1980. Since the agreement came into effect only in July 1977, imports for the year as a whole were still high, around 2 million units. Soon after the negotiations of the OMA, Zenith moved a major portion of its prefinal assembly work offshore, citing increased competition from U.S. offshore plants. Japanese firms were furious.

In March 1977 Zenith amended its antitrust suit to include Sears Roebuck and to require Sanyo to divest Warwick and cancellation of the purchasing agreement between Sanyo and Sears. In April 1977, with regard to the countervailing duty case, the U.S. Customs Court, ruling on Zenith's appeal, ruled unanimously in Zenith's favor. There was an immediate negative reaction from the administration and the press. Japan sent a letter of protest to the State Department, supported by the Council of Permanent Representatives of the eighty-three-nation GATT. The Treasury appealed to the U.S. Court of Customs and Patent Appeals, which in July ruled in

favor of the Treasury. Zenith appealed to the Supreme Court, and briefs were filed in support of Zenith by U.S. Steel, Bethlehem Steel, and COMPACT. In May Zenith agreed to drop Sony from the antitrust suit. In June 1977 Sears filed a counter claim in the Federal Court against Zenith. Sears alleged that Zenith's advertising illegally misled consumers into believing that Zenith's color TV sets and components were entirely U.S.-made.

Meanwhile, the Senate forced the Justice Department to carry out an investigation of the Japanese manufacturers on antitrust grounds. Justice dropped this after a year, saying it had found no evidence of collusion. Several Japanese firms had sent a memo to the Justice Department outlining their case.

1978

Color TV sales were at an all-time high, and small price increases went into effect. After several poor years, Rockwell (Admiral) decided to exit from the TV industry.

RCA. RCA unit sales were up 13 percent, but it was unable to raise prices enough to match inflationary cost increases. RCA introduced the Channel Lock color tuning system, eliminating the need for fine tuning. It began moving from a modular chassis design to a single circuit board concept that would cut the number of parts, improve reliability, and cut costs. RCA also embarked on a two-year program to automate all final assembly and testing operations for color TVs at its Bloomington, Indiana, plant. It used Matsushita technology, which it regarded as the best in the world.

Color picture tubes set new sales records as a result of unprecedented domestic demand and rising sales overseas. RCA negotiated an agreement with the USSR to help set up a color picture tube plant there.

Zenith. Zenith maintained its leadership in the U.S. color and black-and-white TV markets, but experienced market share declines in both. Margins were down in 1978 and early 1979. Zenith introduced its new line of 13-, 17-, 19-, and 25-inch

"System-3" color TVs. The System-3 required fewer components and incorporated a new 100° in-line tube, 100 percent modular chassis, and Color Sentry automatic color control. Of $17 million in capital expenditures, the largest were $6 million related to the System-3 picture tube and chassis and $4 million to acquire, equip, and expand a new chassis plant in Reynosa, Mexico, on the Texas border. Zenith continued to accuse Japanese and other firms of unfair trade practices.

General Electric. GE reported strong gains in sales and earnings in TV. The highlight of new product introductions was the Widescreen 1000 Home Television Theatre, a flat-screened color TV set with a picture three times the size of that on today's standard 25-inch color TV receiver. This unit also used the VIR broadcast controlled color signal system. In early 1978 GE announced that TV set production in Canada would be discontinued.

In late November GE was advised by the U.S. Department of Justice that the department would challenge, if consummated, the previously announced proposal to form a new TV receiver company owned jointly by GE and Hitachi Ltd. of Japan. The proposed agreement was terminated.

Magnavox (North American Philips). Magnavox's unit sales of color TV increased, and penetration increased in the portable and table model categories. However, a loss was registered for the year. Magnavox introduced two new screen sizes—a 9-inch model and a 10-inch model, and installed new 100° in-line picture tubes in all its 19-inch and 25-inch models. A new microprocessor tuning system was incorporated in ten new 25-inch Touch Tune models.

Rockwell (Admiral). Rockwell decided to exit from the U.S. TV business, taking a write-off of $25 million. Rockwell retained the Admiral TV operations for the domestic Canadian and Mexican markets. Admiral's demise was blamed on Japanese price competition. The Taiwan plant was sold to a group of Far Eastern businessmen. Under the terms of the sale, color and black-and-white set production was to continue, though it could not be sold under the Admiral brand name.

GTE-Sylvania. Sylvania reported improvement in sales and earnings through increased sales of TV sets and picture tubes in most major markets, coupled with favorable currency translation effects in Europe. Sylvania continued as the number two U.S. tube producer. However, the TV set business in the United States continued to incur losses. The new Sylvania 19-inch Superset Plus was judged substantially superior in terms of overall picture quality to comparable models of two leading producers. This was used as the basis of a large-scale national advertising campaign.

Japanese and Other Imports. The first full calendar year for which the OMA was in effect was 1978. Japanese imports were below 1.5 million units. However, imports from Taiwan, Korea, Canada, and Singapore all rose significantly. As a result, total imports were almost as high as in 1976 and higher than in 1977. COMPACT urged that OMAs be negotiated with Korea and Taiwan. Discussions with the two countries resulted in agreements in December 1978, limiting exports from them as follows:

> . . . from Taiwan during the period February 1, 1979, to June 30, 1979: 127,000 complete sets and incomplete sets with picture tubes, and 270,000 incomplete sets without picture tubes, and from July 1, 1979 to June 30, 1980, 373,000 complete and incomplete sets with picture tubes, and 648,000 incomplete sets without picture tubes. [Of this latter 648,000 figure, the Taiwan government alloted RCA 540,000.]
>
> . . . from Korea during the period February 1, 1979, to October 31, 1979: 153,000 complete and incomplete sets; and from November 1, 1979 to June 30, 1980: 136,000 complete and incomplete sets.

During the negotiations RCA was anxious to ensure that subassemblies like circuit boards did not get included in the quota. Most of RCA's color circuit boards were assembled in Taiwan (as were all of its black-and-white sets); RCA was the largest single employer in Taiwan. Some U.S. observers argued that one cause for the surge in imports from Taiwan and Korea was Japanese companies diverting U.S. orders to their affiliates in these countries. Another reason was mass merchandisers like Sears and Ward seeking new sources of low-cost supplies. The Japanese indeed participated in Korean, Taiwanese, Canadian, and Singaporean exports to the United States. The only color TV exporting plant in Singapore was owned and controlled by Hitachi. Matsushita had a Canadian facility purchased from Motorola. In the case of Taiwan, the largest complete color TV exporter had always been Admiral, followed by Hitachi. The other significant exporters were Sampo (9.5 percent owned by Sharp) and Tatung (8.3 percent owned by Toshiba). The extent of Japanese control of these firms was not clear.

In Korea the bulk of the output was accounted for by Samsung and Gold Star, both of which were large conglomerates. Sanyo (Japan) had a 40 percent participation in Samsung's color TV venture, while NEC (Japan) owned 20 percent of Gold Star's. However, some observers argued that there was no Japanese control over the Korean companies, with the Japanese participation being limited to technical assistance and providing manufacturing equipment.

After the signing of the OMA with Japan in 1977, all the Japanese manufacturers announced plans to set up plants in the United States. MITI discouraged this, according to press reports, to no avail. In 1978 both Toshiba and Mitsubishi opened facilities in the United States. The Hitachi-GE agreement fell through and Hitachi was building a U.S. plant in California in 1979. Sharp had decided not to build a U.S. plant in 1978 but changed its mind in 1979.

Other Legal Developments. The Treasury was the subject of increasing criticism from the U.S. TV industry for failing to act on the dumping issue. In March the Treasury used a legally untested commodity tax formula to assess $46 million in duties for sets imported in 1972 and the first half of 1973. If the formula held up, approximately $400 million would be due on sets imported since then. The Japanese government protested the use of the formula, calling it incorrect. The Japanese manufacturers refused to pay and lodged protests. The Treasury suspended its assessment of post-1973 liabilities to deal with the protests. Sears was the only major importer to pay in 1978, and that payment was under protest as well. Meanwhile, the Supreme Court heard the countervailing duty case and ruled in favor of the Treasury and against Zenith. The case ended there.

Overview of Product Technology Changes

Picture tubes had changed when the delta three-electron gun configuration was replaced by the in-line configuration. In-line tubes required fewer adjustments and reduced needed circuitry. Changes in the tube mask had led to brighter pictures. The move was pioneered by Sony with its Trinitron set. By 1972 most manufacturers had adopted slotted masks with vertical phosphor stripes, which could be viewed as a variant of Sony's system. Another innovation that gained universal acceptance was surrounding the color phosphor dots on the screen with a black matrix, thus increasing contrast. Zenith's Chromacolor was the first such tube.

Color TV circuitry began to change when transistors first started replacing vacuum tubes in the 1960s. Transistors reduced the power consumption by about 50 percent, increased the reliability, and also opened up the possibility for automated insertion in manufacturing. The next major change was integrated circuits (ICs), which combined the functions of many components. The use of ICs reduced component counts and facilitated automated insertion even more.

In the early 1970s tuners changed from mechanical to electronic, reducing the need for manual adjustments and making "touch tuning" or electronic tuning" possible. Electronic tuning also simplified remote control tuning devices. Until the early 1970s remote control units had operated by using ultrasonics. These units could be fooled by spurious sounds, however, and were increasingly replaced by units that sent their information on infrared light waves.

In 1977 microprocessors began to be used in TVs. With microprocessors, sets could be programmed to turn on and off on different channels at particular times, for example. The capabilities of microprocessor units were expected to continue to expand.

Overview of Process Technology Changes

In the late 1960s the Japanese were by and large regarded as lagging behind their U.S. and European competitors in the areas of set design and labor productivity. By the late 1970s the situation had been reversed. By reducing component counts and aggressively automating production, the Japanese produced a more reliable product and attained a low cost position as shown in Exhibit 25–7.

The genesis of the Japanese advantage was in 1970, when all Japanese color set manufacturers switched to 100 percent solid-state chassis. Subsequently they were able to reduce component counts through extensive use of integrated circuits, early use of in-line tubes, and single circuit board designs. Labor cost savings were achieved by Japanese firms both through reduced component counts and use of automated insertion and testing. In contrast, use of more labor-intensive multiple circuit boards and modules were prevalent in the United States and Europe because they were easier (and less expensive) to service.

Automatic insertion was the most important process technology innovation since the adoption of printed circuit boards. Developed first in the United States in the mid-1950s, the early machines were used en masse by the radio divisions of automobile companies, like GM's Delmonico Division, to insert components into the relatively simple circuit boards used in auto radios. These early machines, however, were incapable of handling the far more complex circuit boards in TVs. As machines were improved during the 1960s and their insertion speeds went up, several U.S. companies, like RCA and Magnavox, experimented with a few units, without success. The machines were plagued by the fact that each machine could handle only a particular shape and size of component, necessitating an entire sequence of machines to insert all the varied components on a circuit board. In addition to the expense, whenever one machine jammed the entire line was held up. Another problem was that manufacturers had not understood how to design their circuit board layouts with the needs of production in mind, and so many of the designs were simply not amenable to automatic insertion.

It was not until 1969 that the first variable center distance (VCD) machine was developed. This could handle any sequence of any components and was easily programmed and controlled via a computer. It could therefore insert nearly all the components on a circuit board. A few U.S. TV companies experimented with these VCDs, but they still hadn't learned how to design to take advantage of automation. At this time the changeover to solid-state also necessitated constantly changing designs, and as a result no economies were achieved. Meanwhile RCA was pursuing its own direction with its ceramic circuit modules, which used a fundamentally different technology. The first U.S. company to use automatic insertion on a plantwide basis was Zenith, which converted its Chicago plant in 1973. Though it seemed to have considerable success, in 1977 Zenith followed the lead of all other U.S. manufacturers and shifted much of its color circuit board production to manual, low wage rate offshore plants. It was only toward the late 1970s that U.S. manufacturers began adopting more automation, including the offshore plants, because of the increased reliability that this led to.

The adoption of automatic-insertion machines, and automation in general, had followed a different pattern in Japan. Around 1969 Hitachi, Matsushita, and TDK (not a TV manufacturer) had developed automatic-insertion machines for their own use. Though Matsushita and TDK also began selling their machines on the open market, most of the other Japanese TV manufacturers began buying U.S.-made VCDs. The Japanese were very successful in meshing circuit board designs with the needs of automation. By the time the oil crisis struck in late 1973, they were ready for a wholesale conversion to automatic insertion. By 1975 the conversion was nearly total, with approximately 80 percent of all components in Japanese sets being inserted by machine. The Japanese also used automation in all their offshore plants in the United States, Europe, and elsewhere.

The switch to transistors, ICs, and automated production had also increased reliability. This was improved even more by the Japanese practice of extensive pretesting of components. Increased reliability allowed the Japanese to switch to the single circuit board designs, because service costs were not nearly so important since the set rarely failed. Single circuit boards further reduced component counts.

Large scale was not necessary for automatic insertion, which was feasible in plants with capacities under 100,000 color sets per year. As plant volume increased, an increasing number of material handling operations could be automated. At volumes of 500,000 or more color sets a year, some Japanese manufacturers had even automated operations such as final assembly, tuning, testing, and packaging. Above 500,000 units per year, however, most experts believed that no further manufacturing economies were gained. Scale could also provide economies of purchasing. Over the 50,000 to 250,000 set per year production range, component costs could be reduced approximately 5 percent for every doubling of volume. The purchasing cost saving was greater for ICs (around 25 percent) and less for color picture tubes.

The Japanese firms emphasized permanent or long-term relationships with their suppliers, unlike U.S. firms, which had multiple suppliers and less permanent relationships. The long-term relationships gave Japanese component manufacturers the incentive to invest in automatic testing equipment and to strive for high component reliability.

Total company production volume became important above the 500,000 unit level for spreading development costs of color picture tubes and IC designs. Development costs for a new color TV model were estimated at $300,000 to $400,000, while retooling costs for producing the model were about $1 million.

By 1979 U.S.-based production was intrinsically no less competitive than the sets imported from Japan, owing to rapid increases in Japanese wage rates.

The U.S. Manufacturers' Shift Overseas

Every major U.S. manufacturer had established manufacturing facilities in low wage rate areas such as Mexico, Taiwan, and Singapore by 1973. The trend had been to start with labor intensive assembly of black-and-white portable TVs and certain other subassemblies such as tuners. This was generally followed by assembly of printed circuit boards and/or modules for color TV, sometimes eventually followed by entire chassis assembly.

In 1978 one source estimated that RCA, GE, GTE, and Zenith had an average of 50 percent of their value added abroad.[17] Table 25–1 gives estimates of when offshore TV-related plants were started by U.S. firms.

In 1979 RCA imported color chassis (incomplete) from its facilities in Taiwan and Mexico, having shifted production in a big way in 1975. Zenith imported color modules from Mexico and Taiwan, having made the move in 1977. GE produced color chassis and parts in Singapore. Magnavox imported from Philips's Taiwan plant. In addition, all black-and-white sets were obtained from offshore plants.

Japanese Manufacturing in the United States

By 1979 all the major Japanese firms were manufacturing color TV sets in the U.S. market. Exhibit 25–8 summarizes their participation. Japanese companies generally sourced their color picture tubes from U.S. companies because of high duties on tubes (15 percent) and relatively high transport costs on the larger tubes, except for Sony, which had its own proprietary tube. Matsushita (Quasar) sourced from both RCA and Sylvania, while Sanyo (Warwick) purchased predominantly from RCA. Sylvania had been Warwick's traditional supplier.

The Japanese had not restricted themselves to

---

[17] *Sources of Competitiveness in the Japanese Color Television and Video Tape Recorder Industry,* Developing World Industry & Technology, Inc.

TABLE 25–1.   **Start-up Dates of Offshore TV Production**

Company	Mexico	Taiwan	Singapore	Hong Kong
RCA	pre-1970	1970	—	—
Zenith	1972	1971	—	—
Motorola	1970	1970	—	—
GTE	1973	1975	—	1969
Philco	—	1966	—	—
Admiral	1974	1967	—	—
GE	—	—	1971	—
Warwick	pre-1970	—	—	—
Magnavox	1972	—	—	—

producing color TVs, and many had begun or were about to begin making a number of other products in the United States, including microwave ovens, stereos, and some appliances, such as vacuum cleaners and small refrigerators.

Recent Legal Developments

The antidumping case had become very complicated. After numerous extensions of the payment deadline, the U.S. Treasury Department had received only $6 million. In May the Electronic Industries Association (EIA) tube division and COMPACT sued the Carter administration to force collection in cash of the $600 million allegedly owed. In June the Treasury asked Justice to collect roughly $40 million. In August the EIA/COMPACT case was rejected for having been filed in the wrong court (District Court instead of Customs). EIA/COMPACT appealed the decision. In September the Justice Department filed seven civil suits to collect the amounts owed. In November the Treasury announced that it had processed the protests and decided that the assessments had to be reduced.

In December EIA and COMPACT petitioned the International Trade Commission to extend the OMAs, arguing that the concept had become effective only in 1979 after Taiwan and Korea also signed. The ITC planned for hearings in March 1980.

EXHIBIT 25-1. Financial Performance of Selected TV Set Competitors, 1970-1978 (dollars in millions)

	1970	1971	1972	1973	1974	1975	1976	1977	1978
General Electric									
Sales	$ 8,726.7	$ 9,425.3	$10,240.0	$11,575.3	$13,413.1	$13,399.1	$15,697.0	$17,519.0	$19,654.0
Depreciation	334.7	273.6	314.3	334.0	376.2	418.6	386.2	522.1	576.4
Net income	328.5	471.8	530.0	585.1	608.1	580.8	930.6	1,008.2	1,229.7
Return on sales (%)	3.8%	5.0%	5.2%	5.1%	4.5%	4.3%	5.9%	6.2%	6.3%
Return on equity (%)	14.2%	18.2%	18.6%	19.6%	19.0%	14.9%	17.7%	14.8%	15.9%
Marketable securities	149.9	35.9	27.3	25.3	57.3	100.3	554.3	560.3	470.3
Debt to total capital	22.4	21.7	23.2	21.1	24.0	20.0	19.8	17.5	12.9
Capital expenditures	581.4	553.1	435.9	598.6	671.8	448.2	740.4	822.5	1,055.1
Dividend payout	.72	.53	.48	.47	.48	.51	.36	.44	.46
Research and development	NA	250.0	300.0	300.7	351.9	357.1	411.5	463.5	520.8
Magnavox[a]									
Sales	$ 547.1	$ 627.9	$ 685.0	$ 620.2	$ 519.1	$ 1,431.0	$ 1,724.0	$ 1,917.0	$ 2,184.0
Depreciation	12.2	12.6	14.5	11.8	13.3	26.7	28.0	31.2	
Net income	27.8	34.7	20.7	53.3	(14.9)	31.4	57.4	61.2	68.0
Return on sales (%)	5.1%	5.4%	2.6%	1.1%	(2.9)%	2.2%	3.5%	3.2%	3.1%
Return on equity (%)	14.9%	17.2%	9.8%	2.6%	(4.5)%	3.6%	6.3%	6.0%	5.7%
Marketable securities	4.04	1.49	—	2.0	—	26.8	28.1	—	—
Debt to total capital	12.25	10.14	9.61	19.04	24.13	28.36	25.63	25.06	31.5
Capital expenditures	17.7	11.2	16.2	3.7	10.9	34.72	37.9	51.2	65.35
Dividend payout	.71	.60	1.03	.25	(1.18)	.43	.26	.42	.33
Research and development	NA	NA	NA	NA	NA	NA	NA	NA	NA
Motorola[b]									
Sales	$ 796.4	$ 926.6	$ 1,163.0	$ 1,203.0	$ 1,367.1				
Depreciation	32.8	34.4	37.9	42.9	43.5				
Net income	24.24	31.75	52.04	82.0	70.78				
Return on sales (%)	3.22%	3.43%	4.47%	5.7%	5.7%				
Return on equity (%)	7.23%	8.82%	12.76%	17.03%	15.66%				
Marketable securities	6.07	4.23	30.1	21.98	7.6				
Debt to total capital	16.95	14.51	15.45	22.31	11.12				
Capital expenditures	33.5	44.1	54.7	92.5	62.3				
Dividend payout	.32	.25	.16	.15	.22				
Research and development	NA	NA	NA	NA	NA				

EXHIBIT 25-1. (continued)

Philco/Ford[c]

	1970	1971	1972	1973	1974	1975	1976	1977	1978
Sales	$14,979.9	$16,430.0	$20,194.0	$23,015.1	$23,620.6				
Depreciation	413.6	823.6	913.3	948.2	923.5				
Net income	515.7	656.7	870.0	906.5	327.1				
Return on sales (%)	3.44%	4.0%	4.31%	3.94%	1.38%				
Return on equity (%)	9.65%	11.92%	15.12%	14.66%	5.17%				
Marketable securities	600.0	795.2	1,107.3	647.8	371.7				
Debt to total capital	7.71	12.63	14.29	13.23	19.13				
Capital expenditures	413.81	823.8	913.5	948.7	924.0				
Dividend payout	.50	.40	.31	.35	.91				
Research and development									

RCA

	1970	1971	1972	1973	1974	1975	1976	1977	1978
Sales	$ 3,317.3	$ 3,529.8	$ 3,838.2	$ 4,246.8	$4,594.3	$ 4,789.6	$ 5,363.6	$ 5,880.9	$ 6,600.6
Depreciation	190.0	201.8	229.9	232.4	259.8	271.7	300.2	332.0	363.8
Net income	91.3	(115.9)	158.1	183.7	113.3	110.0	117.4	247.0	278.4
Return on sales (%)	2.76%	(4.41)%	4.12%	4.32%	2.47%	2.30%	3.33%	4.1%	4.1%
Return on equity (%)	8.13%	10.07%	15.56%	16.45%	9.85%	9.44%	14.4%	18.24%	9.77%
Marketable securities	91.1	91.6	252.2	147.9	167.7	173.8	79.2	204.0	171.0
Debt to total capital	46.81	52.34	51.25	47.23	43.96	44.8	42.89	42.92	41.15
Capital expenditures	557.5	489.7	463.6	621.3	749.4	667.6	767.1	542.5	699.7
Dividend payout	.79	.85	.51	.43	.70	.73	.45	.38	.38
Research and development	126.7	129.6	87.8	103.8	110.1	113.6	111.9	126.5	140.5

Admiral[d]

	1970	1971	1972	1973	1974	1975	1976	1977	1978
Sales	$ 8.73	$ 9.43	$ 10.24	$ 11.58	$ 4,257.0	$ 4,804.0	$ 5,195.0	$ 859.0	$ 5,668.8
Depreciation	8.69	7.58	6.09	6.64	98.30	115.5	118.6	120.4	119.8
Net income	(14.32)	4.82	10.69	9.72	130.3	101.6	122.2	144.1	176.6
Return on sales (%)	(3.89)%	1.18%	2.28%	1.86%	3.06%	2.11%	2.35%	1.33%	3.12%
Return on equity (%)	(18.29)%	6.94%	13.15%	9.8%	12.77%	9.19%	10.61%	11.84%	13.04%
Marketable securities	1.5	—	1.33	2.19	0.8	3.0	9.2	9.6	7.1
Debt to total capital	31.22	32.43	25.91	19.9	35.5	38.8	31.6	39.3	34.18
Capital expenditures	15.79	(5.82)	11.34	13.66	217.3	202.3	98.6	196.0	218.9
Dividend payout	—	—	—	—	.44	.61	.59	.66	.46
Research and development	NA	NA	NA	NA	31.0	77.8	86.3	97.0	124.4

EXHIBIT 25-1. *(continued)*

	1970	1971	1972	1973	1974	1975	1976	1977	1978
GTE-Sylvania									
Sales	$ 3,439.2	$ 3,836.8	$ 4,326.7	$ 5,105.3	$ 5,661.5	$ 5,948.4	$ 6,750.9	$ 7,680.1	$ 8,723.5
Depreciation	354.8	398.6	454.1	523.6	569.2	633.6	722.7	806.3	902.5
Net income	215.5	260.4	295.0	352.1	272.7	388.2	453.2	559.7	627.2
Return on sales (%)	6.3%	6.8%	6.8%	6.6%	6.5%	6.1%	6.3%	6.8%	6.8%
Return on equity (%)	5.78%	9.47%	12.69%	17.65%	16.82%	10.9%	14.46%	15.69%	16.0%
Marketable securities	NA	NA	NA	NA	NA	NA	NA	NA	NA
Debt to total capital	56.7	57.9	56.4	53.9	53.1	51.7	49.5	47.0	46.3
Capital expenditures	1,022.8	1,202.5	1,239.0	1,411.1	1,480.0	1,372.3	1,568.3	1,746.1	2,080.9
Dividend payout	.25	.53	1.09	.55	.47	.48	.38	.54	.55
Research and development	354.8	398.6	454.1	523.6	569.2	633.6	722.7	806.3	902.5
Teledyne[e]									
Sales	$ 1,216.0	$ 1,102.0	$ 1,216.0	$ 1,455.0	$ 1,700.0				
Depreciation	31.8	33.4	36.4	46.3	47.5				
Net income	64.1	56.2	57.4	65.4	31.14				
Return on sales (%)	5.27%	5.1%	4.72%	4.49%	1.83%				
Return on equity (%)	11.75%	9.27%	8.76%	10.71%	6.04%				
Marketable securities	0.42	6.89	9.5	25.3	54.14				
Debt to total capital	25.46	30.99	38.9	44.88	42.32				
Capital expenditures	35.5	23.0	47.5	45.7	30.4				
Dividend payout	.09	.08	.07	.06	.15				
Research and development	NA	NA	NA	NA	NA				
Zenith									
Sales	$ 573.1	$ 613.1	$ 795.9	$ 1,007.2	$ 910.5	$ 900.5	$ 978.2	$ 965.6	$ 980.0
Depreciation	12.5	11.3	13.3	14.4	15.9	15.2	16.8	17.3	16.0
Net income	24.7	37.4	48.6	55.0	13.2	30.8	38.6	(4.7)	23.3
Return on sales (%)	4.3%	5.1%	6.1%	5.5%	1.3%	2.9%	3.9%	(4.9)%	2.4%
Return on equity (%)	11.03%	16.38%	19.82%	20.38%	4.12%	11.2%	13.7%	(1.67)%	6.8%
Marketable securities	83.9	83.1	95.4	13.4	1.13	6.6	28.32	16.03	7.8
Debt to total capital	—	3.21	2.52	2.64	3.52	15.12	14.6	15.68	15.49
Capital expenditures	8.5	13.7	14.6	47.1	40.9	21.3	30.0	22.5	17.1
Dividend payout	.77	.51	.39	.34	2.3	.61	.49	(4.01)	.81
Research and development	NA	NA	NA	NA	NA	NA	NA	NA	NA

[a] Magnavox acquired by North American Philips in 1974. Post-1974 figures include N.A. Philips performance.

[b] Motorola purchased by Matsushita, 1974.

[c] Philco brand name sold to GTE-Sylvania, 1974.

[d] Acquired by Rockwell International, April 1974. Post-1973 figures include Rockwell International performance. Phased out TV operations, 1978.

[e] Packard-Bell, a subsidiary of Teledyne, suspended TV manufacturing in 1974.

SOURCE: Annual reports.

506

EXHIBIT 25-2. *Demand Composition (millions of units)*

	1970	1971	1972	1973	1974	1975	1976	1977	1978
Factory production and imports									
Black-and-white (units)	6.90	7.65	8.24	7.30	6.87	4.42	5.94	6.09	6.73
Color (units)	5.32	7.27	8.85	10.07	8.41	6.22	8.19	9.34	10.67
Black-and-white (dollars)	$ 518.00	$ 621.00	$ 649.00	$ 560.00	$ 543.00	$ 371.00	$ 528.00	$ 542.00	$ 572.00
Color (dollars)	$1684.00	$2355.00	$2825.00	$3097.00	$2658.00	$2121.00	$2860.00	$3269.00	$3736.00
B&W market by type (units)									
Table & portable	6.37	7.33	7.85	6.79	5.79	4.89	5.13	5.62	6.03
Consoles & combinations	.38	.34	.29	.25	.15	.08	.06	.05	.04
Color market by type (units)									
Table & portable	3.01	4.38	5.34	6.08	5.30	4.40	5.43	6.60	7.62
Console	2.27	2.58	2.96	3.12	2.49	2.06	2.25	2.48	2.60
Combinations	.14	.15	.08	.07	.04	.03	.03	.03	.02
Replacement market									
Black-and-white (% of unit sales)	54.00	59.00	58.00	82.00	59.00	53.00	50.00	65.00	63.00
Color (% of unit sales)	39.00	41.00	50.00	60.00	64.00	65.00	64.00	64.00	76.00
Imports (units)									
Black-and-white total	3.60	4.17	5.06	4.99	4.66	2.97	4.33	4.91	5.93
Color total	.91	1.28	1.32	1.40	1.28	1.21	2.83	2.54	2.78
Private label (units)									
Black-and-white, U.S.-made	.17	.40	.54	.46	.37	.24	.14[a]	NA	NA
Black-and-white, imported	1.31	.38	.43	1.06	.66	.74	.70[a]	NA	NA
Color, U.S.-made	.54	.50	.78	.85	1.02	.66	.36[a]	NA	NA
Color, imported	.38	.01	.25	.25	.31	.39	.65[a]	NA	NA
Wholesale price index (1967 = 100)									
Black-and-white portables	94.7	94.9	93.2	91.6	93.2	97.8	95.4	89.4	87.5[b]
Color consoles	88.8	90.2	88.4	85.6	85.0	87.3	87.3	83.7	82.3[b]
Programming:									
Total TV stations on air (no.)	862	881	906	927	938	953	960	972	982
Cable TV systems (no.)	2490	2639	2841	2991	3158	3506	3681	3832	3997
Cable subscribers (millions)	4.5	5.3	6.0	7.3	8.7	9.8	10.8	11.9	13.0
Saturation (% of households owning)									
Black-and-white (total)	98.7	99.8	99.8	99.9	99.9	99.9	99.9	99.9	99.9
1st set	57.9	52.4	45.3	38.3	31.4	28.3	NA	NA	NA
2nd set	36.8	39.4	45.6	52.7	58.3	NA	NA	NA	NA
Color (total)	42.5	51.1	60.7	67.1	71.5	74.4	77.7	81.3	85.2
1st set	37.3	43.1	50.5	57.7	64.7	68.8	NA	NA	NA
2nd set	2.2	2.8	3.9	5.1	6.8	NA	NA	NA	NA

[a] Annualized from nine months.
[b] December.

SOURCES: EIA; U.S. Bureau of the Census; U.S. ITC; *Merchandising;* U.S. Bureau of Labor; *TV Factbook.*

EXHIBIT 25-3. *Distribution Channels for TV, 1976*[a] *(units in thousands)*

Type of Outlet	Color Sets	Black-and-White Sets	Total TV Sales	Percent
Appliance-radio-TV store	3,696	1,715	5,411	42 %
Department store	1,386	935	2,321	18 %
Discount store	539	935	1,474	11.4%
Catalog showroom	154	260	414	3.2%
Furniture store	539	312	851	6.6%
Catalog chains	1,386	1,039	2,425	18.8%
Total for all outlets	7,700	5,195	12,896	100.0%

[a]The distribution of sales by channel was similar in 1977 and 1978.

SOURCE: *Merchandising.*

EXHIBIT 25-4. *U.S. Market Share Estimates*

A. Black-and-White TV (percent of units)

Company or Brand	1970[a]	1971	1972	1973	1974	1975	1976	1977	1978	1979
Zenith	14.5	14.4	13.2	17.0	17.8	17.0	18.0	17.0	17.4	16.05
RCA	12.4	11.1	10.6	12.0	12.0	13.2	14.0	14.0	14.0	14.5
Matsushita										
Panasonic	—	—	10.8	8.0	7.8	6.2	8.0	10.0	8.7	7.4
Quasar						7.1	5.0	5.0	5.5	4.0
Motorola	4.1	3.6	3.8	6.0	6.0					
General Electric	7.6	8.5	9.3	11.0	11.9	11.6	11.0	10.0	9.5	10.0
Sears	6.7	7.2	7.9	9.0	8.8	9.0	9.0	9.8	10.0	9.0
GTE										
Sylvania	—	—	2.45	2.45	2.35	3.5	3.0	2.5	2.0	2.1
Philco						3.5	3.0	2.8	2.4	2.2
Philco-Ford	3.5	3.3	3.3	4.8	4.3					
Sony	—	—	5.1	4.0	3.2	4.1	4.0	4.0	4.0	4.1
Admiral	5.2	4.6	4.6	5.6	5.0	4.0	5.7	4.3	3.4	2.5
Sanyo	—	—	.95	1.5	1.1	1.3	1.35	1.9	2.3	2.9
Montgomery Ward	—	—	1.6	1.7	1.9	1.8	2.7	3.0	2.5	2.5
Sharp	—	—	2.3	2.2	1.8	1.7	2.3	2.5	2.9	2.0
Hitachi	—	—	1.45	1.5	1.9	1.35	1.45	2.2	2.45	2.0
Penncrest (Penney)	—	—	1.65	1.45	1.65	1.6	1.55	1.7	1.9	1.9
Magnavox	4.1	3.9	3.3	4.0	3.1	2.25	2.0	2.0	1.5	1.7
Toshiba	—	—	—	—	—	—	0.5	0.55	0.6	0.5
MGA (Mitsubishi)	—	—	—	—	—	—	0.1	0.3	0.35	0.45
Packard-Bell	—	—	1.0	0.7	0.4	0.1				

[a] Years refer to model years (July to June).

SOURCES: *Television Digest* and others.

B. Color TV (*percent of units*)

Company or Brand	1970[a]	1971	1972	1973	1974	1975	1976	1977	1978	1979
Zenith	20.6	19.9	19.1	22.5	23.8	24.0	23.0	22.0	21.15	20.0
RCA	22.8	20.8	20.5	20.3	20.5	19.0	20.0	20.0	20.0	21.0
Sears	7.1	8.7	8.5	7.8	7.5	8.7	9.0	9.0	8.55	7.9
Magnavox	9.5	10.0	8.9	8.0	6.8	6.6	6.5	7.0	7.0	7.2
Matsushita										
Panasonic	—	—	3.2	2.1	2.0	2.3	2.5	3.0	2.9	2.2
Quasar						5.9	5.0	5.0	5.3	5.0
Motorola	5.7	5.2	7.0	8.0	6.8	—	—	—	—	—
General Electric	4.6	5.2	5.3	6.0	6.0	6.2	5.5	6.0	6.5	6.9
Sony	—	—	3.3	4.0	5.0	5.8	7.0	7.5	6.9	6.5
GTE										
Sylvania	4.6	4.3	4.5	5.0	5.0	4.4	4.5	4.0	3.5	3.9
Philco						1.0	1.5	1.5	1.45	1.2
Philco-Ford	—	—	3.0	2.9	3.1					
Admiral	5.0	4.3	4.2	3.5	3.5	3.0	3.5	2.5	2.4	1.5
Montgomery Ward	—	—	1.0	1.3	1.8	2.4	2.1	2.0	2.0	2.1
Sanyo	—	—	0.5	0.5	0.7	1.2	1.3	1.8	2.0	2.0
Hitachi	—	—	0.7	0.8	0.9	0.8	1.0	1.6	1.65	1.85
Sharp	—	—	0.9	0.9	0.65	0.65	1.7	2.0	2.0	1.5
Pencrest (Penney)	—	—	1.0	1.25	1.3	1.6	1.45	1.45	1.5	1.5
Toshiba	—	—	—	—	—	—	0.65	0.9	1.0	1.0
MGA (Mitsubishi)	—	—	—	—	—	—	0.4	0.8	1.0	1.0
Curtis-Mathes	—	—	—	—	—	—	1.4	1.3	1.2	1.0
Packard-Bell	—	—	0.7	0.7	0.7					

[a] Years refer to model years (July to June)

SOURCES: *Television Digest* and others.

EXHIBIT 25-5. *Import Penetration (units in thousands)*

	1970	1971	1972	1973	1974	1975	1976	1977	1978	1979 (11 months)
Black-and-white sets – total	3,596	4,166	5,056	4,989	4,659	2,975	4,327	4,908	4,931	5,453
Japan	2,467	2,609	1,654	877	775	647	1,385	1,662	1,751	544
Taiwan	} 871 {	208	532	1,235	1,468	566	1,360	1,291	NA }	3,212
using U.S. parts[a]		1,040	2,196	2,071	1,842	1,532	1,265	1,218	NA }	
Korea	} 273 {	44	105	336	403	231	432	765	NA	1,661
Mexico		1	4	–	–	–	–	–	NA	NA
using U.S. parts		309	435	350	30	NA	NA	NA	NA	NA
Color sets – total	914	1,281	1,318	1,399	1,282	1,215	2,834	2,539	2,775	1,309
Japan	850	1,191	1,094	1,058	917	1,042	2,530	2,030	1,430	494
Taiwan	} 52 {	62	130	201	135	76	152	159 }	625	345
using U.S. parts		23	83	124	202	67	75	144 }		
Korea	–	–	10	2	22	22	55	98	435	305
Singapore	–	–	–	–	–	–	3	14	61	68
Canada	11	4	–	1	1	2	16	72	218	88
Black-and-white sets unassembled or unfinished – total	NA	NA	NA	NA	NA	NA	156	105	NA	NA
Taiwan	NA	NA	NA	NA	NA	NA	29	30	NA	NA
using U.S. parts	NA	NA	NA	NA	NA	NA	118	69	NA	NA
Color sets unassembled or unfinished – total	NA	NA	NA	NA	NA	NA	461	692	NA	NA
Japan	NA	NA	NA	NA	NA	NA	152	87	NA	NA
using U.S. parts	NA	NA	NA	NA	NA	NA	–	7	NA	NA
Mexico	NA	NA	NA	NA	NA	NA	5	1	NA	NA
using U.S. parts	NA	NA	NA	NA	NA	NA	298	586	NA	NA

[a] "Using U.S. parts" refers to imports entering under Tariff Provision 807.00, which allows sets using U.S. parts to be charged duty only on the value added abroad.

SOURCE: U.S. Bureau of the Census.

EXHIBIT 25-6. *Effect of Government Policy on Japanese Import Cost Structure*

	12" mono		19" mono		18" color	
	6/30/71	11/1/71	6/30/71	11/1/71	6/30/71	11/1/71
Net FOB price	$43.41	$47.03	$57.32	$62.09	$176.73	$191.45
Freight, insurance, brokers' fees	3.19	3.46	5.75	6.23	10.41	11.28
U.S. import duty (6%)	2.60	2.82	3.44	3.72	10.60	11.49
U.S. import surcharge (10%)	–	4.70	–	6.21	–	19.15
U.S. handling charges	.75	.75	1.99	1.99	2.65	2.65
Net importer cost	$49.94	$58.76	$68.50	$80.24	$200.39	$236.02

SOURCE: *Television Digest.*

EXHIBIT 25-7. *Comparative Cost and Reliability of U.S. and Foreign Color TV Sets, 1977*

A. Comparative color TV Set Costs (*figures on per set basis*)

	Japan	U.S	South Korea	West Germany	U.K.
Average man-hours	1.9	3.6	5.0	3.9	6.1
Employment costs (£/hour)	3.0	2.45	0.3	3.85	1.74
Direct labor costs (£)	5.7	8.8	1.5	15.1	10.6
Material costs (£)	100.0	NA	113.0	119.0	126.0
Plant overheads (£)	11.0	NA	2.0	17.0	20.0
Total production costs (£)	116.7	NA	116.5	151.1	156.5

SOURCE: Casewriter estimates from unpublished internal studies.

B. Comparative Color TV Reliability Measures

	Japan	U.S.	U.K.
Field call rate (calls per set)	.09–.26	1–2	1.2–3
Production fall-off rate (faults per set on assembly line)	.01–.03	1.4–2	1.8–2.9

SOURCE: *Industrial Policy in Japan.*

EXHIBIT 25-8. *U.S. Color TV Production by Japanese Firms (units in thousands)*

	1973	1974	1975	1976	1977	1978	1979	1980	1981
Sony	130	250	275	370	400	450	475	800[a]	
Matsushita	–	–	300	400	460	600	700	720[a]	
Sanyo	–	–	–	–	300	600	680	950[a]	
Toshiba	–	–	–	–	–	60	175	500[a]	
Mitsubishi	–	–	–	–	–	60	120	120[a]	240[a]
Hitachi	–	–	–	–	–	–	20	120[a]	
Sharp	–	–	–	–	–	–	100	360[a]	
	130	250	575	770	1160	1770	2270	3570[a]	

[a]Figures are end-of-year capacities.

SOURCE: Industry interviews.

CASE 26

The Television Set Industry in 1979: Japan, Europe, and Newly Industrializing Countries

While the television set market was maturing in the United States, activity had also been occurring elsewhere in the world. This case describes the development of the TV set markets in Japan and Europe, as well as the positions of the chief European and Japanese TV set competitors. It also describes the recent growth of the industry in other newly industrializing Southeast Asian nations besides Japan. Background data on the TV set industry is contained in Case 24 and Case 25.

Development of the Japanese TV Set Market

As early as 1933 Professor Kenjiro Takayanagi was at work in Japan researching all-electronic television, and Japan began some experimental broadcasting in the late 1930s. As in other countries, however, World War II halted all ideas of commercialization of TV. After the war, with an economy in shambles, Japan's planners decided that promo-

tion of the electronics industry was essential to the nation's progress and sought to start TV broadcasting as soon as possible. In the fall of 1945 the Ministry of Communications (later renamed the Ministry of Postal Services) began efforts to reopen experimental broadcasting. Initially the Occupation Command banned all research on TV and radar, but in June 1946 it relented and allowed research on closed-circuit TV. This was the beginning of postwar TV research in Japan. At the end of 1946 the researchers formed an informal group, which evolved into the Academy of Television in 1948. Later in 1948 manufacturers, namely Toshiba, Nichiden, Victor, and Columbia, formed a group and began conducting experiments in conjunction with NHK (the Japanese Government Broadcasting Network) on closed-circuit TV. This group evolved into a TV Committee, and by February 1950 the Occupation Command had been persuaded to allow over-the-air TV research. Consequently, in February 1950 NHK Technological Research Institute was allowed to open an experimental TV station, broadcasting a picture employing 525 scanning lines. NHK was active in promoting TV through traveling demonstrations around Japan. Manufacturers set out to develop their own TV sets but were plagued by component shortages, the need to divert parts from radio manufacture, and the necessity of importing picture tubes.

In February 1951 TV was demonstrated to the Japanese House of Councillors. In May the House passed a resolution to encourage TV broadcasting—a big step forward. In October 1951 Nippon Television, an independent broadcaster, announced that it was going to set up a TV broadcasting station. In 1952 government, NHK, and industry representatives held discussions on setting a standard for TV broadcasting. The Ministry of Postal Services recommended a bandwidth of 6 MHz, as in the United States, while NHK and the others wanted a 7 MHz bandwidth. The U.S. standard was eventually adopted.

Broadcasting Begins

In July 1952 the first license in Japan was given to the commercial station, Nippon Television. NHK, the government station, received its license on December 26. TV broadcasting began on February 1, 1953, as planned. Many companies had great expectations for the future of TV, and seventy to eighty companies, mainly radio manufacturers, intended to begin manufacturing TV sets. Most of the basic patents on TV were held by three companies: RCA, Philips, and EMI. While Japanese companies had been working on developing TV for several years, they faced considerable difficulties, and in 1952 and 1953 more than forty entered into royalty agreements with RCA to use its patents. On September 15, 1953, the government Committee on Foreign Capital permitted thirty-seven companies to proceed with their plans, wishing to limit investments in TV, and eventually thirty-five manufacturers imported the required technology.

Early TV set prices were extremely high. While the average white-collar worker earned 30,000 yen per month in the early 1950s, TV prices ranged from 175,000 yen for a 14-inch table model TV to 290,000 yen for a 19-inch console. The large receivers that

were on the market in the early days were mostly imported, and those that were not had imported picture tubes. Japanese manufacturers decided to concentrate on 14-inch models because Japanese houses had smaller rooms. By 1954 Japanese companies had developed transformerless TV of the type that Philips was known for in Europe. In 1955 they began using metal cabinets and plastics to reduce costs. As a result TV prices began to fall, and the price of a 14-inch set went from 175,000 yen in 1953 to 70,000 yen in 1957.

Early demand for TV sets was volatile. After several slow years, in the summer of 1955 there was a surge in demand due to the broadcasting of professional wrestling on TV. By the end of the year supply again exceeded demand. Demand picked up in 1956 with the opening of large numbers of local broadcasting stations and continued strongly for a number of years. By 1962, however, no further growth was expected in domestic black-and-white TV shipments due to the high rate of saturation. Replacement and second set purchases were expected to sustain demand but not increase it.

The economy went into recession, and demand for black-and-white sets slumped, hitting a trough in 1965. Replacement sales had not materialized as originally expected. Instead of buying a new set, people simply replaced the picture tube. In 1966 the economy began to recover, and black-and-white sales were aided by rising exports and a rising domestic market for replacements and second sets, particularly transistorized sets. This domestic market continued upward until 1969. After that it was a continuous decline, and black-and-white manufacturers came to rely increasingly on exports. By 1975 black-and-white TV sales in Japan were almost all small, personalized 3-inch and 5-inch sets that began to be combined with cassette players and radios.

Color TV

Research on color TV began in Japan around 1950. In March 1956 NHK held an open house for the general public and demonstrated NTSC (National Television System Committee—the U.S. standard) color TV pictures. In October NHK demonstrated live broadcasting to the general public in Mitsukoshi Department Store, Nahonbashi, Tokyo. In November NHK received a preliminary license for the experimental station with Radio Kyushu TV and Hoddaido TV.

Meanwhile, Japanese TV manufacturers started to produce color TV on an experimental basis. In April 1957 Toshiba made Japan's first 21-inch color TV receiver and exhibited it in public. In collaboration with the Ministry of Postal Services, the Ministry of International Trade and Industry (MITI) established a research committee for color TV that was half government and half private in June 1957. The committee recommended the adoption of the NTSC compatible color system using the VHF band, like that used in the United States. As a result of the committee's findings the Ministry of Postal Services issued formal color standards in June 1960, and in September 1960 NHK, NTV, Radio Tokyo TV, Asahi Hoso, and Yomiuri TV started regular color telecasting.

Manufacturers already had some technological know-how from producing black-and-white TV. In addition research had been going on to produce domestic color TV sets before actual color TV broadcasting started. In early efforts Japanese manufacturers had to depend on the United States for picture tubes and at least ten other important parts. Special emphasis in Japan was put on the development of domestic expertise in color picture tube manufacture. In 1957, under the leadership of the Radio Wave Technology Association, a committee was set up for the trial production of 17-inch color tubes. The committee included TV manufacturers, component manufacturers, NHK, and academics. MITI provided a 30,000,000-yen subsidy. The NHK technology laboratory made a preproduction 17-inch color tube in 1958, and the trial production committee developed an experimental 17-inch unit in 1960.

Manufacturers began selling color TV receivers in early 1960. The price was very high (500,000 yen), because round 21-inch picture tubes were still imported from the United States for these sets, and volumes were low. Models using locally produced 17-inch color tubes began to appear in the market in September 1960 and cost 400,000 yen. While color TV appeared with fanfare, only several hundred sets were produced by all manufacturers combined, and most were sold for business purposes. In

January 1961 Mitsubishi Electric introduced a new 17-inch model at the price of 350,000 yen. Other manufacturers followed suit, and the price went to 300,000 yen. However, demand did not increase.

Manufacturers had continued working on color picture tube development. In August 1961 Toshiba Electric introduced a color set with a 14-inch picture tube for the first time in the world. Subsequently other manufacturers started to develop 14-inch tubes, and by 1962 each major manufacturer had come up with a 14-inch model. In 1961 Sony imported technology from Paramount of America and tried to produce "Chromatron" color receivers. Sony was the only company that refused to enter the color TV market using shadow-mask tubes.

As production know-how accumulated, 14-inch color sets at 198,000 yen began to appear in December 1961. However, color TVs were still four times as expensive as black-and-white models. Furthermore, not enough TV programs were produced in color and color broadcasting time was short. To increase demand, manufacturers and others petitioned for the reduction of the commodity tax paid by manufacturers on color sets. A 30 percent tax was imposed on 17-inch and 21-inch models, and a 20 percent tax on 14-inch models. However, in April 1962 the tax was reduced to 10 percent on models smaller than 20 inches; 21-inch sets (which used imported color tubes) were still taxed at 30 percent.

Realizing the need to popularize color TV, TV set manufacturers formed a committee for TV promotion in March 1963. The committee asked, through the National Diet (legislature), that Japan Telegraph and Telephone Company establish a nationwide microwave network and that color broadcasting be improved and time extended. In May 1963 the industry committee held a color TV festival in Tokyo, inviting not only the general public but also members of the Diet who belonged to the Committee on Communications.

In January 1964 manufacturers were producing about 500 color sets per month. Anticipating stepped-up demand as a result of the 1964 Tokyo Olympics, outputs were increased sharply and picture tubes were in short supply. By mid-1964 a host of different color tube sizes were being produced or under development. Most of Japan's color TV sets and all the new 16-inch tubes (which became almost standard) were made by Toshiba and Matsushita. The 16-inch models sold for 190,000 yen. Hitachi was producing 14-inch and 17-inch models, and Nippon Columbia had an 11-inch shadow-mask tube, and its sets went on sale in July for around 99,000 yen. In April Mitsubishi began selling a 6-inch set for 92,000 yen. While the Olympics had a wide TV audience, they failed to stimulate demand for color TV, and only 5,000 color sets were in use by late 1964, most in hotel lobbies and other public places.

In order to raise demand, it was again thought essential to bring down the price and to reduce the commodity tax in order to popularize color TV. In July 1965 the presidents of Toshiba, Hitachi, Sony, and Mitsubishi, accompanied by the executive director of the industry committee, visited Prime Minister Sato to petition for a reduction in the commodity tax.

Major manufacturers expected to turn out 100,000 color sets in 1965, nearly double their production of 1964. Much of the output was being exported, Toshiba was reported to be selling between 2,000 and 3,000 sets per month to Sears Roebuck & Co. in the United States. In 1966 the economy began to recover from the severe recession of the preceding two years, and the commodity tax was reduced again effective April 1966. That year major manufacturers of color TV rushed to build full-scale specialized factories to prepare for the surge in domestic demand. Until then, manufacturers had been dependent upon exporting, mainly to the United States. In 1966 color was being telecast for nine program hours per day, and this increased to fifteen program hours per day in 1967. Color set production rose dramatically in 1966 to 520,000 sets, of which 240,000 were for domestic consumption. In 1967 production rose further and topped the 1 million mark.

As color TV spread, concern arose over the high power consumption of vacuum tube sets. Manufacturers approached MITI and asked it to sponsor a multicompany project on the use of transistors in color TV circuits. Under this project different companies were assigned to the task of studying transistor applications in different circuits used in color TV. The results of these studies were then circulated among all the companies. Consequently hybrid models began to appear in the market in 1968. In May 1969 the world's first all-transistor color TV was introduced by Hitachi. With nine such models ranging from 13 inches to 25 inches, Hitachi gained considerably in the market. In 1970 most of the important models of all manufacturers became all-transistor. All-transistor models consumed one-half to one-third the power and were more reliable and easier to service. Consequently all-transistor sets spread very rapidly.

Everything progressed smoothly in the Japanese industry until the second half of 1970. Then, dumping allegations in the United States crimped color TV exports. Simultaneously Japanese consumers picked up on the large differences in retail price that U.S. manufacturers claimed existed between a Japanese set sold in the United States and its equivalent sold in Japan. Japanese consumers were also incensed by the dual-pricing system under which color TVs sold through large discount houses (primarily in the cities) retailed at much lower prices than TVs sold through smaller, generally manufacturer-controlled retail outlets in rural areas (the latter sold at manufacturers' list prices). The consumer protest manifested itself in a joint boycott by five consumer groups beginning in September 1970, which cut sharply into domestic color set sales. MITI, concerned by the situation, "suggested" that the list prices be cut by at least 15 percent. In response, each manufacturer announced a reduction in list price between January and March 1971, eroding the differential that had existed under the dual-pricing system. In the fall of 1971 consumers lifted their boycott.

With the end of the boycott domestic shipments recovered, reaching an all-time high in 1971. Meanwhile MITI sponsored another multicompany research project, this time to study the use of integrated circuits in color TV, and in 1971 manufacturers began replacing transistors with integrated circuits (ICs) in the control circuits. Simultaneously, they embarked on programs to rationalize production processes and after-sales service. Manufacturers also sought to stimulate color set demand through technological add-ons. Matsushita introduced infrared remote control, while General had introduced an ultrasonic unit. Sharp had an electronic channel display that flashed the channel number over half the screen momentarily after changing channels. Toshiba and Matsushita introduced digital tuners. Toshiba, Sanyo, and Sony began using wide-angle tubes in their sets. Meanwhile, the use of ICs continued.

In 1973 the oil crisis struck. Raw material prices shot upward, and shortages developed for many items. Manufacturers were forced to raise prices across the board by about 10 percent in January 1974. Coupled with this, the economy went into a serious recession and consumers cut back on durable good purchases. With plunging demand and an inventory overhang of 1 million sets in the market (by some estimates), competition became fierce. Furthermore, the change to a floating exchange rate system after 1973 continuously eroded the competitiveness of Japanese exports.

Faced with uncertain demand, a cost-price squeeze, material shortages, and rising labor costs, Japanese manufacturers desperately tried to suppress rising costs. By increasing the use of ICs and simplifying circuit designs they reduced component counts by more than 30 percent. Whereas in the past manufacturers had partially automated their production process, computer-controlled automatic-insertion machines were now adopted wholesale. These machines inserted more than 100 components on a circuit board, drastically cut man-hours, and boosted reliability at the same time. During this period Japanese color TVs gained prominence internationally for their high reliability.

Domestic shipments recovered somewhat in 1975 and were more or less level in 1976. Manufacturers expanded both set making and color tube capacity in 1976, and that year a record 10.5 million sets were produced. In 1977 exports fell to 414 million units because of the Orderly Marketing Agreement with the United States, and the Japanese economy remained stagnant, so that domestic shipments fell to 5.3 million units. As a result, a severe price war began in the domestic market that continued into 1978.

An important stimulus to color TV demand in the future was expected to be stereo sound capability. NHK, the dominant and noncommercial government-owned station, had been experimenting with multiplex stereo sound since 1970, in conjunction with set manufacturers. Regular broadcasting with this system commenced in late 1978.

The Japanese Market in 1979

Exhibit 26-1 gives data on the TV set production and demand in Japan. By 1978 black-and-white TV demand had declined to below 1 million units, and most black-and-white sets sold in Japan were small combination units with radios and/or cassette tape units. Color TV demand in Japan had peaked in 1973, and by 1978 the Japanese home market was the most saturated in the world. Since 1973 manufacturers had tried to stimulate domestic sales through technological add-ons like remote control, dual-screen sets, microprocessor-based programmable units, and, most recently, sets capable of receiving stereo multiplex sound. Domestic demand was expected to hold steady at around 5 million units in the forseeable future.

Domestic competition in the TV set industry was vigorous and took place along the dimensions of price, promotion and innovation, as in the United States. There was one major difference however, and that lay in the distribution system. Manufacturers used in-house distributors to sell to approximately 61,000 retailers spread throughout the country and approximately 300 discount stores located in large urban centers. Nearly 70 percent of the retailers were manufacturer franchised. A franchised retailer had very close relations with the manufacturer and carried only that manufacturer's products. In return he received liberal discounts, promotional allowances, and so forth, which often permitted him to sell color sets at up to 10 percent below the suggested retail price. Manufacturers also provided extensive credit as well as technical support and undertook heavy national advertising.

The franchise system worked in part because the manufacturers, namely Matsushita, Toshiba, Hitachi, and Sanyo, were all full-line producers making every type of consumer electronic and household appliance. The franchised retailer thus had no need to turn to another manufacturer for any product. He could, of course, carry noncompeting products like cameras, not made by any of the franchisers. The importance of the franchised retailers is evident from the figures in Table 26-1.

As a result, manufacturers were aggressive in organizing franchised retail outlets. In recent years,

TABLE 26–1. Franchised TV Set Retailers in Japan

Company	Approximate Number of Franchised Retailers in 1975	Approximate Domestic Market Share in Color TV, 1975
Matsushita	21,000	30%
Toshiba	12,000	17%
Hitachi	9,000	15%
Sanyo	6,000	12%
Sony	5,000	10%

however, large discounters and retailers with sufficient financial resources of their own had been expanding their own chain store networks and consequently their market shares.

Relations between the government and set manufacturers in Japan were much closer than between the U.S. government and U.S. manufacturers. Some examples of this have already been mentioned, such as R&D funding, demand-stimulating reductions in the commodity tax, and close cooperation between the set makers and NHK, the government-owned broadcasting station.

The government had also played an important part in advancing Japanese exports. In the 1950s Japanese consumer electronics products enjoyed a worldwide reputation for junkiness, and "made in Japan" was synonymous with poor quality. To remedy this situation, in 1957 the government set up the Japan Machinery and Metal Institute (JMMI). JMMI established comprehensive quality standards and testing procedures for all products and provided testing facilities as well. No product could be exported without the JMMI stamp of approval, although this stamp was not required for domestic sales.

In the early days of the Japanese consumer electronics export drive, MITI had used both quantity and price controls to regulate exports. The first such instance was in the late 1950s, when MITI imposed quantity limits on transistor radio exporters, i.e., the trading companies (not on the manufacturers per se), in an effort to prevent excessive competition. With television, however, quantity limits were not used, since whenever MITI thought things were getting out of hand it simply called in all the twenty-odd manufacturers and asked them to exercise restraint. (This latter method was not suited to the

much more fragmented early radio industry.) In the case of television MITI's main control was via the check price system, which set a floor on the price at which TVs could be exported. This was to avoid disrupting the U.S. market. MITI's jawboning and the check price system did not have much effect on the manufacturers, however, since they claimed that MITI did not understand U.S. market conditions. U.S. manufacturers' lack of concern with occasional very low prices on Japanese black-and-white sets in the mid-1960s strengthened the Japanese manufacturers' case. The check price system was abandoned soon after the end of fixed exchange rates in 1973, because floating rates made it too difficult to administer. Furthermore, by then Japan was no longer the only major TV exporter to the United States.

The independence of the Japanese set makers was demonstrated again in the late 1970s. After the negotiation of the OMA in 1977, almost all the Japanese manufacturers that did not already have production facilities in the United States made plans to set up plants. MITI tried to dissuade them—fruitlessly.

TV imports into Japan were basically nil. Though tariffs had been high initially, since the early 1970s they had been comparable to U.S. tariffs. However, two major nontariff barriers were often cited as inhibiting imports. The first was the franchised retailer distribution system, which was very difficult to break into. The second was the certification process. Products imported into Japan required Japan Machinery and Metals Institute approval. JMMI inspection and testing took from two to twelve months (versus two to four for products entering the United States) and had to be done in Japan (versus either the United States or Japan for

U.S. imports). It was acknowledged that Japanese quality specifications and safety standards were more stringent than those in the United States.

Japanese Competitors in 1979

By 1978 there were eleven Japanese manufacturers of TV sets, down from twenty-two in 1963. The top six manufacturers of black-and-white TV accounted for 91 percent of the production value; in color TV the figure was 83 percent; in color and black-and-white picture tubes it was 100 percent. The estimated shares of production (dollars) in Japan for 1977 and 1978 are shown in Table 26–2.

Some leading Japanese firms are briefly profiled below. Financial data on these firms is given in Exhibit 26–2.

Matsushita. Matsushita was Japan's leading manufacturer of consumer electronic products and household durables. It also made communication and measuring equipment, lighting equipment, batteries, industrial equipment (mainly motors), tubes, semiconductors, and other miscellaneous products. Consumer electronic products accounted for approximately 43 percent of total 1978 sales. Approximately 66 percent of Matsushita's sales were in Japan, 18 percent in North America, 5 percent in Europe, 4 percent in Southeast Asia, and 7 percent in the rest of the world. Exports accounted for 27 percent of sales. Matsushita had a stated goal of reducing exports and increasing local production in the countries in which its products were sold.

Matsushita was the world's largest manufacturer of both black-and-white and color TVs under the Panasonic, National, Victor, and Quasar names. Japan Victor Company was a 51 percent subsidiary. Matsushita made all its own picture tubes and semiconductors, supplied all of Sanyo's color picture tubes, and exported some tubes to Southeast Asia and elsewhere. Production of color picture tubes was 250,000 to 300,000 a month.

Matsushita was particularly known for its production orientation; it had designed and made all its own automated production equipment, which it also sold to other manufacturers under the Panasert brand name, including Sony. Matsushita had received much of its early tube technology from NV Philips, which held a minority participation in Matsushita Electronics Corp., a subsidiary that made picture tubes, lamps, vacuum tubes, semiconductors, and other products.

Sony. Sony was founded in 1946 and was still run by the two founders. Of all the Japanese competitors, it was the most highly dependent on consumer electronics, manufacturing TV sets, tape recorders, radios, video tape recorders, audio high-fidelity equipment, and blank audio and video tape. TV accounted for approximately 41 percent of 1978 sales. Sony was the most highly dependent on foreign markets, with only 40 percent of its sales in Japan. Since the Sony line was restricted to consumer electronics only, it lacked the retail strength of its larger full-line competitors in Japan.

Sony started out in tape recorders and then moved into transistor radios, making its own transistors from the very beginning. Sony entered the TV market in 1960, with the first fully transistorized black-and-white TV, a small portable. A year later it started exporting it to the United States under the

TABLE 26–2. **Japanese Market Shares of Top Japanese TV Manufacturers**

	Black-&-White TV Sets		Color TV Sets		Picture Tubes	
	1977	1978(E)	1977	1978(E)	1977	1978(E)
Matsushita	39.0	40.0	24.9	26.1	26.2	20.9
Sony	18.2	17.4	18.1	16.5	9.8	9.7
Toshiba	11.1	12.4	16.4	15.4	30.2	31.5
Hitachi	9.1	10.2	13.5	13.5	24.4	28.3
Sanyo	8.2	7.3	6.0	6.8	—	—
Mitsubishi	NA	NA	4.2	4.6	4.5	5.0
Sharp	5.2	4.2	3.2	3.3	—	—
Nippon Electric	NA	NA	2.8	2.7	4.9	4.6

Sony brand name, resisting OEM sales. In 1968 Sony introduced the novel Trinitron color picture tube, which was an overnight success and remained a proprietary Sony item. Sony's products commanded premium prices because of their high quality. In the late 1970s, however, Sony was experiencing problems because its competitors had caught up in terms of quality.

Toshiba. Toshiba, established in 1875, was engaged in the manufacture of a wide range of consumer products, including TVs, radios and appliances, heavy electrical products such as nuclear reactors, power equipment and locomotives, industrial electronic products such as communication equipment and electronic components, and other products. Consumer products were approximately 38 percent of 1978 sales. Exports were approximately 18 percent of total sales.

Toshiba was distinguished by the fact that it was the largest color picture tube manufacturer in Japan. Producing 350,000 to 400,000 color picture tubes a month, Toshiba supplied its internal needs and those of Sharp, and was a major world exporter. It was also an aggressive innovator in picture tubes.

Hitachi. Hitachi was founded in 1910 to provide an indigenous capability in electrical equipment. By 1978 it was Japan's largest manufacturer of electric utility equipment, industrial machinery, household appliances, and electronic equipment and the seventh largest corporation outside the United States. Consumer products were approximately 22 percent of 1977 sales. Over the past few years Hitachi had made large and successful efforts to increase its computer and semiconductor businesses.

Hitachi had been making color TVs since 1960. It stole a march on the industry and gained share by introducing a complete line of fully transistorized color TVs in 1969. Hitachi had a reputation as an aggressive pricer but not as a strong marketer. It was the only Japanese company that actively used offshore plants (in Taiwan and Singapore) to export color sets to the United States and Europe. Hitachi was the number two color tube producer in Japan, making 300,000 to 350,000 color tubes per month, many of which were exported to world markets.

The European Television Market

As in other markets, European TV got started in earnest after World War II. In 1947 European nations met to adopt a common standard for black-and-white TV. RCA tried to get its 525-line system introduced in Europe but was rejected. The British had been telecasting their 405-line AM sound system since before the war and wanted to continue with it. The French were advocating an 819-line, AM sound, negative modulation system developed by a young French engineer with powerful connections. Philips was pushing a 537-line, FM sound system. The Germans felt that the resolution provided by 537 lines was too low and proposed 625 lines, which Philips agreed to. No European consensus could be achieved, and thus Europe was split into three camps, the United Kingdom, France, and the rest of Europe.

An important factor in popularizing TV was the establishment of a broadcasting interlink among stations. In the United States this had been handled by private industry, notably AT&T and the networks. In Europe, since TV stations were government-owned, the various postal authorities had to agree on setting up interlinks. Philips did a great deal of promotion for such a network. Also, the existence of multiple TV standards required the use of converters. Philips manufactured all the necessary converters and helped set up the interlinks, often subsidizing portions of the cable when local governments ran out of money. The first network broadcast seen all over Europe was Queen Elizabeth's coronation in 1953. Philips was also active in aiding in the construction of TV transmitters all over Europe.

The distribution of TV sets in Europe differed from that elsewhere in the world in a number of respects. Most European countries were small enough so that manufacturers handled distribution, and there was no need for wholesalers. In Germany, though, which had developed historically as a federation of states (e.g., Bavaria), each state was dominated by a long-established wholesaler who had intimate contact with the market and retailers. It was difficult to displace these wholesalers, and the distribution system for TV sets in Germany thus remained primarily two-step. The United

Kingdom also developed its own unique distribution systems—most sets were rentals. Under the rental system the retailer maintained ownership of the set, and the consumer made weekly rental payments. For the consumer this overcame the high initial set costs and the problems of technological obsolescence and service costs. The retailer was allowed to depreciate the sets rapidly under the U.K. tax system. Economies in purchasing and servicing led to the formation of large rental chains, and brand image of the TV manufacturer became relatively unimportant—what was required was an inexpensive, simple, reliable set with easy serviceability.

Rental systems were tried in other countries as well—primarily Scandinavia, Holland, and Germany—but they never caught on. However, TV set retailing elsewhere in Europe did consolidate into chains, which had significant purchasing power with manufacturers. In some instances manufacturers had stepped in and taken over a chain that had been a customer as a result of retirement or other reasons, and in certain markets distribution became partially vertically integrated (particularly in Scandinavia, Holland, and the United Kingdom). Exclusive dealerships were not adopted anywhere in Europe.

Television progressed in Europe as a whole much slower than it did in the United States. Exhibits 26–5 and 26–6 show European TV set demand since 1950. In 1968 the saturation rate varied considerably from country to country, as shown in Table 26–3. More than 90 percent of unit sales in 1968 were in the 17- to 23-inch screen sizes (at an average retail price of $215), with 19-inch sets the leading size. Less than 10 percent of sales were accounted for by large-screen 25-inch sets ($350 to $500). Portable sales were under 3 percent of sales, since only the privileged few could buy these as second sets. All sets sold were table-top models; the console segment never existed in Europe.

Replacement sales had also been slow to develop. Europeans tended to keep their sets for a long time and maintain them very well. In Europe manufacturers and dealers had thought that owners would trade in their sets after five years. In actuality, sets were kept from eight to ten years and meticulously serviced to last up to eleven years or more for good quality sets.

Competition in 1968

The competitors involved in the European TV industry in 1968 are listed in Table 26–4. There were two principal types, multinational companies and essentially national companies.

TABLE 26–3. TV Set Ownership in Europe, 1968

Country	Population (millions)	Sets in Use (millions)	Saturation (percent of households)
Austria	7.3	1.0	48%
Belgium	9.7	1.9	63%
Denmark	4.9	1.2	74%
Finland	4.8	0.92	62%
France	50	8.5	56%
West Germany	60	14.0	69%
Ireland	3	0.4	62%
Italy	53	7.8	55%
Luxembourg	0.34	0.045	42%
Monaco	0.02	0.01	140%
Netherlands	12.7	2.6	75%
Norway	3.8	0.68	53%
Portugal	9.3	0.26	11%
Spain	33	2.7	26%
Sweden	8	2.3	80%
Switzerland	5.9	0.9	49%
U.K.	55	16.0	96%
Total	320.96	61.215	65%

TABLE 26-4. Competitors in the European TV Industry, 1968[a]

The Netherlands	West Germany	United Kingdom	France	Italy
		Manufacturers of Television Sets		
Philips (dominant) (parent of the Philips group)	Allgemeine Deutsche Philips Industrie (25%) (menber of the Philips group) Grundig AEG-Telefunken Standard Elektrik Lorenz (member of ITT Europe) Norddeutsche Mende Rundfunk SABA (controlled by General Telephone & Electronics) KUBA-Imperial (controlled by the General Electric Corporation)	Thorn Electrical Industries (30–35%) (incorporating Baird) Philips Industries-Pye of Cambridge (25%) (members of the Philips group) Rank Bush Murphy (20%) (a division of the Rank Organisation) The General Electric Company (16%)[c] Standard Telephone & Cable (6–8%) (member of ITT Europe)	Radiotechnique (30%) (controlled by Philips)[b] Thomson-Brandt-CSF CGE-Lebon-Lyonnaise (25–30%) Oceanic (10%) (member of ITT Europe)	Philips S.p.A. (large share) (member of the Philips group)
		Manufacturers of Picture Tubes		
Philips (dominant)	Allgemeine Deutsche Philips Industrie (40%) AEG-Telefunken Standard Elektrik Lorenz	Mullard (50%+) (member of the Philips group) Thorn-AEI (45%) (Thorn in association with the General Electric Company)	Radiotechnique (50%+) Compagnie Industrielle Francaise des Tubes Electroniques (controlled by Thomson-Brandt-CSF and CGE-Lebon-Lyonnaise)	Philips S.p.A. (strong number one)

[a] Approximate market shares given in parentheses where known.
[b] Philips owned 53 percent of Radiotechnique. Other Philips units in Europe were 100 percent or close to 100 percent owned.
[c] General Electric Company was not affiliated the the U.S. General Electric Company.

Philips.   Philips had between 25 and 30 percent of the total West European market for black-and-white TV. It was also the chief supplier of black-and-white picture tubes and other components and made every type of TV studio and transmission apparatus. Philips was the only company that was integrated into glass manufacturing. Philips had major TV-related operations in every country shown and also had units in Austria and the Scandinavian countries.

Philips had twelve major product divisions: lighting; glass and allied industries; electronic components and materials; radio, TV, and gramophone; telecommunications and defense systems; electro-acoustics; x-ray and medical apparatus; industrial and professional equipment; data systems; domestic appliances; and pharmaceutical-chemical products. Philips had always been dependent on foreign markets for its business—the Netherlands accounted for only 10 percent of its total sales. It had evolved into a "federation of companies" spread over sixty countries, with centralized control over most engineering and R&D functions and decentralized, country-level control over sales and marketing. Some of the larger country organizations like the United Kingdom and West Germany had developed their own engineering and development groups. Though it was multinational, Philips was viewed more like a national company in every country in which it operated.

Philips had been involved with TV since before the war and had carried on work in secret while occupied by invasion forces. After the war it played an important role in getting war-shattered Europe off to an early start in TV.

As a major supplier of components to other set manufacturers it had also played a key role in disseminating technology. Its role as a supplier of components had also tended to ensure that its competitors were never very different technologically in their sets' designs.

ITT. ITT was involved in the European TV set industry, even though it made no TVs in the United States. ITT's European operations were centered in West Germany, France, Austria, and the United Kingdom, with the first being the largest. The West German operation also made black-and-white picture tubes and was tooling up to produce color picture tubes.

Thorn Electrical Industries. Thorn was a U.K. company engaged in TV, lighting, appliances, electronics, and industrial equipment. The number one spot in the U.K. TV market was held by Thorn, with some 30 to 35 percent of the market. This was after the 1968 merger with Radio Rentals, the country's largest rental chain. Thorn–Radio Rentals controlled about 33 percent of the rental business in the United Kingdom. Thorn also managed a 50–50 joint venture with GE that made 45 percent of Great Britain's black-and-white picture tubes. Since 1959 Thorn had also made TV sets for Philco's international operations. Approximately 75 percent of Thorn's gross cash flow came from TV manufacturing and rental.

GTE had owned a minority interest in Thorn and had hoped to merge with it. After this hope dimmed with the Thorn–Radio Rental merger, GTE divested its holding but continued to supply Thorn with know-how on color picture tubes, which Thorn had just started to make. This was complicated by the fact that Radio Rentals had a 33 percent interest in a new color picture tube venture with RCA. Eventually, Thorn gave up the GTE assistance to form a 51/49 color picture tube venture with RCA.

Rank. Third place in the U.K. TV market was held by the Rank Organisation, with about 20 percent of the market. In 1968 Rank had divested its in-

terests in the rental business, which were too small to operate economically. Rank's main business came from Rank-Xerox, which accounted for nearly 70 percent of its profits.

General Electric Company. The TV division of GEC was fourth, with about a 15 percent share.

Grundig. Grundig was a privately owned company that was a close second behind Philips in the West German black-and-white TV market. It was the most active and aggressive exporter of TV sets from Germany. The company was focused on high-quality consumer electronic products. It bought the bulk of its components from Philips and the remainder from ITT.

Telefunken. Telefunken was in third or fourth place (along with ITT) in the West German market. It made its own black-and-white picture tubes and, besides Philips, was the main component supplier in West Germany. Telefunken held many of the basic patents on the PAL color TV system (to be discussed below). Telefunken was part of AEG-Telefunken, a large electrotechnical concern.

Thomson-Brandt-CSF. Thomson held second place in the French market with a share of between 25 and 30 percent. The company was formed as the result of a 1967 merger between Thomson-Houston-Hotchkiss-Brandt and CSF. A partially owned company, CIFTE (Compagnie Industrielle Française des Tubes Electroniques) made black-and-white picture tubes and had just started color picture tube production. The group was France's chief operator in the field of industrial electronics and was also active in consumer products and appliances, medical electronics, electrical products, armaments, and nuclear engineering, among other things. It was favored by the French government for equipping the national TV network.

Color TV in Europe

Informal discussion on European color TV had been going on since the mid-1950s, and in 1962 study groups were set up to study the specifications of available color systems: the NTSC (National

Television System Committee) system being used in the United States; the French SECAM (Sequential Color Modulation) system; and the German PAL (Phase Alternation Line) system, proposed by Telefunken. PAL and NTSC were largely compatible. In 1962 the NTSC (modified for 625 lines) was by far the best-supported, with the backing of RCA, Philips, the British Broadcasting Corporation (BBC), and U.K. set manufacturers. SECAM had the backing of the French government, while PAL seemed to have only Telefunken (the main patent holder) behind it.[1]

In early 1964 twenty European countries met in London for their fourth annual attempt to choose a system, and got nowhere. After the 1964 London stalemate, the United Kingdom's BBC wanted to push ahead on its own with the NTSC system. The issue of color TV was far more urgent for the United Kingdom than for the Continent as a result of its high saturation rate for black-and-white TV. Despite the fact that unilateral action could damage British exports of sets if the rest of Europe chose another system, the BBC was determined to have color transmission by 1967. France was pushing hard for SECAM and was attempting to get the USSR to adopt it as a way of encouraging other countries to do so as well. In April 1965 the USSR and its satellites accepted SECAM.

In 1966 the European countries met again, in Oslo. A number of countries had indicated their desire to start color broadcasting in 1967, and it was imperative that a decision be reached. Halfway through this meeting the British agreed to switch from NTSC to PAL, and finally PAL was chosen by the majority of delegates. The dissenters were the USSR, France, and a few nations closely aligned politically with France, which stuck with SECAM. Italy and Spain later chose PAL. Europe was thus divided into two camps with incompatible systems; the only commonality was that all colorcasts were to be 625 lines.

The color era in Europe began in the late 1960s. Color set demand in Europe took on many of the same characteristics as black-and-white demand. The bulk of the market had been table models, and no console market of significance had developed. Growth in sales of portable sets was modest and

[1] The key PAL patents would expire between 1979 and 1985 in key European countries.

relatively recent. Most sets were large-screen first sets, and the second set market was estimated at only 1 to 2 percent of demand for Europe as a whole. The replacement market had developed slowly, as consumers repaired their sets rather than bought a new set. Prices for color sets varied considerably from country to country depending on luxury taxes, degree of competition, and extent of interchangeability with sets used in other countries.

TV set distribution patterns had generally been maintained. In the major countries, the majority of distribution was direct to retailers in France, Belgium, Holland, and Austria. In the United Kingdom rental prevailed, while distribution was approximately 40 percent direct and 60 percent through wholesalers in West Germany. Beginning around 1972 dealers throughout Europe formed buying cooperatives, which enhanced their bargaining power.

A second important change in European retailing was the removal of retail price maintenance. This increased competition at the retail level, and retail and manufacturer's margins had dropped. Discount stores had gained in importance. Dealers in Europe carried multiple brands in 1979 (two or three on average) except in France, where dealers carried exclusive brands, like Thomson or Philips.

Japanese Penetration in Europe

Japanese exports of color sets to Europe commenced only in 1970 and were to a large extent regulated by the PAL licensing system. Originally, Telefunken wanted to exclude all Japanese companies from the PAL patents. When Japanese producers threatened to undermine the PAL 625-line standard by flooding the market with cheap sets using circuits that bypassed the PAL patents, Telefunken changed its mind. Hitachi was the first Japanese company to buy the PAL license, in December 1970. However, the Japanese were given the PAL license under conditions far more onerous than those placed on European producers.

For production in Europe, the PAL license placed no limit on set size and quantity, but specified that only 50 percent of sets produced could be exported. For Japanese production, the allowed screen sizes were originally limited to 12 to 16 inches. Though these screen sizes then dominated the Japanese market, European consumers were purchasing predominantly 20-inch to 26-inch sets. In 1974 the Japanese PAL licenses were extended to include up to the 20-inch size, but 20-inch sets were limited to 50 percent of total Japanese exports to Europe. Finally, sales of sets to other manufacturers were forbidden, limiting Japanese producers to selling under their own brands.

The Japanese were also affected by a number of "voluntary" import restrictions. In 1973 the United Kingdom negotiated a Voluntary Restraint Agreement with the Japanese to limit color imports to 10 percent of the U.K. market (and 25 percent for black-and-white). That same year the Benelux countries negotiated an import restraint agreement with the Japanese. Later, the U.K. agreement was extended to Japanese offshore plants in the Far East. Japanese exports to France were not affected by the PAL license conditions. The SECAM patent, held by Cie Française de Television, was freely licensed to anyone who wanted it and was not used as a trade barrier. However, an agreement restricted Japanese color set imports to France to approximately 60,000 units a year.

Japanese color TV penetration in Europe via exports was thus relatively low, and Japanese companies began setting up or acquiring manufacturing bases in Europe. The United Kingdom formed a natural target for the Japanese to initially establish their manufacturing base. The United Kingdom was a large domestic market and was more susceptible to smaller-screen sets than the rest of the Continent. Further, the U.K. retailer and consumer were psychologically more prepared to accept Far Eastern goods than their Continental counterparts because of long-standing trade with Hong Kong. Investment in France was ruled out by its adherence to the SECAM system, and West German investment was made less attractive by extremely high labor costs and severe price competition in the market.

The United Kingdom was made even more attractive by government encouragement and grants to establish plants in economically depressed regions, where labor was cheap and plentiful. Furthermore, the Japanese were comfortable with the English language and more attuned to British/American culture than Continental culture.

Sony led by establishing a plant in Wales in 1973. Sony was welcomed (with subsidies) by the U.K. government, as was Matsushita in 1974. The plants were to use a significant share of U.K. components. However, by the time Hitachi wanted to establish a plant in 1976 the U.K. TV industry and unions launched a protest so vociferous that the government, with much embarrassment, had to withdraw the support and subsidies it had originally promised Hitachi. The U.K. government subsequently encouraged Japanese firms either to take over existing TV plants or preferably to form joint ventures with U.K. firms. Toshiba formed a joint venture with Rank in 1978, with Rank contributing its factories and Toshiba some cash and expertise for a 30 percent share. Hitachi formed a 50/50 joint venture with GEC (U.K.) in 1979, with GEC contributing its plant and Hitachi cash and technology. Mitsubishi purchased a nonoperating TV plant in Scotland in 1979.

On the Continent Japanese companies signed technical assistance agreements with companies in a number of countries. Also, Sony acquired Wega Radio in Germany in 1975, and Sanyo acquired a 34 percent stake in a Spanish company in 1977 and a 30 percent stake in Emerson in Italy in 1978. The latter move aroused interest as being the first major Japanese entry into Europe from the south. Exhibit 26-3 summarizes the Japanese set manufacturing base in Europe as of 1979.

In general, the Japanese plants in Europe had been automated to a lesser degree than the parent plants in Japan, using insertion equipment two or even three generations older. Even so, they were far more automated (especially in insertion) than most other European plants.

The Japanese penetration of European TV markets had been far greater in color picture tubes than in color sets. The boom in the U.K. color TV market in the 1970–73 period placed U.K. manufacturers in the situation of not being able to meet the demand for large (22-inch and 26-inch) tubes. The Japanese, relatively unsuccessful at penetrating the U.K. set market because of PAL license restrictions and links between rental companies and manufacturers, found this an ideal opportunity to penetrate the picture tube market. Since tubes were relatively less labor-intensive than sets, the political problem was less difficult. The Japanese immediately introduced 20-inch and 18-inch tubes into the U.K. market, and despite practically no home market for larger tubes they tooled up to begin supplying 22-inch and 26-inch tubes as well. The Japanese large-tube thrust was also successful on the Continent—so much so that by 1979 they had taken over from RCA and Sylvania as the dominant non-Philips suppliers and also cut into Philips's market share.[2]

In smaller tubes, the market began developing only in the mid-1970s. It was still a small market on the Continent, and opinions differed as to how far the small-set market would develop. European tube makers did not perceive sufficient volume to justify tooling up for small-tube manufacture, and thus all small tubes used in Europe were exported from Japan. The chief exporters were Toshiba and Hitachi. By 1979 Japanese imports accounted for fully one-third of all color picture tubes used in TV sets sold in the European Economic Community.

Hitachi had entered into a joint venture in Finland in 1976 for the production of color picture tubes and was expected to export 600,000 of its 800,000 tubes per year to the rest of Europe or elsewhere. The joint venture was with the Finnish government and a local TV manufacturer. Other than the Hitachi facility, there was no Japanese plant manufacturing picture tubes in Europe. In 1978 it was rumored that Toshiba had obtained permission to set up a color tube plant in Spain, but it had not materialized. There had been a recent outcry by EEC component manufacturers against the high level of Japanese tube penetration. So far no action had been taken.

Product and Process Technology in Europe

European companies had all moved to printed circuit board technology during the black-and-white era, but the move from manual insertion of components to automatic insertion had been slow. In the mid-1970s European manufacturers were rudely jolted by the immense improvements in Japanese color set reliability. Only around 1975 did the major European manufacturers begin seriously to consider automating, and they were then confronted by poor component quality in Europe compared to

what was available in Japan. Thus the component manufacturers, who were mostly associated with set manufacturers, were asked to improve their products. Despite these efforts the level of automation of European producers was still lower in 1979. Philips had begun automating very slowly and was using a total of five or six different systems in different plants. Only since 1978 had it tried to use only one system. The large German companies were only just introducing automation, and Thorn was probably not automated even as of late 1979. European firms also trailed the Japanese in testing technology.

In color picture tubes, Philips began mass producing 26-inch 90° deflection color picture tubes in Europe in 1966, later extended to the 22-inch size. In 1969 Philips was the first company in the world to introduce 110° tubes. Initially produced in the 26-inch size, they were later extended to smaller screens.

In 1972 RCA and the Japanese companies (principally Toshiba and Hitachi) began selling in-line tubes in Europe. In sizes above 20 inches these tubes had 110° deflection, while for 20-inch and smaller tubes the old 90° angle deflection was retained. Philips countered by introducing its own in-line 110° tubes in 1974, and GTE-Sylvania also began making in-lines in Europe. The Philips in-line tubes had thick necks and were not compatible with the RCA and Japanese thin-necked tubes. Tubes with 110° deflection angles proved far more popular in the 22-inch and 26-inch sizes than in the 20-inch and below range. In the late 1970s, after RCA and Japanese 90° in-lines had made inroads in the 20-inch and under tube market, Philips tooled up for the production of 20-inch 90° in-lines at Mullard in the United Kingdom. The first 90° tubes were made in early 1979.

European TV Manufacturers in 1979

In the mid- to late 1960s, nearly all the color TVs in Europe were made by Philips. By 1977, however, market positions had shifted, as shown in Exhibit 26-4. Exhibits 26-5 and 26-6 show European color and black-and-white demand. In the United Kingdom, greatly expanded color programming in 1970 and the abolition of down payment requirements on rentals in 1971 provided a double stimulus

---

[2]In 1974, U.K. component manufacturers tried unsuccessfully to prove that the Japanese were dumping color picture tubes.

to the color TV market. Color set sales boomed and manufacturers scrambled to increase capacity. In particular Mullard (Philips) and Thorn/RCA added greatly to their color picture tube capacity. In December 1973 the government reinstated credit controls, slamming the brakes on the economy, and in 1974 there was color set overcapacity for the first time. Mullard's color tube capacity was 2 million units a year, while Thorn's was 900,000. Thorn never made more than 500,000 tubes per year, and after incurring a loss of £ 4.6 million on color tube production in 1974 it decided to close its plant. A year earlier Thorn had closed its black-and-white tube plant too. Thus Mullard was left as the sole U.K. manufacturer of picture tubes. Thorn purchased color picture tubes from RCA and the Japanese.

The U.K. industry continued in a state of poor profitability until it was racked by a series of consolidations in 1978. Thorn, with 25 percent of the color set market, consolidated its 500,000 set per year production into two plants, closing two others. Decca, with 7 percent of the color set market, closed one of its two factories. Rank, with 7 percent of the market, formed a joint venture with Toshiba, to which Rank contributed its two factories and Toshiba contributed money and technology. Finally, GEC, with about 9 percent of the color set market, formed a joint venture with Hitachi to which GEC contributed its TV plant and Hitachi contributed money and technology. Paralleling this consolidation on the manufacturing side was a steady consolidation on the rental side of the business. Electronic Rentals, a chain 33 percent owned by Philips, increased its market share from 8 to 12 percent through an acquisition. Further moves took place in 1979. ITT closed two of its three U.K. TV plants. Also in 1979 Thorn acquired, for nearly $550 million, the electronics and entertainment company EMI.

The West German color TV market was characterized by every manufacturer's intention to increase market share. As a result there was continuous, unrelenting price-cutting, which resulted in poor profitability for all companies in color sets, especially after market growth slowed in 1974 and beyond. The major realignment that took place in the West German market was Grundig's rise to a strong number one position after a late start, reaching a 25 percent share by 1979, trailed by Philips with 12 to 14 percent. Six or seven other manufacturers followed close behind Philips. In 1978 Nord Mende, with some 10 percent of the West German color set market and 18 percent of the black-and-white market, was acquired by Thomson of France.

Grundig had also made progress during the 1970s toward becoming a multinational. Using an aggressive export drive to gain a foothold, Grundig established a number of plants in various European countries. It also set up a plant in Taiwan to manufacture small-screen black-and-white TVs. Color picture tubes were purchased primarily from Philips.

Grundig had run into profitability problems by 1978, however, and was thin on management. It still bought its components almost completely from Philips, and the two companies had collaborated on various projects, including video tape recorders. In 1979 Philips acquired a 24.5 percent interest in Grundig (higher than this would have run afoul of the German Cartel Office).

Telefunken was another company in trouble. Its color picture tube plant at Ulm, built in 1967, had a capacity of 900,000 tubes per year but was severely underutilized in 1978, operating at only 66 percent of rated output. Furthermore, the parent company AEG had been unprofitable since 1970 and had experienced huge losses in the field of nuclear reactors. As a result, Telefunken entered a joint venture agreement in 1979 with Thomson to operate the tube plant at Ulm, explained in more detail below.

The color set situation in the French market was very different from elsewhere in Europe, because the market was shielded from export interest by the SECAM system. France also established a 60,000 color TV set per year import quota for the Japanese. Market growth in France was gradual because of the high price of color sets. There had been no boom/bust cycle and no capacity overbuilding.

Other than Philips, color picture tubes were made in France by Thomson in a joint venture with RCA (originally 49 percent) called Videocolor. Videocolor built its first plant in Italy in 1969. In 1974 it built a second plant in France. By 1979 after steady investments, the two plants were producing 2.2 million color tubes a year. Thomson had also begun expanding geographically, such as through its acquisition of Nord Mende. Prior to the acquisition Nord Mende had sourced its color tubes from Philips; after the acquisition, it sourced them from Videocolor. In 1979 Thomson entered into a 51/49 joint venture with Telefunken to form Europacolor, a holding company that owned 58 percent of Videocolor, the other 42 percent of which was owned by RCA. Videocolor in turn took over the operation of Telefunken's color picture tube plant at Ulm, thereby obtaining a plant in Germany to augment its existing ones in Italy and France. Videocolor was thus becoming a major open market competitor.

Some experts believed that Philips and Thomson viewed the picture tube part of the business as primary, with sets being important only as outlets for the tubes.

The multinational competitors in Europe underwent substantial shifts during the color era.

ITT. ITT's consumer operations in Europe had suffered losses. In early 1979 ITT held talks with an unspecified company (rumored to be Thomson-Brandt) to form a joint venture to take over the consumer electronics business. During 1979 ITT consolidated its operations by closing three plants in Italy, Austria, and France, and then two more in the United Kingdom, concentrating ITT's 700,000 annual color set production in three plants—one each in the United Kingdom, France, and West Germany. The ITT Esslingen (Germany) color picture tube plant supplied its internal picture tube needs. ITT's commitment to the TV business seemed to have returned after the terminated negotiations.

Philips. Philips had been active in research on color TV from an early stage and was the only company that could make sets for the NTSC, SECAM, and PAL standards. Philips began mass production of rectangular 25-inch 90° color picture tubes in Europe in 1966. Philips had aggressively built color picture tube capacity in the United Kingdom, France, Germany, Austria, and elsewhere. It held about 60 percent of the color picture tube market in Europe and was the world's largest manufacturer of picture tubes. It made its own glass as well. Financial information on Philips is shown in Exhibit 26–2.

In the early 1970s Philips opened an integrated, 4 million unit capacity black-and-white tube plant in Taiwan and began assembling small screen black-and-white TV sets in Singapore. In 1978 black-and-white TV set assembly was shifted to Taiwan, Singapore began making small-screen color TV sets, and the Taiwan tube plant was expanded to make small-screen color tubes as well. Around 1979 Philips began making subassemblies for large-screen color sets in Singapore.

As a result of its historical development, Philips made its products in many plants situated throughout Europe. In the early 1970s Philips went through an extensive process of trying to integrate and rationalize its European operations. This was done by leaving final assembly intact in the local markets but rationalizing component and subassembly production to take advantage of economies of scale. Philips also made a number of acquisitions. In France it acquired the Radiola and Schneider brands. In the United Kingdom, Philips increased its forward integration into the rental business. In the United States Philips acquired Magnavox, and in Germany it acquired an interest in its largest customer, Grundig.

Philips had also been active in new product development. It had pioneered the video tape recorder market in Europe in 1972 and in 1979–80 was preparing to introduce its optical videodisk system into the European market, having already done so in the United States. These products will be discussed below.

Southeast Asian Activity in TV

Japanese manufacturers started setting up TV plants in Southeast Asian countries in the late 1960s, manufacturing essentially for the local markets. Around the same period U.S. manufacturers began setting up assembly plants in Taiwan to make small-screen black-and-white TVs for the U.S. market. By the early 1970s as a result of these U.S. plants and the rise of certain local manufacturers like Tatung and Sampo, Taiwan had overtaken Japan as the leading source of black-and-white TV imports to the United States. Black-and-white picture tubes were originally imported from Japan, but three plants set up in the early 1970s had made Taiwan self-sufficient. These were operated by Chunghwa, which was a Tatung Group company (initially as a joint venture with RCA), Philips, and Clinton, a U.S. firm.

After the negotiation of the Orderly Marketing Agreement between Japan and the United States, certain Taiwanese manufacturers were able to set up color TV joint ventures with Japanese companies to export to the United States. The first was Tatung (8.3 percent Toshiba participation), which began exporting private label sets in 1977. The other major venture was Sampo (9.5 percent Sharp), which began in 1978. That same year Philips began making color picture tubes locally. Mitsubishi, Sanyo, Sharp, and Hitachi exported. During the late 1970s Hitachi was constrained from increasing its exports by a Taiwan government edict. The surge in color TV exports was crimped in 1979 because of the OMA between Taiwan and the United States.

Japanese companies began using their South Korean affiliates in 1973 to export color TVs to the United States on a trial basis, soon after the 17 percent revaluation of the yen against the U.S. dollar. Korean color TV exports became important in terms of magnitude after 1977, when Japanese exports to the United States were restricted by the OMA. The 1978 exports of color TVs were more than four times the 1977 level, with most of the production accounted for by two companies: Samsung (40 percent Sanyo participation) and Gold Star (20 percent NEC participation). Korea National (50 percent Matsushita) and Taihan Electric Wire were also important exporters. Unlike the Taiwanese case, there were no Japanese companies manufacturing CTVs for local Korean consumption, because color broadcasting did not exist. Also, because of Korean government policy, there were no wholly owned Japanese subsidiaries.

The opportunity presented by the Japanese OMA spurred a major capacity expansion in 1978 among the Korean companies. Samsung was to step up output from 300,000 to 500,000 and had long-range plans to double that capacity to 1 million units per year. Gold Star boosted the capacity of its plant at Gumi from 300,000 to 500,000 a year. Korea National expanded its capacity to 360,000 per year. Taihan Electric, which first exported color TV on a trial basis in 1977, completed a new plant in 1978. Dongnam Electric also installed production lines for color TV. All told, it was estimated that South Korean capacity at the end of the year was nearly 2 million color TV sets per year.

Unfortunately, this capacity had not yet been used. In early 1979 the U.S. restricted South Korean color TV imports to approximately 300,000 units under an Orderly Marketing Agreement. This, coupled with certain political events in Korea, threw the entire economy and the TV industry into a recession. Some of the companies were forced to sell off some of their plants, and a government austerity program and spiraling wage rates severely affected the performance of Korean–Japanese joint ventures in 1979.

The Global Picture in 1979

By the end of the 1970s the TV manufacturing industry had become a global industry. Exhibit 26–5 shows the development of the black-and-white and color TV markets in the four key regions of the world. Exhibits 26–6 and 26–7 show the location of production and markets for the principal world competitors as of 1976, the latest year for which such data were available. A number of changes had occurred since 1976 as discussed elsewhere, notably growth in South Korean and Taiwanese color TV, the emergence of RCA as number one in the United States, and major realignments in Europe.

The Future of Television Sets

The television set was expected to improve through continued introduction of IC technology and automated assembly and testing. However, a more revolutionary development was the conversion of sets from analog to digital signals, which would allow a marked improvement in picture quality.

Digital processing was already a reality in phonograph records; the world's first audio record to be produced using digital processing was released in 1979. The next step was to make LPs on which the information itself was recorded digitally. Since late 1978 the Audio "PCM" (pulse code modulation) Council had been meeting to adopt a worldwide standard for PCM records. All the major Japanese consumer electronics companies were on the council, along with RCA, MCA DiscoVision, Philips, AEG-Telefunken, and Thomson-CSF.

One of the impediments to digital processing was the high cost of the large number of digital ICs required. VLSI (very large scale integration) technology, as it developed further, was expected to bring down the cost of the digital circuitry. The centers of VLSI technology today were the United States and Japan. While VLSI innards for digital processing in TVs were still distant, LSI technology had already entered TVs with microprocessor-based programmable systems.

Another thrust of developments would convert the TV screen into the display device of a home information center. Currently two different approaches were being pursued. In one, the source of data would be a data bank maintained at home on a home computer. In the other approach, data would be stored externally and transmitted to the home for display on the TV screen, either as teletext (information broadcast on normal TV signals through the air) or viewdata (information transmitted over telephone lines). Whether the two different approaches—internal data banks versus external data banks—would compete with or complement each other was an open question.

In the home computer approach, the computer would be connected directly to existing TV sets. Home computers could also have their own display tubes, in which case they did not need to be connected to TV sets. However, computer manufacturers would prefer a TV set to reduce the cost of the computers. If home computers using TV sets as display devices develop a significant mass market, this could stimulate the purchase of additional TVs. Home computers were just beginning to take off in 1979.

Teletext and viewdata could be received on existing TV sets by purchasing appropriate decoding units and making some modifications in the sets. Or it was possible that new TV sets could be bought which incorporated these decoders inside them. If the services caught on, people buying sets for the first time would want sets with the decoders included, and set owners might well be spurred to replace them sooner.

Both teletext and viewdata required modifications of the TV set in order to receive, decode, store, and manipulate data. These modifications more than doubled the cost of a set in 1979, but it was expected that volume production might eventually allow either system to be integrated into TV sets for $100 extra. Both teletext and viewdata were pioneered in the United Kingdom, in 1975 and 1979 respectively. Numerous trials were under way throughout the world, involving a number of competing technologies. The United States had been slow to adopt teletext and viewdata technology, with the first teletext broadcasts started in 1977 by Micro-TV. A number of experiments were under way in the United States in 1979. In late 1979 twenty-two large companies, including AT&T, CBS, RCA, Dow Jones, and Texas Instruments, sponsored a comprehensive study to determine the likely effects of teletext and viewdata technology. It was going to affect many people in many ways. Among those expected to be affected were newspapers, publishers, advertisers, communications companies, and electronics companies.

So far the viewdata systems being tested allowed the user to call up specific information on a terminal. When the interactive capability of viewdata was more fully exploited there was no reason why the user would not be able to shop, vote, and communicate with other terminals. This would require the addition of a certain amount of "intelligence" at the terminal, and the result began to look very much like a home computer, which could then use its intelligence to do all sorts of other things around the home.

EXHIBIT 26-1. Japanese TV Production and Demand (units in thousands)

	1953	1954	1955	1956	1957	1958	1959	1960	1961	1962	1963	1964	1965	1966	1967	1968	1969	1970	1971	1972	1973	1974	1975	1976	1977	1978
Black-and-white TVs																										
Production (complete sets)	13	31	137	312	613	1205	2872	3578	4609	4885	4916	5197	4060	5074	5677	6266	7284	6089	5378	4650	3681	3750	3153	4572	4710	4567
Domestic shipments (imputed)[a]	13	31	137	311	607	1190	2845	3533	4515	4623	4230	4213	2603	3231	3754	3505	3997	3715	3936	3188	2273	2389	2287	3606	3683	3852
Exports (complete sets)	–	–	–	1	6	15	27	45	94	262	686	984	1457	1843	1923	2761	3287	2374	1442	1462	1408	1361	866	956	1027	715
To: U.S.	NA	NA	NA	NA	NA	NA	NA	NA	NA	NA	NA	NA	15	33	19	65	175	362	373	626	597	422	482	570	444	666
EEC	NA	NA	NA	NA	NA	NA	NA	NA	NA	NA	NA	NA	13	29	17	58	142	236	226	305	324	257	240	298	186	298
West Germany	NA	NA	NA	NA	NA	NA	NA	NA	NA	NA	NA	NA	2	4	0.4	5	16	80	117	217	219	132	216	230	213	316
U.K.	NA	NA	NA	NA	NA	NA	NA	NA	NA	NA	NA	NA	NA	NA	NA	NA	80	122	51	161	276	216	158	159	173	197
Rest of the world	NA	NA	NA	NA	NA	NA	NA	NA	NA	NA	NA	NA	353	989	656	925	807	886	954	907	799	1192	1158	1651	1577	1435
Exports (chassis and kits)	NA	NA	NA	NA	NA	NA	NA	NA	NA	NA	NA	NA	NA	NA	NA	NA	366	631	732	799	1036	1249	754	1067	1263	875
To: Rest of the world	NA	NA	NA	NA	NA	NA	NA	NA	NA	NA	NA	NA	NA	NA	NA	NA	324	605	702	788	1032	1249	754	1007	1259	875
Production value (billion yen)[b]	NA	NA	NA	NA	NA	NA	NA	NA	NA	NA	NA	NA	NA	NA	NA	NA	192	143	112	92	70	81	83	104	106	97
Export value (billion yen)[c]	NA	NA	NA	NA	NA	NA	NA	NA	NA	NA	NA	NA	NA	NA	NA	NA	69	80	85	71	55	72	65	97	96	87
Color TVs																										
Production (complete sets)	–	–	–	–	–	–	–	–	–	4.4	3.7	57.1	97.5	520	1232	2735	4834	6399	6872	8388	8756	7323	7472	10,531	9632	8549
Domestic shipments	NA	NA	NA	NA	NA	NA	NA	NA	NA	NA	NA	31.3	49.9	242	899	1970	3765	4773	5889	6410	6489	5100	5565	5691	5277	5650
Exports (includes chassis and kits)	NA	NA	NA	NA	NA	NA	NA	NA	NA	NA	NA	17.2	43.3	252	341	769	1003	1008	1577	1849	2092	2289	2756	5251	4423	3609
To: U.S.	NA	NA	NA	NA	NA	NA	NA	NA	NA	NA	NA	NA	NA	240	324	734	935	883	1237	1116	1095	1001	1215	2959	2135	1537
EEC	NA	NA	NA	NA	NA	NA	NA	NA	NA	NA	NA	NA	NA	NA	NA	NA	3	57	NA	51	235	466	351	530	484	542
West Germany	NA	NA	NA	NA	NA	NA	NA	NA	NA	NA	NA	NA	NA	NA	NA	NA	NA	3	NA	28	81	143	98	351	199	214
U.K.	NA	NA	NA	NA	NA	NA	NA	NA	NA	NA	NA	NA	NA	NA	NA	NA	NA	51	NA	161	216	276	158	159	173	197
Rest of the world	NA	NA	NA	NA	NA	NA	NA	NA	NA	NA	NA	NA	NA	12	17	35	68	122	283	498	586	822	1190	1762	1804	1530
Production (chassis and kits)[d]	NA	NA	NA	NA	NA	NA	NA	NA	NA	NA	NA	NA	NA	NA	NA	NA	NA	NA	NA	NA	NA	NA	549	617	242	327
Production value (billion yen)[b]	NA	NA	NA	NA	NA	NA	NA	NA	NA	NA	NA	NA	NA	NA	NA	NA	504	681	608	715	686	615	584	758	701	617
Export value (billion yen)[c]	NA	NA	NA	NA	NA	NA	NA	NA	NA	NA	NA	NA	NA	NA	NA	NA	58	58	90	103	110	137	168	310	262	189

EXHIBIT 26-1. (continued)

	1953	1954	1955	1956	1957	1958	1959	1960	1961	1962	1963	1964	1965	1966	1967	1968	1969	1970	1971	1972	1973	1974	1975	1976	1977	1978
Black-and-white picture tubes																										
Production	10.8	26.9	217	516	908	1453	3211	4185	4921	5694	5798	6375	4540	5640	6895	7183	9539	7896	7004	7453	6474	5970	5079	6448	NA	NA
Export	NA	NA	NA	NA	NA	NA	NA	NA	NA	NA	NA	NA	213	401	486	717	1929	1522	1892	2201	1976	1713	1348	1391	1689	1631
To: U.S.	NA	NA	NA	NA	NA	NA	NA	NA	NA	NA	NA	NA	70	280	265	210	659	373	56	128	141	171	110	248	242	177
EEC	NA	NA	NA	NA	NA	NA	NA	NA	NA	NA	NA	NA	4.5	25	53	36	38	92	133	251	525	462	386	280	258	153
West Germany	NA	NA	NA	NA	NA	NA	NA	NA	NA	NA	NA	NA	4	24	43	23	12	56	93	85	195	250	114	118	129	109
U.K.	NA	NA	NA	NA	NA	NA	NA	NA	NA	NA	NA	NA	0.9	1.5	2	3	1.4	2	8	87	172	105	167	96	83	10
Rest of the world	NA	NA	NA	NA	NA	NA	NA	NA	NA	NA	NA	NA	138.5	96	168	471	1232	1057	1703	1822	1310	1080	852	863	1185	1301
Color picture tubes																										
Production	—	—	—	—	—	—	—	NA	NA	NA	NA	NA	NA	714	1481	3172	5536	6866	7705	9611	11544	9801	9662	14841	14567	14838
Export	—	—	—	—	—	—	—	NA	NA	NA	NA	NA	NA	NA	NA	NA	126	85	295	675	1666	1817	2044	3309	4200	5847
To: U.S.	—	—	—	—	—	—	—	NA	NA	NA	NA	NA	NA	NA	NA	NA	93	32	115	115	94	31	152	183	387	283
EEC	—	—	—	—	—	—	—	NA	NA	NA	NA	NA	NA	NA	NA	NA	4	18	95	317	1058	1099	985	1459	1867	2052
West Germany	—	—	—	—	—	—	—	NA	NA	NA	NA	NA	NA	NA	NA	NA	2	0.5	6	41	167	295	407	631	742	943
U.K.	—	—	—	—	—	—	—	NA	NA	NA	NA	NA	NA	NA	NA	NA	0.6	17	88	274	854	673	500	507	566	444
Rest of the world	—	—	—	—	—	—	—	NA	NA	NA	NA	NA	NA	NA	NA	NA	29	35	85	243	514	687	907	1667	1946	3512
Saturation (% of households owning)[e]																										
Black-and-white TV	NA	NA	NA	NA	NA	NA	NA	NA	NA	NA	NA	NA	NA	NA	96.4	94.7	90.2	82.3	75.1	65.4	55.7	48.7	42.2	38.3	29.6	26.9
Color TV	—	—	—	—	—	—	—	NA	NA	NA	NA	NA	NA	NA	5.4	13.9	26.3	42.3	61.1	75.8	85.9	90.3	93.7	95.4	97.8	97.8

[a] Domestic shipments = production – exports.
[b] Includes chassis and kits 1974 and beyond.
[c] Includes chassis and kits.
[d] Casewriter calculations.
[e] As of February of the following year up to 1976, and March of the following year for 1977 and 1978.

SOURCES: Electronic Industries Association of Japan, (Japanese) Ministry of Finance, MITI.

531

EXHIBIT 26-2. *Financial Performance of Selected Foreign TV Set Competitors, 1966-1977 (millions of yen)*

	1966	1967	1968	1969	1970	1971	1972	1973	1974	1975	1976	1977
Average effective annual exchange rate (yen = 1 U.S. dollar)	360.0	360.0	360.0	360.0	357.6	314.8	302.2	280.0	301.0	305.2	292.8	277.5
Hitachi												
Sales	413,816	491,965	629,685	821,422	1,028,819	1,198,046	1,218,485	1,288,365	1,632,388	1,807,615	1,801,564	2,221,999
Depreciation	22,014	21,339	24,330	28,179	37,560	50,623	56,899	51,636	58,535	64,098	65,513	71,093
Net income	9,628	18,633	27,960	43,111	55,560	51,413	39,630	62,415	79,840	35,138	41,127	70,169
Return on sales (%)	3.60%	4.30%	5.10%	5.30%	4.20%	3.20%	4.80%	4.90%	1.94%	2.30%	3.20%	3.16%
Return on equity (%)	11.70%	16.50%	20.90%	21.70%	16.60%	11.40%	16.10%	17.60%	7.00%	7.80%	12.60%	11.70%
Marketable securities	20,716	27,182	26,198	29,642	29,074	42,059	103,974	144,302	139,911	118,598	177,265	191,037
Debt to total capital	38.5	39.4	37.4	41.5	46.1	43.2	37.3	33.5	35.8	36.3	36.0	34.2
Dividend payout	.45	.26	.21	.20	.28	.37	.24	.19	.43	.31	.20	.22
Matsushita												
Sales	256,534	347,271	467,107	740,526	931,764	947,321	1,046,943	1,257,332	1,450,966	1,385,301	1,707,310	1,949,594
Depreciation	NA	NA	12,872	17,156	23,400	26,975	25,741	25,933	29,296	28,230	32,029	36,918
Net income	16,099	22,019	30,427	63,968	70,434	41,398	69,864	71,980	53,607	31,693	65,667	78,021
Return on sales (%)	5.70%	5.70%	8.10%	8.60%	7.60%	6.20%	6.70%	5.70%	3.70%	2.30%	3.90%	4.10%
Return on equity (%)	20.60%	23.10%	31.50%	31.40%	24.70%	16.70%	16.90%	15.00%	10.10%	5.70%	10.90%	10.30%
Marketable securities	NA	NA	NA	5,944	10,622	34,195	(32,008)	6,325	2,651	6,321	6,717	6,262
Debt to total capital	21.9	20.1	19.7	11.4	10.6	10.7	7.6	5.1	8.2	6.6	9.9	6.0
Dividend payout	.28	.24	.24	.12	.10	.17	.13	.13	.22	.31	.15	.10
Sanyo												
Sales	78,175	108,964	152,524	198,908	235,937	254,085	274,856	303,011	378,377	424,080	545,641	641,639
Depreciation	NA	NA	NA	2,928	4,156	5,366	5,628	6,103	6,560	6,004	6,422	8,127
Net income	2,578	5,003	7,709	9,763	9,732	6,312	4,470	6,122	9,638	3,931	16,397	18,354
Return on sales (%)	4.60%	5.10%	4.90%	4.10%	2.50%	2.00%	2.00%	2.30%	1.90%	0.93%	3.00%	2.86%
Return on equity (%)	NA	NA	NA	21.44%	11.10%	7.60%	9.90%	13.00%	11.20%	5.10%	17.80%	16.30%
Marketable securities[a]	NA	NA	NA	NA	6,525	9,428	17,761	23,623	17,898	43,367	49,089	33,258
Debt to total capital	NA	NA	19.1	19.4	22.4	23.3	19.2	23.1	21.3	24.3	19.8	15.1
Dividend payout	NA	NA	.12	.28	.48	.67	.49	.35	.38	(1.01)	.23	.27

EXHIBIT 26-2. *(continued)*

	1966	1967	1968	1969	1970	1971	1972	1973	1974	1975	1976	1977
Sony												
Sales	46,940	58,403	71,213	108,939	149,173	193,985	245,103	314,061	397,051	409,610	463,528	506,024
Depreciation	1,318	1,665	2,111	2,885	4,987	5,586	5,730	7,481	10,180	10,737	10,644	12,859
Net income	2,747	4,252	4,518	8,683	9,913	12,431	20,014	25,380	24,992	16,313	30,694	34,642
Return on sales (%)	5.70%	7.10%	6.30%	7.70%	6.90%	7.10%	7.70%	8.10%	5.70%	5.60%	6.60%	6.90%
Return on equity (%)	21.50%	27.40%	23.40%	33.90%	27.00%	25.80%	24.10%	23.30%	16.20%	10.00%	16.30%	16.10%
Marketable securities	4,306	802	1,992	1,901	2,875	17,001	16,738	13,336	2,625	18,318	49,266	29,346
Debt to total capital	12.0	15.6	7.7	8.9	5.6	4.4	5.4	2.8	0.75	1.2	1.4	1.1
Dividend payout	.29	.19	.22	.11	.12	.10	.08	.08	.10	.15	.14	.16
Toshiba												
Sales	321,319	395,776	515,554	674,933	807,504	847,016	836,937	967,533	1,185,988	1,223,390	1,317,981	1,384,202
Depreciation	14,597	16,683	19,994	23,356	29,382	34,681	35,228	35,495	43,266	44,262	42,043	43,887
Net income	3,422	9,698	15,664	22,148	19,924	5,120	12,449	19,699	14,052	7,468	(3,939)	3,568
Return on sales (%)	1.10%	2.60%	3.00%	3.30%	2.50%	0.60%	1.50%	2.00%	1.20%	0.61%	(0.30%)	0.26%
Return on equity (%)	3.30%	9.60%	13.50%	16.00%	12.30%	3.10%	7.60%	11.20%	7.50%	3.96%	(2.26%)	0.82%
Marketable securities	10,961	11,516	11,300	14,674	12,795	32,280	31,205	37,514	28,269	29,409	32,523	10,503
Debt to total capital	35.2	36.4	38.4	34.6	37.8	43.3	53.7	50.2	51.6	60.6	61.0	60.7
Dividend payout	1.22	.55	.46	.41	.56	1.63	.59	.53	.83	1.55	(2.48)	2.74
Average effective annual exchange rate (guilder = 1 U.S. dollar)	3.620	3.620	3.620	3.620	3.597	3.245	3.245	2.781	2.781	2.781	2.837	2.837
N.V. Philips (millions of guilders)												
Sales	8,069	8,695	11,596	13,023	15,070	18,200	19,925	22,563	25,288	27,115	30,435	31,164
Depreciation	2,792	2,942	3,635	4,074	4,690	5,931	6,519	7,401	8,684	9,951	10,348	11,328
Net income	301	315	435	519	435	343	717	899	734	384	563	634
Return on sales (%)	3.73%	3.62%	3.75%	3.99%	2.89%	1.89%	3.60%	3.98%	2.90%	1.42%	1.85%	2.03%
Return on equity (%)[b]	6.46%	6.36%	8.48%	7.34%	5.35%	3.78%	6.98%	7.55%	5.38%	2.56%	3.60%	3.89%
Marketable securities	76	80	131	119	82	133	195	223	104	167	225	196
Debt to total capital	23.14	23.99	21.40	16.57	16.81	16.48	15.71	13.25	10.71	10.06	20.28	29.62
Dividend payout[c]	.58	.59	.45	.43	.47	.56	.32	.33	.42	.62	.49	.46

[a] Includes time deposits.

[b] Equity = common stock and retained earnings and surpluses.

[c] Based on dividends paid to Philips Incandescent Lamp Holding Company.

SOURCES: Annual reports, security analyst data.

EXHIBIT 26-3. *Japanese Color Set Production in Europe*

Firm	Facility	Estimated Capacity	Ownership Share (%)
Sony	Bridgend, Wales plant	150,000	100%
	Wega Radio, West Germany	NA	100%
Matsushita	Cardiff, Wales plant	150,000	100%
Toshiba	Rank-Toshiba joint venture	350,000	40%
Hitachi	Hitachi-GEC (U.K.) joint venture	250,000	50%
Sanyo	Aznarez, Spain	100,000	34%
	Emerson, Italy	240,000	30%
Mitsubishi	Haddington, Scotland plant	100,000	100%

SOURCE: Industry sources.

EXHIBIT 26-4. *Estimated European Unit Market Shares in Color TV Sets, 1977*

	West Germany	United Kingdom	France	Italy	Spain
Philips Group	15%	19%	33%	17%	25%
Grundig	26%	1%	11%	19%	16%
Telefunken	11%	1%	4%	11%	11%
ITT	6%	7%	10%	0	5%
Thomson (includes Nord Mende)	11%	0	26%	0	8%
Thorn	0	27%	0	0	0
Japanese	8%	14%	7%	4%	2%
Others	23%	31%	9%	49%	33%

SOURCE: Industry sources.

EXHIBIT 26-5. *European Demand for Black-and-White TV Sets, 1950–1978 (units in thousands)*

	1950	1955	1956	1957	1958	1959	1960	1961	1962	1963	1964	1965	1966
Netherlands	1	45	98	175	162	228	265	285	295	340	355	410	290
Belgium		50	65	100	160	190	230	225	230	230	235	235	210
Western Germany		325	517	666	1207	1534	1378	1476	1482	1545	1819	1945	1855
Italy		123	273	480	564	625	694	876	831	1086	1257	1342	1270
Denmark		15	48	80	123	170	211	193	154	109	106	80	62
Finland			1	3	10	35	65	95	145	150	155	120	95
Norway							7	53	66	96	97	105	100	113
Sweden		10	25	125	235	410	420	365	295	230	225	203	190
Austria		3	4	18	42	70	93	105	90	100	124	148	160
Switzerland		15	10	15	33	49	65	85	95	115	135	145	160
Portugal			2	7	19	15	19	26	26	44	50	67	80
Spain Peninsula		16	20	26	37	53	95	175	260	355	495	645	670
France	7	187	255	323	350	490	639	795	1005	1175	1371	1304	1359
United Kingdom	454	1661	1433	1816	2032	2776	1817	1508	1378	1678	1935	1690	1297
Ireland		5	5	6	11	15	30	40	60	88	70	44	48
Total Europe	462	2455	2756	3840	4985	6667	6074	6315	6442	7342	8437	7478	7859

	1967	1968	1969	1970	1971	1972	1973	1974	1975	1976	1977	1978
Netherlands	262	270	360	373	330	325	303	311	252	243	256	249
Belgium	204	213	230	230	205	189	180	165	145	125	123	120
Western Germany	1557	1918	1906	2107	1918	2024	1905	1830	1550	1390	1294	1267
Italy	1230	1300	1325	1435	1230	1350	1600	1450	1400	1450	1400	1350
Denmark	70	74	75	73	89	70	73	65	53	38	34	28
Finland	85	80	80	75	70	75	75	70	60	60	50	50
Norway	90	70	72	57	64	52	50	43	39	38	33	26
Sweden	170	175	195	210	150	135	115	100	86	80	80	80
Austria	143	177	175	180	170	155	150	150	142	135	135	137
Switzerland	130	161	142	147	137	120	91	90	70	65	49	46
Portugal	94	114	138	133	124	120	142	150	140	200	200	200
Spain Peninsula	635	655	653	630	658	675	707	635	515	480	515	430
Canary Islands							25	25	25	30	25	20
France	1333	1480	1390	1336	1274	1219	1190	1090	1063	1023	881	765
United Kingdom	1330	1769	1705	1812	1764	1825	1400	815	938	1007	1034	1270
Ireland	45	50	59	48	41	49	50	31	26	26	28	30
Total Europe	7378	8605	8505	8846	8224	8383	8056	7020	6504	6390	6137	6068

SOURCE: Industry sources.

EXHIBIT 26-6. *European Demand for Color TV Sets, 1967–1978 (units in thousands)*

	1967	1968	1969	1970	1971	1972	1973	1974	1975	1976	1977	1978
Netherlands	13	29	68	128	187	248	314	415	415	488	506	644
Belgium	1	2	8	25	65	105	170	245	285	310	335	325
Western Germany	146	238	392	626	853	1215	1570	2040	1905	2220	2469	2490
Italy	0	1	6	14	25	45	66	120	240	650	880	1350
Denmark	1	5	16	30	47	78	113	135	185	229	197	163
Finland	0	1	2	7	10	27	44	85	118	149	126	130
Norway	NA	1	2	7	16	44	54	82	117	154	172	140
Sweden	4	43	100	130	205	275	278	338	333	369	329	274
Austria	2	3	17	31	45	89	110	155	182	230	283	263
Switzerland	5	15	38	54	69	115	165	186	175	224	232	244
Spain	NA	NA	NA	NA	NA	5	15	31	85	265	510	650
Canary Islands	NA	NA	NA	NA	NA	NA	NA	NA	5	30	35	35
France	22	57	107	203	321	452	634	670	833	1135	1334	1432
United Kingdom	31	121	157	504	922	1780	2773	2257	1618	1560	1700	1825
Ireland	NA	NA	NA	1	6	9	14	40	38	40	55	80
Total Europe	225	516	913	1761	2771	4485	6329	6801	6536	8058	9175	10,050

SOURCE: Industry sources.

EXHIBIT 26-7.   *Composition of World TV Set Demand*

A. Composition of World Black-and-White
TV Set Demand

UNITS
(MILLIONS)

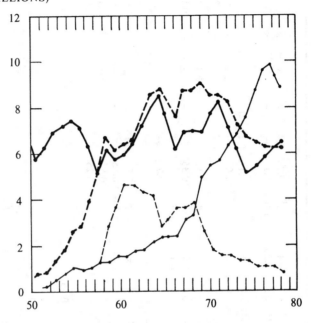

B. Composition of World Color
TV Set Demand

UNITS
(MILLIONS)

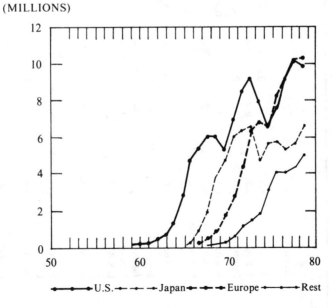

EXHIBIT 26-8. *World Black-and-White TV Positions in 1976 (quantities × 1,000,000)*

Parent Company	Country	Total Production	PROD West Europe[a]	PROD USA	PROD Japan	PROD Taiwan	PROD South Korea	PROD Singapore	PROD Lat. Am.	PROD Rest	SALES West Europe	SALES USA	SALES Japan	SALES Taiwan	SALES South Korea	SALES Singapore	SALES Lat. Am.	SALES Rest	Own Prod. Picture Tubes	Own Prod. Semiconductors
1. Matsushita El, Ind.	Japan	2.5	-	-	1.9	0.1	-	-	0.1	0.4	?[b]	0.7	0.45	x[c]	x	x	0.1	?	yes	yes
2. Philips	Netherl.	1.85	0.8	0.05	-	-	-	0.25	0.5	0.25	1.0	0.1	-	-	-	x	0.55	0.25	yes	yes
3. Sanyo Electrical	Japan	1.15	-	-	0.8	0.35	-	-	-	0.1	?	0.1	0.1	0.05	-	x	?	?	no	yes
4. Zenith	U.S.A.	0.8	-	0.4	-	0.4	-	-	x	x	-	1.0	-	-	-	-	x	0.1	yes	no
5. Toshiba	Japan	0.8	-	-	0.5	-	0.3	-	-	-	?	?	0.2	-	x	-	?	?	yes	yes
6. Samsung	S. Korea	0.75	-	-	-	-	0.75	-	-	-	?	?	-	-	0.3	-	?	?	yes	yes
7. GTE	U.S.A.	0.7	0.15	0.3	-	0.05	-	-	0.1	0.1	0.15	0.35	-	-	-	-	0.1	0.1	yes	no
8. Grundig	W. Germany	0.6	0.5	-	-	-	-	-	-	-	0.5	-	-	-	-	-	-	-	no	yes
9. RCA	U.S.A.	0.6	-	-	-	0.6	-	-	-	-	-	0.7	-	-	-	-	-	-	no	yes
10. Gold Star	S. Korea	0.6	-	-	-	-	0.6	-	-	-	?	-	-	-	0.35	-	?	?	no	yes
11. Hitachi	Japan	0.5	-	-	0.2	0.2	-	0.1	-	x	?	0.1	0.15	x	-	-	x	?	yes	yes
12. Sharp	Japan	0.5	-	-	0.4	-	-	-	-	0.1	?	0.15	x	x	-	x	x	?	no	yes
13. G.E.	U.S.A.	0.5	-	0.4	-	-	-	-	0.1	x	-	0.5	-	-	-	-	0.15	x	no	yes
14. Rockwell	U.S.A.	0.45	-	0.35	-	-	-	-	0.1	-	-	0.25	-	-	-	-	0.05	x	no	yes
15. Ford ("Philco") Lat. Am.	U.S.A.	0.45	-	-	-	-	-	-	0.45	-	-	-	-	-	-	-	0.45	-	no	no
16. AGE/Telefunken	W. Germany	0.4	0.2	-	-	-	-	-	0.1	0.1	0.3	-	-	-	-	-	0.1	0.1	yes	yes
17. Thorn	U.K.	0.4	0.3	-	-	-	-	-	-	0.1	0.4	-	-	-	-	-	-	0.1	no	yes
18. General	Japan	0.4	-	-	0.4	-	-	-	-	-	?	x	x	-	-	-	?	?	no	no
19. Thomson Brandt	France	0.4	0.4	-	-	-	-	-	-	-	0.4	-	-	-	-	-	-	-	yes	yes
20. Sampo	Taiwan	0.4	-	-	-	0.4	-	-	-	-	?	?	-	0.05	-	-	?	?	no	no
21. Tatung	Taiwan	0.4	-	-	-	0.4	-	-	-	-	?	?	-	0.05	-	-	?	?	yes	no
22. Colorado	Brasil	0.35	-	-	-	-	-	-	0.35	-	-	-	-	-	-	-	0.35	-	no	no
23. United Electronics	Taiwan	0.35	-	-	-	0.35	-	-	-	-	?	?	-	-	-	-	?	?	no	yes
24. Shinlee	Taiwan	0.35	-	-	-	0.35	-	-	-	-	?	?	-	x	-	-	?	?	no	no
25. ITT	U.S.A.	0.3	0.3	-	-	-	-	-	-	-	0.3	-	-	-	-	-	-	-	yes	yes

EXHIBIT 26-8. (continued)

		Total Produc-tion	Geographical Spread																Own Production	
			PRODUCTION								SALES								Pic-ture Tubes	Semi-conduc-tors
Parent Company, Country			West Europe[a]	USA	Japan	Tai-wan	South Korea	Singa-pore	Lat. Am.	Rest	West Europe	USA	Japan	Tai-wan	South Korea	Singa-pore	Lat. Am.	Rest		
26. Nordmende	W. Germany	0.3	0.2	—	—	—	—	—	—	0.1	0.2	—	—	—	—	—	—	0.1	no	no
27. Taihan	S. Korea	0.25	—	—	—	—	0.25	—	—	—	?	?	—	—	0.15	—	?	?	no	yes
28. Sony	Japan	0.2	x	—	0.2	—	—	—	—	x	?	0.2	0.1	—	—	—	?	?	yes	yes
29. Nippon Electric	Japan	0.2	—	—	0.2	—	—	—	—	—	?	x	x	—	—	—	?	?	yes	yes
30. Indesit	Italy	0.2	0.2	—	—	—	—	—	—	—	0.2	—	—	—	—	—	—	—	no	no
31. Oscar El.	Taiwan	0.15	—	—	—	0.15	—	—	—	—	?	?	—	—	—	—	?	?	no	no
32. Zanussi	Italy	0.15	0.15	—	—	—	—	—	—	—	0.15	—	—	—	—	—	—	—	no	no
33. Formenti	Italy	0.15	0.15	—	—	—	—	—	—	—	0.15	—	—	—	—	—	—	—	no	no
34. R. Bosch	W. Germany	0.1	0.1	—	—	—	—	—	—	x	0.1	—	—	x	—	—	—	x	no	yes
35. Taiwan Kolin	Taiwan	0.05	—	—	—	0.05	—	—	—	—	?	?	—	—	—	—	?	?	no	no
36. Korea Nat. Electric	S. Korea	0.05	—	—	—	—	0.05	—	—	—	?	?	—	—	x	—	?	?	no	no
37. Washin Sony	S. Korea	0.05	—	—	—	—	0.05	—	—	—	?	?	?	?	x	?	?	?	no	no
38. Rest		3.05	1.35	—	x	x	x	0.05	0.8	0.8	?	?	?	?	?	?	?	?		
Total Free World		21.4	4.8	1.5	4.6	3.3	2.0	0.4	2.65	2.15	6.4	5.2	1.0	0.2	0.85	0.1	2.8	2.4		

[a] Excluding Greece and Turkey.
[b] ? means unknown.
[c] x means fewer than 50,000 sets.

539

EXHIBIT 26-9. World Color TV Positions in 1976

Parent Company	Main Brand Names	Total Sales CTV in Mill. pcs.	SALES Europe	SALES USA	SALES Japan	SALES Lat. Am.	SALES Rest	PROD. Europe	PROD. USA	PROD. Japan	PROD. Lat. Am.	PROD. Rest	Number[a] of Employees	Turnover Total[a] Company	Turnover Of which CTV	CTV as % of Total	Average Turnover per Set	Own Prod. Picture Tubes	Own Prod. Semiconductors
1. Matsushita El. Industrial	National/Panasonic Quasar/Nivico Victor/JVC	3.15	0.15	0.7	1.9	x[b]	0.4	x	0.5	2.6	x	0.2	83.100	5.737	(898)[c]	(16)	(285)	yes	yes
2. Philips	Philips (numerous others)	2.85	1.95	0.45	–	0.15	0.3	2.05	0.45	–	0.15	0.25	391.500	11.522	1.583	14	555	yes	yes
3. Sony	Sony/Wega	1.85	0.25	0.6	0.75	–	0.25	0.05	0.37	1.45	–	x	22.700	1.505	522	35	282	yes	yes
4. Zenith	Zenith	1.6	–	1.4	–	–	0.2	–	1.6	–	–	–	23.365	978	723	74	(400)	yes	no
5. Sanyo El.	Sanyo, priv. label a.o. Silvertone (Sears)	1.55	0.1	0.8	0.4	0.05	0.2	–	0.45	1.2	x	0.1	16.100	1.833	(442)	(24)	(285)	no	yes
6. Tokyo Shibaura El. Co.	Toshiba, priv. label	1.45	0.05	0.35	0.9	–	0.15	–	–	1.6	–	x	105.000	4.460	(413)	(9)	(285)	yes	yes
7. Hitachi	Hitachi	1.4	0.05	0.35	0.7	–	0.3	–	–	1.4	x	0.2	143.000	6.680	(400)	(6)	(285)	yes	yes
8. RCA	RCA	1.3	–	1.2	–	–	0.1	–	1.1	–	–	0.1	110.000	5.329	(520)	(10)	(400)	yes	no
9. Grundig	Grundig/Minerva	0.95	0.95	–	–	–	x	0.95	–	–	–	–	31.400	943	(520)	(55)	(550)	no	no
10. Sharp	Sharp	0.9	x	0.3	0.4	0.1	0.1	–	–	1.0	0.1	x	10.300	807	(257)	(32)	(285)	no	no
11. AEG/Telefunken	Telefunken/Imperial/Kuba	0.6	0.5	–	–	0.1	x	0.5	–	–	0.1	–	161.900	5.351	(330)	(6)	(550)	yes	yes
12. Thorn El. Ind.	Ferguson/HMV/Ultra	0.6	0.5	–	–	–	0.1	0.5	–	–	–	x	81.000	2.795	(171)	(10)	(285)	no	no
13. ITT	Graetz/Oceanic/Schaub Lorenz/Ingelen/ITT	0.6	0.6	–	–	–	x	0.5	–	–	–	–	375.000	11.764	(330)	(3)	(550)	yes	yes
14. GTE	Sylvania/Saba/Philco/	0.6	0.2	0.3	–	–	x	0.25	0.30	–	–	x	194.000	6.750	(220)	(3)	(400)	yes	yes
15. Rockwell	Fleetwood/Empire Admiral, priv. label	0.55	–	0.45	–	x	x	–	0.25	–	x	0.25	119.100	5.220	(220)	(4)	(400)	yes	yes
16. G.E.	General, priv. label	0.5	–	0.4	–	x	x	–	0.35	–	x	x	380.000	15.700	(180)	(1)	(400)	no	yes
17. General	MGA (USA)/Teleton/	0.45	–	0.2	0.1	–	0.1	–	–	0.5	–	–	3.350	257	(114)	(44)	(285)	yes	no
18. Mitsubishi El.	Mitsubishi	0.4	0.05	–	0.2	–	x	–	–	0.4	–	–	67.000	2.273	(100)	(4)	(285)	no	yes
19. Nordmende	Nordmende	0.35	0.3	–	–	–	x	0.35	–	–	–	–	± 6.000	257	(165)	(64)	(550)	yes	no
20. Thomson Brandt	Thomson Brandt Cont. Edison, etc.	0.3	0.3	–	–	–	–	0.35	–	–	–	–	105.600	3.534	(200)	(6)	(665)	no	yes
21. Robert Bosch	Blaupunkt, priv. lab.	0.3	0.3	–	–	–	–	0.35	–	–	–	–	110.900	3.306	(165)	(5)	(550)	yes	no
22. Nippon El. Corp.	NEC	0.2	–	–	0.2	–	–	–	–	0.3	–	–	61.100	1.923	(60)	(3)	(285)	no	yes
23. Luxor	Luxor	0.15	0.15	–	–	–	–	0.15	–	–	–	–						no	no
24. Salora	Salora, UPO	0.15	0.15	–	–	–	–	0.15	–	–	–	–						no	no
25. Rest		2.55	1.35	0.1	–	0.4	0.5	1.65	x	–	0.4	0.65							
Total Free World		24.9	7.9	7.7	5.6	0.8	2.9	7.85	5.35	10.5	0.8	2.00							

[a] Including consolidated subsidiaries.
[b] x means less than 50.000 sets.
[c] ( ) unknown, own approximations.

Index of Cases